## 2006 – 2007
## TOWNSEND PRESS SUNDAY SCHOOL
# COMMENTARY

BASED ON THE INTERNATIONAL LESSON SERIES

### Eighty-sixth Edition

Sunday School Publishing Board
National Baptist Convention, USA, Inc.
Dr. E. L. Thomas, Executive Director

**EIGHTY-SIXTH EDITION • KING JAMES VERSION**

Copyright © 2006

Townsend Press, Nashville, Tennessee. A division of the Sunday School Publishing Board, NBC, USA, Inc. All rights reserved. No part of this book may be reproduced or transmitted in any form by any means, electronic or mechanical, including photocopying, recording, or by any information storage or retrieval system without expressed permission in writing from the Sunday School Publishing Board, 330 Charlotte Avenue, Nashville, Tennessee 37201-1188. E-mail: sspbcustomercare@bellsouth.net.

The *Commentary* lesson expositions have been developed from the International Sunday School Lesson Series, 2004-2007 Cycle, copyright © 2002 by the Committee on Uniform Series of the National Council of Churches USA. The Home Daily Bible Readings are prepared by the Committee on the Uniform Series, copyright © 2004. Used by permission.

Bible passages are taken from the *King James Version* unless otherwise noted.

Unmarked contemporary translation of Scripture or passages marked NRSV are from the *New Revised Standard Version* of the Bible, copyright by the National Council of the Churches of Christ in the USA, and are used by permission.

Scripture quotations marked NIV are taken from the Holy Bible, *New International Version.* Copyright © 1973, 1978, 1984 by International Bible Society. Used by permission of Zondervan. All rights reserved.

Scripture quotations marked NKJV are taken from the *New King James Version.* Copyright © 1982 by Thomas Nelson, Inc. Used by permission. All rights reserved.

Scripture quotations marked NCV are taken from the *New Century Version.* Copyright © 1987, 1988, 1991 by Thomas Nelson, Inc. Used by permission. All rights reserved.

Scripture quotations marked NASB are taken from the *New American Standard Bible,* Copyright © 1960, 1962, 1963, 1968, 1971, 1972, 1973, 1975, 1977, 1995 by The Lockman Foundation. Used by permission.

Scripture quotations taken from *The New Living Translation,* copyright © 1996, are used by permission of Tyndale House Publishers, Inc., Wheaton, Illinois 60189. All rights reserved.

Scripture quotations marked AMP are taken from the *Amplified® Bible,* Copyright © 1954, 1958, 1962, 1964, 1965, 1987 by The Lockman Foundation. Used by permission. (www.Lockman.org)

*Some Scripture passages may represent the writers' paraphrase.

---

*Writers:* Dr. E. Christopher Jackson, Rev. John K. Patterson, Dr. Geoffrey V. Guns, Rev. Derrick Jackson; *Editors:* Rev. Olivia M. Cloud, Rev. Wellington A. Johnson, Sr., Dr. Sherman Tribble, Dr. Gideon Olaleye; *Copy Editors:* Yalemzewd Worku, Tanae McKnight, Lucinda Anderson, Tanya Savory; *Layout Designers:* Royetta Davis, Joyce Evans.

ISBN: 1-932972-31-5

# CONTENTS

Three-year Cycle .................................................................... v
List of Printed Texts ................................................................ vi
Preface ............................................................................ vii
Acknowledgements ................................................................... viii
In Tribute ......................................................................... ix
Know Your Writers ................................................................... x

### Fall Quarter, 2006—*God's Living Covenant*

General Introduction ................................................................ 1

### September: UNIT I—*In Covenant with God*
  3  God's Covenant with Noah (Genesis 9:1-15) ....................................... 3
10  God's Covenant with Abram (Genesis 17:1-8, 15-22) .............................. 10
17  God's Covenant with Israel (Exodus 19:1-6; 24:3-8) ............................. 17
24  Covenant Renewed (Joshua 24:1, 14-24) .......................................... 24

### October: UNIT II—*God's Covenant with Judges and Kings*
  1  God Sends Judges (Judges 2:16-23) .............................................. 31
  8  God Leads Through Deborah (Judges 4:4-10, 12-16) ............................... 38
15  God Answers Samuel's Prayer (1 Samuel 7:3-13) .................................. 45
22  God Covenants with David (2 Samuel 7:8-17) ..................................... 52
29  God Grants Wisdom to Solomon (1 Kings 3:3-14) .................................. 59

### November: UNIT III—*Living as God's Covenanted People*
  5  Elijah Triumphs with God (1 Kings 18:20-24, 30-35, 38-39) ...................... 66
12  Josiah Brings Reform (2 Kings 22:8-10; 23:1-3, 21-23) .......................... 73
19  The People Go into Exile (2 Chronicles 36:15-21; Psalm 137:1-6) ................ 80
26  God Offers Return and Restoration (2 Chronicles 36:22-23; Ezra 1:5-7) .......... 87

### Winter Quarter, 2006–2007—*Jesus Christ: A Portrait of God*

General Introduction ............................................................... 93

### December: UNIT I—*Christ, the Image of God*
  3  Who Is Jesus Christ? (Colossians 1:15-23) ...................................... 95
10  What God Says About Jesus (Hebrews 1:1-9) ..................................... 102
17  Light that Conquers (1 John 1:1–2:5) .......................................... 109
24  The Word Became Flesh (John 1:1-18) ........................................... 116
31  Humiliation and Exaltation (Philippians 2:1-11) ............................... 123

### January: UNIT II—*Christ Sustains and Supports*
  7  "I Am from Above" (John 8:31-38, 48-56, 58-59) ................................ 130
14  Jesus Is Authority and Judge (John 5:19-29) ................................... 137
21  Jesus Is the Bread of Life and Living Water (John 6:34-40; 7:37-39) ........... 144
28  "I Am the Light of the World" (John 8:12-20; 12:44-46) ........................ 151

### February: UNIT III—*Christ Guides and Protects*
  4  "I Am the Good Shepherd" (John 10:1-5, 7-18) .................................. 158

11 "I Am the Resurrection and the Life" (John 11:17-27) . . . . . . . . . . . . . . . . . . . . . . . . . . . . . . . 165
18 "I Am the Way, the Truth, and the Life" (John 14:1-14) . . . . . . . . . . . . . . . . . . . . . . . . . . . . 172
25 "I Am the True Vine" (John 15:1-17) . . . . . . . . . . . . . . . . . . . . . . . . . . . . . . . . . . . . . . . . . . . 179

### Spring Quarter, 2007—*Our Community Now and in God's Future*

General Introduction . . . . . . . . . . . . . . . . . . . . . . . . . . . . . . . . . . . . . . . . . . . . . . . . . . . . . . . . . . . 187

**March: UNIT I**—*Known by Our Love*
 4 The Light of Love (1 John 2:7-11, 15-17) . . . . . . . . . . . . . . . . . . . . . . . . . . . . . . . . . . . . . . . 189
11 The Test of Love (1 John 3:11-24) . . . . . . . . . . . . . . . . . . . . . . . . . . . . . . . . . . . . . . . . . . . . . 197
18 The Source of Love (1 John 4:7-21) . . . . . . . . . . . . . . . . . . . . . . . . . . . . . . . . . . . . . . . . . . . 204
25 The Way to Love (1 John 5:1-12) . . . . . . . . . . . . . . . . . . . . . . . . . . . . . . . . . . . . . . . . . . . . . 211

**April: UNIT II**—*A New Community in Christ*
 1 Christ Is Our King (Revelation 1:8; Luke 19:28-40) . . . . . . . . . . . . . . . . . . . . . . . . . . . . . . 218
 8 Christ Is Risen (Revelation 1:12, 17-18; John 20:11-16, 30-31) . . . . . . . . . . . . . . . . . . . . . 225
15 God Is Worthy of Praise (Revelation 4:1-11) . . . . . . . . . . . . . . . . . . . . . . . . . . . . . . . . . . . . 232
22 Christ Is Worthy to Redeem (Revelation 5:1-5, 11-14) . . . . . . . . . . . . . . . . . . . . . . . . . . . . 239
29 Christ Is Our Protection (Revelation 7:1-3, 9, 13-17) . . . . . . . . . . . . . . . . . . . . . . . . . . . . . 246

**May: UNIT III**—*Living in God's New World*
 6 The Final Banquet (Revelation 19:5-10) . . . . . . . . . . . . . . . . . . . . . . . . . . . . . . . . . . . . . . . 253
13 Our New Home (Revelation 21:1-8) . . . . . . . . . . . . . . . . . . . . . . . . . . . . . . . . . . . . . . . . . . 260
20 God in Our Midst (Revelation 21:9-10, 22–22:5) . . . . . . . . . . . . . . . . . . . . . . . . . . . . . . . . 267
27 Christ Will Return (Revelation 22:6-10, 12-13, 16-21) . . . . . . . . . . . . . . . . . . . . . . . . . . . . 274

### Summer Quarter, 2007—*Committed to Doing Right*

General Introduction . . . . . . . . . . . . . . . . . . . . . . . . . . . . . . . . . . . . . . . . . . . . . . . . . . . . . . . . . . . 281

**June: UNIT I**—*Life as God's People*
 3 Amos Challenges Injustice (Amos 5:10-15, 21-24) . . . . . . . . . . . . . . . . . . . . . . . . . . . . . . . 283
10 Hosea Preaches God's Accusation Against Israel (Hosea 4:1-4; 7:1-2; 12:8-9) . . . . . . . . . . 290
17 Isaiah Calls for True Worship (Isaiah 1:10-11, 14-20) . . . . . . . . . . . . . . . . . . . . . . . . . . . . . 297
24 Isaiah Invites Us to God's Feast (Isaiah 55:1-3a, 6-11) . . . . . . . . . . . . . . . . . . . . . . . . . . . . 303

**July: UNIT II**—*What Does God Require?*
 1 Micah Announces God's Requirements (Micah 3:1-4; 6:6-8) . . . . . . . . . . . . . . . . . . . . . . . 310
 8 Zephaniah Announces God's Justice (Zephaniah 3:1-5, 8-9) . . . . . . . . . . . . . . . . . . . . . . . 317
15 Habakkuk Announces the Doom of the Unrighteous (Habakkuk 2:6-14) . . . . . . . . . . . . . 324
22 Jeremiah Announces the Consequences of Disobedience
    (Jeremiah 7:11-15; 2 Kings 23:36-37) . . . . . . . . . . . . . . . . . . . . . . . . . . . . . . . . . . . . . . . . . 330
29 Jeremiah Invites Jews in Babylon to Trust God (Jeremiah 29:1-14) . . . . . . . . . . . . . . . . . . 337

**August: UNIT III**—*How Shall We Respond?*
 5 Lamentations Urges Hope in God (Lamentations 3:25-33, 55-58) . . . . . . . . . . . . . . . . . . 344
12 Ezekiel Preaches About Individual Responsibility
    (Ezekiel 18:4, 20-23, 30-32) . . . . . . . . . . . . . . . . . . . . . . . . . . . . . . . . . . . . . . . . . . . . . . . . . 351
19 Zechariah Calls for a Return to God (Zechariah 1:1-6; 7:8-14) . . . . . . . . . . . . . . . . . . . . . 358
26 Malachi Describes God's Just Judgment (Malachi 2:17–3:5; 4:1) . . . . . . . . . . . . . . . . . . . . 365

Glossary of Terms . . . . . . . . . . . . . . . . . . . . . . . . . . . . . . . . . . . . . . . . . . . . . . . . . . . . . . . . . . . . . 371

# CYCLE OF 2004-2007

**Arrangement of Quarters According to the Church School Year,
September Through August**

|  | Fall | Winter | Spring | Summer |
|---|---|---|---|---|
| 2004-2005 | The God of Continuing Creation (Bible Survey)<br><br>Theme: Creation | Called to Be God's People (Bible Survey)<br><br>Theme: Call | God's Project: Effective Christians (Romans and Galatians)<br><br>Theme: Covenant | Jesus' Life, Teachings and Ministry (Matthew, Mark, Luke)<br>Theme: Christ |
| 2005-2006 | "You Will Be My Witnesses"<br><br>(Acts)<br><br><br>Theme: Community | God's Commitment—Our Response<br><br>(Isaiah; 1 and 2 Timothy)<br><br>Theme: Commitment | Living in and as God's Creation<br><br>(Psalms, Job, Ecclesiastes, Proverbs)<br>Theme: Creation | Called to Be a Christian Community<br><br>(1 and 2 Corinthians)<br><br>Theme: Call |
| 2006-2007 | God's Living Covenant<br><br>(Old Testament Survey)<br><br><br>Theme: Covenant | Jesus Christ: A Portrait of God<br><br>(John, Philippians, Colossians, Hebrews, 1 John)<br>Theme: Christ | Our Community Now and in God's Future<br><br>(1 John, Revelation)<br><br><br>Theme: Community | Committed to Doing Right<br><br><br>(Various Prophets, 2 Kings, 2 Chronicles)<br><br>Theme: Commitment |

# LIST OF PRINTED TEXTS—2006-2007

The Printed Scriptural Texts used in the *2006-2007 Townsend Press Sunday School Commentary* are arranged here in the order in which they appear in the Bible. Opposite each reference is the page number on which Scriptures appear in this edition of the *Commentary*.

| Reference | Page |
|---|---|
| Genesis 9:1-15 | 3 |
| Genesis 17:1-8, 15-22 | 10 |
| Exodus 19:1-6 | 17 |
| Exodus 24:3-8 | 17 |
| Joshua 24:1, 14-24 | 24 |
| Judges 2:16-23 | 31 |
| Judges 4:4-10, 12-16 | 38 |
| 1 Samuel 7:3-13 | 45 |
| 2 Samuel 7:8-17 | 52 |
| 1 Kings 3:3-14 | 59 |
| 1 Kings 18:20-24, 30-35, 38-39 | 66 |
| 2 Kings 22:8-10 | 73 |
| 2 Kings 23:1-3, 21-23 | 73 |
| 2 Kings 23:36-37 | 330 |
| 2 Chronicles 36:15-21 | 80 |
| 2 Chronicles 36:22-23 | 87 |
| Ezra 1:5-7 | 87 |
| Psalm 137:1-6 | 80 |
| Isaiah 1:10-11, 14-20 | 297 |
| Isaiah 55:1-3a, 6-11 | 303 |
| Jeremiah 7:11-15 | 330 |
| Jeremiah 29:1-14 | 337 |
| Lamentations 3:25-33, 55-58 | 344 |
| Ezekiel 18:4, 20-23, 30-32 | 351 |
| Hosea 4:1-4 | 290 |
| Hosea 7:1-2 | 290 |
| Hosea 12:8-9 | 290 |
| Amos 5:10-15, 21-24 | 283 |
| Micah 3:1-4 | 310 |
| Micah 6:6-8 | 310 |
| Habakkuk 2:6-14 | 324 |
| Zephaniah 3:1-5, 8-9 | 317 |
| Zechariah 1:1-6 | 358 |
| Zechariah 7:8-14 | 358 |

| Reference | Page |
|---|---|
| Malachi 2:17 | 365 |
| Malachi 3:1-5 | 365 |
| Malachi 4:1 | 365 |
| Luke 19:28-40 | 218 |
| John 1:1-18 | 116 |
| John 5:19-29 | 137 |
| John 6:34-40 | 144 |
| John 7:37-39 | 144 |
| John 8:12-20 | 151 |
| John 8:31-38, 48-56, 58-59 | 130 |
| John 10:1-5, 7-18 | 158 |
| John 11:17-27 | 165 |
| John 12:44-46 | 152 |
| John 14:1-14 | 172 |
| John 15:1-17 | 179 |
| John 20:11-16, 30-31 | 225 |
| Philippians 2:1-11 | 123 |
| Colossians 1:15-23 | 95 |
| Hebrews 1:1-9 | 102 |
| 1 John 1:1–2:5 | 109 |
| 1 John 2:7-11, 15-17 | 189 |
| 1 John 3:11-24 | 197 |
| 1 John 4:7-21 | 204 |
| 1 John 5:1-12 | 211 |
| Revelation 1:8 | 218 |
| Revelation 1:12, 17-18 | 225 |
| Revelation 4:1-11 | 232 |
| Revelation 5:1-5, 11-14 | 239 |
| Revelation 7:1-3, 9, 13-17 | 246 |
| Revelation 19:5-10 | 253 |
| Revelation 21:1-8 | 260 |
| Revelation 21:9-10, 22-27 | 267 |
| Revelation 2:1-5 | 267 |
| Revelation 22:6-10, 12-13, 16-21 | 274 |

# PREFACE

The *Townsend Press Commentary*, based on the International Lesson Series, is a production of the Sunday School Publishing Board, National Baptist Convention, USA, Incorporated. These lessons were developed consistent with the curriculum guidelines of the Committee on the Uniform Series, Education Leadership Ministries Commission, National Council of the Churches of Christ in the United States of America. Selected Christian scholars and theologians—who themselves embrace the precepts, doctrines, and positions on biblical interpretation that we have come to believe—are contributors to this publication. By participating in Scripture selection and the development of the matrices for the Guidelines for Lesson Development with the Committee on Uniform Series, this presentation reflects the historic faith that we share within a rich heritage of worship and witness.

The format of the *Townsend Press Commentary* consists of: Unit Title, general subject with age-level topics, printed text from the *King James Version* of the Bible, Objectives of the Lesson, Unifying Lesson Principle, Points to Be Emphasized, Topical Outline of the Lesson, Biblical Background of the Lesson (under discussion), Exposition and Application of the Scripture, Concluding Reflections (designed to focus on the salient points of the lesson), Word Power and the Home Daily Bible Readings. Each lesson concludes with a prayer.

The 2006-2007 *Commentary* features a Glossary of Terms to help readers better understand specific theological terms and biblical issues.

The *Townsend Press Commentary* is designed as an instructional aid for persons involved in the ministry of Christian education. While the autonomy of the individual soul before God is affirmed, we believe that biblical truths find their highest expression within the community of believers whose corporate experiences serve as monitors to preserve the integrity of the Christian faith. As such, the Word of God must not only be understood—it must also be embodied in the concrete realities of daily life. This serves to allow the Word of God to intersect in a meaningful way with our daily lives.

The presentation of the lessons anticipates the fact that some concepts and Scripture references do not lend themselves to meaningful comprehension by children. Hence, when this occurs, alternative passages of Scripture are used, along with appropriate content emphases that are designed to assist children in their spiritual growth.

We stand firm in our commitment to Christian growth, to the end that lives will become transformed through personal and group interaction with the Word of God. The challenge issued by the apostle Paul continues to find relevance for our faith journey: "Do your best to present yourself to God as one approved by him, a worker who has no need to be ashamed, rightly explaining the word of truth" *(2 Timothy 2:15, NRSV).*

# ACKNOWLEDGEMENTS

The *Townsend Press Commentary* is recognized as the centerpiece of a family of church school literature designed especially to assist teachers in their presentation of the lessons, as well as to broaden the knowledge base of students from the biblical perspective. Our mission has been and will always be to provide religious education experiences and spiritual resources for our constituency throughout this nation, as well as many foreign countries. To achieve this end, a collaboration of persons provides the needed expertise in the various areas of the production process. Although under the employ of the Sunday School Publishing Board, personnel too numerous to list approach their respective tasks with the dedication and devotion of those who serve God by serving His people. This *Commentary* is presented with gratitude to God for all those who desire a more comprehensive treatment of the selected Scriptures than is provided in the church school quarterlies, and is intended to be a complementary resource to them.

Our gratitude is hereby expressed to Dr. E. Christopher Jackson (Fall), Rev. John K. Patterson (Winter), Dr. Geoffrey V. Guns (Spring), and Rev. Derek Jackson (Summer) for their devotion in the development of the respective lessons. These writers bring diversity and a broad spectrum of ministerial and educational experience to bear on the exposition and application of the Scripture.

The Sunday School Publishing Board consists of employees with expertise in their assigned area whose self-understanding is that of "workers together with God" and partners with those who labor in the vineyard of teaching the Word of God, in order to make disciples and nurture others toward a mature faith.

Special appreciation is appropriately accorded to Dr. E. L. Thomas, executive director of the Sunday School Publishing Board, for his continued insightful and inspiring leadership and motivation. The determination he exhibits in seeking to meet the needs of our constituency by providing top-quality curriculum materials is not only reflected in this publication, but also pervades all of the other educational resources that are produced for the enrichment and enhancement of the people of God. It is a credit to Dr. Thomas' leadership that the employees have embraced the mission of the Sunday School Publishing Board with a self-perspective that enhances their personal commitment to the cause of Christ. This happens as they interact with one another and intersect with the greater community of faith.

The task in which we are all involved would be meaningless and fruitless if it were not for the many readers for whom this publication has been so diligently prepared. The faithfulness of our constituency has been enduring for over a century. We consider ourselves blessed to be their servants in the ministry of the printed Word exalting the living Word, our Lord and Savior Jesus Christ. We pray that God's grace will complement our efforts so that lives will be transformed within and beyond the confines of classroom interaction—as the Spirit of God manifests Himself through the intersection of teaching and learning. It is our prayer that God may grant each of us the power to live for Him and witness to the saving grace of the One who died for us, even Jesus Christ, our Lord and Savior.

Wellington A. Johnson, Sr.
Managing Editor

# IN TRIBUTE
## to
# The Reverend Ottie L. West, Sr.

~December 18, 1933~     ~January 1, 2006~

For a number of years, the *Townsend Press Commentary* has been edited by the Rev. Ottie L. West, who served with distinction as senior editor at the Sunday School Publishing Board of the National Baptist Convention, USA, Incorporated. Rev. West departed this life on Sunday, January 1, 2006 and was funeralized on Saturday, January 7, 2006. This eighty-sixth edition of the *Commentary* is dedicated to his memory and the untiring efforts he exerted in assuring that this publication was produced as close to perfection as humanly possible. Executive director Dr. E. L. Thomas leads the staff of the Sunday School Publishing Board in paying tribute to Rev. West.

Rev. West's journey through life allowed him to touch many lives, particularly in the fields of education and ministry. He served several institutions of higher learning as an assistant professor of religion and philosophy, dean of men, dean of students, director of teacher training, dean of student personnel, director of human relations and assistant registrar. In ministry, he served as interim pastor of First Baptist Church Capitol Hill, Nashville, Tennessee, on two occasions.

As a reflection of his commitment to the task of senior editor and editor of the *Townsend Press Commentary,* prior to his passing, Rev. West had already started preliminary work on this edition of the publication. It is our fondest hope that the work he has done will speak for him. His spirited energy and unwavering dedication will be greatly missed by all who had the pleasure of knowing him.

# Know Your Writers

**Dr. E. Christopher Jackson**
**Fall Quarter**

Dr. E. Christopher Jackson was born in Chattanooga, Tennessee and is the youngest son of Andrew and Christine Jackson. He received his Bachelor of Arts degree in English Literature from the University of Tennessee-Knoxville. He completed his Master of Divinity degree at Southern Baptist Theological Seminary in Louisville, Kentucky, and his Doctor of Ministry degree at United Theological Seminary in Dayton, Ohio. His ministry experience includes serving in campus ministry at the University of Tennessee and the University of Louisville. Full-time professional Campus Ministry positions include nine years at Lincoln University in Missouri and ten years at Tennessee State University and Fisk University in Nashville. He and his wife founded Creative Ministry Consultants (ministryConcepts.com), which provides seminars, counseling, and ministry consulting on a national basis. Locally, Dr. Jackson serves as a Staff Pastor and Minister of Nurture at the Temple Church.

Dr. Jackson is an accomplished writer and the author of two books, internationally published by Zondervan. His most recent product is *The Couple Game,* a practical communication tool for married couples. He has written for the Baptist World Youth Conference, the Sunday School Publishing Board, and LifeWay. He has been referenced in *Essence* and *Ebony* Magazines. Nationally, he is a frequent facilitator for universities, singles groups, marriage conferences, and various churches.

Dr. Jackson is married to Coreen D. Jackson, Ph.D, whose degree is from Howard University. Their sons are Joshua, Juleon, and Jemiah. International travels include West Africa, the Bahamas, Jamaica, Spain, and Venezuela. One of Dr. Jackson's primary objectives in life is to help other people to discover their life purpose. His personal mission statement is "To honor God, pursue purpose, and empower people through practical and creative ministries of teaching, writing, conferencing, and producing the arts."

**Rev. John K. Patterson**
**Winter Quarter**

Rev. John K. Patterson is a native of Milwaukee, Wisconsin—the son of the late Pastor Genora Patterson and Zenobia Patterson. Pastor Patterson was married in May 1986 to his high school sweetheart, Barbara J. Strickland; they were blessed with two children, Kevin D. and Chanice J. Patterson. Pastor Patterson is a veteran of the United States Army, where he served as a firefighter at Ft. Greeley, Alaska and Ft. Leonard Wood, Missouri.

He was called by God into the preaching ministry in May 1985 and preached his first sermon in July 1985. In September 1987, Pastor Patterson was called as the first pastor of Greater Community Missionary Baptist Church and served as pastor for three years. The Holy Spirit moved him to Springfield, Missouri, where he became the pastor of Greater Metropolitan Missionary Baptist Church and served for seven years. His father, the late Genora Patterson, died in March of 1996 and had been the pastor of Mt. Olive Missionary Baptist Church for thirty-five years. John K. Patterson was offered the pastorate after his father's death and became the pastor in February 1997.

Pastor Patterson is a graduate of Cardinal Stritch University in Milwaukee, Wisconsin with a bachelor's degree in Religious Studies and a master's degree from Trinity Evangelical Divinity School in Deerfield, Illinois in Religious Studies. He is currently working on his doctorate in Leadership and Communications. Pastor Patterson's most recent accomplishments include: serving as vice president of the Wisconsin General Baptist Congress of Christian Education under Congress president Robert Harris and Archie Ivy; former director of the Minister's Union in the Wisconsin General Baptist State Convention, under the leadership of President Joe Games; an instructor in the Wisconsin State Baptist Congress of Christian Education—in which he teaches Christian Ethics and a host of other classes; and the newly-appointed general secretary of the Wisconsin General Baptist Convention by president-elect Dr. E. L. Thomas.

---

### Dr. Geoffrey V. Guns
**Spring Quarter**

Dr. Geoffrey V. Guns is a native of Newport, Rhode Island. He is the son of a retired Baptist pastor and co-pastor. Dr. Guns received his elementary and secondary education in the Norfolk public school system. He earned his B.S. degree in Business Administration from Norfolk State University in 1972.

In 1981, he earned his Masters of Divinity degree from the School of Theology, Virginia Union University, graduating *summa cum laude.* He earned his Doctor of Ministry degree from the School of Religion, Howard University in Washington, D.C. in 1985.

Dr. Guns is the senior pastor of the Second Calvary Baptist Church in Norfolk, Virginia, where he has served for the past twenty-three years. He is active in his denomination, the National Baptist Convention, USA, Inc. Dr. Guns served as the president of the Virginia Baptist State Convention (VBSC) from 1997 to 2001 and is currently the moderator for the Tidewater Peninsula Baptist Association (TPBA).

He has written articles for the *Christian Education Informer* of the Department of

Christian Education of the Sunday School Publishing Board. Dr. Guns serves as vice chairman of the Council of Christian Education for the Department of Christian Education of the Sunday School Publishing Board of the NBC. He works with the Home Mission Board of the NBC and serves as the regional representative for the Southeast region.

He is the author of two books: *Church Financial Management* (1997), which is published by Providence House Publishers; and *Spiritual Leadership: A Practical Guide to Developing Spiritual Leaders in the Church* (2000), published by Orman Press, Inc.

He is married to the former Rosetta Harding of Richmond, Virginia. Mrs. Guns is a licensed social worker and works as a school social worker for the City of Chesapeake public schools. They are the parents of two daughters, Kimberly Michelle Cummings and Nicole Patrice. Dr. and Mrs. Guns have one granddaughter, Kennedy Nicole Cummings.

### Pastor Derrick Jackson
**Summer Quarter**

Pastor Derrick Jackson is a native of Itta Bena, Mississippi, where he received his diploma as valedictorian of Leflore County High School. He is an ordained minister who received the Bachelor of Business Administration in Accounting from Prairie View A&M University in Prairie View, Texas. He also received the Master of Theology degree from Vanderbilt University Divinity School in Nashville, Tennessee.

Pastor Jackson is the current pastor of the First Baptist Church of Gallatin, Tennessee. In addition to serving as pastor, he is vice president of the Middle Region of the Tennessee Baptist Missionary and Education Convention, dean of the East Fork District Association Congress of Christian Education, and president of the African-American Ministerial Fellowship in Gallatin, Tennessee.

Pastor Jackson has received several awards on the local and national levels for his dynamic leadership, his unselfish devotion to the needs of his community, and his keen awareness of the importance of establishing a partnership between the government and the faith community.

Pastor Jackson is married to Laurie Michelle Lanakila of Nashville, Tennessee, and he is the proud father of sons Jeffery and Joshua. Pastor Jackson's life experiences have led him to choose a life motto based on an African-American spiritual: "If I can help someone along the way. . . If I can cheer someone with word of song. . .If I can show someone that he or she is traveling wrong. . . then my living will not be in vain."

# FALL QUARTER—September, October, November 2006

## *God's Living Covenant*

### GENERAL INTRODUCTION

In this quarter, we will focus on the history of covenant. Of ancient origin, the word *convenant* is seldom used to define contemporary relationships, except marriage. In the Old Testament, the Hebrew word *berith,* which is translated "covenant," comes from the root word meaning "to cut." A covenant, therefore, is a cutting—with reference to the cutting or dissecting of animals into two equal parts. The parties in the contract would then walk through the animals to seal the deal (see Genesis 15; Jeremiah 34:18-19). The biblical record reveals that various types of covenants were established—vertically, between God and humanity, and horizontally, between human beings, in marriage, business and friendship.

**Unit I,** *In Covenant with God,* contains four lessons that focus on biblical covenant. The first lesson centers on Noah and the covenant God made with him. It was a covenant that demonstrated God's commitment to be in relationship with humanity. Noah was a unique individual who lived in a generation of wicked people; yet, he did not compromise God's standard. The wickedness of his generation provoked God's wrath, and He resolved to bring an end to Noah's generation; but He allowed respite for 120 years. The people entrenched themselves in sin to the point of no return; however, God favored Noah and his family. The second lesson deals with trusting promises of God. Abraham is our focal point. Abraham becomes an example of those who wait on God to pull them through. Because of God's sure promises, Abraham and his wife received the promise. God brought a son from out of Abraham's loins, and Sarah conceived at an advanced age. This lesson serves as a reminder that there is no biological clock with God's promises. God changed Abram's name to Abraham to seal the covenant made with him. It is an encouragement to those who are waiting on God. Lesson three focuses on Moses, another Old Testament figure whom God used without reckoning on his weakness. Moses served his generation, and through him God delivered to humankind the Decalogue (Ten Commandments). The Decalogue formed the basis for ethical and moral living all over the world today. The fourth lesson explores the story of Joshua, Moses' successor. The Lord used him to lead the Israelites to the Promised Land. Like his predecessor, he did not fail God. He challenged his generation to uphold the tenets of God. Joshua vouched, "as for me and my house, we will serve the Lord." We need leaders like Joshua who will stand tall and call this generation back to God.

**Unit II,** *God's Covenant with Judges and Kings,* is a continuation of the former one, but it is more extensive. As the community of the Israelites grew and became more sophisticated, God continued to extend His unfailing love and mercy to them. It does not mean God is catching up with His creatures, but rather, His love continues to cover our spiritual destituteness. Lesson five focuses on seeking deliverance. The chosen people failed to adhere to the terms of the covenant between them and God; as a result, He allowed enemies to plunder them. But each time they realized their follies and repented, God sent judges to deliver them. Lesson six is unusual because in a patriarchal society, women have no roles in public life. But God used Deborah to accomplish a great feat for His glory. God used Deborah as a judge and commander-in-chief to discomfit King Sisera. Through this act of God, we know that God is no respecter of persons and personality. Lesson seven explores a shift in the socio-political landscape of the Israelites. They demanded a king instead of God-appointed judges. Samuel was dissatisfied with their decision. He cried to the Lord all night, yet God allowed them to choose their own king. We will see in this lesson the commissioning of Israel's first king. God's hand was still mighty on them. Lesson eight centers on a promise you can trust. Saul was the first monarch, but he dishonored God. He did not wholly carry out the instruction of God. Lesson nine is on prayer. There are many facets in prayer, but our focus in this lesson is "God answers prayer." Solomon asked for wisdom at the beginning of his reign. God granted his prayer, including blessings of which he did not ask.

**Unit III,** *Living as God's Covenanted People,* has four sessions. The first two lessons highlight the challenge of living in covenant by focusing on the ministry of Elijah and the kingship of Josiah. Elijah demonstrated the power of God in time of apostasy. God answered his prayer by fire. Crises are means through which God wants to see our faith in action. Josiah started to reign at the age of eight. When he read the book of the law he called for a communal renewal. Lesson twelve focuses on making wrong choices. While in exile, the Israelites chose not to praise God. How many Christians have relocated to new places and then refused to take part in God's work? Stubborn and prideful behavior often leads to painful consequences. The final session ends on a word of hope as it examines the restored covenantal relationship that God offered after Judah returned from exile. God displayed His extravagant mercy when He prompted Cyrus to release the people from exile.

You have heard that knowledge is power, but that is only partially true. Applied knowledge is power. It is hoped that you will take these lessons to heart and apply them to your daily living. One common thread in these thirteen lessons is covenant. God remains faithful to every word He has ever uttered. On many occasions, the Israelites violated the covenant, but God relentlessly pursued them with His love and mercy. We, too, are blessed to be under the covenant which Jesus ratified with His blood.

**Lesson 1**

# God's Covenant with Noah

**September 3, 2006**

**ADULT TOPIC:** Finding Security
**YOUTH TOPIC:** God's Promise to Noah
**CHILDREN'S TOPIC:** God Makes a Promise to Noah

**UNIT I**
In Covenant with God

**CHILDREN'S UNIT**
God's First Covenants

**DEVOTIONAL READING:** Psalm 36:5-9
**BACKGROUND SCRIPTURE:** Genesis 9:1-17
**PRINT PASSAGE:** Genesis 9:1-15

### Genesis 9:1-15—KJV

AND GOD blessed Noah and his sons, and said unto them, Be fruitful, and multiply, and replenish the earth.

2 And the fear of you and the dread of you shall be upon every beast of the earth, and upon every fowl of the air, upon all that moveth upon the earth, and upon all the fishes of the sea; into your hand are they delivered.

3 Every moving thing that liveth shall be meat for you; even as the green herb have I given you all things.

4 But flesh with the life thereof, which is the blood thereof, shall ye not eat.

5 And surely your blood of your lives will I require; at the hand of every beast will I require it, and at the hand of man; at the hand of every man's brother will I require the life of man.

6 Whoso sheddeth man's blood, by man shall his blood be shed: for in the image of God made he man.

7 And you, be ye fruitful, and multiply; bring forth abundantly in the earth, and multiply therein.

8 And God spake unto Noah, and to his sons with him, saying,

9 And I, behold, I establish my covenant with you, and with your seed after you;

10 And with every living creature that is with you, of the fowl, of the cattle, and of every beast of the earth with you; from all that go out of the ark, to every beast of the earth.

11 And I will establish my covenant with you; neither shall all flesh be cut off any more by the waters of a flood; neither shall there any more be a flood to destroy the earth.

12 And God said, This is the token of the covenant which I make

## KEY VERSE

I will remember my covenant, which is between me and you and every living creature of all flesh; and the waters shall no more become a flood to destroy all flesh.
—Genesis 9:15

## OBJECTIVES

**Upon completion of this lesson, the students are expected to:**

1. Understand the purpose, blessing, and provisions of the covenant made by God with Noah and his descendants;

2. Recognize that the covenant required unconditional love for God and obedience to God; and,

3. Understand how the rainbow is a divinely-given symbol of the covenant between God and humanity.

between me and you and every living creature that is with you, for perpetual generations:

13 I do set my bow in the cloud, and it shall be for a token of a covenant between me and the earth.

14 And it shall come to pass, when I bring a cloud over the earth, that the bow shall be seen in the cloud:

15 And I will remember my covenant, which is between me and you and every living creature of all flesh; and the waters shall no more become a flood to destroy all flesh.

## UNIFYING LESSON PRINCIPLE

We all long for some sense of security. What can we trust as being sound and secure? God promised all creation never to send another flood, and the rainbow serves as a reminder that God is keeping this promise.

## POINTS TO BE EMPHASIZED ADULTS/YOUTH

**Adult Key Verse:** Genesis 9:15
**Youth Key Verse:** Genesis 9:11
**Print Passage:** Genesis 9:1-15

—God placed a rainbow in the clouds as a reminder of His covenant with Noah.
—God's covenant was a way of blessing Noah and his descendants by giving them a sense of security.
—The whole world benefits from the covenant God made with Noah.

## CHILDREN

**Key Verse:** Genesis 9:11
**Print Passage:** Genesis 9:1-15

—God made a covenant with Noah never again to destroy the earth by a flood.
—God set the rainbow in the sky as a symbol or reminder of His promise.
—God's covenant with Noah signified that the relationship with Noah and all future generations would continue.
—God promised to supply all of Noah's needs.

## TOPICAL OUTLINE OF THE LESSON

I. INTRODUCTION
   A. The Concept of Covenant
   B. Biblical Background

II. EXPOSITION AND APPLICATION OF THE SCRIPTURE
   A. Blessing and Provisions of the Covenant *(Genesis 9:1-7)*
   B. The Covenant Established *(Genesis 9:8-11)*
   C. Covenant Symbolism *(Genesis 9:12-15)*

III. CONCLUDING REFLECTIONS

## I. INTRODUCTION
### A. The Concept of Covenant

We live in a fast-paced world of instant everything. We have fast food, instant oatmeal, on-line college courses, disposable cameras, and no-fault divorce. The trend of the day leans toward the easy and the temporary. However, just because something is quick does not mean it is quality, and because something is easy does not mean it is excellent. Some things simply cannot be done without the processed seasoning of time and longevity in order to operate effectively. How did we develop this attitude of instantaneous gratification, and how do we get beyond it?

This "gotta-have-it-now" attitude combined with "instant" attitudes and expectations, more often than not are a hindrance to the very binding, everlasting nature of covenant. Many in our modern society enter into contract. Covenant, however, tends to run antithetical to our contemporary understanding of commitment in relationship. Today, a binding agreement is generally implemented as a contract. However, a contract is no substitute for a covenant. Consider the differences between the two: a contract very often is built upon distrust; conversely, a covenant is built upon trust. A contract can be breached or voided by mutual consent, but a covenant is permanently binding. A contract depends on human witnesses. A covenant holds God as its witness. Most importantly, a contract is of human origin; a covenant is divine in nature and substance.

In this lesson, we examine God's covenant with Noah, the first such alliance recorded in the Bible. Like every true covenant, this agreement was filled with powerful promises, precious privileges, and real responsibilities. Unlike human covenants, when God makes a promise, that promise is always lasting and true. God's promises serve as an eternal inheritance and, therefore, are still in effect for God's people today.

## B. Biblical Background

What made Noah so special that the God of the universe would make a major covenantal promise with him and his descendants? Noah was the son of Lamech, who chose the name as a reflection of his circumstances: "Out of the ground that the LORD has cursed this one shall bring us relief from our work and from the toil of our hands" (Genesis 5:29). Noah was also the grandson of Methuselah and the great grandson of Enoch. Genesis 6:8-9 records three characteristics about the life of Noah that set him apart from the rest of the wicked and corrupt generation of his time. Noah found favor in the sight of God because:

1. *Noah was a righteous man.* Righteousness indicates an inner characteristic of right standing with God and sincere obedience to God's commandments.
2. *Noah was blameless in his generation.* What a tremendously powerful commentary on the morality and character of this great patriarch of the faith. In contemporary leadership, more leaders like Noah are needed.
3. *Noah walked with God.* This simply means that this man spoke with God, listened to God and acted in a godly fashion in the everyday events and circumstances of life.

Most of us are capable of acting piously during the relatively short amount of time that we are within the walls of the church building. The challenge to live righteously more often comes when we are at home or school, or in the workplace, community, or social settings.

Noah rose to meet this challenge and spent approximately 120 years publicly obeying a command that he had received from God in private. This command must have seemed outrageous and extremely impractical to onlookers: Build an ocean liner-sized vessel in the middle of an arid, desert climate region. Collect two of all animals on earth and load them into the ark. Ignore the derisive jeers and taunts of your neighbors who did not hear what you heard. Then gather enough food to feed all the animals, pack up your family, board the ark, let God shut the door, and wait for the rain.

Hebrews 11:7 records that because of Noah's faith and obedience, he became an heir to the righteousness that is in accordance to faith. This potentially puts us on a similar level with Noah because we all are capable of such obedience to God. Whether or not we will obey is most often a matter of personal choice. God always rewards sacrifice, and Noah's life is evidence of this fact.

The Bible is full of prime examples of individuals being blessed and favored because they have been faithful and obedient. After the waters came and later subsided and the ark was unloaded, Noah built an altar to the Lord and offered a sacrifice to Him. God's reaction to this seems very human. Genesis 8:21 records that "the Lord smelled a sweet savour; and the Lord said…I will not again curse the ground…as I have done." Consequently, God declared that He would never again bring such destruction upon the earth via flood.

## II. Exposition and Application of the Scripture
### A. Blessing and Provisions of the Covenant *(Genesis 9:1-7)*

**AND GOD blessed Noah and his sons, and said unto them, Be fruitful, and multiply, and replenish the earth. And the fear of you and the dread of you shall be upon every beast of the earth, and upon every fowl of the air, upon all that moveth upon the earth, and upon all the fishes of the sea; into your hand are they delivered. Every moving thing that liveth shall be meat for you; even as the green herb have I given you all things. But flesh with the life thereof, which is the blood thereof, shall ye not eat. And surely your blood of your lives will I require; at the hand of every beast will I require it, and at the hand of man; at the hand of every man's brother will I require the life of man. Whoso sheddeth man's blood, by man shall his blood be shed: for in the image of God made he man. And you, be ye fruitful, and multiply; bring forth abundantly in the earth, and multiply therein.**

The initial blessing by God upon Noah was a pronouncement of God-given capacity and potential. God summoned Noah's ability when He said "be fruitful and multiply." This is the same challenge/command given to Adam and Eve in the Garden of Eden. The Jews interpreted this verse as an express command of God to bear children. But tucked inside this command to be physically fruitful is the divine urging to utilize all of our gifts in order to help humanity and ultimately to produce glory for the kingdom of God. The faithful example of Paul demonstrates the human capacity to be fruitful and make an impact upon the world to the glory of God. His example is encouraging to singles and childless couples alike.

Included in God's blessing was protection from animal enemies (verse 2). Verse 3 has been used by some to legitimize the divine authorization of all animals as fair game for consumption. A similar sentiment is reflected in Acts 11:5-10, which pronounces the cleanliness of all God's creation. There is a clause to this allowance of all meat for food. None of the meat is to be eaten along with the blood of the animal. There was a close ancient association of the blood of an animal or person with the life of that animal or person, as is reflected in verses 4-5. When the blood of an animal or an individual was poured out, that animal or individual always died. The more blood spilled meant the less life left. Consequently, to eat meat with the blood of an animal still inside would be like taking on the life/instincts of that animal. Furthermore, only the barbarians and dabblers in the demonic historically embraced such a practice.

Verse 6 is an adaptation of the ancient social stratagem commonly known as "an eye for an eye." It is a scriptural reminder of the important, divine, and precious nature of human life.

## B. The Covenant Established
*(Genesis 9:8-11)*

And God spake unto Noah, and to his sons with him, saying, And I, behold, I establish my covenant with you, and with your seed after you; And with every living creature that is with you, of the **fowl, of the cattle, and of every beast of the earth with you; from all that go out of the ark, to every beast of the earth. And I will establish my covenant with you; neither shall all flesh be cut off any more by the waters of a flood; neither shall there any more be a flood to destroy the earth.**

The Hebrew word used here to convey the concept of covenant is *beriyth (ber-eeth)*. The powerful and pervasive nature of this covenant is demonstrated in the fact that this covenant applies not only to Noah and his family, but also to the descendants for generations after Noah. This is evidence of the fact that families can be impacted by generational blessings as well as by generational curses.

The word *covenant* used here comes from a root word meaning "to select." It carries a connotation of a pact sealed by cutting the flesh. Of course, any cutting of flesh is accompanied by blood. This sense of covenant was demonstrated at ancient Jewish wedding feasts when the bride and groom would go in to consummate the marital covenant and the wedding guests would wait for the groom to show the bloody sheets that had resulted from the pierced hymen of the virgin bride. Although such customs no longer exist in most contemporary cultures, the serious commitment of the marital covenant continues to apply.

In verse 10, God's favor is extended not only to Noah and his family but also to their livestock. To the average contemporary urban individual, this pronouncement of favor upon the birds, cattle, and other animals with Noah's family may not seem terribly significant. However, one must remember that the people of Noah's time were predominantly agriculturalists and herdsmen. Their livelihood primarily stemmed from the produce of a fruitful land and the commerce from a healthy herd. In America, the sense of appreciation for a bountiful harvest is a sentiment reflected in the traditional Thanksgiving celebration, which was initiated by the Pilgrims.

Scriptural promises of blessings extend to all areas of life, as is seen in Deuteronomy 28:3-4: "Blessed shall you be in the city, and blessed shall you be in the field. Blessed shall be the fruit of your womb, the fruit of your ground, and the fruit of your livestock, both the increase of your cattle and the issue of your flock." It is interesting to note that when it comes to obedience, many people want to obey only in the area of so-called spiritual things, such as weekly church attendance, occasional monetary offerings, and avoidance of the "major" sins. But when it comes to blessings from God, we want to experience them in *every* area of our lives, especially the "secular" areas. When we learn to love God unconditionally and to obey Him unconditionally, we will not have to be concerned about when, where, and how much God will bless us. This truth is affirmed by Jesus in His admonishment to seek first the kingdom of God and God's righteousness (Matthew 6:33). Faithfulness is a characteristic that is inextricably connected to the divine DNA of God. Whatever is fair and whatever is right, God will pay.

## C. Covenant Symbolism *(Genesis 9:12-15)*

**And God said, This is the token of the covenant which I make between me and you and every living creature that is with you, for perpetual generations: I do set my bow in the cloud, and it shall be for a token of a covenant between me and the earth. And it shall come to pass, when I bring a cloud over the earth, that the bow shall be seen in the cloud: And I will remember my covenant, which is between me and you and every living creature of all flesh; and the waters shall no more become a flood to destroy all flesh.**

It was not enough for God to extend a verbal promise of provision for Noah and his descendants. In order to emphasize the importance and significance of this blessing, God provided the rainbow, a beautiful and unique symbol of His promise to never again destroy the earth by means of a flood. One may wonder why it was necessary to provide a symbol when Noah had already received God's Word on the matter. Symbols play an important role in the interaction between God and God's people throughout the entire biblical record. Old Testament sign types included identifying marks, declarations, warnings, proof of assurance, and object lessons. The Sabbath itself was established as a weekly reminder of God's day of rest and of humanity's need to rest. In the New Testament, the ordinance of Holy Communion is a symbolic reminder of the broken body and shed blood of Jesus Christ.

In the covenant of holy matrimony, wedding rings are exchanged as a symbol of the mutual vows shared and permanent promises made between the couple. Wedding rings are usually constructed of durable material such as silver, gold, or platinum, all of which are congruent with the expectation of a long-lasting marital relationship. The daily wearing of these rings serves as a visual and constant reminder to the wearers as well as to other parties that the person has made a permanent promise that is not to be broken.

In the fall of 2005, Hurricane Katrina rocked New Orleans and the Gulf Coast region of the United States. In its wake, the storm left behind destroyed properties, broken levees, and thousands of residents stranded on rooftops due to the massive flood conditions. Perhaps individuals who were directly or indirectly affected by this tragedy may have raised the questions: "What about the rainbow? What happened to God's promise of never destroying the earth by flooding again?" A closer look at the pledge made to Noah will reveal God's provision that *the entire earth* would never again be destroyed by water. One cannot truthfully conclude that every natural calamity is brought about by God in order to make a statement. However, God reserves the right to utilize the movement of the elements at any time in order to secure our attention for a message that needs to be delivered.

## III. Concluding Reflections

One of the most important characteristics of almighty God is that of absolute trustworthiness. Trust is a foundational building block for any functional and quality human relationship. Why is trust so seminal and germane to a divine or human relationship? Trust enables effective communication and distrust deactivates communication. Strong, durable relationships are not formed overnight but require time and experience in order to become seasoned and able to withstand the inevitable storms that accompany any long-term relationship. Developing trust is a primary reason for advertising. Every product wants consumers to trust its product claims. Advertisers boldly proclaim their track record in business, often using terms like "a name you can trust." The false claims of advertisers, politicians, and others have caused many in contemporary society to mistrust what they cannot see and be suspicious of what they do see. If we doubt the words that someone is speaking, a quality relationship can never be established and cultivated.

Noah trusted God, as demonstrated by his obedience in building the ark. There must have been taunting and ridicule as Noah worked on his project, but he kept his focus on the call of God. Similarly, when God calls us to a task today, it may not make sense to others.

The prophet Jeremiah proclaims, "Blessed are those who trust in the Lord, whose trust is the Lord" (Jeremiah 17:17). Those of us who put our trust in Him will not be left without hope—defenseless and insecure. In this we can trust and depend.

## WORD POWER

**Remember (Hebrew: *zakar*)**—this means "to put a landmark that must not be removed; to be mindful perpetually." In essence, God is saying that "I will constantly and perpetually call to mind My covenant." There is no memory lapse with God. To remember is to follow with action (see Genesis 8:1; 9:15).

## HOME DAILY BIBLE READINGS

for the week of September 3, 2006
*God's Covenant with Noah*
Aug. 28, Monday
　—Psalm 36:5-9
　—God Is Gracious
Aug. 29, Tuesday
　—Genesis 7:1-12
　—Noah Enters the Ark
Aug. 30, Wednesday
　—Genesis 7:13-24
　—The Flood Rages
Aug. 31, Thursday
　—Genesis 8:1-12
　—The Water Subsides
Sept. 1, Friday
　—Genesis 8:13-22
　—God Makes a Promise
Sept. 2, Saturday
　—Genesis 9:1-7
　—God Instructs Noah
Sept. 3, Sunday
　—Genesis 9:8-17
　—God Covenants with Noah

## PRAYER

*Lord, we thank You for Your holy Word that reminds us of Your covenantal relationship with us. In Jesus' name, we pray. Amen.*

**September 10, 2006**

**UNIT I**
In Covenant with God

**CHILDREN'S UNIT**
God's First Covenants

## KEY VERSE 💡

Neither shall thy name any more be called Abram, but thy name shall be Abraham; for a father of many nations have I made thee.—Genesis 17:5

## OBJECTIVES

Upon completion of this lesson, the students are expected to:
1. Explore the meaning of trusting in God's promises;
2. Recognize that when God makes a promise He will keep His promise; and,
3. Understand that what is impossible with humanity is possible with God.

Lesson 2

# God's Covenant with Abram

**ADULT TOPIC:** Trusting Promises
**YOUTH TOPIC:** God's Promise to Abram
**CHILDREN'S TOPIC:** God Makes a Promise to Abram

**DEVOTIONAL READING:** Hebrews 6:13-20
**BACKGROUND SCRIPTURE:** Genesis 17
**PRINT PASSAGE:** Genesis 17:1-8, 15-22

### Genesis 17:1-8, 15-22—KJV

AND WHEN Abram was ninety years old and nine, the LORD appeared to Abram, and said unto him, I am the Almighty God; walk before me, and be thou perfect.

2 And I will make my covenant between me and thee, and will multiply thee exceedingly.

3 And Abram fell on his face: and God talked with him, saying,

4 As for me, behold, my covenant is with thee, and thou shalt be a father of many nations.

5 Neither shall thy name any more be called Abram, but thy name shall be Abraham; for a father of many nations have I made thee.

6 And I will make thee exceeding fruitful, and I will make nations of thee, and kings shall come out of thee.

7 And I will establish my covenant between me and thee and thy seed after thee in their generations for an everlasting covenant, to be a God unto thee, and to thy seed after thee.

8 And I will give unto thee, and to thy seed after thee, the land wherein thou art a stranger, all the land of Canaan, for an everlasting possession; and I will be their God.

.....

15 And God said unto Abraham, As for Sarai thy wife, thou shalt not call her name Sarai, but Sarah shall her name be.

16 And I will bless her, and give thee a son also of her: yea, I will bless her, and she shall be a mother of nations; kings of people shall be of her.

17 Then Abraham fell upon his face, and laughed, and said in his heart, Shall a child be born unto him that is an hundred years old? and shall Sarah, that is ninety years old, bear?

18 And Abraham said unto God, O that Ishmael might live before thee!

19 And God said, Sarah thy wife shall bear thee a son indeed; and thou shalt call his name Isaac: and I will establish my covenant with him for an everlasting covenant, and with his seed after him.

20 And as for Ishmael, I have heard thee: Behold, I have blessed him, and will make him fruitful, and will multiply him exceedingly; twelve princes shall he beget, and I will make him a great nation.

21 But my covenant will I establish with Isaac, which Sarah shall bear unto thee at this set time in the next year.

22 And he left off talking with him, and God went up from Abraham.

## UNIFYING LESSON PRINCIPLE

It is difficult to trust a promise that runs counter to our experience and our logic. What promises can we trust? God promised to give Abraham descendants and land, and these promises came true despite Abraham's doubts.

## POINTS TO BE EMPHASIZED ADULTS/YOUTH

**Adult Key Verse:** Genesis 17:5
**Youth Key Verse:** Genesis 17:7
**Print Passage:** Genesis 17:1-8, 15-22

—God makes and keeps His promises, no matter how insurmountable the obstacles may appear.
—God changed Abram's name to Abraham, who was both fearful and faithful when he learned of God's promise.
—God's promise to Abraham was a life-changing commitment; nothing would ever be the same for him.
—God's promise affected not only Abraham, but also his descendants to the end of time.

## CHILDREN
**Key Verse:** Genesis 17:4
**Print Passage:** Genesis 17:1-8, 15-22

—God chose Abram for a special purpose.
—Abram's response to God's covenant was obedience.
—As part of the covenant, God set very specific requirements for Abram to fulfill.
—Like Abram, God's requirements may be difficult to understand; yet, we must be obedient.

## TOPICAL OUTLINE OF THE LESSON

I. INTRODUCTION
   A. Do It the Right Way
   B. Biblical Background
II. EXPOSITION AND APPLICATION OF THE SCRIPTURE
   A. God's Challenges and Blessings *(Genesis 17:1-4)*
   B. God Will Change Your Name *(Genesis 17:5)*
   C. God Will Honor the Covenant *(Genesis 17:6-8)*
   D. Things Impossible with People Are Possible with God *(Genesis 17:15-17)*
   E. Never Presume God's Pathway to Prosperity *(Genesis 17:18-19)*
   F. God's Perfect Will Prevails *(Genesis 17:20-22)*
III. CONCLUDING REFLECTIONS

# I. Introduction
## A. Do It the Right Way

Has someone close to you ever made you a promise, but you were not quite sure that the person making the promise had the wherewithal to back up his or her verbal generosity with realistic action? What may happen in such situations is that the person who received the promise begins to look for other ways to make his or her desire a reality. This is especially true if too much time passes between the time that the promise was extended and the realization of the promise.

There is no right way to do wrong. Even when one's intentions are good, a negative and dishonorable means does not justify a positive and honorable end. If Abram were here, he would be able to provide firsthand testimony to the fact that it is ultimately better to do things God's way because God's way is the best.

Another appropriate lesson we will see in the life of Abram is that we cannot hurry God. We just have to wait for the promise to manifest itself. When that happens, it will eventually be apparent to all that God has moved and that God's will has been accomplished. The absolute best way to build our lives is from the quality materials of trust, hope, and reliance upon the perfect will of God. When our house is built this way, we don't have to fear the storms of life because we know that our house will stand.

## B. Biblical Background

In order to properly understand the promise given to Abram we must rewind the scene to several instances in Abram's life in which blessings and favor were conferred upon him. In Genesis 12, God promised to develop a great nation through the lineage of Abram and Sarai. Abram was blessed by the Priest/King Melchizedek who declared (Genesis 14:19), "Blessed be Abram by God Most High, maker of heaven and earth…." Then in Genesis 15:1, this word of the Lord came to Abram through a vision: "Do not be afraid, Abram, I am your shield; your reward shall be very great." In spite of all the blessings and promises surrounding Abram's life, he remained without a child from his wife Sarai, who was extremely beautiful. Abram obviously realized this because prior to them going into Egypt, Abram asked her to pretend to be his sister rather than his wife so that no one would kill him out of covetousness. Although Sarai was extremely beautiful, she was also extremely barren.

The culture and mentality of Abram's time period were very different from today's norm. During Abram's time, bearing children was a badge of honor that superceded a woman's physical loveliness. When Abram and Sarai did not see the promise of God coming into fruition on their timetable, they attempted to "jump start" God's blessings and promises by having a son through Sarai's maid, Hagar. Whenever we attempt to bypass God's methods in pursuit of God's blessings, we end up disappointed.

# II. Exposition and Application of the Scripture
## A. God's Challenges and Blessings
*(Genesis 17:1-4)*

**And when Abram was ninety years old and nine, the Lord appeared to Abram, and said unto him, I am the Almighty God; walk before**

me, and be thou perfect. And I will make my covenant between me and thee, and will multiply thee exceedingly. And Abram fell on his face: and God talked with him, saying, As for me, behold, my covenant is with thee, and thou shalt be a father of many nations.

Genesis 17 opens with a tremendous command/challenge for the life of Abram. After verifying God's identity to Abram, God presents an overwhelming challenge for this faithful patriarch. This challenge would intimidate the average person: "Walk before me and be blameless." How would you react if God commanded you? Would you complain about the harshness of such a lofty command, or would you accept the challenge and plunge in wholeheartedly with the help of God? In the *King James Version* of the Bible, the Hebrew phrase used here is translated as "be perfect." The word *tamiym* (pronounced taw-meem), which literally refers to "integrity" or "truth," characterizes a life that is without blemish, complete, full, sincere, sound, spotless, undefiled, upright, and whole.

Along with the challenge/command extended to Abram, God also extended a powerful promise: a divine covenant with a provision for innumerable descendants. The culture of that day equated numerous descendents with great honor and prosperity. Other Old Testament Scriptures, such as Psalm 127:3, 5, reflect this notion: "Sons are indeed a heritage from the Lord, the fruit of the womb a reward…Happy is the man who has his quiver full of them."

When Abram heard the word that he would be the ancestor of a multitude of nations, he fell on his face in reaction to God's revelation. This was a common reflex action that indicated Abram's absolute awe and profound humility in response to the outpouring of favor God conferred upon him. It was simply an extension of the practice of "bowing," which is still prevalent in many non-western nations.

### B. God Will Change Your Name
*(Genesis 17:5)*

**Neither shall thy name any more be called Abram, but thy name shall be Abraham; for a father of many nations have I made thee.**

In Old Testament times, a person's name held more meaning than it does today. Contemporary names are commonly given not because they mean something significant, but simply because they have a phonetically interesting sound or a unique spelling. This practice differs from the ancient practice of giving names based upon the projected character of the child or a name given by God to direct one's destiny. When a name is changed in the Scripture, it is an indication of a significant alteration in one's spiritual direction. A familiar New Testament example of a name change is Saul's name change to Paul, though the transition is largely viewed by scholars as a Roman accommodation.

The names Abram and Abraham are quite similar in meaning. According to the *Holman Bible Dictionary,* Abram means "father is exalted," while Abraham means "father of a multitude" (Trent Butler, editor. Nashville: Broadman and Holman, 1991). Perhaps the longer adaptation of this name form is reflective of Abram's addition of descendents—evidence of the sure fulfillment of the patriarch's purpose. From the day that Abram's name was changed to Abraham, any time Sarai and others called out to him, Abraham must have been reminded of

God's promise and covenant, in spite of all circumstances.

## C. God Will Honor the Covenant
   *(Genesis 17:6-8)*

**And I will make thee exceeding fruitful, and I will make nations of thee, and kings shall come out of thee. And I will establish my covenant between me and thee and thy seed after thee in their generations for an everlasting covenant, to be a God unto thee, and to thy seed after thee. And I will give unto thee, and to thy seed after thee, the land wherein thou art a stranger, all the land of Canaan, for an everlasting possession; and I will be their God.**

Several different facets of God's covenant with Abraham are evident throughout this discourse. This covenant was initiated by God and thus can only be fulfilled by God. In the Hebrew mind, a relationship with God was much more objective than this society's subjective personal faith in God. The Hebrew mind and heart is centered on God, and they believed that God is limitless; however, a human being's life is short.

A covenant with God outweighs all other covenants or binding agreements. Any other covenant that exists must be understood, influenced, and executed in concert and in congruence with God's divine covenant. For example, God's divine covenant should make a difference in how one executes a business partnership. This means that because one is a follower of God, his or her business practices will be honest in spite of the fact that more financial profit could potentially be made through dishonest means. God's covenant with Abraham affected and influenced not only him, but also virtually everything Abraham touched for generation upon generation.

## D. Things Impossible with People Are Possible with God *(Genesis 17:15-17)*

**And God said unto Abraham, As for Sarai thy wife, thou shalt not call her name Sarai, but Sarah shall her name be. And I will bless her, and give thee a son also of her: yea, I will bless her, and she shall be a mother of nations; kings of people shall be of her. Then Abraham fell upon his face, and laughed, and said in his heart, Shall a child be born unto him that is an hundred years old? and shall Sarah, that is ninety years old, bear?**

Just as Abram's name change reflected a change in life direction, so did Sarai's name change to Sarah. Like Abraham, the change is grammatically slight, but spiritually huge. Just as it was an honor for a man to have a son, so it was a signal honor for a woman to bear a son for her husband. This honor was many times magnified due to Sarai's advanced age and lifelong barrenness. The fulfillment of God's promise in their lives signaled a turning point from which there was no return. At a stage of life when most people are preparing for the end of life, Abraham and Sarah were preparing for a new life.

When God revealed his incredible plans, Abraham repeated the same physical response he gave in verse 3: he fell on his face. But this time, instead of falling on his face in awe and reverence, he fell on his face in laughter. It may seem hard to imagine that one would actually fall on the floor laughing upon hearing a promise from God, but from a human perspective, Abraham's amusement is understandable. Even in our age of technological advancements, it is difficult to imagine a 90-year-old woman giving birth to a child fathered by a 100-year-old man. Perhaps Abraham's laughter was prompted by incredulity rather than doubt.

Nevertheless, Abraham was depending upon his flesh to understand God's plans. He was demonstrating the very unfaithful exercise of attempting to place God in a box. Too many believers spend their time engaged in trying to shrink God down rather than taking on the greater spiritual challenge of enlarging our vision to see what great things God has in store for us.

### E. Never Presume God's Pathway to Prosperity *(Genesis 17:18-19)*

**And Abraham said unto God, O that Ishmael might live before thee! And God said, Sarah thy wife shall bear thee a son indeed; and thou shalt call his name Isaac: and I will establish my covenant with him for an everlasting covenant, and with his seed after him.**

Surely in his most reasonable tone of voice, Abraham offered God a more practical suggestion for producing descendants. Since Ishmael was already on the scene, he was a good candidate for God to use. Although this plan seemed right, it was not a part of God's perfect plan (Proverbs 16:25). The successful walk of faith calls for us to leave open every possibility for God to move. Abraham doubted the idea that Sarah would conceive. By doubting God, we sometimes closed the door on the possibility for God to act according to His promise. It is important for believers to trust God completely to bring to pass His perfect will. While Abraham's doubt is certainly understandable from a human perspective, as believers we are called to trust in the Lord rather than to rely upon our own understanding (Proverbs 3:5). God's ability far exceeds the human capacity for understanding.

### F. God's Perfect Will Prevails *(Genesis 17:20-22)*

**And as for Ishmael, I have heard thee: Behold, I have blessed him, and will make him fruitful, and will multiply him exceedingly; twelve princes shall he beget, and I will make him a great nation. But my covenant will I establish with Isaac, which Sarah shall bear unto thee at this set time in the next year. And he left off talking with him, and God went up from Abraham.**

In verse 20, God responded to the suggestion made by Abraham regarding Ishmael. The four short words uttered by God are simple but powerful. When God verified that Abraham had been heard, Abraham should have been able to rest in faith and confidence that whatever needed to be done would be accomplished. God's assurance that Ishmael would not be forgotten is proof of the fact that even when we do things that fall short of God's perfect will, God is able to take those less-than-perfect circumstances and turn them into something good. Abraham and Sarah had stepped outside of God's will and involved Hagar in producing an heir from Abraham's seed. God then took this mistake and turned it into a blessing. God's ability to redeem our mistakes when we trust Him should make every child of God glad. Having this assurance should also enable us to boldly step out on faith and not be afraid to attempt great things for God.

The following question is one that commonly appears in motivational literature: "If you had a 100 percent guarantee of success, what feat would you attempt?" This question fits neatly into the biblical concept of divine intervention. When we walk in the will of God, we are guaranteed spiritual success. Even when we miss the will of God, there is a plan in place to incorporate our misses into the grand scheme of life in order to turn something that was negative into something that is positive. Verses 20-21 compare and contrast the difference between a blessing and a covenant. The blessing conferred upon Ishmael in verse 20 was a courtesy extended by God based upon a request from a righteous man. But the covenant conferred upon Abraham was not a response to a request; rather, it was an action initiated by a holy God in relationship with a righteous man.

### III. CONCLUDING REFLECTIONS

God is a covenant-making and a covenant-keeping God. This deep concern with the creation and continuation of covenants is rooted in God's constant yearning for a sincere and lasting relationship with humanity. If there had to be just one characteristic to reflect the inner nature of God, surely that characteristic would be love. Not only does God *have* love and *give* love, God literally *is* love. Consequently, the only way for humanity to experience genuine love is to do so through the auspices of divine love—or *agape*. As we rely on God to help us understand our relationships and our responsibilities in maintaining them, we will then be able to develop covenantal relationships within our marriages, families, churches, and friendships that will bring honor and glory to God.

### WORD POWER

**Anymore** *(owd: ode)*—is translated "anymore." It means "from now on, all life long, hence forth." God puts a perpetual ban on the first name (Abram). A new name, Abraham, is a covenantal name. God would ensure that this new name will be remembered in all generations.

### HOME DAILY BIBLE READINGS

for the week of September 10, 2006
*God's Covenant with Abram*

Sept. 4, Monday
—Hebrews 6:13-20
—God's Promise Is Sure
Sept. 5, Tuesday
—Hebrews 11:8-16
—Abraham Had Heroic Faith
Sept. 6, Wednesday
—Genesis 15:1-8
—God's Promise to Abram
Sept. 7, Thursday
—Genesis 15:12-21
—God Foretells Future Greatness
Sept. 8, Friday
—Genesis 16:1-15
—God Blesses Hagar
Sept. 9, Saturday
—Genesis 17:1-8
—God Covenants with Abraham
Sept. 10, Sunday
—Genesis 17:15-22
—God Promises a Son

### PRAYER

*Thank You for being a God who never fails but who makes good on all Your promises. In Jesus' name, we pray. Amen.*

# Lesson 3

# God's Covenant with Israel

**ADULT TOPIC:** Being Mutually Responsible
**YOUTH TOPIC:** God's Promise to Israel
**CHILDREN'S TOPIC:** The People Promise to Obey God

**September 17, 2006**

**UNIT I**
In Covenant with God

**CHILDREN'S UNIT**
God's First Covenants

**DEVOTIONAL READING:** Psalm 119:33-40
**BACKGROUND SCRIPTURE:** Exodus 19:1-6; 24:3-8
**PRINT PASSAGE:** Exodus 19:1-6; 24:3-8

### Exodus 19:1-6; 24:3-8—KJV

IN THE third month, when the children of Israel were gone forth out of the land of Egypt, the same day came they into the wilderness of Sinai.

2 For they were departed from Rephidim, and were come to the desert of Sinai, and had pitched in the wilderness; and there Israel camped before the mount.

3 And Moses went up unto God, and the LORD called unto him out of the mountain, saying, Thus shalt thou say to the house of Jacob, and tell the children of Israel;

4 Ye have seen what I did unto the Egyptians, and how I bare you on eagles' wings, and brought you unto myself.

5 Now therefore, if ye will obey my voice indeed, and keep my covenant, then ye shall be a peculiar treasure unto me above all people: for all the earth is mine:

6 And ye shall be unto me a kingdom of priests, and an holy nation. These are the words which thou shalt speak unto the children of Israel.

.....

3 And Moses came and told the people all the words of the LORD, and all the judgments: and all the people answered with one voice, and said, All the words which the LORD hath said will we do.

4 And Moses wrote all the words of the LORD, and rose up early in the morning, and builded an altar under the hill, and twelve pillars, according to the twelve tribes of Israel.

5 And he sent young men of the children of Israel, which offered burnt offerings, and sacrificed peace offerings of oxen unto the LORD.

**KEY VERSE**

Moses came and told the people all the words of the LORD, and all the judgments: and all the people answered with one voice, and said, All the words which the LORD hath said will we do.—Exodus 24:3

## OBJECTIVES

**Upon completion of this lesson, the students are expected to:**

1. Recognize that a relationship of commitment with God is dependent upon obedience to God;
2. Understand that God has always worked through a leader or nation to accomplish His purposes on earth; and,
3. Recognize the importance of making a commitment to obey God without reservations.

6 And Moses took half of the blood, and put it in basons; and half of the blood he sprinkled on the altar.

7 And he took the book of the covenant, and read in the audience of the people: and they said, All that the LORD hath said will we do, and be obedient.

8 And Moses took the blood, and sprinkled it on the people, and said, Behold the blood of the covenant, which the LORD hath made with you concerning all these words.

## UNIFYING LESSON PRINCIPLE

Healthy, successful relationships depend on mutual commitment and responsibility. What does it mean to bear mutual responsibility for one another? God's promise in this text called for commitment and respect on both sides: If the people would honor God through obedience, God would treasure the people and set them apart.

## POINTS TO BE EMPHASIZED
## ADULTS/ YOUTH

**Adult Key Verse:** Exodus 24:3
**Youth Key Verses:** Exodus 19:5b-6
**Print Passage:** Exodus 19:1-6; 24:3-8
—The Israelites were to be set apart as God's priestly kingdom.
—The people accepted the words of the covenant and promised to obey them.
—What is the relationship between God's covenant and God's law?
—The Lord, Moses, and the people formally enter into a covenantal relationship.

## CHILDREN

**Key Verse:** Exodus 24:3
**Print Passage:** Exodus 19:1-6; 24:3-4, 7, 12, 15-18
—Israel was chosen by God to become a holy nation.

—Moses served as God's instrument in leading the Israelites to commit themselves to God's covenant.
—God's people need to be reminded of past blessings in their lives.
—Moses recorded the words of the covenant.

## TOPICAL OUTLINE OF THE LESSON

I. INTRODUCTION
  A. The Basis of True Relationship
  B. Biblical Background

II. EXPOSITION AND APPLICATION OF THE SCRIPTURE
  A. The Pilgrimage to Mt. Sinai
    (Exodus 19:1-2)
  B. Provisions of the Covenant
    (Exodus 19:3-6)
  C. Reactions to the Covenant
    (Exodus 24:3-4a)
  D. Symbolic Offering
    (Exodus 24:4b-5)
  E. Components of the Covenant
    (Exodus 24:6-8)

III. CONCLUDING REFLECTIONS

## I. INTRODUCTION
### A. The Basis of True Relationship

Commitment is the cement that bonds real relationships between people. Without commitment, a relationship is only as good as the promises made in the moment. Quality relationships bloom best when planted in the fertile soil of agreements made, promises kept, and trust that is mutually embraced. Temporary relationships may initially appear to be more exciting, but it is those bonds that have hardened over time that are most useful in supporting the weight of heavy-duty relationships.

Many of the principles that are effective in relationships between people are also traceable to the life link between God and humanity. The reason that God created people was because God desired a relationship with His creation. Trees, mountains, and animals were inadequate candidates for mutual love and trust to be developed. Only men and women were created in the image of God and, thus, unlike plants or animals, people possess a piece of God and are able to respond to the love that God exudes. Most essentially, humanity was created with a spirit, a soul, and a rational mind capable of choosing to obey or not to obey. When we choose to obey God, we give pleasure to God like an obedient child gives a parent. When we choose to disobey God, we bring sorrow to the heart of God.

## B. Biblical Background

Without a doubt, the central event recorded in the book of Exodus is the occurrence that gives the book its name. When Moses led the mass exodus from the slavery and injustice suffered in Egypt, this was the beginning of the promise between God and the children of Israel. Promises were made at the beginning, in the middle portion, and during the culmination of this epic journey. The crown jewel event during this historic passage was the crossing of the Red Sea and the drowning of Pharaoh's army. This divine intervention on the part of God emblazoned upon the collective psyche of the people. They were the chosen people of a passionate God who was willing to go to great lengths to protect and provide for a people with whom God was in covenantal partnership. This grand-scale demonstration of God's love struck fear in the hearts of Israel's enemies and solidified their widespread reputation as a people to be feared because of the God they served. Interestingly, Israel herself had to be constantly reminded of the power of God and of the covenant made between them and God, even though they had been eyewitnesses to the great movement of God.

Another major sequence of events within the book of Exodus is the giving and receiving of the Ten Commandments. The covenant made through Moses is represented by a written record of God's love and boundaries for God's people. Even though most of the commandments are expressed with negative phrasing ("Thou shalt not..."), these commandments were not written to place people in bondage. Rather, they were designed to avail Israel of the best life possible. The three major areas addressed by these commandments are the relationship with God, the relationship with self, and the relationship with others. The first commandment summarizes this perspective through basically exhorting the Israelites to love God, love self, and love others.

In the New Testament, this concept is echoed in Matthew 6:33, when Jesus directs His disciples to first seek God's kingdom and God's righteousness; everything else will be added to this central priority. Jesus verbalized this assurance in response to the disciples' inquiry about life's basic provisions, such as food and drink. Jesus was constantly seeking to raise the priority level of His followers. The central message was a covenantal proposal requiring a great deal of faith and trust: "If you trust Me with your life, I will provide whatever you need." Further, in Matthew 22-36-39, Jesus amplifies the commandment that is most important to obey. In John 13:34, Jesus added a new commandment: "Love one another." The disciples' blueprint for loving each other was the example set by Jesus Himself: the willingness to lay down one's very life for a friend. Even beyond this extreme demonstration of commitment, God demonstrated His love toward us in that while sin prevailed in the lives of humanity, Christ willingly died on our behalf (see Romans 5:8).

## II. Exposition and Application of the Scripture
### A. The Pilgrimage to Mt. Sinai
*(Exodus 19:1-2)*

In the third month, when the children of Israel were gone forth out of the land of Egypt, the same day came they into the wilderness of Sinai. For they were departed from Rephidim, and were come to the desert of Sinai, and had pitched in the wilderness; and there Israel camped before the mount.

Mount Sinai holds an important place as a geological structure within biblical history and Israelite heritage. God would make many significant revelations of Himself and His purposes to Israel there. While historians disagree on its precise location, Mount Sinai is located in the south central part of a peninsula in the northwestern end of Arabia. The exact meaning of the name is unclear; but it probably means "shining" and was likely derived from the word *sin*, a Babylonian moon god. In the third month after leaving Egypt, the mass of Hebrews descended upon the *desert of sin* and made camp in front of the mountain. The Desert of Sin is a barren region somewhere west of the Sinai plateau on the Sinai Peninsula and may have been named from the "glare" of its white chalk. In due time, at Sinai the glory of the Lord would shine "like devouring fire on the top of the mount in the eyes of the children of Israel" (Exodus 24:17).

Just prior to arriving at Sinai, the Israelites had camped at Rephidim where there was no water and the people grumbled against Moses. This was the same spot where the Israelites had battled with the Amalakites and the two attendants (Aaron and Hur) held up Moses' hands all day in order for the Israelites to be victorious in the battle.

### B. Provisions of the Covenant
*(Exodus 19:3-6)*

And Moses went up unto God, and the Lord called unto him out of the mountain, saying, Thus shalt thou say to the house of Jacob, and tell the children of Israel; Ye have seen what I did unto the Egyptians, and how I bare you on eagles' wings, and brought you unto myself. Now therefore, if ye will obey my voice indeed, and keep my covenant, then ye shall be a peculiar treasure unto me above all people: for all the earth is mine: And ye shall be unto me a kingdom of priests, and an holy nation. These are the words which thou shalt speak unto the children of Israel.

Moses had the distinct privilege of having had a message dictated to him directly from God. From the mountain, God gave Moses a message directed to the offspring of Jacob. Later called Israel (Genesis 32:28), Jacob was the father of the twelve tribes. As God delivered the message to Moses on Mount Sinai, the power of memory is invoked. Whenever a leader seeks to motivate a large group of people, it is important for the people to be reminded of past victories in order to prepare them for the future. God's deliverance of the people through the Red Sea was certainly a high watermark in Israelite history.

Personal and corporate obedience is a central and significant characteristic in the effective functioning of the covenant. The kind of obedience desired by God has never been, and will never be, a partial type of obedience. True obedience to God should be full and wholehearted. In the sight of almighty God, partial obedience is considered disobedience. Successful obedience requires a commitment to discipline because conforming to the dictates of God can often run counter to the desires of the flesh. Many times we may be faced with a situation that could either please God or please self. When we choose to please God through our obedience He takes notice, the results of which may include spiritual blessings, material blessings, or both. When we choose to be obedient in crucial situations that tempt us to do otherwise, God recognizes and rewards this choice. In the case of the Israelites, the consequence of keeping the covenant was special status in the sight of God among all other nations.

Why did God choose to give favored status to the Israelites? Does God's choice of Israel mean that God loves other nations and peoples less? The Bible affirms that God has generally worked through one leader, one tribe, or one nation to accomplish God's purposes on earth. God's choices throughout biblical and contemporary history have not always been popular with humanity, to be sure. God does not always stipulate the specific reason for selecting certain people and groups for specific tasks. However, we can rest assured that even though God chose Israel as the initial vehicle for the dissemination of divine truth, God extends the same depth of love to all people in all places. God is an equal-opportunity Deity who has made provision for anyone willing to be adopted into the family as heirs and joint-heirs of the promise (see Romans 8:14-17).

## C. Reactions to the Covenant
*(Exodus 24:3-4a)*

**And Moses came and told the people all the words of the Lord, and all the judgments: and all the people answered with one voice, and said, All the words which the Lord hath said will we do. And Moses wrote all the words of the Lord, and rose up early in the morning, and builded an altar under the hill.**

*Decision to Do the Word*—The people gave a unanimous affirmative response to the covenant issued by God and communicated by God's mouthpiece, Moses. Historically, whenever the people of God unify in agreement over a particular directive from God, great things are capable of happening. Unity within the faith community is essential for experiencing maximum spiritual effectiveness. God waits for a positive response to the extended covenant. Not only did the people decide to obey God's Word, they decided to obey *all* that God had spoken. This additional dynamic illuminates the degree of determination within the hearts and minds of the people to completely comply with the covenant communicated by God.

*Decision to Write the Word*—Moses had been trained in the household of an Egyptian king through his adoption by Pharaoh's daughter. Undoubtedly, this privileged life exposed him to formal training and education due any royal relative or immediate family member. The Egyptian culture strongly embraced the practice of preserving history. This is evident from the many archeological discoveries—everything from mummified kings to important life events written in Egyptian hieroglyphics. Moses immediately decided to preserve the words of God through writing. The Bible itself goes to great lengths to emphasize that its writers were only serving as scribes and that almighty God is the primary source for the divine revelation contained therein (1 Peter 1:21). The natural and logical extension of this concept is that even today—whenever God speaks a word of revelation or inspiration—that thought, idea, or vision should be captured on paper or computer and in our hearts. Since the divine revelation of God has not ceased, then neither should the human preservation of that message—for as long as God speaks, we must continue to write the vision and to make it plain so that those in the future may still benefit from the revelation of the past (see Habakkuk 2:2).

### D. Symbolic Offering *(Exodus 24:4b-5)*

**And twelve pillars, according to the twelve tribes of Israel. And he sent young men of the children of Israel, which offered burnt offerings, and sacrificed peace offerings of oxen unto the Lord.**

A major component of the Old Testament worship concept and practice involved the offering of sacrifices. Worship was simply incomplete until some type of sacrificial offering had been made (Leviticus 1-7). Types of offerings included drink offering, vegetable offering, animal offering, trespass offering, peace offering, sin offering, and the free will offering. The latter was offered not in gratitude for specific blessings, but as an expression of one's overwhelming love for God (Leviticus 3). In the case of the animal sacrifice, the blood was sometimes sprinkled on the altar, poured out at the base of the altar, applied to the person sacrificing, sprinkled before the veil of the sanctuary or even taken into the Holy of Holies (Leviticus 16:14). Sometimes, the person sacrificing would slay the animal; at other times, the priest would perform this task. Blood sacrifice was a significant part of Old Testament worship and was an important component of the pilgrimage of God's people.

### E. Components of the Covenant *(Exodus 24:6-8)*

**And Moses took half of the blood, and put it in basons; and half of the blood he sprinkled on the altar. And he took the book of the covenant, and read in the audience of the people: and they said, All that the Lord hath said will we do, and be obedient. And Moses took the blood, and sprinkled it on the people, and said, Behold the blood of the covenant, which the Lord hath made with you concerning all these words.**

The components of the covenant included the blood in the basins and on the altar, the Book of the Covenant, and the blood on the people. In the Old Testament, blood is a symbol of the grace of God in the life of humanity. The blood in the basins and on the altar is linked to a sense of sacrificial cleansing and consecration. The death of the animal is symbolically associated with a substitutionary atonement on behalf of the one offering the sacrifice. The presence of the blood creates a sense of unity and fellowship between the people and the altar. This same blood from an animal that was sprinkled on the altar, as well as on the people, served as a tangible and visual metaphor of connectivity that existed between a holy God and sinful humanity. When burnt offerings were conducted, the fire from the altar *consumed* the part of the animal that was placed there. In like manner, the rest of the meat was consumed by the one sacrificing in the form of a fellowship meal.

## III. Concluding Reflections

Obviously, the level of respect and responsibility attributed to the fatherhood role was much greater in Moses' era than in current times. The father was remembered and referred to for many generations. This was especially true when the father served with honor and left a spiritual legacy for his children to remember. Fathers have the privilege and responsibility to leave a financial and spiritual legacy for their children.

A good man leaves a heritage and an inheritance for his children and for his children's children (Proverbs 13:22). Today's fathers may or may not leave an impressive financial legacy to their offspring, but all fathers can learn to develop and extend a legacy of faith. This kind of legacy costs little money but does involve a huge investment of time, teaching, concern, and spiritual fervor in the discipleship of young lives for the sake of God's kingdom.

## WORD POWER

**All (Hebrew: *Kol*)**—when this word precedes a noun, as in our text today, it expresses a unit and signifies the whole. In essence, when the Israelites said we will obey all (kol), they were saying "we will obey the words of the law unit by unit in its totality."

## HOME DAILY BIBLE READINGS

for the week of September 17, 2006
*God's Covenant with Israel*

Sept. 11, Monday
—Psalm 119:33-40
—Our Pledge to God
Sept. 12, Tuesday
—Exodus 18:13-27
—Moses Chooses Judges
Sept. 13, Wednesday
—Exodus 19:1-9a
—Moses Goes Up to God
Sept. 14, Thursday
—Exodus 19:9b-15
—Preparing for God's Covenant
Sept. 15, Friday
—Exodus 20:1-17
—God Gives the Commands
Sept. 16, Saturday
—Exodus 24:3-8
—The People Vow Loyalty
Sept. 17, Sunday
—Exodus 24:12-18
—Moses Enters God's Presence

## PRAYER

*Lord, in the midst of our challenges and our spiritual growth, please help us to remain consistent in our trust and obedience. In Jesus' name, we pray. Amen.*

**September 24, 2006**

Lesson 4

# Covenant Renewed

**UNIT I**
In Covenant with God

**CHILDREN'S UNIT**
God's First Covenants

**ADULT TOPIC:** Making Life's Choices
**YOUTH TOPIC:** Making the Right Choice
**CHILDREN'S TOPIC:** The People Renew the Covenant

**KEY VERSE**

If it seem evil unto you to serve the LORD, choose you this day whom ye will serve... but as for me and my house, we will serve the LORD.
— Joshua 24:15

**DEVOTIONAL READING:** Psalm 51:1-12
**BACKGROUND SCRIPTURE:** Joshua 24
**PRINT PASSAGE:** Joshua 24:1, 14-24

### Joshua 24:1, 14-24—KJV

AND JOSHUA gathered all the tribes of Israel to Shechem, and called for the elders of Israel, and for their heads, and for their judges, and for their officers; and they presented themselves before God.

.....

14 Now therefore fear the LORD, and serve him in sincerity and in truth: and put away the gods which your fathers served on the other side of the flood, and in Egypt; and serve ye the LORD.

15 And if it seem evil unto you to serve the LORD, choose you this day whom ye will serve; whether the gods which your fathers served that were on the other side of the flood, or the gods of the Amorites, in whose land ye dwell: but as for me and my house, we will serve the LORD.

16 And the people answered and said, God forbid that we should forsake the LORD, to serve other gods;

17 For the LORD our God, he it is that brought us up and our fathers out of the land of Egypt, from the house of bondage, and which did those great signs in our sight, and preserved us in all the way wherein we went, and among all the people through whom we passed:

18 And the LORD drave out from before us all the people, even the Amorites which dwelt in the land: therefore will we also serve the LORD; for he is our God.

19 And Joshua said unto the people, Ye cannot serve the LORD: for he is an holy God; he is a jealous God; he will not forgive your transgressions nor your sins.

**OBJECTIVES**

Upon completion of this lesson, the students are expected to:
1. Explore the importance of deciding to whom they will give allegiance;
2. Recognize God's role in bringing Israel to this place of "promises fulfilled"; and,
3. Recognize the danger of violating the commitment to obey and serve only the Lord.

20 If ye forsake the LORD, and serve strange gods, then he will turn and do you hurt, and consume you, after that he hath done you good.

21 And the people said unto Joshua, Nay; but we will serve the LORD.

22 And Joshua said unto the people, Ye are witnesses against yourselves that ye have chosen you the LORD, to serve him. And they said, We are witnesses.

23 Now therefore put away, said he, the strange gods which are among you, and incline your heart unto the LORD God of Israel.

24 And the people said unto Joshua, The LORD our God will we serve, and his voice will we obey.

## UNIFYING LESSON PRINCIPLE

Life is full of choices. What choice matters most? Joshua told the people that the most important choice they could make was to serve God.

## POINTS TO BE EMPHASIZED
## ADULTS/ YOUTH

**Adult Key Verse:** Joshua 24:15
**Youth Key Verse:** Joshua 24:24
**Print Passage:** Joshua 24:1, 14-24

—God desires commmitment from His people, but will not coerce it.

—Commitments to God need to be renewed at various points in one's faith journey.

—Although the Israelites remembered that God had saved their ancestors from bondage, they were still having problems being loyal to Him.

—The covenant renewal ceremony recounted in Joshua describes what God had already done for the people and what the people pledged to do.

## CHILDREN

**Key Verse:** Joshua 24:24
**Print Passage:** Joshua 24:1-3, 14, 16-17, 18b, 26

—God reminded Israel that He is always faithful to His promises.

—Some of the tribes of Israel had become lax in following God's covenant.

—Joshua led the Israelites to recommit themselves to the covenant made by their ancestors.

—The people were admonished to serve God in sincerity and faithfulness.

## TOPICAL OUTLINE OF THE LESSON

I. INTRODUCTION
  A. Which God Is God?
  B. Biblical Background

II. EXPOSITION AND APPLICATION OF THE SCRIPTURE
  A. Momentous Gathering (*Joshua 24:1*)
  B. A Simple Plan for Certain Success (*Joshua 24:14-15*)
  C. Corporate Cooperation with God (*Joshua 24:16-18*)
  D. Serious Warning Against Apostasy (*Joshua 24:19-20*)
  E. Solemn Resolution Toward Obedient Service (*Joshua 24:21-24*)

III. CONCLUDING REFLECTIONS

## I. INTRODUCTION
### A. Which God Is God?

God has given humanity the capacity to make choices, and life is full of them. Many of our choices make little impact on the rest of our existence. Other choices have tremendous consequences. The color of clothes we choose may not matter much, but the God we serve is a choice that will make a world of difference. Some of the gods that people serve today include the god of money, the god of education, the god of status, the god of material gain, the god of relationships and, without a doubt, the god of self. Although none of these entities are negative in and of themselves, they all must occupy a subordinate role in order for a healthy relationship with God to be developed.

### B. Biblical Background

After inheriting the baton of national leadership from Moses, Joshua led Israel into the Promised Land of Canaan. He established a strong presence in Canaan and solidified their position against encroaching enemy nations. Joshua's trademark battle cry and lifelong mission statement of sorts was "Possess the land." From the beginning of his career to the end, he was on a continuous quest to possess.

As Joshua neared the end of his life and reign as leader of the children of Israel, he began to reflect on his life, his purpose, and his legacy. Quite possibly, Joshua wondered whether he had done enough to insure that the people would stick to the spiritual direction that had been modeled for them. Would the people forsake the God of Moses and turn to the false gods worshiped by neighboring nations? This question weighed hard on the mind of Joshua and he gathered the leaders of Israel to hear the valedictory of a retiring warrior.

## II. EXPOSITION AND APPLICATION OF THE SCRIPTURE

### A. Momentous Gathering *(Joshua 24:1)*

**And Joshua gathered all the tribes of Israel to Shechem, and called for the elders of Israel, and for their heads, and for their judges, and for their officers; and they presented themselves before God.**

Joshua gathered the leaders in Shechem. It was a town in central Canaan and was quite appropriate as the site of a major covenantal renewal due to Shechem's geographical and historical significance. Joshua issued a summons to the leaders, the old men, the judges, and the officials to come to the sacred tent and listen to his message. The text is careful to note that this message is not from Joshua. Joshua served only as a conduit or mouthpiece for the words and commands that originated from the heart and mind of God.

### B. A Simple Plan for Certain Success *(Joshua 24:14-15)*

**Now therefore fear the LORD, and serve him in sincerity and in truth: and put away the gods which your fathers served on the other side of the flood, and in Egypt; and serve ye the LORD. And if it seem evil unto you to serve the LORD, choose you this day whom ye will serve; whether the gods which your fathers served that were on the other side of the flood, or the gods of the Amorites, in whose land ye dwell: but as for me and my house, we will serve the LORD.**

Joshua wasted no words in identifying the pathway for living a life of power, peace, and progress. The components are simple to understand, but are sometimes difficult to achieve on a consistent basis.

*Worship the Lord*—Worshiping God has always been a central component in the lives of God's people. We were created to worship God and to love God forever. Consequently, if we fail to worship God, we are not fulfilling our purpose in life. True worship often involves awareness of one's sin and inadequacy, confession of that sin, an attitude of humility, seeking God's face and openness to God's voice (2 Chronicles 7:14).

*Obey the Lord*—Obedience to God is the litmus test for a life that is sold out to God. To obey means to live in compliance with the laws or requirements of an individual or a governmental system. Spiritually speaking, obedience means "to submit and surrender to the will, rule and reign of God." The type of obedience that God desired from the Israelites and from people today is wholehearted obedience (Deuteronomy 26:16). It is possible for us to obey God, but in a partial, unenthusiastic manner. Wholehearted obedience affirms the worth and value of God's guidelines for living.

*Always Be Faithful*—Followers of God are called to reflect and emulate the attitude and behavior of the Father. God is a faithful God, and God's people are called to be faithful followers. Faithfulness is demonstrated by consistency, but the children of Israel had an erratic record of faithfulness. In hard times they would cry out to God for help; during times of calm, they tended to drift away from God.

*Lose the Idols*—Throughout the Old Testament, the living God consistently displays "zero tolerance" for the worship of idols. Having no other gods before God always has been and always will be a major tenet of what it means to be holy and righteous. On the subject of worshiping God, there is no room for compromise. In many places in Scripture, the people are given an opportunity to choose whether to serve God or to serve idols. This is still the pivotal life decision to be made today. Our choice either produces tragic consequences or yields great rewards.

### C. Corporate Cooperation with God (Joshua 24:16-18)

**And the people answered and said, God forbid that we should forsake the Lord, to serve other gods; For the Lord our God, he it is that brought us up and our fathers out of the land of Egypt, from the house of bondage, and which did those great signs in our sight, and preserved us in all the way wherein we went, and among all the people through whom we passed: And the Lord drave out from before us all the people, even the Amorites which dwelt in the land: therefore will we also serve the Lord; for he is our God.**

When Joshua placed the choice before the people, their response was certain and emphatic. The mere idea or thought of leaving God in order to serve idols seems reprehensible in their sight. The phrase "God forbid" could also be understood as "far be it from us" (NIV) or "we could never worship other gods" (CEV). After confirming their decision in verse 16, the rationale for their choice is introduced in verse 17. This reasoning is threefold: God's liberation, God's demonstration, and God's preservation.

God displayed *liberation* on a grand scale through the deliverance of the Israelites from the hands of their Egyptian oppressors. Forever engrained upon the consciousness of the Israelites was the fact that they once were slaves. To forget their history would open the door to repeating that history. Just as they were determined to remember their enslavement, they were just as driven to remember who liberated them from slavery. This remembrance engendered a perpetual state of gratitude on behalf of the Israelites toward God, whose love was personal enough to care and strong enough to rescue.

God's personal *demonstration* came in the form of great signs and wonders. The twelve plagues that were unleashed upon Egypt were only the beginning of the miracles that took place as a tangible manifestation of God's covenantal relationship with the people. The epic parting of the Red Sea followed these miraculous demonstrations in Egypt. All along the wilderness journey, God demonstrated covenant-keeping commitment through the following:

- the pillar of cloud by day and the pillar of fire by night
- the provision of manna for bread and quail for meat
- the water that emerged from inside the rock
- the miraculous falling down of the walls of Jericho

This sample of the many miracles performed by God served as a constant reminder in the memory of the people that God is indeed a faithful God. To forsake such a great God with such a tremendous track record of proven power would be the mistake of a lifetime. No other god could dare to compare.

When Joshua mentions God's *preservation,* this refers to the many times that God intervened to preserve the Israelites from destruction by enemy nations. As these hundreds of thousands of people meandered through the desert, their reputation preceded them. They were viewed as a threat by nations that were in geographic proximity to their pathway. Even though the Israelites were not as well-armed as neighboring countries, God consistently intervened and protected them from annihilation. God's personal relationship with the people helped them to move beyond religion as ritual. They now understood God as a personal friend who is to be regarded with awe and respect.

### D. Serious Warning Against Apostasy
*(Joshua 24:19-20)*

**And Joshua said unto the people, Ye cannot serve the Lord: for he is an holy God; he is a jealous God; he will not forgive your transgressions nor your sins. If ye forsake the Lord, and serve strange gods, then he will turn and do you hurt, and consume you, after that he hath done you good.**

Israel's easy declaration of allegiance to God must have seemed suspect to Joshua. Perhaps they seemed to give in too easily after having engaged in years of idolatrous worship, so Joshua took a different approach. Joshua made known his reservations about their ability to be faithful to God (verse 19). Rather than employing his usual approach of admonishing them to serve the Lord, however, he emphasized their covenantal obligation of loyalty to Yahweh. The words, *You cannot serve the LORD, for he is a holy God.... He will not forgive your transgressions or your sins* seem incongruent with God's love and faithfulness, which had just been described and discussed at length. The last phrase at the end of verse 19 makes more sense, however, if joined with the next verse without a break in thought. When associated with the following phrase, it begins to yield greater understanding: "If you forsake the Lord and serve foreign gods." Divine forgiveness is possible only through forsaking the false and embracing truth. He warned them of the consequences of covenant violation but also reminded them of the blessings that accompany their fidelity to Him.

The intent of Joshua's indictment was to establish the unworthiness of Israel against the worthiness of their holy God. Joshua was not implying that God was unwilling to forgive Israel; rather, he garnered their attention to let them know that they could present themselves before Yahweh to worship while at the same time worshipping idols. They could not worship idols and then come running back to God in search of His blessings and protection.

At Sinai, God made known His uncompromising position in the eyes of His chosen people. In Exodus 20:5, the Lord unapologetically proclaimed Himself to Israel as a jealous God who would not tolerate their worship of other gods. The characterization of God as jealous does not refer to the kind of petty jealousy that is common among humanity. The Hebrew word used here is *quanna* (pronounced kaw-naw). While the term can be used in a negative way concerning humans, when attributed to God it carries a sense of zeal with regard to one's possession. Additionally, Israel experienced definite benefits from serving a jealous God. One expression of God's jealousy for Israel was His protection of His people from enemies. Thus, God's jealousy included avenging Israel (see Ezekiel 36:6; 39:25; Nahum 1:2; Zechariah 1:14; Zechariah 8:2).

### E. Solemn Resolution Toward Obedient Service *(Joshua 24:21-24)*

**And the people said unto Joshua, Nay; but we will serve the Lord. And Joshua said unto the people, Ye are witnesses against yourselves that ye have chosen you the Lord, to serve him. And they said, We are witnesses. Now therefore put away, said he, the strange gods which are among you, and incline your heart unto the Lord God of Israel. And the people said unto Joshua, The Lord our God will we serve, and his voice will we obey.**

There is a sense that Joshua did not want the people to take for granted the seriousness of this covenantal renewal. Therefore, he made the renewal as difficult as possible for them to agree to its ratification. Anything in life that is gained too easily tends to be undervalued. Once this issue is resolved, the pathway is cleared for the reaffirmation of the covenant. Once the people insisted on serving the Lord, Joshua reminded them that they were *witnesses* against themselves. Joshua utilized a legal analogy in order to graphically describe what the people had just done. It is as if they were all present in a great courtroom scene with Joshua as the attorney, God as judge, and the people as both defendants and witnesses. Their testimony as defendants was heard by themselves as witnesses. These same words can serve to condemn them or to exonerate them, depending on their actions and spiritual choices in the future.

Verse 23 holds the key to spiritual success for the Israelites in the future as well as the key to our spiritual success in the present: Put away the strange gods and incline your heart toward the true God. This two-part assignment must be executed in concert, without excluding either aspect. To leave out one part would cancel the overall effect. If we dispense of strange gods yet fail to embrace the true God, there is a vacuum. Likewise, if we incline our hearts toward the true God but retain the strange gods, there is an insurmountable conflict of interest. When both aspects of this renewed covenant are accomplished, we steadily move closer to the picture of purpose that is painted on the pages of God's divine covenant for God's people.

### III. Concluding Reflections

Why would a covenant need to be renewed? For human beings, familiarity can foster devaluation and neglect.

Sometimes we can be in such close proximity to something that we begin to take that thing for granted. A good example of this phenomenon is marriage. At the beginning of most marriages, the atmosphere is filled with warm thoughts, kind words, surprise gifts, and gentle touches. But as the years go by, an interesting phenomenon can occur—the warm thoughts turn into lukewarm regard, the kind words turn into barked orders and the gifts become obligatory, appearing only on the "expected" occasions, if then.

A marriage is like a living plant that requires regular water and sunshine in order to flourish. Likewise, in our covenantal relationship with God, we must daily renew our commitment to love God with all our hearts, souls, minds, and strength.

### WORD POWER

**Serve (Hebrew: *abad* [aw-bad])**—to serve, be bondsmen, to commit wholeheartedly. Joshua used this word (abad) to declare to the Israelites that he and his family were bond slaves of God.

### HOME DAILY BIBLE READINGS

for the week of September 24, 2006
*Covenant Renewed*

Sept. 18, Monday
 —Psalm 51:1-12
 —Pray for Renewal
Sept. 19, Tuesday
 —Deuteronomy 31:14-23
 —Be Strong and Bold
Sept. 20, Wednesday
 —Joshua 1:1-9
 —God Commands Joshua
Sept. 21, Thursday
 —Joshua 24:1-7
 —Recalling God's Mighty Acts
Sept. 22, Friday
 —Joshua 24:8-13
 —God Gives a Land
Sept. 23, Saturday
 —Joshua 24:14-18
 —Choose Whom You Will Serve
Sept. 24, Sunday
 —Joshua 24:19-24
 —The People Renew Their Vows

### PRAYER

*O Lord, help us to never take for granted our relationship with You. Let us forever walk in the light as You are in the Light. In Jesus' name, we pray. Amen.*

## Lesson 5

# God Sends Judges

**ADULT TOPIC:** Seeking Deliverance
**YOUTH TOPIC:** Judges Bring Justice
**CHILDREN'S TOPIC:** God Sends Leaders for the People

**October 1, 2006**

**UNIT II**
God's Covenant with Judges and Kings

**CHILDREN'S UNIT**
God Sends Judges and Kings

**DEVOTIONAL READING:** Deuteronomy 6:4-9
**BACKGROUND SCRIPTURE:** Judges 2:11-23
**PRINT PASSAGE:** Judges 2:16-23

### Judges 2:16-23—KJV

16 Nevertheless the LORD raised up judges, which delivered them out of the hand of those that spoiled them.

17 And yet they would not hearken unto their judges, but they went a whoring after other gods, and bowed themselves unto them: they turned quickly out of the way which their fathers walked in, obeying the commandments of the LORD; but they did not so.

18 And when the LORD raised them up judges, then the LORD was with the judge, and delivered them out of the hand of their enemies all the days of the judge: for it repented the LORD because of their groanings by reason of them that oppressed them and vexed them.

19 And it came to pass, when the judge was dead, that they returned, and corrupted themselves more than their fathers, in following other gods to serve them, and to bow down unto them; they ceased not from their own doings, nor from their stubborn way.

20 And the anger of the LORD was hot against Israel; and he said, Because that this people hath transgressed my covenant which I commanded their fathers, and have not hearkened unto my voice;

21 I also will not henceforth drive out any from before them of the nations which Joshua left when he died:

22 That through them I may prove Israel, whether they will keep the way of the LORD to walk therein, as their fathers did keep it, or not.

23 Therefore the LORD left those nations, without driving them out hastily; neither delivered he them into the hand of Joshua.

**KEY VERSE**
Nevertheless the LORD raised up judges, which delivered them out of the hand of those that spoiled them.
—Judges 2:16

### OBJECTIVES

**Upon completion of this lesson, the students are expected to:**

1. Learn that rebellion against God carries severe repercussions, such as enemy oppression;
2. Recognize that although the love of God is deep and long, the justice of God is equally as strong; and,
3. Understand that God uses and empowers ordinary people to make a difference in the natural world.

## UNIFYING LESSON PRINCIPLE

We all long to be delivered from desperate situations, even those of our own making. Where can we look for help? Whenever the Hebrew people cried to God, God raised someone (a judge) to save them.

## POINTS TO BE EMPHASIZED
### ADULTS/ YOUTH
**Adult/Youth Key Verse:** Judges 2:16
**Print Passage:** Judges 2:16-23
—God raised up judges to deliver the people from the plunderers of the land.
—During the period of the judges, the Israelites engaged in a cycle of disobedience, despair, and deliverance.

## CHILDREN
**Key Verse:** Judges 2:18
**Print Passage:** Judges 2:6-8, 11-12, 14, 16, 18
—Disobedience and unfaithfulness often bring about disastrous consequences.
—God remains faithful to His covenant, even though the believers do not.
—God sends special people to bring back to God those believers who stray.

## TOPICAL OUTLINE OF THE LESSON

  I. INTRODUCTION
     A. The Depth of God's Love
     B. Biblical Background

 II. EXPOSITION AND APPLICATION OF THE SCRIPTURE
     A. The Judges Deliver; the People Ignore *(Judges 2:16-17)*
     B. God's Pity Versus God's Anger *(Judges 2:18-21)*
     C. This Is Only a Test *(Judges 2:22-23)*

III. CONCLUDING REFLECTIONS

## I. INTRODUCTION
### A. The Depth of God's Love

Have you ever had to forgive someone for the same offense—over and over again? After a while, you probably began to doubt the sincerity of the person's request for forgiveness. Many of us have known a long-suffering spouse who endured infidelity, mistreatment, and neglect, yet continued to give faithful love and service in return. God has loved His people with such devotion despite their sin and idolatry. The cyclical nature of their relationship to God tried His patience many times, but He never wavered in His love for them. The depth of God's love for the Israelites was inexhaustible. Each time God forgave and restored them, they somehow found a way to meander back toward idolatry and moral degradation. The book of Judges portrays the people as pushing God to the point of provocation with their repeated acts of spiritual adultery.

Although God's love is endless and vast, God's grace should never be taken for granted. God's love relationship with humanity consists of mercy as well as justice. If God's love only was extended mercy, the relationship would lean out of control and descend into human lawlessness. If the justice only was in operation, the relationship would veer into the valley of legalism. Thankfully, God's love is balanced with appropriate amounts of mercy and justice so that He can lead us from where we are and into our eternal destiny.

The book of Judges represents the record of how God sent a series of wise judges into the Israelite community to intervene and redirect the attention of the people back toward the things of God. It serves as a reminder for us today that although the love of God is deep and long, the justice of God is equally as strong.

## B. Biblical Background

Historically, the book of Judges takes its name from twelve anointed military and social leaders. God appointed them to deliver His people from those who plundered them. Their period commenced from Joshua's death around 1200 B.C. and continued until Saul became the first king of Israel around 1030 B.C. (1 Samuel 12). The covenant between God and the people was simple: Serve Me and enjoy prosperity; follow other gods and suffer destruction. Such a proposition may seem like a clear-cut choice but the influence of Canaanite culture repeatedly drew the Israelites away from the God of familiarity toward the gods of convenience. The word *Baal* means "lord" and was believed to produce fertility and rain for the soil. *Astoreth* (female consort of *Baal*) was associated with war and fertility. Worship of these gods involved so-called sacred prostitution and even child sacrifice.[1]

The lure of the Canaanite religion lay in its sensual nature and its convenient offering of purported short-range benefits, such as sexual permissiveness, numerous offspring, and successful farming (which translated into increased income). By contrast, God's way involved discipline. Baal's way meant that the people "could remain selfish and yet fulfill their religious requirements. They could do almost anything they wished and still be obeying at least one of the many Canaanite gods."[2] The people continuously repeated the cycles of: (1) rebellion; (2) defeat by enemies; (3) deliverance by a judge; (4) loyalty to God under judge's leadership; and (5) turning away from God after the death of the judge.[3] It would seem that after a few rotations of this same cycle, the nation would have observed this disturbing pattern within their history and adopted measures to halt the cycle. However, this did not occur and the abundant mercy of God was increasingly tried by this idolatrous trend.

The door to idolatry can be opened when a God-fearing generation dies without firmly instilling moral and spiritual values into the minds and lives of their children. Of course, no generation can force the succeeding generation to serve God. But when we do our best to "train up a child in the way he should go," Scripture affirms "when he is old, he will not depart from it" (Proverbs 22:6). God is ever mindful of His covenant. The Israelites forgot what God had done for them. Their fathers served God but this generation had forgotten their past. It was important for them to seek God with all their hearts and souls. The faith of their fathers was a personal faith. They could not and should not depend on it. Each generation must seek God.

## II. Exposition and Application of the Scripture
### A. The Judges Deliver; the People Ignore (Judges 2:16-17)

**Nevertheless the Lord raised up judges, which delivered them out of the hand of those that spoiled them. And yet they would not hearken unto their judges, but they went a whoring after other gods, and bowed themselves unto them: they turned quickly out of the way which their fathers walked in,**

obeying the commandments of the Lord; but they did not so.**

When God desires to intervene into an earthly situation, God often uses a prepared individual as a vessel to communicate a divine message. The people God uses are usually very ordinary people from all walks of life who, sometimes reluctantly, consent to be used by God to make a difference in the natural world. The judges served as one biblical example of how God can choose to use anyone to accomplish godly goals. God does not require great ability in order for one to be effective; a little faith and a commitment to obedience go a long way when used by almighty God.

During the time of the judges, Israel was in a terrible predicament and the Lord was angry (verse 14) because they would not obey. What grand plans their God had for them! But instead of living in victory and prosperity through obedience to Him, they were mired in idolatry, sin and debauchery. Forever at the mercy of their enemies, Israel would cry out to the Lord in troubling times and cavort with idols as their troubles seemed to subside.

During this time, there was a near constant threat of war within any given kingdom. As one group of people raided another, to the victor would go the spoils of the city. Sometimes these spoils included human treasure in the form of wives and slaves. Most cities during this era were built in places that afforded significant physical vantage points as well as sturdy protective walls surrounding the city.

Israel lived under the threat of aggression by the Mesopotamians (3:8), the Moabites (3:12-14), the Midianites, Amalekites and others (6:3), not to mention the Ammonites (10:7) and the Philistines (13:1). Despite their recurring disobedience, God was moved to pity (2:18) because of their condition and sent them judges (verse 16). The judges would be God's chosen vessel of divine deliverance in the period between the leadership of Joshua and the establishment of the kingdom. God equipped the judges with keen military skills and insight that assisted them in successfully defeating the encroaching enemies. When the people followed the instructions of the judges, they were victorious in war.

Even though the judges proved their abilities on the battlefield, the people did not listen to them off the battlefield. The text records that they *lusted after other gods* through bowing down and worshiping them. The analogy and terminology used here carries a connotation of a marital covenant being violated. Throughout the Bible, there are repeated references to God as a husband figure (see Isaiah 54:5 and Hosea 3:1). The relationship between God and God's people is one of intimacy, commitment, love, trust, feelings, faith, and deep care. This picture is not of a God who is distant and abstract, but rather of one who is up close and personal, intensely involved in the everyday lives of the loved ones. Israel was like an unfaithful spouse, wanting all of the benefits of marriage without the commitment.

Despite their having been the beneficiaries of God's providence and loving kindness, the Israelites refused to honor their covenantal relationship with God. He had provided them with all they needed. He had given them victory in battle. By giving them judges, God allowed Israel to enjoy periods of deliverance and rest from their enemies. Instead of continuing in the way of their forebears, the Israelites prostituted themselves with idol worship. But these blessings Israel soon forgot.

### B. God's Pity Versus God's Anger
*(Judges 2:18-21)*

**And when the L**ORD **raised them up judges, then the L**ORD **was with the judge, and delivered them out of the hand of their enemies all the days of the judge: for it repented the L**ORD **because of their groanings by reason of them that oppressed them and vexed them. And it came to pass, when the judge was dead, that they returned, and corrupted themselves more than their fathers, in following other gods to serve them, and to bow down unto them; they ceased not from their own doings, nor from their stubborn way. And the anger of the L**ORD **was hot against Israel; and he said, Because that this people hath transgressed my covenant which I commanded their fathers, and have not hearkened unto my voice; I also will not henceforth drive out any from before them of the nations which Joshua left when he died.**

The spiritual inconsistency of the people tugged at the heart of God. When the people would worship the idols, the anger of the Lord would flare up and Israel's enemies would be allowed to painfully persecute God's people. To Israel, it must have seemed as if the Lord turned aside and looked another way as neighboring countries invaded various tribes of Israel. When this occurred and the people helplessly cried out to God for assistance, the father-spirit of almighty God was touched. As Father, God intuitively moved to the aid of His crying child. Distress signals from a child activate parental instincts, and no matter how disobedient the child has been, the parent cannot help but offer assistance. God's help came in the form of obedient judges who led the people in the ways of the Lord until the judge's death.

During the reign of each judge, the people would experience times of peace and tranquility. There was an absence of war and the presence of prosperity. Under these ideal conditions the people settled into the carefree lifestyle of their idolatrous neighbors. What is it about the absence of struggle that causes people to neglect the very source that made peace possible? Marcus Garvey wisely observed that frequently when there is no struggle, there is no progress. It is almost as if the presence of pain and persecution provides us with a necessary reminder of our personal need for God.

Surely the children of Israel could have benefited from employing the wisdom expressed by Annie S. Hawkes in the third verse of her unforgettable hymn, "I Need Thee Every Hour": "I need Thee ev'ry hour, in joy or pain; Come quickly and abide, or life is vain." Evidently, Hawkes clearly understood the important principle that God's power, presence, and influence are intended for *all* of life. Conversely, Israel refused to live in this awareness, choosing instead to abandon God in times of peace and prosperity and running back to Him when they were in trouble.

Too often we tend to treat God like a spare tire—for use only in emergencies. But God refuses to be a parachute God. We must not just reach for God only when we are falling. If a friend is truly a friend, we would not always wait until we are in desperate need to make contact and nurture an ongoing relationship. God is there in our times of distress, but God is also there for our times of rest.

### C. This Is Only a Test *(Judges 2:22-23)*

**That through them I may prove Israel, whether they will keep the way of the Lord to walk therein, as their fathers did keep it, or not. Therefore the Lord left those nations, without driving them out hastily; neither delivered he them into the hand of Joshua.**

In elementary school, middle school, and high school through college, there is a standard procedure for dispensing knowledge and determining progress. First comes the teaching, and then comes the test. The test is necessary in order to determine how much of the teaching was absorbed. The test is therefore designed to be an accurate barometer of one's progress. If the tests are passed, the student is promoted to a higher level. If the tests are failed, the student must repeat the class. Pity the student who does not study for the test, fails the test, and still expects promotion! Unfortunately, this is the presumptuous attitude that the Israelites frequently projected: "Protect us because we are your people. We know we have not done our spiritual homework, but give us a break…again."

The test given to the Israelites came in the form of God not completely driving out every single idol-worshiping nation that was still left following the death of Joshua. What kind of God would allow trouble to occur in the lives of His own children? Have you ever questioned God about undesirable or tragic events that may have occurred in your life despite the fact that you were living a faithful life of devotion and dedication to God? Matthew 5:45 records that God "makes his sun rise on the evil and on the good, and sends rain on the righteous and on the unrighteous." Just because we are righteous does not mean that we are somehow exempt from pain. One of the primary personal characteristics of a child of God is the presence of joy. Joy and happiness are not the same. Happiness is dependent upon pleasing circumstances. Joy is the ability to stand strong even in the face of devastating circumstances. Happiness therefore is surface and temporary. Joy is lasting and permanent.

Another aspect of this issue of human pain and suffering revolves around the positive outcome of pain. Although Joshua got rid of the majority of the problem, enough of the problem remained to keep the people prayerful and dependent upon God. From this example, we can begin to see a helpful purpose for problems. Problems help to keep us prayerful instead of prideful. Pain enables us to focus on God's sovereignty rather than on our selfishness. When we submit and surrender to God, God has a way of causing all things to work together for our good when we truly love God and are called according to God's purpose (see Romans 8:28). God's ways surpass human understanding and wisdom.

## III. Concluding Reflections

In considering the tenuous nature and pattern exhibited by the Israelites, there is a strong temptation to dismiss them as an ungrounded group of ingrates who were offered everything on a silver platter yet rejected God's goodness in order to do things their way. However, this portrayal is a fairly accurate description of contemporary society.

On September 11, 2001, America suffered a major attack when four commercial airline jets were hijacked and crashed into the World Trade Center towers, the Pentagon, and an open field, resulting in numerous deaths. In the aftermath of that tragedy, churches all over the country experienced a swell in attendance. Crime fell dramatically in many areas. Ministers were asked to offer prayer during prime time news shows without the slightest objection from the atheist or agnostic communities. But as the threat of attack seemed to diminish and the memory of danger began to dim, human interactions in general drifted back to fleshly normality and spiritual abnormality, much the way it was before the tragedy occurred.

The challenge that stands before every generation is the maintenance of faithfulness throughout all of life's situations. Faithfulness is one of the fruits of the Spirit and is an indispensable personal character trait for those who follow Christ. The hope of all Christians is to live faithfully in all things and through all things and eventually hear the Master say: "Well done, good and faithful servant" (Matthew 25:23).

### WORD POWER

**Judge (Hebrew: *Shaphat*)**—the judges in ancient Israel were not like our present-day judges. God, who was not subject to be voted into office by the people, summoned them. The divinely-appointed judges received unusual anointing to tackle the enemies of Israel. God gave them the ability to deliver and rule God's people for a period of time. In the case of Deborah, her activities (as recorded in Judges 4:4) were judicial and constituted a kind of ruling over Israel.

### HOME DAILY BIBLE READINGS

for the week of October 1, 2006
*God Sends Judges*

Sept. 25, Monday
—Deuteronomy 6:4-9
—Love the Lord
Sept. 26, Tuesday
—Psalm 78:1-8
—God and the Hebrew People
Sept. 27, Wednesday
—Psalm 85:4-13
—Prayer for a Nation
Sept. 28, Thursday
—Judges 2:1-5
—Israel Disobeys God
Sept. 29, Friday
—Judges 2:6-10
—A New Generation
Sept. 30, Saturday
—Judges 2:11-15
—Israel Abandons God
Oct. 1, Sunday
—Judges 2:16-23
—Call to Repentance

### PRAYER

*Lord, let us live lives of unswerving faithfulness. In Jesus' name, we pray. Amen.*

---

[1] *NIV Study Bible* (Grand Rapids: Zondervan Publishing House, 1995) p. 329.
[2] *Life Application Bible* (Tyndale House Publishers, Inc. Wheaton, Ill., 1991) Judges 2:17.
[3] *Ibid.*

**October 8, 2006**

**UNIT II**
God's Covenant with Judges and Kings

**CHILDREN'S UNIT**
God Sends Judges and Kings

## KEY VERSES

Barak said unto her, If thou wilt go with me, then I will go: but if thou wilt not go with me, then I will not go. And she said, I will surely go with thee: ... And Deborah arose, and went with Barak to Kedesh.—Judges 4:8-9

## OBJECTIVES

Upon completion of this lesson, the students are expected to:

1. Recognize Deborah's distinctive role in Israel's history;
2. Affirm that God can and does speak through sincere persons; and,
3. Discover that God always has a leader prepared to serve.

Lesson 6

# God Leads Through Deborah

**ADULT TOPIC:** Leadership Counts!
**YOUTH TOPIC:** Deborah: A Strong Leader
**CHILDREN'S TOPIC:** God Chooses Deborah to Lead

**DEVOTIONAL READING:** Psalm 91
**BACKGROUND SCRIPTURE:** Judges 4
**PRINT PASSAGE:** Judges 4:4-10, 12-16

### Judges 4:4-10, 12-16—KJV

4 And Deborah, a prophetess, the wife of Lapidoth, she judged Israel at that time.

5 And she dwelt under the palm tree of Deborah between Ramah and Bethel in mount Ephraim: and the children of Israel came up to her for judgment.

6 And she sent and called Barak the son of Abinoam out of Kedesh-naphtali, and said unto him, Hath not the LORD God of Israel commanded, saying, Go and draw toward mount Tabor, and take with thee ten thousand men of the children of Naphtali and of the children of Zebulun?

7 And I will draw unto thee to the river Kishon Sisera, the captain of Jabin's army, with his chariots and his multitude; and I will deliver him into thine hand.

8 And Barak said unto her, If thou wilt go with me, then I will go: but if thou wilt not go with me, then I will not go.

9 And she said, I will surely go with thee: notwithstanding the journey that thou takest shall not be for thine honour; for the LORD shall sell Sisera into the hand of a woman. And Deborah arose, and went with Barak to Kedesh.

10 And Barak called Zebulun and Naphtali to Kedesh; and he went up with ten thousand men at his feet: and Deborah went up with him.

. . . . .

12 And they shewed Sisera that Barak the son of Abinoam was gone up to mount Tabor.

13 And Sisera gathered together all his chariots, even nine hundred chariots of iron, and all the people that were with him, from Harosheth of the Gentiles unto the river of Kishon.

14 And Deborah said unto Barak, Up; for this is the day in which the LORD hath delivered Sisera into thine hand: is not the LORD gone out before thee? So Barak went down from mount Tabor, and ten thousand men after him.

15 And the LORD discomfited Sisera, and all his chariots, and all his host, with the edge of the sword before Barak; so that Sisera lighted down off his chariot, and fled away on his feet.

16 But Barak pursued after the chariots, and after the host, unto Harosheth of the Gentiles: and all the host of Sisera fell upon the edge of the sword; and there was not a man left.

## UNIFYING LESSON PRINCIPLE

Strong leaders may get results when no one else can. What characterizes a strong leader? Deborah modeled strong leadership by obeying God and supporting Barak with her presence.

## POINTS TO BE EMPHASIZED
## ADULTS/YOUTH

**Adult Key Verse:** Judges 4:8-9
**Youth Key Verse:** Judges 4:4
**Print Passage:** Judges 4:4-10, 12-16
—Despite the perception that the Hebrews were patriarchal, the leadership of Deborah was considered natural.
—Barak's insistence that Deborah accompany him to the battle indicates his trust in God and Deborah.
—In accord with holy war tradition, the Lord dictates tactics and gives assurance of victory.

## CHILDREN

**Key Verse:** Judges 4:9
**Print Passage:** Judges 4:4-10, 12-16
—The Israelites consulted and followed respected leaders such as Deborah.
—Deborah served as a visionary for God in helping Israel.
—A lack of confidence caused Barak to miss out on some of the glory of victory.

## TOPICAL OUTLINE OF THE LESSON

I. INTRODUCTION
  A. God Can Use Anyone
  B. Biblical Background

II. EXPOSITION AND APPLICATION OF THE SCRIPTURE
  A. Deborah: A Woman of Many Roles *(Judges 4:4-5)*
  B. Deborah's Vision: A Call and a Promise *(Judges 4:6-7)*
  C. Deborah and Barak: A Doubt and a Deal *(Judges 4:8-10)*
  D. The Defeat of Sisera *(Judges 4:12-16)*

III. CONCLUDING REFLECTIONS

## I. INTRODUCTION
### A. God Can Use Anyone

Deborah is a memorable biblical personality who stands out because of her character, her dedication to God, and the profound impact she made upon her generation. Like many women both then and now, Deborah handled a wide variety of roles. First, Deborah was a prophetess. This word in Hebrew is *nebiy'ah* (pronounced neb-ee-YAW), which means a woman who is inspired to speak to others on behalf of

God. Other prophetesses mentioned in the Bible include: Miriam (Exodus 15:20); Huldah (2 Kings 22:14-20); Anna (Luke 2:36-38); and four nameless daughters of Phillip the evangelist (Acts 21:9).

In addition to being a prophetess, Deborah was also wife of Lappidoth. The only recorded biblical accomplishment of Lappidoth is that he was the husband of Deborah. Although given what seems like a dubiously honorable mention, Lappidoth must have been a very secure and faithful man to be the spouse of a strong, successful, and powerful wife. The third hat that Deborah wore was that of a judge, and it is this role that we explore in the text.

### B. Biblical Background

Tribal conflict is a central issue in the book of Judges. Three of the primary groups involved in this conflict are the Israelites, the Canaanites, and the Perizzites. The Israelites are perhaps best known for being the "chosen people" of God. The Canaanites were the inhabitants of the land that had been promised to the children of Israel. The Canaanites were present when the Israelites arrived at the border of the city. Canaanites served gods that were very different from the God of Abraham, Isaac, and Jacob. When Israel finally went to possess the Promised Land, not all of the Canaanites were banished. Since some of the Canaanites remained nearby, eventually, components of the Canaanite religious culture began to infiltrate and influence the spiritual practices of the Israelites. It is for this reason that the people began to stray from God's covenant. The Perizzites' name in Hebrew signifies "villager." They were the dwellers of the forest country near Shechem (Joshua 17:15). They are not mentioned in the Table of Nations in Genesis 10 and their origin is obscure. They first appeared in Genesis 13:7 as dwelling in the land together with the Canaanites in Abraham's day. Amorites represented a wide array of non-Israelite nations that lived in Canaan.[1]

The judges themselves were part of God's plan to restore God's people to the right course and to lead them during times of conflict. The judges that are profiled in this biblical book are twelve very different people who at different times rise to God's call of leadership. The judges delivered the people from their oppressors and they pointed the nation back toward their spiritual legacy, which included absolute obedience to God. The list of judges did not include perfect people: Ehud, the assassin, the promiscuous Samson, and the power-hungry Abimelech, who murdered his own brothers in order to attain his desires. But God is good; God saw in them what human eyes could not see. Despite their faults they were submissive to God, and God used them.[2]

## II. Exposition and Application of the Scripture

### A. Deborah: A Woman of Many Roles
*(Judges 4:4-5)*

**And Deborah, a prophetess, the wife of Lapidoth, she judged Israel at that time. And she dwelt under the palm tree of Deborah between Ramah and Bethel in mount Ephraim: and the children of Israel came up to her for judgment.**

Deborah's role as a judge involved inspiration, encouragement, discernment, empowerment, instruction, and decision making. Deborah had to strike a delicate balance between sensitive, godly obedience and shrewd military strategy. She was a prick for the moral conscience of the Israelite people, but she was also a mighty conqueror of the opposing forces. Whenever the people had interpersonal disputes, they came to Deborah to have them settled. Consequently, her spiritual gifts of faith, administration and discernment worked together to provide the people with direction, protection and correction. Possibly, she held court under a palm tree because the process of judging many different cases in the hot sun all day required much time and attention. A nice palm tree would have been a very welcomed respite from the sun.

### B. Deborah's Vision: A Call and a Promise *(Judges 4:6-7)*

**And she sent and called Barak the son of Abinoam out of Kedesh-naphtali, and said unto him, Hath not the LORD God of Israel commanded, saying, Go and draw toward mount Tabor, and take with thee ten thousand men of the children of Naphtali and of the children of Zebulun? And I will draw unto thee to the river Kishon Sisera, the captain of Jabin's army, with his chariots and his multitude; and I will deliver him into thine hand.**

The concept of Holy War is present throughout the Old Testament. There was a broad, clear-cut sense of the forces of evil and forces of good doing battle against each other. In this era of "an eye for an eye and a tooth for a tooth," there was little room for a neutral zone. In many instances, people were given the opportunity to choose service to God or allegiance to foreign gods. Those who failed to side with God were unceremoniously annihilated. Holiness, godliness, and ministry, therefore, became associated with conflict for the cause and killing for the kingdom. It is this historical foundation that caused the people of Jesus' day to expect the Messiah to come as a military deliverer and conquering king rather than a Suffering Servant and a baby born in a manger. Surely the Messiah could not be a carpenter's son-turned-unconventional Jewish rabbi who speaks about love, peace, and forgiving one's enemies.

After receiving a divine directive from the Lord, Deborah shared her vision with Barak, the son of Abinoam from Kadesh in Naphtali. The name Barak means "lightning" or "thunderbolt." When Deborah wanted to speak to Barak, she did not go to him but rather summoned him to come to her. Barak complied with her request, and from this action it should be inferred that Deborah possessed great power, authority, and respect. Military leaders of that time did not instantly respond to just anybody's summons, and most especially a woman. Usually, the person who issued a summons was considered higher ranking than the one who had been summoned.

Notice how Deborah prefaced her message to Barak by identifying the originator of the information. Deborah's manner of speaking reflects her familiarity with royal leadership, military ranking, and spiritual authority. During the time she lived, a distasteful message delivered to a military ruler could jeopardize the life of the messenger. Surely, Deborah was never in any danger of being harmed by Barak, but she did go to great lengths to make it clear that she was only the messenger. Deborah realized that the message she must deliver potentially could endanger the lives of 10,000 troops. Therefore, she put an end to possible speculation, secondary strategies, and contrasting opinions: This was a message from the Lord.

When it came to Israel's wins and losses in holy war, there was always a big zero in the "lost" column whenever God was on their side. Whenever God said "Go and fight," the battle was already won, regardless of the enemy troop's size and military prowess. Thus, Deborah prefaced her words to Barak with a divine disclaimer: "The Lord, the God of Israel, commands you…." This was not a suggestion for Barak. This was not some clever idea that popped into the head of a female judge with nothing better to do. God said it, so Barak needed to do it.

The assignment for Barak was not general and broad. This word from the Lord was pointed and specific. Today, God can and does still speak through true prophets who are able to deliver the words that are ordained by God. But so-called prophets whose motives are questionable at best deliver other modern-day prophecies. Sometimes their prophecies are so general that the law of averages would make their prediction possible within a sizable margin of the hearers. But Deborah was a genuine prophet whose concern was not self-profit. Deborah's message covered all the "who, what, where and why" bases necessary for success on the battlefield:

Who: Barak along with 10,000 troops from Naphtali and Zebulun;
What: Take battle positions;
Where: Mount Tabor
Why: I (God) will give him (Sisera) into your hands.

It would seem that a message with such specificity would imbue the receiver of the message with all the confidence necessary to go forth and fight in faith. Although Barak was actually the battle leader, in Barak's eyesight, Deborah's spiritual presence carried a greater impact than his own army's military compentencies.

## C. Deborah and Barak: A Doubt and a Deal *(Judges 4:8-10)*

**And Barak said unto her, If thou wilt go with me, then I will go: but if thou wilt not go with me, then I will not go. And she said, I will surely go with thee: notwithstanding the journey that thou takest shall not be for thine honour; for the LORD shall sell Sisera into the hand of a woman. And Deborah arose, and went with Barak to Kedesh. And Barak called Zebulun and Naphtali to Kedesh; and he went up with ten thousand men at his feet: and Deborah went up with him.**

Barak's response to Deborah's revelation is an indication of Barak's trepidation. Although he complied with God's command, he attached a human proviso just in case God's plan failed to unfold—asking Deborah to accompany him. Barak essentially accepted God's promise on a conditional basis. How often have we consciously or unconsciously said, "Yes God, I will obey Your request … after I have tried it my way for a while"? Or, perhaps we have responded, "Yes God, I will do what you say just as long as you let someone else come to keep me company." This is provisional obedience. Provisional obedience is conditional obedience, and conditional obedience is essentially disobedience.

Was Barak a coward? Was he a doubter

of God's promise? Was Barak simply being a wise leader by making sure that Deborah's hearing from God was clear and accurate? We cannot with certainty discern what was in the heart of this man. We can only use his example to examine our own hearts and determine our own rationale for responding or failing to respond when we receive a summons from God.

As the messenger of God, judge/prophetess Deborah accepted Barak's conditional response and consented to be his personal escort on the battlefield. However, as Barak did not comply without condition, the outcome of the effort would not be without condition. The prize trophy in the culture of war is the killing or the capture of the leader for the opposing army. If the enemy is defeated and the leader escapes, there is satisfaction in the general victory but disappointment in the specific failure. God chastises us in very appropriate ways. The "punishment" perfectly fits the "crime." Barak was told by God to go into battle and God would deliver the enemy into his hands. Barak consents to God's command provided that a woman will accompany him in battle as his human security blanket. God's response to Barak's response was this: "Yes, you will still win the battle, but the credit for acquiring the prime game piece will go to a woman." Essentially, God was pleased with Barak's consent, but displeased with Barak's condition.

### D. The Defeat of Sisera *(Judges 4:12-16)*

**And they shewed Sisera that Barak the son of Abinoam was gone up to mount Tabor. And Sisera gathered together all his chariots, even nine hundred chariots of iron, and all the people that were with him, from Harosheth of the Gentiles unto the river of Kishon. And Deborah said unto Barak, Up; for this is the day in which the Lord hath delivered Sisera into thine hand: is not the Lord gone out before thee? So Barak went down from mount Tabor, and ten thousand men after him. And the Lord discomfited Sisera, and all his chariots, and all his host, with the edge of the sword before Barak; so that Sisera lighted down off his chariot, and fled away on his feet. But Barak pursued after the chariots, and after the host, unto Harosheth of the Gentiles: and all the host of Sisera fell upon the edge of the sword; and there was not a man left.**

Having heard that Barak had gone up to Mt. Tabor, Sisera mustered all the surrounding kings and they brought their respective troops—with Sisera believing that with his immense hosts he would defeat the army of the Lord. Deborah and Barak stationed their bands on the road summit of Tabor. The stage was set and Deborah issued a command to Barak: "Up! For this is the day on which the Lord has given Sisera into your hand. The Lord is indeed going out before you" (verse 14). With the courage of the Lord in him, Barak charged into the battlefront. The Lord threw Sisera's army into confusion by orchestrating a supernatural panic, which caused them to commit mass suicide (see Judges 4:16). Even the stars in their courses fought against the army of Sisera (see Judges 5:20). Barak relentlessly pursued the chariot of Sisera as they fled northward; others were forced to go to the western part of Kishon and drowned. God had fought for His people. The Lord is able to defeat any enemy who is opposing the work of God.

## III. Concluding Reflections

In reviewing this lesson, one thing should be abundantly clear: it is not easy being a leader. Leadership calls for making instantaneous decisions that may significantly affect others for a lifetime. That is why not everyone is called to be a leader.

Some may look at this list and wonder: With expectations such as these, who then can be a leader? Whatever God desires, God designs. Whatever God requires, God supplies. God always has a remnant and will never run out of qualified people prepared to serve in a spiritual leadership capacity. We can learn from life and from other scriptural examples that God can transform a life from "messed up to blessed up." Spiritual leadership should be bathed in prayer and directed by God. God equips whom God uses. Spiritual leaders must strike the delicate balance between their spiritual calling and their earthly setting.

We can learn a great deal from the lives of Deborah as well as Barak. If you had to compare your own life, character, and motives to one of them, to whom would you most closely compare yourself? Do you see in yourself strong leadership traits like those of Deborah? Do you hear from God clearly and fearlessly communicate God's message? Or are you skeptical like Barak when you hear a word from the Lord? Do you second-guess the strength, the accuracy of God's power, or God's prophet, God's prophetess, or God's promises?

The presence of faith pleases God and the absence of faith displeases God.

## WORD POWER

**Lightning *(Barak)*** —names in the Israelites' culture are significant. The hope of a father is wrapped in the name of the child. A child is expected to exemplify the meaning attached to his or her name. Ironically, Barak (lightning) abdicated the power implied by his name.

## HOME DAILY BIBLE READINGS

for the week of October 8, 2006
*God Leads Through Deborah*

Oct. 2, Monday
—Psalm 91
—The God in Whom I Trust
Oct. 3, Tuesday
—Psalm 27:1-6
—Wait for God's Guidance
Oct. 4, Wednesday
—Judges 3:7-11
—Othniel Judges Israel
Oct. 5, Thursday
—Hebrews 11:1-2, 32-34
—Courageous Leaders
Oct. 6, Friday
—Judges 4:1-10
—Deborah Leads the People
Oct. 7, Saturday
—Judges 4:12-16
—Success Assured
Oct. 8, Sunday
—Judges 5:1-12
—Deborah's Song of Praise

## PRAYER

*Dear Lord, we pray for our spiritual leaders. In Jesus' name, we pray. Amen.*

---

[1] *The Learning Bible* (New York: American Bible Society, 2000) Judges p. 437, 441.
[2] *(NIV Study Bible/Judges,* p. 452).

## Lesson 7

# God Answers Samuel's Prayer

**October 15, 2006**

**ADULT TOPIC:** Prayer Makes the Difference
**YOUTH TOPIC:** Samuel Prays for Help
**CHILDREN'S TOPIC:** Samuel Prays and God Answers

**UNIT II**
God's Covenant with Judges and Kings

**CHILDREN'S UNIT**
God Sends Judges and Kings

**DEVOTIONAL READING:** Psalm 31:14-24
**BACKGROUND SCRIPTURE:** 1 Samuel 7:3-13
**PRINT PASSAGE:** 1 Samuel 7:3-13

### 1 Samuel 7:3-13—KJV

3 And Samuel spake unto all the house of Israel, saying, If ye do return unto the LORD with all your hearts, then put away the strange gods and Ashtaroth from among you, and prepare your hearts unto the LORD, and serve him only: and he will deliver you out of the hand of the Philistines.

4 Then the children of Israel did put away Baalim and Ashtaroth, and served the LORD only.

5 And Samuel said, Gather all Israel to Mizpeh, and I will pray for you unto the LORD.

6 And they gathered together to Mizpeh, and drew water, and poured it out before the LORD, and fasted on that day, and said there, We have sinned against the LORD. And Samuel judged the children of Israel in Mizpeh.

7 And when the Philistines heard that the children of Israel were gathered together to Mizpeh, the lords of the Philistines went up against Israel. And when the children of Israel heard it, they were afraid of the Philistines.

8 And the children of Israel said to Samuel, Cease not to cry unto the LORD our God for us, that he will save us out of the hand of the Philistines.

9 And Samuel took a sucking lamb, and offered it for a burnt offering wholly unto the LORD: and Samuel cried unto the LORD for Israel; and the LORD heard him.

10 And as Samuel was offering up the burnt offering, the Philistines drew near to battle against Israel: but the LORD thundered with a great thunder on that day upon the Philistines, and discomfited them; and they were smitten before Israel.

### KEY VERSE

Samuel took a sucking lamb, and offered it for a burnt offering wholly unto the LORD: and Samuel cried unto the LORD for Israel; and the LORD heard him.
—1 Samuel 7:9

### OBJECTIVES

Upon completion of this lesson, the students are expected to:

1. Learn that prayer is the spiritual exercise of communicating with God;
2. Understand that prayer should be a continuous attitude that pervades the atmosphere of our entire lives; and,
3. Discover that God draws near to help those who call upon Him from a sincere heart.

11 And the men of Israel went out of Mizpeh, and pursued the Philistines, and smote them, until they came under Beth-car.

12 Then Samuel took a stone, and set it between Mizpeh and Shen, and called the name of it Eben-ezer, saying, Hitherto hath the LORD helped us.

13 So the Philistines were subdued, and they came no more into the coast of Israel: and the hand of the LORD was against the Philistines all the days of Samuel.

## UNIFYING LESSON PRINCIPLE

Praying for others shows our concern for them and, on some level, engages us with their plight. What are the effects of praying for others? Samuel prayed for the Israelites when they were threatened by the Philistines, and God saved them.

## POINTS TO BE EMPHASIZED
## ADULTS/ YOUTH

**Adult Key Verse:** 1 Samuel 7:9
**Youth Key Verse:** 1 Samuel 7:8
**Print Passage:** 1 Samuel 7:3-13

—What role did Samuel play in ancient Israel?
—What does this story suggest about how God responds to prayer?
—What role did Samuel play in ancient Israel?

## CHILDREN

**Key Verse:** 1 Samuel 7:9
**Print Passage:** 1 Samuel 4:1; 7:5-13

—The Israelites depended upon a strong leader, Samuel, to intercede on their behalf with God.
—Samuel demonstrated the power of prayer.
—Samuel set up a stone to remind the people that God had helped them.

## TOPICAL OUTLINE OF THE LESSON

I. INTRODUCTION
  A. A Look at Prayer
  B. Biblical Background

II. EXPOSITION AND APPLICATION OF THE SCRIPTURE
  A. Rejecting Baalism and Embracing God *(1 Samuel 7:3-4)*
  B. The Petition, the Sacrifice, and the Confession *(1 Samuel 7:5-6)*
  C. Fearfulness Induces Prayerfulness *(1 Samuel 7:7-8)*
  D. An Interrupted Sacrifice and a Military Slaughter *(1 Samuel 7:9-11)*
  E. Here I Raise My Ebenezer *(1 Samuel 7:12-13)*

III. CONCLUDING REFLECTIONS

## I. INTRODUCTION
### A. A Look at Prayer

This week's lesson showcases a powerful example of effective prayer. There is a colossal difference between reading about the power of prayer and personally experiencing the power of prayer. When we approach the subject of prayer from a purely academic perspective, we learn a great deal about technique but very little about results. The best way to learn about prayer is to pray. Prayer is the spiritual exercise of communicating with God. There are many different types of prayer, including corporate prayer, intercession, confession, thanksgiving, petition, and others. Although people may like the idea of receiving automatic, guaranteed answers to their prayers, only God can determine the answers. However, there are certain spiritual prerequisites to prayer that place God's people in the prime position to speak to God and receive answers from God.

The Bible affirms that powerful prayer is largely dependant on the personal characteristics of the petitioner. Below is a partial list of characteristics that are identified in Scripture as creating an atmosphere conducive for effective answers to prayer.

James 5:16 declares, "The effectual fervent prayer of a righteous man availeth much." From this we see that effective prayer is intense rather than lackadaisical. It also comes from a person whose life conforms to the guidelines of God.

James 1:6-7 can be summarized by stating that whenever we ask God for something, we must ask in faith without wavering. Persons who doubt cancel their own answer to prayer. People who believe boost their chances of receiving an answer.

First Thessalonians 5:17 simply says to pray without ceasing. This helps us to understand that prayer is not just an event that occurs at a particular point in our lives when we happen to be in need. Prayer should be a continuous attitude that pervades the atmosphere of our entire lives.

Samuel was a man whose life reflected characteristics that placed him in a position to receive answers from God. As we read about his life, let us pay close attention to his words and his ways in order to apply his principles to our own lives.

## B. Biblical Background

Throughout his life, Samuel experienced a variety of roles and responsibilities. He was a judge, a prophet, a priest, and a counselor. As a child, he was brought to the temple by his mother Hannah and dedicated to the service of God. As a young man, he heard the voice of God calling him into service. He answered that call and was faithful as Eli's assistant. God promoted him to more responsible positions; some distinctive occurrences in his life include the following:

- Samuel commissioned Israel's first two kings that created the transition from a theocracy to a monarchy.
- Samuel helped to unify Israel and to transform them from loosely-organized tribes to a solid center of power.
- Samuel was the last in the line (two centuries) of Israel's judges and is listed in the Hall of Faith (Hebrews 11).
- Samuel failed to influence his own two sons, Joel and Abijah, into an obedient relationship with God.

We learn from Samuel that lasting and significant accomplishments in life are directly related to a person's relationship with God. A person cannot toy with his or her relationship with God in this one life. In Samuel's life, we also see that personal character is significantly more important than personal accomplishment.[1]

What is it about being unique that sometimes causes people and nations to want to conform themselves to be like others? In spite of Samuel's stellar example of what it means to be a man of God, the people of Israel insisted upon having a king like the surrounding nations. Both Samuel and God reluctantly consented, and Israel's request was finally granted. Little did they know that this request would open the door for future failure and great disappointment on the part of the kings, as well as for hardship for the people. The people of Israel would be forced to learn the hard way that there is no better leader than God. People are limited; God is unlimited.

## II. Exposition and Application of the Scripture
### A. Rejecting Baalism and Embracing God
*(1 Samuel 7:3-4)*

**And Samuel spake unto all the house of Israel, saying, If ye do return unto the Lord with all your hearts, then put away the strange gods and Ashtaroth from among you, and prepare your hearts unto the Lord, and serve him only: and he will deliver you out of the hand of the Philistines. Then the children of Israel did put away Baalim and Ashtaroth, and served the Lord only.**

In the midst of their oppression by their archenemies—the Philistines—Israel "lamented after the Lord" (verse 2). By nature, the heart of God is soft and sensitive toward those who honestly and fervently cry out for His assistance. Throughout Scripture, there is a pattern of God drawing near to help those who call upon God with a sincere heart. A legitimate cry of distress represents a golden opportunity for God to display His power and rescue His people.

As God's mouthpiece, Samuel offered the Israelites a spiritual solution to their Philistine problem. This offer contained conditions as well as a guarantee. The guarantee represented exactly that for which Israel had been praying—deliverance from their enemies. However, the conditions had to be met before the guarantee was made good. The conditions given to the Israelites are basically the same as God gives to us today.

- *Return to the Lord*—Israel's return to God simply represented a reclaiming of the spiritual fervor and commitment that had been lost through distractions, backsliding, preoccupation with the world, and generally taking God for granted. A similar sentiment is echoed in the book of Revelation, where John writes to the church in Ephesus, "But I have this against you, that you have abandoned the love you had at first" (Revelation 2:4). When we leave our spiritual home and behave like a prodigal, the loving Father continuously longs for the day that the wandering child will come back home.

- *With all your heart*—Not only does God want us to repent, God wants us to come home with all of our hearts. A halfhearted return is almost worse than no return at all, because a halfhearted return increases the likelihood of another episode of falling away. God is able to accomplish so much more with us when God is assured of our whole hearts.

- *Put away the strange gods*—This request seemed to be a constant refrain when the judges made requests of the people on behalf of God. A "strange god" both then and now represents anything and anyone who comes between the true God and us. Strange gods distract our attention from God and inhibit our spiritual progress. God can tolerate much from His people, but the serving of strange gods does major collateral damage to our covenantal relationship with God.

- *Prepare your hearts unto the Lord*—The way that we prepare our hearts unto the Lord is by taking the time to consciously and intentionally put God at the top of our priority list. Preparing our hearts unto God includes saturating ourselves in the Word and ways of God. Heart preparation involves an adjustment of our attitudes and priorities to a point of readiness to receive and obey whatever God commands.

- *Serve God only*—As if to make sure that the Israelites comprehended the message, Samuel reemphasized the fact that this "marriage" between God and the children of Israel was an exclusive, lifelong covenantal commitment. Exclusive commitment to God enables exclusive benefits from God. When the Israelites entered Canaan, they were experienced as herdsmen. Consequently, they were forced to depend upon the conquered Canaanites for expert instruction on raising crops. When they entered the land they learned the religious observances that were believed to be essential to their success in the new land. Unfortunately, they attempted to blend worship of Yahweh with Baalism. This mixture of religions is called syncretism. It was a serious menace to the religion and morals of Israel, and was sternly opposed by the prophets.

### B. The Petition, the Sacrifice, and the Confession *(1 Samuel 7:5-6)*

**And Samuel said, Gather all Israel to Mizpeh, and I will pray for you unto the Lord. And they gathered together to Mizpeh, and drew water, and poured it out before the Lord, and fasted on that day, and said there, We have sinned against the Lord. And Samuel judged the children of Israel in Mizpeh.**

When the people met God's condition for divine intervention, Samuel agreed to intervene on their behalf. After all of the people were gathered at Mizpah, Samuel offered a prayer of petition and intercession. Mizpah is associated with the word "watchtower." If indeed there was a watchtower in Mizpah, it might have come in handy as a location high enough to adequately address such a great number of people. It also may have been a good vantage point to keep an eye on any advancing enemies as well.

Pouring out water is a practice that is not common elsewhere in the Scripture. It may have been a symbolic and sacrificial gesture held over from the wilderness experience since water there was such a valuable resource. Another aspect of their sacrifice was the fast that was called and implemented on that day. The fast allowed the people to deny physical gratification and concentrate solely on the very serious commitment they were making to God.

Operating hand in hand with the sacrifice of the people was the confession of the people. Open and honest confession creates an atmosphere and mindset of liberation. As David articulates so well throughout the Psalms, silence and hidden sin stagnate the spiritual process of healing and forgiveness. But openness and transparency activate the spiritual process and allow forgiveness to occur so the believer can move forward toward his or her destiny.

### C. Fearfulness Induces Prayerfulness *(1 Samuel 7:7-8)*

**And when the Philistines heard that the children of Israel were gathered together to Mizpeh, the lords of the Philistines went up against Israel. And when the children of Israel heard it, they were afraid of the Philistines.**

**And the children of Israel said to Samuel, Cease not to cry unto the LORD our God for us, that he will save us out of the hand of the Philistines.**

The reason that the children of Israel had gathered to request God's assistance was because of the oppression of the Philistines. Now that they were petitioning God for relief, a major attack was staged by the very enemies they were asking God to harness. Sometimes, when we make a move toward God it seems that all that the devil has to offer breaks loose on us; instead of things getting better, they appear to get worse. The news of the Philistines' mounting presence struck fear in the hearts of the people; but instead of allowing fear to paralyze them, they drew closer to God. It is noteworthy that the people did not pray to God for themselves. Instead, they appealed to Samuel to pray for them. This request reflects faith that is still in infancy. Although it is always good to have a designated spiritual leader to prayerfully intervene on our behalf, it is better to have a relationship with God that enables us to reach God for ourselves.

### D. An Interrupted Sacrifice and a Military Slaughter *(1 Samuel 7:9-11)*

**And Samuel took a sucking lamb, and offered it for a burnt offering wholly unto the LORD: and Samuel cried unto the LORD for Israel; and the LORD heard him. And as Samuel was offering up the burnt offering, the Philistines drew near to battle against Israel: but the LORD thundered with a great thunder on that day upon the Philistines, and discomfited them; and they were smitten before Israel. And the men of Israel went out of Mizpeh, and pursued the Philistines, and smote them, until they came under Beth-car.**

It was common to have a lamb offered as a sacrifice to God. In this case, the lamb was extremely young because it was still dependent on its mother's milk. Sacrifices throughout the Old Testament took different forms according to various customs and cultures, including:

- *Gifts and Tributes*—These offerings were given as an expression of thanksgiving.
- *Covenant and Communion*—These sacrifices forged or reaffirmed ties of kinship and undergirded political alliances.
- *Sin Offerings and Guilt Offerings*—These sacrifices involved instances in which there had been moral or physical contact with impurity or an infraction that required divine mediation.

When the Philistines interrupted the worship of God, the wrath of God was manifested and the result was their utter annihilation. God spoke displeasure through the natural auspices of overwhelmingly loud thunder. The fear that had been in the hearts of the Israelites was multiplied in the hearts of the Philistines, and the confusion that resulted proved to be their downfall.

### E. Here I Raise My Ebenezer *(1 Samuel 7:12-13)*

**Then Samuel took a stone, and set it between Mizpeh and Shen, and called the name of it Eben-ezer, saying, Hitherto hath the LORD helped us. So the Philistines were subdued, and they came no more into the coast of Israel: and the hand of the LORD was against the Philistines all the days of Samuel.**

In an effort to symbolize and never forget the great move of God that occurred at Mizpeh, Samuel erected a stone between Mizpeh and Shen. Samuel called the name of the stone *Ebenezer*. This is interpreted, "stone of help." This was their recognition of God's hand in their history. Whatever might happen to them as a nation in the future, here was a clear and decisive recognition: *Hiterto hath the Lord helped us.* It is important to recall, acknowledge, and affirm how God has undeniably intervened during times of trouble and challenge. When we see how God intervenes, our faith is strengthened and we are better able to face the challenges of the future. We can know that if God has delivered once, God certainly can deliver again.

## III. Concluding Reflections

The Israelites' miraculous deliverance from the Philistines occurred many years ago, but the story holds relevance for us today. Just as the Israelites were tempted to be spiritually syncretistic, so are we today. Syncretism, used in this context, involves the meshing of meaning, symbolism, and morality from a variety of spiritual persuasions. Syncretism occurred because it was easy, convenient, and popular. Some of the things about serving God today can be difficult, inconvenient, and unpopular. Consequently, God becomes displeased when we opt for worldly ways that are in direct conflict with obedience to God. History has proven something that is forever true: God's way is always the best way.

## WORD POWER

**Cried (Hebrew: *za'ak*)**—there are different ways of crying. The word used here depicts a cry of anguish. Samuel was fully aware of the predicament of the Israelites. He cried *(Za'ak)* from his heart and God hears such cries from His anointed. Danger was looming, and the best action was not only to sacrifice but cry unto the Lord.

## HOME DAILY BIBLE READINGS

for the week of October 15, 2006
*God Answers Samuel's Prayer*

Oct. 9, Monday
—Colossians 4:2-6
—Call to Prayer
Oct. 10, Tuesday
—Psalm 31:14-24
—The Psalmist Prays
Oct. 11, Wednesday
—1 Samuel 1:21-28
—Hannah Pays Her Vows
Oct. 12, Thursday
—1 Samuel 2:1-11
—Hannah Prays
Oct. 13, Friday
—1 Samuel 3:1-10
—The Lord Calls Samuel
Oct. 14, Saturday
—1 Samuel 7:2-6
—Israel Returns to God
Oct. 15, Sunday
—1 Samuel 7:7-13
—The Lord Helps the Hebrew People

## PRAYER

*Dear God, please give us a spirit of discernment to detect ways that Your standards are being compromised by our thoughts, words, or behavior. In Jesus' name, we pray. Amen.*

---

[1] *Life Application Study Bible*, p. 541.

**October 22, 2006**

## Lesson 8

**UNIT II**
God's Covenant with Judges and Kings

**CHILDREN'S UNIT**
God Sends Judges and Kings

# God Covenants with David

**ADULT TOPIC:** A Promise You Can Trust
**YOUTH TOPIC:** David's Everlasting Kingdom
**CHILDREN'S TOPIC:** God Makes a Promise to David

**KEY VERSE**

Thine house and thy kingdom shall be established for ever before thee: thy throne shall be established for ever.
— 2 Samuel 7:16

**DEVOTIONAL READING:** Psalm 5
**BACKGROUND SCRIPTURE:** 2 Samuel 7
**PRINT PASSAGE:** 2 Samuel 7:8-17

### 2 Samuel 7:8-17—KJV

8 Now therefore so shalt thou say unto my servant David, Thus saith the LORD of hosts, I took thee from the sheepcote, from following the sheep, to be ruler over my people, over Israel:

9 And I was with thee whithersoever thou wentest, and have cut off all thine enemies out of thy sight, and have made thee a great name, like unto the name of the great men that are in the earth.

10 Moreover I will appoint a place for my people Israel, and will plant them, that they may dwell in a place of their own, and move no more; neither shall the children of wickedness afflict them any more, as beforetime,

11 And as since the time that I commanded judges to be over my people Israel, and have caused thee to rest from all thine enemies. Also the LORD telleth thee that he will make thee an house.

12 And when thy days be fulfilled, and thou shalt sleep with thy fathers, I will set up thy seed after thee, which shall proceed out of thy bowels, and I will establish his kingdom.

13 He shall build an house for my name, and I will stablish the throne of his kingdom for ever.

14 I will be his father, and he shall be my son. If he commit iniquity, I will chasten him with the rod of men, and with the stripes of the children of men:

15 But my mercy shall not depart away from him, as I took it from Saul, whom I put away before thee.

16 And thine house and thy kingdom shall be established for ever before thee: thy throne shall be established for ever.

**OBJECTIVES**

Upon completion of this lesson, the students are expected to:

1. Recognize that one of life's most important considerations is our desires centering in God's will;
2. Learn that the divine instrument for blessing God's people was the family and lineage of David; and,
3. Understand God's promise to forever remain faithful to the covenant being made with the house of David.

**17** According to all these words, and according to all this vision, so did Nathan speak unto David.

## UNIFYING LESSON PRINCIPLE

Trustworthy promises mean more to us than ones easily broken. What is an example of a promise we can trust? God promised to secure David's lineage and throne, and Christians celebrate the eternal nature of this promise as fulfilled in Jesus Christ.

## POINTS TO BE EMPHASIZED ADULTS/YOUTH

**Adult/Youth Key Verse:** 2 Samuel 7:16
**Print Passage:** 2 Samuel 7:8-17

—God reserves the right to discipline David's heirs.
—The prophet Nathan revealed God's covenant to David.
—What does this passage suggest about David and his relationship with God?

## CHILDREN

**Key Verse:** 2 Samuel 7:16
**Print Passage:** 2 Samuel 7:8-17

—God's promise to David includes a place where Israel can live in safety.
—God is a trustworthy God who keeps His promises.
—God promises an eternal love.

## TOPICAL OUTLINE OF THE LESSON

I. Introduction
   A. Determining the Will of God
   B. Biblical Background

II. Exposition and Application of the Scripture
   A. Remembering the Past Gives Perspective to the Present *(2 Samuel 7:8-9)*
   B. Remembering the Past Gives Perspective to the Future *(2 Samuel 7:10-11)*
   C. A Faithful Life Yields a Fruitful Legacy *(2 Samuel 7:12-13)*
   D. God Establishes a Family Tie *(2 Samuel 7:14-15)*
   E. Promise of an Everlasting Kingdom *(2 Samuel 7:16-17)*

III. Concluding Reflections

## I. Introduction
### A. Determining the Will of God

It has been said that good is the enemy of the best. Sometimes we can invest a great deal of time and energy into things that are admirable, but not necessarily beneficial to God's kingdom or to ourselves. We may desire to accomplish great works for ourselves, for others, and even for God. Our motives may be completely pure, but the most important factor to consider is whether or not our desire is at the center of God's will. Scripture records that " 'All things are lawful', but not all things are beneficial. 'All things are lawful', but not all things build up" (1 Corinthians 10:23). How do we determine if something is truly the will of God?

In 2 Samuel 7, King David had conquered all neighboring contenders and the kingdom was calm. This position of dominance allowed David to reflect on more idealistic objectives. He realized that his palace was a fine house made of cedar but the ark of God was still surrounded by curtains. His altruistic idea was to construct a grand house for God. When he shared his vision with Nathan the prophet, Nathan initially encouraged David to move forward with his plans because God was with David. This incident is an example of how we can have an idea or a desire that is personally honorable but not spiritually plausible. We can even receive confirmation through a person whom we consider to be close to God, but this does not always mean our plan is from God. Thankfully, Nathan did not stop with his first response. He was spiritually mature enough to admit he had made a mistake in his initial answer to David.

No matter how long we have been walking with the Lord, there is always room to grow. Being a disciple of Jesus Christ is such an awesome experience because we never arrive at a spiritual plateau where we can rest upon our accomplishments. There is always more to learn about the Lord and more to do for the Kingdom. Although God affirmed David's idea, God had to make an adjustment in order for David's vision to be properly aligned with God's plan. Our very best thought, idea, or plan will fail if it is not aligned with God's plan. God's ways are much higher than our ways. Proverbs 16:9 reminds us that "The human mind plans the way, but the LORD directs the steps."

## B. Biblical Background

Second Samuel begins by outlining David's grief over the death of Saul. Even though Saul had sought David's life, David had so much respect for spiritual authority that he refused to attempt retaliation against Saul, nor would he allow anyone else to do so. After David became king of Judah, there were seven years of war against Ish-bosheth, the son of Saul. Eventually, David was made king over all Israel and Jerusalem became the capitol of the unified nation.

The Old Testament is a detailed record of God's specific plan for blessing God's people. God's instrument for blessing God's people was the family and lineage of David. Second Samuel 7 records the first in an extensive series of promises regarding an eternal king who would emerge from the seed of David. Below are examples of these prophecies:

"Thy throne shall be established for ever" (2 Samuel 7:16).

"If thou wilt walk before me, as David thy father walked…Then I will Establish the throne of thy kingdom, according as I have covenanted with David thy father" (2 Chronicles 7:17-18).

"Unto us a child is born, unto us a son is given: and the government shall be upon his shoulder…there shall be no end, upon the throne of David" (Isaiah 9:6-7).

Why was the family of David extended the honor of being used by God to bring blessings to the world and to give us the Messiah? David was deemed to be a man after God's own heart. He was a radical worshiper who was not intimidated by other people's opinion of his intense worship of God. Even when David committed grievous sin, he was sensitive enough to the Spirit of God to heed the corrective offered by God's prophet. He repented of his sins and sought God's forgiveness. David had a heart and soul wholly devoted to God. In a world of idolatry, and amid a nation that was prone to turn away from God, David stood like a rock for God. It was the divine plan of God that through one family every other nation of the world would be blessed.

## II. Exposition and Application of the Scripture
### A. Remembering the Past Gives Perspective to the Present
*(2 Samuel 7:8-9)*

**Now therefore so shalt thou say unto my servant David, Thus saith the Lord of hosts, I took thee from the sheepcote, from following the sheep, to be ruler over my people, over Israel: And I was with thee whithersoever thou wentest, and have cut off all thine enemies out of thy sight, and have made thee a great name, like unto the name of the great men that are in the earth.**

Sometimes it is good to be reminded of our past in order to properly understand and contextualize our present circumstances. When God initially exposed David via the prophet Nathan, David spent the majority of his days in isolation, with no company other than the sheep he tended in the pasture. Occasionally, David performed some act of valor, such as killing a lion or a bear while tending to his father's sheep. However, there was no one there to applaud him, to appreciate him or to even corroborate his exciting stories. The only witnesses were the smelly sheep, David himself, and God. It was God who passed over royal families and trained warriors to reach into the pasture and pull out David to lead, protect, and represent the people of God. Only God could take a boy who leads sheep and promote him to a man who leads a nation. Jogging David's memory by reminding him of God's past provisions was a technique used by God to prepare David for the veto of his idea. A subtle undertone here is the assurance of God's love. If God did not love David, God would not have chosen David.

Not only did God choose David (verse 8), but God also provided *presence, protection,* and *prominence.* Throughout the majority of his life, whenever David attempted something, he always succeeded. This phenomenon can be traced to the perpetual presence of God in David's life. Even when the odds against David were devastating, with the presence of God he always prevailed. God's presence with David also translated into military protection. The hand of the Lord eradicated all of David's enemies in an era when there were constant contenders to a king's throne. The enemies eventually realized that fighting against David would be a losing battle. The same principle can apply to believers today: If God is for us, who can be against us? Finally, God's presence with David elevated David's name to a place of great historical prominence. Not every disciple of Jesus Christ is guaranteed a prominent position in history from an earthly perspective. But if our names are recorded in the Lamb's Book of Life, we automatically become prominent people. Being spiritually prominent does not necessarily mean we will be socially popular or financially wealthy. But divine relationship is more valuable than financial prosperity. To be counted in the company of God is a priceless privilege. If the Father owns everything, and the child is in right relationship with the Father, that means the child has direct access to everything deemed appropriate by the Father.

### B. Remembering the Past Gives Perspective to the Future (2 Samuel 7:10-11)

**Moreover I will appoint a place for my people Israel, and will plant them, that they may dwell in a place of their own, and move no more; neither shall the children of wickedness afflict them any more, as beforetime, And as since the time that I commanded judges to be over my people Israel, and have caused thee to rest from all thine enemies. Also the Lord telleth thee that he will make thee an house.**

When we remember what God has done in the past, it serves as an encouragement for God's work in the future. As David entered a contemplative period of his life, he was reminded of how God had provided for them in the past. The logical conclusion should be a sense of trust in God's ability to make good on these plans and prophecies for the future. Promises made by God are promises that will be fulfilled by God.

In order to develop a sense of permanence and longevity, God decided to appoint a place of worship for the people in order to plant them forever. In the past, the people and their leaders never knew when the nation might be attacked. Therefore, it was necessary to have a mobile temple that was always ready to be moved at a moment's notice. But since God had brought peace to the camp, the permanent building could be established. A place of worship that is "planted" should be able to yield more "fruit" than a place of worship that is mobile.

### C. A Faithful Life Yields a Fruitful Legacy (2 Samuel 7:12-13)

**And when thy days be fulfilled, and thou shalt sleep with thy fathers, I will set up thy seed after thee, which shall proceed out of thy bowels, and I will establish his kingdom. He shall build an house for my name, and I will stablish the throne of his kingdom for ever.**

One of the concerns of Old Testament culture was the type of legacy one would leave. This notion is reflected in Proverbs 13:22: "The good leave an inheritance to their children's children." The cultural importance of memory is also reflected in the kings and pharaohs' preoccupation with embalming and erecting statues, monuments, buildings, and regal tombs. The pursuit of immortality is timeless. God's promise was that David's son would carry on the business of the kingdom and that he would oversee the construction of the temple.

Solomon's temple would prove to be one of unsurpassed beauty, splendor, and grandeur. Solomon used expert Phoenician workers and 30,000 forced laborers to construct the temple. Seven years were required to complete the building of the temple, and Solomon took thirteen additional years to erect a series of palaces and other royal buildings adjoining the temple. "Everything was richly trimmed in gold, especially the holy of holies, with its six hundred talents of fine gold.... Even the nails were made of gold, some weighing as much as fifty shekels... For good measure, precious stones were plentifully sprinkled round about."[1] Although the permanent temple contained such lavish appointments, the spectacle of the design was not the original purpose of the temple as reflected in 2 Samuel 7:13.

The purpose, as expressed here by God, was to "build a house for my name." We must never allow the surface trimmings of a building to distract from the central purpose of God's house—to worship and concentrate on the King of kings and the Lord of lords.

### D. God Establishes a Family Tie
*(2 Samuel 7:14-15)*

**I will be his father, and he shall be my son. If he commit iniquity, I will chasten him with the rod of men, and with the stripes of the children of men: But my mercy shall not depart away from him, as I took it from Saul, whom I put away before thee.**

In this spiritual proposal, God promises to forever remain faithful to the covenant being made with the house of David. A foundational relationship in life is the bond that exists between a father and a son. Family ties between father and son extend beyond the surface relationships of acquaintances. Expectations and commitment levels extend far beyond the average. This is a bond that cannot be severed, even when the other party in the covenant does not fulfill the terms of the agreement. Foreknowing the problems that would arise in his relationship with Solomon, God established the certainty of discipline when iniquity occurs. Several Scriptures refer to the parallel between the disciplines extended to a wayward child by a concerned father (see Deuteronomy 8:5; Proverbs 13:24; Hebrews 12:6-7). Although godly discipline can sometimes be misunderstood as anger or hatred, it is actually a parent's *failure* to discipline a child that is an indication of disdain.

The most important aspect of God's promise to David was God's insistence that God's mercy would never depart from the house of David. Certainly, fresh in David's memory must have been the fact that God's Spirit once had led Saul but later departed because of Saul's disobedience. One of the saddest verses in the Bible records God's withdrawal from someone whom God once led: "Now the spirit of the Lord departed from Saul, and an evil spirit from the Lord tormented him" (1 Samuel 16:14). Since God is sovereign, God is capable of harnessing anything—including a troubling spirit—for God's divine purposes.

### E. Promise of an Everlasting Kingdom
*(2 Samuel 7:16-17)*

**And thine house and thy kingdom shall be established for ever before thee: thy throne shall be established for ever. According to all these words, and according to all this vision, so did Nathan speak unto David.**

Although this text focuses on the lineage of David, there was a long-standing belief in David's everlasting kingdom in a physical sense. This belief persisted even after the downfall of David's dynasty during the period of the Exile. Israel's hope then centered on the coming of David's greater son. Without the proper interpretation of God's promises, the expectations of people can easily be intertwined and combined with the stated promises of God. The result of this combination can be the creation of flawed and false information about God. A true promise can become an untrue myth if the true promise is not properly understood and interpreted. That is why it is so important not to add or subtract from the promises of God (Luke 16:17). This is why we are encouraged in 2 Timothy to diligently demonstrate our commitment to "rightly dividing" or correctly interpreting the Word of God (2 Timothy 2:15). The only truly everlasting throne is the throne of God (see Psalm 45:6). The good news today is that God has made it possible for all believers to live forever. We are able to last forever when we accept Jesus Christ, who freely offers to us the gift of everlasting life (see John 3:16).

## III. Concluding Reflections

This chapter of 2 Samuel helps us to properly understand the difference between the physical temple and God's spiritual temple. The permanent physical temple would replace and improve upon the curtained temple of the portable structure and lacked significant emphasis upon beauty and aesthetics. The temple played an important role in the life of the Israelites. It unified them around a common course—that is, worshiping God. But Jesus Christ gave a new understanding of the temple of God. Our bodies are the temple of the Lord. Where two or three gathered together, He said, "I am in your midst." The apostle Paul affirms that we should glorify God with our bodies.

## WORD POWER

**Forever (Hebrew: *ad-olaam*)**—this word is used twice in 2 Samuel 7:16. Some news is too good to be true. As mundane modern people, this promise seems too good to be true, but it is the promise of God to David. The first part *(ad)* means duration, lasting perpetually. The second word *(ol-aam)*, means "to continue without end." No earthly power could stop the fulfillment of God's promise to David. This promise is fulfilled in the Lord, Jesus Christ.

## HOME DAILY BIBLE READINGS

for the week of October 22, 2006
*God Covenants with David*

Oct. 16, Monday
 —1 Samuel 16:1-13
 —Samuel Anoints Young David
Oct. 17, Tuesday
 —1 Samuel 16:14-23
 —David's Lyre Soothes Saul
Oct. 18, Wednesday
 —1 Samuel 17:32-37
 —David Protects the Sheep
Oct. 19, Thursday
 —Psalm 5
 —A Cry for Help
Oct. 20, Friday
 —2 Samuel 2:1-7
 —Judah Anoints David King
Oct. 21, Saturday
 —2 Samuel 7:8-17
 —God's Promises to David
Oct. 22, Sunday
 —2 Samuel 7:18-29
 —David Speaks to God

## PRAYER

*O Lord, let us not become so caught up in church busyness that we neglect to accomplish the mandatory church business of loving You, loving others, and loving ourselves.*

---

[1] *Interpreter's Dictionary, Temple,* p. 538.

# Lesson 9

# God Grants Wisdom to Solomon

**October 29, 2006**

**ADULT TOPIC:** God Answers Prayer
**YOUTH TOPIC:** Wisdom to Rule
**CHILDREN'S TOPIC:** God Makes Solomon Wise

**UNIT II**
God's Covenant with Judges and Kings

**CHILDREN'S UNIT**
God Sends Judges and Kings

**DEVOTIONAL READING:** Psalm 119:97-104
**BACKGROUND SCRIPTURE:** 1 Kings 3
**PRINT PASSAGE:** 1 Kings 3:3-14

## 1 Kings 3:3-14—KJV

3 And Solomon loved the LORD, walking in the statutes of David his father: only he sacrificed and burnt incense in high places.

4 And the king went to Gibeon to sacrifice there; for that was the great high place: a thousand burnt offerings did Solomon offer upon that altar.

5 In Gibeon the LORD appeared to Solomon in a dream by night: and God said, Ask what I shall give thee.

6 And Solomon said, Thou hast shewed unto thy servant David my father great mercy, according as he walked before thee in truth, and in righteousness, and in uprightness of heart with thee; and thou hast kept for him this great kindness, that thou hast given him a son to sit on his throne, as it is this day.

7 And now, O LORD my God, thou hast made thy servant king instead of David my father: and I am but a little child: I know not how to go out or come in.

8 And thy servant is in the midst of thy people which thou hast chosen, a great people, that cannot be numbered nor counted for multitude.

9 Give therefore thy servant an understanding heart to judge thy people, that I may discern between good and bad: for who is able to judge this thy so great a people?

10 And the speech pleased the Lord, that Solomon had asked this thing.

11 And God said unto him, Because thou hast asked this thing, and hast not asked for thyself long life; neither hast asked riches

## KEY VERSE

Behold, I have done according to thy words: lo, I have given thee a wise and an understanding heart; so that there was none like thee before thee, neither after thee shall any arise like unto thee.—1 Kings 3:12

## OBJECTIVES

Upon completion of this lesson, the students are expected to:

1. Understand that nothing can take the place of total obedience to the will of God;
2. Recognize God's ability to supply our needs; and,
3. Learn that when we are aligned with God's will/purpose, we will receive what we request, plus a great deal more.

TOWNSEND PRESS COMMENTARY | 59

for thyself, nor hast asked the life of thine enemies; but hast asked for thyself understanding to discern judgment;

**12** Behold, I have done according to thy words: lo, I have given thee a wise and an understanding heart; so that there was none like thee before thee, neither after thee shall any arise like unto thee.

**13** And I have also given thee that which thou hast not asked, both riches, and honour: so that there shall not be any among the kings like unto thee all thy days.

**14** And if thou wilt walk in my ways, to keep my statutes and my commandments, as thy father David did walk, then I will lengthen thy days.

## UNIFYING LESSON PRINCIPLE

Most people want to understand the world around them and learn to make wise choices in it. What is the source of such wisdom? Solomon gained his tremendous wisdom by asking God for it, and God granted his prayer.

## POINTS TO BE EMPHASIZED
## ADULTS/YOUTH

**Adult Key Verse:** 1 Kings 3:12
**Youth Key Verse:** 1 Kings 3:9
**Print Passage:** 1 Kings 3:3-14

—Solomon connects wisdom with both ruling well and living well.
—Solomon understands that the king serves God.
—Solomon understands that God grants him authority and ability to rule.

## CHILDREN

**Key Verse:** 1 Kings 3:12
**Print Passage:** 1 Kings 3:3-14

—God is a powerful God who can grant all requests.
—God answers the prayers of those who are young, as He did with Solomon.
—God is pleased with a humble heart.

## TOPICAL OUTLINE OF THE LESSON

I. INTRODUCTION
  A. The Source of Morality
  B. Biblical Background

II. EXPOSITION AND APPLICATION OF THE SCRIPTURE
  A. Intensive Devotion, Expensive Exceptions *(1 Kings 3:3-4)*
  B. A Blank Check from God *(1 Kings 3:5)*
  C. Solomon's Appreciation Verbalized *(1 Kings 3:6)*
  D. Solomon's Humility Displayed *(1 Kings 3:7-8)*
  E. Solomon's Wise Request *(1 Kings 3:9)*
  F. God's Blessing for Solomon's Sacrifice *(1 Kings 3:10-11)*
  G. The Value of a Wise and Understanding Heart *(1 Kings 3:12-14)*

III. CONCLUDING REFLECTIONS

## I. INTRODUCTION
### A. The Source of Morality

How does one determine what makes right, right, and what makes wrong, wrong? What is the source of a person's system of ethics? Some base their ethics and morality upon how they feel at the moment. Others base truth upon what is written in God's Word. Still others take a combined approach and base their decisions upon God's Word, mingled with what seems most practical, convenient, and humanly feasible. What are the advantages and disadvantages of these different approaches to morality? Those who base their ethics solely upon personal feelings are at the mercy of their whims. Their approach allows their beliefs to change without warning. Those who base their ethics upon the written promises in the Word of God can expect to experience an abundant life of obedience and blessings, as promised by God. The third category is the most complicated category because it seeks in vain to retain the best benefits of both worlds. This approach desires the stability of God's promises combined with the convenience of worldly ways. Scripture issues a warning about such spiritual ambivalence: "I know your works; you are neither cold nor hot. I wish that you were either cold or hot" (Revelation 3:15).

This third flawed and fatal approach to morality and ethics is, unfortunately, the approach adopted by Solomon. While Solomon respected and embraced the godly ways of his father, David, at the same time he made substitutions for the proper place of worship and allowed the influence of foreign gods to filter into the environment.

## B. Biblical Background

The books of 1 and 2 Kings were once a single work. They were divided into two books in the Septuagint, possibly for reasons of convenience. Both books are over twenty chapters long. The author of this book is unknown, but the date of its writing has been placed at about 600 B.C., not long after the death of Josiah. As its title suggests, Kings offers a chronology of kings in Israel's history. Two separate lines of kings are mentioned (1 Kings 12:1—2 Kings 17:41). One of the universal principles expounded in 1 and 2 Kings relates to the recognition and elevation of monotheism. Kings introduces a strong sense of standards reflected in the habits, history, and standards of Yahweh. Yahweh's standards relate to a wide variety of topics, including worship, sexuality, sacrifice, justice, and forgiveness.

Solomon is the king profiled in this. No other king in history, can compare to the economic scope and vast impact of Solomon's kingdom. Solomon was an advanced thinker who reflected the unique gift of wisdom given to him by God. He excelled in the subjects of botany, zoology, architecture, poetry, finance, and philosophy. First Kings reflects the events and accomplishments that took place during the United Kingdom in Israel (1:1—11:43).

Under Solomon's leadership, Israel was able to eliminate opposition to the throne, construct the temple that David was not allowed to build, and establish a strong national military. Even with so many things going well for Solomon, he eventually allowed his love for business, commerce, and foreign women to distract him from wholeheartedly following God.

Although Solomon was known as the wisest man who ever lived, his wisdom must have been primarily in the governmental arena. When it came to finances and managing a nation and her people, Solomon chose wisely. But in matters related to being a godly man, a husband, and a father, Solomon often chose foolishly. It somehow seems impossible for a man who is so wise to make such unwise decisions. This should be a reminder to all followers of Christ—we can never become so comfortable and assured of our place in Christ that we neglect our need for continually growing in Him and remaining spiritually watchful.

## II. Exposition and Application of the Scripture

### A. Intensive Devotion, Expensive Exceptions *(1 Kings 3:3-4)*

**And Solomon loved the Lord, walking in the statutes of David his father: only he sacrificed and burnt incense in high places. And the king went to Gibeon to sacrifice there; for that was the great high place: a thousand burnt offerings did Solomon offer upon that altar.**

Similar to his father in many ways, Solomon was a man plagued by a tendency toward duplicity. Although his love and devotion to God was genuine and intense, he also had a persistent tendency toward moral and spiritual compromise. Perhaps this is a good example of the sins of the father being visited upon the next generation.

Both then and now, the tremendous impact and influence of a father's example is undeniable. Solomon inherited and replicated much of his father David's positive traits as well as the negative characteristics. Verse 3 of today's text identifies an example of how Solomon straddled the spiritual fence. Although he offered sacrifices and burnt incense to God, he did so in a dubious location. The "high places" were local hill shrines originally belonging to the Canaanites. Of course, the God of Israel had not been worshiped at these places. Hence, they retained an atmosphere of idolatry. The amount and extent of Solomon's offering was, without a doubt, extreme. Like his father, David, whose worship was so intense that he danced out of his clothes, Solomon did not just offer one burnt offering, or ten, or even a hundred. Solomon offered a thousand burnt offerings at Gibeon.

### B. A Blank Check from God *(1 Kings 3:5)*

**In Gibeon the Lord appeared to Solomon in a dream by night: and God said, Ask what I shall give thee.**

Suppose God appeared to us in a dream following worship. In the dream, God asked us to name any request and it would be surely granted. What would we request? Undoubtedly, many of us would request money, power, fame, health, or long life. For some, God's open request may seem oddly uncharacteristic of God. Such a reaction to God's generosity toward God's children is an indication that the true characteristics of God are not fully known. Two Scriptures from the Old and New testaments serve as evidence of the generous nature of God:

*Old Testament*—"Delight thyself also in the Lord; and he shall give thee the desires of thine heart. Commit thy way unto the Lord; trust also in him; and he shall bring it to pass" (Psalm 37:4-5).

*New Testament*—"If ye then, being evil, know how to give good gifts unto your children, how much more shall your Father which is in heaven give good things to them that ask him?" (Matthew 7:11).

God has no problems getting good things into the hands of obedient children because God also realizes that those hands are only a distribution station to touch the lives of others who are in need. Solomon is not the only one to receive a "blank check" from God. In fact, every believer has this opportunity available. Jesus said, "If ye abide in me, and my words abide in you, ye shall ask what ye will, and it shall be done unto you" (John 15:7). The reason that Jesus was able to make such a broad, open-ended statement is because of the spiritual condition applied at the beginning of the statement. Jesus knows that if we truly do abide, remain, and live within His will, whatever we ask of Him will already be in line with His desires. It is much like an obedient son asking to accompany his father on a job-related project or a star, high school student requesting extra homework.

### C. Solomon's Appreciation Verbalized
   *(1 Kings 3:6)*

**And Solomon said, Thou hast shewed unto thy servant David my father great mercy, according as he walked before thee in truth, and in righteousness, and in uprightness of heart with thee; and thou hast kept for him this great kindness, that thou hast given him a son to sit on his throne, as it is this day.**

After God asked Solomon to name his request, Solomon did not give a direct response. He first exercised a bit of spiritual diplomacy and genuine appreciation through acknowledging God's great mercy and kindness displayed toward his father and toward himself. God appreciates good manners, too. David was well-known for his psalms filled with words of thanksgiving. When Jesus healed the ten lepers he took notice of the one who returned to express appreciation. When we pray, it is wise not to begin and end the prayer with nothing in between but requests or "gimmes." Genuine thanksgiving gets God's attention. God wants to know that His relationship with us is based upon more than God's ability to supply our needs and wants.

God is concerned with the inner character of a person. The three characteristics of David that are identified in Solomon's response are David's truthfulness, righteousness, and uprightness of heart with God. These are the qualities that gain God's attention and capture God's heart.

### D. Solomon's Humility Displayed
   *(1 Kings 3:7-8)*

**And now, O LORD my God, thou hast made thy servant king instead of David my father: and I am but a little child: I know not how to go out or come in. And thy servant is in the midst of thy people which thou hast chosen, a great people, that cannot be numbered nor counted for multitude.**

Solomon displays his sense of humility through the phrase: "I am but a little child: I know not how to go out or come in." This statement reveals Solomon's sense of divine call to a super-human task. At this point of his life, Solomon was between twelve and twenty years old. His confession reveals his overwhelming sense of dependence on God. Solomon overemphasizes his own weakness in order to magnify God's strength. Personal humility is an important characteristic of effective spiritual leadership. This approach is almost completely opposite from the world's perspective. But Scripture corroborates this principle in Luke 14:11, which essentially holds that the person who exalts self will eventually be brought low, but the one who is humble will be exalted by God. Jesus Himself told His disciples that He did not come to be served, but to serve. Whoever desires to be the greatest should become the servant (Matthew 23:11).

### E. Solomon's Wise Request *(1 Kings 3:9)*

**Give therefore thy servant an understanding heart to judge thy people, that I may discern between good and bad: for who is able to judge this thy so great a people?**

In the true spirit of a humble servant, Solomon does not ask God for selfish and superficial supplies. Solomon's simple request is for an understanding heart. This request echoes the sentiments later recorded in Proverbs 4:5: "Get wisdom, get understanding: forget it not; neither decline from the words of my mouth." A heart of understanding is a necessary component for successfully judging a vast nation of people. A clear sense of discernment and understanding is not only useful and important for the king of a nation, it is also an invaluable asset for everyday people. Solomon demonstrated his keen sense of discernment in perhaps his most notable decision when he accurately judged the birth mother in a dispute over a child (see 1 Kings 3:16-28). Although Solomon was a king, his strong desire to judge accurately is somewhat a continuation of the tradition of Israel's long line of great judges.

### F. God's Blessing for Solomon's Sacrifice *(1 Kings 3:10-11)*

**And the speech pleased the Lord, that Solomon had asked this thing. And God said unto him, Because thou hast asked this thing, and hast not asked for thyself long life; neither hast asked riches for thyself, nor hast asked the life of thine enemies; but hast asked for thyself understanding to discern judgment.**

Throughout Scripture and contemporary history, God has always had a marvelous way of doing exceedingly, abundantly above all we can ask or think (see Ephesians 3:20). All that God needs from us is simple cooperation with God's will and ways. Solomon could have asked for so many things. God had put no restrictions on his request. He is pleased when we choose spiritual blessings over those of a temporal nature. Undoubtedly, the Lord was pleased with Solomon's humility regarding the task before him. Solomon was more concerned with leading his people than with accomplishing self-centered goals. Whenever we sincerely say "yes" to God through our words, will, and actions, we position ourselves to be blessed in ways that we could never imagine, according to God's abundance.

### G. The Value of a Wise and Understanding Heart *(1 Kings 3:12-14)*

**Behold, I have done according to thy words: lo, I have given thee a wise and an understanding heart; so that there was none like thee before thee, neither after thee shall any arise like unto thee. And I have also given thee that which thou hast not asked, both riches, and honour: so that there shall not be any among the kings like unto thee all thy days. And if thou wilt walk in my ways, to keep my statutes and my commandments, as thy father David did walk, then I will lengthen thy days.**

When Solomon aligned himself with God's mind, he received what he requested, plus a great deal more. God greatly rewarded Solomon because, instead of being self-centered, Solomon exhibited a Kingdom-centered mentality. This same principle is still in operation today. When we dare to seek first God's kingdom and God's righteousness, all the other things will be added (Matthew 6:33). Making God the top priority in life is by far the wisest decision one could ever make. Walking in godly ways and obeying God's commandments produces a life worth living.

## III. Concluding Reflections

As we study the life of Solomon and compare it to that of David, we are able to see patterns of generational curses and generational blessings. Undoubtedly, Solomon must have been negatively influenced by the polygamy that was practiced by his father, David. On the positive side, Solomon seemingly inherited David's strong love for God, as reflected through his worship. This paradigm can serve as an important lesson for us today as we endeavor to raise positive children in the midst of negative influences. Because of people's tendency to replicate their home environment, when we nurture children, we are making a statement and an impact upon many generations to come. We can leave an imprint of pain or we can leave a legacy of love for the things of God. Children are gifts and assets entrusted to us by God. Like every other gift or asset we receive, we must eventually give full account to God of our stewardship.

## WORD POWER

**I have done (Hebrew: *asah*)**—this means "to fashion, to accomplish." God is the one speaking to Solomon. As far as God is concerned, the request of Solomon has been accomplished. The statement "I have done" is cast in a perfect tense, meaning Solomon should have no doubt about his request.

## HOME DAILY BIBLE READINGS

for the week of October 29, 2006
*God Grants Wisdom to Solomon*

Oct. 23, Monday
—Proverbs 1:1-7
—The Incomparable Worth of Wisdom
Oct. 24, Tuesday
—Job 28:12-28
—Where Is Wisdom Found?
Oct. 25, Wednesday
—Psalm 119:97-104
—Add to Wisdom Understanding
Oct. 26, Thursday
—1 Kings 1:28-40
—Solomon Chosen to Be King
Oct. 27, Friday
—1 Kings 3:3-9
—Solomon Requests Wisdom
Oct. 28, Saturday
—1 Kings 3:10-15
—God Answers Solomon's Request
Oct. 29, Sunday
—1 Kings 4:29-34
—Solomon Was Wise

## PRAYER

*Lord, thank You for the gift of abundant life. In Jesus' name, we pray. Amen.*

**November 5, 2006**

Lesson 10

# Elijah Triumphs with God

**UNIT III**
Living as God's Covenanted People

**CHILDREN'S UNIT**
Living as Covenant People

**ADULT TOPIC:** Depending on God's Power
**YOUTH TOPIC:** Elijah Scores a Victory
**CHILDREN'S TOPIC:** Elijah Takes a Stand

**DEVOTIONAL READING:** Psalm 86:8-13
**BACKGROUND SCRIPTURE:** 1 Kings 18:20-39
**PRINT PASSAGE:** 1 Kings 18:20-24, 30-35, 38-39

## KEY VERSE

When all the people saw it, they fell on their faces: and they said, The LORD, he is the God; the LORD, he is the God.
—1 Kings 18:39

## OBJECTIVES

Upon completion of this lesson, the students are expected to:
1. Recognize that God often uses the natural elements to get the world's attention;
2. Understand that we must make a personal choice whether to serve God or to serve our own way of thinking; and,
3. Realize that Elijah wanted God to answer by fire so that the hearts of the people would be turned back to God.

### 1 Kings 18:20-24, 30-35, 38-39—KJV

20 So Ahab sent unto all the children of Israel, and gathered the prophets together unto mount Carmel.

21 And Elijah came unto all the people, and said, How long halt ye between two opinions? if the LORD be God, follow him: but if Baal, then follow him. And the people answered him not a word.

22 Then said Elijah unto the people, I, even I only, remain a prophet of the LORD; but Baal's prophets are four hundred and fifty men.

23 Let them therefore give us two bullocks; and let them choose one bullock for themselves, and cut it in pieces, and lay it on wood, and put no fire under: and I will dress the other bullock, and lay it on wood, and put no fire under:

24 And call ye on the name of your gods, and I will call on the name of the LORD: and the God that answereth by fire, let him be God. And all the people answered and said, It is well spoken.

.....

30 And Elijah said unto all the people, Come near unto me. And all the people came near unto him. And he repaired the altar of the LORD that was broken down.

31 And Elijah took twelve stones, according to the number of the tribes of the sons of Jacob, unto whom the word of the LORD came, saying, Israel shall be thy name:

32 And with the stones he built an altar in the name of the LORD: and he made a trench about the altar, as great as would contain two measures of seed.

33 And he put the wood in order, and cut the bullock in pieces, and laid him on the wood, and said, Fill four barrels with water,

and pour it on the burnt sacrifice, and on the wood.

34 And he said, Do it the second time. And they did it the second time. And he said, Do it the third time. And they did it the third time.

35 And the water ran round about the altar; and he filled the trench also with water.

.....

38 Then the fire of the LORD fell, and consumed the burnt sacrifice, and the wood, and the stones, and the dust, and licked up the water that was in the trench.

39 And when all the people saw it, they fell on their faces: and they said, The LORD, he is the God; the LORD, he is the God.

## UNIFYING LESSON PRINCIPLE

Sometimes we realize we need to depend on a power greater than ourselves. On what power can we depend? At a very critical moment, Elijah depended on God's power, and he was not disappointed.

## POINTS TO BE EMPHASIZED ADULTS/YOUTH

**Adult Key Verse:** 1 Kings 18:39
**Youth Key Verse:** 1 Kings 18:37
**Print Passage:** 1 Kings 18:20-24, 30-35, 38-39

—Elijah challenged the people to decide whom they were going to worship.
—Elijah doused the entire offering in water so that no one could claim that the fire was accidental or magic.

## CHILDREN

**Key Verse:** 1 Kings 18:21
**Print Passage:** 1 Kings 18:20-24, 30-35, 38-39
—God answers the prayers of His people.
—The Israelites recognized God's power when God answered with fire.

## TOPICAL OUTLINE OF THE LESSON

I. INTRODUCTION
  A. Levels of Faith
  B. Biblical Background

II. EXPOSITION AND APPLICATION OF THE SCRIPTURE
  A. Elijah Proposes a Divine Duel *(1 Kings 18:20-24)*
  B. Elijah Sets the Stage for Yahweh's Fiery Work *(1 Kings 18:30-35)*
  C. The Fire Falls, the People Fall, the False Prophets Fall *(1 Kings 18:38-39)*

III. CONCLUDING REFLECTIONS

## I. INTRODUCTION
### A. Levels of Faith

Have you ever had an experience that helped you to know beyond any doubt whatsoever that God is God? Until such an experience occurs, one's faith will remain somewhat weak and wavering. There is something about personal experience that adds a quality unsurpassed by any other occurrence. Three sequential levels of faith may be described as traditional/habitual faith, academic/head knowledge faith, and personal/experiential faith.

*Traditional/habitual faith* is a belief system that depends largely upon what has been handed down from one's elders. This category represents those who have been raised in and around the church. The exterior things of God have become a normal and expected part of this person's tradition.

This is an unmistakable "cultural Christian" who is now comfortably accustomed to Christ. The next category characterizes one who possesses *academic/head knowledge* faith. Possessing academic knowledge about God is a good thing, as long as one's quest for God does not stop in the middle of a Bible commentary or a Bible research paper. There is a considerable, qualitative difference between head knowledge and heart knowledge. Pure head knowledge is moved and motivated by facts; pure heart knowledge is moved and motivated by faith. Pure head knowledge focuses on impressing others; pure heart knowledge focuses on impressing God. We are called to be doers of the Word, not hearers only who deceive themselves. The third category showcases personal/experiential faith. For this individual, God is a wonderful, multifaceted friend, Jesus serves as an everyday example of how to live, and the Holy Spirit is constantly guiding and empowering toward life's ultimate purpose.

Anyone who witnessed what happened with Elijah on Mt. Carmel should have come away with a strong sense of *personal/experiential faith*. This kind of faith is unshakable, even in stormy weather, because it is rooted in the things that God has already done. Today's lesson is a prime example of what happens when traditional/habitual faith in an idol god competes against personal/experiential faith in the living God who answers with results.

### B. Biblical Background

Elijah had prophesied that there would be no dew or rain in the land for some years. God was displeased with the trend of the people, which had drifted toward widespread Baal worship. When the prophecy of a drought was delivered to King Ahab, the king was obviously displeased. Rain was essential for growing crops and watering animals. After delivering his prophecy, Elijah was directed to seclude himself near the brook Cherith, where he was fed by ravens until the brook dried up. After that, Elijah was directed to a widow's house in Zerephath where a miraculous supply of staples came from God as a result of the woman's obedience (17:9-16). After being out-of-sight for quite some time, Elijah suddenly appeared to Ahab, who greeted him with the question, "Is it you, you troubler of Israel?" True prophets of God tend to disturb worldly smugness and godless complacency. When the world ignores God, God often uses the natural elements to get its attention. This can occur through a flood or through its opposite—a drought.

Elijah boldly refused to engage in a trivial exchange of insults with Ahab. Instead, he challenged the prophets of Baal to a duel of sorts. The place: Mt. Carmel. The contest: determine which god/God was powerful enough to ignite a sacrifice with fire. The stakes: the God who was victorious would be served and obeyed by all the people. Neither God nor the Word of God needs to be defended. Instead of defending God, believers need only unleash the power of God and allow it to prove its own point. Elijah set up the perfect contest to unleash the power of God and allow the people to reach their own conclusions. Baal was considered the sky god who influenced fertility and controlled the weather. Elijah's God was known as the Creator of the earth and the

One who controlled the rain. Elijah's God was even rumored to have rolled back the water of the Red Sea to allow the Israelites safe passage. God and Baal could not both be right, and this contest would expose the truth. God desires to use our lives like a stage on which the power of God can be displayed.

Mt. Carmel is located on a ridge that is bordered by the Mediterranean Sea on the northwest and the Plain of Esdraelon on the southeast. Its southernmost side was considered the most fertile strip of land in the entire country. The word *Carmel* means "the garden land." The actual site of Elijah's contest, which can still be toured today, is commonly identified with El-Muhraka, i.e, "place of burning." The site features a platform just below the summit on the southern edge, some 1,600 feet above sea level, with the brook Kishon below, and near to the (priest's mound), the traditional site of the slaughter of the priests of Baal.

## II. Exposition and Application of the Scripture
### A. Elijah Proposes a Divine Duel
*(1 Kings 18:20-24)*

**So Ahab sent unto all the children of Israel, and gathered the prophets together unto mount Carmel. And Elijah came unto all the people, and said, How long halt ye between two opinions? if the Lord be God, follow him: but if Baal, then follow him. And the people answered him not a word. Then said Elijah unto the people, I, even I only, remain a prophet of the Lord; but Baal's prophets are four hundred and fifty men. Let them therefore give us two bullocks; and let them choose one bullock for themselves, and cut it in pieces, and lay it on wood, and put no fire under: and I will dress the other bullock, and lay it on wood, and put no fire under: And call ye on the name of your gods, and I will call on the name of the Lord: and the God that answereth by fire, let him be God. And all the people answered and said, It is well spoken.**

After the people and the Baal prophets were gathered at Mt. Carmel, Elijah placed a choice before the people: choose Baal or choose God. This is the universal, quintessential choice before all of humanity. This decision represents the great divide; once this choice is made, many of life's other choices become much simpler. The characteristic that makes humanity so unique is this freedom of choice. God could have created us as human robots, but the option of choice is what makes love more meaningful. If we were forced to love God and each other, that kind of love would not be very personal. God has always given us a choice. In the Garden of Eden, Adam and Eve had a choice to obey the guidelines of God and prosper, or to disobey those guidelines and suffer. In the wilderness, Moses gave the children of Israel the choice to worship artificial gods or to obey the God who delivered them from Egypt. Today, we still must individually make the choice to serve God or to serve our own way of thinking. This is life's most significant decision and it yields life's most significant results.

After Elijah issued this very simple and clear choice to the people, their response was the sound of silence. Here was the opportunity of a lifetime and they chose not to choose. One of the most distasteful flavors in the mouth of God is the flavor of wavery or indecision. God has little tolerance for those who want a little bit of God, when convenient, and a little bit of worldliness and idolatry whenever the mood strikes. Elijah characterizes this type of lifestyle as "hesitating between two opinions." When selecting whom we will serve in life, *not* deciding is a decision itself.

Verse 22 highlights what appears to be stark odds involved in this spiritual battle between 850 pagan prophets, 450 prophets of Baal, plus 400 prophets of Asherah—and God's one. Not only was this a spiritual battle, but a political one as well because these pagan prophets enjoyed the protection and company of Queen Jezebel. However, Elijah understood the truth that God, plus none, is still a majority. Although God prefers to use us, God is not forced to do so. The contest proposed by Elijah, while not equitable, was simple and straightforward. Thus, the people were compelled to approve it. Unlike Elijah's initial challenge to the people to choose which God they would follow, this contest to determine which deity would answer by fire required no personal commitment on the people's part.

The prophets of Baal expended a great deal of time, energy, and even blood in their vain attempt to contact their god. What an unfortunate waste of resources on the part of these prophets! Their god was silent because it was a deity made from human hands. In our contemporary world, the gods we may be tempted to follow are not idols of wood or stone. Today, we are tempted by gods of power, politics, connections, status, materialism, vanity, and the almighty dollar. These gods are just as dangerous as the Baals of ancient times because they cause us to depend on something other than the true and living God. Serving other gods is futile; during times of crisis and desperation, these gods will be silent. They can offer no true answers, no guidance, and no wisdom.

The efforts of the Baal prophets to prompt their god into action lasted almost the entire day. However, no amount of volume or physical gyration could infuse life into a dead god. Perhaps the people stayed for this entire spectacle because they were being entertained by the antics of the false prophets. By the time the false prophets finished cutting themselves and jumping on the altar, the altar was broken and in need of repair.

### B. Elijah Sets the Stage for Yahweh's Fiery Work *(1 Kings 18:30-35)*

**And Elijah said unto all the people, Come near unto me. And all the people came near unto him. And he repaired the altar of the Lord that was broken down. And Elijah took twelve stones, according to the number of the tribes of the sons of Jacob, unto whom the word of the Lord came, saying, Israel shall be thy name: And with the stones he built an altar in the name of the Lord: and he made a trench about the altar, as great as would contain two measures of seed. And he put the wood in order, and cut the bullock in pieces, and laid him on the wood, and said, Fill four barrels with water, and pour it on the burnt sacrifice, and on the wood. And he said, Do it the second time. And they did it the second time. And he said, Do it the third time. And they did it the third time. And the water ran round about the altar; and he filled the trench also with water.**

Elijah was intentional in preparing the altar that would receive God's fire. He beckoned the people to come near to him so that they could verify that no tricks were being played with the altar preparation. The twelve stones used to construct the altar were symbolic of the twelve tribes of Israel. It should have reminded the people of their rich heritage and of the many powerful ways that God had provided for them in the past. Forgetting one's history and spiritual heritage can be potentially devastating to one's future. To add to the difficulty of a burning altar, Elijah constructed a water-filled trench around the altar. In addition to this, he commanded that a total of twelve barrels of water be poured on the bullock and on the wood. (Notice the uniform usage of the number *twelve.*) In the presence of a drought, one wonders from what source such a significant amount of water could have been attained. Perhaps servants secured it from the Mediterranean Sea.

As recorded in 1 Kings 18:35-37, in Elijah's prayer just before the sacrifice occurred, he began "reminding" God and reminding himself of exactly who God was and what God had done in the past. Remember, God's past works give us encouragement about what God can do in the present. Elijah reminded God that God reigned supreme in Israel, that Elijah was God's mouthpiece, and that this whole contest was God's idea in the first place. Elijah wanted God to answer by fire—not just to prove God's power, but also that the hearts of the people would be turned toward God once again (verse 37).

### C. The Fire Falls, the People Fall, the False Prophets Fall *(1 Kings 18:38-39)*

**Then the fire of the Lord fell, and consumed the burnt sacrifice, and the wood, and the stones, and the dust, and licked up the water that was in the trench. And when all the people saw it, they fell on their faces: and they said, The Lord, he is the God; the Lord, he is the God.**

Undoubtedly, the fire that fell on Mt. Carmel that day was like nothing that any of the onlookers had ever seen. One of the identifying characteristics or "trademarks" of work done by God is that it is often "overdone." This term is used in a positive manner to describe a God who often does exceedingly, abundantly above all that we could ever possibly ask or think. As we sometimes say today, "When God shows up, God shows out!" The God of Abraham, Isaac, and Jacob is the God of more than enough. There is absolutely nothing average or mediocre about God. Even the very name of God is not merely good; God's name is excellent. Whether in creation or in destruction, God's work is convincingly complete and tremendously thorough.

Finally, it was God's turn to demonstrate His power on Mount Carmel in the presence of 850 pagan priests, many more curious people, and one faithful prophet. With His name and sovereignty on the line in the eyes of the people, the great God of heaven and earth stepped up to the plate of opportunity and dealt a mighty blow to the prevailing circumstances. Not only did the fire burn up the sacrificed animal—the wood, the dirt, and the stones were also consumed. This fierce fire even licked up the water that ordinarily should have put the fire out. After God send down fire from the sky, the people fell to their knees and acknowledged the great and awesome power of God. That day, the prophets of Baal also fell. They were forced to pay a high price for bowing down to a god other than the Most High.

## III. Concluding Reflections

When Elijah asked the Israelites to choose between serving God or serving Baal, to them it may have seemed like a small decision. In reality, it was the most significant choice they ever could have made. One step toward God is a blessed step in the right direction. But one step away from God is a fatal step in the wrong direction. The third choice that some make of staying in the middle ground of faith is perhaps the worst option of all. Those who straddle the spiritual fence may unwittingly lull themselves into a false sense of security because they are constantly comparing themselves to others who may seem more ungodly than them. Those who model this mindset must remember that the benchmark of true spirituality and submission to God is not other people, but the example of Jesus Christ and the Word of God.

When we learn to trust God with the seemingly insignificant, everyday matters in our lives, then we will be better able to flow into the larger destiny that God has in store. When we realize that God is not out to get us but to give us, then we will voluntarily release our hold on the reigns of our lives and gladly give them over to the One who knows the way home. One genuine experience with God can revolutionize one's life irrevocably. The God of Elijah is always ready to demonstrate divine power through the life of anyone willing to surrender to God's agenda.

## WORD POWER

**They fell (Hebrew: *naphal-naw-fal*)**—when the people saw the real God in action, their response was total reverence to the God of Elijah. The Hebrew word *(naphal)* is cast in imperfect tense; the action was spontaneous. When the fire consumed the sacrifice and the water, they were terrified. They were not commanded to fall down. When was the last time you were amazed with an action of God?

## HOME DAILY BIBLE READINGS

for the week of November 5, 2006
*Elijah Triumphs with God*

Oct. 30, Monday
    —Psalm 145:1–7
    —God Is Great
Oct. 31, Tuesday
    —Psalm 86:8-13
    —None Is like God
Nov. 1, Wednesday
    —Psalm 93
    —God's Majesty and Might
Nov. 2, Thursday
    —1 Kings 18:17-24
    —Who Is the Powerful God?
Nov. 3, Friday
    —1 Kings 18:25-29
    —Elijah Taunts the Baal Worshipers
Nov. 4, Saturday
    —1 Kings 18:30-35
    —Elijah Built an Altar to God
Nov. 5, Sunday
    —1 Kings 18:36-39
    —Elijah Prays, God Acts

## PRAYER

*Lord, direct our pathways as we trust in You with all our hearts. In Jesus' name, we pray. Amen.*

## Lesson 11

# Josiah Brings Reform

**ADULT TOPIC:** Seeking Renewal
**YOUTH TOPIC:** Josiah Brings Renewal
**CHILDREN'S TOPIC:** Josiah Remembers the Covenant

**November 12, 2006**

**UNIT III**
Living as God's Covenanted People

**CHILDREN'S UNIT**
Living as Covenant People

**DEVOTIONAL READING:** Psalm 103:1-18
**BACKGROUND SCRIPTURE:** 2 Kings 22–23
**PRINT PASSAGE:** 2 Kings 22:8-10; 23:1-3, 21-23

### 2 Kings 22:8-10; 23:1-3, 21-23—KJV

8 And Hilkiah the high priest said unto Shaphan the scribe, I have found the book of the law in the house of the LORD. And Hilkiah gave the book to Shaphan, and he read it.

9 And Shaphan the scribe came to the king, and brought the king word again, and said, Thy servants have gathered the money that was found in the house, and have delivered it into the hand of them that do the work, that have the oversight of the house of the LORD.

10 And Shaphan the scribe shewed the king, saying, Hilkiah the priest hath delivered me a book. And Shaphan read it before the king.

· · · · ·

AND THE king sent, and they gathered unto him all the elders of Judah and of Jerusalem.

2 And the king went up into the house of the LORD, and all the men of Judah and all the inhabitants of Jerusalem with him, and the priests, and the prophets, and all the people, both small and great: and he read in their ears all the words of the book of the covenant which was found in the house of the LORD.

3 And the king stood by a pillar, and made a covenant before the LORD, to walk after the LORD, and to keep his commandments and his testimonies and his statutes with all their heart and all their soul, to perform the words of this covenant that were written in this book. And all the people stood to the covenant.

· · · · ·

21 And the king commanded all the people, saying, Keep the passover unto the LORD your God, as it is written in the book of this covenant.

### KEY VERSE

The king stood by a pillar, and made a covenant before the LORD, to walk after the LORD, ... to perform the words of this covenant that were written in this book. And all the people stood to the covenant.— 2 Kings 23:3

### OBJECTIVES

**Upon completion of this lesson, the students are expected to:**

1. Learn that God's Word was designed to change people.
2. Discover that God desires us to grow spiritually; and,
3. Recognize that we need not be ashamed of embracing and believing God's Word.

22 Surely there was not holden such a passover from the days of the judges that judged Israel, nor in all the days of the kings of Israel, nor of the kings of Judah;

23 But in the eighteenth year of king Josiah, wherein this passover was holden to the LORD in Jerusalem.

## UNIFYING LESSON PRINCIPLE

Life provides us with many opportunities for second chances and other forms of renewal. What spurs us to seek renewal? Reading the book of the covenant drove Josiah to lead the people in a magnificent ceremony of covenantal renewal.

## POINTS TO BE EMPHASIZED
## ADULTS /YOUTH

**Adult/Youth Key Verse:** 2 Kings 23:3
**Print Passage:** 2 Kings 22:8-10; 23:1-3, 21-23

—Unlike his father Amon, Josiah "did what was right in the sight of the Lord."

—Josiah made a covenant to follow the book of the Law, and the people joined in the covenant.

## CHILDREN

**Key Verse:** 2 Chronicles 34:2
**Print Passage:** 2 Chronicles 34:1-3, 8, 14b-16a, 30-31

—Josiah was eight years old when he became king, and sixteen years old when he began to seek God.

—After the book of the Law was found, Josiah and the people renewed their covenant with God.

## TOPICAL OUTLINE OF THE LESSON

**I. INTRODUCTION**
 A. The Power of the Word of God
 B. Biblical Background

**II. EXPOSITION AND APPLICATION OF THE SCRIPTURE**
 A. The Book of the Law Is Found
 (2 Kings 22:8-10)
 B. Hearing the Word of God from the Lips of the Leader
 (2 Kings 23:1-3)
 C. A Grand Celebration of Passover
 (2 Kings 23:21-23)

**III. CONCLUDING REFLECTIONS**

## I. INTRODUCTION
### A. The Power of the Word of God

There is a light-giving quality about reading the Bible. One may wonder how the Word of God is specifically different from other types of literature. Other literature is limited in its ability to exact positive change in the lives of people. But the Word of God was designed to touch the hearts of people in ways that produce genuine and dramatic results.

God's Word is universal in scope and is able to illuminate truth as well as expose error—regardless of age, race, color, or creed. Like dynamite, even if God's covenant Word was packed away and stored for many years, it would still accomplish its work when properly ignited.

The Word is essential to faith. We know that without faith it is impossible to please God (Hebrews 11:6). We also know that faith comes by hearing, and hearing by the

Word of God (Romans 10:17). Reading the Word ignites truth and effectively unleashes it to accomplish the necessary task. The Word is able to comfort the afflicted and afflict the comfortable. It is living, active, and sharper than a two-edged sword. "All scripture is given by inspiration of God, and is profitable for doctrine, for reproof, for correction, for instruction in righteousness" (2 Timothy 3:16).

When the Word of God is a low priority in our lives, we are highly susceptible to the attacks of the enemy. But when we are properly armed with God's Word (the sword of the Spirit), we can successfully protect ourselves against spiritual attacks. Self-motivation can be useful at times and positive thinking is nice, but there is no substitute for a daily dose of the Word. The Bible is God's love letter to God's loved ones. It is not enough to read it once a month or even once or twice per week. Hiding God's Word in our hearts and minds through memorization is the process that helps to vaccinate us against the virus of sin. Memorization makes the Word portable and instantaneously useful whenever needed.

Spiritual maturity is the process of becoming one with the Spirit of God and the Word of God. We move from just hearing the Word, to reading the Word, to studying the Word, to meditating on the Word, to memorizing the Word, and, most importantly, to doing the Word. Just as Jesus is the divine incarnation of God's Word, so we are called to be God's living letters. God's truth and witness should clearly be seen whenever people look at our lives.

## B. Biblical Background

Once a united kingdom, Israel was now divided into the two kingdoms of Israel and Judah for over 100 years. The book of 2 Kings demonstrates what happens to those who follow God and what becomes of those who choose to follow a false god. Unfortunately, very few people from Israel, the northern kingdom, and Judah, the southern kingdom, followed God. Their kings led them astray. The evil kings were shortsighted and self-centered. They thought they could control their nations' destinies by importing other religions, forming unholy alliances with pagan nations, and prospering themselves. The good kings among them spent most of their time undoing the evil done by their predecessors.

The name Josiah literally means "founded of Jah" (Jah is a prefix for Jehovah). Josiah ascended the king's throne at the young age of eight years old. Although his father and grandfather had been very wicked, Josiah did what was right in the sight of the Lord without wavering. He was the sixteenth king of Judah and was a part of the southern kingdom. His father was Amon, his mother Jedidah, and his son was Jehoahaz. There seems to have been a morally unstable up-and-down spiritual pattern among the kings of Judah during this period. Josiah's father was disobedient; Josiah was obedient, and then Josiah's son was disobedient. It would seem like a spiritually strong king would be sure to transmit that same type of character and legacy to his children—especially to the heir to the throne.

One of the biggest mistakes of great leaders is the failure to train potential successors to continue the vision and work once the initial leader has departed. This failure of great leaders to prepare for their succession seems to be a pattern throughout Scripture. Eli, the priest, had two sons who were to succeed him, but they behaved irresponsibly even while in training. Because of Eli's failure to discipline his sons, God disciplined Eli. Throughout human history, the failing of many great spiritual leaders has been tending to the things of God and leaving little time to properly train their own children. Although spiritual leadership is very important, we cannot place the total blame on spiritual leaders for our failure to follow God.

After Solomon's kingship, 209 years passed before the Assyrians destroyed Israel. The Babylonians overtook Jerusalem after 345 years. When God's repeated warnings to rid the nation of idolatry went unheeded, God was forced to allow unholy nations to take over or destroy what had originally been built for the purpose of glorifying God.

## II. Exposition and Application of the Scripture
### A. The Book of the Law Is Found
*(2 Kings 22:8-10)*

**And Hilkiah the high priest said unto Shaphan the scribe, I have found the book of the law in the house of the LORD. And Hilkiah gave the book to Shaphan, and he read it. And Shaphan the scribe came to the king, and brought the king word again, and said, Thy servants have gathered the money that was found in the house, and have delivered it into the hand of them that do the work, that have the oversight of the house of the LORD. And Shaphan the scribe shewed the king, saying, Hilkiah the priest hath delivered me a book. And Shaphan read it before the king.**

As renovation of the temple was taking place, Hilkiah, the high priest, discovered the book of the Law in the house of the Lord. How ironic it is for the spiritual leader to find the Bible in the house of God! How could a book that was so spiritually important have been physically misplaced? Perhaps the book was not very highly regarded and was stored away and forgotten like yesterday's news clippings. Perhaps in their zeal to preserve its historic pages and to protect its storied legacy, the priests sealed the Law in a special, protected environment and neglected to tell their successors. Whatever the reason, the book that was intended to be widely broadcast among the people had somehow become secluded and forgotten among the dilapidated rubble of the temple.

With the current number of Bibles in print and our easy access to the Word of God via radio, television, and the Internet, perhaps it would be hard to imagine the Bible becoming lost in this generation. But when was the last time you memorized a new Bible verse? How often have you been guilty of doing or saying something wrong, knowing full well what the Bible says on the matter? It is quite possible for us to carry a Bible under our arms and to wear a cross around our necks and still not have the Word in our hearts. The purpose of having God's Word in writing was not to be displayed in the showcase of a museum. God's Word was designed to be showcased in the lives of the saints so that those people who pass by the display window of our lives are able to clearly see that the Spirit of God resides in us.

When King Josiah heard the Word of God for the first time, its power was so overwhelming that Josiah literally tore his royal robes. Today it might seem odd for someone to tear an article of clothing in reaction to hearing Scripture read. But in Josiah's era, tearing one's clothes represented deep, extreme, inexpressible negative feelings. The first biblical instance of clothing being torn occurs in Genesis, when Reuben and Jacob tore their clothing in anguish over the disappearance of Joseph (see Genesis 37:29, 34). A New Testament example of rending (tearing) robes occurred with the chief priest, who tore his robes when he believed that Jesus had blasphemed (Matthew 26:65). Josiah had a heart so sensitive to the Spirit of God that when the Word of God made contact with his heart, there was an immediate chemical-like reaction. This positive example represents a challenge for us today. God desires us to grow spiritually to the extent that our Scripture reading directly impacts our practical reality. When our daily reading begins to impact our daily walk, the Spirit of God can then easily and effectively use us, much like the potter fashions clay upon a potter's wheel.

## B. Hearing the Word of God from the Lips of the Leader *(2 Kings 23:1-3)*

**And the king sent, and they gathered unto him all the elders of Judah and of Jerusalem. And the king went up into the house of the Lord, and all the men of Judah and all the inhabitants of Jerusalem with him, and the priests, and the prophets, and all the people, both small and great: and he read in their ears all the words of the book of the covenant which was found in the house of the Lord. And the king stood by a pillar, and made a covenant before the Lord, to walk after the Lord, and to keep his commandments and his testimonies and his statutes with all their heart and all their soul, to perform the words of this covenant that were written in this book. And all the people stood to the covenant.**

Josiah was not content to confine the Word and its effects to a personal revelation. Josiah was powerfully compelled to communicate the truth of God's Word to all those within his circle of influence. As a king, Josiah's sphere of influence included a diversity of people—the elders and inhabitants of Judah and Jerusalem, and the priests and the prophets. It is a noteworthy feat for Josiah to have been able to assemble such a wide cross section of Israel's people, even in the midst of a divided kingdom. When it comes to hearing the truth of God's Word, artificial barriers such as age, race, class, and nationality are made irrelevant and insignificant. Josiah had his personal priorities in order, and at the very top of his priority list was absolute and uncompromised obedience to the Word of God.

Every leader—from a parent, to a work supervisor, to a governmental official, to a minister—has the right and the responsibility to lead people in accordance with the principles of God's Word. When this is acknowledged and accomplished, these leaders have truly understood and accepted the leadership model of the human authority living under divine authority. No one can rise so high on the leadership ladder that submission to God is no longer needed.

Josiah was extremely wise and practical in his acute understanding of human nature. His perspective was that mere reading of the Word is insufficient and unproductive.

After the people heard the Word, the next step was personal commitment. Josiah asked the people to promise in the Lord's name to faithfully obey the Lord and to follow His commands. The covenant of God is activated at the level of personal commitment and implementation. Far too many people hear the Word and give mental assent, but little else. The people agreed to do "everything written in the book." Some may argue that this agreement was solicited under the pressure of the king. This may or may not be true. Perhaps the reading of God's Word had the same impact on the people as it had on Josiah. But if they were simply agreeing due to pressure from the king, it was better for the king to pressure the people to do right rather than to pressure them into doing evil. The priorities of a leader tend to have a great and powerful impact on the persons being led.

### C. A Grand Celebration of Passover
*(2 Kings 23:21-23)*

**And the king commanded all the people, saying, Keep the passover unto the LORD your God, as it is written in the book of this covenant. Surely there was not holden such a passover from the days of the judges that judged Israel, nor in all the days of the kings of Israel, nor of the kings of Judah; But in the eighteenth year of king Josiah, wherein this passover was holden to the LORD in Jerusalem.**

The celebration of Passover is related to the deliverance of the children of Israel from Egypt. During the last plague, when lamb's blood was sprinkled over the door- posts of the Israelite households, the death angel would pass over that particular dwelling and spare the life of the firstborn (see Exodus 12:12-27). Passover was designed to be an annual observance for the entire nation to remember, reflect, and rejoice in their deliverance by almighty God. Part of the celebration involved a reenactment of the events of that fateful night—eating the bitter herbs and the unleavened bread. In Exodus 13, Moses gave very detailed instructions regarding celebration of Passover. Even before they physically departed from Egypt, Moses evidently realized that the people would tend to forget their slavery experience. Remembering one's deliverance experience serves as an insurance policy against a repeat bondage experience. Since many of the more recent kings of Judah and Israel had not strictly adhered to the righteous ways of the Lord, it is quite likely that the Passover celebration had not occurred regularly, as it had during the days of the righteous judges.

It is a wise thing for any covenant we make to be periodically renewed. There is a tendency for time and toil to take its toll on our memory, and even the best intentions of yesteryear suffer significantly at the hands of Father Time. Since the adage still holds true that familiarity breeds contempt, there is a need to recall and renew our covenant with God, with our spouses, and with our church family, and any other spiritual covenantal relationship. Such a renewal is a fresh reminder of the original commitment.

### III. CONCLUDING REFLECTIONS

Reading God's Word is designed to be an engaging, exciting, and inviting experience. God's Word was not designed to be read in a distant and detached manner. The great prophets and patriarchs of the Bible were consumed with the Word of God. If we approach the Word with a positive, expectant attitude, through the Holy Spirit the Bible will open itself to us.

A passive approach to reading the Bible leads to a passive response in real life. But an active approach to reading the Bible leads to an active response in real life. An active approach includes some of the following activities:

- Maintaining a personal, subjective perspective in reading rather than a detached, objective perspective.
- Immediately applying the Word rather than addressing it later in life or thinking it applies to someone else.
- Actively searching for promises to apply, sins to confess, qualities to adopt or avoid, and growth areas in which to engage.
- Reserving a daily time and place to meet with God, put on the whole armor and receive your marching orders for the day.
- Memorize specific passages that particularly apply to your life.
- Allow the Word of God to permeate your thoughts and decisions as you daily apply the Word to all facets of your life.

When we embrace the Word of God as did King Josiah, the Word will work wonders in our lives. Embracing and believing God's Word is the key to true success in life. Let us learn an important lesson from the life of Josiah—when it comes to worship, there is no room for compromise. Anything that remotely resembles an idol in our lives must immediately be destroyed so that God's purpose for our lives will proceed and succeed.

## WORD POWER

**Covenant (Hebrew:** *beriyth*)—originally it meant to cut in two, or to divide. Making a covenant involved killing an animal and the two parties would walk between the slain animal. The interpretation is that should either of the parties fail to keep the terms of the covenant, the offending party would suffer the same fate as the animal.

## HOME DAILY BIBLE READINGS

for the week of November 12, 2006
*Josiah Brings Reform*

Nov. 6,  Monday
  —Psalm 103:1-12
  —God Restores Us
Nov. 7,  Tuesday
  —Psalm 32
  —Renewal in the Lord
Nov. 8,  Wednesday
  —Joel 2:12-17
  —Return to the Lord
Nov. 9,  Thursday
  —2 Kings 22:1-7
  —Josiah Made King of Judah
Nov. 10, Friday
  —2 Kings 22:8-13
  —A Lost Book Is Found
Nov. 11, Saturday
  —2 Kings 23:1-5
  —The People Renew Their Covenant
Nov. 12, Sunday
  —2 Kings 23:21-25
  —Celebrate the Passover

## PRAYER

*Lord, if there is anything in our lives that challenges Your position of supreme authority, let it be unmercifully destroyed so that Your will and Your purpose may prevail.*

**November 19, 2006**

## Lesson 12

# The People Go into Exile

**UNIT III**
Living as God's Covenanted People

**CHILDREN'S UNIT**
Living as Covenant People

**ADULT TOPIC:** Making Wrong Choices
**YOUTH TOPIC:** Exile in Babylon
**CHILDREN'S TOPIC:** Jeremiah Delivers God's Message

**DEVOTIONAL READING:** Proverbs 1:20-33
**BACKGROUND SCRIPTURE:** 2 Chronicles 36:15-21; Psalm 137
**PRINT PASSAGE:** 2 Chronicles 36:15-21; Psalm 137:1-6

## KEY VERSE

By the rivers of Babylon, there we sat down, yea, we wept, when we remembered Zion.
— Psalm 137:1

### 2 Chronicles 36:15-21; Psalm 137:1-6—KJV

15 And the LORD God of their fathers sent to them by his messengers, rising up betimes, and sending; because he had compassion on his people, and on his dwelling place:

16 But they mocked the messengers of God, and despised his words, and misused his prophets, until the wrath of the LORD arose against his people, till there was no remedy.

## OBJECTIVES

**Upon completion of this lesson, the students are expected to:**

1. Recognize that our life choices are directly connected to our life consequences;

2. Learn that one of the primary character traits of God is that of love and compassion; and,

3. Understand that God's message to His people is that on the very day that we hear His voice, we should not harden our hearts.

17 Therefore he brought upon them the king of the Chaldees, who slew their young men with the sword in the house of their sanctuary, and had no compassion upon young man or maiden, old man, or him that stooped for age: he gave them all into his hand.

18 And all the vessels of the house of God, great and small, and the treasures of the house of the LORD, and the treasures of the king, and of his princes; all these he brought to Babylon.

19 And they burnt the house of God, and brake down the wall of Jerusalem, and burnt all the palaces thereof with fire, and destroyed all the goodly vessels thereof.

20 And them that had escaped from the sword carried he away to Babylon; where they were servants to him and his sons until the reign of the kingdom of Persia:

21 To fulfil the word of the LORD by the mouth of Jeremiah, until the land had enjoyed her sabbaths: for as long as she lay desolate she kept sabbath, to fulfil threescore and ten years.

.....

BY THE rivers of Babylon, there we sat down, yea, we wept, when we remembered Zion.

**2** We hanged our harps upon the willows in the midst thereof.

**3** For there they that carried us away captive required of us a song; and they that wasted us required of us mirth, saying, Sing us one of the songs of Zion.

**4** How shall we sing the LORD's song in a strange land?

**5** If I forget thee, O Jerusalem, let my right hand forget her cunning.

**6** If I do not remember thee, let my tongue cleave to the roof of my mouth; if I prefer not Jerusalem above my chief joy.

## UNIFYING LESSON PRINCIPLE

Stubborn and prideful behavior often leads to painful consequences. What price is paid for such foolish choices? After Israel and Judah consistently rebelled against God, the people went into exile. There they longed for the relationship they had had with God.

## POINTS TO BE EMPHASIZED ADULTS/YOUTH

**Adult/Youth Key Verse:** Psalm 137:1

**Print Passage:** 2 Chronicles 36:15-21; Psalm 137:1-6

—Rejection of the messages of the prophets was common in Judah.
—God provided an element of hope for the people, although He punished them.
—In exile, the people mourned for their homeland and the life they once knew.

## CHILDREN

**Key Verse:** Jeremiah 1:5

**Print Passage:** 2 Chronicles 36:11-13, 17-20; Jeremiah 1:4-8

—Disrespecting God's prophet is like disrespecting God.
—Like God did for Jeremiah, God has plans for each of us and cares for us as we discover what those plans are.

## TOPICAL OUTLINE OF THE LESSON

### I. INTRODUCTION
A. Spiritual Cause and Effect
B. Biblical Background

### II. EXPOSITION AND APPLICATION OF THE SCRIPTURE
A. Divine Compassion for the People *(2 Chronicles 36:15)*
B. The People Reject God's Warnings *(2 Chronicles 36:16)*
C. Can God Use an Enemy to Accomplish Divine Purpose? *(2 Chronicles 36:17-21)*
D. The Mourning After *(Psalm 137:1-2)*
E. An Insulting Request *(Psalm 137:3-4)*
F. Remembering Jerusalem *(Psalm 137:5-6)*

### III. CONCLUDING REFLECTIONS

## I. INTRODUCTION
### A. Spiritual Cause and Effect

Our choices in life are directly connected to our consequences in life. Almost everything that happens within the physical universe is directly linked to a system of cause and effect. For example, when water from the rain consistently runs across bare topsoil, erosion occurs because the topsoil is stripped of essential nutrients and much of the dirt is washed away to another area. In order to remedy erosion and retain topsoil, grass or crops must be systematically planted to keep the ground from being removed by the rain.

Over the years, Israel had suffered a kind of spiritual erosion. Due to the corruption of their leadership, the people had been led astray. The rich topsoil of righteousness and faith, so carefully nurtured by the judges, had gradually disappeared due to the erosive effects of willful sin and blatant disobedience condoned by Israel's kings. In the physical sense, the process of ground erosion can be so gradual that it is almost unnoticeable. Likewise in the spiritual realm, our spiritual foundation can gradually slip away undetected unless a plan is implemented to protect us from such perils. Although God desires the best for us, every generation must eventually reap whatever they sow. When we sow disobedience, we must reap pain. But when we sow obedience, we reap a harvest of blessings.

### B. Biblical Background

The Hebrew title for this book is "the events of the days or times." Chronicles was written many decades ago, yet many of the attitudes and character traits that plagued the Hebrews are the same ones that prove problematic today. This is evidence of the fact that this basic human nature has still remained the same. The writer of Chronicles relied on many different sources to compile the material contained in the texts. At least one half of the material was excerpted from 1 and 2 Samuel and 1 and 2 Kings. Other sources include the Pentateuch, Judges, Ruth, Psalms, Isaiah, Jeremiah, Lamentations, and Zechariah. Several themes and issues are evident throughout the books of 1 and 2 Chronicles. The following list reflects some of those themes:

- David's preparation for the temple and Solomon's building of the temple
- The Law and the prophets as major forces in the life, history, and future of Israel
- Unrepentant sin and idolatry within a nation that inevitably lead to divine retribution and punishment
- The eternal hope and expectation of the Promised Messiah

Second Chronicles 36:14-16 provides a thumbnail sketch of events that led to the downfall of Judah and Israel. This destruction did not happen overnight. Although God is slow to anger and quick to forgive, there must be divine punishment for blatant and repetitious spiritual disobedience. The increasing unfaithfulness exhibited was not limited to the people but also included the priests. The idolatrous influence of the godless culture not only permeated their lifestyles, but also the temple worship.

God initially felt sorry for the people and commissioned several prophets to repeatedly warn the people of their sins. Not only were these warnings unheeded, but the people derided and insulted the prophets of God. After being ignored and unheeded for such a protracted period of time, God's righteous indignation mushroomed from warning mode into full action. The result was the utter devastation and eventual destruction of the people, the temple, and the city.

## II. Exposition and Application of the Scripture

### A. Divine Compassion for the People
*(2 Chronicles 36:15)*

**And the Lord God of their fathers sent to them by his messengers, rising up betimes, and sending; because he had compassion on his people, and on his dwelling place.**

One of the primary character traits of God is the characteristic of love, which yields divine compassion. The very nature and character of God is pure love. In many instances throughout biblical history, the people rebelled against godly leadership and disregarded prophetic calls to reform their wicked ways. Although the divine anger of God was provoked many times and God was tempted to wipe His own people off the face of the earth, there always seemed to be a sense of determination smoldering within the heart of God. Despite Israel's gross disobedience, God determined there was still an opportunity for their redemption if they would only repent and ask for forgiveness.

There are two primary human relationships that serve as effective analogies for helping us to comprehend God's persistent love. The first human bond that gives us a glimpse into God's love is the love of a devoted parent to a child. Healthy parental love is irresistible, ingrained, and instinctive. It is not usually something that must be learned in a classroom; it is not easily deterred or discouraged. No matter how terrible a son or daughter may behave, that parent still loves and cares for that child. The parent views the child with an eye that looks beyond faults and sees needs. Positive parenting means working hard to uncover the sometimes hidden qualities of one's offspring.

The other human relationship that illustrates God's love for Israel is the ideal relationship between a husband and a wife. Only a marital relationship calls for two people to love and to cherish each other for better or for worse, for richer or for poorer, in sickness and in health, so long as they both shall live. Marriage is an extreme risk because there is no guarantee that the other person will not radically change the very next day after the vows are taken. Unfortunately, in the cases of Judah and Israel, there was only one willing party in their relationship. As the one who would not relinquish His obligation to the covenant, God sent Israel many prophets and messages, some at the very beginning of their apostasy, and others afterward, 'till the very day of their captivity.

### B. The People Reject God's Warnings
*(2 Chronicles 36:16)*

**But they mocked the messengers of God, and despised his words, and misused his prophets, until the wrath of the Lord arose against his people, till there was no remedy.**

Old Testament prophets were considered God's official mouthpieces. When the prophets spoke, they communicated the oracles of God. Those who heeded the words of the prophets received the benefits of the prophets' wisdom and insight from God. Prophets were sternly charged to speak only what they heard from God—nothing more and nothing less.

Not even kings were above the scathingly direct messengers of God's Word. After King David committed adultery and murder, God sent Nathan to expose his transgressions and to call him to repentance. Since David had a heart that was tender and receptive to the Word of God, David was able to humble himself, ask for forgiveness, and receive God's blessed restoration. If a king could listen to a prophet and profit, then certainly the people could follow this wise royal example. King David proved that no one is exempt from the need to heed God's call to repentance. Not only did the people refuse to hear the prophets, but the people added an additional provocation by laughing at the prophets, ignoring them, and insulting them. Although the capacity of God is extensive, there is a limit to God's tolerance, and the people of Judah definitely crossed the line. The unenviable result was the frightful predicament of their being sinners in the hands of an angry God.

### C. Can God Use an Enemy to Accomplish Divine Purpose? *(2 Chronicles 36:17-21)*

**Therefore he brought upon them the king of the Chaldees, who slew their young men with the sword in the house of their sanctuary, and had no compassion upon young man or maiden, old man, or him that stooped for age: he gave them all into his hand. And all the vessels of the house of God, great and small, and the treasures of the house of the Lord, and the treasures of the king, and of his princes; all these he brought to Babylon. And they burnt the house of God, and brake down the wall of Jerusalem, and burnt all the palaces thereof with fire, and destroyed all the goodly vessels thereof. And them that had escaped from the sword carried he away to Babylon; where they were servants to him and his sons until the reign of the kingdom of Persia: To fulfil the word of the Lord by the mouth of Jeremiah, until the land had enjoyed her sabbaths: for as long as she lay desolate she kept sabbath, to fulfil threescore and ten years.**

When Judah had passed beyond the point of no return, God used an ungodly king as the primary instrument to bring retribution upon Judah and Jerusalem. For some, this apparent liaison between a good God and a pagan king may seem like a strange and unorthodox mixing of moral agents. But just because God chose to use King Nebuchadnezzar to attack Jerusalem does not mean that God had descended to the same moral plane as Nebuchadnezzer. Since the entire city had to be purged, God allowed him to kill everyone in the city. It would not have been spiritually plausible for a righteous, godly dweller of the city to kill his fellow residents…some of which could possibly have been neighbors and close relatives.

The primary reason why God could use an enemy to destroy a once holy city is because God is sovereign. God's sovereignty means that God can do anything—without first asking or receiving our permission or anyone else's, for that matter. If God can use an enemy, can't God use a woman? If God can use a woman, can't God use a child? If God can use a child, can't God use a flawed man? There are documented scriptural examples for each of these instances. The destruction of Jerusalem represented many years of neglecting and rejecting the will of God. Not only were the buildings destroyed and many of the people killed, but the survivors were made slaves.

In their quest for economic gain, Judah had ignored the need for the land to rest periodically. Instead, they planted continuously and stripped the land of its much-needed nutrients. After Nebuchadnezzar's invasion, Judah became a wasteland for the next seventy years, according to Jeremiah's prophecy (Jeremiah 25:11). Although this was a sad turn of events, God was already at work in the process of restoring the land and restoring the people. The national pursuit of righteousness is a picture of beauty. But the nation that embraces sin results in the opposite portrait of utter devastation.

### D. The Mourning After *(Psalm 137:1-2)*

**By the rivers of Babylon, there we sat down, yea, we wept, when we remembered Zion. We hanged our harps upon the willows in the midst thereof.**

This psalm, written by an anonymous writer, begins with the melancholy strains of lament. Psalm 137 stands in stark contrast to the preceding psalm. Psalm 136 exudes a consistent and continuous tone of rhythmic euphoria and exaltation all throughout. But Psalm 137 presents a vivid portrait of the personal psychology and inner mood of the Jews during the Babylonian exile. Even though they were experiencing great trials and tribulation, they remained committed to their faith and to their national heritage. Sometimes outer persecution and hard times are the catalysts used to expose inner values that have previously been concealed.

The introduction of Psalm 137 is beautifully poetic. The reader is impressed by the fresh, vivid, and emotional appeal of this ballad-like psalm. However, most of us are blind to the real purpose, which it is meant to serve. It is properly a cursing or imprecatory psalm. Psalm 137 is a beautiful, but painful, literary masterpiece full of rich and historically-illustrative expression. The pain comes from the regret over Israel's sad predicament of captivity, as contrasted with its great spiritual heritage of the past.

### E. An Insulting Request *(Psalm 137:3-4)*

**For there they that carried us away captive required of us a song; and they that wasted us required of us mirth, saying, Sing us one of the songs of Zion. How shall we sing the LORD's song in a strange land?**

The tears of the captives were produced by the memory of the past. They cried because they realized what was, and what could still be, if not for disobedience. Although the tears were real, they were too late. Their musical harps were retired because the conditions of their captivity were not exactly conducive to mirth and glee. The cruel request of the captors to ignore their feelings and sing godly songs in an ungodly environment wounded their psyche and stirred their grief, homesickness, and indignation. To sing the Lord's songs in a strange land would be to desecrate the songs. Foreign land is idolatrous and profane; therefore, singing those songs there was tantamount to insulting God.

### F. Remembering Jerusalem *(Psalm 137:5-6)*

**If I forget thee, O Jerusalem, let my right hand forget her cunning. If I do not remember thee, let my tongue cleave to the roof of my mouth; if I prefer not Jerusalem above my chief joy.**

The curse issued by the psalmist was not pronounced upon an enemy, but rather upon the psalmist himself, should he dare to forget Jerusalem and fail to prioritize such an important component of national legacy. The psalmist embraced the philosophy that unless a person is willing to die for something that person is not fit to live. Unfortunately, it took a national tragedy of epic proportion for the people of Israel to realize that God's exaltation of them would occur only when they humbled themselves and submitted to God. When we seek first God's kingdom and God's righteousness, everything else that is needed will eventually be added unto us.

## III. Concluding Reflections

Even one little step away from God is a huge step in the wrong direction. God's sheep hear God's voice and will not follow another shepherd. Most sheep don't suddenly bolt and run away from the shepherd. Most sheep get lost in the slow grazing process, and after several absentminded hours they eventually find themselves a far distance from the shepherd. God's message to God's people is that in the very day that we hear God's voice, we should not harden our hearts. A hard heart is as useless as a piece of hardened clay. What God desires is a soft and pliable heart that can be molded and shaped into a vessel dedicated to God's glory.

While the children of Israel were in route to the Promised Land, there were many occasions during which God communicated specific messages to them. God's Word was consistently ignored and disregarded. Consequently, God punished the obstinate people by allowing them to wander aimlessly in the desert for forty years. When that faithless generation finally died out, Joshua's generation literally walked into the blessing of the Promised Land.

Today, if we desire to experience the complete provisions of our spiritual inheritance, we must heed the voice of God the first time we hear it.

## WORD POWER

**We sat down (Hebrew:** *yashab)*—to sit down in this context refers to a condition of the heart. It does not mean literal sitting. Altogether they had conditioned their minds not to sing in a foreign land. When there were occasions for them to sing they refused.

## HOME DAILY BIBLE READINGS

for the week of November 19, 2006
*The People Go into Exile*

Nov. 13, Monday
    —Proverbs 1:20-33
    —Embrace Wisdom
Nov. 14, Tuesday
    —Proverbs 8:32-36
    —Key to the Good Life
Nov. 15, Wednesday
    —Jeremiah 1:11-19
    —Jeremiah Prophesies Judgment
Nov. 16, Thursday
    —Jeremiah 25:1-11
    —Jeremiah Predicts Jerusalem's Fall
Nov. 17, Friday
    —2 Chronicles 36:11-14
    —Zedekiah Rebels Against God
Nov. 18, Saturday
    —2 Chronicles 36:15-21
    —Jerusalem Falls
Nov. 19, Sunday
    —Psalm 137
    —Psalm of Remorse

## PRAYER

*When You speak to us, Lord, let us hear You and fear You. When You direct our paths, let us follow. When You feed us, let us heed You. In Jesus' name, we pray. Amen.*

## Lesson 13

# God Offers Return and Restoration

**November 26, 2006**

**ADULT TOPIC:** Experiencing Forgiveness
**YOUTH TOPIC:** Coming Home!
**CHILDREN'S TOPIC:** God's People Return Home

**DEVOTIONAL READING:** Jeremiah 29:10-14
**BACKGROUND SCRIPTURE:** 2 Chronicles 36:22-23; Ezra 1:5-7
**PRINT PASSAGE:** 2 Chronicles 36:22-23; Ezra 1:5-7

### 2 Chronicles 36:22-23; Ezra 1:5-7—KJV

22 Now in the first year of Cyrus king of Persia, that the word of the LORD spoken by the mouth of Jeremiah might be accomplished, the LORD stirred up the spirit of Cyrus king of Persia, that he made a proclamation throughout all his kingdom, and put it also in writing, saying,

23 Thus saith Cyrus king of Persia, All the kingdoms of the earth hath the LORD God of heaven given me; and he hath charged me to build him an house in Jerusalem, which is in Judah. Who is there among you of all his people? The LORD his God be with him, and let him go up.

· · · · ·

5 Then rose up the chief of the fathers of Judah and Benjamin, and the priests, and the Levites, with all them whose spirit God had raised, to go up to build the house of the LORD which is in Jerusalem.

6 And all they that were about them strengthened their hands with vessels of silver, with gold, with goods, and with beasts, and with precious things, beside all that was willingly offered.

7 Also Cyrus the king brought forth the vessels of the house of the LORD, which Nebuchadnezzar had brought forth out of Jerusalem, and had put them in the house of his gods.

**UNIT III**
Living as God's Covenanted People

**CHILDREN'S UNIT**
Living as Covenant People

### KEY VERSE

Thus saith Cyrus king of Persia, All the kingdoms of the earth hath the LORD God of heaven given me; and he hath charged me to build him an house in Jerusalem... Who is there among you of all his people? The LORD his God be with him, and let him go up.
—2 Chronicles 36:23

### OBJECTIVES

Upon completion of this lesson, the students are expected to:

1. Recognize the importance of returning to the things of God;
2. Recognize God's power over earthly authority; and,
3. Discover that God's goodness and mercy will follow us all the days of our lives.

## UNIFYING LESSON PRINCIPLE

Many people experience forgiveness after they have done something wrong. How do we experience God's forgiveness? The Israelites knew God had forgiven them when they were allowed to return home and rebuild.

## POINTS TO BE EMPHASIZED
### ADULTS/YOUTH
**Adult/Youth Key Verse:**
2 Chronicles 36:23
**Print Passage:** 2 Chronicles 36:22-23; Ezra 1:5-7

—Not all of the people returned to Judah, only those "whose spirit God had stirred."

—What role did Cyrus play in the rebuilding of the temple in Jerusalem?

—God intervenes in human history to bring about change.

## CHILDREN
**Key Verse:** Ezra 1:5
**Print Passage:** 2 Chronicles 36:22-23; Ezra 1:5-7

—Cyrus, a political authority, recognized that God was the ultimate authority.

—God often uses inner change (attitudes, beliefs, and desires) to accomplish positive outer actions.

## TOPICAL OUTLINE OF THE LESSON
**I. INTRODUCTION**
   A. The Challenge of the Future
   B. Biblical Background

**II. EXPOSITION AND APPLICATION OF THE SCRIPTURE**

   A. God Blesses Judah Through an Ungodly King *(2 Chronicles 36:22-23)*
   B. God Specializes in Fixing Hearts *(Ezra 1:5)*
   C. Material Goods Used for Spiritual Purposes *(Ezra 1:6)*
   D. God's Preservation and Restoration *(Ezra 1:7)*

**III. CONCLUDING REFLECTIONS**

## I. INTRODUCTION
### A. The Challenge of the Future

The opportunity to return home to someone or something that was left behind many years ago can be a challenging and bittersweet experience. Even though home is said to be the place where the heart is, time and distance can make the heart grow fonder. There is a sense of comfort, lure, and leisure that attaches itself to the familiar. One's present circumstances can sometimes outweigh and override one's devotion and loyalty to one's roots. In that vein, it is possible for slavery to become so comfortable and familiar that the steps necessary to achieve freedom seem like too great an effort.

The Jewish expatriates in Babylon had similar choices. They could remain in the familiar and relatively friendly confines of unholy Babylon, or they could turn their hearts toward home and lay a foundation for the next generation by helping to restore the ruins of Jerusalem. If you were in a similar situation, what would you do? Many Jews chose to go to Jerusalem, but many chose to remain in Babylon. The journey back to Jerusalem was difficult, dangerous, and expensive, lasting over four months. Travel conditions were poor and hazardous, and the surrounding countryside was in ruins. The people living in the area were hostile. Persian records indicate that many Jews in captivity had accumulated great wealth. Therefore, returning to Jerusalem would have meant giving up everything they had and starting over.

There are many spiritual parallels and comparisons in the Jews' dilemma. When we are "captured" by sin, there is sometimes a tendency for us to be lulled into a sense of emotional resolve. It may seem easier to remain in sin than to exert the effort to return to the things of God. This is a familiar tactic of the enemy that must not be tolerated. No matter how difficult returning to God may seem initially, God's way is always the best way. The permanent rewards of the Light always outweigh the temporary fireworks of darkness.

### B. Biblical Background

Leviticus 26:27-45 predicts the captivity of Israel that occurs in 2 Chronicles. The prophecy reveals how God's people would be banished from their homeland as punishment for their disobedience. The book of 2 Chronicles seems as if it will end on a very somber note of curses and prophecies of desolation; however, the final two verses conclude the book on a positive and uplifting note of hope. This is a trend employed throughout Scripture. Regardless of how harsh and punitive a Scripture passage may read, there is an eventual reprieve and an opportunity for repentance and forgiveness.

The book of Ezra is probably not named for the author but, rather, for the principal character in the narrative. The unknown author is referred to as the Chronicler and is probably responsible for 1 and 2 Chronicles, Ezra, and Nehemiah. All of these writings contain many of the same issues, interests, points of view, and theological and ecclesiastical conceptions. The book of Ezra was written to assist the Jerusalem Jews in understanding their rich heritage and identity as people of God. Ezra and Nehemiah were originally the same book and they provide extremely important information on Israel's history between 538 and 430 B.C. During this period, the Jews began a reformation following the Babylonian exile. Ezra was a priest and the foremost spiritual leader of his time. Ezra, along with Nehemiah, who was appointed governor, was largely responsible for the development of the newly-formed Jewish community.

## II. Exposition and Application of the Scripture
### A. God Blesses Judah Through an Ungodly King *(2 Chronicles 36:22-23)*

**Now in the first year of Cyrus king of Persia, that the word of the Lord spoken by the mouth of Jeremiah might be accomplished, the Lord stirred up the spirit of Cyrus king of Persia, that he made a proclamation throughout all his kingdom, and put it also in writing, saying, Thus saith Cyrus king of Persia, All the kingdoms of the earth hath the Lord God of heaven given me; and he hath charged me to build him an house in Jerusalem, which is in Judah. Who is there among you of all his people? The Lord his God be with him, and let him go up.**

Just as God used King Nebuchadnezzer to attack and destroy Jerusalem, God used another non-Jewish leader, King Cyrus, to facilitate the renovation and restoration of Jerusalem. Truly the heart of the king is in the hand of the Lord; this is God's world and God can use anyone to fulfill His purposes on earth. Even before King Cyrus was born, Jeremiah had prophesied that King Cyrus would release the captives from Judah. This clearly demonstrates God's sovereign power over earthly authority. Cyrus made his written proclamation the year after Babylon was conquered, which was forty-eight years after the temple was destroyed (see 36:18-19). King Cyrus ruled the Persian Empire from 549 to 530 B.C. His most significant military victory was the capture of Babylon. After defeating the Babylonians, the Persians sought to develop a sense of loyalty on behalf of those conquered peoples by allowing and encouraging them to return to their original homelands.

During the time that Judah was in exile, the Israelites were a privileged and protected people. The treatment and liberties extended to Judah were very different from the experience of typical captive nations. The kingdom of Judah was afforded numerous perks: they had their own communities and schools; they had freedom of worship and as such the hope for restoration of David's throne was alive; the scribes and priests were allowed to continue teaching the Law; and after their return from Babylon, their lives were centered on teaching God's Word.

The great and powerful King Cyrus openly attributed his world-renowned military and political success to the Lord, the God of heaven. No matter how many accomplishments we may achieve in life, we should never become so far removed that we neglect to acknowledge God as the source of our help. Humility is an indispensable characteristic to any leader's ultimate success.

### B. God Specializes in Fixing Hearts (Ezra 1:5)

**Then rose up the chief of the fathers of Judah and Benjamin, and the priests, and the Levites, with all them whose spirit God had raised, to go up to build the house of the LORD which is in Jerusalem.**

The heads of household from Judah and Benjamin took the initiative for the restoration of Jerusalem and the temple. These individuals established an important precedent for spiritual leadership among present-day households. It is the husband's responsibility to be the spiritual leader of the home. Far too many of today's husbands and fathers are spiritually AWOL (absent without leave). There are great privileges that come with being a husband and a father, but there are also great responsibilities. The priests and Levites joined the heads of the various households in returning to rebuild Jerusalem. Although these individuals fell into different categories, the one thing that was common among them was that their hearts were all moved to action by the power of God.

Sometimes, life's situations and circumstances seem beyond our control. In Israel's case, only God could touch the heart of the pagan king to release the captives, and only God could move on the hearts of comfortable captives to leave Babylon's convenience and commit to rebuilding the

Jerusalem ruins. Most people are limited to affecting others from the outside, but God specializes in making a difference on the inside. Outside change is usually topical and temporary; inside change is permanent and lasting.

## C. Material Goods Used for Spiritual Purposes *(Ezra 1:6)*

**And all they that were about them strengthened their hands with vessels of silver, with gold, with goods, and with beasts, and with precious things, beside all that was willingly offered.**

The articles that were collected for the purpose of returning to Jerusalem and rebuilding the temple were strictly of a material nature: gold, silver, livestock, gifts, and offerings. Although these articles possessed no inherently spiritual significance, their spiritual value was reflected in their purpose. The purpose of a thing reflects and transforms its value and worth. These articles were collected to be used for a godly purpose—a purpose that was aligned and in spiritual sync with the kingdom of God.

Some Christians may pray to God for material possessions, such as money, cars, houses, or other material goods. God's primary concern, however, is not that our lives are inundated with many things. God's concern is that the things we possess be used for Kingdom purposes. Perhaps more of our prayers would be answered if we would realign our priorities to reflect the sentiments reflected in the Lord's Prayer: "Thy Kingdom come, God's will be done right here on earth, just as it is in heaven." In heaven, God's will is always accomplished. As "subjects" of God's kingdom, we would do well to discover God's existing will and join God in the process of fulfillment. When this occurs, our prayers will change from self-centered requests to those that benefit others as well, just as Solomon's prayer (1 Kings 3) regarding his needs was for the benefit of his people. We should make our specific requests known unto God, and trust God to fulfill them.

## D. God's Preservation and Restoration *(Ezra 1:7)*

**Also Cyrus the king brought forth the vessels of the house of the LORD, which Nebuchadnezzar had brought forth out of Jerusalem, and had put them in the house of his gods.**

All of the 5,400 articles that had been taken by King Nebuchadnezzar from the temple in Jerusalem were kept safe in Babylon. While in Babylon, they were placed in the temple of King Nebuchadnezzar's god. This might seem like a blasphemous gesture, but if it had not occurred, perhaps the temple articles would have been lost or destroyed during the period of the captivity. God used another ungodly king, Cyrus, to safely return the sacred articles to Jerusalem.

This is yet another example of God allowing *all things* to work together for good to them that love God and those who are *called* according to God's purpose. If we look at the destruction of Jerusalem in isolation, we may not be able to see any practical or spiritually-redeeming value. But if we look at the total picture in retrospect, we can clearly see the hand of God at work. What does it mean to be called? A good question for every Christian is: "Would you consider yourself to be called?" Most people associate the term "called" with calling to preach the Gospel. This is only partially true. Every Christian is called to proclaim the Gospel, for these are the very words of the Great Commission recorded in Matthew 28:19-20. However, not every believer is given the gift to preach from a pulpit inside a church. Since most non-Christians never venture inside a church building, one easily understands why God would equip believers with a wide variety of gifts to be used in diverse ways—but with the same intent: to communicate the Good News of Jesus Christ to a world in great need of God's love.

## III. Concluding Reflections

Our bodies and our very lives are temples of God. What is the status of your temple? Is it fully functional and standing strong, or is it seriously suffering from spiritual neglect? Perhaps it has a beautiful exterior; but is the foundation weak? Are you dependent upon someone else to maintain your temple, or have you assumed personal responsibility to operate your temple in a way that is pure and pleasing to the Lord? Honest answers to these questions and others will help us to remain vigilant in living lives that are full of power, purpose, victory, and abundance.

It is comforting to know that even when God is forced to discipline and punish people, the heart of God is still soft, the mind of God is still planning, and the protection of God is still activated. Situations and circumstances may arise in life when God is forced to cut us. But, we can rest assured that God's cuts are always for healing, not killing. God is not out to get us, but to give us.

## WORD POWER

**Let him go (Hebrew: *'alah*)**—the statement made by Cyrus is not a command; it is a general proclamation. It is an advisement for people to go if they so choose. This explains the reason why some of them choose to remain behind. The word "let" used by English translators makes the proclamation an advisement.

## HOME DAILY BIBLE READINGS

for the week of November 26, 2006
*God Offers Return and Restoration*

Nov. 20, Monday
—Psalm 57
—Prayer for Deliverance
Nov. 21, Tuesday
—Isaiah 57:14-19
—God Promises to Lead and Heal
Nov. 22, Wednesday
—Psalm 130
—God Forgives
Nov. 23, Thursday
—Jeremiah 29:10-14
—God's Plan Revealed
Nov. 24, Friday
—2 Chronicles 36:22-23
—King Cyrus Plans to Rebuild
Nov. 25, Saturday
—Ezra 1
—The Exiles Return
Nov. 26, Sunday
—Ezra 5:7b-14
—Rebuilding the Temple

## PRAYER

*Lord, please let us clearly hear Your voice when You warn us of our wandering. Remind us of the consequences of a hardened heart. In Jesus' name, we pray. Amen.*

# WINTER QUARTER—December 2006, January, February 2007

## *Jesus Christ: A Portrait of God*

### GENERAL INTRODUCTION

This quarter has three units that present Jesus Christ and provide insight into His work. The lessons afford a theological framework for understanding where Jesus came from, as well as a practical perspective on what He came to accomplish.

**Unit I,** *Christ, the Image of God,* has five lessons designed to be an appropriate Advent/Christmas study. The first lesson begins with the basic question: Who is Jesus Christ? The second lesson explores what God has to say relative to Jesus' identity. The third lesson examines Jesus as the light that comes to conquer. The fourth lesson (Christmas) focuses on Jesus as the Word becoming flesh to live among humankind. The final lesson looks at how the issues of humiliation and exaltation converge in Jesus as depicted in passages from various New Testament letters.

Lesson 1—people struggle sometimes with understanding who God is. There is a scriptural basis for answering this question. The Colossians passage affirms that Jesus, the Son of the Most High God, is both human and divine, and that He reveals God to us. The Luke passage describes the birth of John the Baptist who became a powerful witness to Jesus as the Son of God. Lesson 2—people have varying ideas about Jesus Christ: where He came from, how He is related to God, and how He is able to reveal God to us. The writer of Hebrews affirms that Jesus Christ came from God and is superior to the angels. Lesson 3—people seek meaningful relationships that add to their self-esteem and self-worth. Where can we cultivate such a relationship that is always affirming and self-enhancing? John tells us that in God there is found the type of relationship that not only reveals our need for a life-changing encounter with God, but also provides the benefits of a relationship that contributes to our spiritual maturity. The Matthew passage shows how Joseph's relationship with God and Mary led him to care for her and her child. Lesson 4—people need to feel that God is with them. What does it mean for God to enter our world? John suggests that in Jesus Christ, God entered into human existence in order to bring humanity back into relationship with God. Lesson 5—some people misinterpret humility as a sign of weakness, while others embrace it to the point that they become proud of their humility. Is it possible to balance humility with an appropriate level of self-esteem? Pointing out that Jesus Christ achieved the perfect balance between humility and exaltation, Paul urges Christians to take on the mind of Christ.

**Unit II**, *Christ Sustains and Supports,* has four lessons that focus on various "I am" statements in the gospel of John. The first two lessons establish that Jesus has the power to sustain and support us because He came from above as our authority and judge. The last two lessons explore Jesus' concept of Himself as the Bread of Life, Living Water, and the Light of the world. In each lesson, we see that Jesus addresses the deepest needs of the human heart. Lesson 6—human beings often seek help when trying to free themselves from destructive behavioral patterns. What source of help is available to us when we seek freedom from sin? John says that we are made free in Christ, who is from above, and emphasizes that Jesus Christ, our Savior, is indeed God's Son. Lesson 7—many times, we question the appropriateness of a particular judgment or decision. Is it possible for decisions to be unbiased and completely fair? John says that Jesus has authority that comes directly from God; because God and Jesus are perfect, their decisions are perfect. Jesus' authority was directly demonstrated when He healed the lame man on the Sabbath. Lesson 8—people constantly search for those experiences and possessions that can provide satisfaction and fulfillment. Can we discover someone or something that can provide spiritual satisfaction? Jesus portrayed Himself as the life-giver in whom there is complete satisfaction. Lesson 9—the fear or avoidance of darkness is a common experience for many people. Is there any light available that can dispel the spiritual darkness in which many people find themselves? John says that the light Jesus provides reaches into areas of our lives where physical light cannot reach. The healing of the blind man was one way that Jesus manifested Himself as the Light of life.

**Unit III**, *Christ Guides and Protects,* has four lessons that also focus on the "I am" sayings as recorded in John. These lessons explore particularly Jesus' relationship to believers from a corporate perspective. In the first lesson, we see Jesus as the Good Shepherd of the flock. The second lesson examines Jesus as the Resurrection and the Life, while the third lesson looks at Jesus as the Way, the Truth and the Life. The final lesson explores how we remain vitally alive as a faith community by being connected to Jesus, the True Vine. Lesson 10—people seek protection from those elements that pose a threat to their well-being. Is it possible to find protection in our fearful world? Jesus uses the image of the shepherd to imply that He provides spiritual protection for His people. Lesson 11—everyone eventually experiences the death of a family member or an acquaintance. We are encouraged by the fact that Jesus taught that death is not a permanent reality for those who have developed a personal relationship with Him through faith, because He has power over death. Lesson 12—all of us at some time have been lost or needed direction. Jesus says that He is the Way, and all other directions for life are to be found through Him. Lesson 13—we are all born to be in relationships with others; we need these relationships to be productive.

**Lesson 1**

# Who Is Jesus Christ?

**December 3, 2006**

**ADULT TOPIC:** Seeking Reconciliation
**YOUTH TOPIC:** Double Agent
**CHILDREN'S TOPIC:** Good News for Elizabeth and Zechariah

**DEVOTIONAL READING:** Isaiah 9:2-7
**BACKGROUND SCRIPTURE:** Colossians 1
**PRINT PASSAGE:** Colossians 1:15-23

## Colossians 1:15-23—KJV

15 Who is the image of the invisible God, the firstborn of every creature:

16 For by him were all things created, that are in heaven, and that are in earth, visible and invisible, whether they be thrones, or dominions, or principalities, or powers: all things were created by him, and for him:

17 And he is before all things, and by him all things consist.

18 And he is the head of the body, the church: who is the beginning, the firstborn from the dead; that in all things he might have the preeminence.

19 For it pleased the Father that in him should all fulness dwell;

20 And, having made peace through the blood of his cross, by him to reconcile all things unto himself; by him, I say, whether they be things in earth, or things in heaven.

21 And you, that were sometime alienated and enemies in your mind by wicked works, yet now hath he reconciled

22 In the body of his flesh through death, to present you holy and unblameable and unreproveable in his sight:

23 If ye continue in the faith grounded and settled, and be not moved away from the hope of the gospel, which ye have heard, and which was preached to every creature which is under heaven; whereof I Paul am made a minister.

**UNIT I**
Christ, the Image of God

**CHILDREN'S UNIT**
Good News for Everyone

**KEY VERSES**

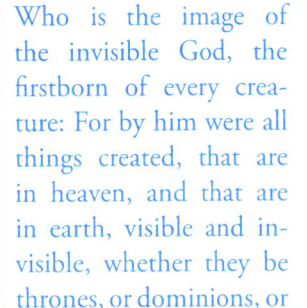

Who is the image of the invisible God, the firstborn of every creature: For by him were all things created, that are in heaven, and that are in earth, visible and invisible, whether they be thrones, or dominions, or principalities, or powers: all things were created by him, and for him.
—Colossians 1:15-16

**OBJECTIVES**

Upon completion of this lesson, the students will know that:

1. Jesus Christ, the Son of God, is both human and divine;
2. Jesus Christ—in His humanity—reveals God to us in a palatable way; and,
3. Jesus Christ is the mediator and instrument of reconciliation.

## UNIFYING LESSON PRINCIPLE

People sometimes struggle with understanding who God is. Is there a means by which we can obtain this understanding? The Colossians passage affirms that Jesus, the Son of the Most High God, is both human and divine, and that He thus reveals God to us. The Luke passage describes the birth of John the Baptist, who became a powerful witness to Jesus as the Son of God.

## POINTS TO BE EMPHASIZED
## ADULTS/YOUTH

**Adult/Youth Key Verse:** Colossians 1:15-16
**Print Passage:** Colossians 1:15-23

—The church owes its existence to Christ, who is her Head.

—All persons have been reconciled with God through the cross of Christ.

—Our reconciliation to God hinges on our faithfulness to the Gospel.

—Paul proclaimed that Jesus the Messiah was co-creator of the universe with God.

## CHILDREN

**Key Verse:** Luke 1:13
**Print Passage:** Luke 1:5-13, 24-25, 59-64

—Zechariah and Elizabeth, who were devout and obedient to God, prayed for a son.

—An angel informed Zechariah that Elizabeth would bear a son, who was to be named "John," which means "the Lord is gracious."

## TOPICAL OUTLINE OF THE LESSON

I. **INTRODUCTION**
   A. The Person of Christ
   B. Biblical Background

II. **EXPOSITION AND APPLICATION OF THE SCRIPTURE**
   A. Who Is Christ? *(Colossians 1:15-17)*
   B. Christ as Head of the Church *(Colossians 1:18-19)*
   C. Christ Reconciles All Things to God *(Colossians 1:20-23)*

III. **CONCLUDING REFLECTIONS**

## I. INTRODUCTION
### A. The Person of Christ

Have you ever been told that you look like and act like your father? If you have, basically what the person was saying was that you have some characteristics that resemble those of your father. In most cases, people don't mind when others recognize the physical or personality traits that link them to a parent. As followers of Jesus Christ, we should be especially pleased when we are able to reflect the characteristics of our heavenly Father.

Paul explained the image of God in Christ; not as an intellectual discourse on the creative aspects of God's incarnation, but rather as a statement formed by faith. For now, the incarnation of Christ is a mystery; this is how the Trinity or the Godhead must be explained. Jesus provides a unique glimpse of God and helps us better understand the work of the Godhead.

Today's lesson will disclose the three distinctive aspects of the person of Christ, the preexistence of Christ, the co-existence of Christ, and the incarnation of Christ. These three distinct aspects are valuable to the Christian faith, for nestled in them is the reconciliation of humanity back to God.

## B. Biblical Background

The book of Colossians is one of four prison epistles; Ephesians, Philippians, and Philemon are the other three. During Paul's stay in Ephesus, a man named Epaphras received Jesus Christ as his Lord and Savior. Epaphras went back to his home in Colossae, where he proclaimed Christ and, by all accounts, was the pastor of a church. Epaphras shared with Paul what was happening at the Colossian church—that false teachers were seeking to make Christianity philosophical and therefore open to debate, rather than transformational. Paul was compelled to clarify the theology of the believers in Colossae by focusing on the person and mission of Christ.

Christology (i.e., the study of Christ), as expressed in this writing, is foundational to the Christian faith. Paul was disturbed by the influx of false teaching called Gnosticism, which had crept into the Colossian church. Essentially, the heretical teachers denied the humanity of Christ. Their false teaching espoused the belief that one could not know God personally because His body was not real; it only appeared to be so.

From their perspective, God must be understood through reason and intellect. This teaching denied divine creation of the world, as well as Christ's incarnation into a physical body.

In combating this issue, the apostle Paul addressed three distinctive perspectives of the person of Christ that would dispel any attack on the Christian faith: Christ's pre-existence, Christ's co-existence, and Christ's incarnation. Each of these perspectives sheds more light on the person of Christ and gives more insight into the mystery of the Godhead.

## II. Exposition and Application of the Scripture

### A. Who Is Christ? *(Colossians 1:15-17)*

**Who is the image of the invisible God, the firstborn of every creature: For by him were all things created, that are in heaven, and that are in earth, visible and invisible, whether they be thrones, or dominions, or principalities, or powers: all things were created by him, and for him: And he is before all things, and by him all things consist.**

Who is Christ? Paul had to address this question because of the circulation of the false doctrine called Gnosticism. Paul addressed the personhood of Christ by evaluating Christ from the image of God. The identity of Christ can be seen in the image of the invisible God. The identity of Christ is revealed in the shared nature of God and Christ.

That Christ is the visible manifestation of God is imperative to belief in Him as the Son of God. Paul acknowledges that God is invisible; however, Paul refutes the notion that He is only an image by using the phrase, "the firstborn of every creature." In Adam Clarke's work on the book of Colossians, he notes that there is a Jewish term, *becoro shel olam*, which means "the firstborn of all the world, or of all the creation, to signify his having created or produced all things."[1] As the "firstborn," Christ was not only pre-existent to creation, but also a full participant in the creative activity of the Godhead. The fact that Christ is a visible image of God in creation is terribly significant because it signals Christ's role at the beginning of time and His continual creative role in human history.

Colossians 1:16-17 reveals four critical things concerning the nature and work of Christ: (1) Christ is the Creator of the universe; (2) All things in the universe were created by Him; (3) All things were made for His pleasure and plan; (4) Only He can ensure their continuance.

The Christian doctrine of creation is foundational, for it rests upon the premise that God is the Creator and Sustainer of all. Paul argued that creation is not only in the sole province of God, but that Christ, as the visible part of the Godhead, created all parts of the cosmos. When one accepts the notion that God (i.e., Christ) is creator of the stars, moons, planets, water, earth, and so forth, it clearly suggests that believers can trust the events that occur within these realms. Planets were planned, stars were designed, and heavens came into being as a part of the express plan of the Creator. No other hypothesis is sufficient to convince the believer of how the world came into being. So when one prays in the name of Jesus about the events and wonder of the cosmos, He understands; for He made it.

Secondly, Paul argues that all things in the universe were created by Him. In following the logic of the Genesis creation account (see Genesis 1), Paul separates the cosmos from the things in the cosmos. It seems apparent that the apostle followed this scheme because it not only suggests the orderly manner in which God (Christ) caused things to come into being, but it also ties everything to Himself. Since everything is tied to God, one can pray about everything.

By arguing that all things were made for God, Paul essentially asserts that God (Christ) is the object and subject of creation. Creatures are made to serve the creator. Believers often approach God as though He exists to serve human whims and caprices; the petitions of believers are often mired in selfish aims. Paul's assertion that all things were made *for* God is vital to understanding that humanity exists for God; God does not exist for humanity.

The apostle argues that God is the essential element of all that exists. This is not to be confused with pantheism, which suggests that all things are essentially godly. Instead, Paul asserted that creation continues to be sustained by Christ. He not only created water, but also restrains its destructive flow so that His children might enjoy a fresh moment of grace.

---

[1] Adam Clarke, *Commentary on the Whole Bible: The Book of Colossians.*

Another aspect of who Christ is can be seen in His co-existence with God. Several Scriptures unveil Christ's identity through His co-existence with the Father. Genesis 1:26 alludes to the co-existence of God and Christ in creation, especially in the creation of humanity. So from Paul's perspective, he sees Christ present from the beginning, working with God in those things that were being created.

John 14:7-15 is one portion of the Scriptures that speaks of the oneness of the Father and the Son; here we see mutuality and the interaction between both. In John 8:28, Jesus states that He does nothing on His own, but that all things come from God the Father. In John 17:11, Jesus prays for His disciples, "that they may be one, as we are." Jesus realized that He was a human being, with all of its frailties—hunger, sorrow, pain—and emotions. He also recognized His divinity—the God who could feel the pain, the sorrow, the joy, and the hunger of His creation.

Philippians 2:5-6 offers insight into the co-existence of God in Christ. Jesus could have divulged His full identity, but instead humbled Himself by taking off the image of the true God and putting on the form of a servant, in the likeness of man. Notice the word *likeness*; unlike the word *image* found in our text, *likeness* means "replica or copy." God replicated Himself through incarnation and became flesh; however, after He humbled Himself to death and the cross (see Philippians 2:8), God "highly exalted Him" and gave Him a name that was above every name.

The last aspect of the divinity of Christ can be seen in His incarnation. He became flesh, as John 1:14 states, and lived among humans as the only begotten of the Father. He became a model of what the first Adam should have been. In 1 Corinthians 15:20-27, Scripture speaks of the incarnation of Christ, being the "firstfruits of them that slept," overcoming death and the grave, as well as having all things under His feet.

Paul had to enlighten the Colossian church because the evidence given by the false teachers had intellectualized Christ—which could appeal to their rational minds if they did not receive the incarnate Christ by faith.

### B. Christ as Head of the Church
*(Colossians 1:18-19)*

**And he is the head of the body, the church: who is the beginning, the firstborn from the dead; that in all things he might have the preeminence. For it pleased the Father that in him should all fulness dwell.**

Christ is not only the image of the invisible God incarnate and creator of everything that exists, He is also the founder, organizer and head of the church. Paul pointed to Christ's role for good reason—there would be no church if Jesus, the Lamb of God, had not given His life for her. Therefore, the body of Christ has her genesis in Him. Without Christ, the church would not exist, so it should be understood that Jesus should have preeminence since He gave His life for the church. Nothing should overshadow Him, for He is the foundation of the church.

As the head, Christ sets the standard for the church. He establishes order, and members of His church should embrace that order and put Him in His rightful place. There is no agenda that takes precedence over His agenda. Verse 19 emphasizes that it pleases the Father that the fullness of His presence dwells in the express image of Jesus, as well as within the church—the *ekklesia* (the called-out).

### C. Christ Reconciles All Things to God (Colossians 1:20-23)

**And, having made peace through the blood of his cross, by him to reconcile all things unto himself; by him, I say, whether they be things in earth, or things in heaven. And you, that were sometime alienated and enemies in your mind by wicked works, yet now hath he reconciled In the body of his flesh through death, to present you holy and unblameable and unreproveable in his sight: If ye continue in the faith grounded and settled, and be not moved away from the hope of the gospel, which ye have heard, and which was preached to every creature which is under heaven; whereof I Paul am made a minister.**

Having firmly established the identity of Christ as both human and divine, and that He established the church—what was Christ's mission? Paul entreated the readers to know Christ and His mission through the way of the cross. The cross is the place of redemption for humankind; therefore, it would be the place where the healing of this fractured relationship must begin. Verse 20 imputes all things to God because peace was made through the blood of Christ. This imputing comes through reconciliation; it is a relational term. It depicts a relationship that was once fractured, and then is mended. This reconciliation was to reconnect humanity with God. According to 2 Corinthians 5:18-19, God does not ascribe the trespasses of the world to the people; God uses the ministry of reconciliation to reconnect all things back to Himself.

Why was this necessary? God is a relational God, and He wants to be in relationship with His creation—especially humankind. Therefore, Gnosticism can be refuted, because we can know God apart from reason and intellectual thought: for He reveals Himself to all through His Word. Paul portrays God as one who is in love with humankind. Out of this love He seeks to forgive humanity and to present humanity as holy and blameless in His sight. Paul helped the Colossian believers to understand that this would only happen if they continued in the faith and walked and believed in the Gospel.

## III. Concluding Reflections

The fact that Christ is both human and divine was a key issue that the church of Paul's day struggled to grasp. This issue continued to plague believers in succeeding centuries as evidenced in councils in Nicea and Chalcedon and the subsequent creeds that emerged from the church leaders. It was important to for the people to understand this wonderful blessing.

This understanding continues to be vital for contemporary believers, because we can easily dismiss God's creative activity in our lives. It is a divine Christ who blesses us; in His humanity He identifies with our cause. Liberation theologians such as James H. Cone, J. Deotis Roberts, Emily Townes, and others have understood this notion and applied this idea to their important work. Activist preachers such as Martin Luther King Jr., Kelly Miller Smith Sr., and Joseph Lowery have helped us understand this dual-natured diety who makes certain that "the vicious vicissitudes of life are not ultimate or final because He sits high and looks low." A detached divinity might be sympathetic but would never move out of His comfort zone to offer comfort to the dying children of Dafur, offer balm to the AIDS-riddled residents of Southern Africa, or give peace to the war-ravaged Iraqis. A Christ that is both human and divine is sorely needed for hope and help in the present age.

## WORD POWER

**Eikon**—the word "icon" is derived from the Greek word *eikon*. It means "a likeness, resemblance, carbon copy." It means one in whom the likeness of anyone is seen. It also means, "a being corresponding to the original." In our study today, Christ is the EIKON—Image—the Being compatible to God.

## HOME DAILY BIBLE READINGS

for the week of December 3, 2006
*Who Is Jesus Christ?*

Nov. 27, Monday
 —Luke 1:5-20
 —An Angel Promises

Nov. 28, Tuesday
 —Luke 1:21-25
 —Elizabeth Is with Child

Nov. 29, Wednesday
 —Luke 1:67-80
 —A Father Sings His Praise

Nov. 30, Thursday
 —Matthew 3:1-6
 —John Prepares the Way

Dec. 1, Friday
 —Isaiah 9:2-7
 —A Son Is Promised

Dec. 2, Saturday
 —Colossians 1:9-14
 —Into the Kingdom of His Son

Dec. 3, Sunday
 —Colossians 1:15-23
 —Who Jesus Is

## PRAYER

*God, we thank You for comforting us when we experience anxiety. We thank You for directing us when we lose our way. Lord, we also thank You for teaching us how to receive results for believing in You. We ask that You would continue to help us to grow in wisdom so that we may continue to work in truth and life. We love You, God, for Your goodness. We pray this, in Jesus' name. Amen.*

**December 10, 2006**

Lesson 2

## UNIT I
Christ, the Image of God

## CHILDREN'S UNIT
Good News for Everyone

# What God Says About Jesus

**ADULT TOPIC:** Learning About God
**YOUTH TOPIC:** Jesus: The Reflection of God
**CHILDREN'S TOPIC:** Good News for Mary

**DEVOTIONAL READING:** Luke 1:46-55
**BACKGROUND SCRIPTURE:** Hebrews 1
**PRINT PASSAGE:** Hebrews 1:1-9

## KEY VERSES

God, who at sundry times and in divers manners spake in time past unto the fathers by the prophets, Hath in these last days spoken unto us by his Son, whom he hath appointed heir of all things, by whom also he made the worlds.
—Hebrews 1:1-2

## OBJECTIVES

Upon completion of this lesson, the students will know that:
1. Jesus came from God and is superior to the angels;
2. Jesus is God's exact counterpart; and,
3. God's final revelation to humanity came through His Son, Jesus Christ.

### Hebrews 1:1-9—KJV

GOD, WHO at sundry times and in divers manners spake in time past unto the fathers by the prophets,

2 Hath in these last days spoken unto us by his Son, whom he hath appointed heir of all things, by whom also he made the worlds;

3 Who being the brightness of his glory, and the express image of his person, and upholding all things by the word of his power, when he had by himself purged our sins, sat down on the right hand of the Majesty on high;

4 Being made so much better than the angels, as he hath by inheritance obtained a more excellent name than they.

5 For unto which of the angels said he at any time, Thou art my Son, this day have I begotten thee? And again, I will be to him a Father, and he shall be to me a Son?

6 And again, when he bringeth in the firstbegotten into the world, he saith, And let all the angels of God worship him.

7 And of the angels he saith, Who maketh his angels spirits, and his ministers a flame of fire.

8 But unto the Son he saith, Thy throne, O God, is for ever and ever: a sceptre of righteousness is the sceptre of thy kingdom.

9 Thou hast loved righteousness, and hated iniquity; therefore God, even thy God, hath anointed thee with the oil of gladness above thy fellows.

## UNIFYING LESSON PRINCIPLE

People have varying ideas about Jesus Christ—where He came from, how He is related to God, and how He is able to reveal God to us. Is there a definitive concept about Jesus? The writer of Hebrews tells us that Jesus Christ came from God and is superior to the angels. The Luke passage tells how God selected Mary to bear the Christ child.

## POINTS TO BE EMPHASIZED ADULTS/YOUTH

**Adult Key Verses:** Hebrews 1:1-2
**Youth Key Verse:** Hebrews 1:2
**Print Passage:** Hebrews 1:1-9

—The writer of Hebrews used Old Testament texts to prove that Jesus came from God and is superior to the angels.
—The Hebrews who had been converted to Christianity were being persecuted by Gentile authorities.
—The book of Hebrews argues that it would be a serious mistake to abandon the superior faith of Jesus to return to the inferior faith of Israel.

## CHILDREN

**Key Verse:** Luke 1:35
**Print Passage:** Luke 1:26-38; Hebrews 1:1-2

—An angel announced to Mary that she would bear God's Son who would fulfill God's promise to send a redeemer.
—Mary's response to the angel's announcement revealed her humility and faithfulness to God.

## TOPICAL OUTLINE OF THE LESSON

I. **INTRODUCTION**
   A. Christ: God's Spokesman to the World
   B. Biblical Background

II. **EXPOSITION AND APPLICATION OF THE SCRIPTURE**
   A. God's Method of Operation *(Hebrews 1:1-2)*
   B. Jesus, God's Express Image *(Hebrews 1:3)*
   C. The Superiority of Christ *(Hebrews 1:4-9)*

III. **CONCLUDING REFLECTIONS**

## I. INTRODUCTION
### A. Christ: God's Spokesman to the World

"Actions speak louder than words." This saying implies that what a person does communicates louder than what that person says. In this Scripture passage, the writer unveils God's method of delivering His message to humanity. In times past, God spoke through the prophets; He now speaks through Jesus Christ, His Son.

God is meticulous in His approach to expressing Himself to humanity; therefore, He has used various mediums in times past and present to deliver His Word to the world. They include the spoken Word (prophets); the written Word (Scripture); and the Living Word (Jesus Christ). God has not only been meticulous in His methods of communicating with humanity; He has given all authority to His Son Jesus, as His exact image (see Colossians 2:9). Jesus Christ is "the express image" of God as well as the *expression* of God. He is not only the fleshly representation of God, but He is also the very Word of God.

God has not only been exacting in His way of communicating His Word with humanity, He has given authority to His Son Jesus, as His exact image—the mystery of which lies within the Trinity. First John 5:7 states that "there are three that bear record in heaven; the Father, the Son (the Word) and the Holy Ghost; and these three are one." This is necessary to note because in this nugget of Scripture lies the deity of Christ.

This lesson will encompass how God first established His method of operation through the patriarchs, the prophets and finally through His Son, Jesus. Then we will visit Christ, the express image of God. Finally, we will see the superiority of Jesus in the world and among the angels.

### B. Biblical Background

The authorship of Hebrews has been a topic of debate from the earliest times. The author uses Judaism—and its religious ceremonies and traditions—to demonstrate that Christ is a better sacrifice. Since Christ is superior to the Law and the prophets, He is worthy of worship and faithfulness.

The writer's concern was that believers remain faithful to Christ and His teaching. Nothing is superior to Him. The first chapter of Hebrews lays the foundation for what is to come within this book and is a helpful reminder of Christ's identity and power. It is much like going to the movie theater and viewing trailers of upcoming movies before the feature presentation is shown. The reader is entreated to enjoy this great salvation through Christ and His person; for without Him no one can be saved.

The intended audience of Hebrews needed reassurance that Christ is the promise of the Father, and that in Him alone is the fullness of God expressed. The message of Hebrews emphasizes that Jesus Christ is above all that came before Him and any that would come after Him. He is better than the angels and better than the system of sacrificial sin offerings that preceded Him. Christ is the ultimate and final sacrifice; animal sacrifices are no longer needed. Christ took care and became the sacrifice once and for all—for all.

## II. Exposition and Application of the Scripture
### A. God's Method of Operation
*(Hebrews 1:1-2)*

**God, who at sundry times and in divers manners spake in time past unto the fathers by the prophets, Hath in these last days spoken unto us by his Son, whom he hath appointed heir of all things, by whom also he made the worlds.**

The writer of the book of Hebrews addressed himself to Jews that were dispersed and living outside of Judea. While he and his intended readers were aware of the fact that God had acted in Hebrew history, he wanted them to understand that God, through Jesus Christ, had done a new and superior thing. As the book opens, the writer acknowledges that God has revealed Himself at various times and in a number of circumstances. He has revealed Himself in the patriarchs and the prophets. This certainly would sound a responsive chord within the bosom of baptized believers who were of Jewish lineage. These Hebraic worshipers rehearsed the stories of Abraham, Isaac, Jacob, and others. They breathed the words of Isaiah, Daniel, Ezekiel, Amos, Hosea, and others whose prophetic witness revealed the arm of the Lord. They told their children of that wonderful covenant that established and distinguished them as God's people. Nonetheless, God had a more excellent Heir to His legacy of grace. This appointed Heir was no mere mortal but was none other than the second person of the Godhead, Jesus Christ. He was a superior presenter of the things of God because He was God.

The fact that God spoke through His Son is important because it established the order by which spiritual knowledge was discerned. The Jewish believers had been exposed to a number of truths throughout their history as well as through revisionist writers. However, the writer of Hebrews wanted them to know that Jesus Christ was the ultimate standard. He did not discount the contributions of the past nor discard the teachings of old, for they pointed to Christ. Thus, Christ was and is superior to them because they merely pointed to the truth; they did not embody the truth.

Jesus was a superior to the patriarchs and the prophets; He was the Creator, while they were only creatures. He was not only *heir* of all things, but was also the *maker* of all things. The writer of Hebrews was consistent with the apostle Paul in his teaching that Christ was a full participant in the creative activity of the Godhead (see Colossians 1:15-17). This included the things of the world, but also the worlds themselves. Notice the use of the plural, "worlds" (verse 1). The plural form is utilized because the ancients thought of the heavenly, the earthly, and the underworld as distinct realms. Since Christ formed these worlds, He is superior to anything in them. These worlds were made by Him, and were and are sustained by Him.

### B. Jesus, God's Express Image
*(Hebrews 1:3)*

**Who being the brightness of his glory, and the express image of his person, and upholding all things by the word of his power, when he had by himself purged our sins, sat down on the right hand of the Majesty on high.**

Christ is not only the express image of God, but He is also the expression of God. Scripture teaches that Christ is God, as referenced by Colossians 1:15-17. However, a definition for the "express image" must be asserted before we can conclude with Hebrews 1:3. An "express image" is like the stamp of a notary public: when it is pressed onto paper, the imprint of the stamp appears on the paper where the stamp was pressed. In similar fashion, Christ in the life of an individual leaves an indelible imprint of God. This truth is referenced by 2 Corinthians 5:17: "If any man be in Christ, he is a new creature: old things are passed away; behold, all things are become new." Ephesians 2:10 also affirms Christ's image on a believer's life: "We are his workmanship, created in Christ Jesus." Further, 2 Corinthians 4:7 states: "But we have this treasure in earthen vessels, that the excellency of the power may be of God, and not of us."

Jesus is the image, or the exact representation, of God in the flesh—the embodiment of God in divine nature. The exactness of God in Christ not only demonstrates His deity, but also describes His expression. Jesus is the expression of God in love. Romans 5:8 (NKJV) states: "God demonstrates His own love toward us, in that while we were still sinners, Christ died for us." Jesus gave His life for the sins of the world; therefore, all who receive Christ as Lord have life. Love was the major motivation for this sacrifice and is one of the many attributes of God. The sacrifice of Christ's death on the cross portrays both God's love and His justice—His love in that His life was sacrificed for our sins, and His death in that He was the payment for the penalty of sin (Romans 6:23).

### C. The Superiority of Christ
*(Hebrews 1:4-9)*

**Being made so much better than the angels, as he hath by inheritance obtained a more excellent name than they. For unto which of the angels said he at any time, Thou art my Son, this day have I begotten thee? And again, I will be to him a Father, and he shall be to me a Son? And again, when he bringeth in the first begotten into the world, he saith, And let all the angels of God worship him. And of the angels he saith, Who maketh his angels spirits, and his ministers a flame of fire. But unto the Son he saith, Thy throne, O God, is for ever and ever: a sceptre of righteousness is the sceptre of thy kingdom. Thou hast loved righteousness, and hated iniquity; therefore God, even thy God, hath anointed thee with the oil of gladness above thy fellows.**

The author paints a picture for believers of both Jewish and Gentile backgrounds: Christ is better. In the first two verses, the author gives a history lesson on how God spoke in times past. However, in the last days, God speaks through His Son, Jesus Christ. Although the prophets and their contribution to God's people were divinely authentic, Jesus is the fulfillment of the Old Testament prophecy and the embodiment of the Law. Therefore, God sent His Son into the world to communicate His message: "And the Word became flesh..." (John 1:14, NRSV).

Moreover, He was superior to any sacrifice offered in the past because He could purge sins. The word used for "purge" in this text is *katharisimo*. The meaning behind it was well known to Jewish persons. It meant a cleansing, a purification—a ritual purgation or washing in one of two settings:

a. the washing of the Jews before and after their meals.

b. Levitical purification of women after childbirth.

In the first of these two instances, all persons of Jewish heritage would understand the importance of this practice. In the second instance, since all did not have children, it was well established in the Levitical code that women cleanse themselves. By using this word, *katharisimo*, the writer implied that all have the need for cleansing, but only Christ can serve as the superior priest to make this happen. Thus, in the setting of the book of Hebrews, *katharisimo* meant a cleansing from the guilt of sins wrought by the expiatory sacrifice of Christ. Since Christ singularly could effect this purging, He was superior to any and all comers. Furthermore, once He completed this important work, He joined the Almighty in majestic splendor by taking a seat at the right hand of God.

The Hebrews writer explained that the Jews were compelled by Judaist ceremonies, traditions, and the Law, so it was important to assure his audience that Christ—the Word, God's express image—was better than the prophets, better than the angels, better than pagan gods, or Gnostic theories—better than anything. It is through Jesus Christ that a person is saved. The angels have no idea of the concept of redemption. Therefore, they are not connected with humanity and the need to be redeemed. However, Jesus understood the need for humankind to be redeemed. Therefore, Jesus felt the hurt and pain of humans from two perspectives: from a divine perspective and from a human perspective. From the divine perspective, Christ was and is involved in the pain of humanity; He felt the sorrow and the hurts that plague humanity. From a human perspective, Christ is in touch with the feelings of human beings—He experienced pain and temptation (Matthew 4).

He was and is superior because He, being God, loved righteousness and hated iniquity. This is important to point out because of His holiness, which is one of His divine attributes. Jesus identifies with these divine attributes and has been anointed with the Spirit to set at liberty those who have been incarcerated by sin. This idea is referenced by the mission statement of Christ—found initially in Isaiah 61:1-2, and read by Jesus in Luke 4:18-19—which emphasizes His duty to set at liberty those who were bound. This also authenticates the word of the prophets and fulfillment in Christ.

Christ is superior because He is the only hope for humanity. God has given humankind the opportunity to see Him in fleshly form to give us hope. Matthew 11:28-30 gives humankind an open invitation to experience the rest of God. Acts 4:12 states: "Neither is there salvation in any other: for there is none other name under heaven given among men, whereby we must be saved." There is no one else like Jesus; He is the best that God has, and Jesus gave His best to everyone.

## III. Concluding Reflections

Learning about God and acquiring intimate knowledge of Him should be the goal of every believer. Learning about God begins with understanding how God communicates with us. God speaks through His Son Jesus Christ, the Word that became flesh who is active and present in the lives of every born-again believer.

Living in a world of great religious diversity, it is imperative that Christian believers know the superiority of Jesus to other faith claims. There are modern Christians who erroneously believe that Jesus is but one viable faith option. Thus, they embrace thoughts, beliefs, and practices from other streams of thought and philosophy. While Christians need not be imperialistic about our precious faith or hateful in our expression of it, we need to know why Christ is the answer to our problems. This is of particular significance in the African American community. As the Islamic faith proselytizes actively in our neighborhoods, we need to know that what we have is right and good. More than ever, our people must understand that, "Can't nobody do me like Jesus!" Nature and good people may point the way to God. However, those who truly want to see God must look to Jesus, because He is the *imagio dei*, the express image of God.

## WORD POWER

**Incarnation**—this word is not in the Bible; however, the inference is derived from passages in Scripture, such as Roman 8:3; Ephesians 2:15; and Colossians 1:22. "Incarnation" is a theological word, referring to the coming of God into the world as a human being in the person of Jesus.

## HOME DAILY BIBLE READINGS

for the week of December 10, 2006
*What God Says About Jesus*
Dec. 4, Monday
   —Matthew 12:15-21
   —Jesus, the Promised One
Dec. 5, Tuesday
   —Luke 1:26-33
   —You Will Name Him Jesus
Dec. 6, Wednesday
   —Luke 1:34-38
   —Jesus, Son of God
Dec. 7, Thursday
   —Luke 1:46-55
   —Mary Sings Her Joy
Dec. 8, Friday
   —Matthew 17:1-5
   —Listen to Him!
Dec. 9, Saturday
   —Hebrews 1:1-9
   —God's Anointed Son
Dec. 10, Sunday
   —Hebrews 1:10-14
   —More than the Angels

## PRAYER

*Father, we thank You for Your Word, which helps us learn more about You and thus grow closer to You. As we continue to grow, may we never lose sight of what You did in sending Your Son to die for our sins. Your love is evident, and we give You the praise for all You have done. In Jesus' name, we pray. Amen.*

**Lesson 3**

# Light that Conquers

**December 17, 2006**

**ADULT TOPIC:** Walking in the Light
**YOUTH TOPIC:** Jesus: The Light of the World
**CHILDREN'S TOPIC:** Good News for Joseph and Mary

**UNIT I**
Christ, the Image of God

**CHILDREN'S UNIT**
Good News for Everyone

**DEVOTIONAL READING:** Ephesians 5:8-14
**BACKGROUND SCRIPTURE:** 1 John 1:1–2:6
**PRINT PASSAGE:** 1 John 1:1–2:5

### 1 John 1:1–2:5—KJV

THAT WHICH was from the beginning, which we have heard, which we have seen with our eyes, which we have looked upon, and our hands have handled, of the Word of life;

2 (For the life was manifested, and we have seen it, and bear witness, and shew unto you that eternal life, which was with the Father, and was manifested unto us;)

3 That which we have seen and heard declare we unto you, that ye also may have fellowship with us: and truly our fellowship is with the Father, and with his Son Jesus Christ.

4 And these things write we unto you, that your joy may be full.

5 This then is the message which we have heard of him, and declare unto you, that God is light, and in him is no darkness at all.

6 If we say that we have fellowship with him, and walk in darkness, we lie, and do not the truth:

7 But if we walk in the light, as he is in the light, we have fellowship one with another, and the blood of Jesus Christ his Son cleanseth us from all sin.

8 If we say that we have no sin, we deceive ourselves, and the truth is not in us.

9 If we confess our sins, he is faithful and just to forgive us our sins, and to cleanse us from all unrighteousness.

10 If we say that we have not sinned, we make him a liar, and his word is not in us.

## KEY VERSE

This then is the message which we have heard of him, and declare unto you, that God is light, and in him is no darkness at all.—1 John 1:5

## OBJECTIVES

**Upon completion of this lesson, the students will know that:**

1. In the Bible, the image of light is used to symbolize all that is right and good, while darkness symbolizes all that is wrong and evil;

2. Confession of sin results in forgiveness, while denial of our sin continues our disharmony with God; and,

3. Our obedience to God will increase our spiritual maturity.

MY LITTLE children, these things write I unto you, that ye sin not. And if any man sin, we have an advocate with the Father, Jesus Christ the righteous:

2 And he is the propitiation for our sins: and not for ours only, but also for the sins of the whole world.

3 And hereby we do know that we know him, if we keep his commandments.

4 He that saith, I know him, and keepeth not his commandments, is a liar, and the truth is not in him.

5 But whoso keepeth his word, in him verily is the love of God perfected: hereby know we that we are in him.

## UNIFYING LESSON PRINCIPLE

People seek meaningful relationships that add to their self-esteem and self-worth. Where can we cultivate such relationships that are always affirming and esteem-enhancing? John tells us that in God there is found the type of relationship that not only reveals our need for a life-changing encounter with God, but also provides the benefits of a relationship that contributes to our spiritual maturity. The Matthew passage shows how Joseph's relationships with God and Mary led him to care for her and her child.

## POINTS TO BE EMPHASIZED
## ADULTS/YOUTH

**Adult Key Verse:** 1 John 1:5
**Youth Key Verse:** 1 John 1:7
**Print Passage:** 1 John 1:1–2:5
— The Word of life of whom the writer of 1 John witnesses was Jesus Christ.
— "Light" and "darkness" are common biblical metaphors for those who abide in God and those who do not, respectively.
— Confession of sin results in God's forgiveness, while denial of our sin continues our disharmony with God.
— The facts about Jesus, as expressed in the Bible, must be accepted by faith.

## CHILDREN

**Key Verse:** Matthew 1:20-21
**Print Passage:** Matthew 1:18-25; 1 John 1:5
— When our decisions affect the lives of others, we should always seek God's guidance before we take action.
— God ordains marriage and instructs parents to provide for the needs of their children.

## TOPICAL OUTLINE OF THE LESSON

I. Introduction
   A. Jesus Christ, the Life and Light
   B. Biblical Background

II. Exposition and Application of the Scripture
   A. A Witness to the Word
      *(1 John 1:1-2)*
   B. Links in the Chain of Fellowship
      *(1 John 1:3-4)*
   C. Conditions of Fellowship
      *(1 John 1:5-10)*
   D. Evidence of Fellowship
      *(1 John 2:1-5)*

III. Concluding Reflections

# I. INTRODUCTION
## A. Jesus Christ, the Life and Light

There are several metaphors used in the Bible to express the life of the believer—*running, wrestling, fighting,* and *standing* are among them. The metaphors for this lesson are *walking, light,* and *darkness.* As a biblical metaphor, "walking" addresses the conduct and the behavior of the believer. One is either walking closer to God or farther away from Him. Another metaphor used in this context is *light.* This metaphor is used to describe Christ, the church, and the believers in Christ. In the Bible, the word *light* implies "understanding, wisdom, and enlightenment." The last metaphor mentioned in this text is *darkness,* the opposite of light. Darkness represents that which is void of wisdom, understanding, and enlightenment. Those who are not walking in the light are walking in darkness, separated from God.

The descriptions of the metaphors in 1 John 1 are referenced by Jesus Christ—who declares Himself to be the Light—and John, who witnesses to that Light. Christ is both life and light, and those who receive Christ are alive because of Him and have light because He shines within them.

Three distinctive threads are found in 1 John—life, light and love. All three ideas epitomize who Jesus Christ is. John the apostle contends that if there is no Living Word there is no life, and if there is no life, there is no light—and if neither light nor life exist, then there is no love!

## B. Biblical Background

It is generally accepted that the same person who wrote this epistle was the author of the gospel bearing the same name. In reading 1 John it is all but impossible not be reminded constantly of the gospel of John.

Little is known of the time and place of the writing of 1 John, and there is much conjecture on the subject. Some contemporary critics have supposed that 1 John was originally a part of the gospel of John and in some way became detached; others assert that 1 John was sent *as an epistle* at the same time with the gospel and to the same persons. Some scholars speculate that 1 John was written before the destruction of Jerusalem (A.D. 70); some think it was written long after, when John was an old man.

Despite what is not known, it is clear that the apostle John wrote this book with the intended purpose of giving his readers a clear visualization of life in fellowship with God and Christ, but also with the eyewitnesses and other believers. In this epistle, John emphasizes having fellowship, the importance of knowing Christ, and realizing love as the staple characteristics of the believer. John writes this book for the church at-large, so that all who would believe will see the light and walk therein.

# II. EXPOSITION AND APPLICATION OF THE SCRIPTURE
## A. A Witness to the Word *(1 John 1:1-2)*

**That which was from the beginning,**

**which we have heard, which we have seen with our eyes, which we have looked upon, and our hands have handled, of the Word of life; (For the life was manifested, and we have seen it, and bear witness, and show unto you that eternal life, which was with the Father, and was manifested unto us.)**

As the first epistle of John begins, the author establishes that what he is about to share is not only revealed knowledge, but also experiential testimony. He uses three key phrases to ground his testimony: *we have heard…we have seen with our own eyes…and our hands have handled the Word of life*. It is important to note that John had firsthand knowledge of Jesus, for he was the beloved disciple of the Lord. He had heard the teachings of Christ with his own ears. He had listened while persons marveled at the Master Teacher. He had heard the gracious wisdom from the Sage who pre-dated Abraham and Aristotle. He had taken note of the failed counter-arguments levied by His detractors.

John did not have to overhear the old story, for he heard it fresh. He had seen the gospel lived out in the experience of One who was hailed as a hero one day and branded as a criminal just a few days later. He saw the Gospel being lived out by One who counseled others to turn the other cheek and then gave His own life for the ungrateful. John saw the empty tomb, that powerful and wondrous symbol of an all-powerful Christ. More importantly, he had seen and touched a risen, living Lord.

This firsthand testimony was essential to the early church, for it established Christianity as a historical faith. The basis of the claim of the church could be traced to the eyewitness accounts of persons who knew Jesus intimately. Jesus was not only tied to events and places, but also to people who would not recant their stories, even in the face of their own demise. Although John did not die as a martyr like other disciples, he did endure persecution because of his discipleship. Despite these trials, he continued to identify himself as a primary witness of Jesus. Belief in eternal fellowship with the Father and His Son was the bedrock of his unshakeable testimony of faith. No heresy could stand against an irrefutable observer.

The parentheses in verse 2, as shown in the KJV, signal that what was stated in verse 1 is made clearer here. Jesus is God, and John firmly stands on his eyewitness account of that fact. God manifested Himself in human flesh, through Jesus Christ, and was justified by the Spirit. The true characteristics of this incarnate God could be attested to by those who had seen Him, and who had remained with Him. John could and did give personal testimony to the fact that the Word of God had appeared in human form. This was done in order to make possible eternal life to all humanity, through the redemption of His blood.

### B. Links in the Chain of Fellowship
*(1 John 1:3-4)*

**That which we have seen and heard declare we unto you, that ye also may have fellowship with us: and truly our fellowship**

is with the Father, and with his Son Jesus Christ. And these things write we unto you, that your joy may be full.**

The Word not only gives life, light, and love, but also provides fellowship. This fellowship is like a chain with both horizontal and vertical links. Believers are connected to the apostles as fellow believers, and to the Father and Son for the fullness of their joy in the faith.

The horizontal link connects the present-day believer to the apostles. The apostles, who were eyewitnesses, proclaimed and wrote about what they had seen and heard. Because of their eyewitness experience, all who believed their witness would be linked to the fellowship. This horizontal link is inclusive of all those who believe the testimony of the apostles. The vertical link connects the believer to the Father and the Son through faith. However, the Bible affirms that one cannot have true fellowship with the Father and the Son apart from true fellowship with fellow believers.

The horizontal and vertical links to fellowship result in fullness of joy (verse 4). When the believer is in fellowship with others who have received Christ, and in fellowship with the Father and Son, then the result is fullness (i.e., completeness), which gives a spiritual satisfaction that words cannot describe.

## C. Conditions of Fellowship
*(1 John 1:5-10)*

**This then is the message which we have heard of him, and declare unto you, that God is light, and in him is no darkness at all. If we say that we have fellowship with him, and walk in darkness, we lie, and do not the truth: But if we walk in the light, as he is in the light, we have fellowship one with another, and the blood of Jesus Christ his Son cleanseth us from all sin. If we say that we have no sin, we deceive ourselves, and the truth is not in us. If we confess our sins, he is faithful and just to forgive us our sins, and to cleanse us from all unrighteousness. If we say that we have not sinned, we make him a liar, and his word is not in us.**

John declares that God is light! Light represents understanding, wisdom and enlightenment. The message is part of the light, but one has to understand the message. How does one see what John is saying? Jesus asked Martha, "Did I not tell you that if you believed, you would see the glory of God?" (John 11:40, NRSV).

There is an old saying, "Seeing is believing." But for those who claim to be of the household of faith, the opposite is true: "Believing is seeing." In this context, "seeing" is understanding. With spiritual sight, believers walk in the light of God's Word. If we walk in the light as He is in the light, we have fellowship with Him and with one another, and the blood of Jesus Christ His Son cleanses us from all sin (see John 1:7). The believer who walks in the light continually applies the Word to his or her life as the Lord continues to reveal His Word.

Verse 6 emphasizes that fellowship does not happen if one does not walk in the truth. Without walking in the light and truth, there is no fellowship with one another or with God. John states (verse 7) that our fellowship with others and the forgiveness of our sins is a manifestation of having fellowship with Jesus Christ.

The light illuminates sin; if one is to have fellowship with God, one must allow the light of the Word to expose personal sin. In fact, if we do not admit that we have sinned, Scripture says that we deceive ourselves, and the truth is not in us. Those who do not confess their sins are walking in darkness; therefore, they have no fellowship with God. But there is good news! John gives all believers a means of egress, or a way out of darkness (verse 9). God extends His faithfulness to those who seek to walk in the light, and is fair to all who will confess their transgressions to Him; the result is forgiveness and cleansing of all sins and unrighteousness.

### D. Evidence of Fellowship
*(1 John 2:1-5)*

**My little children, these things write I unto you, that ye sin not. And if any man sin, we have an advocate with the Father, Jesus Christ the righteous: And he is the propitiation for our sins: and not for ours only, but also for the sins of the whole world. And hereby we do know that we know him, if we keep his commandments. He that saith, I know him, and keepeth not his commandments, is a liar, and the truth is not in him. But whoso keepeth his word, in him verily is the love of God perfected: hereby know we that we are in him.**

When a person is charged with a crime, the plaintiff needs someone to plead his or her case. The accused seeks a lawyer who has expertise in the area of jurisprudence. In the same manner, believers have the privilege of expert representation for their sins. When believers sin, they have spiritual representation with the Father in Jesus Christ, the righteous one. This is evidence of fellowship with God and gives believers help in times of trouble. In explaining this, the writer asserts that Jesus is the *propitiation for our sins* (1 John 2:2). The Greek noun for "propitiation" is *hilasmos*, meaning appeasing or expiating. In Jewish culture, a propitiation used the cover of the ark of the covenant in the Holy of Holies. This was sprinkled with the blood of the expiatory victim on the annual Day of Atonement—hence, the lid of expiation or the propitiatory. Jesus Himself was that blood victim, offered on behalf of a sinful humanity so that humanity could have eternal life.

Another key component giving evidence of fellowship is that no one can experience fellowship alone. When believers keep God's commandments, the love of God is perfected or matures in them (see 1 John 2:5). According to John 13:34, Jesus gave the believers a new commandment: love one another as Christ loved them. Simply put, the love demonstrated among believers proves that there is fellowship between those believers and God.

### III. Concluding Reflections

The interplay between light and darkness in the book of 1 John is fascinating. As Christians we are admonished to stay away from the shadows of darkness. As persons of the modern age, we can easily be confronted by the glaring light of media exposure. The scandals of the modern age abound—not simply because people are living more wickedly, but because the technology of a tell-all world often leaves people without the comfort of shadows for sin. Private darkness becomes public embarrassment.

Certainly, for reasons far beyond these, it is preferable to walk in light rather than darkness. But God is not like the unforgiving and unrelenting public. His light is to cleanse and purge, yet He stands ready to forgive and reconcile. Fellowship results in the love of God made perfect within the believer. This fellowship breeds forgiveness and reconciliation among God's people.

The Advent season is a time to reflect and rejoice because the invitation to walk in the light will be open to all. Everyone will have fellowship with the One who is soon to come! This love enriches the fellowship and increases the bonds of peace between believers. "Hark the herald angels sing, Jesus, the light of the world!" He is the ever-shining light in the lives of believers.

## WORD POWER

**Life (Greek: *Zoe*)**—it is a life of vitality free from pain, anxiety, sickness and oppression. This is the life that Christ offers to those who come to Him—a life that is devoted to God. This would be a life blessed both in this world, and eternally.

**Life (Greek: *Bios*)**—a word used to denote life. It is used to refer to animals or to reflect a limited life.

## HOME DAILY BIBLE READINGS

for the week of December 17, 2006
*Light that Conquers*

Dec. 11, Monday
—Matthew 1:18-25
—An Angel Speaks to Joseph

Dec. 12, Tuesday
—2 Peter 1:16-21
—Eyewitnesses of God's Majesty

Dec. 13, Wednesday
—2 Corinthians 4:1-6
—We Preach Jesus Christ

Dec. 14, Thursday
—Ephesians 5:8-14
—Live as Children of Light

Dec. 15, Friday
—1 John 1:1-4
—Jesus Is the Word of Life

Dec. 16, Saturday
—1 John 1:5-10
—Walk in the Light

Dec. 17, Sunday
—1 John 2:1-6
—Following Jesus

## PRAYER

*Our Father, we ask that You will help us walk in the light. We have a need to walk closer with You, and we want to experience life through You. We ask that You will perfect Your love in us through the relationship that we have with our brothers and sisters. In Jesus' name, we pray. Amen.*

**December 24, 2006**
*(Christmas Eve)*

## Lesson 4

### UNIT I
Christ, the Image of God

### CHILDREN'S UNIT
Good News for Everyone

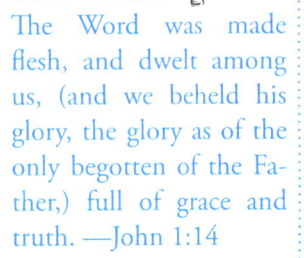

# The Word Became Flesh

**ADULT TOPIC:** Receiving the Word
**YOUTH TOPIC:** Jesus: God with Us
**CHILDREN'S TOPIC:** Good News for the Shepherds

### KEY VERSE
The Word was made flesh, and dwelt among us, (and we beheld his glory, the glory as of the only begotten of the Father,) full of grace and truth. —John 1:14

**DEVOTIONAL READING:** Isaiah 53:1-6
**BACKGROUND SCRIPTURE:** John 1:1-34
**PRINT PASSAGE:** John 1:1-18

### John 1:1-18—KJV

IN THE beginning was the Word, and the Word was with God, and the Word was God.

2 The same was in the beginning with God.

3 All things were made by him; and without him was not any thing made that was made.

4 In him was life; and the life was the light of men.

5 And the light shineth in darkness; and the darkness comprehended it not.

6 There was a man sent from God, whose name was John.

7 The same came for a witness, to bear witness of the Light, that all men through him might believe.

8 He was not that Light, but was sent to bear witness of that Light.

9 That was the true Light, which lighteth every man that cometh into the world.

10 He was in the world, and the world was made by him, and the world knew him not.

11 He came unto his own, and his own received him not.

12 But as many as received him, to them gave he power to become the sons of God, even to them that believe on his name:

13 Which were born, not of blood, nor of the will of the flesh, nor of the will of man, but of God.

### OBJECTIVES
Upon completion of this lesson, the students will know that:

1. God entered into the human experience in order to bring humanity back into relationship with Him;
2. Jesus Christ is the Word by which God created everything and through whom God gives everyone life; and,
3. Jesus Christ is the connection between perfect divinity and sinful humanity.

14 And the Word was made flesh, and dwelt among us, (and we beheld his glory, the glory as of the only begotten of the Father,) full of grace and truth.

15 John bare witness of him, and cried, saying, This was he of whom I spake, He that cometh after me is preferred before me: for he was before me.

16 And of his fulness have all we received, and grace for grace.

17 For the law was given by Moses, but grace and truth came by Jesus Christ.

18 No man hath seen God at any time; the only begotten Son, which is in the bosom of the Father, he hath declared him.

## UNIFYING LESSON PRINCIPLE

People need to feel that God is with them. What does it mean for God to enter our world? John suggests that in Jesus Christ, God entered into human experience as a human in order to bring humanity back into relationship with divinity. The Luke passage gives the details of Jesus' birth (children's lesson).

## POINTS TO BE EMPHASIZED ADULTS/YOUTH

**Adult/Youth Key Verse:** John 1:14
**Print Passage:** John 1:1-18
—The Word is the supreme revelation of God.

—God became flesh so that human beings might know Him.

—To affirm that Jesus is the life, light, and salvation of the world is a negation of all religions except Christianity.

—In Genesis 1:1, God brings physical light. In John 1:1, Christ brings spiritual light.

## CHILDREN

**Key Verse:** Luke 2:11
**Print Passage:** Luke 2:1-20; John 1:1, 4
—God has unusual ways of communicating His Word and His works.
—The greatest event in history, the birth of God's Son, occurred in humble surroundings.
—God calls people from all walks of life, including those who are disenfranchised.

## TOPICAL OUTLINE OF THE LESSON

I. INTRODUCTION
   A. Receiving the Word
   B. Biblical Background

II. EXPOSITION AND APPLICATION OF THE SCRIPTURE
   A. The Pre/Co-Existence of the Word *(John 1:1-5)*
   B. The Deity of the Word in Flesh *(John 1:6-14)*
   C. The Fullness of the Word *(John 1:15-18)*

III. CONCLUDING REFLECTIONS

## I. INTRODUCTION
### A. Receiving the Word

Words are used to communicate thoughts or ideas. As the communicator structures the words, he or she conveys the thoughts to be communicated. But unless the words can be understood by the hearers, the message is lost. In this passage of Scripture, God is the Communicator and Jesus is the Word, the means of communication. He is the means God used to transmit a divine message to an unholy people.

What does it mean to receive the Word? Receiving the Word means that one opens his or her mind to comprehend or understand the message of God—that one accepts Jesus Christ as the message of God.

John's introduction directs the reader to the divinity of Jesus, the Christ. His focus has led many scholars to believe that John's was the last gospel written of the four.

John is intent on providing the reader with his view of the deity of Christ. John wrote a prologue in which God, the Great Communicator, introduces the reader to the beginning, with emphasis on the Word, which is Jesus Christ. John's gospel also provides an epilogue that offers the believer hope in the pending return of Christ. Therefore, in celebrating His coming, believers can also rejoice in the knowledge of His victorious return.

### B. Biblical Background

This Gospel places emphasis on the deity of Christ, the witness of John the Baptist, and it shines light on the sacrifice of Christ on the cross and His resurrection. In all of this, God is communicating, through John the apostle, the love that He has for the world; He communicates His love for the world through the Word, Jesus Christ, and His hope is that the world would receive the Word as the answer.

To give emphasis to his message, John uses his gospel to highlight segments of our Savior's life that most clearly display His divine power and authority. This includes Jesus' own words regarding His nature and the power of His death as atonement for the sins of the world. By giving cursory treatment to the events recorded by the other evangelists, John gave testimony that their narratives were and are true and sure. John devoted his attention to the particulars omitted in the other gospels, many of which are exceedingly important.

John concentrates on the ministry of the Word. He understands that the Word is the hope of the world, and the Word gives life to the world. In fact, the portrait that John paints is intended to show Christ as the express image of God, as in Hebrews 1:3. Nothing else would or will do to save the world.

## II. Exposition and Application of the Scripture

### A. The Pre/Co-Existence of the Word (John 1:1-5)

**In the beginning was the Word, and the Word was with God, and the Word was God. The same was in the beginning with God. All things were made by him; and without him was not any thing made that was made. In him was life; and the life was the light of men. And the light shineth in darkness; and the darkness comprehended it not.**

John's opening statement is what Paul calls the mystery of godliness (1 Timothy 3:16). In the opening verse of the gospel of John, God reveals the identity of the Word.

He declares that the Word, Jesus Christ, existed from the very beginning. In other words, God validates Himself and at the same time validates the Word (1 John 5:7). He reveals the Word as having existed from the very beginning. Genesis 1:1 begins in a similar fashion; it states, "In the beginning God created. . . ." God and the Word were in the beginning. Scripture states: "...without him was not any thing made that was made" (John 1:3).

In the opening of both Genesis and John, there is no distinction given to God and the Word as Creator; His pre-existence is important to the world because His pre-existence is an extension of His deity. Nothing was before Him, and nothing will be after Him!

What is the significance of the co-existence of God and the Word? The co-existence of God and the Word reveals the unity between the Father and the Son. To state this in a more precise way, the Word's co-existence with the Father actually gives a glimpse into the Trinity. The Word was in the beginning, and the Word was God; moreover, the Word was with God. The word "with" is crucial to John's purpose. "With" puts the Word and God face to face with one another! The three components of the Trinity make up the Godhead. Each is distinct, but vital to the work and persona of the Godhead.

Not only do God and the Word co-exist, but together they bring light to a dark world. We learned in last week's lesson that light signifies understanding, wisdom and enlightenment. What this world did not have was light! It was not the physical light of the sun, but the spiritual light of understanding, wisdom, and enlightenment that was lacking. The Word would bring enlightenment and understanding to the world.

However, the world was unable to understand what God was doing in regard to reestablishing His relationship with humanity. Only through the Word could this be done. Through the collaborative effort of God and the Word, God sent His only Son. The world needed Jesus, the light of the world! The Word did not come to condemn the world, but rather so that the world would be saved. The fulfillment of the Law was manifested through the Word.

God and the Word gave the world hope, and it is through their co-existence that this hope was made manifest. In verse 4, John states that in the Word is life and the life is the light of humankind! This hope of life can only be found in the Word, and without the Word there is no hope for the world.

### B. The Deity of the Word in Flesh
*(John 1:6-14)*

**There was a man sent from God, whose name was John. The same came for a witness, to bear witness of the Light, that all men through him might believe. He was not that Light, but was sent to bear witness of that Light. That was the true Light, which lighteth every man that cometh into the world. He was in the world, and the world**

**was made by him, and the world knew him not. He came unto his own, and his own received him not. But as many as received him, to them gave he power to become the sons of God, even to them that believe on his name: Which were born, not of blood, nor of the will of the flesh, nor of the will of man, but of God. And the Word was made flesh, and dwelt among us, (and we beheld his glory, the glory as of the only begotten of the Father,) full of grace and truth.**

The prologue of the gospel of John provides a perfect introduction to the book. After the opening section, the writer provides an earthly prologue to the ministry of Jesus—the witness of John the Baptist. John the Baptist loudly proclaimed that he was not that promised Light, but rather that he came to bear witness to that Light. John came to prepare the way for the coming of Christ through his preaching. John preached repentance and regarded himself as only a voice crying in the wilderness.

Humankind's perception of God was and is limited. There was no divine perception due to human understanding; and human understanding was and is limited without divine perception. The refusal to receive Jesus was their rejection of Him, and their rejection of Him was the evidence of their closed minds. This numbed their understanding of the Light of the World and gave opportunity to those that were not Christ's own to receive Him (i.e., Gentiles). A mind closed to the deity of Christ kept the Jews in darkness.

The phrase, "cometh into the world," employed by John in verse 9, was a common rabbinical saying to express every human being. Christ's coming benefitted and benefits every person ever born. And, just as we are exposed to the light of the world upon being born out of the womb of darkness, our spiritual rebirth in Jesus Christ allows the heavenly light to peer into the human soul. We do not have this light ourselves, but Christ mercifully gives it to us. The Law had given much light in itself, but it shone only upon the Jews, and even then only as much as they would receive it. The superior light of the Gospel is to be scattered over the face of the whole earth.

Verse 14 deals with the Word taking on human form. The One who was present from the beginning of time, the One who was with God and who was God, became flesh. The theological term for the Word that was made flesh and dwelt among us is "incarnation." As John writes, he discloses the revelation of the Word that was unveiled to humankind in Christ, as the only begotten of the Father. John was among the disciples privileged to witness Christ's glory at the Transfiguration—a glory that no mere human being could manifest. While God dwelled in the tabernacle among the Jews, the priests saw His glory. While Jesus dwelled on earth among humankind, His glory was manifested in His profound words and His miraculous acts. Through John's own experience, he could testify, unequivocally, that there was no one there like Christ—there was none before, and there will be none after Him. He is full of grace and truth.

## C. The Fullness of the Word
*(John 1:15-18)*

**John bare witness of him, and cried, saying, This was he of whom I spake, He that cometh after me is preferred before me: for he was before me. And of his fulness have all we received, and grace for grace. For the law was given by Moses, but grace and truth came by Jesus Christ. No man hath seen God at any time; the only begotten Son, which is in the bosom of the Father, he hath declared him.**

As John nears the conclusion of the first chapter, he leaves the reader to recognize the eternal existence of the Word. When the recipient of the Word receives Him, he or she receives the fullness of grace (unmerited favor) from God and is allotted grace from the Son of God, the Word (verse 16). This is not just for the moment; this is eternal and speaks of the eternal existence of the Word! The Word, or God, is infinite; the Word was in the beginning when God spoke.

John the Baptist had preached about Jesus before Jesus appeared, but John the apostle could give a personal account regarding the One about whom the Baptist had preached. His coming brought an outpouring of grace, which continues with more grace added fresh daily to the grace already bestowed (verse 16). This inestimable favor stands in direct contrast to the Law, which had served its purpose for its time. The Law of Moses elicited a consciousness among God's people regarding their sin and need of redemption. Moses had given the Law to God's chosen; Christ gives grace and opens the way for all who believe to be heirs of the kingdom. Understanding the superiority of grace moved the apostle Paul to refer to the Law and the prophets as "shadow," and the Gospel as "substance" (Colossians 2:17).

Moses and others heard his voice, and saw the cloud and the fire, but these were only the symbols of God's presence. Only Christ has seen God. Jesus had knowledge of God that no human being could claim or comprehend—not Abraham, Isaac, Jacob, Moses, or any of the ancient prophets. Therefore, by His Word and Spirit, only Christ can lead us to the true knowledge of God. True and full knowledge of God comes only through his Son.

## III. Concluding Reflections

One of the dilemmas of the modern age is how to communicate in language that is politically correct. One of the most telling examples of the difficulty of this circumstance is during the Christmas season. In recent years, there has been so much emphasis on not offending others that Christmas, for some, has been reduced to just another celebration.

Christians should celebrate and remember that the Word became flesh in the coming of Jesus Christ was not only an awesome gift, but one that should be celebrated with the full joy that any believer can muster. No matter what the rest of the world does to celebrate the season, or for whatever reason they do so, Christmas is more than a time of warm feeling, generous giving, and fellowship. Had God not come to us, there would be no Christmas. Such a statement may not be considered politically correct, but it is doctrinally accurate.

Christians celebrate the fact that the True Light has come into the world! No longer are we forced to live in spiritual darkness. Jesus, the light of the world, is still the reason for the season!

## WORD POWER

**Word (Greek: *logos*, transliterated)**— This means the personal Word. It is God's distinct and super-infinite personality. The Logos is completely God in all essence. In the gospel of John, Logos denotes the essential Word of God, Jesus Christ. He is personal wisdom and power in union with God, and his minister in creation and government of the universe. For the cause of all the world's life both physical and ethical, He put on human nature in the person of Jesus the Messiah for the salvation of humanity. Logos is the second person in the Godhead, and shines forth conspicuously from His words and deeds.[1]

**Spoken Word (Greek: *Rhema*, transliterated)** — that which is or has been uttered by the living voice, thing spoken, a word or any sound produced by the voice and having definite meaning; what is uttered in speech or writing.

---

[1] Thayer and Smith. "Greek Lexicon entry for Logos". "The New Testament Greek Lexicon."

## HOME DAILY BIBLE READINGS

for the week of December 24, 2006
*The Word Became Flesh*

Dec. 18, Monday
—Luke 2:1-7
—Jesus Is Born
Dec. 19, Tuesday
—Luke 2:8-20
—Angels and Shepherds Celebrate
Dec. 20, Wednesday
—Romans 1:1-5
—Called to Belong to Jesus Christ
Dec. 21, Thursday
—Ephesians 1:3-10
—God's Plan for Us
Dec. 22, Friday
—John 1:1-9
—The Word Sent by God
Dec. 23, Saturday
—John 1:10-18
—The Word Became Flesh
Dec. 24, Sunday
—Isaiah 42:5-9
—New Things I Now Declare

## PRAYER

*God, the Creator of all, help us to receive Your Word as the answer to the world. We want to thank You for Your Word, who became flesh, and dwelt among us. We also thank You for the testimony of the apostles, who endured persecution so that we could hear the Good News of the Cross and Christ. We love You, Lord, and we receive Your Son. We pray this in the name of Jesus. Amen.*

Lesson 5

# Humiliation and Exaltation

**December 31, 2006**

**ADULT TOPIC:** Keeping the Balance
**YOUTH TOPIC:** Imitating Christ
**CHILDREN'S TOPIC:** Good News for the Wise Men

**UNIT I**
Christ, the Image of God

**CHILDREN'S UNIT**
Good News for Everyone

**DEVOTIONAL READING:** 1 Peter 3:8-12
**BACKGROUND SCRIPTURE:** Philippians 2:1-11
**PRINT PASSAGE:** Philippians 2:1-11

## Philippians 2:1-11—KJV

IF THERE be therefore any consolation in Christ, if any comfort of love, if any fellowship of the Spirit, if any bowels and mercies,

2 Fulfil ye my joy, that ye be likeminded, having the same love, being of one accord, of one mind.

3 Let nothing be done through strife or vainglory; but in lowliness of mind let each esteem other better than themselves.

4 Look not every man on his own things, but every man also on the things of others.

5 Let this mind be in you, which was also in Christ Jesus:

6 Who, being in the form of God, thought it not robbery to be equal with God:

7 But made himself of no reputation, and took upon him the form of a servant, and was made in the likeness of men:

8 And being found in fashion as a man, he humbled himself, and became obedient unto death, even the death of the cross.

9 Wherefore God also hath highly exalted him, and given him a name which is above every name:

10 That at the name of Jesus every knee should bow, of things in heaven, and things in earth, and things under the earth;

11 And that every tongue should confess that Jesus Christ is Lord, to the glory of God the Father.

## KEY VERSE

Let nothing be done through strife or vainglory; but in lowliness of mind let each esteem other better than themselves.
—Philippians 2:3

## OBJECTIVES

**Upon completion of this lesson, the students will know that:**

1. Having the mind of Christ helps His followers in reaching balance between humility and exaltation;
2. Having the mind of Christ enables believers to find unity in the body of Christ (the church); and,
3. Our relationship in Christ should motivate believers to place the needs of others above our own.

## UNIFYING LESSON PRINCIPLE

Some people avoid humility as a sign of weakness, while others embrace it to the point that they become proud of their humility! Is it possible to balance a sense of humility with an appropriate level of self-esteem? Pointing out that Jesus Christ achieved the perfect balance between humility and exaltation, Paul urges Christians to take on the mind of Christ. Matthew's account of the wise men presents a vivid illustration of powerful people humbly worshiping the Christ child.

## POINTS TO BE EMPHASIZED ADULTS/YOUTH

**Adult Key Verse:** Philippians 2:3
**Youth Key Verse:** Philippians 2:5
**Print Passage:** Philippians 2:1-11

—Paul told the Philippians that his joy would be complete when they were of one mind.
—Paul quoted an early hymn to say that Jesus gave up His power in heaven to live as a servant to others; thus, He was highly exalted.
—Having the mind of Christ allows for unity amid diversity.
—Christ is our model for a healthy concept of humility.

## CHILDREN

**Key Verse:** Matthew 2:11
**Print Passage:** Matthew 2:1-11; Philippians 2:5-7, 9-11

—We worship God when we willingly give God what is valuable to us.
—God is almighty and worthy of the best that we have to give.
—We exhibit humility as we trust and obey God.
—God rewards humility.

## TOPICAL OUTLINE OF THE LESSON

I. **INTRODUCTION**
   A. Keeping Your Head Straight
   B. Biblical Background

II. **EXPOSITION AND APPLICATION OF THE SCRIPTURE**
   A. The Spirit of Fellowship and Humility *(Philippians 2:1-4)*
   B. Christ: The Embodiment of Fellowship and Humility *(Philippians 2:5-8)*
   C. The Result of Fellowship and Humility *(Philippians 2:9-11)*

III. **CONCLUDING REFLECTIONS**

## I. INTRODUCTION

### A. Keeping Your Head Straight

Have you ever heard the adage, "Keep your head on straight"? In essence, it is saying that one should not look at things as they seem to be, but rather to be rooted and grounded in what is true and right. In Philippians 2, the apostle Paul is encouraging believers to keep their heads on straight for the sake of Christian fellowship. In order to experience fellowship, there must be more than one person involved. With collective involvement, there will be more than one thought, more than one point of view; however, there also may be attitudes that conflict with one another. Therefore, if believers are to emulate their role model, which is Christ, they must follow His example of humility and fellowship, and have a sense of oneness of purpose, though they may not always agree.

What is the end result of "keeping your head on straight" or keeping balance? Keeping things in proper faith perspective means that Jesus Christ is exalted, and God is glorified. This mindset does not come naturally, but is the work of the Holy Spirit in one's life. Without the work of the Holy Spirit in our lives there is imbalance, and when there is imbalance there is danger of falling away from the fold.

### B. Biblical Background

Paul wrote the epistle to the Philippians while he was a prisoner in Rome. The exact date cannot be ascertained, but general consensus among scholars is that it was written around A.D. 62. The basic thrusts of the epistle are twofold: (1) It demonstrates the adequacy of Jesus Christ for all experiences of life. (2) It is an epistle of appreciation to the church of Philippi for their encouragement and their financial assistance to Paul during his confinement.

The book of Philippians is also a book of warning. Paul cautions the church against Judaizers who were seeking to discredit Christ and devalue the priceless gift of grace that is extended to all who would receive Christ Jesus. Paul was full of pride and love for the church of Philippi. He had started the Philippian church while on his second missionary journey. They had a teachable spirit and were committed to obeying what they were taught. This church was seeking to follow the example of Christ as described in Paul's teaching.

Paul encouraged them by example to be content no matter what their circumstance. Paul's perspective was that his trials were only temporary, and no matter what, he knew how to praise the Lord in all things. Paul then made a powerful statement of confidence in the faith: "I can do all things through Christ which strengtheneth me" (Philippians 4:13). Paul was emphasizing to the church of Philippi that all things are accomplished through Christ Jesus.

Philippians is filled with joyful statements that encourage believers to be steadfast in their fellowship with each other and with the Lord. In this epistle, Paul helps contemporary Christians to know that Christ gives joy and triumph in various circumstances of life.

## II. Exposition and Application of the Scripture

### A. The Spirit of Fellowship and Humility *(Philippians 2:1-4)*

**If there be therefore any consolation in Christ, if any comfort of love, if any fellowship of the Spirit, if any bowels and mercies, Fulfil ye my joy, that ye be likeminded, having the same love, being of one accord, of one mind. Let nothing be done through strife or vainglory; but in lowliness of mind let each esteem other better than themselves.**

**Look not every man on his own things, but every man also on the things of others.**

Paul had an agenda in writing this chapter to the church at Philippi. His agenda was to encourage the believers there to find comfort in belonging to Christ and the love that Christ displays for all. Therefore, Paul advised them that if they wanted to please him, they must learn to be Christ-like—agreeable, loving and unified in purpose. That is to say that fellowship with one another is crucial to imitating Christ. This fellowship leads to oneness that sets believers apart for a common purpose.

The spirit of fellowship is the ability to work together through conflict and trial to accomplish a mission. When people work together in fellowship, having the same mind, the same love, and being of one accord, the spirit of fellowship abides. Evidence of this spirit of fellowship can be observed in Acts 2, when the church came together on one accord in the Upper Room. Paul merely emphasized the fellowship of believers in hope that they would be encouraged to be like Christ.

Where there is fellowship, there has to be humility. The spirit of fellowship cannot exist if there is no humility. The spirit of fellowship has to be agreeable. If one is unwilling to be humble, conflict is inevitable. Humility does not insist on its own way; but rather, it is willing to compromise for the good of all involved. The impetus of humility is love. Paul wanted to impress upon the church of Philippi that everything should be done in humility, not for personal glory or in an attempting to trespass on the things of others.

By emphasizing cooperation and humility, Paul set the stage for the understanding that no member of the body of Christ is at liberty to live for self or disregard the wants of others. Out of his great love for the Philippians, Paul wanted to ensure that the narrow spirit of selfishness did not intrude upon their fellowship. The spirit of humility, in cooperation with the spirit of fellowship, enabled the church to identify with Christ. Paul, then, pushed his agenda in hopes that the church of Philippi would conform to the image of Christ.

### B. Christ: The Embodiment of Fellowship and Humility
*(Philippians 2:5-8)*

**Let this mind be in you, which was also in Christ Jesus: Who, being in the form of God, thought it not robbery to be equal with God: But made himself of no reputation, and took upon him the form of a servant, and was made in the likeness of men: And being found in fashion as a man, he humbled himself, and became obedient unto death, even the death of the cross.**

If the believer is going to enjoy the spirit of fellowship and the spirit of humility, there is a need to see these attributes demonstrated. Verse 5 is a transition to show the church of Philippi that fellowship and humility are consistent with the attitude of Christ. Jesus demonstrated fellowship with His Father, but He also displayed humility when He washed the feet of His disciples (John 13:5).

Paul showed where these attributes were modeled (verse 6). Paul drew the conclusion that Jesus is God; therefore, He would not take away from God. Or as the Scripture declares, He "thought it not robbery to be equal with God" here on earth. Jesus would have been within His right to be who He was (i.e., God), but it was His love for all that made Him choose otherwise. He humbled Himself by making Himself nothing (i.e., of no reputation), and He became a servant. He used His equality with God as an opportunity to empty Himself.

Jesus demonstrated His humility by demonstrating His humility and servitude to God through His obedience—even to death on the cross. The Greeks had two words for "form," one of them referring to mere external appearance, as when a mirage takes the appearance of water. The other suggests that the appearance is the true revelation of the object itself, the form participating in the reality. It is the second word (*morphe*) which Paul here employs.[1]

Jesus emptied Himself, which means He could have shown His power, but His mission was to die (Romans 5:8). Working in obedience to the will of the Father was the only way that the salvation of humankind could be accomplished. Jesus and the Father are one; so He could not work on a separate or selfish agenda. Therefore, Jesus chose to divest His divinity in order to submit to the humility of death on the cross.

---

[1] John A. Knight, Beacon Bible Commentary, Vol. IX, Philippians (Kansas City, Missouri: Beacon Hill Press, 1965), p. 381.

Jesus had to strip Himself of His insignia of majesty to submit to death on the cross. The humility that Jesus demonstrated was for the benefit of the world.

Jesus assumed the posture of ordinary human life—subjecting Himself to His earthly parents, working as a carpenter, going to the synagogues, washing His disciple's feet. He demonstrated humility to both God and humankind. Paul makes mention of what Christ did because this was connected to the fellowship that God wanted to have with humanity. In fact, death expresses the climax of Jesus' obedience. His obedience to death was necessary for humankind to have fellowship with God. So it was through His humility that the conflict (sin) that existed between humankind and God opened the way for fellowship.

## C. The Result of Fellowship and Humility *(Philippians 2:9-11)*

**Wherefore God also hath highly exalted him, and given him a name which is above every name: That at the name of Jesus every knee should bow, of things in heaven, and things in earth, and things under the earth; And that every tongue should confess that Jesus Christ is Lord, to the glory of God the Father.**

Results are the conclusion of a planned course of action. In this case, the obedience of Christ resulted in the exaltation of His name. This was not just a prestigious ceremony bestowed upon a common man: God, the Son's name, is above every name (Hebrews 2:9)! The name "Jesus" is the most significant name in all the earth, for His name represents the Messiah, the Kinsmen Redeemer of all humankind. Jesus was the sacrificial Lamb who died for the sins of the world. There was and is no other like Him. He was given divine privilege by the Father for meritorious service in the line of duty. He is the only one who could have died, arisen from the dead, and made the declaration that He was coming back again (Acts 4:10). General Douglas Macarthur made a declaration similar to this when he was fired by President Dwight Eisenhower: "I shall return"; however, no one heard from him on a significant level after that. Jesus, however, will return!

Paul made reference to the fact that since the name of Jesus is above every other name, "at the name of Jesus every knee should bow, of things in heaven, and things in earth, and things under the earth; and that every tongue should confess that Jesus Christ is Lord, to the glory of God" (Philippians 2:10-11). Nothing is more profound than what Paul says here—that Christ, because of His obedience, is Lord. That, "He is Lord," which suggests He is worthy of worship in heaven and on earth, as well as under the earth. Further investigation of this Scripture concludes that because of His name, angels worship Him, humans worship Him, and those who are dead, as well as those in hell, will worship Him. This will bring glory to the Father.

Paul is emphasizing that if Christ can humble Himself and have fellowship with the Father through obedience, then we too need to imitate the model that Christ left behind.

## III. Concluding Reflections

The title of the introduction is "Keeping Your Head Straight." The question we must ask is: What does this phrase mean? An old Chinese adage says, "If you stop at every dog that barks, you will never reach your destination." The insight of this saying is helpful because as we look in the mirror, our reflections may not be what they ought to be. For every believer there must be a balance—connecting to others through fellowship and having the humility to understand one's limitations. Where there is no humility, there is no fellowship, and when there is no fellowship, conflict does not get resolved.

Few things are more painful to observe than a church in conflict. It saddens the entire body of Christ when believers quarrel, engage in litigation, or even perform acts of violence. Such conflict moves those outside the body to retort, "Why bother going to church when they treat each other worse than people on the street?"

Nothing on earth is more lovely or enjoyable than true fellowship among believers in Jesus Christ. Paul knew this, and therefore encouraged the church of Philippi to enjoy fellowship and humility. In order to accomplish this, they needed to take on the mind of Christ and conform themselves to His image. This is only possible if believers operate from the position of like-mindedness, having the same love, being of one accord in Christ.

What makes this possible? Being of one mind is made possible by the balance between who one is, along with one's limitations, and who one will become as the person proceeds toward being more and more like Christ. Believers in Christ must be able to see themselves as they are. Not only that, they must not think of themselves more highly than they ought. In fact, they need to esteem others higher than themselves. This balance is difficult, especially in this modern age of self-aggrandizement.

Believers who desire to keep the balance must be obedient to the Father and die to self in order that the greater good of others may become the vanguard of fellowship. This brings glory and honor to God and makes believers light in this post-modern time. This should be the end result for all believers—to bring glory to God and thereby please Him!

## WORD POWER

**Divest/Empty (Greek: *Kenosis*)**—this is an important word in our lesson today. It is the act of emptying oneself of everything that one possesses. It is divesting oneself of privileges that one has, and also means "to ruin, destroy, or come to nothing." This is what Jesus Christ did for our sakes, not for God's sake.

## HOME DAILY BIBLE READINGS

for the week of December 31, 2006
*Humiliation and Exaltation*

Dec. 25, Monday
—Matthew 2:1-11
—The Magi Gives Honor

Dec. 26, Tuesday
—Luke 2:22-38
—Jesus Is Presented

Dec. 27, Wednesday
—Hebrews 2:5-13
—Jesus, Our Brother

Dec. 28, Thursday
—Hebrews 2:14-18
—Christ, Our Great High Priest

Dec. 29, Friday
—1 Peter 3:8-12
—Unity of Spirit

Dec. 30, Saturday
—Philippians 2:1-5
—Be Like Christ

Dec. 31, Sunday
—Philippians 2:6-11
—Jesus Emptied Himself

## PRAYER

*God, we thank You for Your grace and Your mercy, but most of all we thank You for Your Son Jesus who became flesh for us to teach us a lesson on fellowship and humility. Lord, keep reminding us to walk humbly with each other, and to be of one mind to bring glory to Your name. We praise You and love You. In Jesus' name, we pray. Amen.*

**January 7, 2007**

## UNIT II
Christ Sustains and Supports

## CHILDREN'S UNIT
We Believe in Jesus

## KEY VERSES

Then said Jesus to those Jews which believed on him, If ye continue in my word, then are ye my disciples indeed; And ye shall know the truth, and the truth shall make you free.—John 8:31-32

## OBJECTIVES

Upon completion of this lesson, the students will know that:

1. Divine help is available to every person who seeks freedom from sin;
2. When we receive Jesus Christ as Savior and Lord we are made free from sin; and,
3. Obedience to Jesus Christ releases believers from the bondage of sin and the hold of death.

# Lesson 6

# "I Am from Above"

**ADULT TOPIC:** Be Free!
**YOUTH TOPIC:** Be Free!
**CHILDREN'S TOPIC:** Jesus Is God's Son

**DEVOTIONAL READING:** John 14:23-31
**BACKGROUND SCRIPTURE:** John 8:31-59
**PRINT PASSAGE:** John 8:31-38, 48-56, 58-59

## John 8:31-38, 48-56, 58-59—KJV

31 Then said Jesus to those Jews which believed on him, If ye continue in my word, then are ye my disciples indeed;

32 And ye shall know the truth, and the truth shall make you free.

33 They answered him, We be Abraham's seed, and were never in bondage to any man: how sayest thou, Ye shall be made free?

34 Jesus answered them, Verily, verily, I say unto you, Whosoever committeth sin is the servant of sin.

35 And the servant abideth not in the house for ever: but the Son abideth ever.

36 If the Son therefore shall make you free, ye shall be free indeed.

37 I know that ye are Abraham's seed; but ye seek to kill me, because my word hath no place in you.

38 I speak that which I have seen with my Father: and ye do that which ye have seen with your father.

. . . . .

48 Then answered the Jews, and said unto him, Say we not well that thou art a Samaritan, and hast a devil?

49 Jesus answered, I have not a devil; but I honour my Father, and ye do dishonour me.

50 And I seek not mine own glory: there is one that seeketh and judgeth.

51 Verily, verily, I say unto you, If a man keep my saying, he shall never see death.

52 Then said the Jews unto him, Now we know that thou hast a devil. Abraham is dead, and the prophets; and thou sayest, If a man keep my saying, he shall never taste of death.

53 Art thou greater than our father Abraham, which is dead? and the prophets are dead: whom makest thou thyself?

54 Jesus answered, If I honour myself, my honour is nothing: it is my Father that honoureth me; of whom ye say, that he is your God:

55 Yet ye have not known him; but I know him: and if I should say, I know him not, I shall be a liar like unto you: but I know him, and keep his saying.

56 Your father Abraham rejoiced to see my day: and he saw it, and was glad.

. . . . .

58 Jesus said unto them, Verily, verily, I say unto you, Before Abraham was, I am.

59 Then took they up stones to cast at him: but Jesus hid himself, and went out of the temple, going through the midst of them, and so passed by.

## UNIFYING LESSON PRINCIPLE

Human beings often seek help when trying to free themselves from destructive behavioral patterns. What source of help is available to us when we seek freedom from sin? John says that we are made free in Jesus, who is from above. The John passage underscores that Jesus, our Savior, is indeed God's Son.

## POINTS TO BE EMPHASIZED ADULTS/YOUTH

**Adult Key Verse:** John 8:31-32
**Youth Key Verse:** John 8:36

**Print Passage:** John 8:31-38, 48-56, 58-59
—The Jewish people denied and their heritage as slaves (their sinfulness).
—Believing that Jesus is from God and that He is truth sets us free from sin.
—Obedience to Christ releases us from the hold of death.
—Speaking the truth in Christ may open believers to ridicule or attack as it did Jesus.

## CHILDREN

**Key Verse:** John 1:34
**Print Passage:** John 1:19-20, 29-34
—God appointed a messenger to announce the coming of God's Son, Jesus.
—God sent His Son to earth to die for our sins.
—God gave John a sign so that John would know that Jesus was God's Son.

## TOPICAL OUTLINE OF THE LESSON

I. **INTRODUCTION**
   A. Seeking Freedom
   B. Biblical Background

II. **EXPOSITION AND APPLICATION OF THE SCRIPTURE**
   A. The Concept of Truth and Freedom *(John 8:31-32)*
   B. The Absence of Freedom *(John 8:33-38)*
   C. The Means of Freedom *(John 8:48-56, 58-59)*

III. **CONCLUDING REFLECTIONS**

## I. INTRODUCTION
### A. Seeking Freedom

"Freedom is relative." This quote from an anonymous theologian of the twentieth century means that, depending on whom the person is, freedom may not be freedom. Simply put, there is no such thing as absolute freedom; all freedom is contingent on something or someone.

It is not the intent of Scripture to entrap the believer in a "box" of do's and don'ts; rather, we are free as long as we abide within the safe boundaries of obedience to the Word of God.

True freedom is having a clear conscience with no sense of guilt for sinful thoughts or actions; one's mind and thought pattern is free of all ill will and negativity. How does one get to this point? As Christians, our freedom is extreme sensitivity to the will of God which is revealed in the Word of God. This is a delicate situation in one's spiritual life. Acts 24:16 states, "And herein do I exercise myself to have always a conscience void of offence toward God, and toward men." That's freedom!

In John 8:32, Jesus tells us how to experience freedom: "Ye shall know the truth, and the truth shall make you free." Here, the truth is both the Living Word and the written Word. To know the truth here is not just information, but relation. Freedom is relative!

### B. Biblical Background

In recording the words of Jesus, John seems to be more emphatic in his approach in this particular passage of Scripture. In fact, his emphasis is placed on two components: freedom and truth. What Jesus says about these two vital components is that when believers know the truth, it will make them free. A feeling of ease rests with the believer who knows the truth, and when a believer has an intimate knowledge of the truth, freedom makes its abode within him or her. However, the question is: Who has the privilege of knowing the truth? The answer to that question is forthcoming; however, keep in mind that no one can get to God unless he or she comes through the Son.

Jesus recognized that some of the Jews thought that because of their lineage they were already free; they felt that they were not in bondage. They even said that they had never experienced bondage before. But Jesus was not talking about physical bondage—He was speaking of spiritual bondage. Freedom, in Jesus' estimation, has nothing to do with the ability to move around freely or being under the control of someone else. Jesus' point was that the one who commits sin is in bondage.

As today's passage of study opens, Jesus has been victorious in yet another round with the Pharisees and scribes. After challenging anyone who claimed to be without sin to stone the woman caught in adultery, the Jewish leaders were convicted by their own consciences to depart. Jesus then focused His attention on those who professed to believe in Him, teaching them how to attain true freedom from sin.

Jesus not only revealed sin as the slave master that held them in bondage; He also gave them the prescription to experience truth, thus allowing them the opportunity to taste true freedom. But because they rejected Him, Jesus stated that the truth was hidden from them; therefore, they could not experience freedom. All they needed to do to be free was receive Jesus!

## II. Exposition and Application of the Scripture
### A. The Concept of Truth and Freedom
(John 8:31-32)

**Then said Jesus to those Jews which believed on him, If ye continue in my word, then are ye my disciples indeed; And ye shall know the truth, and the truth shall make you free.**

Discipleship is determined by one's beliefs. Jesus makes a statement of contingency that would determine whether one was His disciple or not (verse 31): "If ye continue in my word, then are ye my disciples indeed." The word "indeed" has a more profound meaning: it not only speaks of being a disciple in word, but also in fact or in truth. When one continues in the Word, he or she is, without question, one of Jesus' disciples. It is imperative for every would-be follower of Christ to know that discipleship comes with a price, which is obedience to the Word of God. Living a rebellious life is indicative of an unregenerate mind. A rebellious life is evidence that one has not had an encounter with Jesus Christ. He says, in essence, "If you are my disciples you will keep my commandments." Believers are made free when they accept Christ and live according to the truth He set before us.

Finally, notice the word "make" in verse 32. The word as used here implies that the truth confirms God's revelation in the believer, and then it conforms the believer to the Truth. Therefore, when Jesus said, "If you continue in my word . . . then you shall know the truth," that is the confirmation.

Human truth is fallible, and therefore, cannot be trusted completely. The truth found in Jesus Christ, however, is the truth of God. Truth in the Bible does not mean conformity to some external standard, but rather is focused on faithfulness or reliability. God's faithfulness is not measured by an external standard; God *is* the standard. God's truth can be depended on for all time.

### B. The Absence of Freedom
(John 8:33-38)

**They answered him, We be Abraham's seed, and were never in bondage to any man: how sayest thou, Ye shall be made free? Jesus answered them, Verily, verily, I say unto you, Whosoever committeth sin is the servant of sin. And the servant abideth not in the house for ever: but the Son abideth ever. If the Son therefore shall make you free, ye shall be free indeed. I know that ye are Abraham's seed; but ye seek to kill me, because my word hath no place in you. I speak that which I have seen with my Father: and ye do that which ye have seen with your father.**

Jesus was a great listener, and as He formed His discourse pertaining to the truth and freedom, He listened to what those He was teaching had to say. It is normal for people to respond quickly when they think they have an understanding of what is being taught. Often, hastiness is the rule, and in this case, as Jesus was teaching, it was no different. The Jewish believers naively responded to Jesus that, as seeds of Abraham, they were never in bondage. They couldn't help but wonder, "What do you mean that we shall be made free? How is it that you see us in bondage?" They saw bondage in the physical sense—bondage that required a slave-taskmaster relationship. However, Jesus was not speaking of this type of bondage. Jesus was speaking of spiritual bondage, in which sin is the taskmaster. Jesus says that whoever commits sin is a servant, or a slave to sin. Even more, a servant or a slave is not a permanent member of the family, but the Son is. And those whom the Son—the heir—makes free are free indeed.

Jesus made the charge that these people sought to kill Him because the Word, or the truth that He spoke, had no place in them. The truth that Jesus spoke was not received; therefore, freedom was absent. Jesus attempted to make known to them the mystery of God, which was encapsulated in Him. However, they could not see the truth because they were bound by the sinfulness of the flesh. Their rejection of Jesus proved that they were unable at that time to experience freedom; therefore, they were subject to the will of the flesh. Nothing is more confining than being bound by the flesh, because the flesh is limited to the carnal and can be blind to the spiritual. But Jesus reminded them that their forefathers had acted in the same way.

Jesus told them that they could be free, if they would open their minds to change. However, instead of being grateful, they were indignant when they heard the truth about spiritual freedom. The elders could not understand real freedom. Jesus took time to explain it to them, yet they plotted to kill Him. True spiritual freedom comes when one allows the Word of God to dwell in one's heart and lives according to its precepts.

### C. The Means of Freedom (John 8:48-56, 58-59)

**Then answered the Jews, and said unto him, Say we not well that thou art a Samaritan, and hast a devil? Jesus answered, I have not a devil; but I honour my Father, and ye do dishonour me. And I seek not mine own glory: there is one that seeketh and judgeth. Verily, verily, I say unto you, If a man keep my saying, he shall never see death. Then said the Jews unto him, Now we know that thou hast a devil. Abraham is dead, and the prophets; and thou sayest, If a man keep my saying, he shall never taste of death. Art thou greater than our father Abraham, which is dead? and the prophets are dead: whom makest thou thyself? Jesus answered, If I honour myself, my honour is nothing: it is my Father that honoureth me; of whom ye say, that he is your God: Yet ye have not known him; but I know him: and if**

**I should say, I know him not, I shall be a liar like unto you: but I know him, and keep his saying. Your father Abraham rejoiced to see my day: and he saw it, and was glad....Jesus said unto them, Verily, verily, I say unto you, Before Abraham was, I am. Then took they up stones to cast at him: but Jesus hid himself, and went out of the temple, going through the midst of them, and so passed by.**

The truth sometimes has an adverse effect on the people toward whom it is directed; these verses are further proof of that. Faced with the truth, the Jews had been placed on the defensive. They were insulted by the words Jesus spoke. They called Him both a Samaritan and a person possessed by a devil. For a Jew to be called a Samaritan was a terrible insult. Jesus didn't respond to being called a Samaritan; however, He did respond to the insinuation that He was possessed by a demon. His response was that His freedom was evident because He honored His Father. Jesus said that they dishonored Him, meaning that as God in the flesh, He was not received in the manner that He should have been. He was extending the truth to them; however, they didn't receive that truth. They could not see the means from which their freedom would come.

Freedom comes when the desire to live in obedience to God's Word outweighs one's will to become a servant to sin. It is the Word that shapes one's thoughts and actions in a positive way. In fact, Jesus stated that He did not seek to glorify Himself; there was only one who sought and judged: the Father. He saw and sees the bondage that those who are restricted spiritually are in; but Jesus said that those who hear, adhere to, and keep His sayings would not see death; they would have eternal life.

The Jewish listeners were insulted by Jesus' exhortation to keep His sayings, because He claimed to be greater than Abraham and to know him better than they did. Jesus said that He would be a liar if He said He didn't know God, just like they were. Jesus said Abraham was nothing like them, for he was free to rejoice in the day that he saw Jesus. Jesus was the truth, the revelation of God in the flesh, but they would not receive Him as the truth, the means of their freedom, because of His words that convicted them in their sins.

The means of salvation of the world was before them, but they couldn't see it because they would not receive the words of Jesus. To be free, one must receive Christ as the one who existed before the beginning. He was before Abraham, before Isaac, before Jacob, and even before Adam. Time cannot keep Him bound, but time is in His hands—for He is God, the means of freedom for all humanity.

### III. Concluding Reflections

A young man walked down the aisle to join the church one Sunday. Clearly, he had lived a difficult life. He was not an old man, but the years had weathered his appearance. Upon giving his testimony, the man shared his history of drug and alcohol abuse. Then he said, "I'm tired. I'm just tired." Clearly, this man longed for freedom from his current lifestyle, and he believed that through Christ he could be free indeed.

Truth is a necessary component of freedom from sin. Jesus offered freedom to the Jews, but they turned it down because of the bondage that they were in. What makes this lesson relevant today is that there are people who occupy the pews of the church and are seemingly connected, but they are not free. They claim that they come from a great religious tradition; however, they are not free in that their thoughts and actions don't line up with the truth. These groups of people are not enjoying the freedom Christ brings.

Though the truth confirms God's will, there are those who don't conform, and because of that, they are not free. Being free is contingent upon continuing in the Word, and through that truth we will be free indeed.

## WORD POWER

**Truth (Greek: *Aletheia*)**—the truth as taught in the Christian religion, respecting God and the execution of His purposes through Christ, and respecting the duties of man, opposing the superstitions of the Gentiles and the inventions of the Jews, and the corrupt opinions and precepts of false teachers, even among Christians

**Continue (Greek: *Meno*)**—This is a word in our key verse. It means to abide continually, without interruption. It is to count the cost of discipleship and yet not be moved by the demands. Words that are synonymous are dwell, endure, stand, and tarry.

## HOME DAILY BIBLE READINGS

for the week of January 7, 2007
*"I Am from Above"*

Jan. 1, Monday
—John 1:19-28
—A Voice in the Wilderness

Jan. 2, Tuesday
—John 1:29-34
—Jesus Is the Lamb of God

Jan. 3, Wednesday
—Matthew 13:11-17
—Promises Fulfilled

Jan. 4, Thursday
—John 14:23-31
—Jesus Gives Peace

Jan. 5, Friday
—Matthew 11:1-6
—Jesus Is the Christ

Jan. 6, Saturday
—John 8:31-38
—Jesus Promises Freedom

Jan. 7, Sunday
—John 8:48-59
—Jesus Speaks of Eternal Life

## PRAYER

*God our Father, we give You praise for liberty in Christ Jesus, for we understand that it was through what He did, and through Your Word, that we are made free. Keep us ever so mindful of the truth so that we will conform to Your will, and that our lives will confirm Your salvation in us. We pray this in Jesus' name. Amen.*

## Lesson 7

# Jesus Is Authority and Judge

**ADULT TOPIC:** Ultimate Fairness
**YOUTH TOPIC:** Justice for All
**CHILDREN'S TOPIC:** Jesus Heals a Lame Man

**DEVOTIONAL READING:** 2 Timothy 4:1-5
**BACKGROUND SCRIPTURE:** John 5:19-29
**PRINT PASSAGE:** John 5:19-29

### John 5:19-29—KJV

19 Then answered Jesus and said unto them, Verily, verily, I say unto you, The Son can do nothing of himself, but what he seeth the Father do: for what things soever he doeth, these also doeth the Son likewise.

20 For the Father loveth the Son, and sheweth him all things that himself doeth: and he will shew him greater works than these, that ye may marvel.

21 For as the Father raiseth up the dead, and quickeneth them; even so the Son quickeneth whom he will.

22 For the Father judgeth no man, but hath committed all judgment unto the Son:

23 That all men should honour the Son, even as they honour the Father. He that honoureth not the Son honoureth not the Father which hath sent him.

24 Verily, verily, I say unto you, He that heareth my word, and believeth on him that sent me, hath everlasting life, and shall not come into condemnation; but is passed from death unto life.

25 Verily, verily, I say unto you, The hour is coming, and now is, when the dead shall hear the voice of the Son of God: and they that hear shall live.

26 For as the Father hath life in himself; so hath he given to the Son to have life in himself;

27 And hath given him authority to execute judgment also, because he is the Son of man.

### January 14, 2007

**UNIT II**
Christ Sustains and Supports

**CHILDREN'S UNIT**
We Believe in Jesus

### KEY VERSE

Verily, verily, I say unto you, He that heareth my word, and believeth on him that sent me, hath everlasting life, and shall not come into condemnation; but is passed from death unto life.
—John 5:24

### OBJECTIVES

**Upon completion of this lesson, the students will understand:**

1. Jesus' authority and relationship to God: believers can know the Father through the Son;

2. Believers have hope and security for the future because of our faith in Christ; and,

3. The determining factor in the eternal judgment is whether we accept or reject Jesus in this life on earth.

28 Marvel not at this: for the hour is coming, in the which all that are in the graves shall hear his voice,

29 And shall come forth; they that have done good, unto the resurrection of life; and they that have done evil, unto the resurrection of damnation.

## UNIFYING LESSON PRINCIPLE

Many times, we question the fairness or appropriateness of a particular judgment or decision. Is it possible for decisions to be unbiased and completely fair? John says Jesus has authority that comes directly from God; because God and Jesus are perfect, their decisions are perfect. Jesus' authority was directly demonstrated when he healed the lame man on the Sabbath.

## POINTS TO BE EMPHASIZED
## ADULTS/YOUTH

**Adult Key Verse:** John 5:24
**Youth Key Verse:** John 5:27
**Print Passage:** 5:19-29

- The words of Jesus were spoken in response to the accusation that He had made Himself equal with God.
- While Christianity is rooted in Judaism, the distinction for the Christian faith is belief in Jesus as the Promised Messiah.
- Statements such as the ones made in the print passage earned Jesus the reputation of being a blasphemer.
- Revelation 20:4-6 and 11-15 validate Jesus' claim about his role in the judgment.

## CHILDREN

**Key Verse:** John 5:9

**Print Passage:** John 5:1-9

- God wants us to desire to be whole.
- As part of His ministry, Jesus helped those who were hopeless and helpless.
- God wants us to demonstrate our faith in Jesus Christ by being obedient.
- God uses people to provide us with unexpected blessings.

## TOPICAL OUTLINE OF THE LESSON

I. INTRODUCTION
   A. Understanding Final Judgment
   B. Biblical Background

II. EXPOSITION AND APPLICATION OF THE SCRIPTURE
   A. Indelible Impression of God (*John 5:19-22*)
   B. Reverencing the Righteous Judge (*John 5:23-26*)
   C. Final Authority (*John 5:27-29*)

III. CONCLUDING REFLECTIONS

## I. INTRODUCTION
### A. Understanding Final Judgment

At a very young age, children learn to say, "No fair!" upon witnessing what they feel to be an injustice against themselves or someone else. The naiveté that is a natural part of their developmental process compels them to believe that everyone deserves to be and will be treated fairly. Too soon they learn that this is hardly the case in life. Because human beings are sinful and fallible, people are often subjected to unfair treatment, sometimes through no fault of their own. The practice of fairness, from the human perspective, is inexact and imperfect. Because of our faulty decision-making capabilities, some innocent persons have been executed or imprisoned for crimes they did not commit. Such injustices result from our imperfections, and often leave us wondering whether fairness is even humanly possible.

Ironically, the truth of life is exactly as young children believe—every person deserves to and will be treated fairly—and this truth will be made manifest at the final judgment. Every person will find justice and ultimate fairness in God. Jesus has the final word and is the final authority. It is gratifying to know that Jesus, who knows all things—even the hearts of all people—will deal fairly with all humanity.

This lesson explains that ultimate fairness comes from Christ, who is the righteous Judge; His judgments are unparalleled because they are perfect; He knows the thoughts and intents of our hearts (Hebrews 4:12). Ultimate fairness is found in Christ!

### B. Biblical Background

The events that lead up to Jesus' discussion of judgment and the resurrection can almost be deemed humorous, as it is revelatory of human nature. Prior to this dialogue with the Pharisees, Jesus had healed the man who had been paralyzed for thirty-eight years. He had spent nearly four decades lying on a mat (KJV: bed). After his encounter with the Son of God, the man was able to walk for the first time in his life. Having followed Jesus' instructions to pick up his mat and walk, the man encountered the Jewish religious leaders. Their spiritual blindness was so dense that they could not bring themselves to rejoice at the man's healing. Instead, they chastised the man for breaking the Law by carrying his mat on the Sabbath!

Already enraged that Jesus had broken the Sabbath, these men became even more indignant when Jesus claimed God as His Father, thus equating Himself with God. Jesus then began His discourse on His relationship to His Father and His role in the judgment. The Pharisees were judging the healed man and Jesus with their limited perspective and knowledge, which was solely based on the Law. Jesus, having full view and understanding of the final judgment, sought to enlighten them regarding this judgment.

The gospel of John captures the humanity as well as the deity of Christ through His power to be a fair and impartial judge to all humanity. This fairness cannot be understood from a human perspective; it must be understood from the spiritual perspective. The fairness of Christ enables Him to judge not only the actions, but also the thoughts and the intents of all persons (Hebrews 4:12).

## II. Exposition and Application of the Scripture

### A. Indelible Impression of God (John 5:19-22)

**Then answered Jesus and said unto**

them, Verily, verily, I say unto you, The Son can do nothing of himself, but what he seeth the Father do: for what things soever he doeth, these also doeth the Son likewise. For the Father loveth the Son, and showeth him all things that himself doeth: and he will shew him greater works than these, that ye may marvel. For as the Father raiseth up the dead, and quickeneth them; even so the Son quickeneth whom he will. For the Father judgeth no man, but hath committed all judgment unto the Son.

The Jews had a long tradition of referring to God as "our Father." When Jesus taught his disciples to pray he taught them to address God as "our Father." But in verse 17, Jesus had referred to God as "My Father." Jesus laid claim to a relationship between Himself and God in which the terms "father" and "son" took on a degree of identity as to denote equal authority and power.

God leaves a lasting impression on those who receive Him. In fact, God made a lasting impression on the world through sending His Son, Jesus, whom Hebrews 1:3 states is "the express image of his person." Jesus is God's certified stamp and, therefore, whatever God is, His Son Jesus is; He is the very imprint or impression of God.

Jesus declared in verse 19 that He can do nothing of Himself; what He sees the Father do, He in turn does. Again, this lesson reiterates lessons 1-4, wherein Jesus is acknowledged as the very image of God, not a replica or a copy. This is what John is establishing through the words of Christ. There is a mutuality that exists between the Father and the Son; the world is the benefactor of this mutuality because as humanity honors God, they in turn honor Christ. However, in the same breath, those who dishonor God dishonor Christ.

When Jesus made this declaration, hearing meant much more than simply understanding the meaning of the words and doing nothing with them—it meant responding to the words and conforming to what they meant. When one responds positively to Jesus' words, there is an indelible impression made. In other words, no one who comes in contact with Jesus remains the same, because of the certified stamp that has been placed on his or her heart! God's name is written on the hearts of the righteous.

### B. Reverencing the Righteous Judge (John 5:23-26)

**That all men should honour the Son, even as they honour the Father. He that honoureth not the Son honoureth not the Father which hath sent him. Verily, verily, I say unto you, He that heareth my word, and believeth on him that sent me, hath everlasting life, and shall not come into condemnation; but is passed from death unto life. Verily, verily, I say unto you, The hour is coming, and now is, when the dead shall hear the voice of the Son of God: and they that hear shall live. For as the Father hath life in himself; so hath he given to the Son to have life in himself.**

God has committed all judgment to His Son, Jesus Christ. Therefore, Christ ought to be revered as the righteous Judge.

This reverence should not only honor God, but should also honor Christ. How does one honor Christ? One honors Christ by first receiving Him as God in the flesh (see John 1:14) and by receiving His words (see John 6:63).

Receiving Christ as God in the flesh is necessary in revering Him as the righteous judge, because God has committed all judgment to Him. Jesus proclaimed that just as the Father raises the dead and gives them life, so also the Son gives life to whom He wishes. Jesus was not claiming to be an instrument in God's hand for restoring the dead to normal life, as was Elijah; rather, Jesus boldly asserts in verse 24 that He is the grantor of eternal life. And it is not merely that eternal life is granted to those who believe in him, as though it were some type of ticket system; it is that Jesus exercises the divine prerogative itself of imparting this life. He has the power and he has the authority because it is given to him by God the Father.

In revering Him as the righteous judge, one should reverence His authority. Notice that He quickens, or makes alive, those whom He chooses; this testifies to the fact that God has committed everything to Jesus' hand. Not only does this show His authority, but His sovereignty. Christ does only what His Father does; therefore, He uses sovereignty to get things accomplished.

Finally, one who honors Christ honors Him by receiving His words (John 5:24). This is to say that persons are made alive through receiving the words of Christ and by believing in the One who sent Him. When one honors Him, eternal life is the aftereffect. In fact, Jesus says in John 6:63, "The words that I speak unto you, they are spirit, and they are life." The power of the Word affects one's life; for these words are not just vowels, consonants, and syllables—they are God's statements that give life.

Jesus will judge the world in righteousness. What does that mean? Jesus has the authority to do this because He was commissioned by His Father to do so. To repeat something that was written earlier, in order for fairness to be ultimate, the final authority has to come from the Final Authority. Decisions of fairness are executed by Jesus, the righteous Judge who has the power to make such judgment a reality.

### C. Final Authority (John 5:27-29)

**And hath given him authority to execute judgment also, because he is the Son of man. Marvel not at this: for the hour is coming, in the which all that are in the graves shall hear his voice, And shall come forth; they that have done good, unto the resurrection of life; and they that have done evil, unto the resurrection of damnation.**

The topic for this lesson is "Ultimate Fairness." Further investigation suggests that the word *ultimate* means "final," and *fairness* means "judgment." As was stated in the last outline, Jesus has final authority to judge the world in righteousness (John 5:27). How will this final judgment take place? Jesus unveils the plan for the judging of the world through two resurrections.

In John 5:28, Jesus states that He will speak the Word, and those in the graves will hear His voice. What one should notice here is that the Word will speak the Word and those who are dead shall be made alive for the purpose of judgment. The Jewish teachers anticipated a day when God's ability to grant life and execute judgment would unite into one great moment; this would be the consummation of history. Jesus inserts Himself directly into this picture. In this message is an echo of Daniel 7:13: "An hour is coming, in which all who are in the tombs will hear my voice, and will come forth; those who did the good deeds to a resurrection of life, those who committed the evil deeds to a resurrection of judgment." Jesus revealed that inasmuch as God the Father has given the Son the right to impart life, He also has given him the authority of judgment.

Hebrews 9:27 states that it is appointed once for all human beings to die, and then comes the judgment. Jesus the righteous judge had the first word in creation, and He will have the final word in judgment. John 5:29 provides the reader a view of how this resurrection will take place. The first resurrection will be of those who have done well; they will receive life; they are the ones who have received the words of Christ, and the One who sent Him.

The second resurrection is slated for those who have done evil; they will receive damnation. These are those persons who have not received the Word of Christ and the One who sent Him. There are two prerequisites for receiving life. One prerequisite is the receiving, or hearing, of the Word. This hearing requires action on our part. This means that there must be adherence to the words spoken by Christ. The next prerequisite is to believe in He who sent Christ. If one is to experience eternal life, one must believe that God is the One who sent Jesus.

Jesus' judgment is final. This is essential to understand, for final judgment means that there will be no further judgments after He pronounces His judgment. Unlike our system of judgment, which is imperfect, the judgment executed by Christ is without error. Everyone will spend eternity somewhere, whether in heaven or in hell. Christ will not make any mistakes; no one will find later that they were unjustly accused—for all deeds done in the body are being recorded in the Lamb's Book of Life. Thus, this judgment is fair and final.

### III. Concluding Reflections

In *Men at Work: The Craft of Baseball* (Macmillan Publishing Company, 1990), author George Will writes: "Baseball umpires are carved from granite and stuffed with microchips...they are professional dispensers of pure justice. Once when Babe Pinelli called Babe Ruth out on strikes, Ruth made a populist argument. Ruth reasoned fallaciously (as populists do) from raw numbers to moral weight: "There's 40,000 people here who know that last one was a ball, tomato head." Pinelli replied with the measured stateliness of John Marshall:

"Maybe so, but mine is the only opinion that counts." The same is true concerning the final judgment. There will be only one opinion that counts—the one belonging to the Ultimate Judge and dispenser of justice.

Humans are prone to error because of their prejudices and their inability to see the intent of the heart, as well as the dimension of thought. Because of these flaws, fairness from the human perspective misses its mark because of limited understanding and practice. However, from the perspective of the righteous Judge, Jesus Christ, fairness is not conceptual; it is who Christ is. He is the ultimate Judge. He is the final Authority and has the authority to make the final decision on everything. Nothing gets by Him—no lying, no deception, nothing!

The apostle Paul says, "Wherefore God also hath highly exalted him, and given him a name which is above every name" (Philippians 2:9). What is this name that is above every other name? Paul reveals the answer in verse 11: "And that every tongue should confess that Jesus Christ is Lord, to the glory of God the Father."

## WORD POWER

**Believe (Greek: *Pisteuo*)**—it is one thing to hear the word of God; the most important thing is to believe. In the original language, *believe* means "to be persuaded, have implicit confidence in, reliance without shadow of doubt." This word *pisteuo* appears ninety-nine times in John's gospel.

## HOME DAILY BIBLE READINGS

for the week of January 14, 2007
*Jesus Is Authority and Judge*

Jan. 8, Monday
  —John 5:1-9
  —Jesus Heals a Lame Man

Jan. 9, Tuesday
  —John 3:31-36
  —Whom God Has Sent

Jan. 10, Wednesday
  —John 4:19-26
  —I Am the Christ

Jan. 11, Thursday
  —Matthew 7:24-29
  —Jesus Taught with Authority

Jan. 12, Friday
  —2 Timothy 4:1-5
  —Christ Will Judge

Jan. 13, Saturday
  —John 5:19-23
  —Honor the Son

Jan. 14, Sunday
  —John 5:24-30
  —Jesus Speaks of Judgment

## PRAYER

*Our Father, we pray to You because we know that Your Son has ultimate authority over the world. Nothing gets past Him, and as a result He is fair in all that He does. Teach us, O Lord, to honor You, and in honoring You we honor Your Son. Thank You for who You are, and for Your love and patience with us. Keep us, we pray. In Jesus' name, we pray. Amen.*

**January 21, 2007**

Lesson 8

# Jesus Is the Bread of Life and Living Water

**UNIT II**
Christ Sustains and Supports

**CHILDREN'S UNIT**
We Believe in Jesus

**ADULT TOPIC:** Lasting Results
**YOUTH TOPIC:** Jesus: Life-Giving Bread and Water
**CHILDREN'S TOPIC:** Jesus Saves

**DEVOTIONAL READING:** Ephesians 3:14-21
**BACKGROUND SCRIPTURE:** John 6:25-59; 7:37-39
**PRINT PASSAGE:** John 6:34-40; 7:37-39

**KEY VERSE**
Jesus said unto them, I am the bread of life: he that cometh to me shall never hunger; and he that believeth on me shall never thirst. —John 6:35

## John 6:34-40; 7:37-39—KJV

34 Then said they unto him, Lord, evermore give us this bread.

35 And Jesus said unto them, I am the bread of life: he that cometh to me shall never hunger; and he that believeth on me shall never thirst.

36 But I said unto you, That ye also have seen me, and believe not.

37 All that the Father giveth me shall come to me; and him that cometh to me I will in no wise cast out.

38 For I came down from heaven, not to do mine own will, but the will of him that sent me.

39 And this is the Father's will which hath sent me, that of all which he hath given me I should lose nothing, but should raise it up again at the last day.

40 And this is the will of him that sent me, that every one which seeth the Son, and believeth on him, may have everlasting life: and I will raise him up at the last day.

.....

37 In the last day, that great day of the feast, Jesus stood and cried, saying, If any man thirst, let him come unto me, and drink.

38 He that believeth on me, as the scripture hath said, out of his belly shall flow rivers of living water.

**OBJECTIVES**
Upon completion of this lesson, the students will know that:
1. Jesus—the Life Giver—provides complete satisfaction to those who receive Him;
2. As the Bread of Life and Living Water, Jesus presents Himself as the provider to all human needs; and,
3. As the source of life, Jesus' provision for humanity extends from this life into eternal life.

39 (But this spake he of the Spirit, which they that believe on him should receive: for the Holy Ghost was not yet given; because that Jesus was not yet glorified.)

## UNIFYING LESSON PRINCIPLE

People constantly search for those experiences or possessions that can provide satisfaction and a sense of fulfillment. Can we discover someone or something that can provide spiritual satisfaction? John suggests that Jesus portrays Himself as the Life Giver in whom there is complete satisfaction.

## POINTS TO BE EMPHASIZED ADULTS/YOUTH

**Adult/Youth Key Verse:** John 6:35
**Print Passage:** John 6:34-40; 7:37-39
—Bread is often used as a biblical metaphor for basic human sustenance.
—In His teaching, Jesus often used water as a metaphor for the Holy Spirit.
—On the last day of Festival of Booths, Jesus invites all those who are thirsty to come to Him.
—In fulfilling both hunger and thirst, Jesus postures Himself as the provider of all human needs.
—Jesus is the "manna" that will never allow believers to go hungry.

## CHILDREN

**Key Verse:** John 6:40
**Print Passage:** John 6:22-24, 35-40
—Jesus teaches us that we need rest after we minister to the needy.
—The crowd searched for Jesus because they wanted Him to give them more food to eat.
—Jesus wants us to believe in Him so that He can bless us with all that will meet our needs.
—God the Father and Jesus the Son work together to fill the needs of all who believe in Jesus.

## TOPICAL OUTLINE OF THE LESSON

I. **INTRODUCTION**
   A. The Sustenance of Life
   B. Biblical Background

II. **EXPOSITION AND APPLICATION OF THE SCRIPTURE**
   A. Jesus, the Bread of Life *(John 6:34-35)*
   B. The Focus of Christ *(John 6:36-38)*
   C. The Father's Will Toward the Believer *(John 6:39-40)*
   D. The Divine Invitation *(John 7:37-39)*

III. **CONCLUDING REFLECTIONS**

## I. INTRODUCTION
### A. The Sustenance of Life

Food and water are two primary needs of the body. A proper diet as well as adequate hydration of the body helps to sustain and maintain it. Without food and water, the human body begins to malfunction and wither away.

Just as the body needs the physical nourishment of both food and water, it must also be spiritually nourished. This is referenced by what Jesus said in Matthew

4:4 and Luke 12:23. Believers and non-believers alike need to be fed spiritually. People are looking for something to fill the spiritual void in their lives.

In this lesson, Jesus offers both believers and non-believers bread and water to sustain them spiritually. He offers spiritual nourishment for life as well as a well-balanced meal that will build one's faith, hope, and love for God and all people. This bread that He offers is Himself, the Word, and His words, as well as living water, quench the thirst for righteous living that will flow from one's belly. This water is a perpetual well that flows within. It is self-contained, through the Holy Spirit, and will never run dry as long as one believes.

Jesus said (Matthew 5:6): "Blessed are they which do hunger and thirst after righteousness: for they shall be filled." One must develop an appetite for Jesus and His words, as well as a thirst for righteousness, if one's needs are to be satisfied. All one needs to do in order to be filled is: (1) come to Jesus hungry—not for the things of this world, but for the Word and His words; and (2) possess the thirst to walk in righteousness. Jesus offers life to all that will receive Him and His words, as well as the One who sent Him.

## B. Biblical Background

This Scripture contrasts the characteristics of physical bread and that of spiritual bread. The opening verses of John 6 reveal that Jesus had fed 5000 people with two fish and five barley loaves. This satisfied their physical hunger; but physical bread cannot satisfy the soul.

The Old Testament states that God provided the Israelites with manna, a bread-like substance that God miraculously provided for them in the wilderness (Exodus 16:4; Numbers 11:7-9). Manna kept them alive while they journeyed toward the Promised Land. This grain-like substance, considered to be food from heaven, nurtured their physical bodies, but it also nurtured their spiritual bodies, serving as a constant reminder of God's providential care. In the New Testament, God provided humanity with spiritual sustenance in the form of Jesus Christ. The manna which had sustained the Israelites in the wilderness also foreshadowed Christ, the true Bread from heaven. This Bread gives the believer life (John 6:33, 35) as he or she journeys toward the land that Jesus is preparing for those who love Him (John 14:1-3).

Jesus is not only the Bread of Life; He declared that He is living water. Those who believe in Him would never thirst again. When one places his or her trust in Him, one will find complete satisfaction. Complete satisfaction is found in walking in righteousness. John sought to show what believers can experience when they come and partake of the Word and His words.

The Jewish custom of breaking bread together was significant because it was a sign of a covenant. When one comes to Jesus, there is a covenant being established between Jesus and the one who surrenders to Jesus.

John 7:37–39 takes on its meaning in the context of a dramatic ceremony performed during the Feast of Tabernacles. In the ceremony, the priest took a golden pitcher, went down to the Pool of Siloam, and filled the pitcher with water. He carried the pitcher back through the Water Gate and up to the temple altar where it was poured out as an offering.

## II. Exposition and Application of the Scripture
### A. Jesus, the Bread of Life
*(John 6:34-35)*

**Then said they unto him, Lord, evermore give us this bread. And Jesus said unto them, I am the bread of life: he that cometh to me shall never hunger; and he that believeth on me shall never thirst.**

Whenever Jesus taught, especially when He used parables, there were some who did not understand His message. Often, He was not speaking about the physical context; instead, He addressed matters in a spiritual context by using everyday examples. He spoke on earthly things that must be understood from a spiritual perspective. While the crowd that followed Him was interested in His ability to supply physical bread, Jesus had something far more significant in mind which He revealed to them by pointing to Himself.

The crowd had witnessed His feeding more than 5000 people. These people were full, but not satisfied. They wanted bread, but what Jesus said to them caused them to say, "Lord, evermore give us this bread" (verse 34). They had a certain reverence, but they did not fully understand what Jesus meant. They considered the regularity with which God had provided the manna for their ancestors in the wilderness, and this prompted them to say, *show us the bread*, or more accurately, "evermore give us this bread." They wanted another miracle. Adherents to Judaism had the expectation that when the Messiah came He would feed them with manna, as was done when the children of Israel were in the wilderness. Since they were at least considering the idea that Jesus might be the Messiah, this request could have possibly been a proof text to attest to His messianic claim. However, Jesus wanted to provide them with life and not just full bellies. He offered them Himself, as the answer for what they needed; Jesus proclaimed, "I am the bread of life: he that cometh to me shall never hunger" (John 6:35). Jesus sought to satisfy them completely, but they had to surrender themselves to Him. One cannot be completely satisfied until one comes to Jesus and surrenders his or her life to Him, knowing that He can completely satisfy one's hunger as well as give him or her true life.

### B. The Focus of Christ *(John 6:36-38)*

**But I said unto you, That ye also have seen me, and believe not. All that the Father giveth me shall come to me; and him that cometh to me I will in no wise cast out. For I came down from heaven, not to do mine own will, but the will of him that sent me.**

In this lesson, notice Jesus' focus in inviting the people to come to Him. It was not His intent that any should be left hungry. However, He did recognize that there were those who rejected Him. They did not believe, even though they had seen Him. Yet, He never lost sight of the fact that they also needed to be fed. In fact, He would not cast them out. The allusion to being cast out suggested that those who had come may be as beggars to the home of a nobleman. This person could serve as a benefactor or behave churlishly, rejecting their attempts to be fed. Jesus made it clear that His bread was available to all who truly wanted it. The manna fed only a restricted group of people.

Jesus' commitment to the world is focused and intense. His prayer in the Garden of Gethsemane illustrates this, as He prayed for all to receive fellowship with God through Himself. His intensity can be seen on the Cross as He asked the Father to "forgive them, for they know not what they do." He is intense about the salvation of the world and His intensity cannot be questioned, for it has been demonstrated by His own blood.

Jesus loves all and wants all to partake of the Bread of Life and have their thirst quenched through their belief. He is calling: *whosoever will let him come, come and drink from the fountain freely, a fountain that never runs dry*. This dual metaphor of bread and water is an apt characterization of what Jesus truly offers, for one cannot live physically or spiritually without proper sustenance. Jesus is focused and willing to receive anyone who desires to come to Him and receive the Bread of Life.

### C. The Father's Will Toward the Believer *(John 6:39-40)*

**And this is the Father's will which hath sent me, that of all which he hath given me I should lose nothing, but should raise it up again at the last day. And this is the will of him that sent me, that every one which seeth the Son, and believeth on him, may have everlasting life: and I will raise him up at the last day.**

What is the will of the Father concerning those who believe? Three issues are highlighted in verses 39 and 40; verse 40 is merely an amplification of verse 39. First, Jesus would lose nothing as a result of His work and would be fully validated by His resurrection. Secondly, everyone who saw Jesus would believe on Him. Thirdly, those who believe will have life everlasting.

It is God's will that everyone who believes in Jesus will be redeemed and will enjoy the fruits of resurrection. As a Jewish person, Jesus was familiar with the tenet in Judaism that only the righteous would be resurrected. The will of the Father is for those who receive Jesus Christ by making a declaration of faith to be raised up! This is exciting news for all who believe. Jesus gave His life, so that all that believe would have everlasting life (see Romans 5:8). Those who receive Christ will not be lost—because of what He has already done and what He will do when He raises all who believe on the last day. The will of the Father is that corruption will cease and incorruption shall reign; hatred shall cease and love shall reign—for it is God's will toward the believer.

Jesus is content with fulfilling His Father's will. Therefore, God seeks to win humanity through the persistence of the Son. His commitment to humankind is relentless; therefore, He is willing to go all the way to the Cross and die for the sake of humanity, because of the love that He has for His creation. Belief in the Son is necessary to receive everlasting life.

### D. The Divine Invitation (John 7:37-39)

**In the last day, that great day of the feast, Jesus stood and cried, saying, If any man thirst, let him come unto me, and drink. He that believeth on me, as the scripture hath said, out of his belly shall flow rivers of living water. (But this spake he of the Spirit, which they that believe on him should receive: for the Holy Ghost was not yet given; because that Jesus was not yet glorified.)**

Jesus offers a personal invitation to all who are thirsty to come to Him and drink. Believers who drink will never thirst again. He calls all to come and drink freely from the fountain that never runs dry. This is a divine invitation because when one comes to Jesus, it is a walk toward the divine, a journey toward God in the flesh. Nothing is more satisfying for believers than to come to Jesus and allow Him to fill them.

When Jesus approached the woman at the well (John 4), His invitation was so thirst-quenching that she felt the need to go back into her own hometown and tell others to come and see this Man whose discernment was miraculous. Her invitation was to see the divine, and taste and see that the Lord is good. All who believe are given this same invitation, and all those who receive Him have the same opportunity to invite others to experience the sweet waters of righteousness.

Lastly, Jesus stated that for those who believe in Him (in accordance with Scripture), "Out of his belly shall flow rivers of living water" (verse 38). It is through the belief of those in Christ that a perpetual river of living water will flow. This flowing river describes the attitude of the believers; there is an attitude of joy that flows no matter what happens around them. This is the result of being in Christ; in fact, this is the lasting result of coming to Christ and believing. This joy makes one alive, invigorated, and excited. The lasting result is everlasting life!

## III. Concluding Reflections

"Oh the world is hungry for the living bread…." These words, as penned by Johnson Oatman, certainly reflect the condition of modern life. The world is hungry, but often that hunger is unsatisfied because the world fills it with junk food.

There is a story about a young man who joined a gang. Initially, he was afraid of the violence of the lifestyle, but he eventually got acclimated to it. Unfortunately, his ways caught up to him, and he was standing before a judge. He had killed a policeman and was convicted of first-degree murder. As he stood before the court, his parents quietly wept as they awaited the sentence. The judge asked him if he wanted to address the court before sentencing. The young felon said, among other things, that he had joined a gang because it made him feel powerful and loved. After he finished his statement, the judge reviewed his record. He noted that the young man had once been active in his local church. The judge shook his head in disbelief. This young man had everything to satisfy his hunger—a good family, introduction to Christ at an early age, a decent education, a good home, and other things not normally associated with people who get off the right track. He was hungry, but like the prodigal, he chose to satisfy his longings with junk food.

The old saying, "You are what you eat," is certainly true in the physical realm, but it is also true of the spiritual realm. Those who subsist on the junk food of life will not reap the benefits as do those who feast on the Bread of Life and Living Water, for they shall never hunger or thirst.

## WORD POWER

**Cometh/come (Greek: *erkhomai*)**—this, in the original language, carries the idea of "come by yourself with all your heart and soul." It involves a personal decision. It is a coming out of darkness into the light. The promise follows the invitation, which is: "One who cometh shall never be hungry."

## HOME DAILY BIBLE READINGS

for the week of January 21, 2007
*Jesus Is the Bread of Life and Living Water*
Jan. 15, Monday
—Ephesians 3:14-21
—May Christ Dwell Within
Jan. 16, Tuesday
—John 6:16-24
—Do Not Be Afraid
Jan. 17, Wednesday
—John 6:25-34
—Jesus, the Heavenly Bread
Jan. 18, Thursday
—John 6:33-40
—I Am the Bread of Life
Jan. 19, Friday
—John 6:41-51
—Sustained by Living Bread
Jan. 20, Saturday
—Isaiah 49:7-13
—Sing for Joy
Jan. 21, Sunday
—John 7:37-41
—Living Water

## PRAYER

*God, we thank You that Your Son gives us sustenance because He is the Bread of Life. We are thankful that as we come to Him we are able to drink water that will satisfy us. Please help us to stay faithful to Your Word—as we walk in adherence to what it says—and keep us humble, seeking the continual move toward perfection. Lastly, O Lord, we thank You for the living rivers of water that flow in every believer, that keep us ever so mindful that You are there. We love You and adore You, O Lord. We pray this in Jesus' name. Amen.*

**January 28, 2007**

Lesson 9

# "I Am the Light of the World"

**ADULT TOPIC:** Overcoming Darkness
**YOUTH TOPIC:** Jesus: Our Light in the Darkness
**CHILDREN'S TOPIC:** Jesus Brings Light

**UNIT II**
Christ Sustains and Supports

**CHILDREN'S UNIT**
We Believe in Jesus

**DEVOTIONAL READING:** Isaiah 35:3-10
**BACKGROUND SCRIPTURE:** John 8:12-20; 12:44-46
**PRINT PASSAGE:** John 8:12-20; 12:44-46

### John 8:12-20; 12:44-46—KJV

12 Then spake Jesus again unto them, saying, I am the light of the world: he that followeth me shall not walk in darkness, but shall have the light of life.

13 The Pharisees therefore said unto him, Thou bearest record of thyself; thy record is not true.

14 Jesus answered and said unto them, Though I bear record of myself, yet my record is true: for I know whence I came, and whither I go; but ye cannot tell whence I come, and whither I go.

15 Ye judge after the flesh; I judge no man.

16 And yet if I judge, my judgment is true: for I am not alone, but I and the Father that sent me.

17 It is also written in your law, that the testimony of two men is true.

18 I am one that bear witness of myself, and the Father that sent me beareth witness of me.

19 Then said they unto him, Where is thy Father? Jesus answered, Ye neither know me, nor my Father: if ye had known me, ye should have known my Father also.

20 These words spake Jesus in the treasury, as he taught in the temple: and no man laid hands on him; for his hour was not yet come.

.….

### KEY VERSE

Then spake Jesus again unto them, saying, I am the light of the world: he that followeth me shall not walk in darkness, but shall have the light of life.
—John 8:12

### OBJECTIVES

**Upon completion of this lesson, the students will know that:**

1. Believers can find direction in the light of Christ for making important life decisions;

2. Those who believe in Jesus come out of spiritual darkness and become children of the Light; and,

3. Jesus' disciples are expected to reflect His light in the world.

44 Jesus cried and said, He that believeth on me, believeth not on me, but on him that sent me.

45 And he that seeth me seeth him that sent me.

46 I am come a light into the world, that whosoever believeth on me should not abide in darkness.

## UNIFYING LESSON PRINCIPLE

The fear or avoidance of darkness is a common experience for many people. Is there any light available that can dispel the spiritual darkness in which so many people find themselves? John says that the light Jesus provides reaches into areas that are out of bounds for physical light. The healing of the blind man was one way Jesus manifested Himself as the Light of life.

## POINTS TO BE EMPHASIZED ADULTS/YOUTH

**Adult/Youth Key Verse:** John 8:12
**Print Passage:** John 8:12-20; 12:44-46

—On the first day of the feast, the moon rose at sunset, so there was no time that was completely dark that day.
—The coming of the light is a metaphor for the coming of salvation.
—Jesus said that He is the ultimate revelation of God. He came into the world to reveal God's way to all who believe in Him.
—Those who believe in Jesus come out of the darkness and become children of the light.
—Jesus' claim to be the Light of the world compares with God's being the guiding light of Israel as a pillar of fire, leading them through the wilderness.

## CHILDREN

**Key Verse:** John 8:12
**Print Passage:** John 8:12; 9:1-12, 35-38

—Jesus wants us to follow in the way or the light that He offers us.
—Jesus healed the blind beggar so that the people could see God's goodness.
—Some people did not believe that Jesus healed the blind man.
—When we know that Jesus has healed us, we will worship Jesus.

## TOPICAL OUTLINE OF THE LESSON

I. INTRODUCTION
    A. Overcoming Darkness
    B. Biblical Background

II. EXPOSITION AND APPLICATION OF THE SCRIPTURE
    A. Christ: The Light of the World (John 8:12-14)
    B. Christ and His Witness (John 8:15-20)
    C. Seeing Is Believing (John 12:44-46)

III. CONCLUDING REFLECTIONS

## I. INTRODUCTION
### A. Overcoming Darkness

The term "overcoming darkness" may seem obscure, but it means much, much more than turning on a switch to bring light into a dark room. One must have light within in order to overcome the darkness without. A simple example of this is when people get out of bed at night to use the bathroom. They don't have to turn on the light because they know the way; therefore, they have light within, although the darkness is all around them.

Many blind persons are able to live independently—they know what they want to do, where they want to go, and how to get there. Consider the accomplishments of Helen Keller, Fannye Crosby, Ray Charles, and Stevie Wonder. Each of them managed to overcome living in physical darkness and live productive lives. None of them allowed darkness to serve as a hindrance; instead, they chose to be led by the light that lies within. John 11:9-10 states: "If any man walk in the day, he stumbleth not, because he seeth the light of this world. But if a man walk in the night, he stumbleth, because there is no light in him." A person may be surrounded by darkness, but the light within does not permit the darkness around to deter that person because he or she has light within.

## B. Biblical Background

The Pharisees were relentless in their attempts to entangle Jesus in debate on issues of the Law. They were unwilling to let go of what Jesus had come to fulfill—the Law. When Jesus would mention His name in conjunction with the Father, they took offense that He was making Himself equal to the Father—to the Jewish leaders this was blasphemy. This caused them to oppose Jesus and conspire to kill Him; but it was not His time yet.

Not only did they debate the Law, but they also debated His identity. This is why they wanted to kill Him, believing that He was blasphemous in His assessment of Himself. They told Him that the record He bore of Himself was not true. Undaunted by their opposition of Him, Jesus continued to express that not only is He God's Son, but He is also God! Jesus knew who He was, and what His mission was while here on earth.

If anyone should have known who Jesus was, it was the Pharisees. The Scriptures declare who He was; however, they were blinded spiritually because of their dependence on and trust in physical sight. What they saw was Joseph and Mary's son, a carpenter; they missed that He was the Son of God. John unveiled, through the words of Jesus, that the attitude of walking in light or darkness is the acceptance or rejection of Him as the promised Messiah.

The metaphors of darkness and light were used by Jesus to illustrate a spiritual truth, and that truth is that those who walk in darkness do so not because they have no other choices, but because they love darkness rather than light (John 3:19).

## II. Exposition and Application of the Scripture
### A. Christ: The Light of the World
*(John 8:12-14)*

**Then spake Jesus again unto them, saying, I am the light of the world: he that**

followeth me shall not walk in darkness, but shall have the light of life. The Pharisees therefore said unto him, Thou bearest record of thyself; thy record is not true. Jesus answered and said unto them, Though I bear record of myself, yet my record is true: for I know whence I came, and whither I go; but ye cannot tell whence I come, and whither I go.

When one makes a statement of declaration, the person is merely telling those who will listen who he or she is. In fact, in 1776, the nascent republic of America wrote what was known as the "Declaration of Independence." In this declaration, the leaders addressed the nature of this "upstart" republic and its purpose, and declared for itself freedom from England. War ensued because England did not want to accept the declaration coming from the newly-formed republic. Just as there were those that did not accept the Declaration of Independence, there were those that did not accept the declaration from Jesus.

Jesus made a declaration to the Pharisees: "I am the light of the world: he that followeth me shall not walk in darkness, but shall have the light of life" (John 8:12). This statement bruised some sensibilities because of who they considered Jesus to be. They knew Him as the carpenter's son, not as the Light of the world. Therefore, His statement produced conflict.

Jesus' declaration helps us to see how significant He is to our lives and our existence. In fact, light is synonymous with life (See John 1:4). The sun is the source of light for the solar system and, as such, is the source of life, for nothing living can do without it, animal or vegetable. So like the sun, Jesus brings light and life to all. The reference in Malachi 4:2 applies here, for He is "the Sun of righteousness." That is, He is the source, sustenance, and supplier of righteousness. He brings us the ultimate light—the light of God which leads to eternal life. This is His promise when He said, "he that followeth *(believes in)* me shall not walk in darkness, but shall have the light of life."

Jesus was saying that He is the fulfillment of what they had been waiting for; they needed to follow Him so that they would not walk in darkness. To the Pharisees, this was an insult because what Jesus was in fact saying to them was that they were walking in darkness. The questions that would be asked were: "Why do I need to follow you? In fact, where are you going? And lastly, who do you think you are?" The Pharisees believed that they were good Jews—they knew the Law; therefore, they thought that they followed the Law. However, they used the Law to define sin rather than to guide them along the path of righteousness.

They didn't realize they needed to follow Jesus because He was God's answer to the Law, and the fulfillment thereof. Their eyes deceived them and they missed an opportunity to follow Jesus. Jesus wanted them to walk in the light of faith in Him, rather than in darkness of their limited knowledge.

Still, they had another problem: Where was Jesus going? Jesus was attempting to lead them to the light and to life. Jesus was leading them to the understanding of God's plan and eternal life. This was what the Pharisees wanted—to have life eternal—but because they were walking in darkness, they were unable to understand what Jesus was indeed saying to them.

Jesus declared Himself the Light of the World. Darkness cannot comprehend the light; therefore, those who were in darkness did not receive the Light. Jesus was declaring that He was the one who would bring understanding to them. This light would not be an outer expression, but rather, an inward reflection of the light that guides everyone who accepts the Light of the World. Their unbelief would not allow them to see this; therefore, they questioned His declaration. They questioned Him not only because they didn't believe Him, but also because Jesus had no witness to corroborate His claim—as Mosaic Law required. Without saying it, they were asking, "Where are your witnesses?" Jesus then told them that His record is true, because He knows both where He came from and where He is going. His next statement was that they could not do the same. Jesus was before the beginning and He is the ending—but they had no idea.

## B. Christ and His Witness
*(John 8:15-20)*

**Ye judge after the flesh; I judge no man. And yet if I judge, my judgment is true: for I am not alone, but I and the Father that sent me. It is also written in your law, that the testimony of two men is true. I am one that bear witness of myself, and the Father that sent me beareth witness of me. Then said they unto him, Where is thy Father? Jesus answered, Ye neither know me, nor my Father: if ye had known me, ye should have known my Father also. These words spake Jesus in the treasury, as he taught in the temple: and no man laid hands on him; for his hour was not yet come.**

Who could verify Jesus' claim to be the Light of the world? None of the Pharisees could do it, nor would they have wanted to. Jesus stated that they judged Him with their physical sight—connecting Him with His earthly father, mother, and siblings—and that is where they stopped. But there were some things that their physical sight could not reveal to them. There are people who are blinded because of their eyes. If one is to be able to see spiritually, one cannot depend on what one sees physically. Physical sight can be deceptive at times and should never be the measure of drawing conclusions.

There's an old saying, "Believe only half of what you see and none of what you hear." We should not draw conclusions based solely on what we see. Appearances can be deceiving and should not always be used as final evidence. Jesus understood the Law of having the testimony of two witnesses. Jesus had His heavenly Father to substantiate His claims. However, Jesus said, "I bear witness of Myself, and My Father does too."

If they had known Him, they would have known His Father. God stands as the witness for the Son, and this can be seen throughout Scripture. When John the Baptist baptized Jesus in the Jordan River, the voice of God said, "This is my beloved Son." On the Mount of Transfiguration, when Peter said, "It is good for us to be here…," God said, "This is my beloved Son in whom I am well pleased; hear ye him." The Father stands up for the Son as His witness. Though Jesus was under the threat of death, He continued His ministry in public (see John 7:26). But they could do nothing to Him because "his hour was not yet come" (see John 7:6, 8, 30). They could not arrest Him, try Him, punish Him, or kill Him until "his hour" came. Nothing happens but that which is according to the perfect timing of God. Let us always remember that "Everything occurs on time!"

## C. Seeing Is Believing
*(John 12:44-46)*

**Jesus cried and said, He that believeth on me, believeth not on me, but on him that sent me. And he that seeth me seeth him that sent me. I am come a light into the world, that whosoever believeth on me should not abide in darkness.**

There is an old adage that goes "Seeing is believing." That is to say, if we see something, we can believe it. Eyes can be deceiving; however, the "seeing" that is being used here is seeing from the spiritual perspective. Those who believe in Him do not believe in what they see; rather, they are believing in what they don't see, which is the One who sent Him. Jesus shows to the world His deity by saying, through implication, "I am God in the flesh. I am the express image of God in fullness. I AM THAT I AM"—in the Old Testament (Exodus 3:14); "I am the Way"—in the New Testament (John 14:6); and today, "I am the Light of the world." The Light in Jesus is the fullness of God, and without that Light, all would walk in darkness.

Seeing the Light of Christ in a believer is the ability to possess understanding and wisdom. Jesus has come so that no one would have to suffer in darkness; all one needs to do is believe in Him, and the Light will begin to shine. With the Light that leads, even if one cannot physically see one can know the way. This Light never goes out and needs no replacement. It is guaranteed to last forever. The only way one can overcome darkness is through belief in the One who is the Light of the world—for in Him, there is no darkness. With so much darkness expressed in unbelief, ignorance, and spiritual blindness, He gave His listeners another chance to embrace Him as the light. In these three verses, the word "believeth" is emphasized. Jesus did not want them or us to "abide in darkness." In verses 35-36, He stressed that He, "the light," would not be long with them. He challenged them to "walk while ye have the light." The urgency of the opportunity is expressed (see 2 Corinthians 6:2).

## III. Concluding Reflections

One of life's greatest tragedies is for people to live in darkness when they could live in the light. A woman named Rose Crawford had been blind for fifty years. Then she had an operation in a hospital in Ontario, Canada. The operation was successful. Rose wept tears of joy when—for the first time in her life—her eyes beheld a beautiful world of form and color. Interestingly, at least two decades of the half century Rose had spent in blindness had been unnecessary. At the age of thirty, she hadn't known that surgical techniques had been developed that could restore her vision. She had assumed there was nothing that could be done for her condition. So much of her life could have been different, had she known the truth.

When we know and receive the truth about salvation through Jesus Christ, we are no longer in darkness. Still, Scripture states that there are people who love darkness rather than light. The probability for stumbling is great for one who chooses to walk in darkness. But the one who chooses to walk by the aid of the light walks with sure footing because, there, his or her path is illuminated. The 'Light' of Christ illuminates understanding and wisdom in this dark world, and enlightens believers to the will and intentions of God.

## WORD POWER

**Follow (Greek: *Akoloutheo*)**—means "to be in the same way with a master, mentor, or leader." In Christian usage, it means "to follow with the intention of becoming like Christ."

## HOME DAILY BIBLE READINGS

for the week of January 28, 2007
*"I Am the Light of the World"*

Jan. 22, Monday
—Isaiah 35:3-10
—Promises for God's People

Jan. 23, Tuesday
—Matthew 4:12-17
—Jesus Brings Light

Jan. 24, Wednesday
—John 9:1-11
—Jesus Heals a Blind Man

Jan. 25, Thursday
—John 9:35-41
—Who Is the Son of Man?

Jan. 26, Friday
—Ephesians 5:15-21
—Knowing God's Will

Jan. 27, Saturday
—John 8:12-20
—Jesus Is the World's Light

Jan. 28, Sunday
—John 12:44-50
—I Have Come as Light

## PRAYER

*Our Father, we thank You for giving us the Light of the world. We are thankful because in Christ we are able to see where You are leading us. Keep us in the Light, O Lord, which guides us through this dark world. We pray in Jesus' name! Amen.*

**February 4, 2007**

Lesson 10

UNIT III
Christ Guides and Protects

# "I Am the Good Shepherd"

CHILDREN'S UNIT
We Believe in Jesus

**Adult Topic:** Protection from Evil
**Youth Topic:** Whose Sheep Are You?
**Children's Topic:** Jesus Protects Us

**Devotional Reading:** Isaiah 40:10-14
**Background Scripture:** John 10:1-18
**Print Passage:** John 10:1-5, 7-18

**KEY VERSE**

I am the good shepherd: the good shepherd giveth his life for the sheep.
—John 10:11

### John 10:1-5, 7-18—KJV

VERILY, VERILY, I say unto you, He that entereth not by the door into the sheepfold, but climbeth up some other way, the same is a thief and a robber.

2 But he that entereth in by the door is the shepherd of the sheep.

3 To him the porter openeth; and the sheep hear his voice: and he calleth his own sheep by name, and leadeth them out.

4 And when he putteth forth his own sheep, he goeth before them, and the sheep follow him: for they know his voice.

5 And a stranger will they not follow, but will flee from him: for they know not the voice of strangers.

. . . . .

7 Then said Jesus unto them again, Verily, verily, I say unto you, I am the door of the sheep.

8 All that ever came before me are thieves and robbers: but the sheep did not hear them.

9 I am the door: by me if any man enter in, he shall be saved, and shall go in and out, and find pasture.

10 The thief cometh not, but for to steal, and to kill, and to destroy: I am come that they might have life, and that they might have it more abundantly.

11 I am the good shepherd: the good shepherd giveth his life for the sheep.

12 But he that is an hireling, and not the shepherd, whose own

**OBJECTIVES**

Upon completion of this lesson, the students will know that:

1. Jesus, the Good Shepherd, provides spiritual protection for for those who trust in Him;

2. As the Good Shepherd, Jesus willingly gave His life for His sheep; and,

3. Believers can trust the voice of Jesus, the Good Shepherd, to protect them from spiritual danger.

the sheep are not, seeth the wolf coming, and leaveth the sheep, and fleeth: and the wolf catcheth them, and scattereth the sheep.

13 The hireling fleeth, because he is an hireling, and careth not for the sheep.

14 I am the good shepherd, and know my sheep, and am known of mine.

15 As the Father knoweth me, even so know I the Father: and I lay down my life for the sheep.

16 And other sheep I have, which are not of this fold: them also I must bring, and they shall hear my voice; and there shall be one fold, and one shepherd.

17 Therefore doth my Father love me, because I lay down my life, that I might take it again.

18 No man taketh it from me, but I lay it down of myself. I have power to lay it down, and I have power to take it again. This commandment have I received of my Father.

## UNIFYING LESSON PRINCIPLE

People seek protection from those elements that pose a threat to their well-being. Is it possible to find protection in our fearful world? Jesus uses the image of a shepherd to imply that He provides spiritual protection for people.

## POINTS TO BE EMPHASIZED ADULTS/YOUTH

**Adult/Youth Key Verse:** John 10:11
**Print Passage:** John 10:1-5, 7-18

—Shepherds were familiar figures in Palestine and were ever present to protect.
—In the Old Testament, God is pictured as a shepherd.
—Shepherding practices during biblical days provided the internal meaning of Jesus' story.
—The role of the shepherd paints a picture of the believer's relationship with Christ as leader, guide, and protector.

## CHILDREN

**Key Verse:** John 10:27
**Print Passage:** John 10:11-18

—Jesus presented Himself as The Good Shepherd appointed by God—in contrast to the self-appointed false shepherd.
—As the Good Shepherd, Jesus would willingly give His life for His sheep.
—Jesus clearly proclaimed His power over death through His willingness to lay down His life and His power to take it up again.

## TOPICAL OUTLINE OF THE LESSON

I. **INTRODUCTION**
   A. Safety from Peril Is Provided by Divine Providence
   B. Biblical Background

II. **EXPOSITION AND APPLICATION OF THE SCRIPTURE**
   A. Distinguishing the Shepherd from the Thief/Robber *(John 10:1-5)*
   B. The Intent of the Shepherd and the Thief/Robber *(John 10:7-11)*
   C. The Approved Shepherd *(John 10:12-18)*

III. **CONCLUDING REFLECTIONS**

## I. INTRODUCTION

### A. Safety from Peril Is Provided by Divine Providence

This lesson deals with the parable of the Good Shepherd. In this parable, Jesus explained the three major responsibilities of a shepherd: to protect the sheep; to lead the sheep; and to feed the sheep. The lesson today concentrates on the aspect of safety and protection.

The key element that should be grasped in this parable is that the shepherd is responsible for the sheep, so he shows his concern and care for them. The shepherd is Christ, who guides His sheep and watches them. But He is also concerned about those who get near them. The sheep are those who have professed belief in Christ, those who need a shepherd to lead and guide them. The next character the parable mentions is that of the thief. The thief is anyone who does not have the best interest of the sheep at heart; he or she seeks to deceive the sheep. It must be asserted that while the thief may be the devil or another entity, he is at the center of what happens; he uses various means of deception to blind the sheep, including using other sheep. What are the perils that the sheep face? The sheep may meet a predatory element that seeks to lead them away from the flock—and from the protection of the shepherd—to kill, steal, and destroy the sheep. The shepherd has to be knowledgeable regarding food and water supplies for the sheep, lest they die. That is why it is vital for the sheep to allow the shepherd to lead them.

### B. Biblical Background

The parable is a tool used by Jesus to illustrate spiritual truth; however, the parable is a metaphor that leads one into a relationship with Christ. In this parable, Jesus communicates His concern and care for the sheep; it is common knowledge that the shepherd continuously lays his life on the line for the sheep.

A shepherd has three major responsibilities: to lead, feed, and protect the sheep. At the forefront of these responsibilities is protecting the sheep. Therefore, in the parable, the shepherd carries a rod with a crook in it (see Psalm 23:4). The shepherd's protection deters thieves who seek to steal the sheep and destroy them; furthermore, the shepherd protects them from wild animals, as David did (1 Samuel 17:34-36).

The root meaning of the Greek word used here for shepherd (*poimhn*) means "to protect." Jesus applies it to Himself in verse 16 and implies it in verse 2. Jesus' describing Himself as the Good Shepherd draws a sharp contrast to His love and compassion for humanity versus the legalism offered by the Pharisees. Chapter 10 opens on the heels of Jesus having healed the man born blind. Instead of rejoicing at the man's blessing and praising Jesus for His mercy and kindness, the Pharisees responded with judgment and narrow, legalistic thinking.

The duties of a shepherd in open country like Palestine were quite arduous. Their job duties included leading the flock from the fold, marching ahead until they reached the spot where they were to be pastured. Here, he watched them all day, ever watchful of straying sheep and crafty predators. If for some reason any eluded his watch and wandered away, the shepherd would search diligently until he found them and brought them back. Sheep also require a generous water supply; the shepherd had to guide them either to a running stream or to wells dug in the wilderness and furnished with troughs. At night, he brought the flock home to the fold, counting them as they passed under the rod at the door to assure himself that none were missing. But his labors did not always end with sunset. He had to guard the fold through the dark hours from the attack of wild beasts or the wily attempts of the prowling thief.

Like the shepherds of ancient Palestine, Jesus is the Good Shepherd who cares for and protects His sheep.

## II. Exposition and Application of the Scripture

### A. Distinguishing the Shepherd from the Thief/Robber (John 10:1-5)

**Verily, verily, I say unto you, He that entereth not by the door into the sheepfold, but climbeth up some other way, the same is a thief and a robber. But he that entereth in by the door is the shepherd of the sheep. To him the porter openeth; and the sheep hear his voice: and he calleth his own sheep by name, and leadeth them out. And when he putteth forth his own sheep, he goeth before them, and the sheep follow him: for they know his voice. And a stranger will they not follow, but will flee from him: for they know not the voice of strangers.**

Jesus provided believers with guidelines for distinguishing the shepherd from the thief. The first distinguishing characteristic of the thief is that he does not enter at the door; he finds some other way in which to enter. Since thieves do not want to be caught, they often use an alternate means of entry in order to avoid detection. Thieves generally work through the means of stealth. This is how the enemy works; the enemy is anyone who seeks to destroy God's people. The enemy desires to come in without being noticed so that he can overwhelm unsuspecting sheep. Jesus alerted believers to the tricks and the deceptions of the thief so that they would not be deceived.

In contrast to the thief, the shepherd enters at the door. He does not need to find a way to enter other than the door, for his intentions are honorable and without deception. In fact, Jesus says that the porter, or the one responsible for watching the door, actually opens the door to the shepherd. This is crucial because it implies that the porter knows the shepherd and his motives, so he freely opens the door for him and the sheep. The shepherd and the porter working cooperatively is characteristic of how the Godhead works in tandem.

The next distinguishing characteristic is voice recognition. The sheep are sensitive to the voice and even the steps of the shepherd. The sheep know the shepherd's voice, as well as how He walks; therefore, they will not follow a stranger. Those who belong to the Lord know His voice. The Good Shepherd has a relationship with the sheep, and this relationship is demonstrated through His care for them.

The fact that the shepherd knows who belongs to him suggests a close relationship between the shepherd and his sheep. As for the thief, the sheep do not recognize his voice; therefore, when he approaches, the sheep move away from him. Likewise, believers in Christ have a relationship with Him that is intimate and endearing. When sheep have grown accustomed to the loving and caring ways of their shepherd, they will not follow a stranger. Compassion for helpless animals is a marked characteristic of biblical people. The birth of offspring in a flock often occurred far off on the mountainside. In these cases, the shepherd would carefully guard the mother during her helpless moments. Following the birth, the shepherd would pick up the lamb and carry it to the fold. For the few days until it was able to walk, he might carry it in his arms or in the loose folds of his coat. Jesus is concerned with keeping His sheep safe; He does not want the sheep to be deceived and walk away from the flock, putting themselves in harm's way.

### B. The Intent of the Shepherd and the Thief/Robber *(John 10:7-11)*

**Then said Jesus unto them again, Verily, verily, I say unto you, I am the door of the sheep. All that ever came before me are thieves and robbers: but the sheep did not hear them. I am the door: by me if any man enter in, he shall be saved, and shall go in and out, and find pasture. The thief cometh not, but for to steal, and to kill, and to destroy: I am come that they might have life, and that they might have it more abundantly. I am the good shepherd: the good shepherd giveth his life for the sheep.**

In these verses, Jesus transitioned the metaphor from being the shepherd to being the door. The door (Jesus Christ) knows that those that came before Him were both robbers and thieves. There is a difference between a thief and a robber; a thief is sneaky, and moves about quietly. The robber, on the other hand, will strong-arm. He is not sneaky; rather, he is bold and diabolical. There is no hidden agenda: he comes to rob, to take—and to do it all by force.

As the door, Jesus declared that if anyone enters through the door, he or she shall be saved and shall go in and out and find pasture (Psalm 23). Since Jesus is both Shepherd and door, it implies the completeness of His protection and guardianship. He trusted no other one to take care of His sheep. By being the door, Jesus ensures that the sheep safely abide.

The intent of the thief/robber is to kill, steal, and destroy. He wants to kill the sheep, he wants to steal the sheep, and he wants to destroy the future of the sheep. Jesus countered the thief's motives by saying that He has come that His sheep might have life, and have it more abundantly. The door allowed the sheep to come in and saves them from the thief/robber. In fact, behind the door is a place of safety. Jesus offers safety to all who come to Him.

Lastly, the intent of the Good Shepherd is to give His life for the sheep. Here,

Jesus spoke of the future events surrounding Him and His death. His commitment to the sheep is so intense that He would much rather lay down His life for the sheep than have any of them perish. The Good Shepherd desires that none would perish, but that all would come to repentance.

### C. The Approved Shepherd
(John 10:12-18)

**But he that is an hireling, and not the shepherd, whose own the sheep are not, seeth the wolf coming, and leaveth the sheep, and fleeth: and the wolf catcheth them, and scattereth the sheep. The hireling fleeth, because he is an hireling, and careth not for the sheep. I am the good shepherd, and know my sheep, and am known of mine. As the Father knoweth me, even so know I the Father: and I lay down my life for the sheep. And other sheep I have, which are not of this fold: them also I must bring, and they shall hear my voice; and there shall be one fold, and one shepherd. Therefore doth my Father love me, because I lay down my life, that I might take it again. No man taketh it from me, but I lay it down of myself. I have power to lay it down, and I have power to take it again. This commandment have I received of my Father.**

Jesus mentioned the hired workers that do not own any of the sheep, but are present because they are paid to do a job. Because they are merely earning a living, they are not totally concerned about the welfare of the sheep. This hireling sees the wolf and flees. He does not care for the sheep; he only cares for himself. This hireling may not be the devil. However, one can rest assured that the devil is at the core of the evil that happens.

Jesus was concerned about the sheep, and the relationship that they have. The truth of this statement was found in what Jesus said in verse 14: "I am the good shepherd, and know my sheep, and am known of mine." Jesus is personally and intimately involved with His sheep. His love for the sheep is mirrored by the love that He shared with His Father. The love He has for His Father moved Him to lay down His life for the world.

Jesus stated that He has other sheep that are not of the Jewish fold; there is another fold that will hear His voice, and there will be one fold and one shepherd. This other fold is considered to be the Gentiles, who would receive Him as their shepherd. The Good Shepherd, Jesus Christ, then made a statement of prophecy: He would lay down His life that He might take it up again. As the approved Shepherd, Jesus was willing to die for the sheep, not because people said that they would kill Him, but because He was obedient to His Father. The approved Shepherd gives life to His sheep through His death and resurrection.

### III. Concluding Reflections

A pastor who was leading a very difficult church had prayed that God would release him from his post. Even though he had prayed concerning accepting this charge, it had become unbearable to him. One day, another minister met with the troubled pastor and casually mentioned that he, too, would love to pastor some day. The beleaguered pastor replied that there was no hour like the present hour and literally gave his colleague the church without regard to his original calling! Having put the church in the hands of one who wanted the post, the liberated pastor went on his way.

Sometime later, the newly-liberated pastor ran into his colleague. The colleague confessed that he was seeking refuge by searching for a replacement and had not been at the church in several weeks. Hearing this, the former pastor returned with great reluctance.

While this story sounds incredible, it is true. The sad fact is that this local congregation had no real under-shepherd. They only had a hired hand. Because of this, many souls may have been lost or damaged because of their lack of true shepherding.

Unfortunately, many congregations seeking leadership are swayed by hirelings disguised by a charismatic personality and enlivened preaching and singing. However, a true shepherd can be recognized by whether he or she demonstrates a call to care for the needs of the flock, and not simply to entertain the flock.

## WORD POWER

**Abundance/Fullness (Greek: *Perissos*)**—this means "a life with advantage." It is a life of super abundance in quality. It is a life full of joy and protection. Compare this to the plan of Satan—who comes to steal, kill, and destroy. Satan will not negotiate his plan. Jesus did not make a promise that He would not fulfill (see John 10:10).

## HOME DAILY BIBLE READINGS

for the week of February 4, 2007
*"I Am the Good Shepherd"*

Jan. 29, Monday
—Isaiah 40:10-14
—God Tends His Flock
Jan. 30, Tuesday
—Ezekiel 34:1-6
—A Warning to False Shepherds
Jan. 31, Wednesday
—Ezekiel 34:11-16
—I Will Shepherd My Sheep
Feb. 1, Thursday
—Ezekiel 34:25-31
—You Are My Sheep
Feb. 2, Friday
—John 10:1-5
—The Sheep Know Their Shepherd
Feb. 3, Saturday
—John 10:7-11
—I Am the Good Shepherd
Feb. 4, Sunday
—John 10:12-18
—The Shepherd Suffers for the Sheep

## PRAYER

*Father, we thank You for the Good Shepherd, who protects us from those who intend to inflict harm on us. Lord, we thank You because You watch over us and keep us and guide us. Father, let us be ever so mindful of Your goodness and keep us in the path. We pray in the name of Jesus. Amen.*

**Lesson 11**

February 11, 2007

# "I Am the Resurrection and the Life"

**ADULT TOPIC:** Life After Death
**YOUTH TOPIC:** Life in Christ Conquers Death
**CHILDREN'S TOPIC:** Jesus Gives Us Life

---

**DEVOTIONAL READING:** Jude 17-23
**BACKGROUND SCRIPTURE:** John 11:1-44
**PRINT PASSAGE:** John 11:17-27

## John 11:17-27—KJV

17 Then when Jesus came, he found that he had lain in the grave four days already.

18 Now Bethany was nigh unto Jerusalem, about fifteen furlongs off:

19 And many of the Jews came to Martha and Mary, to comfort them concerning their brother.

20 Then Martha, as soon as she heard that Jesus was coming, went and met him: but Mary sat still in the house.

21 Then said Martha unto Jesus, Lord, if thou hadst been here, my brother had not died.

22 But I know, that even now, whatsoever thou wilt ask of God, God will give it thee.

23 Jesus saith unto her, Thy brother shall rise again.

24 Martha saith unto him, I know that he shall rise again in the resurrection at the last day.

25 Jesus said unto her, I am the resurrection, and the life: he that believeth in me, though he were dead, yet shall he live:

26 And whosoever liveth and believeth in me shall never die. Believest thou this?

27 She saith unto him, Yea, Lord: I believe that thou art the Christ, the Son of God, which should come into the world.

---

**UNIT III**
Christ Guides and Protects

**CHILDREN'S UNIT**
We Believe in Jesus

**KEY VERSE**

Jesus said unto her, I am the resurrection, and the life: he that believeth in me, though he were dead, yet shall he live.
—John 11:25

**OBJECTIVES**

**Upon completion of this lesson, the students will know that:**

1. Jesus taught that death is not a permanent reality for those who trust in Him;

2. Jesus' promise of resurrection for all believers can been seen in the resurrection of Lazarus; and,

3. Believers can find comfort in knowing that Jesus is with us as we face issues related to both life and death.

## UNIFYING LESSON PRINCIPLE

Everyone eventually experiences the death of a family member or acquaintance. What does Jesus teach about death? Jesus taught that death is not a permanent reality for those who have developed a personal relationship with Him through faith, because He has the power to overcome death.

## POINTS TO BE EMPHASIZED ADULTS/YOUTH

**Adult/Youth Key Verse:** John 11:25
**Print Passage:** John 11:17-27
—Martha was accusatory of Jesus for His late arrival and for the death of her brother.
—The Jews believed that one's soul stayed near the grave for three days in hopes that it could return to the body.
—The raising of Lazarus is often interpreted in light of Jesus' own resurrection from the dead.
—Jesus' close, personal relationship with Mary, Martha, and Lazarus reveals His humanity, while His raising of Lazarus demonstrates His power over the natural order.
—The Jews believed that the soul stayed near the body for three days, but left on the fourth day when decomposition set in.

## CHILDREN

**Key Verse:** John 11:25
**Print Passage:** John 11:1-4, 21-36, 38-44
—Even those who are close to Jesus are affected by sickness.
—Martha had faith in Jesus' ability to prevent death, but was not aware of His ability to reverse death.
—Jesus revealed through words and actions His power over life and death.

## TOPICAL OUTLINE OF THE LESSON

I. **INTRODUCTION**
   A. Dying to Live Again
   B. Biblical Background

II. **EXPOSITION AND APPLICATION OF THE SCRIPTURE**
   A. Jesus Arrives! *(John 11:17-20)*
   B. Martha Demonstrates Her Sorrow *(John 11:21-23)*
   C. Jesus Gives Life and Hope *(John 11:24-27)*

III. **CONCLUDING REFLECTIONS**

## I. INTRODUCTION

### A. Dying to Live Again

This lesson will examine a phase of theology called "eschatology." Eschatology is the study of last or final things, and plays a prominent role in New Testament teaching and religion. Therefore, it is incumbent upon all people, especially Christians, to take a serious look at life and, equally as important, death.

Death is not always easy to accept, especially when the one who died made an impact on the lives of other people. The death of Lazarus was no different. Not only was he the only brother of Mary and Martha, he was also a beloved friend of Jesus. Imagine the emptiness that was felt by the sisters. Jesus felt their pain, but He also saw beyond their sorrow—He saw resurrection.

Jesus used the death of Lazarus to teach His disciples an invaluable lesson—death is not the conclusion for those in Christ. Jesus sees death as merely the passageway to eternal life. Knowing that Christ abides within makes death a welcomed visitor to those who believe in Him. When one experiences a full life, that is wonderful, but the beauty of living is dying, to live again.

### B. Biblical Background

The gospel of John redefines death and life in relationship to Jesus. In the fourth gospel, especially, the very way that hearers respond to Jesus is a matter of life and death (see John 5:24). The account of Lazarus's resurrection from the dead makes this point rather dramatically. It was upon Lazarus's death that Jesus proclaimed Himself the resurrection and the life, and that all those who believe in Him shall never die.

Rising from the dead to live again was a belief that was held among many of the Israelites, although it was not a universal conviction. It was a more important article of faith among the Christians, as Paul argued in 1 Corinthians 15. Resurrection is not only projected in the New Testament, but further investigation of this subject unearths that it was written of in the Old Testament. Several Old Testament passages address the concept of resurrection prior to Christ's appearance in the flesh, including Psalm 71:20 and Hosea 13:14. However, most biblical references to the Resurrection are found in the New Testament (Matthew 28; Mark 16:1-14; Luke 24:1-46; John 11:1-44; 20:1-31; 1 Thessalonians 4:13-18).

The New Testament distinctively defines human life, death, and resurrection in light of Jesus' life, death, and resurrection. Thus, death is distinguished from its normal context at the end of life and placed in the very middle of life—in Christ we die and are raised as we commit our lives to Him. Looking at death and resurrection from a Christian perspective gives those who believe in Christ hope that leads to life everlasting.

## II. Exposition and Application of the Scripture

### A. Jesus Arrives! *(John 11:17-20)*

**Then when Jesus came, he found that he had lain in the grave four days already. Now Bethany was nigh unto Jerusalem, about fifteen furlongs off: And many of the Jews came to Martha and Mary, to comfort them concerning their brother. Then Martha, as soon as she heard that Jesus was coming, went and met him: but Mary sat still in the house.**

People die all the time; but the pain of death is felt more keenly when it is a member of the family or a close friend. The death of a brother or a sister is usually quite sorrowful. This sorrow can be increased if the sibling was the only brother or sister that person had. Martha and Mary were stricken with grief because of the death of their only brother. There were people who arrived at their house to comfort both Martha and Mary, but they were not the people whom they were looking to receive. Martha and Mary were hoping for Jesus to come! They waited four days for Jesus to arrive, and finally, on that fourth day, He showed up. When Martha heard that Jesus was coming, she couldn't wait for Him to come to the house; she was so anxious that she went to meet Him.

By contrast, Mary stayed at home. In the *King James Version*, the word *still* is italicized, indicating that it is not original to the text but is added for amplification and understanding. That Mary *sat still in the house* may refer to her having taken the common posture of grief among the Jews—that of sitting (see Job 2:8; Ezekiel 8:14). At times, this grief posture was so intense that the grieving person was rendered immovable or transfixed. John may have used this expression to convey that the depth of Mary's grief rendered her unable to move (see also Ezra 9:3,4; Nehemiah 1:4; Isaiah 47:1).

Martha's grief was more visible. She suggested to Jesus that if He had been there, her brother would not have died. Misplaced blame is often a part of the grieving process. Jesus didn't fire back a retort, nor did He rebuke her. Instead, He was moved to comfort her by telling her that her brother would live again.

Two things happened when Jesus arrived. First, Jesus paid attention to Martha's grief and pain. Jesus knows the pain of grief. He hurts with those who hurt; He suffers with those who suffer. In fact, He cares and is willing to assist with the pain. The second thing that happened was that Jesus comforted her by telling her that her brother would live again. He would have had limited opportunity to use this teaching, had she not been familiar with some teaching on resurrection prior to this painful period. Even as Jesus comforted her, Martha still felt the pain of loss, which blinded her to what Jesus was really trying to tell her.

Feelings of loss can interrupt one's life and restrict the desire to engage in even the simplest activity. Even while we are in sorrow, Jesus still seeks to comfort our grief. He wants to comfort and put at ease those who need to experience relief from their afflictions.

Lastly, Jesus will help to calm the anxiety that accompanies those who are grieving. Whenever someone important to us passes away, we are often left with feelings of uncertainty regarding the future. A child may wonder what life will be like without a parent. A bereaved spouse may wonder about his or her ability to raise a child as a single parent. The sudden death of a pastor may cause a church in the middle of a building program to wonder about its future.

While it is normal, even healthy, to grieve the loss of a loved one, Jesus desires that we look beyond this life to the future

He has in store for those who believe in Him. He seeks to instill confidence in His ability to give life even after death. This is what He sought to do with Martha during their discussion.

## B. Martha Demonstrates Her Sorrow (John 11:21-23)

**Then said Martha unto Jesus, Lord, if thou hadst been here, my brother had not died. But I know, that even now, whatsoever thou wilt ask of God, God will give it thee. Jesus saith unto her, Thy brother shall rise again.**

Martha's sorrow was demonstrated through her words: "Lord, if you had been here, my brother would not have died" (John 11:32, NRSV). This statement suggests that her grief was personal, because even though she had a sister, she didn't say *our* brother—she said, *my* brother. When people experience grief, they usually take it personally: the loss is felt in a most personal and intimate way. Nobody's grief or suffering is more debilitating than their own. Martha did not get indignant with Jesus; however, her voice suggested that she was hurting. She knew that if Jesus would speak to the Father, He would give Him what He asked. She was hurting and wanted her pain alleviated.

The Jewish Mishnah teaches that the soul stays near the body for three days. And on the fourth day, after the body sinks into decomposition, the soul finally faces reality and departs. The fact that Lazarus had been in the tomb four days meant that, according to Jewish thought, the situation was hopeless. Lazarus's soul had departed and there was no way Jesus could perform a healing miracle now. Given this belief, Martha's words in verse 22 indicate her faith in Jesus, despite her pain and lack of understanding. Apparently, Martha still had a glimmer of faith that Jesus possessed the power to go to the Father and receive whatever He asked for—including breathing life into a hopeless situation.

Not every believer could stand next to a brother's grave and express the type of faith in God that Martha did. Her statement was that she believed that Jesus could raise her brother, but also that she would trust Jesus even if He didn't. A woman was talking to a friend whose young son had cancer. Seeking to encourage the mother, she said, "Perhaps God will be good and heal your son." The mother replied, "God is good whether he heals my son or not." That is what Martha was saying: "Even now I believe that You can do anything."

Jesus responded that her brother would live again. Martha could not see the here-and-now, but by faith she saw the hereafter. It is difficult to see the now when one is consumed by grief. There are times when a person's need is urgent. There are times when one needs Jesus to come right now and ease the pain. The future was the resurrection of those who die in Christ. Jesus was not speaking of the future but the right now. Jesus wanted to immediately impact her life by giving back the life of her brother.

The friendship that existed between Christ and this family was genuine. Jesus stayed at their house, He ate with them, and He, too, was affected by the death of Lazarus—even though He would soon change the situation.

## C. Jesus Gives Life and Hope
(John 11:24-27)

**Martha saith unto him, I know that he shall rise again in the resurrection at the last day. Jesus said unto her, I am the resurrection, and the life: he that believeth in me, though he were dead, yet shall he live: And whosoever liveth and believeth in me shall never die. Believest thou this? She saith unto him, Yea, Lord: I believe that thou art the Christ, the Son of God, which should come into the world.**

When one is grieving, hope often seems distant. However, in the midst of Martha's grief, Jesus brought her hope. Jesus makes this audacious statement: "I am the resurrection and the life." That is to say, Jesus is not only hope, but also the life that she was seeking.

In the initial conversation between Martha and Jesus, Martha had hoped that Jesus would have been there earlier to intervene. But, in this second part of their conversation, Martha has a different response concerning the death of her brother—hope in God's promises. Martha answered, "I know he will rise again in the resurrection at the last day." Martha probably knew from Daniel 12 that in the last day, those whose names are found in the book will be delivered. She probably also remembered God's promises in Isaiah 65:17, 19 (NIV): "Behold, I will create new heavens and a new earth….the sound of weeping and of crying will be heard in it no more."

Although she grieved, Martha did not have to worry, because Jesus was present to restore life. Her brother was dead, but the resurrection that she hoped for in the future would be made manifest in the now.

After hearing Jesus' statement, Martha confessed her belief that He is the Christ, the Son of God. The Son of God is humanity's hope for life. Without Him, hope in eternal life is non-existent. Most, if not all, people have experienced a sense of hopelessness. Death and dying have a way of making people feel that way; however, Jesus is committed to those who believe in Him. Hope in Him leads to life—in the present and in the future

Lastly, the hope of life after death is what all believers have to look forward to. It is through this belief that one keeps trusting and believing in Christ. No matter how life looks, every believer is encouraged by the Christ, who is the "I AM" of all life—the Bread of Life, the Good Shepherd, the Way, the Truth, and the Life—and in today's lesson, the Resurrection and the Life.

## III. Concluding Reflections

John 11 reveals that Jesus deals sensitively with the pain of those for whom He cares. This is a good lesson for those who offer fast judgments on the lives of others. Everyone experiences grief from a variety of "deaths" in life, not just physical ones—death of a marriage, death of a career, death of a reputation, death of physical vitality, death of mental agility, and so forth.

Jesus is the door to life—both a full and abundant life on earth, and when we leave earth headed for our eternal home: heaven. When we place our faith in Him and what He did on Calvary, then we have the hope He offers to all who will take it. Our hope cannot be found in trying to live a good life. Our hope for eternity lies neither within us nor in anything we can do, but in Christ alone. Hope is available for everyone, through Jesus.

There are a number of popular thinkers who suggest that everyone who dies will be allowed to enter heaven. This status is given to all, according to the popular opinion, regardless of belief or lifestyle. There was a rap song recorded in the mid-1990's that contemplated the eschatological question, "Do G's (ganstas) go to heaven?"

Everybody who dies does not go to a better place. Belief in Jesus as the source of resurrection is what makes the difference in where one spends eternity. This truth must be proclaimed, for it will make the difference for those who want to live in the age that will never end.

## WORD POWER

**Resurrection (Greek:** *anastasis*)—two words: *ana* means "up"; *histemi* means "to cause to stand." Jesus Christ says, "I am the author of resurrection. I will cause anyone who believes in me to stand up on that day." There will be a physical standing up from death. That is real resurrection.

## HOME DAILY BIBLE READINGS

for the week of February 11, 2007
*"I Am the Resurrection and the Life"*

Feb. 5, Monday
—Jude 17–24
—Christ Offers Eternal Life

Feb. 6, Tuesday
—Proverbs 8:22-32
—The Way of Righteousness

Feb. 7, Wednesday
—John 11:1-7
—Jesus Delays

Feb. 8, Thursday
—John 11:8-16
—Jesus Goes to Bethany

Feb. 9, Friday
—John 11:17-27
—I Am the Resurrection

Feb. 10, Saturday
—John 11:28-37
—Jesus Comforts Mary

Feb. 11, Sunday
—John 11:38-44
—Jesus Raises Lazarus

## PRAYER

*Father, thank You for life, and our existence; we ask that You will teach us how to live, so that we can die only to live again. Our hope is in Christ, who is the giver of life to all those who believe on Him. We believe in the Resurrection, and we look forward to living with You and reigning with You. Help us to love You more than life itself, so that our lives become an extension of the hope we have in Your Son Jesus. Again, we thank You and praise Your name, for we pray this in Jesus' name. Amen.*

**February 18, 2007**

## Lesson 12

# "I Am the Way, the Truth, and the Life"

**UNIT III**
Christ Guides and Protects

**CHILDREN'S UNIT**
We Believe in Jesus

ADULT TOPIC: A Guide for Life
YOUTH TOPIC: Jesus Is the Way
CHILDREN'S TOPIC: Jesus Shows Us the Father

**KEY VERSE**

Jesus saith unto him, I am the way, the truth, and the life: no man cometh unto the Father, but by me.—John 14:6

DEVOTIONAL READING: Ephesians 4:17-24
BACKGROUND SCRIPTURE: John 14:1-14
PRINT PASSAGE: John 14:1-14

### John 14:1-14—KJV

LET NOT your heart be troubled: ye believe in God, believe also in me.

2 In my Father's house are many mansions: if it were not so, I would have told you. I go to prepare a place for you.

3 And if I go and prepare a place for you, I will come again, and receive you unto myself; that where I am, there ye may be also.

4 And whither I go ye know, and the way ye know.

5 Thomas saith unto him, Lord, we know not whither thou goest; and how can we know the way?

6 Jesus saith unto him, I am the way, the truth, and the life: no man cometh unto the Father, but by me.

7 If ye had known me, ye should have known my Father also: and from henceforth ye know him, and have seen him.

8 Philip saith unto him, Lord, shew us the Father, and it sufficeth us.

9 Jesus saith unto him, Have I been so long time with you, and yet hast thou not known me, Philip? he that hath seen me hath seen the Father; and how sayest thou then, Shew us the Father?

10 Believest thou not that I am in the Father, and the Father in me? the words that I speak unto you I speak not of myself: but the Father that dwelleth in me, he doeth the works.

**OBJECTIVES**

Upon completion of this lesson, the students will know that:

1. Jesus is the Way, and believers can trust that all direction for life is found through Him;
2. God's purpose for sending Jesus into the world was to show us the way to His truth; and,
3. Believers can trust Jesus' promise to fulfill whatever is asked in His name, in concert with the will of the Father.

11 Believe me that I am in the Father, and the Father in me: or else believe me for the very works' sake.

12 Verily, verily, I say unto you, He that believeth on me, the works that I do shall he do also; and greater works than these shall he do; because I go unto my Father.

13 And whatsoever ye shall ask in my name, that will I do, that the Father may be glorified in the Son.

14 If ye shall ask any thing in my name, I will do it.

## UNIFYING LESSON PRINCIPLE

We all at some time have been lost or needed direction, either physically or spiritually. Where can we turn for guidance at those times? Jesus says He is the way and all other directions for life are to be found through Him.

## POINTS TO BE EMPHASIZED
## ADULTS/YOUTH

**Adult/Youth Key Verse:** John 14:6
**Print Passage:** John 14:1-14

—The Jews believed that there are different levels of life in heaven; "many rooms" imply that there is plenty of space in heaven for everyone.
—A Greek word used to describe Jesus is "prodromos" (Hebrews 6:20). In the Roman army, the prodromoi were the reconnaissance troops that went ahead of the main army.
—In the statement to Thomas (verse 6), Jesus combines three of the great basics of the Jewish religion.
—Jesus comforts His disciples shortly before He is arrested and condemned to death.
—Believers can see the works of God through the Son Jesus.

## CHILDREN

**Key Verse:** John 14:9
**Print Passage:** John 14:1-14

—According to Jesus, there is abundant room in the Father's kingdom for all who belong to Him.
—Jesus promised that He is preparing an eternal home for His disciples and that He will come back for them.
—Jesus' accomplishments provide adequate proof that the Father was and is in Him and He is in the Father.
—Jesus' access to the Father provides Christians with the privilege of making requests of the Father.

## TOPICAL OUTLINE OF THE LESSON

I. INTRODUCTION
   A. A Sure Guide for Life
   B. Biblical Background

II. EXPOSITION AND APPLICATION OF THE SCRIPTURE
   A. Jesus Comforts the Disciples *(John 14:1-2)*
   B. Jesus Offers Directions and Directives *(John 14:3-9)*
   C. The Results of Belief *(John 14:10-14)*

III. CONCLUDING REFLECTIONS

## I. INTRODUCTION
### A. A Sure Guide for Life

A well-known actress once made the following comment on her beliefs about religion and spirituality: "I consider myself a spiritual person. I believe in an idea of God, although it's my own personal ideal. I find most religions interesting, and I've been to every kind of denomination: Catholic, Christian, Jewish, Buddhist. I've taken bits from everything and customized it." The sentiment of this young actress mirrors what many in our modern society do—they pick and choose parts of different faith systems to create their own beliefs and practices. Why do human beings feel free to pick and choose their beliefs like a religious smorgasbord? Such arrogant thinking emanates out of the fact that our society denies the existence of absolute Truth.

This lesson will deal with directions, directives, and the Director of one's life. In either an active or a latent way, everyone's life incorporates these three things. The intent of this lesson is to steer learners to the right Director, the one Director, who will give believers the right directives and point them in the right direction. Jesus, as the Director, seeks to lead all those who will follow to heaven, as only He can. Anyone who is going to make it to heaven needs to understand that the Director knows the way; He is the Way.

### B. Biblical Background

This passage of Scripture is often read at funerals because it offers comfort to those who are grieving the loss of a loved one. There is nothing more soothing than these words of Jesus: "Let not your hearts be troubled." They have the power to take all of the sorrow and the sadness out, because they give all who will hear a point of reference on which to focus. Jesus wants His believers to focus on His truth—the truth—rather than on death, or on what one believes.

John 14:6 contains a figure of speech unique to the Greek language and one that does not translate into English very well. In most English versions of the Bible, Jesus reveals, "I am the way *and* the truth and the life." In understanding these words in English, the insertion of "and" doesn't appear to enhance the meaning of Jesus' words. In fact, it may even seem redundant. However, there is an expression in Greek which involved this phrase; the way, truth, and life are not co-equal terms. Instead, truth and life describe what the way is. In essence, Jesus is the way to truth and life. According to the *Concordia Study Bible* (Concordia Publishing House, 1986), Jesus was saying: "I am the way [to the father] in that I am the truth and the life."[1] The difference is subtle, but apparent.

In order to adequately explain the impact of Jesus' words in John 14, the previous chapter must be referenced. In John 13, the disciples experienced the exaltation of the Passover meal with the Savior, their Last Supper, the perplexing exit of Judas from their midst, and the confusing conversation of Jesus. They thought that they would always be with Him, but His words to them signaled a departure from them that they had not anticipated. In the latter portion of John 13, Peter not only expressed his gross misunderstanding of the love ethic of Jesus, but also how he would miss the mark. Even though Peter declared that he would lay down his own life to defend Jesus, Jesus asserted that Peter would thrice deny him.

This was the backdrop to the gracious words spoken in John 14. John 13 speaks of death; John 14 speaks of Life. John 13 deals with temporary trouble. John 14 deals with permanent solutions.

## II. Exposition and Application of the Scripture

### A. Jesus Comforts the Disciples

*(John 14:1-2)*

**Let not your heart be troubled: ye believe in God, believe also in me. In my Father's house are many mansions: if it were not so, I would have told you. I go to prepare a place for you.**

John 14 begins with wonderful words of comfort, "Let not your heart be troubled, ye believe in God; believe also in me." This was a direct word of comfort spoken to Peter and the other disciples who desperately needed clarity for their confusion. This clarity would come from their belief in God and Jesus. The Greek word translated "believe" in verse 1 is *pisteuo*; it suggests trust or faith in someone or something. Another emphasis of the text is to have confidence in God and Jesus. The urgency of Jesus' words and the impending hour of His passion strongly suggest the imperative mood of the verb. Jesus could give such a speech to His disciples because they had seen Him deliver in strange and various circumstances. He who was the apex of belief in God could urge others by both precept and example, for His very life breathed belief in His Father.

Jesus' promise of mansions also offered comfort to those who had followed Him from place to place without so much as the comforts of foxes and birds. The mansions, or places of abode, of which Jesus spoke have been prepared as a result of His leaving the earthly realm. The Greek word, *hetoimazo*, is a verb that is translated "prepare" in this text. *Strong's New Testament Lexicon* suggests two applications of this verb. First, it is drawn from the Eastern custom of sending workers to level the roads and make them passable prior to royalty making their journeys. Secondly, it suggests that it takes mental preparation for us to give the Messiah a fit reception and secure His blessing. Here, it is not the servants who are sent to make the way passable for the King. In Jesus' case, it is the King who makes the way passable for His servants. What an awesome statement of comfort! Once our human minds are prepared, we can adequately and completely receive the Messiah. However, it is through the initiative of God that such action takes place. Jesus made it clear that He was not abandoning them. Instead, He was providing new opportunity.

### B. Jesus Offers Directions and Directives (John 14:3-9)

And if I go and prepare a place for you, I will come again, and receive you unto myself; that where I am, there ye may be also. And whither I go ye know, and the way ye know. Thomas saith unto him, Lord, we know not whither thou goest; and how can we know the way? Jesus saith unto him, I am the way, the truth, and the life: no man cometh unto the Father, but by me. If ye had known me, ye should have known my Father also: and from henceforth ye know him, and have seen him. Philip saith unto him, Lord, shew us the Father, and it sufficeth us. Jesus saith unto him, Have I been so long time with you, and yet hast thou not known me, Philip? he that hath seen me hath seen the Father; and how sayest thou then, Shew us the Father?

Besides offering comfort, Jesus offers direction. The Master Teacher offered His disciples guidance that would comfort them to help them overcome the anxiety that they were feeling. There is nothing like experiencing anxiety without direction or a course of action. It can be frustrating, it can be scary, and it can be overwhelming. The good news is that no one has to go through the frustration of experiencing anxious moments without help; Jesus gives those who will believe the direction they need to make it. First, He tells His believers not to worry; He is coming back to receive all those who believe in Him. Essentially, Jesus is saying: "Wait for me; I know that trouble may fill your heart, but know this: I am coming back." This is a point of assurance; the direction or the guidance He gives is to assure believers that He is coming back. There are those who will challenge that guidance, but every believer in Him needs to trust Him and hold fast to what the Lord has said—"Just wait."

Secondly, Jesus invites all who will receive Him to follow so that they will know where to go. A person cannot know the way to his or her destination unless he or she pays attention to the Way. When a person is willing to follow the Way, Christ directs them to Truth and to Light. Therefore, every believer who follows Christ is walking in truth and light—for Jesus is the Way, the Truth, and the Life.

Finally, Jesus directs them to know that He is God! Belief in Jesus is connected to belief in God. If one wants to be headed in the right direction, it is contingent on his or her belief. All Christians have to believe this in order for them to experience eternal life. This should be the end result of the Christian's belief—to experience eternal life. Christ offers this direction; those who are in Christ simply need to follow where He is leading.

### C. The Results of Belief (John 14:10-14)

Believest thou not that I am in the Father, and the Father in me? the words that I speak unto you I speak not of myself: but the Father that dwelleth in me, he doeth the works. Believe me that I am in the Father, and the Father in me: or else believe me for the very works' sake. Verily, verily, I say unto you, He that believeth on me, the works that I do shall he do also; and greater works than these shall he do; because I go unto my Father. And whatsoever ye shall ask in my name, that will I do, that the Father may be glorified in the Son. If ye shall ask any thing in my name, I will do it.

What is the end result of belief? Many children believe that when they lose a tooth, if they put it under their pillow the tooth fairy will come and replace the tooth with money. During Christmas, children believe that if they have been good the whole year that Santa will leave presents under the tree for them after they have gone to sleep. These beliefs are based on myths; they have no truth to sustain them. They are used to illustrate that every belief is rooted in one's desire for positive results. However, belief in Christ is different. He has promised that if we believe in Him we can ask for anything and He will do it. Belief is the ability to trust without hesitation—to have confidence without doubt. This is necessary if one is to see the results of one's belief. Notice that, in verse 12, Jesus stated that as a result of their belief, those who believe shall do even greater works than He. All Christians should look forward to the results of their belief, because Jesus promises that great things will manifest.

Faith must be at work if one is to experience results. In whom or what should one have faith? Faith in Jesus is essential to experiencing eternal life. Every believer must understand that obstacles will seek to impede the progress of the faithful. But when believers are relentless and determined to experience the results that faith brings, we can do all things according to His will. Jesus said that whatever we ask in His name, He would do. Nothing is impossible for one who has faith in the Lord, for He makes the impossible possible.

Even having the assurance of His promise, however, there are times when our faith becomes shaky. At one time or another, most believers experience a faith shortage; however, believers should always consider the Christ who places before every person the opportunity to experience the hope of eternal life.

## III. Concluding Reflections

Jesus has given us a unique promise and an exclusive claim. Jesus bridges the gap between God and humanity by being both fully God and fully human. Jesus has become the bridge that fills the gap, and He is the promise that offers us direction for life. Jesus is our path through the difficulties and trials of life. Jesus cleared us a path that cuts through the power of sin and the penalty of death. Jesus is the Way, and He is our guide for a divine direction.

Living in a diverse, pluralistic society is often challenging. This is especially true for modern Christians. The question is often raised as to how one may be respectful of the claims of others without compromising the claims of Christianity. But Jesus' bold claim does not fit within our pluralistic society that encourages tolerance of all beliefs. Jesus unapologetically postures Himself as the Way, the Truth, and the Life—not a way, a truth, and a life. But He did not stop there; Jesus also said that no one would come to the Father God except through Him. Jesus leaves no room for the inclusive mentality that believes all paths will lead to God. Jesus' bold and awesome declaration stands in stark contrast to others because He, singularly, has resurrection power to back up His claim. No other religious leader or thinker has this trump. Thus, the modern Christian need not flinch. He is the Way!

Jesus makes an exclusive claim to the path to salvation; however, He leaves room for all to come to Him. Paul said in Romans 10:9-10: "If you confess with your mouth, 'Jesus is Lord,' and believe in your heart that God raised him from the dead, you will be saved. For it is with your heart that you believe and are justified, and it is with your mouth that you confess and are saved."

## WORD POWER

**Forerunner (Greek: *sprodromos*)**—Hebrews 6:20 uses this word to describe Jesus. In the Roman army, the *prodromoi* were the reconnaissance troops that went ahead of the main army to blaze a trail. As our *Prodromos*, Jesus has gone before us to prepare for us a place to abide with Him in heaven.

**Way, Truth, and Life**—these are three important words. Before each word is a definite article—*the*. Because each noun has the article attached to it, it emphasizes that there is no other way to God. No other religion has access to God. Definite articles make these nouns definite. The way to God is not pluralistic.

## HOME DAILY BIBLE READINGS

for the week of February 18, 2007
*"I Am the Way, the Truth, and the Life"*

Feb. 12, Monday
 —Hebrews 10:19-23
 —A New and Living Way
Feb. 13, Tuesday
 —John 18:33-40
 —Jesus Testifies to the Truth
Feb. 14, Wednesday
 —2 Timothy 1:8-14
 —Jesus Has Brought Life
Feb. 15, Thursday
 —Ephesians 4:17-24
 —Turn from Darkness
Feb. 16, Friday
 —3 John 2-8
 —Walking in the Truth
Feb. 17, Saturday
 —John 14:1-7
 —Jesus Is the Way
Feb. 18, Sunday
 —John 14:8-14
 —The Son Reveals the Father

## PRAYER

*God, we thank You for comforting us. We thank You for directing us when we lose our way. But Lord, we also thank You for teaching us how to receive results for believing in You. We ask that You would continue to help us to grow in wisdom so that we may continue to walk in truth and life. We pray this in Jesus' name. Amen.*

---

[1] http://www.sermoncentral.com/sermon.asp?SermonID=67340&ContributorID=3397

## Lesson 13

# "I Am the True Vine"

**February 25, 2007**

**ADULT TOPIC:** Secure Connections
**YOUTH TOPIC:** Connected to the Vine
**CHILDREN'S TOPIC:** Jesus Loves Me

**DEVOTIONAL READING:** Psalm 1
**BACKGROUND SCRIPTURE:** John 15:1-17
**PRINT PASSAGE:** John 15:1-17

### John 15:1-17—KJV

I AM the true vine, and my Father is the husbandman.

2 Every branch in me that beareth not fruit he taketh away: and every branch that beareth fruit, he purgeth it, that it may bring forth more fruit.

3 Now ye are clean through the word which I have spoken unto you.

4 Abide in me, and I in you. As the branch cannot bear fruit of itself, except it abide in the vine; no more can ye, except ye abide in me.

5 I am the vine, ye are the branches: He that abideth in me, and I in him, the same bringeth forth much fruit: for without me ye can do nothing.

6 If a man abide not in me, he is cast forth as a branch, and is withered; and men gather them, and cast them into the fire, and they are burned.

7 If ye abide in me, and my words abide in you, ye shall ask what ye will, and it shall be done unto you.

8 Herein is my Father glorified, that ye bear much fruit; so shall ye be my disciples.

9 As the Father hath loved me, so have I loved you: continue ye in my love.

10 If ye keep my commandments, ye shall abide in my love; even as I have kept my Father's commandments, and abide in his love.

## UNIT III
Christ Guides and Protects

## CHILDREN'S UNIT
We Believe in Jesus

## KEY VERSE

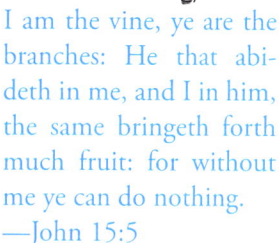

I am the vine, ye are the branches: He that abideth in me, and I in him, the same bringeth forth much fruit: for without me ye can do nothing.
—John 15:5

## OBJECTIVES

**Upon completion of this lesson, the students will know that:**

1. Being connected to Jesus is essential if we are to be productive in our lives;
2. God works in the lives of believers to nurture and prepare them to bear more fruit; and,
3. We receive the power to do good from our relationship with Jesus Christ.

11 These things have I spoken unto you, that my joy might remain in you, and that your joy might be full.

12 This is my commandment, That ye love one another, as I have loved you.

13 Greater love hath no man than this, that a man lay down his life for his friends.

14 Ye are my friends, if ye do whatsoever I command you.

15 Henceforth I call you not servants; for the servant knoweth not what his lord doeth: but I have called you friends; for all things that I have heard of my Father I have made known unto you.

16 Ye have not chosen me, but I have chosen you, and ordained you, that ye should go and bring forth fruit, and that your fruit should remain: that whatsoever ye shall ask of the Father in my name, he may give it you.

17 These things I command you, that ye love one another.

## UNIFYING LESSON PRINCIPLE

We are all born to be in relationships with others, and we need them to be productive. Is there a relationship that can serve as a model for all others? John says that being connected to Jesus is essential if we are to be productive in our lives.

## POINTS TO BE EMPHASIZED ADULTS/YOUTH

**Adult Key Verse:** John 15:5
**Youth Key Verse:** John 15:4
**Print Passage:** John 15:1-17

—As long as we stay connected to the vine (Jesus), we are capable of producing fruit.
—Jesus used the model of the vine, the vine grower, and the branches to talk about God (the vine grower), Jesus the Christ (the vine), and believers (the branches).
—The allegory of the vine defines Jesus' relationship with His followers.

## CHILDREN

**Key Verse:** John 15:9
**Print Passage:** John 15:1-17

—The vine, a symbol of the nation of Israel, was imprinted on Maccabean coins, and was an important part of Jewish imagery.
—God works in the lives of believers to posture them and prepare them to bear more fruit.
—The relationship of believers to Jesus Christ is pictured as branches to the vine.
—Our productivity as Christians is dependent on the maintenance of our relationship with Jesus Christ.
—The relationship that we have with God through Jesus Christ is a reality because Jesus Christ died for us.

## TOPICAL OUTLINE OF THE LESSON

I. INTRODUCTION
   A. Secure Connection
   B. Biblical Background

II. EXPOSITION AND APPLICATION OF THE SCRIPTURE
   A. The Need for Relationship *(John 15:1-8)*
   B. The Fruitful Vine *(John 15:9-12)*

C. The Fruit of Relationship
*(John 15:13-17)*

### III. CONCLUDING REFLECTIONS

### I. INTRODUCTION
#### A. Secure Connection

"Secure connection" has become a household phrase in recent years—most often used to describe a Web site or page that has been configured to minimize the possibility of intrusion by Internet hackers and predators. Two thousand years ago, Jesus used the example of a secure connection in nature to describe the surety of a relationship with Him. As a vine is to its branches, so believers are securely connected to our Savior.

As branches of the Master Vine, believers are not only connected to Christ, they are also connected to others. For various reasons, within these connections unhealthy relationships sometimes develop. This happens when branches get bruised or choked up by vines and are not immediately attended to. Thus, it is important, if not imperative, to do some weeding and pruning to save bruised branches or relationships. Pruning is sometimes painful, but it can serve to repair the relationship/connection. This is what happens to branches when they are connected to the vine. When a branch is not connected to the vine, it is cut off from the source of life, and sometimes has to be grafted in.

#### B. Biblical Background

The vine, a symbol of the nation of Israel, was imprinted on Maccabean coins. This was an important part of Jewish imagery. A great golden vine held a prominent place in the temple at the front of the holy place. The vines of Palestine were popular because of their abundant growth and for the immense clusters of grapes they produced. These were sometimes carried on a staff between two men, as in the case of the spies (Numbers 13:23), and this has been done in some instances in modern times. Although vines grew all over Palestine, they required a lot of attention. If left alone, a vine produced fruitless growth. The illustration of the vine and the branches is a graphic description of the union between Christ and Christians. There is a direct correlation between producing fruit and whatever is asked in Jesus' name.

The thought-provoking symbol of the vine in this parable suggests the relationship between Christ and the Christian, the fruit of which is love. This can be connected to what Paul said in his letter to the Galatians (see 5:22-23), which stated that the fruit of the Spirit is love. However, there are some by-products of that fruit, such as joy, peace, long-suffering, gentleness, goodness, faith, meekness, and temperance. The vine and the branches working together can bring forth fruit that can be seen in a number of forms.

## II. Exposition and Application of the Scripture

### A. The Need for Relationship
(John 15:1-8)

I am the true vine, and my Father is the husbandman. Every branch in me that beareth not fruit he taketh away: and every branch that beareth fruit, he purgeth it, that it may bring forth more fruit. Now ye are clean through the word which I have spoken unto you. Abide in me, and I in you. As the branch cannot bear fruit of itself, except it abide in the vine; no more can ye, except ye abide in me. I am the vine, ye are the branches: He that abideth in me, and I in him, the same bringeth forth much fruit: for without me ye can do nothing. If a man abide not in me, he is cast forth as a branch, and is withered; and men gather them, and cast them into the fire, and they are burned. If ye abide in me, and my words abide in you, ye shall ask what ye will, and it shall be done unto you. Herein is my Father glorified, that ye bear much fruit; so shall ye be my disciples.

When man was created in Genesis 1:26, he was created to be a relational being. In fact, after God created all of the creatures of the field, the fowl of the air, and the fish of the sea, He recognized that human beings needed companionship. Human beings have need for relationship, not only in the physical sense, but also in the spiritual sense in their relationship with the Lord. Jesus injects in John familiar symbolism of the vine, the branches and the gardener or husbandman. The Vine is Christ, the branches are the believers in Christ, and the Gardener is God.

Jesus distinguishes Himself as the True Vine. He is not like that wild vine that deceived Elijah's protégés who gathered the gourds from it (2 Kings 4).

The vine's connection to the branches is vital, for it is through this connection that the branches are nourished. The vine nourishes the branches through providing the branches with what they need to live. The branches move, live, and have their being because of the vine. If the branches are disconnected from the vine, the branches will wither and die. When one is disconnected from Christ, life will cease if he or she is not grafted back into the vine.

The vine and the branches are not the only things in relationship here; there is also a relationship between the branches. As long as these branches stay connected to one another, the relationship can be fruitful; however, when there is no connection between the branches, the relationship is bruised and needs immediate attention. The immediate attention that the branch needs will keep the branch from drying out and dying.

God, the Gardener, is responsible for caring for the branches. He sees the bruised branches and seeks to rectify the problem by pruning the branches. This is to say that those branches, which are disconnected from the vine and from the other branches, are pruned so they won't affect the other branches. God knows how to prune, and He makes no mistakes as it pertains to those who are dying because of their disconnection. That is why it is so necessary for the branches to abide in the vine—so that they can bear fruit.

A key issue in this relationship between the branch and the vine is the will of the branch to abide or live in the vine. Verse 7 notes that if one abides in Jesus then one has the right to ask for what one will. However, it is imperative that one abides in Him regardless of circumstance. Moreover, the word of Jesus must abide in the believer. Once the word abides in the believer, it controls one's heart, thinking, and actions. This inextricably ties the believer to the Lord in a dependent relationship where the will of the believer is subject to the will of the Vine, which is subject to the will of the Gardener. Some erroneously believe that one can simply ask for whatever he or she wants without regard to the will of God. Asking for things, thoughts, and desires is always subject to the veto power of the Vine, which is subject to the veto power of the Gardener. However, since the thinking of the branch is ultimately influenced by the Vine, he or she always seeks the guidance of the Vine.

**B. The Fruitful Vine** *(John 15:9-12)*

**As the Father hath loved me, so have I loved you: continue ye in my love. If ye keep my commandments, ye shall abide in my love; even as I have kept my Father's commandments, and abide in his love. These things have I spoken unto you, that my joy might remain in you, and that your joy might be full. This is my commandment, That ye love one another, as I have loved you.**

What does a fruitful branch look like? A fruitful branch is connected to the vine; therefore, as the vine nourishes the branches, the branches bring forth the fruit in its season. This connection is crucial because all of the branches exist in a network of feeding one another, as the vine sends nourishment to the whole. The gardener wants the branches to bring forth much fruit, but the only time this is possible is when the branches abide in the vine. This means that the connection between the branches and the vine determines the yield that can be expected.

In Palestine, after the grapes had set on the branches, the vines were pruned (Leviticus 25:4; Isaiah 18:5; John 15:1-2). This process produced stronger branches and a greater fruit yield. The pruned branches were useless except as fuel (see Ezekiel 15:2-8).

What happens to the branches that do not yield fruit? They are not productive because they are not working in relation to one another. They are not working together to use the strength and nourishment that comes from the vine. Somehow the connection between the branches is fractured. Therefore, the Gardener has to prune the branches; those that are not bringing forth fruit He throws into the fire. The fire symbolizes hell, and this suggests that God will have no tolerance for those who separate themselves from Him.

Two things are absolutely necessary to our salvation: first, that we remain closely connected to Christ by faith and love, and live in and for Him; second, that we continually receive from Him the power to do good. Not even the strongest, most fruitful branch can bear fruit by itself, through its own juice derived from the vine. And, as the branches cannot survive unless connected to and working in harmony with the Vine, neither can believers bear fruit without the True Vine.

What needs to be done to ensure the fruitfulness of the branches? There should be a sense of necessity among the branches: every branch should see that the other branches are important and vital to the plant as a whole. Nothing is more frustrating than to see those who should be bringing forth fruit—those who are talented and blessed—not living up to their potential. The potentiality of the branches is dependent upon the connection that exists amongst them.

It also must be understood that pruning is a necessary part of gardening. Growth cannot occur without occasional pruning, for there are deadened spots and dying leaves that are a part of every believer's life from time to time. Some issues that occur do not require destruction, but, rather, pruning.

### C. The Fruit of Relationship
*(John 15:13-17)*

**Greater love hath no man than this, that a man lay down his life for his friends. Ye are my friends, if ye do whatsoever I command you. Henceforth I call you not servants; for the servant knoweth not what his lord doeth: but I have called you friends; for all things that I have heard of my Father I have made known unto you. Ye have not chosen me, but I have chosen you, and ordained you, that ye should go and bring forth fruit, and that your fruit should remain: that whatsoever ye shall ask of the Father in my name, he may give it you. These things I command you, that ye love one another.**

Jesus' teaching that there is no greater love than to lay down one's life is utterly revolutionary. It not only flies in the face of conventional human thought, but it also provides a mode of relationship that is rare and special. After describing the close connection that must exist between Him and His disciples, Jesus further taught that His disciples are His friends if they keep His commandments. Notice Jesus described them as friends and not learners. This was a critical element that helped believers understand that dependency on Jesus is not designed to make them underlings; rather, it is to make us like Him.

What is the fruit of relationship? The fruit of relationship is found in the love that the branches have for the vine, and the love that the branches have for one another. A beautiful plant is full when there is unity between the branches and the vine. This is to say that all of the branches are nourished—none of the branches take from the other branches, but they share the nourishment that the vine gives. The plant, when there is much fruit on it, seems happy, and its colors are more vibrant; that is what love looks like. Love is full, vibrant, and refreshing.

These verses describe the many privileges that come as a result of the connection of the branches abiding in the vine. The *first privilege* (promotion) is for our possessions. We are called friends and no longer servants. The difference between the two is that friends are entitled to certain privileges—servants are not.

The *second privilege* (position and purpose) is for our participation. We are "chosen" and "ordained" by the Lord. The word "chosen," speaks of our position, and "ordained" speaks about purpose.

The *third privilege* (prayer) is for our provision—"Whatsoever ye shall ask of the Father in my name, he may give it you" (verse 16). Prayer is our greatest privilege. Asking the Father in His name is another important privilege, and it is designed that "he may give it you." When we ask in His name we line up with His will.

The fruit of relationship is love; therefore, one should remember what Paul has said about love and fruitfulness. In Galatians 5:22, Paul uses the term *fruit* of the Spirit. Notice that Paul does not use the plural version of fruit, which is often misread as fruits. He says "fruit," which suggests there is only one fruit, and that is love. These are by-products of love, which have long-lasting, far-reaching effects.

The church ought to demonstrate this love from branch to branch. The older saints used to say that love ought to flow from heart to heart and breast to breast; love should touch somebody. Love should govern our relationships and feed the hungry from the fruit on the branches.

## III. Concluding Reflections

When Jesus utilized the metaphor of the vine and the branches, He was giving further encouragement to His disciples. As they tried to deal with the announcement of His departure and all the ramifications related to it, He shared with them some of the richest truths and teachings of His ministry. Jesus had already introduced them to the Comforter (14:16), the Strengthener, and the Helper (the Holy Spirit), who is the Spirit of truth (14:17). He is called "the Holy Ghost" (14:26). His ministry would consist of dwelling with them and being "in" them (14:17). He will teach them all things and bring to their remembrance all the things that Jesus had taught them (14:26). It was Jesus' purpose not to leave them comfortless ("orphans"). The Holy Spirit would be the one who would protect, provide, and prepare for them, perfect them, and be productive through them.

When Jesus used the illustration of the vine and branches, He was presenting a dramatic picture of the nourishing, nurturing, protecting, and productive relationship between the vine and the branches. This relationship could also be considered essential.

This illustration was designed to give inspiration and further encouragement to the concerned and troubled disciples. The picture of this connectedness would encourage them to be faithful, as they are being fruitful. It would reassure them of the continued sustaining relationship between them and their Master. Hopefully, it has done the same for you as you have studied this awesome lesson.

One of the painful processes of life is pruning. Loss of jobs, relationship issues, deaths of loved ones, and catastrophic or degenerative illnesses can often be challenging issues that threaten us at the very core of our existence. Sometimes God Himself is the sender of such circumstances. However, His intent is never to destroy, but rather, to provide the privilege of growth and development.

Some find God in painful pruning periods. Others draw closer because they recognize their own limitations and need to be connected to the True Vine.

Have you been able to see His will for your life more clearly as the result of an episode of pruning? It is only through our connection to the True Vine that we are able to blossom and develop as we should in order to produce our maximum amount of fruit for the Kingdom.

## WORD POWER

**Without (Greek: *Ean + me*)**—the word "without" is derived from two Greek words: *ean,* which denotes uncertainty or impossibility, and *me,* which means "not." It also means, "God forbid." When the two words come together, *ean+me*, it translates as "virtually impossible." If one is not abiding in Christ, it is impossible to be a fruitful Christian (John 15:5).

## HOME DAILY BIBLE READINGS

for the week of February 25, 2007
*"I Am the True Vine"*

Feb. 19, Monday
—Matthew 13:18-33
—How the Word Grows
Feb. 20, Tuesday
—John 17:13-19
—Jesus Prays for His Followers
Feb. 21, Wednesday
—1 John 2:24-29
—Abide in Christ
Feb. 22, Thursday
—2 John 7-11
—Continue in Christ's Teachings
Feb. 23, Friday
—Psalm 1
—The Blessed
Feb. 24, Saturday
—John 15:1-8
—I Am the True Vine
Feb. 25, Sunday
—John 15:9-17
—Love One Another

## PRAYER

*Father, we thank You for relationship; we ask that our relationship with Jesus, Your Son, will allow us to show our love for those who are connected with us in life. We need to be free to connect with others to ensure that we become what You want us to be, so that we may bring forth the fruit. We pray that this fruit will bring You glory and glory to Your Son Jesus. We pray this in Jesus' name. Amen.*

# SPRING QUARTER—March, April, May 2007

## *Our Community Now and in God's Future*

### GENERAL INTRODUCTION

This quarter has three units. The first unit interprets the meaning of God's love for people today based on Scripture passages from 1 John. Units II and III draw on passages from Revelation to explore the new community in Christ and how believers will live in God's New World.

**Unit I,** *Known by Our Love,* has four lessons. Each lesson attempts to interpret the meaning of God's love and how it defines our relationships with one another. These lessons explore love as a light in our dark world of evil and hate, our hope for experiencing love in its purest form, the source of love we need and long for, and ways of loving as we ourselves would like to be loved. Lesson 1—the way individual persons treat other people is often a good indication of how they really feel about them. This raises a caution for Christians because we cannot claim to love God and then treat one another shabbily—love of God and love of neighbor are inseparable. Lesson 2—even people who love each other sometimes react angrily or harshly toward one another. John acknowledges that while we are all prone to emotional lapses and roller coasters, it is by our overall abiding love that God judges us, not by occasional failures. The story about the widow's coin in Mark underscores the belief that every loving deed is of great importance to God. Lesson 3—as human beings, we need several kinds of love to become healthy and whole persons. God, who first loved us, is the source of the caliber of love that enables our ability to love one another with divine love. Jesus' command to feed His sheep shows that our love for Him is intimately connected to our loving care for others. Lesson 4—people want to believe that life can go on after physical death. John affirms that our victorious faith in Jesus Christ will grant us eternal life and empower us to love in the way that God wants. The Mark passages tell us that Jesus is the Messiah, who calls us to love and follow Him.

**Unit II,** *A New Community in Christ,* has five lessons. The first lesson (Palm Sunday) celebrates Jesus as our ruler. The lesson for Easter establishes that we are reborn as a community through Jesus' resurrection and that this community has life after death. The third lesson focuses on the community's worship of God. The last two lessons center on Jesus as the one who redeems and protects the new community. Lesson 5—people will easily rally behind a leader that they trust and love. The Revelation passages affirm that Jesus is the Ruler of all rulers. Luke's account of the triumphal entry into Jerusalem describes a time when Jesus' kingship was symbolically demonstrated to the world. Lesson 6—people long to hear good news, especially if it transforms their lives for the better. The belief that Jesus conquered sin and death is the transforming good news about which we celebrate Easter—the ongoing presence of the resurrected Christ in the lives of believers. Lesson 7—most people want to worship someone or something larger and more powerful than themselves. Revelation 4 describes how God is worthy of worship from all beings in heaven and earth. The Ephesians passage and Revelation 2:3 show that we worship and honor God by persevering in love and kindness toward others. Lesson 8—most people want to know that there is a possibility for forgiveness when they do something wrong or make a mistake. What guarantee of forgiveness do we have? Revelation 5 reassures us that the Lamb, who is worthy of our praise, has redeemed us. Paul's letter to the Philippians encourages them to act as redeemed people by showing love to one another, and Revelation 2:19 says that God knows when we act this way. Lesson 9—most people long for a sense of security and safety. Where can we look for protection? The vision in the seventh chapter of Revelation affirms that the Lamb who redeemed them protects God's people. Paul's letter to the Colossians describes some characteristics of those who have been redeemed, and Revelation 3:3 adds that God knows their deeds.

**Unit III,** *Living in God's New World,* has four lessons. The first lesson presents the promise of life with God after death. The second lesson describes the home that God will eventually make for the community of faith, while the third lesson explores the presence of God in the midst of that new home. The final lesson focuses on Christ's return. Lesson 10—most people want to belong to a community that gives meaning to their lives. The description of the marriage feast of the Lamb and His bride illustrates that the church is a holy community in which we can find meaning for our lives. Revelation 7 and Psalm 148 underscore how worship and celebration among heavenly beings parallel celebration among believers on earth. Lesson 11—everyone wants a home in which he or she can be safe from hunger, loneliness, thirst, and pain. Revelation 21 says that the new heaven and the new earth will be a home like this. The Mark passage presents a foreshadowing of this aspect of the new age, as we see Jesus feeding the multitude and eliminating their hunger. Lesson 12—people long for true peace, wholeness, and safety in their lives. Revelation 21 affirms that those who dwell in God's New Jerusalem will experience these things, because God and the Lamb will be permanently in their midst. Lesson 13—most people would like to live in a world in which happy endings always come to pass, and one can trust that everything will be all right in the end. In spite of the reality of this world, Revelation 22 tells us to trust that Jesus Christ will come again and that His coming will transform everything into the ultimate happy ending for us; we can live now as if this were already accomplished.

## Lesson 1

# The Light of Love

**ADULT TOPIC:** Love Is Light
**YOUTH TOPIC:** Turn on Your Heart Light
**CHILDREN'S TOPIC:** God's Children Love One Another

---

**DEVOTIONAL READING:** 1 Peter 4:1-11
**BACKGROUND SCRIPTURE:** 1 John 2:7-17
**PRINT PASSAGE:** 1 John 2:7-11, 15-17

### 1 John 2:7-11, 15-17—KJV

7 Brethren, I write no new commandment unto you, but an old commandment which ye had from the beginning. The old commandment is the word which ye have heard from the beginning.

8 Again, a new commandment I write unto you, which thing is true in him and in you: because the darkness is past, and the true light now shineth.

9 He that saith he is in the light, and hateth his brother, is in darkness even until now.

10 He that loveth his brother abideth in the light, and there is none occasion of stumbling in him.

11 But he that hateth his brother is in darkness, and walketh in darkness, and knoweth not whither he goeth, because that darkness hath blinded his eyes.

.....

15 Love not the world, neither the things that are in the world. If any man love the world, the love of the Father is not in him.

16 For all that is in the world, the lust of the flesh, and the lust of the eyes, and the pride of life, is not of the Father, but is of the world.

17 And the world passeth away, and the lust thereof: but he that doeth the will of God abideth for ever.

### UNIFYING LESSON PRINCIPLE

The way individual persons treat other people is often a good indication of how they really feel about them. What caution does this raise for us as Christians? John says that we cannot claim

---

**March 4, 2007**

**UNIT I**
Known by Our Love

**CHILDREN'S UNIT**
A Special Letter

### KEY VERSE

He that loveth his brother abideth in the light, and there is none occasion of stumbling in him.
—1 John 2:10

### OBJECTIVES

**Upon completion of this lesson, the students are expected to:**

1. Understand that love was the central reason Jesus Christ came into the world;

2. Recognize that obedience to the commandments of God was the first criteria for having a genuine relationship with God; and,

3. Understand that the believer's life should be a living testimony of the life and love of Jesus Christ.

to love God and then treat one another shabbily, because love of God and love of our neighbor are inseparable. Indeed, we are able to truly love one another because the light of the divine love has made us all children of God.

## POINTS TO BE EMPHASIZED
## ADULTS/YOUTH
**Adult/Youth Key Verse:** 1 John 2:10
**Print Passage:** 1 John 2:7-11, 15-17
—The old and new commandments are used as the framework in which to contrast love and light with darkness and hate.
—There is a connection between loving God and loving others.
—How do "light" and "darkness" relate to faith and disbelief?

## CHILDREN
**Key Verse:** 1 John 4:7
**Print Passage:** 1 John 2:12-14; 3:1
—God demonstrates love for children in many ways and expects children to love others the same way.
—Love can extend to all creation, including animals, plants, and the environment.
—Love, not hate, is the key to living by God's rules.
—God communicates love for us through letters.

## TOPICAL OUTLINE OF THE LESSON
I. INTRODUCTION
  A. A Life Governed by Love
  B. Biblical Background

II. EXPOSITION AND APPLICATION OF THE SCRIPTURE
  A. An Old Commandment in a New Form *(1 John 2:7-8)*
  B. Abiding in the Light *(1 John 2:9-11)*
  C. Love Not the World *(1 John 2:15-17)*

III. CONCLUDING REFLECTIONS

## I. INTRODUCTION
### A. A Life Governed by Love

What does it mean to be a Christian? What are the prerequisites for living a life that is well-pleasing in the sight of God? What are the key character traits of a man or a woman who claims to be a Christian? The New Testament spells out the answer to these questions—it is living a life governed by the principle of love. Love was and still is the central reason Jesus Christ came into the world (see John 3:16). One day, a Jewish scribe asked Jesus, "Master, which is the first commandment?" Jesus responded by telling him that we are to first love God with all of our hearts, minds, and souls. The second is like the former, but it applies more to loving our neighbor as ourselves (see Mark 12:28-31). Love is the supreme virtue because it identifies us as children of God. "God is love" is the fundamental declaration of the Scriptures and one of the hallmarks of true righteousness.

### B. Biblical Background

This lesson begins a new unit, which is a brief study of the epistle of 1 John. Unlike the letters of the apostle Paul, these letters were not addressed to a particular congregation. Hence, they are relevant to every age. The epistle of 1 John is part of the corpus of New Testament writings written by the apostle John. The letters were written in the first century some time around A.D. 85-90. Furthermore, John wrote as an eyewitness of the ministry of Jesus (see 1 John 1:1-2). John's writings are referred to as the Johannine writings; those include the gospel of John and the three letters that bear his name—1, 2, and 3 John.

One of the questions that we must raise in our study of these short, yet important, New Testament letters is this: What occurred in John's day and in the church that prompted him to write as he did? The church was beset with several controversies that can only be deduced from reading the letter. The internal harmony of the congregation was disrupted as the leaders struggled with a host of issues that threatened to tear the church apart.

John wrote with the intention of strengthening the relational bond of love within the congregation and correcting some of the spiritual deficiencies that the Holy Spirit revealed to him regarding the church. John expressed his thoughts through the use of clear dualism. We see this in how he developed his arguments and train of thought. There are the contrasts of light versus darkness, love versus hate, obedience versus disobedience, and worldliness versus holiness. For John, there were no gray areas—either one lived totally and absolutely for Jesus or one did not. We too are so challenged in our generation.

## II. Exposition and Application of the Scripture

### A. An Old Commandment in a New Form (1 John 2:7-8)

**Brethren, I write no new commandment unto you, but an old commandment which ye had from the beginning. The old commandment is the word which ye have heard from the beginning. Again, a new commandment I write unto you, which thing is true in him and in you: because the darkness is past, and the true light now shineth.**

In verse 7, John began a discussion about the second criterion that identifies the true Christian who lives in the light of Jesus Christ. In the previous section, verses 1-6, John stated that obedience to the commandments of God was the first criterion for having a genuine relationship with God. If we say that we have fellowship with God and fail to keep the commandments, we are no more than liars, and the truth is not in us (verse 4). John wrote that the presence of love is the one trait that identifies us as true disciples of Jesus Christ (verse 5).

John used the term of endearment, "brethren," in addressing his audience. The *New Revised Standard Version* translates the Greek word in the text with the word "beloved." John spoke to the members of the church as one who knew them intimately and had a genuine interest in their spiritual well-being. Clearly, the central concern of every church leader is the spiritual welfare of the members. The word "brethren" is used more than 231 times throughout the New Testament to show a variety of family and relational connections.

John reminded the church of a new commandment that was, in fact, a commandment that already had been established. It was one that they had heard from the beginning, dating back to the Old Testament (see Leviticus 19:18; Deuteronomy 6:5). First, the commandment to love was firmly rooted in the Jewish Torah, which specifically required Jews to love their neighbors as well as strangers living in their midst. Second, the ethical teaching regarding the practice of love was one of the central tenets of the teachings of Jesus (see Matthew 5:43ff.). Jesus showed men and women how to live in word as well as in deed. He taught His disciples how to live out this ethic of love in practical ways: i.e., by not becoming angry at one another without a cause, bearing false witness against others, or seeking to retaliate against people who had wronged them (see Matthew 5:22, 38ff.).

The commandment to love was a new commandment written to the church (verse 8). The word translated "new" from the Greek *kainos* means "that which has never been seen before." *Kainos* refers to the quality of newness. In what way is this commandment new? First, the new commandment to love had its beginning in Jesus Christ. When we look at the life of Jesus, we see God in the flesh demonstrating to us what it means to love (see John 1:14; 2 Corinthians 8:9). In Him we see the very fullness of God's love reaching its zenith at the cross (see John 3:16; Romans 5:8). The Cross is the clearest visible demonstration of God's sacrificial love for His creation. How do we live out the ethic of love today? We must be intentional in our relationship and in our efforts to love others as Christ loves us. There always must be a desire for reconciliation between estranged believers (see Matthew 5:24; 2 Corinthians 5:18-20). Believers have to look at their actions and weigh them against the teachings of the New Testament. Is there something in our behavior, actions, or words that points to inconsistency in our walk with Jesus Christ, particularly in our relationships? When we identify the inconsistencies, we must quickly correct them through prayer, fasting, and obedience to the Word of God.

Second, the new commandment is grounded in the willingness of Jesus to submit totally and absolutely to the will of the Father (see John 8:29). There was never any doubt in the heart or mind of Jesus regarding the Father's will for His life on earth. He had come for one purpose and one purpose only: to give His life as ransom for the sin of the world (see Luke 19:10 and John 12:27). We become like Jesus when we imitate His life of obedience to the will of the Father (see Luke 6:46-49; John 8:31; Colossians 1:9-10). The believer's life should be a living testimony of the life and love of Jesus Christ. How do we live in obedience to God's Word? We must love other believers as God loves us and gave His Son to redeem us from the penalty of sin and death.

John wrote that the darkness has passed away (verse 8). To be in darkness is to live in a state of separation from God (see Ephesians 4:18). Darkness represents the kingdom and rule of Satan in the lives of men and women. Disobedience and ignorance of God's ways and Word are characteristics of a life in darkness. In contrast to the darkness, to know Jesus Christ is to live in the light. Jesus Christ is the Light of the world, and He has come into the world to lead us from darkness into the light.

## B. Abiding in the Light *(1 John 2:9-11)*

**He that saith he is in the light, and hateth his brother, is in darkness even until now. He that loveth his brother abideth in the light, and there is none occasion of stumbling in him. But he that hateth his brother is in darkness, and walketh in darkness, and knoweth not whither he goeth, because that darkness hath blinded his eyes.**

It is difficult for some non-Christians to believe that Christians can sometimes have bitter disagreements and conflicts. Yet, sadly enough, this is true more often than we all would like to admit. Christians do disagree and we do fall out of fellowship with each other at times. The question is: What should be the standard and norm for our conduct and relationship with other believers? In verse 9, John came right to the point—if we hate our brother or sister we are in the darkness. How can one claim fellowship with Jesus Christ and hate another believer? John said that person is in darkness. One would be no different and no better than the person who has never made a profession of faith in Jesus Christ.

John used the word "hate," which is a very strong word, to describe the conflict between believers within the church. The word "hate" in the Greek text is a present active participle, meaning that it depicts a continuous attitude of indifference and hostility between persons. There are occasions when members of congregations have longstanding disagreements that have become ingrained in the fabric of the church. These are congregations that are held hostage by individual disagreements that are never resolved. Disharmony, discord, and disruption of the fellowship are often signs of this type of behavior. How can a local congregation resolve this type of conflict? Clearly, the leaders must become proactive in seeking to lead the congregation and the persons involved to understand what Jesus taught about resolution of congregational differences (see Matthew 18:15-17, 21-22).

In verse 9, John describes the persons who claim to be Christians, yet whose lifestyles reflect something entirely different. They may look, sound, and act like Christians, but John says they are not Christians according to the standard of love of the body. "He that saith he is in the light, and hateth his brother, is in darkness even until now." John did not "pull any punches." If one hates a brother or sister, he or she is in darkness. Hatred causes us to "stumble." The Greek word for "stumble" is *skandalon,* and gives us the English word "scandal." It refers to something that entraps or causes one to sin or fall into error. Hatred of others causes a multitude of problems and sins. Believers must be discerning of the subtle tricks and snares of the devil, especially in his attempts to destroy, disrupt, and dishonor our relationships within the body of Christ. John helps us to see that love is the one grace that covers a multitude of faults and sins within the local assembly (see Ephesians 4:31-32).

## C. Love Not the World *(1 John 2:15-17)*

**Love not the world, neither the things that are in the world. If any man love the world, the love of the Father is not in him. For all that is in the world, the lust of the flesh, and the lust of the eyes, and the pride of life, is not of the Father, but is of the world. And the world passeth away, and the lust thereof: but he that doeth the will of God abideth for ever.**

The word "flesh" in this instance stands for everything that is part of humanity's lower nature. The word "flesh" is found in both the Old Testament and the New Testament. In the Old Testament, "flesh" describes humanity and all of God's creatures. It is never used in the Old Testament to denote the sinful side of a man or woman. For example, the psalmist says that it is better to put trust in God than in humanity (see Psalm 118:4-6). Isaiah 40:6 states that "all flesh" is as the grass. He means every living creature on the face of the earth is as limited and as fragile as grass. When cut off from its source of life, the blade will perish. *Flesh* in the Old Testament further denotes the very limited and finite nature of humanity. According to Jeremiah 17:5, we should not put trust in humankind, because human beings are limited and prone to failure. "Thus says the LORD, 'Cursed is the man who trusts in mankind And makes flesh his strength, And whose heart turns away from the LORD'" (NASB).

John wrote that we are not to love the world or the things that are in the world. This is an imperative statement. It is a non-negotiable command that leaves the believer with absolutely no options. We are not to fall in love with the world. We live in the world but we are not to love it. How do we understand this seeming contradiction? John uses the Greek word "cosmos" *(kosmos)*. This is the root word for "cosmetic." The reference is to the things that are in the world—that is, lust, unholy ambition, and seeking after pleasures. These are instruments of Satan to lure Christians away from the straight path of righteous living. Does God intend that we separate ourselves completely from our environment and live in isolated conclaves as monks? We must love the people of the world who have been created in the image of God. However, we should not love the very world systems *(kosmos)* that are organized to live in rebellion against God and His Word. The reason a believer cannot love the world is because love of the world sets us against God. "If anyone loves the world, the love of the Father is not in him" (1 John 2:15, NIV). Jesus said, "No one can serve two masters; for either he will hate the one and love the other, or else he will be loyal to the one and despise the other. You cannot serve God and mammon" (Matthew 6:24, NKJV). A second reason John gives for not loving the world is seen in its transitory nature. The world is passing away (verse 17). Everything has its day and time, but it passes away—as with all things created (see Ecclesiastes 3:1ff.).

In verse 16, we see a threefold manifestation of evil: "the lust of the flesh, and the lust of the eyes, and the pride of life." The first of these dangers is from "the lust of the flesh."

In the phrase "the lust of the flesh," lust refers to a deep craving, a desire for things that are forbidden. "The lust of the flesh means the unlawful desire produced by that lower nature. The lust of the flesh includes every desire and appetite centered in humanity's physical nature."

The second danger is from "the lust of the eyes." This is the danger of being moved and impressed by the outward show of things and possessions. The eyes are often the source of our desires and ultimately the cause of our stumbling (see Genesis 3:6). The sin here is one of greed and covetousness, which is aroused by what we see. How easily are the unspiritual and the carnal Christian impressed by things and the outward show? The lures and enticements of Madison Avenue and mass marketers of the American dream quickly deceive some. The more we see the more we want (see Ecclesiastes 1:8; Proverbs 27:20). We can be deceived into thinking that we must have everything we see. The desire for the things of this world can stand between God and us. The lust of the eyes was the beginning of King David's plunge into sin, which led to murder, lying, conspiracy, adultery, and political corruption at the highest levels of Israelite society (see 2 Samuel 11:1–12:13). David's lust brought numerous personal heartaches and pain upon himself and his family. As a result of his sin, God declared that the sword would never leave his house. His family's legacy would be one of violence and death (see 2 Samuel 12:10).

The third danger is from "the pride of life." Pride refers to being a braggart or being one who boasts about what one has. The spirit of "pride" leads us to boast about what we have and our personal achievements in an effort to impress other people. In one sense, "pride of life" refers to boastful egoism.

Paul reminds us that we are not to think more highly of ourselves than we ought to think (see Romans 12:3). We can become too boastful—too big for God to get any glory out of our lives. Satan can fill our hearts with a spirit of pride that produces a false sense of security and accomplishment. We can feel that all that we are—all that we have achieved—is the result of our individual abilities and intellect. Having this attitude ensures that striving to acquire material possessions aids in the development of a vain spirit. The things of this world—the pride that we have in what we have acquired or achieved—can become the very things that block our spiritual development. They can become the very things that Satan uses to keep us stunted and disinterested in the things of the Kingdom. Paul said (1 Timothy 6:9-10), "But those who desire to be rich fall into temptation, into a snare, into many senseless and hurtful desires that plunge men into ruin and destruction. For the love of money is the root of all evils; it is through this craving that some have wandered away from the faith and pierced their hearts with many pangs" (RSV).

### III. Concluding Reflections

One of the great marvels of twentieth-century engineering is the airplane. The airplane has given us the capability to travel anywhere in the world within twenty-four hours. This engineering marvel has made the world smaller and more accessible. However, instead of increased understanding and cooperation among the peoples of the world, we see more fragmentation and divisiveness. The nations of the world have become colder and more distant. The world is full of people who are seeking to be loved. Many will go to any length and make any sacrifice to be loved by anyone. God has created us to live in loving relationships with other human beings. When our relationships are healthy, satisfying, and fulfilling, we feel complete. But for many people, the opposite is more the rule than the exception. They live in broken and damaged relationships void of real love. Similarly, there are congregations that are filled with people who have not learned to love as Christ loved.

This lesson challenges us to look at our relationships and encourages us to examine our hearts to see if we are the reasons why our relationships are so poor. How can Christians become more influential in the spread of the love of God in the world? Are we living in such a way that there is a difference between us and persons who are not believers in the Lord Jesus Christ? Do we live in love? Do we truly love other believers as we claim? Are our lives governed by the spiritual grace of love? And how do we know if we are living in love according to the teachings of Jesus Christ? These are questions that every believer should raise for him- or herself.

## WORD POWER

**Loveth *(Greek: agapao)*** —this is the word that serves as glue for this lesson. The word *agapao*, in the original, means "keep on loving." It is a continuous action. It is the love that God has for us as human beings. This love allows the sun to shine, the moon to shine, and the stars to still be in place. This love is not based on feeling. It does not change like clouds. This love takes pleasure in human beings, is prized above other things, and is unwilling to abandon or do without. This is what we are called to do.

## HOME DAILY BIBLE READINGS

for the week of March 4, 2007
*The Light of Love*

Feb. 26, Monday
    —2 Peter 1:5-11
    —Partakers of the Divine Nature
Feb. 27, Tuesday
    —Romans 12:9-21
    —Living in Love
Feb. 28, Wednesday
    —Romans 13:8-14
    —Fulfilling the Law in Love
Mar. 1, Thursday
    —Galatians 5:13-26
    —Serve with Love
Mar. 2, Friday
    —1 Peter 4:1-11
    —Love Deeply
Mar. 3, Saturday
    —1 John 2:7-11
    —Called to Live in Love
Mar. 4, Sunday
    —1 John 2:12-17
    —Live for God

## PRAYER

*Heavenly Father, Creator of all life, create within us clean and pure hearts. May we see Your example of selfless love and make it our standard for living in the world. Forgive us of every sin that separates us from You. In the name of Jesus Christ, we pray. Amen.*

## Lesson 2

# The Test of Love

**ADULT TOPIC:** Striving for Pure Love
**YOUTH TOPIC:** Love in Action
**CHILDREN'S TOPIC:** God's Children Share with Others

---

**DEVOTIONAL READING:** 1 Corinthians 13
**BACKGROUND SCRIPTURE:** 1 John 3
**PRINT PASSAGE:** 1 John 3:11-24

### 1 John 3:11-24—KJV

11 For this is the message that ye heard from the beginning, that we should love one another.

12 Not as Cain, who was of that wicked one, and slew his brother. And wherefore slew he him? Because his own works were evil, and his brother's righteous.

13 Marvel not, my brethren, if the world hate you.

14 We know that we have passed from death unto life, because we love the brethren. He that loveth not his brother abideth in death.

15 Whosoever hateth his brother is a murderer: and ye know that no murderer hath eternal life abiding in him.

16 Hereby perceive we the love of God, because he laid down his life for us: and we ought to lay down our lives for the brethren.

17 But whoso hath this world's good, and seeth his brother have need, and shutteth up his bowels of compassion from him, how dwelleth the love of God in him?

18 My little children, let us not love in word, neither in tongue; but in deed and in truth.

19 And hereby we know that we are of the truth, and shall assure our hearts before him.

20 For if our heart condemn us, God is greater than our heart, and knoweth all things.

21 Beloved, if our heart condemn us not, then have we confidence toward God.

22 And whatsoever we ask, we receive of him, because we keep his commandments, and do those things that are pleasing in his sight.

---

**March 11, 2007**

**UNIT I**
Known by Our Love

**CHILDREN'S UNIT**
A Special Letter

### KEY VERSE

Beloved, now are we the sons of God, and it doth not yet appear what we shall be: but we know that, when he shall appear, we shall be like him; for we shall see him as he is. —1 John 3:2

### OBJECTIVES

Upon completion of this lesson, the students are expected to:

1. Explore the premise that love is one of the visible manifestations of righteousness;

2. Recognize the need to be more patient, loving, and sincere in our relationships with each other; and,

3. Understand that we are to love one another, which is an ethical and biblical obligation and is the product of new life in Jesus Christ.

23 And this is his commandment, That we should believe on the name of his Son Jesus Christ, and love one another, as he gave us commandment.

24 And he that keepeth his commandments dwelleth in him, and he in him. And hereby we know that he abideth in us, by the Spirit which he hath given us.

## UNIFYING LESSON PRINCIPLE

Even people who love each other sometimes react angrily or harshly to one another. When we fail to show pure love to one another, what does that say about ourselves as Christians? John acknowledges that we are all prone to such emotional lapses, yet he encourages us to keep striving for purity in our love—because it is by our overall abiding love that God judges us, not by our occasional failures. The story of the widow's coin in Mark underscores that every loving deed, however slight it may seem to others, is of great importance to God.

## POINTS TO BE EMPHASIZED
## ADULTS/YOUTH

**Adult Key Verse:** 1 John 3:2
**Youth Key Verse:** 1 John 3:18
**Print Passage:** 1 John 3:11-24

—Believers are challenged as children of God to be like God, who is love.
—A strong test of love is obedient action. One must love in both word and deed.
—Who is our model for loving others?

## CHILDREN

**Key Verse:** 1 John 3:18
**Print Passage:** Mark 12:41-44; 1 John 3:18

—Jesus used parables to teach biblical truths, such as unselfish love for others.
—Sometimes, those with the most material things are unwilling to share their wealth with others.
—Those who seemingly have the least are often willing to share their meager resources with one another.
—Some wealthy people did not demonstrate the same unselfish love as the widow.

## TOPICAL OUTLINE OF THE LESSON

I. INTRODUCTION
   A. The Importance of Love in the Body
   B. Biblical Background

II. EXPOSITION AND APPLICATION OF THE SCRIPTURE
   A. The Essence of the Gospel Message *(1 John 3:11-12)*
   B. The Evidences of Having Received Eternal Life *(1 John 3:13-18)*
   C. The Effects of Our Confidence in God *(1 John 3:19-24)*

III. CONCLUDING REFLECTIONS

## I. INTRODUCTION
### A. The Importance of Love in the Body

In the previous lesson, we learned that the apostle John was used by the Holy Spirit to address relational issues among the believers of his faith community. The disputes that erupted among the saints needed to be addressed before they exploded into more serious disruptions. Many times, members do not address relational issues in the local church as promptly as we should. This lesson speaks quite clearly to believers today about the need to be more patient, loving, and sincere in our relationships with each other. Many times, relationships among Christians can be shallow, empty, and void of genuine love.

John helps us to discover anew the importance of love, which is the unifying mark of the believer's life.

Further, John wants believers to understand the importance of living and behaving consistently with their professions of faith. John shows us that we do not have to live a weak and ineffective life, but rather, we can be strong in Jesus Christ and full of the Holy Spirit. In today's lesson, we will see how John developed further his teachings regarding living out the Christian ethic of selfless love. The love that John is referring to is not superficial; rather, it is a deep love for others. It is the love that we see in God and Jesus Christ. Love is one of the visible manifestations of righteousness (see 1 John 2:29). Jesus Christ is our model for how to live a righteous life that is completely submitted to the Father's will.

### B. Biblical Background

John reminds us that we are children of God who one day will be living reflections of the transformed and glorious nature of the resurrected Christ (1 John 3:1-2).

The apostle John was concerned about the spiritual life of the people of his day. During John's ministry, many people were being deceived by false apostles, prophets, and even some who claimed to be the Christ (see 1 John 3:7). As previously mentioned, John pointed out that the believer's life is a visible manifestation of the life of Jesus Christ. Life in the Spirit means that we are walking in the light as He is in the light. To say we have been born again and still walk in spiritual darkness means that we have not been born again (see Romans 8:4-8). A growing Christian draws closer to Jesus Christ every day and is a living reflection of Him.

## II. Exposition and Application of the Scripture

### A. The Essence of the Gospel Message (1 John 3:11-12)

**For this is the message that ye heard from the beginning, that we should love one another. Not as Cain, who was of that wicked one, and slew his brother. And wherefore slew he him? Because his own works were evil, and his brother's righteous.**

John obviously laid much emphasis on love. He wanted his readers to pay attention to how Jesus displayed love in His teachings and interactions with people (John 13:34-35; 15:12-19; 17:26). The practice of love is seen in how the first disciples of Jesus related to one another and shared together in the breaking of bread and in the spread of the Gospel (see Acts 2:41-47).

The Bible says that this is the message from the beginning—"love one another." This ethic of love is John's reflection on Jesus' life during His earthly ministry. This was not a new message, but rather, one that was well-tested and proven over a long period of time (see 1 John 2:7). The message that we are to love one another is an ethical and biblical obligation, and it is the product of our new life in Jesus Christ. There are no conditions, options, alternatives, or circumstances under which we are to debate whether or not we will love another believer; rather, our love must always be unconditionally given. There are no strings attached to Christian love.

John believed that when we hate other believers, it is the same as committing murder. All believers in Jesus Christ have the same spiritual heritage, which is the heritage of love. Therefore, to hate another human being is a manifestation of a godless life. Every evil act in the world today is the manifestation of the devil's presence. Whether we witness it in corporate greed that rips off the company's shareholders, the consuming public, or in cheating the government in lost taxes, it is evil. We see hatred in the tyrants who rule with heavy hands in various parts of the globe. We see it in the pettiness that grips congregations that resort to backbiting and negative attitudes toward one another. For John, it was all the same. There is one source: the devil. The message we preach and teach today is the same one proclaimed in those days: God is love, and in Him there is no darkness (see John 3:16-17).

### B. The Evidences of Having Received Eternal Life *(1 John 3:13-18)*

**Marvel not, my brethren, if the world hate you. We know that we have passed from death unto life, because we love the brethren. He that loveth not his brother abideth in death. Whosoever hateth his brother is a murderer: and ye know that no murderer hath eternal life abiding in him. Hereby perceive we the love of God, because he laid down his life for us: and we ought to lay down our lives for the brethren. But whoso hath this world's good, and seeth his brother have need, and shutteth up his bowels of compassion from him, how dwelleth the love of God in him? My little children, let us not love in word, neither in tongue; but in deed and in truth.**

John wrote to people who appeared to be surprised that they were not listed among the most popular people of that day. He wanted to know why anyone would be surprised that they were hated (verse 13). Often the issue is not about how people treat us, but rather, how we respond to ill treatment. During the latter days of the first Christian century, the church experienced an onslaught of persecution and stress. All of it was the result of their faith in the Lord Jesus Christ. Many Christians were persecuted because they refused to bow down and worship Caesar. The Jews persecuted Christians as well.

If the world hated Jesus Christ, it stands to reason that the more a person imitates His life, the greater the animosity that will be shown toward him or her. Jesus warned His disciples that if the world hated Him it would hate them as well (John 15:20). John enumerated what he deemed was evidence that we have received eternal life from Jesus Christ and that we are living that life now.

The first of these evidences is love of the brethren. Love of the brethren is irrefutable evidence that we have been born again. We have complete assurance that we have passed from death to eternal life (verse 14).

John used the Greek word *oida* ("know") [pronounced–oy-da], which literally refers to knowing without any shadow of doubt that something is true. This is different from *ginosko* ("know"), which means "surface knowledge." We know for a fact that we have been born from above. In John's view, love of the brethren indicates that "We have passed from death unto life." The believer has literally made a spiritual journey from one state of being to another. This phrase was used to refer to moving from one place or region to another. Failure to love our brothers or sisters is evidence that we are still abiding in the realm of spiritual darkness and death. Hatred reflects a condition of still being lost in sin.

Hating our brothers and sisters makes us murderers (verse 15). It is impossible for anyone who hates another believer (or anyone for that matter) to say that Jesus Christ lives within his or her heart. The hatred that John writes about was not a one-time event; the word he used was in the present active tense, meaning that it is a current, ongoing attitude of indifference to others. Evidently, there were people in the congregation who were having ongoing differences and conflicts that manifested themselves throughout the congregation.

The evidence that God loves us is His personal sacrifice in the death of Jesus upon the cross. "God is love" is one of the central tenets of the Christian faith. How do we know that God loves us? Jesus Christ died for us (1 Corinthians 15:3-4).

The knowledge of God's love is knowledge that we are intimately acquainted with. We know of God's love. We do not just perceive it but we know *(oida)* it for certain. Jesus Christ died for sinners. And because Jesus died for us, He is also our model for what it means to be selfless in our giving. We reach the pinnacle of self-giving when we are willing to sacrifice ourselves for others (see John 15:12-13).

John stated the third piece of evidence for a changed life in the form of a question (verse 17): "But whoso hath this world's good, and seeth his brother have need, and shutteth up his bowels *of compassion* from him, how dwelleth the love of God in him?" In the first century, many Christians were poor and destitute because of persecution, yet they did whatever was necessary to see that the poor among them were provided for (see Matthew 19:21; Acts 2:45; 4:34; Galatians 6:10). Likewise, there were some who had wealth and the means to provide for the care of others who were less fortunate.

The Bible tells us that our works echo our relationship with God. Jesus ministered among the poor and expected His disciples to do the same. Therefore, the practicality of our love is not revealed in our words but in our deeds (verse 18). Right deeds are based upon what the believer has been taught. Truth refers to that which has been taught and then becomes a part of the lives of believers through daily practice.

### C. The Effects of Our Confidence in God *(1 John 3:19-24)*

**And hereby we know that we are of the truth, and shall assure our hearts before him. For if our heart condemn us, God is greater than our heart, and knoweth all**

**things. Beloved, if our heart condemn us not, then have we confidence toward God. And whatsoever we ask, we receive of him, because we keep his commandments, and do those things that are pleasing in his sight. And this is his commandment, That we should believe on the name of his Son Jesus Christ, and love one another, as he gave us commandment. And he that keepeth his commandments dwelleth in him, and he in him. And hereby we know that he abideth in us, by the Spirit which he hath given us.**

This section is among the most difficult verses in the entire epistle of 1 John to interpret and explain because of the complexities associated with the translation of the text from Greek to English. The questions of interpretation have focused on whether verse 18 should be placed with verses 19-24 or verses 13-17 because of its reference to truth as a basis of faith. New Testament scholars differ and many suggest that one consult various English versions to get a sense of how they have been translated. For our purposes here, verse 18 speaks more to what follows than to the previous verses.

John wrote, "Hereby we know that we are of the truth . . .because we keep his commandments and do those things that are pleasing in his sight" (verses 19a, 22). Everything that comes between these two statements parenthetical statements that further explain John's point. Obedience to the commandments of God produces inner, personal assurance that we have been born again and are righteous before Him. Everything hinges on love for God.

There are occasions when we look at our personal walk with God and cannot find anything that we consider to be pleasing in the eyes of God. There are periods when we appear to be walking in dry places—when God's grace appears to be absent and there is nothing experientially that readily points to our growth in Him. John said that if we are feeling condemned by our hearts, we can gain new confidence from God because He knows us and will never condemn us unjustly (see Psalm 139:1-6). God knows when we have done our best in the work of ministry. He will never forget our work and labors of love (see Hebrews 6:10). John remarked that the assurance of answered prayer is one of the primary indicators of a growing and vibrant relationship with God (verse 22). Later, John will qualify his affirmation about answered prayer in 1 John 5:14 by reminding the saints that answered prayer is always the result of praying in accordance with the will of the Father.

John summarized his discussion about obedience to the commandments of God in this way: first, that we believe in the name of His Son, Jesus Christ. The act of faith or expressing confidence in the name of Jesus Christ is a one-time act that continues throughout our lives. For John, nothing could come between him and the absolute confidence he had in Jesus Christ. In order to gain more understanding in this matter, see Romans 8:34-39. Second, John said that believers are to keep the commandments. This is a restatement of that entire thought John had been focusing on throughout this passage.

Verse 24 concludes the passage by reiterating that when we are obedient to God, it is an indication that we are abiding in Him and He in us. The final witness of our new life in Christ is the witness of the

Holy Spirit, who testifies within us that we are the sons and daughters of God (see John 15:26; 16:13-14).

## III. Concluding Reflections

Congregational conflict has become increasingly more prevalent today. One of the biggest causes of congregational conflict is change. As we approached the end of the last century and the start of a new century and a new millennium, the landscape of the Christian church in America experienced significant shifts in worship styles, in music tastes, in dress codes, and in the organizational structure of the local church. All of these issues have produced disagreements so deep that congregations have split—even cutting their ties with traditional denominational affiliations.

Is disagreement ever out of place in a congregation? Yes! However, wherever people gather there may be disagreement. The challenge that congregational leaders face is having the skill and temperament to lead the members through a healthy process of remaining true to the Word of God while working out differences. This lesson has taught us that love is the key to overcoming difficulties in any congregation. A healthy congregation is one in which the members' love for each other grows out of their love for God.

## WORD POWER

**Know (Greek: *oida; ginosko*)**—these two words are translated "know"; therefore, they demand consideration. *Oida* (know), on the first hand, carries the idea of fullness of knowledge—knowing something perfectly and intimately. On the other hand, *ginosko* (know) suggests progress in knowledge as a child continues to have knowledge of parents (e.g., "I begin to know (*ginosko*), and I know *(oida)* him.") John, in this passage, used *oida* in a plural sense—meaning that all the disciples know Jesus Christ.

## HOME DAILY BIBLE READINGS

for the week of March 11, 2007
*The Test of Love*
Mar. 5, Monday
 —1 Corinthians 13
 —Love Is Eternal
Mar. 6, Tuesday
 —John 13:31-35
 —Jesus Commands Us to Love
Mar. 7, Wednesday
 —Mark 12:38-44
 —A Widow's Gift of Love
Mar. 8, Thursday
 —1 John 3:1-5
 —God Loves Us
Mar. 9, Friday
 —1 John 3:6-10
 —Avoid the Wrong
Mar. 10, Saturday
 —1 John 3:11-15
 —Evidence of New Life
Mar. 11, Sunday
 —1 John 3:16-24
 —Love as Christ Loves

## PRAYER

*Heavenly Father, grant that the love of Your Son Jesus Christ may live in us. Forgive us every sin that separates us from You. In the name of Jesus Christ, we pray. Amen.*

March 18, 2007

Lesson 3

**UNIT I**
Known by Our Love

# The Source of Love

**CHILDREN'S UNIT**
A Special Letter

**ADULT TOPIC:** Showing Divine Love
**YOUTH TOPIC:** Blessed by Love
**CHILDREN'S TOPIC:** God's Children Care for Others

**KEY VERSE**

We love him, because he first loved us.—1 John 4:19

**DEVOTIONAL READING:** John 21:15-19
**BACKGROUND SCRIPTURE:** 1 John 4:7-21
**PRINT PASSAGE:** 1 John 4:7-21

### 1 John 4:7-21—KJV

7 Beloved, let us love one another: for love is of God; and every one that loveth is born of God, and knoweth God.

8 He that loveth not knoweth not God; for God is love.

9 In this was manifested the love of God toward us, because that God sent his only begotten Son into the world, that we might live through him.

10 Herein is love, not that we loved God, but that he loved us, and sent his Son to be the propitiation for our sins.

11 Beloved, if God so loved us, we ought also to love one another.

12 No man hath seen God at any time. If we love one another, God dwelleth in us, and his love is perfected in us.

13 Hereby know we that we dwell in him, and he in us, because he hath given us of his Spirit.

14 And we have seen and do testify that the Father sent the Son to be the Saviour of the world.

15 Whosoever shall confess that Jesus is the Son of God, God dwelleth in him, and he in God.

16 And we have known and believed the love that God hath to us. God is love; and he that dwelleth in love dwelleth in God, and God in him.

17 Herein is our love made perfect, that we may have boldness in the day of judgment: because as he is, so are we in this world.

18 There is no fear in love; but perfect love casteth out fear: because fear hath torment. He that feareth is not made perfect in love.

**OBJECTIVES**

Upon completion of this lesson, the students are expected to:

1. Recognize that to love is to live and express through our lives the character of God's divine nature and presence in our lives;
2. Understand that the essence of the believer's life is found in love; and,
3. Recognize that when we do not love it is a clear indication that we do not know God.

19 We love him, because he first loved us.

20 If a man say, I love God, and hateth his brother, he is a liar: for he that loveth not his brother whom he hath seen, how can he love God whom he hath not seen?

21 And this commandment have we from him, That he who loveth God love his brother also.

## UNIFYING LESSON PRINCIPLE

As human beings, we need several kinds of love to become healthy, whole persons. What is the source of our ability to love one another with divine love? John says our love for one another comes from God, who first loved us, and from the Spirit who abides with us. Jesus' command to feed His sheep shows that our love for Him is intimately connected to our loving care for others.

## POINTS TO BE EMPHASIZED
## ADULTS/YOUTH

**Adult Key Verse:** 1 John 4:19
**Youth Key Verse:** 1 John 4:16b
**Print Passage:** 1 John 4:7-21

—Many experience God's love as both comforting and correcting.

—Perfect love casts out fear.

—Love and hate cannot abide together.

## CHILDREN

**Key Verse:** John 21:16c
**Print Passage:** John 21:15-17; 1 John 4:21

—Christian leaders are called to show compassion to those who follow them, especially the young and new converts.

—Some Christian leaders and others have trouble understanding what God expects of them.

—God takes care of the basic needs of those who follow Him.

## TOPICAL OUTLINE OF THE LESSON

I. INTRODUCTION
  A. The Essence of the Believer's Life
  B. Biblical Background

II. EXPOSITION AND APPLICATION OF THE SCRIPTURE
  A. The Appeal to Love One Another *(1 John 4:7-12)*
  B. The Basis of the Believer's Love *(1 John 4:13-16)*
  C. The Power of Perfect Love *(1 John 4:17-21)*

III. CONCLUDING REFLECTIONS

## I. INTRODUCTION
### A. The Essence of the Believer's Life

This is probably one of the most well-known and most widely-read chapters in the New Testament. It contains some of the most beloved and quoted verses in the New Testament, especially verse 18: "There is no fear in love; but perfect love casteth out fear: because fear hath torment. He that feareth is not made perfect in love." Each verse in this chapter captures, in some way, an aspect of the Bible's teaching about the nature of selfless love. It is as though John was eagerly waiting to get to this point in his letter. In the two previous lessons, John helped us see that love is the foundation and essence of the fulfillment of God's commandment to love one another (1 John 2:7-17). Further, the practice of love is the one true identifying mark of the believer's life (see John 13:34-35).

This third passage on love sums up all that the apostle John taught and believed about God—namely that God is love and that love expresses itself through concrete actions.

John stated that anyone who affirms that Jesus Christ came in the flesh is of God and knows God (see 1 John 4:2). This confession is fundamental to authentic Christianity.

## B. Biblical Background

Love was the primary foundation in the relational life of the early Christian church. Love is the bond that holds believers together through trial and tribulation. Without the unbreakable bond of love, it is doubtful that the Christian faith would have survived beyond the first and second centuries.

Our understanding of the word "love" must be grounded in the understanding of the first-century Christian church. There are three distinct words used in the Greek language for love: the first two are found in the New Testament; the third is not found in the New Testament at all. The first and most frequently-used word for "love" is *agape* (or agapao); it is the word that is used exclusively when referring to the love of God. It is also the word that the early Christians used to define and describe the limitless, unfettered love of God.

The second word used in the New Testament for love is *philia*, or *phileo*, and it refers to friendship. This word is used to describe the friendly relationship that exists between two people, whether they be male or female (see Matthew 10:37; John 5:20; 11:3; 16:27).

The third word for love is *eros*. This word is not found in the New Testament, yet it was a very important word in the Greek language and culture. It is the expressing of the love that God intended to exist between Adam and Eve (see Genesis 2:21-24).

In John's letter, *agapeo* is the ultimate expression of love; God is the ultimate model of how to live in His love. Finally, we learn how to love other human beings who are created in the very image of God.

## II. Exposition and Application of the Scripture
### A. The Appeal to Love One Another (1 John 4:7-12)

**Beloved, let us love one another: for love is of God; and every one that loveth is born of God, and knoweth God. He that loveth not knoweth not God; for God is love. In this was manifested the love of God toward us, because that God sent his only begotten Son into the world, that we might live through him. Herein is love, not that we loved God, but that he loved us, and sent his Son to be the propitiation for our sins. Beloved, if God so loved us, we ought also to love one another. No man hath seen God at any time. If we love one another, God dwelleth in us, and his love is perfected in us.**

John began this passage with a note of personal affection toward the letter's recipients. He referred to them as "beloved," which has in it the idea of esteem, favor, and love. He appealed to the believers of his day to love one another (verse 7). The language is inclusive: "let us." This was not something that John would exclude himself from doing. In this passage, John piled one thought about love upon another. It is as though he was building a house and each phrase was a brick laid upon the foundation.

He made five declarations about love and God. First, believers are to love one another. Throughout the epistle, John reiterated this one commandment. Second, love has its origin in the very nature of God—because love is of God. Human beings did not invent nor create love; it is from God. Third, everyone who loves is born of God. This is a thought that John returned to in greater detail in 5:1. Love is both the product of the new birth and a result (see John 3:16). Love is one of the nine fruits of the Holy Spirit (see Galatians 5:22f.). The presence of the Holy Spirit in a person's life is evidence of a life that has been transformed and made new in Jesus Christ. For believers, love is natural to who we are in Christ. Fourth, to love is to know God. The Greek word for "know" is *ginosko*, and it refers to firsthand knowledge. It is experiential knowledge. This is not just head knowledge or knowledge that is gained from secondhand experience. Rather, when we come to truly know God, our deepest desire is to be like Him. Fifth, anyone who does not love does not know God. When we do not love, it is a clear indication that we do not know God.

In verse 9, John said that God's love toward humanity was visibly demonstrated. God made it known that He loved the world by what He did on our behalf. He revealed His true nature for all to see. Jesus came into the world for a clearly-defined purpose: that we might find life more abundantly through Him (see verse 9). God did not just give anything and anybody; He gave His greatest gift—His only begotten Son—so that we might live eternally through Him. God's gift of life through Jesus Christ is an unparalleled act of grace.

God's manifested love toward us places each believer under obligation to love others. Paul wrote to the Galatians that they were obligated to do good to all people, and especially to those who were of the household of faith (see Galatians 6:10). There is a great lesson to be learned from doing good to other believers. When we see and feel the deep sense of obligation that the love of God places upon us to love others, it should change our attitude and behavior toward other people.

John wrote (verse 11), "Beloved, if God so loved us, we ought also to love one another." The force of the statement is expressed in the word "ought." This is a very strong word in the Greek language; it literally refers to being in debt or owing money to someone. It has in it the idea of one's obligation to pay that which is owed. Yet, God's Word says we ought to love one another. How much clearer can this be?

When we fail to love, we demonstrate that we have not taken hold of the divine love. God's love is perfected or reaches its fullness in us when we love others (verse 12). Loving other believers, and people in general, is not an option for Christians; yet many of us treat others as though it is optional. We ought to love others as Christ loves us and gave Himself for us.

### B. The Basis of the Believer's Love (1 John 4:13-16)

**Hereby know we that we dwell in him, and he in us, because he hath given us of his Spirit. And we have seen and do testify that the Father sent the Son to be the Saviour of**

the world. **Whosoever shall confess that Jesus is the Son of God, God dwelleth in him, and he in God. And we have known and believed the love that God hath to us. God is love; and he that dwelleth in love dwelleth in God, and God in him.**

In this passage, John pointed to four signs that are the basis of the believer's love. First, we have the Holy Spirit (verse 13). Second, we have the apostolic eyewitness of the ministry of Jesus Christ as Savior of the world (verse 14). Third, we have the believer's confession of Jesus as the Son of God (verse 15). Fourth, we discover God's love for us (verse 16).

John begins by declaring that the Holy Spirit is the evidence upon which we come to know that we dwell in Him and He dwells in us (verse 13). John's use of the present tense—"hereby know we"—indicates that he was talking about a current experience that they were living in. This was not something that had happened in the past and thereby the event was over. John pointed out that we know these things to be true now. "We dwell in Him, and He in us."

Verse 13 reiterates John's affirmation in 3:24 of the bestowal of the Holy Spirit as evidence of our relationship with the Father. God has given us His Spirit. He is God's gift to the believer and, hence, to the entire body of Christ. In fact, He is the very seal of our redemption in Christ (see Ephesians 1:13; 4:30). Our relationship with the Father is not based upon feelings, emotions, or words. Rather, we know that we have been saved because of God's presence living in us and working through us.

Verse 13 also raises a serious question for the believer. What does it mean to be spiritual? If God has given us His Spirit—who lives in us and works through us—how then do we know that we possess Him? This is particularly important given that so many people confuse emotional responses with genuine spirituality.

What then does it mean to be spiritual? Spirituality is doing all of the things that are necessary to develop, cultivate, and maintain a deep, abiding relationship with the Lord Jesus Christ (see Romans 8:1-5; Galatians 5:16, 22-26). We are spiritual to the extent that we live in submission to the will of the Lord Jesus Christ at all times. Verse 14 says that the witness of the apostles was further evidence of the truth of God's love for the world.

Verse 15 points back to the first statements of John in verse 2: "Hereby know ye the Spirit of God: Every spirit that confesseth that Jesus Christ is come in the flesh is of God." John stated that "whosoever" proclaims Jesus to be the Son of God has God living in him or her. The word "confess" points back to a specific point in time when a man or woman made this declaration of the Sonship of Jesus Christ. For anyone to confess Jesus Christ as the Son of God in the first Christian century meant death (see Revelation 2:13).

God's Spirit dwells in anyone who makes this fundamental confession of faith in Jesus as the Son of God. It is this affirmation of faith that unites all Christians around the world into one global body of Christ (see Ephesians 4:1-6). What does it mean in our lives to confess Jesus Christ to be the Son of God?

The passage concludes with a summary statement regarding the love of God, which reflects that something took place in the past and it is continuing right up to that present moment. John wrote that we knew of God's love in the past and we continue to know it today. Because God never changes, His love for each of us abides forever.

## C. The Power of Perfect Love
(1 John 4:17-21)

**Herein is our love made perfect, that we may have boldness in the day of judgment: because as he is, so are we in this world. There is no fear in love; but perfect love casteth out fear: because fear hath torment. He that feareth is not made perfect in love. We love him, because he first loved us. If a man say, I love God, and hateth his brother, he is a liar: for he that loveth not his brother whom he hath seen, how can he love God whom he hath not seen? And this commandment have we from him, That he who loveth God love his brother also.**

John continues to make his point by turning to what can be termed "the power of perfect love." Perfect is not to be understood as flawless; rather, the Greek word is *telioo* (pronounced tel-i-o-o), and it refers to something that has been brought to an end, has been completed, or is fully developed (see Hebrews 13:21; James 2:22). In some instances, *telioo* is used to indicate maturity, as in the statement of Jesus in Matthew 5:48: "Be ye therefore perfect, even as your Father which is in heaven is perfect." When the Day of Judgment dawns, John declared that we would be able to stand boldly before God's throne, free of condemnation. Boldness is a word that John used on three other occasions in this epistle—2:28; 3:21; and 5:14. In these verses, the word "confidence" is used. Love gives us confidence because we are like Jesus Christ, who is our Advocate with the Father, as well as our example for overcoming the world.

Perfect love—or love that is completely developed—is not characterized by fear or a spirit of fear. In fact, it is the very thing that casts out fear. Because we are the object of God's love and recipients of His grace, we have no need to live in fear. The reason we live without fear points back to the love of God. We did not love God first; He loved us first and without condition. "We love him, because he first loved us" (verse 19).

For John, there were no gray areas: either one loves or one does not love. In verse 20, he expressed what surely must have been a critical issue facing the church at that time—individual members claiming to love God, while hating others in the fellowship. How true this is even in our time; we can claim unequivocally that we love God, and yet will not speak to other believers who share the same pew. The Bible says to such people, "You are a liar." This is a very strong word and refers to someone who breaks faith. When we love God we must love our brothers and sisters in the faith. This is God's timeless commandment to every believer across the ages.

## III. Concluding Reflections

Conflict, confusion, unfounded rumors, and disagreements over congregational direction and pastoral leadership are all too common in America's churches. Many times, the cause of disagreements that erupt among Christians can be insignificant. Yet, these trivial issues can catapult congregations into a period of devastating spiritual decline. What happens to the spiritual climate of a congregation when the members do not love and are constantly involved in disagreements? What happens to the credibility of congregational spiritual leaders when they are always at the center of confusion? How do we avoid these disruptive episodes that bring havoc to congregations? God's Word is our guide. This lesson points out, as did the previous lessons, that love is the true foundation for a healthy congregational life. When the people of God love genuinely and deeply, reconciliation between believers is a living reality and not just another Bible lesson. Do we practice love? Are we open to real reconciliation? Are we serious enough about our relationship with God that we seek to maintain the unity in the bond of peace?

God has shown by His example what it means to love even the most unlovable person when He gave Jesus Christ to be the ransom for the sin of the whole world. When we love, we demonstrate to the world that God's Spirit lives in us.

## WORD POWER

**Love (Greek: *agapao*)**—in our Key Verse, "love" appears two times, but each serves different functions. The first love means "at present, we love Him." This love is viewed as occurring in actual time. This may change because of adverse circumstances. However, the second is in aorist tense. It means, "the love of God is not based on mood." In other words, His love does not suffer mood swings. He loved us, He loves us, and He will continue to love us.

## HOME DAILY BIBLE READINGS

for the week of March 18, 2007
*The Source of Love*
Mar. 12, Monday
 —Romans 5:1-11
 —Be Reconciled to God
Mar. 13, Tuesday
 —Matthew 5:21-26
 —Be Reconciled to One Another
Mar. 14, Wednesday
 —John 21:15-19
 —Care for One Another
Mar. 15, Thursday
 —1 Timothy 6:11-19
 —Investing in Eternity
Mar. 16, Friday
 —1 John 4:7-12
 —Knowing God Through Love
Mar. 17, Saturday
 —1 John 4:13-17
 —God Is Love
Mar. 18, Sunday
 —1 John 4:18-21
 —Love Brothers and Sisters

## PRAYER

*Heavenly Father, thank You for loving us in spite of our brokenness and sinfulness. You loved us with an everlasting love and showed us by the sacrifice of Your only Begotten Son that love is more than a word. May we be more willing to practice the teaching of Your Son to give ourselves in selfless love. Forgive us of every sin that separates us from You. In the name of Jesus Christ, we pray. Amen.*

# Lesson 4

# The Way to Love

**March 25, 2007**

**ADULT TOPIC:** The Way to Love and Life
**YOUTH TOPIC:** Live Forever in Love
**CHILDREN'S TOPIC:** God's Children Follow Jesus

**UNIT I**
Known by Our Love

**CHILDREN'S UNIT**
A Special Letter

**DEVOTIONAL READING:** John 17:1-5
**BACKGROUND SCRIPTURE:** 1 John 5:1-12
**PRINT PASSAGE:** 1 John 5:1-12

## 1 John 5:1-12—KJV

WHOSOEVER BELIEVETH that Jesus is the Christ is born of God: and every one that loveth him that begat loveth him also that is begotten of him.

2 By this we know that we love the children of God, when we love God, and keep his commandments.

3 For this is the love of God, that we keep his commandments: and his commandments are not grievous.

4 For whatsoever is born of God overcometh the world: and this is the victory that overcometh the world, even our faith.

5 Who is he that overcometh the world, but he that believeth that Jesus is the Son of God?

6 This is he that came by water and blood, even Jesus Christ; not by water only, but by water and blood. And it is the Spirit that beareth witness, because the Spirit is truth.

7 For there are three that bear record in heaven, the Father, the Word, and the Holy Ghost: and these three are one.

8 And there are three that bear witness in earth, the spirit, and the water, and the blood: and these three agree in one.

9 If we receive the witness of men, the witness of God is greater: for this is the witness of God which he hath testified of his Son.

10 He that believeth on the Son of God hath the witness in himself: he that believeth not God hath made him a liar; because he believeth not the record that God gave of his Son.

11 And this is the record, that God hath given to us eternal life, and this life is in his Son.

12 He that hath the Son hath life; and he that hath not the Son of God hath not life.

**KEY VERSE**

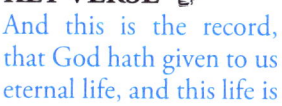

And this is the record, that God hath given to us eternal life, and this life is in his Son.
—1 John 5:11

**OBJECTIVES**

Upon completion of this lesson, the students are expected to:

1. Explore the importance of faith as the means on entering into a right relationship with God through Jesus Christ;
2. Recognize that if we love God, we must also love those whom the Father loves and who have been born of Him; and,
3. Recognize that our faith in the risen Christ guarantees our victory over the world.

## UNIFYING LESSON PRINCIPLE

People want to believe that life can go on after physical death. What hope of life after death can we find in Jesus Christ? John affirms that our victorious faith in Jesus Christ will grant us eternal life and empower us to love in the way that God wants. The Mark passages tell us that Jesus is the Messiah, who calls us to love and follow Him; according to the 1 John passage, those who do will have eternal life.

## POINTS TO BE EMPHASIZED
### ADULTS/YOUTH

**Adult/Youth Key Verse:** 1 John 5:11
**Print Passage:** 1 John 5:1-12

—What does being born of God mean?
—How does Christ empower us to overcome the sin and the evil in the world?
—What is the importance of the three witnesses—Spirit, water, and blood—testifying to the truth?

### CHILDREN

**Key Verse:** Mark 8:29
**Print Passage:** Mark 1:16-18; 8:27-29; 1 John 5:13

—God continues to select the most unlikely persons to help spread the Gospel message.
—The first disciples recognized Jesus as one worthy to be followed.
—Those whom Jesus called were already busily working at their jobs.

## TOPICAL OUTLINE OF THE LESSON

**I. Introduction**
  A. A Right Relationship with God
  B. Biblical Background

**II. Exposition and Application of the Scripture**
  A. Born to Love *(1 John 5:1-3)*
  B. Faith that Overcomes the World *(1 John 5:4-5)*
  C. The True Witnesses *(1 John 5:6-12)*

**III. Concluding Reflections**

## I. Introduction
### A. A Right Relationship with God

Christians hold different opinions on a variety of issues. Some Christians claim to be politically and socially conservative, while others declare themselves to be liberal. We differ over which form of church government is more biblical (i.e., Episcopal—bishop-led church; papal or Roman Catholic—pope-led church; Presbyterian—elected board of elders lead the church; or congregational—people make decisions in a gathered assembly).

But there is one thing that Christians are decidedly unified about, and that is the death, burial, resurrection, ascension, and return of Jesus Christ. Without question, all Christians believe that Jesus of Nazareth was crucified on a Roman cross and that His death was a vicarious atonement for the sins of the whole world. We believe unanimously that Jesus was buried and that on the third day God raised Him from the dead (see Matthew 28:1-8; Acts 2:31-32; 1 Corinthians 15:1-6). We believe that Jesus ascended back to heaven and one day He will return with all of the holy angels to take His people to be with Him in heaven forever (see Acts 1:11; 1 Thessalonians 4:13-17; Revelation 7:9-17).

Today's lesson is the culmination of our study of 1 John. In the previous three lessons, we examined the apostle John's teachings regarding the importance of love as the foundation of congregational life. For John there were no gray areas—either one was saved or one was still a sinner. The evidence of one's salvation was seen in two areas: obedience to the commandments of God, and love for the brethren. This lesson focuses on faith as the means to entering into a right relationship with God through Jesus Christ.

## B. Biblical Background

What were the circumstances that the Christian church faced during the time that the apostle John wrote this epistle? As we have learned throughout this brief study of 1 John, believers in those days experienced a tremendous external threat.

During the outbreak of persecution, many of the believers who lived in Jerusalem migrated to other parts of the Roman Empire to escape the threats. By the time John wrote his epistles, the center of the Christian church had shifted from Jerusalem to Antioch of Syria, Ephesus, and, to a lesser extent, to Alexandria, Egypt, and Rome. Christian tradition has it that John left Jerusalem shortly after the resurrection of Jesus Christ and migrated north and west, eventually settling in Ephesus, where he lived to a ripe-old age.

At the time John wrote his epistle, Christians were facing a far greater threat than outside hostility. They were torn apart from within by members who held beliefs that were antithetical to the doctrine of the apostles, which centered on the death, burial, resurrection, and ascension of Jesus (see Acts 2:42). This heresy came to be known as gnosticism.

The early Christians believed that Jesus was both human and divine at the same time. Unless these false beliefs of gnosticism were addressed and corrected, the Christian faith ran the risk of becoming a religious movement based upon false teachings and practices. This is the chief benefit of John's writings. He helps us understand the importance of confronting false beliefs before they take hold in the lives of believers.

## II. Exposition and Application of the Scripture
### A. Born to Love *(1 John 5:1-3)*

**Whosoever believeth that Jesus is the Christ is born of God: and every one that loveth him that begat loveth him also that is begotten of him. By this we know that we love the children of God, when we love God, and keep his commandments. For this is the love of God, that we keep his commandments: and his commandments are not grievous.**

John remarked that whoever believes that Jesus is the Christ is born of God (verse 1). "Christ" is the Greek translation of the Hebrew word for *Messiah.* Early Christians proclaimed that Jesus was the Messiah (i.e., God's anointed). John stated that the act of believing in the messianic mission of Jesus is a continuous activity. That is to say, it is the very act of believing in Jesus that shows our true spiritual nature—that we have been born again. It is the act of remaining steadfast in one's resolve to follow Jesus in the midst of trials that also validates the new birth. It is clearly true that we are born again by an act of faith (see Romans 10:9ff; Ephesians 2:8-10); nevertheless, saving faith is just the beginning of the Christian life. Continuous faith in the risen Christ reflects the life of God in us as we live in obedience to His Word and will.

Faith and love go hand in hand; therefore, to be born again expresses itself through selfless love of God. Moreover, it is further seen in our love for the children of God. If we love the Father, we love those whom the Father loves and who have been born of Him. How can someone be a member of a local congregation and dislike others who are part of the community of faith and family of God? Verse 2 points to further evidence of the new birth. First, we love God, which is the first and greatest commandment. Second, we keep His commandments (see Joshua 1:5-10). We are called to live and walk in absolute obedience to His will. Obedience identifies us with Jesus, who always did those things that pleased the Father (see John 8:29; 14:15; 15:10). The believer should thrive to live a life that is fruitful and well-pleasing to God (see John 15:1-8; Colossians 1:9-10).

John declared that God's commandments are not grievous (Greek—*barus*, meaning "heavy, burdensome, or stern"). The Christian life is not burdensome. During His earthly ministry Jesus drew a clear line of distinction between His teachings and those of the scribes and Pharisees. The latter made it difficult to live for God. They placed heavy burdens and demands upon the people, many of whom became discouraged and did not try to serve God (see Matthew 23:1-5, 13). Jesus called men and women to follow Him and to take up His yoke and burden, which were much easier to receive and carry.

Christians in the modern era face a tremendous challenge in the area of love for one another, let alone those outside of their individual fellowships. We often hear people praying, "God, give us more love for each other." The very words of the petition are filled with doubt about one's relationship with the Father. Asking for more love to fill our hearts is contrary to the teachings of Scripture. If we keep His commandments and have been born again, love is a natural by-product of the Spirit's presence in our hearts.

### B. Faith that Overcomes the World (1 John 5:4-5)

**For whatsoever is born of God overcometh the world: and this is the victory that overcometh the world, even our faith. Who is he that overcometh the world, but he that believeth that Jesus is the Son of God?**

John returned to the concept of overcoming the world, a theme that he discussed earlier in 2:15-17 about worldliness. The new birth gives us the power to overcome the world. How do we overcome the world? Authentic spiritual transformation is the key to overcoming the lures and traps of the world. Our faith in the risen Christ guarantees our victory over the world. Faith in the power of God gives us certainty in our battles against the demonic schemes of the devil (see Ephesians 6:10-12). "World" is used in Scripture to denote and represent all of the believer's external obstacles and opposition. The "world" denotes every hindrance that seeks to stop what God is doing in the lives of believers.

The lures and the things of this world can pull us away from our commitment to Jesus Christ. Money, silver, and gold can consume us (see Matthew 6:19-20). It is not the possession of money or the riches of this world that drain and drown the presence of God's Spirit; rather, it is the love of money that is the root of all evil (see Joshua 7:10-26; 1 Timothy 6:9-10). There are many people who believe that money can solve all of their problems and every human and social problem that exists. Money can solve many problems, but it cannot restore broken relationships, save from destructive attitudes and behaviors, restore trust, or rebuild shattered marriages.

The things of this world, the pride that we have in what we have acquired or achieved, can become the very things that block our spiritual development. Satan will use every tactic at his disposal to keep us spiritually stunted and disinterested in the things of the kingdom of God. Possessions and materialism are enormous roadblocks for many believers (see Luke 12:13-21; 1 Timothy 6:9-10).

Here are some helpful suggestions on how to overcome the world and the attacks of the devil. First, study the Scriptures to seek spiritual guidance on how to deal with worldliness.

Second, review the three areas of worldly lust discussed in 1 John 2:15-17. We should take a serious look at our personal characters and lifestyles. Are there things that we can see that indicate that Satan is seeking to erect a spiritual stronghold in some area of our lives?

Third, recognize the things, traps, and enticements that Satan uses. Understand the power of temptation and how Satan uses it.

Finally, we must make a conscious effort to list the areas of our lives where we have been vulnerable to worldly passions and attacks, and face our weaknesses and learn the value of flight (see 1 Corinthians 6:18; 1 Timothy 6:11). How do we combat these subtle distractions of the devil? Jesus appeared on the earth as a living human being. He was at once both God and man. John referred to His humanity when he used the earthly name Jesus, and His deity is expressed through His messianic title of Son of God. John says that it is our faith in the Lord Jesus Christ that gives us the victory.

### C. The True Witnesses *(1 John 5:6-12)*

**This is he that came by water and blood, even Jesus Christ; not by water only, but by water and blood. And it is the Spirit that beareth witness, because the Spirit is truth. For there are three that bear record in heaven, the Father, the Word, and the Holy Ghost: and these three are one. And there are three that bear witness in earth, the spirit, and the water, and the blood: and these three agree in one. If we receive the witness of men, the witness of God is greater: for this is the witness of God which he hath testified of his Son. He that believeth on the Son of God hath the witness in himself: he that believeth not God hath made him a liar; because he believeth not the record that God gave of his Son. And this is the record, that God hath given to us eternal life, and this life is in his Son. He that hath the Son hath life; and he that hath not the Son of God hath not life.**

At the heart of this paragraph is the overarching question of the quality of our personal witness to the life and love of God in Christ. Verse 6 continues John's argument against the rise and spread of the heresy of gnosticism (see the Biblical Background section of this lesson). Jesus came into the world as God's remedy for human sin and rebellion. John asserted that He came by water and the blood. How are we to understand what John meant by the words, "He that came by water and blood. . . not by water only, but by water and blood?" On the one hand, John may be referring to his personal witness of the crucifixion of Jesus in John 19:34-35, where he saw blood mixed with water flow from the pierced side of Jesus. On the other hand, these symbols of water and blood point back to the historical events of the baptism and Crucifixion. Jesus did not become the Son of God at His baptism, but was from the beginning. He did not come to die as a martyr, but to destroy the works of Satan by shedding His own blood for our sins. The Holy Spirit bore witness to both the baptism and the crucifixion of Christ.

What and who constitutes a credible witness? Verses 7-9 are clearly allusions to the Mosaic tradition that prescribed the conditions under which a person could be convicted of wrongdoing. There had to be two or more credible witnesses who personally saw the offense take place (see Deuteronomy 17:6; 19:15-16).

Verse 7 points to the threefold witness of Jesus in heaven. It appears that John points to three credible witnesses in heaven that validate that Jesus Christ is the Son of God. First, there is the witness of the Father. Second, there is the witness of the Word, who is the Son. John clearly had in view the fact of Jesus' resurrection, which validated His witness. Third, there is the witness of the Holy Spirit. The verse ends with the declaration that the three witnesses are in agreement with each other.

In verse 8, John points to the three witnesses in the earth that bear witness to the Sonship of Jesus Christ. These three witnesses are the Spirit, the water, and the blood. The latter two have already been discussed in detail in the exposition of verse 6. Again, these three are in agreement. We must not assume that John had in view the development of some Trinitarian doctrine of the Godhead. John does make it clear that if men and women were willing to trust the witness of other human beings, they should be that much more willing to trust the witness of God, which is far greater than any earthly witness.

Belief in the Sonship of Jesus Christ is evidence of the Holy Spirit abiding and living in the heart of the confessor. His internal witness is the Holy Spirit (verse 10). Doubt and disbelief say that one believes God is a liar because one has turned away from His witness. In verses 11 and 12, four statements are made about eternal life. First, God is the Giver of eternal life. It comes to us as a gift of God's grace and is a further expression of His love (see John 3:16). God alone is its source, and no amount of good deeds can supplant that (see Ephesians 2:8-10). Second, eternal life is in His Son. The reference is to the work of Christ as Savior of the world. Eternal life is not found anywhere else in the world. Eternal life begins here and now and refers more to the quality of life than its length. It is a present reality the moment one repents and accepts Jesus Christ as Lord of his or her life. Third, possession of the Son as Lord means that one has eternal life, and that without Him there is no life.

## III. Concluding Reflections

At what point does a church or a Christian begin to look like an organization or a person who reflects more of the culture than Jesus Christ? Worldliness has been a continuing challenge for believers since the earliest days of the Christian faith. Today, we hear echoes of the church becoming more worldly when questions are raised about what constitutes true worship. At the center of many of these debates is the choice of music for a church's worship service. Granted, music that does not highlight the teachings of Scripture, Jesus Christ, the love of God, or the work of the Holy Spirit may be more reflective of the contemporary culture and less of the Bible. Secular music—where a few words have been changed, but the overall tune and tone remains the same—may not be appropriate for a church worship service. Yet, at the same time, music that is more Euro-centric and less Afro-centric is not holier if it does not minister to the spiritual needs of the congregation and honors God. We must be clear about the differences between individual, personal preferences and what Scripture mandates. Today's lesson has taught us that worldliness is an attitude and disposition of heart and mind that is more centered in the culture and not in the Christ.

## WORD POWER

**Record (Greek: *marturia*)**—in the Key Verse, marturia was translated by the *King James Version* as "record." This word has shades of meanings. The clause could be read as: this is the evidence, witness, testimony, or declaration of fact. In essence, John is saying that his writing about Christ is a declaration of fact. The fact of the matter is: Christians have eternal life.

## HOME DAILY BIBLE READINGS

for the week of March 25, 2007
*The Way to Love*
Mar. 19, Monday
 —Mark 1:16-20
 —Jesus Calls Disciples
Mar. 20, Tuesday
 —John 3:16-21
 —God's Love Saves Creation
Mar. 21, Wednesday
 —John 17:1-5
 —Jesus Seeks the Father
Mar. 22, Thursday
 —Romans 8:9-17
 —We Belong to God
Mar. 23, Friday
 —Galatians 4:1-7
 —We Are God's Heirs
Mar. 24, Saturday
 —1 John 5:1-6
 —Love God's Children
Mar. 25, Sunday
 —1 John 5:7-13
 —God Gives Eternal Life

## PRAYER

*Heavenly Father, grant us to know the difference between Your ways and the world's ways. Forgive us of every sin that separates us from You. In the name of Jesus Christ, we pray. Amen.*

**April 1, 2007**

Lesson 5

# Christ Is Our King

**ADULT TOPIC:** Yielding to Christ's Lordship
**YOUTH TOPIC:** Blessed Is the King!
**CHILDREN'S TOPIC:** Jesus Is King!

**DEVOTIONAL READING:** Psalm 118:21-28
**BACKGROUND SCRIPTURE:** Revelation 1:1-8; Luke 19:28-40
**PRINT PASSAGE:** Revelation 1:8; Luke 19:28-40

## UNIT II
A New Community in Christ

## CHILDREN'S UNIT
More Special Letters to Churches

## KEY VERSE
Saying, Blessed be the King that cometh in the name of the Lord: peace in heaven, and glory in the highest.
—Luke 19:38

## OBJECTIVES
Upon completion of this lesson, the students are expected to:
1. Learn that Christians affirm that Jesus of Nazareth is both Christ and Lord;
2. Recognize that in Christ we experience the forgiveness of sins through His sacrifice; and,
3. Understand that praise of God's might and power gives us the courage to face the enemies of our Lord Jesus Christ.

### Revelation 1:8; Luke 19:28-40—KJV

8 I am Alpha and Omega, the beginning and the ending, saith the Lord, which is, and which was, and which is to come, the Almighty.

.....

28 And when he had thus spoken, he went before, ascending up to Jerusalem.

29 And it came to pass, when he was come nigh to Bethphage and Bethany, at the mount called the mount of Olives, he sent two of his disciples,

30 Saying, Go ye into the village over against you; in the which at your entering ye shall find a colt tied, whereon yet never man sat: loose him, and bring him hither.

31 And if any man ask you, Why do ye loose him? thus shall ye say unto him, Because the Lord hath need of him.

32 And they that were sent went their way, and found even as he had said unto them.

33 And as they were loosing the colt, the owners thereof said unto them, Why loose ye the colt?

34 And they said, The Lord hath need of him.

35 And they brought him to Jesus: and they cast their garments upon the colt, and they set Jesus thereon.

36 And as he went, they spread their clothes in the way.

37 And when he was come nigh, even now at the descent of the mount of Olives, the whole multitude of the disciples began to rejoice and praise God with a loud voice for all the mighty works that they had seen;

38 Saying, Blessed be the King that cometh in the name of the Lord: peace in heaven, and glory in the highest.

39 And some of the Pharisees from among the multitude said unto him, Master, rebuke thy disciples.

40 And he answered and said unto them, I tell you that, if these should hold their peace, the stones would immediately cry out.

## UNIFYING LESSON PRINCIPLE

People will easily rally behind a leader that they trust and love. Who is the ultimate such leader for us? The Revelation passages affirm that Jesus, who encompasses all things, is the Ruler of all rulers. Luke's account of the triumphal entry into Jerusalem describes a time when Jesus' kingship was symbolically demonstrated to the world.

## POINTS TO BE EMPHASIZED
## ADULTS/YOUTH

**Adult/Youth Key Verse:** Luke 19:38
**Print Passage:** Revelation 1:8;
Luke 19:28-40
—In response to God's saving act on our behalf, praise and thanksgiving are appropriate.
—Onlookers welcomed Jesus because they believed Him to be the Messiah.
—Jesus is the ruler of a spiritual kingdom, which transcends the physical.

## CHILDREN

**Key Verse:** Luke 19:38
**Print Passage:** Revelation 1:4-5a;
Luke 19:28-38
—God's messengers are given everything they need to be successful.
—God exalts those who serve Him with meekness and humility.

—The disciples praised Jesus for all of His powerful deeds.
—Jesus, our King, deserves praise at all times, in all places, and by all people.

## TOPICAL OUTLINE OF THE LESSON

### I. INTRODUCTION
   A. The King Is Here!
   B. Biblical Background

### II. EXPOSITION AND APPLICATION OF THE SCRIPTURE
   A. Jesus Will Come Again (Revelation 1:8)
   B. Preparations for the King's Entry (Luke 19:28-35)
   C. Praise for the King (Luke 19:36-40)

### III. CONCLUDING REFLECTIONS

## I. INTRODUCTION
## A. The King Is Here!

Christians everywhere affirm that Jesus of Nazareth is both Christ and Lord, and that His redemptive work at Calvary was the fulfillment of God's eternal plan—from the foundation of the world—to save humanity (see Ephesians 1:4; Revelation 13:8). Luke reports that Jesus arrived in the precincts near Jerusalem after leaving Jericho, where He had a successful, though short, period of ministry. Going to Jerusalem had been His primary goal very early in His ministry (see Luke 9:51). The triumphal entry marks the culmination of three years of active ministry for the Lord. We are certain of its historical validity because it is reported by the other three gospel writers (see Matthew 21:1-9; Mark 11:1-10; John 12:12-15).

The procession of Jesus into Jerusalem began at Bethphage, which is located about two miles southeast of Jerusalem. The route that Jesus would have taken crosses near the summit of the Mount of Olives and descends along a winding road, past a Jewish cemetery, the Garden of Gethsemane, through the Kidron Valley, and into the city—through either the Zion Gate or the Dung Gate. We are not certain through which gate Jesus entered the city, but these appear to be the most likely ones, given their proximity to the temple area.

Jesus proceeded toward the city riding on a colt, in a way that fulfilled the ancient messianic prophecies of Zechariah 9:9. The message would have been very clear to the people who accompanied Jesus and His disciples: Behold, the Messiah is coming; prepare the way for the Lord (see Malachi 3:1ff.). As they made their way down the side of the mountain, the people who accompanied Him praised God with loud voices for all of the mighty deeds that they had seen (see Psalm 118). No doubt there was growing excitement that the long-awaited Messiah had finally come! Rome's rule and dominance would be thrown off and Israel would once again be a free sovereign nation.

Our lesson today comes from two passages of the New Testament. The first is Revelation 1:8, where the apostle John has a revelation of the risen and triumphant Christ. In the first passage, we hear the God of creation proclaiming His sovereignty over the universe. In Him, we experience the forgiveness of sins through the sacrifice of His dear Son, Jesus Christ. The second passage takes us back to the triumphal entry of the Lord into Jerusalem. We witness the start of the events that led to the crucifixion of our Lord Jesus Christ as Saviour of the world.

## B. Biblical Background

One of the themes of today's lesson is the Jewish belief in the Messiah. The early Christian church believed and preached that Jesus was the fulfillment of every prophecy concerning the Messiah (see Acts 2:31-36). During the time of Jesus' ministry, there were several messianic movements circulating throughout Israel (see Acts 5:33-37). All of these movements had a major impact upon the life of the Jewish nation. The concept of the Messiah was a very important development in Israel—for it was the belief in the Messiah that provided the hope Israel needed to sustain itself during its days of trial and difficulty, particularly during the time of the Babylonian exile and the period following the return of the exiles. One of the prevailing beliefs was that the Messiah would come as a King.

The concept of the Messiah as a King probably did not develop in the thinking of Israel until some time during or after the reign of King David. The belief was that the King-Messiah would be a son of David.

After the time of David, all of the prophets interpreted the covenant between God and David in messianic overtones. They all made references to the promise made by God to David (see Isaiah 11:1, 10; Jeremiah 23:5; 33:15, 17, 22; Ezekiel 37:24; Hosea 3:5; Amos 9:11; Micah 5:2-5; Zechariah 12:8). David was the ideal king. He had been chosen by God, over his other brothers, to lead God's people. He was not the oldest, nor the tallest, but he was God's choice.

God promised that David's throne would be permanent. One of David's heirs would sit upon his throne forever (see 2 Samuel 7:13). The Babylonian Exile (2 Kings 24-25) effectively ended the Davidic line of kings, but not the lineage of David.

The belief in the Messiah as the son of David was very much alive during the time of the ministry of Jesus. In fact, Jesus was referred to as the Son of David (see Matthew 9:27; Luke 18:38). The ministry of Jesus was steeped with messianic overtones and excitement (see Matthew 11:2-6; Luke 7:16-23). Jesus never used the title of Messiah/Christ to refer to Himself. During His trial by the Jewish Sanhedrin Court, one of the charges against Him was His claim of being the Christ (see Luke 22:66-67). Yet, He never answered His accusers.

There was clearly an expectation that the long-awaited Messiah had appeared in Jesus of Nazareth. On the road to Jerusalem, as they were entering the city on what has come to be known as Palm Sunday, the crowd greeted Jesus as the coming King-Messiah (Luke 19:37-38). Yet, He came not as a conquering Soldier-King, but as the Prince of Peace.

## II. Exposition and Application of the Scripture
### A. Jesus Will Come Again
*(Revelation 1:8)*

**I am Alpha and Omega, the beginning and the ending, saith the Lord, which is, and which was, and which is to come, the Almighty.**

A fundamental declaration of Christian belief is that one day Jesus Christ will return for His church (see 1 Thessalonians 4:13-17; Revelation 1:7). The first time Jesus came into the world was as a babe—humble and helpless. When He appeared in Jerusalem the first time as God's ambassador of peace and goodwill, He rode upon a lowly colt. In the final appearance of the Christ, He will come, riding upon the clouds and surrounded by all of the holy angels. Jesus will come again! Jesus made the Second Coming a centerpiece of His message (see Matthew 16:28; 24:27, 30, 37, 39, 44; 25:13, 31; 26:64; Luke 22:69). At His ascension on Mount Olivet, an angel of the Lord declared that the same Lord the disciples witnessed rise into the clouds would come again in the same manner (see Acts 1:11).

Sometime during the latter days of the first century A.D., God gave John a revelation of the things that are to come during the time immediately preceding the return of Christ. In verse 8, we see the divine seal of confirmation: "I am Alpha and Omega, the beginning and the ending, saith the Lord, which is, and which was, and which is to come, the Almighty." God spoke to John regarding the certainty of what he had just heard and what he was about to hear and see. This verse is one of the most significant in the book of Revelation. It is a verse where Jesus personally speaks to John about who He is. We learn several things about Jesus Christ. He is Alpha and Omega, the first and last letters of the Greek alphabet. The fact is that everything has its origin in Jesus Christ as God. History and time are both subject to Him. Thus, He is both beginning and ending at the same time.

Jesus is the One "which is, which was, and which is to come." This further describes His place in history. One day, Christ will come and take us to be with Him forever in glory. Finally, He is the Almighty (Greek–*pantokrator,* a compound word that means "one who has complete power and authority"). None supersedes nor surpasses Him in power, authority, or sovereignty.

### B. Preparations for the King's Entry
 (Luke 19:28-35)

**And when he had thus spoken, he went before, ascending up to Jerusalem. And it came to pass, when he was come nigh to Bethphage and Bethany, at the mount called the mount of Olives, he sent two of his disciples, Saying, Go ye into the village over against you; in the which at your entering ye shall find a colt tied, whereon yet never man sat: loose him, and bring him hither. And if any man ask you, Why do ye loose him? thus shall ye say unto him, Because the Lord hath need of him. And they that were sent went their way, and found even as he had said unto them. And as they were loosing the colt, the owners thereof said unto them, Why loose ye the colt? And they said, The Lord hath need of him. And they brought him to Jesus: and they cast their garments upon the colt, and they set Jesus thereon.**

After teaching the Parable of the Pounds, either in Jericho or along the way, Luke stated that Jesus made the steep climb up toward Jerusalem. This would be the final time that He would visit Jericho and travel the old road that ran from the Jordan Valley up to Jerusalem. John reported that Jesus had arrived six days prior to the celebration of Passover and that He went first to Bethany, where He spent some days before His triumphal entry (see John 12:1).

Jesus sent two of His unnamed disciples into the village of Bethphage to bring back the donkey that would carry Him into the city. The question—"How did Jesus know where to send the disciples?"—has been the subject of some discussion among Christians. We do not know all of the details surrounding the preparations made by Jesus prior to the day of the procession. Some said Jesus could have pre-arranged the colt to be present, or Jesus could have had a family friend of Lazarus and his sisters pre-position the colt for Him. We believe that Jesus is fully God and, therefore, by divine intuition He knew that there was a colt tied for His use at the moment. The disciples were given clear instructions as to what to look for: an animal that had been tied and one on whom no man had ever ridden. If they were questioned regarding their actions, they were to respond by telling those who asked that the Lord had need of the colt. The events unfolded just as Jesus had stated. They were asked about their actions. The disciples responded just as they had been told. The disciples were never portrayed as being defiant, indifferent, or disobedient to any request that Jesus made of them. They were always willing to follow Jesus, even when they did not fully understand what was going on. It is doubtful whether they fully understood what was about to happen. Sometimes, God will lead us to get involved in activities that serve His purpose, but which we do not fully comprehend. The disciples brought the colt to Jesus, and He sat on it.

The procession to Jerusalem began on the Mount of Olives. Clearly, there were messianic overtones in the procession down the Mount of Olives. At the base of the mountain, not more than a few hundred yards from the Eastern Gate of Jerusalem, is the Garden of Gethsemane. This is a place that was well-known by Jesus and His disciples and was more than likely visited by Jesus during His ministry, especially when He traveled to Jerusalem for the annual feasts (see Luke 22:39-40; John 8:1). Its proximity to Jerusalem makes it one of the ideal locations to view the city, especially the temple mount—where the second temple was built by Zerubbabel and Jeshua sometime shortly after the return from Babylon (see Ezra 4:1ff; Zechariah 4:1ff.).

### C. Praise for the King (Luke 19:36-40)

**And as he went, they spread their clothes in the way. And when he was come nigh, even now at the descent of the mount of Olives, the whole multitude of the disciples began to rejoice and praise God with a loud voice for all the mighty works that they had seen; Saying, Blessed be the King that cometh in the name of the Lord: peace in heaven, and glory in the highest. And some of the Pharisees from among the multitude said unto him, Master, rebuke thy disciples. And he answered and said unto them, I tell you that, if these should hold their peace, the stones would immediately cry out**.

Luke's description of the event varies slightly from that of Mark (11:1-10) and of Matthew (21:1-9). As a sign and show of deep respect and honor, the people spread their garments along Jesus' pathway. Mark and Matthew also state that the people spread out branches of trees in the way. Just as they reached the summit and the point at which they would begin to go down toward Jerusalem, the city came into view. This initial view is of the eastern end, close to where the ancient city of David was located. They saw the first signs of the city and broke forth in jubilant praise.

The praise was not coming from an unknown group of people. These were the Lord's disciples, many of whom had followed along with Him from Galilee. There were also hundreds of pilgrims who were on their way to Jerusalem for the celebration of the annual Passover, who were among those shouting "Hosanna!" The whole multitude of the disciples began to celebrate and praise God with loud voices. Unlike today—wherein some Christians may consider vocal expressions of thanksgiving or loud shouts of praise unnecessary—here Jesus gladly received it. They were praising God for all of the mighty works that they had seen. This more than likely refers to the totality of the demonstrations of power manifested through the life and ministry of Jesus in Galilee. Further, they rejoiced greatly, saying, "Blessed is the King that cometh in the name of the Lord." Their proclamations spoke of a heavenly kingdom where peace and harmony prevailed.

The Pharisees who were part of the throng requested that Jesus rebuke His disciples. They wanted them to stop this vocal demonstration of praise. Was their request centered on the possibility that Jesus would lead a revolt? Certainly, that was not the case. Unlike the Sadducees, who courted

Rome's favor, the Pharisees were adamantly opposed to Roman rule. They no doubt felt that praise should go to God and God alone. They did not acknowledge that Jesus was God in human flesh. Jesus responded that if the disciples held their peace, the stones would immediately cry out.

## III. Concluding Reflections

What is true worship? Is it ever appropriate to express our gratitude to God through emotional outbursts? Some people would argue that emotionalism is never appropriate and, furthermore, it is not a true gauge of a person's heart. Others would argue just the opposite. Biblical praise and worship was always demonstrative. Jesus accepted and encouraged public displays of love and reverence for God through vocal expressions of praise. Praise of God's might and power gives us the courage to face the enemies of our Lord Jesus Christ. In the book of Psalms we are encouraged to praise God with loud voices.

The lessons are clear. First, there are times when we are called to serve the Master in ways that we do not understand. Our response must be complete. Second, as witnesses of the mighty deeds of God, we are summoned to give His name the highest praise and glory. Third, our obedience will one day lead to the opportunity to permanently join the procession of saints who will march into the great celestial city of God.

## WORD POWER

**I am the Alpha and the Omega**—Revelation 1:8 arrests our attention. In contemporary English, it reads, "I am the A and the Z." The definite article (the) points out the particularity of Jesus: no other gods besides Him. The verse goes further to lay emphasis by saying, the One who is, was and is to come. Finally, the word "Almighty" (Greek, *pantokrato*) [Pan-all; krato-ruler] caps it all. It means "the One who holds sway over all things." He has dominion over all. He is the One that is coming.

## HOME DAILY BIBLE READINGS

for the week of April 1, 2007
*Christ Is Our King*

Mar. 26, Monday
    —1 Peter 2:4-10
    —Jesus Is the Cornerstone
Mar. 27, Tuesday
    —Hebrews 3:1-6
    —Jesus, God's Son
Mar. 28, Wednesday
    —Matthew 21:14-17
    —Children Praise Jesus
Mar. 29, Thursday
    —Psalm 118:21-28
    —Give Thanks
Mar. 30, Friday
    —Luke 19:28-34
    —The Lord Needs It
Mar. 31, Saturday
    —Luke 19:35-40
    —Blessed Is the King
Apr. 1, Sunday
    —Revelation 1:1-8
    —Christ Will Return

## PRAYER

*Heavenly Father, Your name is worthy of the highest honor and praise. We bless You for the assurance You have given of Your abiding presence always. Forgive us of every sin that separates us from You. In the name of Jesus Christ, we pray. Amen.*

**Lesson 6**

*April 8, 2007*
*(Easter)*

# Christ Is Risen

**ADULT TOPIC:** Discovering Resurrection
**YOUTH TOPIC:** Alive Forever!
**CHILDREN'S TOPIC:** Jesus Lives!

**UNIT II**
A New Community in Christ

**CHILDREN'S UNIT**
More Special Letters to Churches

**DEVOTIONAL READING:** Romans 14:7-12
**BACKGROUND SCRIPTURE:** Revelation 1:9-20; John 20:1-18, 30-31
**PRINT PASSAGE:** Revelation 1:12, 17-18; John 20:11-16, 30-31

### Revelation 1:12, 17-18; John 20:11-16, 30-31—KJV

12 And I turned to see the voice that spake with me.

.....

17 And when I saw him, I fell at his feet as dead. And he laid his right hand upon me, saying unto me, Fear not; I am the first and the last:
18 I am he that liveth, and was dead; and, behold, I am alive for evermore, Amen; and have the keys of hell and of death.

.....

11 But Mary stood without at the sepulchre weeping: and as she wept, she stooped down, and looked into the sepulchre,
12 And seeth two angels in white sitting, the one at the head, and the other at the feet, where the body of Jesus had lain.
13 And they say unto her, Woman, why weepest thou? She saith unto them, Because they have taken away my Lord, and I know not where they have laid him.
14 And when she had thus said, she turned herself back, and saw Jesus standing, and knew not that it was Jesus.
15 Jesus saith unto her, Woman, why weepest thou? whom seekest thou? She, supposing him to be the gardener, saith unto him, Sir, if thou have borne him hence, tell me where thou hast laid him, and I will take him away.
16 Jesus saith unto her, Mary. She turned herself, and saith unto him, Rabboni; which is to say, Master.

.....

### KEY VERSES

When I saw him, I fell at his feet as dead. And he laid his right hand upon me, saying unto me, Fear not; I am the first and the last: I am he that liveth, and was dead; and, behold, I am alive for evermore, Amen; and have the keys of hell and of death.
—Revelation 1:17-18

### OBJECTIVES

Upon completion of this lesson, the students are expected to:
1. Learn that God used John the revelator to write a message of hope to Christians;
2. Recognize that Resurrection Sunday is the culmination of God's plan on the earth to rid the world of sin; and,
3. Underscore the fact that Christ's resurrection assures us of eternal life.

30 And many other signs truly did Jesus in the presence of his disciples, which are not written in this book:

31 But these are written, that ye might believe that Jesus is the Christ, the Son of God; and that believing ye might have life through his name.

## UNIFYING LESSON PRINCIPLE

People long to hear good news, especially if it transforms their lives for the better. What transforming good news do we have to celebrate this Easter? John's account of the resurrection tells us that Jesus has conquered sin and death on our behalf, and the personal witness in Revelation attests to the ongoing presence of the resurrected Lord in the lives of believers.

## POINTS TO BE EMPHASIZED
## ADULTS/YOUTH

**Adult Key Verses:** Revelation 1:17-18
**Youth Key Verse:** Revelation 1:18
**Print Passage:** Revelation 1:12, 17-18; John 20:11-16, 30-31

—Mary did not find what she expected when she went to the tomb.
—Jesus' death has far-reaching implication for all creation because sin and death have been defeated.
—Although Jesus' voice was recognizable, He was also so transformed that Mary did not immediately realize who was speaking to her.
—The resurrection of Jesus Christ is central to the Good News because it serves as proof of the power of God.

## CHILDREN

**Key Verse:** Revelation 1:18
**Print Passage:** Revelation 1:12, 17-18; John 20:11-16, 30-31

—The Christian conversion experience sometimes evokes fear and disbelief.
—Jesus died, but now He lives forever.
—When a loved one dies, crying helps to assuage the grief.
—Because of fear and anxiety, our lives can sometimes lack the proper focus or clarity.

## TOPICAL OUTLINE OF THE LESSON

I. INTRODUCTION
   A. Death Is Not Final
   B. Biblical Background

II. EXPOSITION AND APPLICATION OF THE SCRIPTURE
   A. A Vision of the Risen Lord *(Revelation 1:12, 17-18)*
   B. The Good News of the Empty Tomb *(John 20:11-16)*
   C. The Witness of the Gospel *(John 20:30-31)*

III. CONCLUDING REFLECTIONS

## I. INTRODUCTION
### A. Death Is Not Final

Many people view death as the last great frontier of the unknown. The world is full of people who face the prospect of death with fear and uncertainty. Many pastors have shared what they observed in the final stages of life with many people. They have watched with great awe and respect those who depart this world with a deep abiding faith and hope in Jesus Christ. Likewise, they have been privy to the final days of persons who were weak in faith and faced death with trepidation and a sense of gloom.

The scriptural readings for today's lesson come from the book of the Revelation of Jesus Christ and the gospel of John. As an apostle of the Lord Jesus Christ, John was both a witness to the humiliating and excruciating death of Jesus on the cross and of the joy that surrounded His resurrection. The central affirmation of today's lesson is that Jesus Christ lives now and forever.

## B. Biblical Background

God gave the Revelation of Jesus Christ to John the apostle while he was an exile on Patmos (see Revelation 1:1). The revelation occurred on the Lord's Day (Sunday). The book of Revelation uses language that is highly figurative and has many images and allusions that refer back to events, places, or acts that are found in the Old Testament. We will see their use in this week's lesson.

The apostle John was probably the last of the original twelve disciples of Jesus to die. He wrote Revelation while imprisoned on the Island of Patmos, which is located in the Aegean Sea, about forty miles off the coast of modern-day Turkey. Patmos was a rocky and rugged island and suitable for criminals. It was used by Roman emperors as a place of punishment. Christians were considered criminals because they refused to acknowledge the emperor as lord. For this reason, Domitian—the emperor at this time—banished John to Patmos. Anyone who would not bow to Caesar's image was considered disloyal and in rebellion against the empire. Consequently, many Christians were persecuted, and John was among them. John's vision of the risen Christ reinforced his hope that one day Jesus would take all Christians to be with Him in heaven. God used John to write a message of hope to Christians living during a difficult period of history. There are several sacred places on the Island of Patmos that venerate the life and time that John spent there.

The second biblical text is taken from John's account of the Resurrection Story. Each of the gospel writers identifies Mary Magdalene as the first woman who met and saw the risen Lord (see Matthew 28:1; Mark 16:1; Luke 24:10; John 20:1). Mary of Magdala became the first witness of the resurrection of the Lord Jesus Christ. She owed much to the Savior. Hence, out of respect she came to the tomb to anoint the body of the Lord. Instead of finding a dead body, she came face-to-face with the risen Christ. Her witness of the risen Christ brought hope and encouragement to the disciples of the Lord, whose lives sank into utter despair when they saw Him led away and crucified among common criminals.

## II. Exposition and Application of the Scripture
### A. A Vision of the Risen Lord
*(Revelation 1:12, 17-18)*

**And I turned to see the voice that spake with me. . . .And when I saw him, I fell at his feet as dead. And he laid his right hand upon me, saying unto me, Fear not; I am the first and the last: I am he that liveth, and was dead; and, behold, I am alive for evermore, Amen; and have the keys of hell and of death.**

John was in the Spirit when the vision of the resurrected Christ began. It began as a great voice that sounded like a trumpet declaring that He was the Alpha and the

Omega (see Revelation 1:11). John turned to see where the voice was coming from (verse 12). Verses 13-16 describe what he saw. From that description there is no doubt that John realized he was once again seeing the risen Christ. This time it was not as the One who had just been raised from the dead. Jesus Christ was now the Sovereign Lord ruling the universe. The sight was so dazzling that John was completely immobilized and fell at the feet of Jesus as one who was dead. Why did Jesus Christ reveal Himself only to John? John was the leader of the church in Ephesus and the last remaining historical link to the life and ministry of Jesus Christ when He walked the earth. John was highly regarded among the saints throughout Asia, and his witness would be credible and highly cherished.

How are we to understand the reference to death in verse 17a? The language of Revelation is highly figurative; thus, it speaks more to John having been completely overcome by the presence of Jesus Christ. Falling down at the feet of Jesus was a sign of respect, reverence, and worship (see Revelation 4:10; 5:8, 14). Jesus Christ laid His right hand upon John. What is the significance of the right hand and how do we understand the act of laying on of hands? God's right hand is the hand of strength and authority. God does mighty things through His right hand (see Exodus 15:6; Deuteronomy 33:2; Psalm 18:35; 118:15). The laying on of hands was the manner in which a person was commissioned and set apart for a particular task. It also signifies the passing on of spiritual authority to act or speak on behalf of the one sending another (see Numbers 27:18ff; Mark 16:18; Acts 6:6; 13:3; 1 Timothy 4:14; 2 Timothy 1:6; Hebrews 6:2). Jesus informed John of His identity: "I am the First and the Last." All things have their origin in Him and they will culminate in Him. He controls all of the circumstances of our lives; therefore, we must never allow doubt and fear to discourage us.

Verse 18 tells John why he must not fear the Roman authorities nor the things that were about to come upon the church. Jesus was alive! He is alive today! Because Jesus lives the Roman threats amounted to nothing. Even if His followers were killed, the living Lord guaranteed them that death would not overcome them. He alone holds the keys of death and hell.

### B. The Good News of the Empty Tomb (John 20:11-16)

**But Mary stood without at the sepulchre weeping: and as she wept, she stooped down, and looked into the sepulchre, And seeth two angels in white sitting, the one at the head, and the other at the feet, where the body of Jesus had lain. And they say unto her, Woman, why weepest thou? She saith unto them, Because they have taken away my Lord, and I know not where they have laid him. And when she had thus said, she turned herself back, and saw Jesus standing, and knew not that it was Jesus. Jesus saith unto her, Woman, why weepest thou? whom seekest thou? She, supposing him to be the gardener, saith unto him, Sir, if thou have borne him hence, tell me where thou hast laid him, and I will take him away. Jesus saith unto her, Mary. She turned herself, and saith unto him, Rabboni; which is to say, Master.**

Each of the gospel writers records the events of the first Easter with little variance. (Read the Resurrection accounts in the

Synoptic Gospels to see if you can discern the differences.) These are not contradictions, but rather are additions to what is the most important event in the Christian faith: the resurrection of Jesus of Nazareth from the dead. The accounts of each gospel writer add to the body of our understanding of this momentous event. By John's account, very early on the first day of the week, which is Sunday, Mary came to the tomb of Jesus by herself. She came to pay final respects, since Jesus had been quickly and hastily buried on Friday—which was the day of preparation for the Passover. Passover began at sunset on Friday and lasted until sunset on Saturday. The Day of Passover would not have been an appropriate time to visit a cemetery, since such a visit would have rendered her unclean and unfit to participate in the Passover. Jesus' tomb was located in a garden, which was very near the place of the Crucifixion (see John 19:42). Mary went and looked into the tomb. When she did not see the body of the Lord she ran and told Peter and John, who accompanied her back to the tomb. They found it just as Mary had declared. Upon entering, they too were puzzled by the absence of Jesus' body. John reported that they did not yet understand the Scriptures—that Jesus must be raised from the dead (John 20:9). The two disciples then returned to their homes; however, unlike them, Mary lingered at the tomb weeping and sobbing over the death of her Lord. At this point, she was confused. Not only was Jesus' body missing—she also had no idea as to where they had taken Him.

Mary stooped down and looked into the tomb. This time she saw two angels standing dressed in white. One was standing in the place where Jesus' head would have laid, and the other was at the place where His feet would have been. One of the angels spoke and asked Mary why she was weeping. The angel's question appears to be insensitive, given that cemeteries are places of great anguish. She was weeping because she did not know where her Lord had been laid. Her response is framed in such a way as to assume that the people who had moved Jesus' body were the same ones who had conspired to have Him killed.

As she was about to leave the gravesite, Mary turned around and saw a man standing in close proximity. She did not know that it was Jesus. Remember, it was very early in the morning and quite possibly still dark enough that facial features may not have been entirely clear. There may have been an early-morning fog hanging over the garden tomb area, or her eyes may have been wet with tears and her vision blurry. Whatever the case, she did not recognize the person she encountered. Jesus asked two questions: "Why are you weeping? And who are you looking for?" Mary thought that she was speaking to the gardener. Just as she had done with the two angels, she wanted to know where He might have taken Jesus' body (John 20:15b).

When Jesus called her name she recognized the voice. Jesus had said on one occasion during His ministry of preaching, teaching, and healing that His sheep knew the sound of His voice and that a stranger they would not follow (see John 10:4-5, 27).

When Mary turned around and saw Jesus all of her heartbreak vanished. She cried out "Rabboni," which is an Aramaic title of deep honor and respect. Mary must have fallen down at His feet and began to embrace Jesus, grabbing His leg in a show of reverence and worship. He told her not to touch Him. He had not yet ascended to His Father. How are we to understand the prohibition not to touch Jesus? Jesus was no longer flesh and blood, though He had the appearance of a human being. His resurrection changed the way He would relate to the disciples. He must continue to be about His Father's business, yet He was no longer of this world. He must depart to return to the Father in heaven.

Mary was commissioned to go and tell the disciples that Jesus was alive and that He would ascend to His Father in heaven. This is not to be understood as the Ascension taking place at that moment. We know that Jesus was on the earth forty full days prior to His ascension (see Acts 1:3). Mary left the presence of the Lord and went and found the disciples. She told them everything that had happened and what Jesus had said and done.

### C. The Witness of the Gospel
*(John 20:30-31)*

**And many other signs truly did Jesus in the presence of his disciples, which are not written in this book: But these are written, that ye might believe that Jesus is the Christ, the Son of God; and that believing ye might have life through his name.**

John added a summary statement about the purpose of his gospel. He pointed out that his account of the life and ministry of Jesus in no way captured all that can be said and known about Jesus. John knew more than he wrote. How can one capture in words the work and words of Jesus Christ? John wrote just enough to spur faith and to increase the faith of believers in his day and for generations to come. Jesus did many signs in the presence of His disciples. Signs are markers of authentication that God has anointed a person for a particular task or has sent him or her on assignment. The miracles of Jesus were the signs of His authority and power. That Jesus performed countless miracles is well-attested in the Synoptics.

The gospel of John was written for the express purpose of being a witness to the greatest event in human history. Three reasons are stated for his witness. First, it was written that we might believe. What did John mean? If a person has never come to a saving faith in Jesus Christ, reading this gospel will cause him or her to reach that decision. On the other hand, if one is saved, then reading this gospel will cause one to continue in the faith.

Second, John stated that belief is to be specific—that Jesus is both the Christ (the promised Messiah, God's Anointed One) and Son of God. The triumphal procession revealed Him as Messiah and the resurrection revealed Him as the Son of God. Jesus was God incarnate living among His creation to redeem the world from the curse of the Law (see John 1:14). He was not just a son, but God's only begotten Son (see John 3:16).

Finally, John wrote so that we might come to see that in Jesus Christ we have life through His name. Life is to be understood in two dimensions. First, in Jesus Christ, we come to know the true meaning of life as we live it day to day. Jesus once said that we must take care that the things of this world do not get in the way of our seeing our purpose (see Luke 12:15). The other dimension of life is eternal life—this is life after physical death. This is the believer's great hope—that in Jesus Christ we come to know life now and in the future.

## III. Concluding Reflections

This generation of Christians is becoming increasingly more secular than spiritual. As the standard of living increases and people become more affluent, God and their relationship to Jesus Christ becomes less and less of a priority. Christians must become more willing to share their personal testimonies of faith with family and friends. Christ's resurrection assures us of eternal life, and that alone is a gift worth more than anything we can ever own.

When we are face-to-face with life-and-death situations, we come to the realization that material possessions are not all there is to life. There is a deeper dimension to living that comes when we discover that Jesus Christ gives us hope beyond this life. Death is a certainty for all of us. The question is: Will we be prepared to meet the Lord Jesus Christ at the judgment seat?

## WORD POWER

**Fear Not (Greek: *me, phobu*)**—this is the root word for "phobia." It means dread, terrified, inwardly frightened, alarmed, or dreadful. In the Key Verse (Revelation 1:17), fear *(phobu)* is preceded by a negative not (Greek: me). The combination of these words means that John should not entertain any form of fear, inwardly or outwardly. John needed this message of assurance because of the weight of the message he was about to receive. It was also a **command**; therefore, John must write it and transmit it without fear.

## HOME DAILY BIBLE READINGS

for the week of April 8, 2007
*Christ Is Risen*

Apr. 2, Monday
—Luke 22:7-23
—This Is My Body
Apr. 3, Tuesday
—Romans 14:7-12
—Jesus Is Lord of All
Apr. 4, Wednesday
—John 20:1-9
—Mary Finds an Empty Tomb
Apr. 5, Thursday
—John 20:10-18
—Jesus Appears to Mary
Apr. 6, Friday
—John 20:19-23
—Jesus Appears to His Disciples
Apr. 7, Saturday
—John 20:24-31
—Jesus Appears to Thomas
Apr. 8, Sunday
—Revelation 1:9-12a, 17-18
—Jesus, the First and Last

## PRAYER

*Heavenly Father, we give You thanks for the gift of eternal life through Your Son, Jesus Christ. May we appreciate and value our new relationship in You enough that we will share our witness with others. Forgive us of being selfish in sharing You. Forgive us of every sin that separates us from You. In the name of Jesus Christ, we pray. Amen.*

**April 15, 2007**

**UNIT II**
A New Community in Christ

**CHILDREN'S UNIT**
More Special Letters to Churches

**KEY VERSE**

Thou art worthy, O Lord, to receive glory and honour and power: for thou hast created all things, and for thy pleasure they are and were created.
—Revelation 4:11

**OBJECTIVES**

Upon completion of this lesson, the students are expected to:
1. Learn that worship enables us to center our thoughts, hearts, and minds on God;
2. Understand that there are times when God will show things to prepare us for challenges that lie ahead; and,
3. Discover that a true worshiper comes before the presence of God in absolute humility and reverence.

Lesson 7

# God Is Worthy of Praise

**ADULT TOPIC:** Worshiping God Alone
**YOUTH TOPIC:** Sing Praise!
**CHILDREN'S TOPIC:** Jesus Lives in You

**DEVOTIONAL READING:** Psalm 111
**BACKGROUND SCRIPTURE:** Revelation 4
**PRINT PASSAGE:** Revelation 4:1-11

### Revelation 4:1-11—KJV

AFTER THIS I looked, and, behold, a door was opened in heaven: and the first voice which I heard was as it were of a trumpet talking with me; which said, Come up hither, and I will shew thee things which must be hereafter.

2 And immediately I was in the spirit: and, behold, a throne was set in heaven, and one sat on the throne.

3 And he that sat was to look upon like a jasper and a sardine stone: and there was a rainbow round about the throne, in sight like unto an emerald.

4 And round about the throne were four and twenty seats: and upon the seats I saw four and twenty elders sitting, clothed in white raiment; and they had on their heads crowns of gold.

5 And out of the throne proceeded lightnings and thunderings and voices: and there were seven lamps of fire burning before the throne, which are the seven Spirits of God.

6 And before the throne there was a sea of glass like unto crystal: and in the midst of the throne, and round about the throne, were four beasts full of eyes before and behind.

7 And the first beast was like a lion, and the second beast like a calf, and the third beast had a face as a man, and the fourth beast was like a flying eagle.

8 And the four beasts had each of them six wings about him; and they were full of eyes within: and they rest not day and night, saying, Holy, holy, holy, Lord God Almighty, which was, and is, and is to come.

9 And when those beasts give glory and honour and thanks to him that sat on the throne, who liveth for ever and ever,

**10** The four and twenty elders fall down before him that sat on the throne, and worship him that liveth for ever and ever, and cast their crowns before the throne, saying,

**11** Thou art worthy, O Lord, to receive glory and honour and power: for thou hast created all things, and for thy pleasure they are and were created.

## UNIFYING LESSON PRINCIPLE

Most people want to worship someone or something larger and more powerful than themselves. Who or what is truly worthy of our worship? Revelation 4 describes how God, glorious on the divine throne, is worthy of worship from all beings in heaven and on earth. The Ephesians passage and Revelation 2:3 show that we worship and honor God, who knows all we do, by persevering in love and kindness to others.

## POINTS TO BE EMPHASIZED
## ADULTS/YOUTH

**Adult/Youth Key Verse:** Revelation 4:11
**Print Passage:** Revelation 4:1-11
— The true worship of God occurs in heaven; earthly worship is an imitation of this worship.
— Worship is to turn away from all created things and offer reverence to the Creator.
— God alone is worthy of our worship and praise.
— Those who have gone before have given us an example of the importance of worshiping God.
— The imagery of Revelation suggests that we will spend eternity in worshiping God.

## CHILDREN

**Key Verse:** Ephesians 4:32
**Print Passage:** Ephesians 4:25–5:2; Revelation 2:3
— As Christians, we have the responsibility to support and share with one another.
— Our words and actions demonstrate whether we are serving God.
— We should never grow weary of living righteous lives.
— Even the vilest sinner has an opportunity to be transformed.

## TOPICAL OUTLINE OF THE LESSON

I. **Introduction**
   A. The Importance of Worship
   B. Biblical Background

II. **Exposition and Application of the Scripture**
   A. An Open Door to Heaven *(Revelation 4:1)*
   B. A Vision of the Throne of God *(Revelation 4:2-6)*
   C. A Vision of Heavenly Worship *(Revelation 4:7-11)*

III. **Concluding Reflections**

## I. Introduction
### A. The Importance of Worship

One of the ways that people grow spiritually is through active participation in corporate worship. What is meant by the phrase "active participation"? Active participation implies being totally involved in worship services with our souls, hearts, and might. It is especially critical that new believers learn the importance of participation in regular, weekly worship. Worship enables believers to center their thoughts, hearts, and minds on God and away from themselves. Worship is the most important activity that Christians engage in each week.

Worship is important for three reasons. First, the Bible teaches that we are to worship God and serve Him only. There should be nothing and no one that comes between the believer and the Lord God. God is the object of all worship and praise (see Exodus 20:1-5; Deuteronomy 26:10; 1 Chronicles 16:28-29; Psalm 95:6; Isaiah 66:23; Matthew 4:10).

Second, worship is always a celebration of the mighty acts of God in our lives. Worship is our time to "dance and praise God" (see 2 Samuel 6:14; Psalm 149:3; 150:4). Praise will be a natural by-product of our celebration of God's goodness and mercy.

Third, worship is important because in the context of worship we are encouraged, stimulated to action, and loved by other saints. In worship, the saints encourage one another, inspire one another, and provoke one another to good deeds in ministry. We should spend time thinking about and reflecting on the things that God has done in our lives. The people of the Bible celebrated God in many demonstrative ways. They used singing, dancing, musical instruments, and shouting to celebrate the things that God had done in their lives.

### B. Biblical Background

Today's lesson comes from the book of Revelation. Revelation is one of the most difficult books in the Bible to understand or interpret. Why? Primarily because the book makes extensive use of ancient Jewish symbolism, allusions, and similes, and many Christians do not take the time to try and understand their correct meaning and interpretation. However, when one removes the covering of the symbolism and imagery, the book becomes easier to read, interpret, and comprehend. It has been a great source of comfort to believers since the day the Lord God gave it to John to preserve in writing.

The book of Revelation is a type of biblical writing that is called "apocalyptic." In fact, the very first word in the book is *apokalupsis* (pronounced a-poc-ka-lip-sis), which translates into the word *revelation* ("unveil"). Revelation is a book that reveals the will and plan of God for creation. It was never intended to be a mystery, nor was it to be shrouded under a cloak of religious darkness and secrecy. Revelation is a book given by God to John for the purpose of strengthening and encouraging the beleaguered church in the latter days of the first Christian century (1:9). John remarked that Jesus Christ is the First and Last of our faith; hence, He is both content and source in Revelation (1:8).

Chapter 4 begins the third major section of the revelation of Jesus Christ as John received it on the Island of Patmos. It covers all of the things that are written in the book—beginning at 4:1 and concluding with 20:15.

John was translated by spiritual experience to the very throne of God. There, he observed the most central truth of the Bible: God is still on the throne. God is the Supreme Ruler of the universe and He holds the key to the consummation of the ages (see Psalm 103:19; Isaiah 40:25-31).

## II. Exposition and Application of the Scripture
### A. An Open Door to Heaven
*(Revelation 4:1)*

**After this I looked, and, behold, a door was opened in heaven: and the first voice which I heard was as it were of a trumpet talking with me; which said, Come up hither, and I will shew thee things which must be hereafter.**

Chapter 4 begins the portion of Revelation that is considered to be prophetic, which looks toward the consummation of the ages. Even though it is prophetic it was also a letter written to encourage Christians living in Asia under the tyranny of the Roman emperor, Domitian. As we read through and examine the chapter, it is critical that we not make assumptions about the meaning of various words and phrases. We must bear in mind that this is apocalyptic writing and it conveys truth through the use of imageries and symbols. Remember to separate what John saw from what he heard.

"After this. . ." refers to John having completed the portion of the letter sent to the Seven Churches of Asia. The phrase also introduces what is about to come next. He looked and there in front of him "a door was opened in heaven," (verse 1) and he heard the same voice that spoke to him as from the beginning telling him to write. This open door to heaven is not to be equated with the open door that was given to the church at Philadelphia (see Revelation 3:8). Their open door was an invitation to reach into the interior of Asia Minor and spread the Gospel of Jesus Christ.

John was caught up in an unusual, ecstatic spiritual experience when he was invited to "Come up hither." This voice also sounded like a trumpet and commanded that he come up there where he would be shown the things which must be hereafter. Two things are of note here. First, the command to "come up hither" is not a reference to the rapture of the church. Some interpreters have incorrectly seen this as the rapture, but there is no mention of anyone else in this passage but John. Second, it speaks to the prophetic tone of the book and looks back into the lives of ancient Hebrew prophets who had similar experiences. In Amos 3:7, we are reminded that God does nothing first without revealing it to His prophets: "Surely the Lord God will do nothing, but he revealeth his secret unto his servants the prophets." (See also Jeremiah 1:11-16.) John was about to be an eyewitness to the unfolding drama of the end of the ages. There are times when God will show things to prepare us for challenges that lie ahead.

### B. A Vision of the Throne of God
*(Revelation 4:2-6)*

**And immediately I was in the spirit: and, behold, a throne was set in heaven, and one sat on the throne. And he that sat was to look upon like a jasper and a sardine stone: and there was a rainbow round about the throne, in sight like unto an emerald. And round about the throne were four and twenty seats: and upon the seats I saw four and twenty elders sitting, clothed in white raiment; and they had on their heads crowns of gold. And out of the throne proceeded lightnings and thunderings and voices: and there were seven lamps of fire burning before the throne,**

**which are the seven Spirits of God. And before the throne there was a sea of glass like unto crystal: and in the midst of the throne, and round about the throne, were four beasts full of eyes before and behind.**

Immediately, John was in the Spirit and he saw a throne standing in heaven and the one who sat upon the throne. The word *throne* is found more than 176 times in the Bible, and thirteen times it is written as either "throne" or "thrones" in chapter 4 alone (verses 2-6, 9-10, NRSV). The throne (Greek: *thronos*) is the seat of power and authority. This is God's throne. There is nothing that happens on earth or in heaven of which God is not aware. He sees and senses even the most secret plots of evil men and women. The vision John saw attests to the sovereignty of God over the universe. Caesar ruled from a throne terrorizing and persecuting Christians, but God's throne stands above every earthly throne and authority (see Ephesians 1:19-23). The image of God's throne being surrounded by attendants and the heavenly host is found in the Old Testament. In 1 Kings 22:19 (NRSV), we read, "Then Micaiah said, 'Therefore hear the word of the Lord: I saw the Lord sitting on his throne, with all the host of heaven standing beside him to the right and to the left of him.'" This verse attests to the importance of God's throne.

John's description is framed in the language of metaphor. God is like a jasper stone, a sardius stone—and He has the appearance of an emerald rainbow. Attempts have been made to uncover the meaning of the stones, which in reality can never be truly known with any degree of certainty. However, they are mentioned in Exodus 28:17-19 as one of the twelve stones in the breastplate of the high priest. The stones symbolize the beauty, majesty, and preciousness of the throne of God, and the awesomeness of being in His presence.

The throne is surrounded by twenty-four seats, and seated upon them are twenty-four elders clothed in white garments with golden crowns upon their heads. How are we to understand the image of the twenty-four elders? Some have suggested been that they represent the twelve tribes of Israel and the twelve apostles. This could be, but John was not told who they were. The twenty-four elders represent the redeemed Old Testament and New Testament saints. There is nowhere in the Bible where the term "elder" was used for angels or other heavenly beings. Angels never wear crowns or occupy thrones; they are messengers (Greek: *angelos*). The twenty-four elders wear white garments, which symbolize purity and holiness. The crown symbolizes victory that has been gained by the saints over persecution and death. The Greek word for "crown" is *stephanos* (pronounced stef-an-os), and it refers to the garland or wreath that was given to the victor in the Greek games. The believers in Christ will receive a crown that will symbolize their steadfastness and faithfulness to Jesus Christ (see 1 Corinthians 9:25; 2 Timothy 4:8; James 1:12; 1 Peter 5:4; Revelation 2:10).

Proceeding out of the throne were sounds of thunder and lightning, which are often associated with the presence of God and His mightiness (see Psalm 77:18; 104:7; Revelation 14:2). There were seven lamps burning before the throne that were the seven Spirits of God. Fire and the oil (to fuel the flame) are also symbols of the Holy Spirit. This symbolizes the perfect spiritual presence of God (see Psalm 19:7-12).

## C. A Vision of Heavenly Worship
*(Revelation 4:7-11)*

**And the first beast was like a lion, and the second beast like a calf, and the third beast had a face as a man, and the fourth beast was like a flying eagle. And the four beasts had each of them six wings about him; and they were full of eyes within: and they rest not day and night, saying, Holy, holy, holy, Lord God Almighty, which was, and is, and is to come. And when those beasts give glory and honour and thanks to him that sat on the throne, who liveth for ever and ever, The four and twenty elders fall down before him that sat on the throne, and worship him that liveth for ever and ever, and cast their crowns before the throne, saying, Thou art worthy, O Lord, to receive glory and honour and power: for thou hast created all things, and for thy pleasure they are and were created.**

Verse 7 says, "And the first beast was like a lion, and the second beast like a calf, and the third beast had a face as a man, and the fourth beast was like a flying eagle." The term "beast" may be better translated by the word "creature," because beast denotes some similarity with the beast of chapters 13-15. The four beasts have been interpreted in several ways. The first is that of a lion. We know that the lion is the king of the woods. No other beasts come close to him in strength and authority. Regarding the divine administration, this would signify that He who sits on the throne is the Ruler over all. His dominion is absolute and entire. The second beast is like a calf. A calf symbolizes firmness, endurance, and strength. But pertaining to Him who sat on the throne, it would denote stability, firmness, and perseverance. These are qualities that are found abundantly in the divine governance. The third beast had a face like a man. The human part here denotes intelligence. The meaning of this regarding divine governance is that the operations of God are conducted with intelligence and wisdom. This symbol helps us to know that the divine administration is not the result of any coincidence. The fourth beast was like a flying eagle. All birds fly, but the eagle is a different class. The eagle is distinguished among birds for speed, power, and elevation of its flight. None among the feathered race is so majestic and grand in its ascent toward the sun. This aspect symbolizes the rapidity with which the commands of God are executed. It also depicts that the purposes of God are carried out with promptness. Nothing can stand in the way of God when He is ready to execute His plans.

Each of the four beasts had six wings, and they were full of eyes within. This picture is found in Ezekiel 10:1-12, especially verse 12—where he sees a cherub who is full of eyes. These creatures could see everything in all directions. They could see things coming before many creatures could. They each had six wings which hark back to the seraphim of Isaiah 6:2 and points to their mobility and readiness to do the Lord's bidding at any moment. They are servants of the Lord God—ready and willing to serve at any moment.

Above all else the four living creatures are worshipers who model the essence of true worship. A true worshiper comes before the presence of God in absolute humility and reverence. Here we see a beautiful image of worship that is continuous. They sing and rest neither night nor day. The Psalmist reminds us of what our attitude should always be when we come to worship. "Come, let us worship and bow down: let us kneel before the LORD our Maker. For He is our God; and we are the people of His pasture, and the sheep of His hand" (Psalm 95:6-7).

The book of Revelation is filled with the beauty and awestruck majesty of worship. Worship is the believer's grand and glorious right and opportunity to say to the world and the demonic powers of darkness: Our God is an awesome God.

## III. CONCLUDING REFLECTIONS

What does it mean to worship God? To "worship" means "to ascribe worth to God, who deserves adoration and praise." We worship God because He is worthy. We worship Him because He is our Creator, Sustainer, and Provider. Worship is never designed to appeal to the audience or to appease the personal preferences of humans. Worship is always designed with God as the audience.

When believers enter into worship that is centered on God, they leave with a deep sense of God's presence. Real worship introduces us to the transcendent power of an omnipotent God. In worship, believers find strength, hope, joy and encouragement for their personal journeys.

## WORD POWER

**Worship (Greek: *proskuneo*)**—worship involves some physical actions. In the Middle East, to worship is to fall on the knees and touch the ground with the forehead as an expression of profound reverence. In the New Testament, worship involves kneeling or prostration to express respect, or to make supplication to God. In modern times, we seldom fall on our knees. The Word of God says "God is spirit, and those who worship him must worship in spirit and truth" (John 4:24, NRSV). The most important thing is our hearts before God.

## HOME DAILY BIBLE READINGS

for the week of April 15, 2007
*God Is Worthy of Praise*

Apr. 9, Monday
—Psalm 145:8-12
—Praise to a Gracious God
Apr. 10, Tuesday
—Psalm 111
—Great Is Our God
Apr. 11, Wednesday
—Ephesians 3:7-13
—God's Eternal Purpose
Apr. 12, Thursday
—Jeremiah 10:6-10
—None Is like God
Apr. 13, Friday
—Ephesians 4:25–5:2
—Live a Life of Love
Apr. 14, Saturday
—Revelation 2:1-7
—Endure Hardships
Apr. 15, Sunday
—Revelation 4
—God Is Worthy of Praise

## PRAYER

*Heavenly Father, we are grateful that in You the whole universe finds its meaning. Open our eyes that we may see the beauty of Your holiness. Forgive us of every sin that separates us from You. In the name of Jesus Christ, we pray. Amen.*

**April 22, 2007**

**Lesson 8**

# Christ Is Worthy to Redeem

**ADULT TOPIC:** Redeemable
**YOUTH TOPIC:** Praise the Worthy One!
**CHILDREN'S TOPIC:** Jesus Wants Us to Be Faithful

**DEVOTIONAL READING:** Psalm 107:1-9
**BACKGROUND SCRIPTURE:** Revelation 5
**PRINT PASSAGE:** Revelation 5:1-5, 11-14

## Revelation 5:1-5, 11-14—KJV

AND I saw in the right hand of him that sat on the throne a book written within and on the backside, sealed with seven seals.

2 And I saw a strong angel proclaiming with a loud voice, Who is worthy to open the book, and to loose the seals thereof?

3 And no man in heaven, nor in earth, neither under the earth, was able to open the book, neither to look thereon.

4 And I wept much, because no man was found worthy to open and to read the book, neither to look thereon.

5 And one of the elders saith unto me, Weep not: behold, the Lion of the tribe of Juda, the Root of David, hath prevailed to open the book, and to loose the seven seals thereof.

......

11 And I beheld, and I heard the voice of many angels round about the throne and the beasts and the elders: and the number of them was ten thousand times ten thousand, and thousands of thousands;

12 Saying with a loud voice, Worthy is the Lamb that was slain to receive power, and riches, and wisdom, and strength, and honour, and glory, and blessing.

13 And every creature which is in heaven, and on the earth, and under the earth, and such as are in the sea, and all that are in them, heard I saying, Blessing, and honour, and glory, and power, be unto him that sitteth upon the throne, and unto the Lamb for ever and ever.

14 And the four beasts said, Amen. And the four and twenty elders fell down and worshipped him that liveth for ever and ever.

**UNIT II**
A New Community in Christ

**CHILDREN'S UNIT**
More Special Letters to Churches

**KEY VERSE**

Every creature which is in heaven, and on the earth, and under the earth, and such as are in the sea, and all that are in them, heard I saying, Blessing, and honour, and glory, and power, be unto him that sitteth upon the throne, and unto the Lamb for ever and ever.

—Revelation 5:13

**OBJECTIVES**
Upon completion of this lesson, the students are expected to:
1. Recognize that God has a complete plan for the universe;
2. Learn that the believers bear the seal of the Holy Spirit, who attests to the Father's ownership; and,
3. Understand that Jesus as the Lamb has earned the right to receive praise.

## UNIFYING LESSON PRINCIPLE

Most people want to know that there is a possibility for forgiveness when they do something wrong or make a mistake. What guarantee of forgiveness do we have? Revelation 5 reassures us that the Lamb, who is worthy of our praise, has redeemed us. Paul's letter to the Philippians encourages them to act as redeemed people by showing love to one another, and Revelation 2:19 says that God knows when we act in this way.

## POINTS TO BE EMPHASIZED
### ADULTS/YOUTH
**Adult Key Verse**: Revelation 5:13
**Youth Key Verse:** Revelation 5:12
**Print Passage:** Revelation 5:1-5, 11-14
—God's saving mystery is symbolized in the scroll; only Jesus Christ is able to make the mystery of God's purpose known.
—The slain Lamb is evidence of God's saving purpose for all creation.
—Jesus is the redeemer of all creation and is worthy of our praise.
—The book of Revelation was written during a time of severe persecution and was intended to encourage those suffering for Christ.

### CHILDREN
**Key Verse:** Revelation 2:19
**Print Passage:** Philippians 1:1-11; Acts 16:13-15; Revelation 2:19
—Christian perfection can be obtained through the continuous study of biblical truths and through insights gained by the indwelling of the Holy Spirit.
—All Christians should dedicate their works to the honor and glory of God.

—God knows our works and expects our works to increase as our faith increases.
—No one and no thing can stop the work of God's church.

## TOPICAL OUTLINE OF THE LESSON
### I. INTRODUCTION
  A. The Song of Redemption
  B. Biblical Background

### II. EXPOSITION AND APPLICATION OF THE SCRIPTURE
  A. A Book Sealed with Seven Seals (Revelation 5:1)
  B. Who Is Worthy? (Revelation 5:2-5)
  C. The Voices of Praise (Revelation 5:11-14)

### III. CONCLUDING REFLECTIONS

## I. INTRODUCTION
### A. The Song of Redemption

The apostle Paul declared, in his epistle to the church of Rome, that "all have sinned, and come short of the glory of God" (Romans 3:23.) This sad but true statement gives an accurate assessment of the human condition. However, the lesson for today provides hope for believers—in that it emphasizes the redemptive possibilities for humanity through Jesus Christ. The book of Revelation emphasizes hope, in both a temporal sense and an eternal one—for there is an inextricable tie that binds the two together. This lesson focuses on the eternal by providing an account of judgment for saints. The deeds of the saints are accounted for by God and will be shared in the last judgment. There is joy expressed over the worthiness of the Lamb who was slain for the sins of the saints. These saints and other heavenly beings will join in a mighty chorus of celebration. The basis for this celebration is the redemption of God's children.

As persons who had endured persecution, it is wonderful to know that God's redemptive plan included them. Just as this word of encouragement gave hope to the ancient believers, it should give fuel to the faith of modern Christian people that God will trade our trouble for eternal triumph. Angels cannot sing the song of the blood washed, but the children of Adam can sing, "I have been redeemed."

### B. Biblical Background

Chapter 5 continues the vision of heaven and the scene of the throne room of God. The same heavenly and angelic beings found in chapter 4 are present in this chapter as well—the four living creatures and the twenty-four elders. Added to this group are multitudes upon multitudes of angels. The action of the vision shifts from the One seated upon the throne to the Lamb who stands in the midst of the elders around the throne.

John saw a book (more properly called a scroll) sealed with seven seals. God, who was sitting upon the throne, was holding the book in His right hand. The seven-sealed book is one of the dominant themes of the chapter. It is referred to in eight of the fourteen verses in the chapter. A strong angel asked if there was anyone worthy to open the book. No one was found worthy, which prompted John to weep bitterly. The Lamb took the scroll and opened it. At that point, the heavenly chorus of angels, the twenty-four elders, and the four living creatures all broke out in jubilant praise of the Lamb. Jesus Christ is the Lamb who is worthy to open the seven-sealed book. He is the subject of the chapter and the object of the heavenly praise. All who form the heavenly court bow before His presence.

## II. Exposition and Application of the Scripture
### A. A Book Sealed with Seven Seals (Revelation 5:1)

**And I saw in the right hand of him that sat on the throne a book written within and on the backside, sealed with seven seals.**

The vision of chapter 4 continues in chapter 5 with the words, "Then I saw in the right hand of Him who sat on the throne a scroll with writing on both sides and sealed with seven seals" (NIV). The focus of this chapter shifts to the scroll, and especially to the One who is worthy to open the scroll.

God was holding in His right hand a scroll that was completely filled on the front and back. We learned previously that the right hand is the hand of authority and power (see Exodus 15:6). The back of a scroll was used only when there was not enough room on the front for all that needed to be said. In the ancient times, when a scroll was completed it was fastened with strings, and the strings were sealed with hot wax at the knots. The seven seals are a security measure to make sure that the contents of the document are not revealed before their time.

John alluded to an image that is also present in the prophetic writings of Ezekiel 2:9-10: "And when I looked, behold, an hand was sent unto me; and, lo, a roll of a book was therein; And he spread it before me; and it was written within and without: and there was written therein lamentations, and mourning, and woe." On the scroll of Ezekiel, God revealed that lamentations, mourning, and woe were about to be released upon Judah and that it would be more than anything they had ever seen or experienced (see also Isaiah 29:11-12).

What is the picture of this document with seven seals? First, seven is the number of perfection and completion. The seven seals symbolize the book's complete security. No unauthorized individual can open it without revealing that the book has been opened. The book represents the perfectly prepared plan of God for all creation. The scroll is rolled to conceal the contents of the seventh seal, then rolled and sealed to conceal the contents behind the sixth seal and so on until there are seven seals on the scroll, with the first seal on the outside of the document.

In this revelation of the scroll with seven seals, we see that God has a complete plan for the universe. From the fall of Adam and Eve to the cross upon which Christ was crucified—up to this present hour—God has a plan for the universe. God has plans for every person born, just as He had plans for the Jews who remained in Jerusalem and those who were in exile in Babylon (see Jeremiah 29:10-11). The scroll was complete and could not be compromised before the time to reveal its contents. What is a seal? Historically (in the ancient worlds), seals were used by kings to indicate their authority and to show ownership or the completion of a transaction (see Jeremiah 32:6-13; Daniel 6:17). The idea of 5:1 is that God has a book in which the history of the universe is already written. The fact is, only God can hold the scroll in His right hand. We must bear in mind that the emphasis is not on the content of the scroll, but on its seals and the One who is capable of opening it.

### B. Who Is Worthy?
*(Revelation 5:2-5)*

**And I saw a strong angel proclaiming with a loud voice, Who is worthy to open the book, and to loose the seals thereof? And no man in heaven, nor in earth, neither under the earth, was able to open the book, neither to look thereon. And I wept much, because no man was found worthy to open and to read the book, neither to look thereon. And one of the elders saith unto me, Weep not: behold, the Lion of the tribe of Juda, the Root of David, hath prevailed to open the book, and to loose the seven seals thereof.**

Next, John saw a strong angel who inquired with a loud voice, "Who is worthy to break the seals and open the scroll?" Some scholars believe that the strong angel is either Gabriel or Michael the archangel. He appears again in 10:1-2 and 18:21. Archangels often appeared when God had major assignments (see Revelation 12:7ff.). We are not sure of the identity of this angel. All we know is that He is a strong messenger of God. "And no one in heaven, or on the earth, or under the earth, was able to open the book, or to look into it" (NRSV). There was no one anywhere—not in heaven, on the earth, or under the earth—that was worthy to open the scroll.

Why was there no one to open the seal? It is because the seals revealed God's eternal plan for salvation and the release of

His wrath upon the world. Throughout all of the annals of time and eternity there was no one who met the qualifications to open the book. From Adam to John the Baptist, none stood the test of worthiness. From John up to this present moment, no one was worthy to open the book. When no one was found, John began to weep bitterly, loudly, and profusely. "And I began to weep greatly, because no one was found worthy to open the book, or to look into it." The weeping of John revealed a deep sense of despair and brokenness when he saw that no one could open the book. He cried out. The Greek word that is used here has a preposition *(ek-*out) attached at the beginning of the word "weep." *Eklaio* (pronounced eklah-yo) in this verse is the same word used in Jesus' crying over Jerusalem (Luke 19:41) and Peter's despair over denying Jesus on the night He was betrayed (Luke 22:62).

Was there no one who could open the book? Why did John weep loudly? In Revelation 4:1, there is a promise that says, "Come up hither, and I will shew thee things which must be hereafter." The weeping of John was not ordinary weeping. Looking to the preposition (ek-out) gives understanding as to what type of crying took place. There are three possibilities:
A. The fact that no one was worthy to open the scroll became a heavy burden for John.
B. The promise to see the future might now be denied.
C. Finally, the cessation of history was now indefinitely postponed.

John's weeping may be regarded as an example of the deep agony and grief that people often experience when all efforts to penetrate the future fail. Pastors and church leaders have—at one time or another—experienced such frustrations. Individual Christians of all ages have come to a point when divine help did not come at the time they needed it most. We see that John kept on weeping profusely and loudly.

### C. The Voices of Praise
*(Revelation 5:11-14)*

**And I beheld, and I heard the voice of many angels round about the throne and the beasts and the elders: and the number of them was ten thousand times ten thousand, and thousands of thousands; Saying with a loud voice, Worthy is the Lamb that was slain to receive power, and riches, and wisdom, and strength, and honour, and glory, and blessing. And every creature which is in heaven, and on the earth, and under the earth, and such as are in the sea, and all that are in them, heard I saying, Blessing, and honour, and glory, and power, be unto him that sitteth upon the throne, and unto the Lamb for ever and ever. And the four beasts said, Amen. And the four and twenty elders fell down and worshipped him that liveth for ever and ever.**

In this section, John referred to something he saw and heard. Throughout heaven the voices of many angels were heard. This is a number that John was unable to capture in words. He simply heaped ten thousand upon ten thousand multiplied by thousands and thousand more. These combined voices included the angels around the throne, the living creatures, the twenty-four elders joined by a host made up of tens of thousands of creatures in heaven worshiping and singing praises to the Lamb. These countless angels joined in unison, declaring with a loud voice the worthiness of the Lamb because of the redemption He has accomplished. Revelation 5:12 says,

*"Worthy is the Lamb that was slain
to receive power and riches and wisdom
and might and honor and
glory and blessing."*

The heavenly hosts sing a sevenfold acclamation of praise to the Lamb. The praise is not given to just anyone, but to the Lamb (see John 1:29, 36; Acts 8:32; 1 Peter 1:19). The image of the Lamb as Victor and not victim appears twenty-four times throughout Revelation (see 5:6, 8, 12-13; 6:1, 16; 7:10, 14, 17; 12:11; 13:8, 11; 14:1, 4, 10; 15:3; 17:14; 19:7, 9; 21:22-23; 22:1). Jesus was God's perfect sacrifice, whose blood cleanses the world of its sin. The Lamb has earned the right to receive the sevenfold acclamation of praise because of His great work at Calvary. Therefore, what is rendered is no more than what is due Him. This joint worship of the Father and the Lamb testifies to the deity of Jesus Christ.

The first four acclamations of praise celebrate the attributes of Christ; the final three render unto Him the praise that is due His name. Power translates as the word *dunamis,* and refers to the inherent ability to achieve results. Riches refer to great abundance. Its use here suggests an eternal wealth unlike the world's riches as seen in Revelation 18:17—where the great city of Babylon is destroyed and her riches plundered. The riches of Christ are of far greater value and will last into eternity. Jesus Christ is both the power of God and the wisdom of God (1 Corinthians 1:24). In Him dwells the fullness of the Godhead. Strength is another word for power in the New Testament that captures a different dimension of God's power. God has power, but He also has the strength to exercise His sovereign will through His power.

In the great cosmic conflict in heaven, the dragon and his angelic hosts were not strong enough to overcome the power of Michael and the angels of heaven (see Revelation 12:7ff.). Honor has in it the idea of deference and respect. Christ receives respect for His accomplished work of redemption. He did what no one else could do. Glory comes from the Greek word *doxa,* and means "to shine or glow brilliantly." Christ is exalted and is made to shine brilliantly before the universe. Blessing comes from *eulogia* and literally means "to speak well of." It is another way of speaking about praise of God. When we eulogize someone it is a statement of affirmation and warmth that is rendered to expound his or her attributes.

Every living creature in heaven and earth will bow before the Lamb and acknowledge His Lordship (see Philippians 2:9-11). The only beings who will not bow are the demonic angels who rebelled against God's sovereign authority and were thrown out of heaven. The tens of thousands (not literal, but figurative) will join together and sing a great chorus of praise to the Lamb.

*"To Him who sits on the throne,
and to the Lamb, be blessing and
honor and glory and dominion
forever and ever."* (Revelation 5:13)

The scene concludes with the four living creatures and the twenty-four elders falling down and worshiping Him, who lives forever and ever. They say Amen, meaning, "so let it be as it was stated."

## III. Concluding Reflections

The redemption of humanity is made clear in the worship of Christ. In no other setting can humanity truly celebrate the uniqueness of God's goodness towards the children of God. This affirmation is so vital to the life of the believer because it underscores that God will right every wrong and will vindicate the evil endured by the faithful. The African-American church has lifted up this continuing tenet of liberation by just letting the faithful know that "Jesus will fix it, after while," and that "Trouble don't last always."

As modern Christians in Asia, South America, and parts of Africa endure persecution expressly for their Christian stance, the promise of redemption signals God's grace. The triune God reigns eternally. Tyrants come and go, but God lives and rules forever. We must celebrate with the saints in order to announce to Satan and His cohorts that their time is short.

## WORD POWER

**Blessing (Greek: *eulogia*), honor (Greek: *time*), glory (Greek: *doxa*), and power (Greek: *krato*)**—these are the four Greek words in our Key Verse. These are the words John heard when the combined choir of heavenly hosts gathered to praise the Lamb and the One sitting on the throne. These words are reserved for the almighty God and His Son for what He has done, and for what is about to happen at the close of this age. The word translated "power" *(kratos)* is better translated "might," "dominion," or "vigor."

## HOME DAILY BIBLE READINGS

for the week of April 22, 2007
*Christ Is Worthy to Redeem*

Apr. 16, Monday
—Psalm 107:1-9
—Thanks for Redemption

Apr. 17, Tuesday
—Hebrews 9:11-15
—Serving the Living God

Apr. 18, Wednesday
—1 Peter 1:13-21
—Life in Exile

Apr. 19, Thursday
—Psalm 40:1-5
—Praise for Redemption

Apr. 20, Friday
—Philippians 1:3-11
—That Your Love May Overflow

Apr. 21, Saturday
—Revelation 5:1-5
—The Scroll Is Opened

Apr. 22, Sunday
—Revelation 5:11-14
—Worthy Is the Lamb

## PRAYER

*O God, we thank You for Jesus, the Lamb of God, being the viable vehicle of redemption. His substitutionary death is the only way that we could have been redeemed. Help us to walk, believe, and live, in the wonderful light of redemption. In the matchless name of Jesus, we pray. Amen.*

**April 29, 2007**

Lesson 9

UNIT II
A New Community in Christ

CHILDREN'S UNIT
More Special Letters to Churches

# Christ Is Our Protection

**ADULT TOPIC:** Source of Security
**YOUTH TOPIC:** Perfect Security
**CHILDREN'S TOPIC:** Jesus Knows Our Work

**DEVOTIONAL READING:** Psalm 121
**BACKGROUND SCRIPTURE:** Revelation 7
**PRINT PASSAGE:** Revelation 7:1-3, 9, 13-17

## KEY VERSE

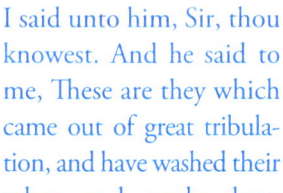

I said unto him, Sir, thou knowest. And he said to me, These are they which came out of great tribulation, and have washed their robes, and made them white in the blood of the Lamb.—Revelation 7:14

## OBJECTIVES

Upon completion of this lesson, the students are expected to:
1. Understand that God is our source of security and protection;
2. Recognize that God is the One who keeps His people from the hand of the enemy; and,
3. Learn that the innumerable multitudes are the ones who have come through the tribulation.

### Revelation 7:1-3, 9, 13-17—KJV

AND AFTER these things I saw four angels standing on the four corners of the earth, holding the four winds of the earth, that the wind should not blow on the earth, nor on the sea, nor on any tree.

2 And I saw another angel ascending from the east, having the seal of the living God: and he cried with a loud voice to the four angels, to whom it was given to hurt the earth and the sea,

3 Saying, Hurt not the earth, neither the sea, nor the trees, till we have sealed the servants of our God in their foreheads.

.....

9 After this I beheld, and, lo, a great multitude, which no man could number, of all nations, and kindreds, and people, and tongues, stood before the throne, and before the Lamb, clothed with white robes, and palms in their hands.

.....

13 And one of the elders answered, saying unto me, What are these which are arrayed in white robes? and whence came they?

14 And I said unto him, Sir, thou knowest. And he said to me, These are they which came out of great tribulation, and have washed their robes, and made them white in the blood of the Lamb.

15 Therefore are they before the throne of God, and serve him day and night in his temple: and he that sitteth on the throne shall dwell among them.

16 They shall hunger no more, neither thirst any more; neither shall the sun light on them, nor any heat.

17 For the Lamb which is in the midst of the throne shall feed

them, and shall lead them unto living fountains of waters: and God shall wipe away all tears from their eyes.

## UNIFYING LESSON PRINCIPLE

Most people long for a sense of security and safety. Where can we look for protection? The vision in Revelation 7 affirms that God's people are protected by the Lamb who redeemed them. Paul's letter to the Colossians describes some characteristics of those who have been redeemed, and Revelation 3:8 adds that God knows their deeds.

## POINTS TO BE EMPHASIZED
## ADULTS/YOUTH

**Adult Key Verse:** Revelation 7:14
**Youth Key Verse:** Revelation 7:17a
**Print Passage:** Revelation 7:1-3, 9, 13-17
—God's seal protects our souls, but it does not shield us from physical harm.
—The faithful are innumerable rather than just a redeemed few.
—Salvation is from God; it is not the role of saints to conquer their enemies.
—Despite persecution and martyrdom, the early Christians affirmed Jesus as Redeemer and Protector.

## CHILDREN

**Key Verse:** Revelation 3:8
**Print Passage:** Colossians 1:1-12; Revelation 3:8
—The basis of Christian hope has its foundation in the living Word.
—Spiritual wisdom and understanding stem from the indwelling of the Holy Spirit.
—Christian believers can draw others to Christ by demonstrating an intimate knowledge of God, and through good works.
—God opens doors of opportunity for true believers to witness to the world.

## TOPICAL OUTLINE OF THE LESSON

  I. Introduction
    A. The True Source of Security
    B. Biblical Background

 II. Exposition and Application of the Scripture
    A. The Seal of the Living God (Revelation 7:1-3)
    B. The Great Multitude (Revelation 7:9)
    C. The Great Tribulation (Revelation 7:13-14)
    D. The Ministry of the Lamb (Revelation 7:15-17)

III. Concluding Reflections

## I. Introduction
### A. The True Source of Security

The early part of the twenty-first century can best be described as a time of tremendous change coupled with unbridled conflict across the globe. Look on any continent and one will find a host of challenges and concerns that leave us wondering about the peace and stability of the world. The security of the entire world is at stake. Many people are asking questions about their personal safety. Where can we go to find protection from the continuing encroachment of evil's presence? Who will protect us from terrorism? Who will protect us from criminals in our midst? Who will protect us from the withering effects of economic upheaval? Who will protect us from the ever-looming threats of pandemic diseases? The bird flu is threatening our existence and the government has no answer.

The lesson today teaches us that God is our source of security and He will protect His people. During the first Christian century, Christians faced a continuing threat of persecution at the hands of the Romans. Insecurity was real in that day. The vision of Revelation 7 affirms that the Lamb who redeemed them protects God's people. God's protection and presence is one of the fundamental affirmations of the Scriptures. It is a fact that runs throughout the Bible—beginning in Genesis and finding its ultimate completion in the consummation of the ages as described in Revelation.

### B. Biblical Background

Chapter 7 is an interlude between the sixth and seventh seal and the blowing of the sixth and seventh trumpets of chapters 8-11. The interlude stands over against the instability that the believers of John's day found themselves facing and pointed out that God is sovereign and in complete control of everything that was happening. In this vision, John saw two multitudes: one consisted of 144,000 people, comprised of 12,000 from each of the twelve tribes of Israel; the other was a great multitude standing before the throne of the living God. This was a number that no one could count. The people who made up this great innumerable multitude came from every nation on the face of the earth.

Who were the people in the vision who overcome during the period of great tribulation? They were the ones who bear the seal of the Lord on their foreheads. The Revelation of Jesus Christ as given to John is deep with allusions to the Old Testament. There is a reference to God executing fierce wrath upon Jerusalem for her sins and the perversion that was in the city (see Ezekiel 9:1-8). Only the people with the mark of God were spared and did not have to face the punishment that was being meted out.

## II. Exposition and Application of the Scripture
### A. The Seal of the Living God
*(Revelation 7:1-3)*

**And after these things I saw four angels standing on the four corners of the earth, holding the four winds of the earth, that the wind should not blow on the earth, nor on the sea, nor on any tree. And I saw another angel ascending from the east, having the seal of the living God: and he cried with a loud voice to the four angels, to whom it was given to hurt the earth and the sea, Saying, Hurt not the earth, neither the sea, nor the trees, till we have sealed the servants of our God in their foreheads.**

John saw four angels standing at the four corners of the earth holding back the four winds from destroying the earth. There are those who would like to discredit the Bible, postulating that this verse is pre-scientific. They are claiming that the Bible assumes that the world is flat. However, in Revelation 20:8, John used the same Greek word, *tessaras gnonias,* translated as "four quarters of the earth." In modern times, mariners and geologists call it the four quadrants of the compass, or the four directions. We also could refer to it as points of the compass. The winds blew out from the four corners of the earth. These winds are powerful forces that can destroy the earth, but are restrained from their natural flow by the four angels. Believers must always be aware that regardless of how powerful the force or great the situation they encounter, God is greater. He can restrain the powers of darkness from the wicked schemes they perpetrate against the saints.

Wind is often used in the Old Testament and in Jewish apocalyptic writings as a metaphor for God's judgment (see Exodus 14:21ff; Jeremiah 4:11-12; 51:16; Hosea 13:15). The wind is a metaphorical symbol of the presence of the Holy Spirit's might to bring spiritual life to the dead (see Ezekiel 37:9-10; John 3:1-8; Acts 2:1-4).

John saw another angel ascending from the east. This angel had the seal of the living God and he cried with a loud voice to the four other angels, saying, "Do not harm the earth or the sea or the trees, until we have sealed the bond-servants of our God on their foreheads." Seals in the ancient world were used to show the ownership of a thing, person, or place. We currently are sealed with the Holy Spirit as down payment of our eventual complete redemption. This act of sealing by the Holy Spirit belongs to every believer when that person is saved. However, believers in Christ must not be careless. This sealing is both a comfort and challenge to us; we are comforted because we know we belong to Him, but it is a challenge in that we must depart from all appearances of evil (see 2 Timothy 2:19). God's seal would come into play again in chapter 13, when the unbelievers and unrepentant receive the seal of the beast (see Revelation 13:16-17).

The seal of the living God would protect and keep these servants of the living Lord from the perilous days that were about to come. John saw that these sealed saints would be given God's divine protection from the awesome days of tribulation that will be unleashed on the earth.

The four angels are told to hold back the winds until the saints have been sealed. What is the significance of God doing this? The answer is to be found in the mercy and grace of God. God would not allow the winds of trouble to blow into the lives of His people until they had been thoroughly prepared. He was not going to keep them from the trials and tribulation. In the letter to the church in Philadelphia, Jesus told the saints that they would have trials for ten days, and the ones who overcame would receive a crown of life (see Revelation 2:10-11).

### B. The Great Multitude *(Revelation 7:9)*

**After this I beheld, and, lo, a great multitude, which no man could number, of all nations, and kindreds, and people, and tongues, stood before the throne, and before the Lamb, clothed with white robes, and palms in their hands.**

"After this I looked, and there was a great multitude that no one could count, from every nation, from all tribes and peoples and languages, standing before the throne and before the Lamb, robed in white, with palm branches in their hands." (7:9, NRSV). Who are these uncountable people? These are a variety of Gentile nationalities that have responded to the Gospel and are saved. This incalculable number of saints are glorifying God. They are crying with loud voices and celebrating the One sitting on the throne. They are joined by all of the angels, the elders, and the four beasts. Every nation, kindred, people, and tongue indicates that there will be people from every nation on the earth in heaven. This clearly speaks to both the task of the church and the penetration of the message of Jesus Christ into the remotest parts of the earth. People are clothed in white, which symbolizes purity, holiness, and victory over trial. The palms branches in their hands and their shout are akin to the voice on Jesus' entry to Jerusalem. Also, these branches symbolize the very blessedness of God. In Leviticus 23:40-42, palm branches were part of the annual celebration of the Feast of Booths. Psalm 92:12 states that palms symbolize prosperity and peace. In John 12:12-13, the people laid palm branches in the path of Jesus as He came down the side of the Mount of Olives and they hailed Him as the King of the Jews.

### C. The Great Tribulation
*(Revelation 7:13-14)*

**And one of the elders answered, saying unto me, What are these which are arrayed in white robes? and whence came they? And I said unto him, Sir, thou knowest. And he said to me, These are they which came out of great tribulation, and have washed their robes, and made them white in the blood of the Lamb.**

In verse 13, John continued to witness sights and sounds he had never seen nor heard before. One of the elders asked him if he knew these people who were standing around the throne, bowing on their faces and celebrating the One sitting on the throne. The specific reference is to the people who are arrayed in white robes with palms in their hands. Where did they come from?

"Sir, thou knowest" is John's response. In John's answer there is a reflection of Ezekiel's response to God's question: "Son of man, can these bones live?" (Ezekiel 37:3). Who are they? These are the ones who have come up through the Great Tribulation, washed their robes, and made them white in the blood of the Lamb. One can hardly imagine how a robe could be washed in red blood and be made white. Jesus' death was not the death of a common criminal, though they crucified Him between two thieves (see Luke 23:33). His death was vicarious—that is, He died for sinners, not for transgressions committed by Him. His blood cleanses from all unrighteousness and makes us whole. A Lamb would hardly expect to be a victor, but that is precisely what Jesus became through His obedience. Further, the symbolism of blood-washed robes is intended to show the identification of the victors with Jesus Christ. Like Jesus, who was martyred, His followers will face the searing flames of persecution; and many will die. But, it is their death that connects them to the victorious Christ (see Galatians 2:20ff.).

There is probably no subject that has generated more debate and discussion among Christians than the Great Tribulation. Will they or will they not go through this period of great trial? Much of the debate has grown up over the last 140 years.

The best approach to the question is to simply take John's witness as given by the angel of the Lord—and then we will understand the fullness of the revelation in God's own time. Much of the current belief or thinking about the Second coming of Christ stems from the popular *Left Behind* book and the subsequent video series. Remember: these are dramatic and literary presentations that often take licenses for the purpose of telling a story.

Whenever it comes, the Great Tribulation will be a period of cataclysmic change, unprecedented suffering, untold cosmic disturbances, and woe heaped upon woe—all of which will precede the Second Coming of Christ to judge the earth. John had in view the time of great tribulation that Jesus spoke about (see Matthew 24:21; Mark 13:19). However, John did not mention a length of time for the period of tribulation. The question for the interpreter of Revelation is this: Will the saints be taken out of the world prior to this great tribulation period or after? John states that this massive multitude of saints will pass through a period of great trial and tribulation. The seal of the living God is what protects them during this time. It does not prevent people from having trials and tribulations; rather, it keeps them while they go through the trials. What is the lesson for twenty-first-century Christians? We must learn, as did the first Christians, that to completely trust God is to believe that He will protect and keep us in moments of great conflict. Those that come out of tribulation show that God's mercy is present even in wrath.

### D. The Ministry of the Lamb
*(Revelation 7:15-17)*

**Therefore are they before the throne of God, and serve him day and night in his temple: and he that sitteth on the throne shall dwell among them. They shall hunger no more, neither thirst any more; neither shall the sun light on them, nor any heat. For the Lamb which is in the midst of the throne shall feed them, and shall lead them unto living fountains of waters: and God shall wipe away all tears from their eyes.**

Because they have come through the period of great tribulation, the gathered multitude stands victoriously before the throne of God. The word "serve" is translated from a Greek word that means "to worship." The service of the saints will be to worship day and night. The reference to night is not a physical night, but is intended to show that heaven will be a place of continuous worship before the throne. Time will not be a factor in eternity because time does not exist in the spiritual realm of God's existence. Just as 2 Peter 3:8 proclaims, "that one day is with the Lord as a thousand years, and a thousand years as one day." This is not a literal reference; it speaks to the endless nature of eternity.

The Lamb who is in the midst of the saints not only receives their praise and worship, but ministers to their needs. "Dwell among them" comes from a word that means "tabernacle." It alludes back to several passages in the Old Testament beginning with God's command to Moses to build a tabernacle to be the dwelling place of the Lord God among His people (see Exodus 25:8; 29:45; Ezekiel 37:27; John 1:14). The Lamb will permanently tabernacle among His people, ministering to them as they serve Him day and night.

Verses 16 and 17 are further evidences of John's abundant knowledge of the prophecies of the Old Testament and of him walking in that tradition (see Revelation 1:3). There are allusions to Isaiah 25:8 and 49:10. The Lamb will satisfy every need and will heal every hurt and heartache. They will no longer suffer rejection, persecution, sickness, and deprivation. The Lamb who dwells in their midst removes everything that hinders their worship.

## III. Concluding Reflections

Insecurity abounds in the world around us. There is nothing that can be done to prevent the unthinkable from happening. Many people spend precious time trying to shield themselves from trials and tribulations. The reality is that such trials and tribulations will come. For the believer in the Lord Jesus Christ there is always the hope that God will one day rescue us from the trials of life. The blessed hope of the church is that one day the Lord will come and take us to live forever with Him in heaven. The believer does not know when that will occur, but one must always be prepared for that moment.

Finally, God is the One on whom we depend for protection. This lesson today reminds us that no matter how grave the times, God will protect and preserve those who belong to Him. The seal of His ownership is the Holy Spirit, who seals us for that blessed day of redemption. In Him we have complete victory!

### WORD POWER

**Seal (Greek: *sphragis*)**—it is a signet that proves ownership. It is a sign that anything is confirmed, approved, and authenticated. Regarding the seal in our lesson, Jesus Christ Himself was sealed. "God the Father has set His seal on Him" (John 6:27). We (Christians) are sealed with the Holy Spirit as a down payment on our final redemption. We are already confirmed and approved by God.

### HOME DAILY BIBLE READINGS

for the week of April 29, 2007
*Christ Is Our Protection*

Apr. 23, Monday
    —Colossians 1:3-8
    —Thanks for Faithful Followers
Apr. 24, Tuesday
    —Psalm 121
    —The Lord Will Keep You
Apr. 25, Wednesday
    —Psalm 3
    —God Is Our Deliverer
Apr. 26, Thursday
    —Psalm 34:1-10
    —God Is Good
Apr. 27, Friday
    —Revelation 3:7-13
    —Protection in Trials
Apr. 28, Saturday
    —Revelation 7:1-3, 9-10
    —Salvation Belongs to God
Apr. 29, Sunday
    —Revelation 7:11-17
    —The Lamb on the Throne

### PRAYER

*Lord God, grant that we may come to know the assurance of Your protection and learn to rest in Your eternal promises to us. Forgive us our sins. In the name of Jesus Christ, we pray. Amen.*

Lesson 10

May 6, 2007

# The Final Banquet

**ADULT TOPIC:** Finding Community
**YOUTH TOPIC:** A Great Party!
**CHILDREN'S TOPIC:** Everyone Will Praise God

**UNIT III**
Living in God's New World

**CHILDREN'S UNIT**
Life in God's New World

**DEVOTIONAL READING:** Psalm 148:1-14
**BACKGROUND SCRIPTURE:** Revelation 19
**PRINT PASSAGE:** Revelation 19:5-10

### Revelation 19:5-10—KJV

5 And a voice came out of the throne, saying, Praise our God, all ye his servants, and ye that fear him, both small and great.

6 And I heard as it were the voice of a great multitude, and as the voice of many waters, and as the voice of mighty thunderings, saying, Alleluia: for the Lord God omnipotent reigneth.

7 Let us be glad and rejoice, and give honour to him: for the marriage of the Lamb is come, and his wife hath made herself ready.

8 And to her was granted that she should be arrayed in fine linen, clean and white: for the fine linen is the righteousness of saints.

9 And he saith unto me, Write, Blessed are they which are called unto the marriage supper of the Lamb. And he saith unto me, These are the true sayings of God.

10 And I fell at his feet to worship him. And he said unto me, See thou do it not: I am thy fellowservant, and of thy brethren that have the testimony of Jesus: worship God: for the testimony of Jesus is the spirit of prophecy.

### KEY VERSE

I heard as it were the voice of a great multitude, and as the voice of many waters, and as the voice of mighty thunderings, saying, Alleluia: for the Lord God omnipotent reigneth.
—Revelation 19:6

### OBJECTIVES

**Upon completion of this lesson, the students are expected to:**
1. Learn that fellowship is the foundation of a healthy congregational life;
2. Recognize that heaven is the perfect place for worship and also the ultimate demonstration of how believers should live together on the earth; and,
3. Understand that God's people will reverence and adore Him for His great act of deliverance.

### UNIFYING LESSON PRINCIPLE

Most people want to belong to a community that adds meaning to their lives. What community can provide this for us? The description of the marriage feast of the Lamb and His bride in Revelation 19 illustrates that the church is a holy community in which we can find the ultimate meaning for our lives. Revelation 7 and Psalm 148 underscore this by showing how worship and celebration among believers on earth is paralleled by worship and celebration among the heavenly beings.

## POINTS TO BE EMPHASIZED ADULTS/YOUTH
**Adult Key Verse:** Revelation 19:6
**Youth Key Verse:** Revelation 19:9
**Print Passage:** Revelation 19:5-10
—Worship among heavenly beings is paralleled by worship among human beings.
—Christians are part of the community of a great multitude.
—The marriage of the Lamb is a time to celebrate.
—The eschatological end to history will find Jesus as Ruler over all creation.

## CHILDREN
**Key Verse:** Psalm 148:1
**Print Passage:** Revelation 7:11-12; Psalm 148:1-3, 7, 10-13
—God, the Creator, deserves our praise and honor.
—God is worthy to be worshiped and praised by everything in heaven and on earth.
—All things, both the animate and inanimate, bear witness to God's greatness and offer praise.
—God can be praised verbally and nonverbally.

## TOPICAL OUTLINE OF THE LESSON
### I. Introduction
A. The Framework for Fellowship
B. Biblical Background

### II. Exposition and Application of the Scripture
A. The Call to Worship *(Revelation 19:5-6)*
B. The Marriage of the Lamb *(Revelation 19:7-8)*
C. Invitation to the Marriage Supper *(Revelation 19:9-10)*

### III. Concluding Reflections

## I. Introduction
### A. The Framework for Fellowship

Fellowship is the foundation of a healthy congregational life. Fellowship strengthens ministry teams and church leaders, empowering them to become more focused on the mission of the church. As leader and ministry leaders work together, they become more productive, efficient, and effective as a congregation. Yet, the church cannot encourage healthy relationships while the members live in isolation from one another. As believers grow, it is critical that they continue to build the kind of fellowship that fosters healthy relationships. There is always a need to discover new creative ways of bringing about social interaction and connection in a world that prizes privacy.

In today's lesson, we learn that Christian community exists not only on the earth, but also in heaven. Heaven is not only the perfect place for worship, but is also the ultimate demonstration of how believers should live together on the earth. One day, God will unite Christians from every nation, race, ethnic group, and tongue around the throne to celebrate the marriage feast of the Lamb and the bride. As we live, awaiting the final consummation of the ages, we will find our greatest fulfillment in devoted service to the Lord Jesus Christ.

## B. Biblical Background

At long last that "great whore Babylon" falls under the mighty weight of God's judgment (Revelation 18:9-19). For John, Babylon was a fitting symbol of the power of Rome—with its massive naval force and nearly invincible army. The Roman Empire was one of the greatest earthly kingdoms in history. Under the Romans, Christians endured repression and oppression by people who believed that Caesar was to be worshiped as a god. Babylon represents every demonic and satanic power that seeks to oppress and stifle the work of God's kingdom on earth.

With Babylon's demise, the end of time is near and God's people break forth with jubilant acclamations of praise. Chapter 19 (see verses 1, 3, 4, 6) is full of the shouts of "Alleluia" by the saints in heaven. *Alleluia* is the word for "Praise the Lord," and is used frequently in Psalms 113, 118, 135, 146, and 148–150. John witnessed God being praised for His salvation, glory, and power (Revelation 19:2). All of the creatures of heaven lend their voices in celebration of God's great act of redemption and vindication (19:3). God is praised because His judgments are true and just. God is praised because the judgment of Babylon brings an end to the trials of His people on the earth. He is praised because He has redeemed the saints from the hands of their enemies and He has vindicated the work of Jesus Christ at Calvary.

## II. Exposition and Application of the Scripture
### A. The Call to Worship
*(Revelation 19:5-6)*

**And a voice came out of the throne, saying, Praise our God, all ye his servants, and ye that fear him, both small and great. And I heard as it were the voice of a great multitude, and as the voice of many waters, and as the voice of mighty thunderings, saying, Alleluia: for the Lord God omnipotent reigneth.**

Shortly after the chorus of praise broke out in heaven, a voice echoed from the throne of God calling upon all of the saints on the earth to praise the Lord. Who are these saints on the earth? The opinions are divided, depending on the believer's view of the rapture of the church—whether it is prior to the Great Tribulation (pre-tribulation), in the middle of the tribulation (mid-tribulation), or at the end of the tribulation (post-tribulation). For John, these kinds of arguments were not at the center of the prophecy he received. The one thing we are sure of is that John saw a great multitude of worshipers on the earth. As said earlier, there came a voice commanding the saints to praise the Lord. This was probably the voice of one of the twenty-four elders or one of the mighty angels who spoke from time to time. The words are addressed specifically to those who are the bondservants of the Lord. The title "servant of the Lord" is one of the greatest titles that any saint can bear, for it connects one with a lineage and heritage of some of the greatest persons in history (i.e., Abraham, Moses, Paul, and Martin Luther King, Jr.). The summons is to "Praise our God." Our God is to be distinguished from the gods of the Romans and Greeks. Domitian (ca. 81-96) was the first Roman emperor to declare himself to be a god. He had temples built in his honor. Ephesus, the city of John's latter years in ministry, was one of the cities where Domitian had a temple built in his honor.

Prior to the consummation, there will be a time when men and women will worship and bow down before the great beast, the Antichrist (see Revelation 13:8). The defeat of Satan and the demonic powers of darkness will usher in a new time of worship and praise by the people of God on the earth. John saw a time when the people of God will celebrate the true and living God on the earth.

The people who worship God are His servants and those who fear Him. Romans considered the worship of Jesus Christ to be an affront to the power of the emperor. In spite of the emperor's threat, John saw a community of believers made up of people from all nations and peoples of the earth worshiping and praising God. These worshipers were all the same, and the barriers that have divided them have disappeared (see Galatians 3:28; Ephesians 2:14-16). The praise of the people of God sounded as though it were a single voice. John described it using three examples. First, it sounded like a great multitude (see Revelation 7:9ff). Second, it sounded like the sound of mighty rushing waters. The sound of Niagara Falls might come close to giving one an example of what rushing waters sound like. Finally, it sounded like loud peals of thunder. This magnificent voice of praise declared that God was to be praised because He is the omnipotent God. He is not to be compared to the petty tyrants of the earth who are all transitory figures on the stage of time, but as the sovereign and supreme Ruler of the universe. He is the King of kings and the Lord of lords (see Revelation 17:14).

There are several important lessons that John points out to us. First, God is the only one to be worshiped (see Exodus 20:3; Jeremiah 25:6). John saw a day when men and women would no longer bow before gold, silver, and precious stones. They would no longer worship power and all of the things that are man-made. When Jesus Christ shall come, the true worship will take place.

Second, worship is a communal event wherein the people of God celebrate the acts of God. It is not the domain of a few super-spiritual, highly-charged emotional saints, but the right and privilege of all of God's people (Psalm 148). In worship, all of the social, economic, educational, and political barriers that have divided people are broken down.

Third, worship celebrates the salvation, power, and glory of God—who does great and marvelous things. True worship is a noisy event, punctuated by loud manifestations of joy and excitement (see Psalm 95:1-6).

### B. The Marriage of the Lamb
*(Revelation 19:7-8)*

**Let us be glad and rejoice, and give honour to him: for the marriage of the Lamb is come, and his wife hath made herself ready. And to her was granted that she should be arrayed in fine linen, clean and white: for the fine linen is the righteousness of saints.**

Marriage in many societies has become a shameful thing. There is "drive-by" marriage in the western world. A man and a woman can walk to the courthouse at any time and be joined together by a government official. Contrariwise, in Jewish culture there was no more joyful occasion than a wedding. Verse 7 introduces one of the most majestic metaphors in the New Testament for describing the relationship between Jesus Christ and His church. The language of marriage and love has a rich history in the Scriptures.

In the New Testament, the metaphor of the church as the bride of Christ is found in several places. In His teachings, Jesus taught a parable about ten virgins who were preparing to meet the bridegroom. In Ephesians 5:25-32, an earthly marriage is compared to the heavenly marriage between Christ and His church. The love that Christ had for the church is evidenced by the sacrifice of His own blood on her behalf. John wrote that the great multitude that praised the Lord for His victory over the whore of Babylon must now praise Him for the coming marriage between Jesus Christ and the church. "Let us be glad and rejoice, and give honour to him: for the marriage of the Lamb is come, and his wife hath made herself ready" (verse 7). The bride appears arrayed in the finest garments. Fine linen was the most costly of fabrics. It was made in Egypt and appears first in the Scriptures in connection with the construction of the tabernacle (see Exodus 25:4; 28:5, 39; 35:6, 23, 25, 35). There is a contrast to the fine linen worn by the great whore of Babylon in 18:12 and fine linen worn by the pure and chaste bride of Christ.

The garments are clean and white. White is the color of purity and denotes that which is without blemish. The bride of Christ is clean (Greek: *katharos*; literally means "to cleanse from all corrupt desires and unrighteousness"). Jesus said that His disciples are cleansed through the Word (see John 15:3; also Ephesians 5:26). Believers are cleansed of all unrighteousness by the blood of Jesus Christ. Through the washing of regeneration we are made fit to be partakers with all of the saints in light (see Titus 3:5). The sacrificial death of Jesus Christ on the cross made it possible for us to experience forgiveness and wholeness. "But if we walk in the light, as he is in the light, we have fellowship one with another, and the blood of Jesus Christ his Son cleanseth us from all sin" (1 John 1:7).

The lessons from this passage are obvious. First, one of the central tasks of the leadership of the local church is to prepare the saints to meet Jesus Christ. Christ is coming to seek a church that will appear without spot or wrinkle. Second, there is an individual responsibility that each believer has to do all that he or she can to live so that Jesus will be pleased when He appears. We must live in holy and righteous ways because we have been saved—not with corruptible seed, but through the incorruptible Word of God (see 1 Peter 1:18-19). Third, the saints exhibit righteousness by the life they live and works that they do. Their holy living is a preparation for the coming marriage. This anticipated consummation will take place—and though it sounds too good to be true, it will happen.

### C. Invitation to the Marriage Supper
*(Revelation 19:9-10)*

**And he saith unto me, Write, Blessed are they which are called unto the marriage supper of the Lamb. And he saith unto me,**

**These are the true sayings of God. And I fell at his feet to worship him. And he said unto me, See thou do it not: I am thy fellowservant, and of thy brethren that have the testimony of Jesus: worship God: for the testimony of Jesus is the spirit of prophecy.**

John looked back to the beginning of the book in Revelation 1:11 and 1:19, where he was told to write down what he saw and send it to the seven churches. The words that John received are the true words of the living God. This is possibly a reference to all that is in the book or has reference to the particular vision he is about to receive. John stated that those who were invited to attend the marriage feast are the blessed. The invitation came in the form of a call. They were called to the marriage supper. They were blessed because the mere fact of the invitation means that they had finally overcome and their time of reward had come. "Blessed" is used in a technical sense in this passage to denote that it is one of seven blessings pronounced throughout the book. Seven is the number of perfection or completion. Therefore, the blessing of being invited to the marriage supper is one of the seven great blessings in the book of Revelation.

There are six other occasions in which John wrote about the blessings bestowed upon the people of God. Who are these blessed people? In Revelation, they are blessed for overcoming the enemies of God. In Revelation 1:3, we read, "Blessed is he that readeth, and they that hear the words of this prophecy, and keep those things which are written therein: for the time is at hand". (See Revelation 14:13; 16:15; 19:9; 20:6; 22:7; 22:14 for the other places where it is used.) They are blessed because they have been invited to the marriage supper. In the Gospels, there are two parables told by Jesus about a marriage supper. In Matthew 22:1-14, a rich man prepared a marriage feast for his son. He invited many guests. Inviting many guests testifies to the importance of marriage in Jewish culture. In all of His teachings about the wedding supper, Jesus taught that only those who were invited and properly attired would be invited into the marriage supper. The invitation is the acceptance of God's free gift of salvation and grace. The garments are the fruits of righteousness and holiness.

We are not told who John fell down to worship, but the context of the passage helps us a great deal. It was neither before the Lord Jesus Christ nor before the throne of God. It was either before one of the great angels, one of the four creatures around the throne, or one of the twenty-four elders. Whoever it was, John was told not to bow to him, for he was nothing more than a servant of the Lord like John. Why did John fall down before the angel or creature? Maybe it was because of the great message of hope he had just received. He had been privileged to witness the final consummation of the ages and the events surrounding the end of time. He may have been completely moved by such and felt compelled to worship the one bringing him the message.

There are several lessons from this text that speak to us in our generation. First, God calls us into relationship with Himself and His Son. We are called to work out our salvation in fear and trembling. We are called to walk worthy of our vocation. We are called to glorify His name. Secondly, worship is always given to God, the Creator.

In our day, we have transformed men and women of the faith into mini-gods by worshiping them, catering to them, and according them a status of respect that is beyond what Scripture teaches. This is not to denigrate men and women of the clergy, but we must be careful to not deify our spiritual leaders.

## III. Concluding Reflections

Often, it is assumed that fellowship is automatic in the local church once a person officially joins. However, the conclusion of new membership sessions and the extension of the right hand of fellowship do not ensure fellowship. Instead, true fellowship in the church is a precious and rare commodity, for too many Christians value individuality over relationships. It is not surprising that even the divorce rate among believers in the modern church is astronomical, since relationships are not valued. It is the sacred duty of the local body of Christians to develop programs that will enhance true communal spirit.

It could be argued that many church disputes have their origin in not being able to live together in Christian fellowship, but Christ has called us to love each other. The marriage of the Lamb is ahead, and only those who purify themselves will take part in it. The goal of Christians is not simply to make it to heaven as individuals; it should be a group attainment. In our Key Verse, we read, "And I heard as it were the voice of a great multitude...saying, Alleluia...." Heaven is a place for multitudes of saints. We need to begin experiencing a foretaste of heaven while we occupy these mortal bodies here on earth.

## WORD POWER

**I heard (Greek: *ekousa*)**—it is "to hear distinctly by the ear what is said in one's presence." In this case, there is no intermediary. John heard a tumultuous sound saying "Alleluia: for the Lord God omnipotent reigneth." John was not hallucinating. The word "heard" in Greek is cast in the indicative mood, which means it is a real event.

## HOME DAILY BIBLE READINGS

for the week of May 6, 2007
*The Final Banquet*

Apr. 30, Monday
  —Matthew 22:1-14
  —Parable of the Wedding Banquet
May 1, Tuesday
  —Revelation 15:1-5
  —The Song of the Lamb
May 2, Wednesday
  —Revelation 11:15-19
  —He Will Reign Forever
May 3, Thursday
  —Psalm 148:1-6
  —The Heavens Praise
May 4, Friday
  —Psalm 148:7-14
  —The Earth Praises
May 5, Saturday
  —Revelation 19:1-5
  —Hallelujah!
May 6, Sunday
  —Revelation 19:6-10
  —Give God Glory

## PRAYER

*Dear Lord and Father, thank You for the privilege of having fellowship with You. Help us to be a balm to bless others, and allow us the grace and space to be used as Your instruments. In Jesus' name, we pray. Amen.*

**May 13, 2007**

**Lesson 11**

**UNIT III**
Living in God's New World

**CHILDREN'S UNIT**
Life in God's New World

# Our New Home

**ADULT TOPIC:** The Eternal Home
**YOUTH TOPIC:** A Fresh Start
**CHILDREN'S TOPIC:** Everyone Will Be Full

**DEVOTIONAL READING:** 2 Peter 3:10-18
**BACKGROUND SCRIPTURE:** Revelation 21:1-8
**PRINT PASSAGE:** Revelation 21:1-8

**KEY VERSE**

I heard a great voice out of heaven saying, Behold, the tabernacle of God is with men, and he will dwell with them, and they shall be his people, and God himself shall be with them, and be their God.—Revelation 21:3

**OBJECTIVES**

Upon completion of this lesson, the students are expected to:
1. Learn that God has prepared a new home for His children;
2. Discover that God will one day create a new heaven and a new earth free of sin and Satan; and,
3. Recognize that true worship will take place in the very presence of the Living God.

### Revelation 21:1-8—KJV

AND I saw a new heaven and a new earth: for the first heaven and the first earth were passed away; and there was no more sea.

2 And I John saw the holy city, new Jerusalem, coming down from God out of heaven, prepared as a bride adorned for her husband.

3 And I heard a great voice out of heaven saying, Behold, the tabernacle of God is with men, and he will dwell with them, and they shall be his people, and God himself shall be with them, and be their God.

4 And God shall wipe away all tears from their eyes; and there shall be no more death, neither sorrow, nor crying, neither shall there be any more pain: for the former things are passed away.

5 And he that sat upon the throne said, Behold, I make all things new. And he said unto me, Write: for these words are true and faithful.

6 And he said unto me, It is done. I am Alpha and Omega, the beginning and the end. I will give unto him that is athirst of the fountain of the water of life freely.

7 He that overcometh shall inherit all things; and I will be his God, and he shall be my son.

8 But the fearful, and unbelieving, and the abominable, and murderers, and whoremongers, and sorcerers, and idolaters, and all liars, shall have their part in the lake which burneth with fire and brimstone: which is the second death.

## UNIFYING LESSON PRINCIPLE

Everyone wants a home in which he or she can be safe from hunger, thirst, and pain. Where does such a home exist? Revelation 21 says that the new heaven and new earth will be a home like this. The Mark passage, especially in tandem with Revelation 7:16–17, presents a foreshadowing of this aspect of the new age when we will see Jesus feeding the multitude and eliminating their hunger.

## POINTS TO BE EMPHASIZED ADULTS/YOUTH

**Adult Key Verse:** Revelation 21:3
**Youth Key Verse:** Revelation 21:5
**Print Passage:** Revelation 21:1-8

— God's purpose is the renewal and redemption of all creation.
— God enables the faithful to be victorious over sin through faith.
— Those who are unfaithful to God will not enter the New Jerusalem.
— God will take away our pain and wipe away our tears.

## CHILDREN

**Key Verse:** Revelation 7:16
**Print Passage:** Mark 6:32-44; Revelation 7:16-17

— Jesus supplies spiritual food for those who hunger and thirst for righteousness.
— God satisfies our spiritual and physical hunger.
— Crowds sometimes follow charismatic leaders and trust them even when they are misguided.
— Jesus' message and actions give direction to those who are seeking fulfillment.

## TOPICAL OUTLINE OF THE LESSON

I. **INTRODUCTION**
   A. The Believers' New Home
   B. Biblical Background

II. **EXPOSITION AND APPLICATION OF THE SCRIPTURE**
   A. A New Heaven and a New Earth *(Revelation 21:1-2)*
   B. The Blessedness of God's Presence *(Revelation 21:3-4)*
   C. All Things New *(Revelation 21:5-7)*
   D. The Second Death *(Revelation 21:8)*

III. **CONCLUDING REFLECTIONS**

### I. INTRODUCTION
### A. The Believers' New Home

Today's lesson teaches us that God has prepared a new home for His children. The people of John's day had experienced persecution, trial and intense tribulations. God used the book of Revelation to encourage believers that, in God's plan and timing, all things would work together for their good. John received a vision in which God will one day create a new heaven and a new earth. In that blessed place the saints of God will experience the joy and majesty of God. The apostle Paul stated it best in Romans 8:18: "For I reckon that the sufferings of this present time are not worthy to be compared with the glory which shall be revealed in us." Heaven is the consummation of the blessed hope of the believer's new life in Jesus Christ.

## B. Biblical Background

In this week's lesson, we move closer to the end of days and the beginning of God's plan—that will commence with the coming of the new heaven and new earth. Prior to the commencement of the end of days there will be the final judgment of Satan, who will be bound and cast into the bottomless pit (20:1-3). This will be followed by the millennial reign of Jesus Christ upon the earth for a thousand years (20:4-5). Those who are part of the millennial reign of Christ will be the martyrs who have not denied the name of the Lord Jesus Christ and who loved not their own lives. They will reign, but the end will not come yet. Satan will have one last opportunity and be set loose on the earth for a period of time. Why this happens John does not reveal; he simply says that he is loosed for a period to continue his tactics of deception of the nations.

The final judgment will begin with the dead—both small and great—standing before the Great White Throne of God to give an account of the deeds done in the body (see Matthew 25:31-46; Romans 14:10; Philippians 2:8-11; 2 Corinthians 5:10). Anyone whose name is not found written in the Book of Life is cast into the lake of fire with Satan and his demonic hosts (20:14-15). The conclusion of the judgment sets the stage for the establishment of God's eternal kingdom in heaven and on earth.

## II. Exposition and Application of the Scripture

### A. A New Heaven and a New Earth
*(Revelation 21:1-2)*

**And I saw a new heaven and a new earth: for the first heaven and the first earth were passed away; and there was no more sea. And I John saw the holy city, new Jerusalem, coming down from God out of heaven, prepared as a bride adorned for her husband.**

When the final judgment has taken place and the saints of God are freed from the tyranny and oppression of Satan, the kingdom of God will come. What John was about to see stood out in bold relief against what he had just seen—the lake of fire with its victims being tormented forever. This is a place where they would find no relief.

There is a new vision of a new reality that was about to unfold before his very eyes. In this new reality, it is possible that John looked back to the prophetic words of Isaiah and saw their fulfillment in this vision given him by God. God had revealed to the prophet Isaiah that He was going to recreate the universe, beginning with heaven (see Isaiah 65:17-18).

John saw "a new heaven and a new earth." The former heaven and earth had passed away; there was no more sea. What will this new heaven and earth look like and be like? Some interpreters see this as a literal new heaven and a literal new earth. Others see it as a representation of the redeemed people of God who will gather together around God's throne. It is possible that the new heaven and the new earth will be a reflection of both. We are not told how this take place, and it will remain a mystery to us until the day it is revealed. What is clear is that God has planned a new creation for the saints.

The word "new" is the key to our interpretation of this verse. New (Greek: *kainos*) is used in the sense of something that is new in respect to time. In other words, it is something that has never been seen before. The new birth is "kainos"—new—because in the moment of conversion we become persons who have never been seen before (see 2 Corinthians 5:17). But the question remains as to why God created a new heaven and a new earth.

The new earth will be new like heaven. We are not told what it will be like, and anything we say about its nature and location will, at best, be mere speculation. For this, too, we must await the final revelation of God's plan of redemption.

John said that there will be no more sea. In the Jewish mind, the sea represented separation and evil—the source of the satanic beast (Revelation 13:1). The sea is a symbol of chaos and is considered to be the world of the unknown. Moreover, John saw a New Jerusalem coming down from heaven dressed as a bride going forth to her wedding. This is the Jerusalem of hope (Hebrews 12:22); this is Jerusalem above (Galatians 4:26); this is our true place of citizenship (Philippians 3:20). This is not a city like the former Babylon, which was the cesspool of sin and oppression. This is the New Jerusalem—the city of God. For every believer who has asked the question of why evil is allowed to run rampant and unchecked in the world, here is the answer. God has a plan and time when Satan's reign of terror will end, and the bliss of His eternal kingdom will unfold before our eyes. This world is imperfect, yet God has purposed a day when that which is known in part will become completely visible to us. In the coming New Jerusalem, we have something totally unique: a perfect, sinless, and pure community of the righteous.

### B. The Blessedness of God's Presence (Revelation 21:3-4)

**And I heard a great voice out of heaven saying, Behold, the tabernacle of God is with men, and he will dwell with them, and they shall be his people, and God himself shall be with them, and be their God. And God shall wipe away all tears from their eyes; and there shall be no more death, neither sorrow, nor crying, neither shall there be any more pain: for the former things are passed away.**

A great voice is heard to thunder from heaven, giving a sterling confirmation of the promise of a new heaven and the new earth. Whose voice is this? It is probably a voice of one of the angels. The voice declares, "Behold the tabernacle of God is with men, and He shall dwell with them. . . ." These words are an allusion to the establishment of the first tabernacle, which was the sign of God's presence with Israel in the wilderness. This presence was symbolized by the Tent of Meeting and the ark of the covenant (see Exodus 25:1-22; 29:43-45). The first tabernacle was a temporary dwelling place for God's glory. The tabernacle was a sign of the covenantal relationship between God and Israel. It was where the people met God and came to know His love and experience His grace.

God Himself will dwell among His people. There will no longer be a longing after the presence of God; the saints will enjoy—unlimited—the unmingled presence of the Creator. God will personally be with them, and He will be their God. These are reflections on the passages that describe the rise of the beast of the sea and the beast of the earth that deceive the world into bowing before them (Revelation 13:1ff.). On that day, true worship will take place, not in a church building, a synagogue, nor on a mountain, but in the very presence of the living God.

John said God will one day wipe away all the tears of the saints. He will take away every reason for sorrow and sadness and remove the seasons of pain forever. The end of all sorrow is characterized in the words, "no more death, neither sorrow, nor crying, neither shall there be any more pain." All of these are scenes that the saints of that day had been keenly aware of—given the nature and severity of Rome's persecution of Christians. God's presence among the saints will make up for their sufferings. It will be all consummated by the passing away of everything that looks like the former world. We have seen saints suffer devastating sickness, pain, death, and sorrow upon sorrow. Life brings its share of sorrows. Jesus said that in this life we would have untold trials and tribulations, but we are to be of good cheer because He has overcome the world.

### C. All Things New *(Revelation 21:5-7)*

**And he that sat upon the throne said, Behold, I make all things new. And he said unto me, Write: for these words are true and faithful. And he said unto me, It is done. I am Alpha and Omega, the beginning and the end. I will give unto him that is athirst of the fountain of the water of life freely. He that overcometh shall inherit all things; and I will be his God, and he shall be my son.**

Finally, God speaks and declares that it is all accomplished. John said that the voice he heard came specifically from He who sat upon the throne. Up to this present time, the voices had come out of heaven and around the throne. But the One on the throne now says, "Behold." It is a command to take a look. Something new has been created. John is asked to take a preview of it. When a new movie is about to be released, some people are invited to a preview showing. This is what God asked John to do. God approved the new thing He had created and said, "It is done." First, the statement is used in the perfect tense. It means that the New Jerusalem is ready. The words that John received are true and faithful. They are from God Himself and, as such, they can be relied upon (see Joshua 1:5). The Scriptures make it plain that God cannot lie (see Titus 1:2; Hebrews 6:18). One of the attributes of God is expressed in these words: God is faithful (see 1 Corinthians 1:9; 10:13).

Second, what John had witnessed and heard is the final consummation of the ages. There is nothing else that would be shown to him. He could share this message of hope with the beleaguered saints throughout Asia. Third, God declared Himself to be the Alpha and the Omega. He is the beginning and the ending. Everything began with Him and every event that occurs in the middle of time is under His sovereign control. He would have the final say on how things would all end. Fourth, He alone is able to satisfy the longing and thirst of the people of the world. He would give the thirsty person to "drink of the fountain of the water of life freely."

Water is irreplaceable; without it, one cannot live. It is the source of life and was viewed by the ancients as a great blessing of God. Heaven was believed to be filled with rivers of living waters (Psalm 46:4). John alluded to some points made by Jesus that He was the water of life and that He would be in men and women as a well of water springing up into everlasting life. Jesus offered men and women the living water (see John 4:10; 7:38; compare Psalm 23:2; Isaiah 49:10; 55:1). Again, there is the confirmation of the promise of Sonship with God. The overcomers would become the sons and daughters of God. Although there were problems aplenty in the churches, God still would reward them all for overcoming the searing fires of trial. He or she who overcomes shall inherit all things, no doubt a reference to all that had been mentioned in the Book and what was yet to be mentioned.

The twenty-first century is an age of great advancement. Our economy has produced the highest standard of living of any nation on the earth. This has led many people to trust in themselves and their own abilities to obtain personal wealth for themselves. The book of Revelation points out that all of these are fleeting against the backdrop of the final judgment. There are some things that money cannot buy—now or in the life to come.

### D. The Second Death *(Revelation 21:8)*

**But the fearful, and unbelieving, and the abominable, and murderers, and whoremongers, and sorcerers, and idolaters, and all liars, shall have their part in the lake which burneth with fire and brimstone: which is the second death.**

The passage concludes with a reminder to the saints that some people will not make it into the New Jerusalem, nor will they see the new heaven and the new earth. John uses what one would consider to be a typical list of vices which are found throughout the New Testament epistles, particularly in the writings of Paul (see Romans 1:29-31; Ephesians 4:25-32; Colossians 3:5-8; 1 Timothy 1:9-10; James 3:14-16; compare with Revelation 9:21; 22:15). Lists of virtues and vices were common throughout the development of the Christian faith and were often used as a means of teaching what acceptable conduct was and what it was not.

It is interesting that leading the list of undesirable traits is fear. The KJV uses the word "fearful," but a word that better approximates the meaning in Greek is the word "coward." The NRSV reads, "But as for the cowardly...," which is in contrast to those in verse 7 who are the overcomers. Why would John put cowardice in first place? One need look no farther than the historical and cultural context. He had been exiled to Patmos for preaching the Gospel of Jesus Christ and taking a stand against emperor worship (see 1:9). In each of the seven letters to the churches, there is a call to overcome (see the previous section).

Every one of these traits on the list is found in some form in the book of Revelation: unbelieving (9:20-21); abomination (17:4-5); murderers (6:9); whoremongers (19:2); sorcerers (9:21); idolaters (13:4); liars (3:9). The list is not intended to serve as the final list of those who will be excluded from the celestial city. It serves as a sign that people who engage in similar types of conduct whose names do not appear in the Lamb's Book of Life will end up in the lake of fire, along with Satan and the hosts of hell. This will be an even more tragic death, referred to as the second death.

## III. Concluding Reflections

One of the signs of our times is the very fickle nature of some members of the household of faith. Many are very easily offended, hurt, discouraged, drawn away, distracted, and deceived by any new religious fad or trend that comes along. So many of us are always in a hurry to rush to worship and conclude it so that we can get on with the rest of our weekend. One of the unfortunate realities of our tradition is the absence of African Americans on the mission field in Africa and the Caribbean, and in Latin and South America. Why won't we go? It is because of fear or, as John would term it, cowardice. How would John view Christians of our day? He possibly might think that we are no more than cowards. Could any believer among us today have been a Christian during the time that John wrote Revelation?

## WORD POWER

**With (Greek: *meta*)**—the word has three spelling forms with different meanings in the original (Greek: meta, sun, pros). John carefully chose his word. The Greek word he used in our Key Verse today is *meta*, which means that Christ will dwell in the midst of the saved ones. He will be in their company. This is where we get our words *metaphysics, metaphor,* and so forth. "Pros" is used in John 1:1. The Word was with (pros) God, meaning the Word was face-to-face in the presence of God. The other word, *sun*, becomes *syn* in English. This is where we get the words *synagogue, synthesis,* and so forth.

## HOME DAILY BIBLE READINGS

for the week of May 13, 2007
*Our New Home*

May 7, Monday
    —Philippians 3:17-21
    —Our Citizenship Is in Heaven
May 8, Tuesday
    —1 Corinthians 15:20-28
    —The Coming of the Kingdom
May 9, Wednesday
    —2 Corinthians 5:1-10
    —Our Heavenly Dwelling
May 10, Thursday
    —Hebrews 11:10-16
    —Longing for a New Home
May 11, Friday
    —2 Peter 3:10-18
    —The Day of the Lord
May 12, Saturday
    —Isaiah 65:17-19, 23-25
    —New Heavens and a New Earth
May 13, Sunday
    —Revelation 21:1-8
    —God Will Dwell Among Us

## PRAYER

*Lord God, Creator of the ends of the earth, teach us to be bold soldiers for You. May we fully embrace the example of our Lord who was a true and faithful witness. Grant us the courage to stand for You and with others who live in lands where religious persecution is a way of life. Forgive us of our sins. In the name of Jesus Christ, we pray. Amen.*

**Lesson 12**

# God in Our Midst

**May 20, 2007**

**UNIT III**
Living in God's New World

**ADULT TOPIC:** Living in Our New Home
**YOUTH TOPIC:** Home, but Not Alone!
**CHILDREN'S TOPIC:** Everyone Will Be Made Well

**CHILDREN'S UNIT**
Life in God's New World

**DEVOTIONAL READING:** Ephesians 1:15-23
**BACKGROUND SCRIPTURE:** Revelation 21:9–22:5
**PRINT PASSAGE:** Revelation 21:9-10, 22–22:5

## KEY VERSE

There shall be no night there; and they need no candle, neither light of the sun; for the Lord God giveth them light: and they shall reign for ever and ever.
—Revelation 22:5

### Revelation 21:9-10, 22–22:5—KJV

9 And there came unto me one of the seven angels which had the seven vials full of the seven last plagues, and talked with me, saying, Come hither, I will shew thee the bride, the Lamb's wife.

10 And he carried me away in the spirit to a great and high mountain, and shewed me that great city, the holy Jerusalem, descending out of heaven from God.

.....

22 And I saw no temple therein: for the Lord God Almighty and the Lamb are the temple of it.

23 And the city had no need of the sun, neither of the moon, to shine in it: for the glory of God did lighten it, and the Lamb is the light thereof.

24 And the nations of them which are saved shall walk in the light of it: and the kings of the earth do bring their glory and honour into it.

25 And the gates of it shall not be shut at all by day: for there shall be no night there.

26 And they shall bring the glory and honour of the nations into it.

27 And there shall in no wise enter into it any thing that defileth, neither whatsoever worketh abomination, or maketh a lie: but they which are written in the Lamb's book of life.

.....

AND HE shewed me a pure river of water of life, clear as crystal, proceeding out of the throne of God and of the Lamb.

2 In the midst of the street of it, and on either side of the river,

## OBJECTIVES

**Upon completion of this lesson, the students are expected to:**

1. Recognize that God has prepared a place of perfect peace and rest for us;
2. Learn that the new city where the saints will dwell more than makes up for their lifetime of pain and suffering; and,
3. Understand that in the New Jerusalem the very presence of the Lord God Almighty and the Lamb would be evident.

was there the tree of life, which bare twelve manner of fruits, and yielded her fruit every month: and the leaves of the tree were for the healing of the nations.

3 And there shall be no more curse: but the throne of God and of the Lamb shall be in it; and his servants shall serve him:

4 And they shall see his face; and his name shall be in their foreheads.

5 And there shall be no night there; and they need no candle, neither light of the sun; for the Lord God giveth them light: and they shall reign for ever and ever.

## UNIFYING LESSON PRINCIPLE

People long for true peace, wholeness, and safety in their lives. Will this ever be possible? Revelation 21 says that those who dwell in God's New Jerusalem will experience these things, because God and the Lamb will be permanently in their midst. Luke's account of the healing of the woman on the Sabbath foreshadows the wholeness that will come in that day, when Jesus makes all things new.

## POINTS TO BE EMPHASIZED
## ADULTS/YOUTH

**Adult/Youth Key Verse:** Revelation 22:5
**Print Passage:** Revelation 21:9-10–22:5
—The cube-shaped New Jerusalem is a metaphor for perfection.
—Because there is no sin in the new city, humankind has access to the Tree of Life.
—Life in the holy city will be a complete contrast to life here on earth.

## CHILDREN

**Key Verse:** Revelation 21:5
**Print Passage:** Luke 13:10-17; Revelation 21:5a
—God empowers Christian disciples to heal the sick and perform other miracles.
—As Christian disciples, we should exhibit caring concern for others at all times.
—Sometimes, we live contrary to what our roles as Christian disciples require of us.
—Sometimes, church members are so focused on church tradition that they miss opportunities for Christian witness and ministry.

## TOPICAL OUTLINE OF THE LESSON

### I. Introduction
  A. Life in a New World
  B. Biblical Background

### II. Exposition and Application of the Scripture
  A. A Vision of the Bride of Christ (Revelation 21:9-10)
  B. Life in the New City (Revelation 21:22-27)
  C. The River of Life and Tree of Life (Revelation 22:1-5)

### III. Concluding Reflections

## I. Introduction
### A. Life in a New World

What would it be like to live in a world free of violence and hatred? It is difficult to imagine such a time. We all would like to live in a world that is free of violence, pain, suffering, famine, sickness, and the things that produce fear in the hearts of people. We would all like to live in a world where peace and sharing are the norm and not the exception. Unfortunately, the reality is just the opposite. The lesson today from Revelation 21 teaches us that God has prepared a place of perfect peace and rest for us. In God's New Jerusalem, we will dwell in safety and security, free from the ravages of sin's destructive power and all of the ills it produces.

## B. Biblical Background

Today's lesson introduces us to greater details regarding the holy city, the New Jerusalem that John saw descending from heaven. In the previous lesson, we learned that God showed John a New Jerusalem dressed as a bride adorned for her husband. In this vision, John saw it coming down from heaven. Hence, it was not a city designed and built by humans. This new city was a stark contrast to the city known as "the great whore Babylon." Ancient leaders prided themselves on building magnificent cities. During his lifetime, Herod the Great built the city of Caesarea Maritima from the ground up. It was one of Israel's most fabulous port cities. Unlike it, the New Jerusalem would not be designed by human hands but by the hand of God.

Today, Jerusalem is one of the great cities of the world; however, it does not rank among the top twenty cities of the world in terms of population, economics, culture, politics or fashion. Jerusalem is a special city because it is the only city in the world where God identified Himself with the people who lived there. It was the religious and political capital of Israel for hundreds of years. Jerusalem is mentioned more than 800 times in the Scriptures—and it was there, just outside the city walls, where Jesus was crucified.

John provided a captivating and majestic view of the holy city. Its beauty far outstrips his ability to capture in words its magnificence. John saw a city that was a perfect square of 1,500 miles on each side. It was large—with twelve gates made of pure pearl, and three gates on each side. The walls are made of jasper and the streets are paved with pure gold. It is a city of great and inestimable value. God has spared nothing for those who have not denied His name and have been true and faithful until the end. This new city where the saints abound will make up for their lifetimes of pain and suffering. John saw what the prophets of old longed to see, a day when Jerusalem would return to its heyday of beauty, reverence, and holiness (see Isaiah 61:1-4).

## II. Exposition and Application of the Scripture
### A. A Vision of the Bride of Christ
*(Revelation 21:9-10)*

**And there came unto me one of the seven angels which had the seven vials full of the seven last plagues, and talked with me, saying, Come hither, I will shew thee the bride, the Lamb's wife. And he carried me away in the spirit to a great and high mountain, and shewed me that great city, the holy Jerusalem, descending out of heaven from God.**

John received a guided tour of the new city of Jerusalem. The guide was one of the seven angels who had held one of the seven vials full of the last plagues (see Revelation 16:1-17). We are not told which of the angels because it is incidental to what John saw. In Revelation, angels are not named unless they are one of the archangels, such as Michael. The angel summoned John to accompany him and he would be shown the beauty of the bride, the Lamb's wife (verse 9). He was carried away in the Spirit (1:10; 4:2; 17:3; compare with Ezekiel 37:1ff).

The use of the past tense to describe the angel as one that had the seven vials of plagues indicated to John that the final judgment and period of tribulation had ended. The believers of John's day could take hope and be encouraged that regardless of how difficult their time of trial and tribulation, it would end at some point. God had fixed a time and season when their days of mourning would be turned to peace and their ashes to joy (see Isaiah 65:17-20).

The reference to Jesus as the Lamb of God appears thirty-one times in the New Testament. The title "Lamb" is used exclusively to refer to the sacrificial death of Jesus on the cross. Jesus was God's perfect sacrifice who was without spot or blemish, who shed His precious blood for others (see 1 Peter 1:19). His crucifixion was a vicarious death for the sin of the whole world (see John 1:29, 36). In Acts 8:32, Jesus appeared as the Lamb that was slaughtered. As the Lamb, He was the only One who could take the Book sealed with seven seals and open it (5:7-8). He also received the praise and adoration from the twenty-four elders and the four living creatures. The great multitude that no man could number stood before Him and the throne bowing in worship and adoration (7:9). Michael, the archangel, and his angels overcame the power of the dragon through the blood of the Lamb and the witness of their testimonies (12:7, 11). Those who would seek to usurp the power and throne of God tried to deceive the world by impersonating the Lamb (13:8, 11). The Lamb stood on Mount Zion, victoriously gathered with 144,000 with the name of the Father written on their foreheads (14:1). The dragon tried one final time to come against the Lamb, but was soundly defeated because the Lamb is the Lord of lords and King of kings (17:14).

The metaphor of the church as the bride of Christ came into use very early in the Christian tradition. It was used by Jesus to talk about His relationship to the new people of God and their need to be personally prepared for His return (see Matthew 25:1-13). It was His sacrifice as the Lamb that gave Him the right of possession of the church to be His bride.

The angel carried John to a high mountain and showed him the great city of Jerusalem descending from heaven. Jerusalem is surrounded by mountains—the Mount of Olives (see Matthew 20). Mount Zion and Mount Moriah are the two principal peaks upon which the city rests. On Mount Carmel, Elijah defeated the prophets of Baal (see 1 Kings 18:1ff.). Mountains are pictures of strength and are from time to time used as a symbol of the strength, protection, and holiness of God (see Psalms 30:7; 48:1; 125:1-2; Isaiah 30:29). It was believed early in Hebrew history that the messianic kingdom would be established upon the mountains around Jerusalem (see Isaiah 2:2; 25:6).

### B. Life in the New City
*(Revelation 21:22-27)*

**And I saw no temple therein: for the Lord God Almighty and the Lamb are the temple of it. And the city had no need of the sun, neither of the moon, to shine in it: for the**

**glory of God did lighten it, and the Lamb is the light thereof. And the nations of them which are saved shall walk in the light of it: and the kings of the earth do bring their glory and honour into it. And the gates of it shall not be shut at all by day: for there shall be no night there. And they shall bring the glory and honour of the nations into it. And there shall in no wise enter into it any thing that defileth, neither whatsoever worketh abomination, or maketh a lie: but they which are written in the Lamb's book of life.**

Verses 11-21 describe the measurements of the city and the distances of walls surrounding the city. The outward beauty captures the eyes; however, there is no temple in the new city (verse 22). It was one of the first things that John noticed. There are four reasons why there is no temple. First, the original temple was the place where God promised to meet His people. It was the place of the daily and annual sacrifices. God had chosen that to be the place where He would be open and attentive to the needs of His people. Second, the temple was the dwelling place of the glory of God. The Shekinah of God radiated from that place and Israel knew that whenever they looked upon the temple God was protecting and providing for them. They would no longer need to come to a place to meet God. His presence would abide with them forever. In the New Jerusalem, the very presence of God Almighty and the Lamb would be ensured.

Third, there would no longer be a need to seek God's presence or His face for guidance. The tabernacle, which was the forerunner to the temple, represented the place where the people went for guidance and direction. Moses would gather the nation at the doorway of the tent of meeting so that they might hear from God. From here they followed the presence of the Lord to the Promised Land. In the New Jerusalem, there would be no need to follow God to the Promised Land. When the saints land safely there, they will be forever in the presence of the Lord. Fourth, Satan and demonic powers of darkness have been defeated; therefore, there is no longer an evil presence in the world.

John saw that there was no longer a sun or moon. There was no longer a need for light from the heavenly bodies because the One who had created the light would serve as the light. The light comes from the very glory of God and the Lamb, who fill the city (verse 23). God is light and in Him there is no darkness. He created the light, and the sun to shine by day and the moon by night. With His presence, there would be no need to have reflective light.

John, in verses 24-26, alludes back to the prophecies of Isaiah in 60:1-5. The nations will gather and give glory to God's name. The world's leaders will lead the procession of people who come to worship at the feet of the Lamb. This is a further rebuke of the beast that emerges from the sea with ten horns, seven heads, and ten diadems on each of the horns impersonating the true King (see 13:1-11). The Eternal King of the universe who sits upon the throne of heaven is the true King of kings and Lord of lords. Kings will come and bow at His feet (verse 24).

John saw a city whose gates were always open. In the ancient world, gates were the most important security feature of the city's walls. They were used to keep the wild animals from entering at night and to protect the cities from invaders. They also were used to control access into and out of the city. The saints are free to enter the New Jerusalem at any time. The gates were not shut because there was no night there. The light of the eternal city comes from the radiant presence of God.

The new holy city will be free of anything that is defiled. John saw a renewed emphasis on God's holiness and purity. God is holy, and there is neither uncleanness nor blemish in Him. Nothing unclean, unholy, or impure can enter the New Jerusalem. This includes all who work abominations, liars, and those who have been identified as unholy throughout the Book. The only ones allowed in the New Jerusalem are those whose names appear in the Lamb's Book of Life.

### C. The River of Life and Tree of Life (Revelation 22:1-5)

**And he shewed me a pure river of water of life, clear as crystal, proceeding out of the throne of God and of the Lamb. In the midst of the street of it, and on either side of the river, was there the tree of life, which bare twelve manner of fruits, and yielded her fruit every month: and the leaves of the tree were for the healing of the nations. And there shall be no more curse: but the throne of God and of the Lamb shall be in it; and his servants shall serve him: And they shall see his face; and his name shall be in their foreheads. And there shall be no night there; and they need no candle, neither light of the sun; for the Lord God giveth them light: and they shall reign for ever and ever.**

John saw water that was crystal clear, pure, and free from any sediments or anything else that would pollute it. Without a stable, safe, and secure supply of water, no city could survive. Here, the water meets all of the qualifications necessary to have a surviving city. The source of this water is not an aqueduct that brings the water from an underground spring or river, but rather, it comes from the very throne of God and from the Lamb.

This water gives life because it is from the source of all life. There is a tree, which is the Tree of Life. John saw a time when the saints would never fear the prospect of death. God planted a tree in the midst of the city of paradise, which is the Tree of Life. It bears twelve different kinds of fruit every month. There is never a need to wait for a season to harvest the fruit; every thirty days new and fresh fruit is produced. The Tree of Life and river of life are both symbols that refer to the endless nature of life in eternity. There are leaves on the tree, which are for the healing of the nations. This does not mean that heaven will be filled with people who become sick from time to time. It is language that expresses, in earthly images, what the glory of heaven will be like. There will never be a time when sickness, pain, disappointment, or despair will be present. The environment will be perfect. As stated in verse 3, there will be complete removal of curses. All will be healed by the glorious presence of God and the Lamb.

In the final consummation of the ages, the finished work of Jesus Christ will find its ultimate completion. In Galatians 3:13, the apostle Paul wrote that "Christ hath redeemed us from the curse of the law, being made a curse for us: for it is written, Cursed is every one that hangeth on a tree." Again, John continues to reiterate that the presence of the throne of God and the Lamb will be the focus. In this glorious city, the servants of God will serve Him and Him alone. Nothing and no one will vie for their loyalty. They will see His face. Unlike Moses—when he was told not to look upon the face of God—in the New Jerusalem the saints will be able to look upon His face and presence and have no fear of death (see Exodus 33:20, 23). The New Jerusalem is a city without night or any other form of darkness; God is the source of the celestial city's light. The saved will reign forever and ever with Him and the Lamb (21:5).

## III. Concluding Reflections

The Apocalypse of John provides believers of every age a wonderful opportunity to reflect upon the future home of believers. In this age, where the faith is presented to have immediate relevance, Christians can sometimes lose sight of the fact that our claim has eternal ramifications and not simply immediate consequences. To know that God has fashioned the faithful for eternity is a sobering and uplifting thought. It also should cause a liberating shout, for it positions believers to receive every delight that heaven has to offer. In these days of crass consumerism, where the mind is set on earthly pleasure, it is good to know that there is an eternal treasure.

## WORD POWER

**No, nay (Greek: *ouk*)**—Some words are too little in spelling form—like no—but their meaning is significant. In the Key Verse, the word "no" precedes light. There are two words for no: *me,* pronounced (may); and *ouk,* (sometimes ou or ouch); this is a qualified negation which expresses an absolute denial. Light as we know it here is nonexistent in heaven. The light there is Christ Himself.

## HOME DAILY BIBLE READINGS

for the week of May 20, 2007
*God in Our Midst*

May 14, Monday
—Ephesians 1:15-23
—The Hope of Our Calling
May 15, Tuesday
—Isaiah 60:18-22
—The Glory of the Lord
May 16, Wednesday
—Hebrews 12:22-28
—An Unshakable Kingdom
May 17, Thursday
—2 Corinthians 3:7-18
—The Hope of Glory
May 18, Friday
—Revelation 21:9-14
—John Sees the Heavenly City
May 19, Saturday
—Revelation 21:22-27
—God Will Be the Light
May 20, Sunday
—Revelation 22:1-5
—Blessings to Come

## PRAYER

*Dear Lord Jesus, we thank You for the home beyond the skies that You have provided for us. Help us to live before You so that we will be fit to receive the mansions in the sky and bid farewell to every tear; wipe our weeping eyes. In Your precious name, we pray. Amen.*

**May 27, 2007**

Lesson 13

**UNIT III**
Living in God's New World

**CHILDREN'S UNIT**
Life in God's New World

# Christ Will Return

**ADULT TOPIC:** The Ultimate Happy Ending
**YOUTH TOPIC:** He's Back!
**CHILDREN'S TOPIC:** Everyone Will Be Happy

**DEVOTIONAL READING:** John 16:17-24
**BACKGROUND SCRIPTURE:** Revelation 22:6-21
**PRINT PASSAGE:** Revelation 22:6-10, 12-13, 16-21

**KEY VERSE**

He which testifieth these things saith, Surely I come quickly. Amen. Even so, come, Lord Jesus.
—Revelation 22:20

**OBJECTIVES**

Upon completion of this lesson, the students are expected to:
1. Learn that Jesus Christ will one day come into the world and take us to live forever with Him;
2. Recognize that faithfulness to Jesus Christ is a central theme of the book of Revelation; and,
3. Discover that the coming of the Lord will signal a time of judgment for the unrepentant, but a time of reward for the saints.

### Revelation 22:6-10, 12-13, 16-21—KJV

6 And he said unto me, These sayings are faithful and true: and the Lord God of the holy prophets sent his angel to shew unto his servants the things which must shortly be done.

7 Behold, I come quickly: blessed is he that keepeth the sayings of the prophecy of this book.

8 And I John saw these things, and heard them. And when I had heard and seen, I fell down to worship before the feet of the angel which shewed me these things.

9 Then saith he unto me, See thou do it not: for I am thy fellowservant, and of thy brethren the prophets, and of them which keep the sayings of this book: worship God.

10 And he saith unto me, Seal not the sayings of the prophecy of this book: for the time is at hand.

· · · · ·

12 And, behold, I come quickly; and my reward is with me, to give every man according as his work shall be.

13 I am Alpha and Omega, the beginning and the end, the first and the last.

· · · · ·

16 I Jesus have sent mine angel to testify unto you these things in the churches. I am the root and the offspring of David, and the bright and morning star.

17 And the Spirit and the bride say, Come. And let him that heareth say, Come. And let him that is athirst come. And whosoever will, let him take the water of life freely.

18 For I testify unto every man that heareth the words of the prophecy of this book, If any man shall add unto these things, God shall add unto him the plagues that are written in this book:

19 And if any man shall take away from the words of the book of this prophecy, God shall take away his part out of the book of life, and out of the holy city, and from the things which are written in this book.

20 He which testifieth these things saith, Surely I come quickly. Amen. Even so, come, Lord Jesus.

21 The grace of our Lord Jesus Christ be with you all. Amen.

## UNIFYING LESSON PRINCIPLE

Most people would like to live in a world in which happy endings always come to pass, and one can trust that everything will be all right in the end. Given the reality of this world, however, what happy ending can we ever trust to come to pass? Revelation 22 tells us to trust that Jesus Christ will come again and that His coming will transform everything into the ultimate happy ending for us. John 16 echoes this by pointing to the permanent joy we already have because of the Resurrection, and Revelation 21:3–4 reminds us that the new age will be a time without sorrow or mourning.

## POINTS TO BE EMPHASIZED ADULTS/YOUTH

**Adult/Youth Key Verse:** Revelation 22:20
**Print Passage:** Revelation 22:6-10, 12-13, 16-21

—The hope of Christ's second coming inspires our worship.
—The images (plagues, seals, Tree of Life, holy city) are concepts employed to convey God's mystery.
—Christ is present in the proclaimed Word, yet He is not present in the sense of His rule on earth.
—Given that two thousand years have passed, how might we interpret Jesus' words that He is coming again?

## CHILDREN

**Key Verse:** Revelation 21:4
**Print Passage:** John 16:16-20, 22; Revelation 21:3-4

—Belief in Jesus Christ comes by faith, not by rational thinking.
—We will experience everlasting joy when Jesus returns.
—There will be no sickness, pain or death when Jesus returns.
—The trouble experienced by believers is the precursor to a glorious future if believers remain faithful to Christ Jesus.

## TOPICAL OUTLINE OF THE LESSON

I. INTRODUCTION
   A. A Happy Ending?
   B. Biblical Background

II. EXPOSITION AND APPLICATION OF THE SCRIPTURE
   A. The Faithful and True Prophecy *(Revelation 22:6-10)*
   B. The Lord Is Coming *(Revelation 22:12-13)*
   C. Come, Lord Jesus *(Revelation 22:16-21)*

III. CONCLUDING REFLECTIONS

## I. Introduction
### A. A Happy Ending?

In this lesson, we come to a conclusion that life will have a happy ending for all of God's people. Regardless of how difficult and challenging life may be, the end will be worth the wait. Jesus Christ will one day come into the world and take us to live forever with Him. This is the point we explore today as we conclude our brief survey of Revelation.

### B. Biblical Background

In this passage of study, John has come to the final vision of the Revelation of Jesus Christ. In the previous lesson, we were introduced to the Tree of Life and the river of the water of life. In his final vision, John saw the Lamb of God standing in the midst of the new city, Jerusalem.

The closing verses of Revelation are called the epilogue, and they serve to bring to a fitting close the sights and sounds John saw and heard. They are the final words found in the Bible. John's message of hope was initially read by people who were yearning for the day of the Lord. Even so, come Lord Jesus.

## II. Exposition and Application of the Scripture
### A. The Faithful and True Prophecy
   (Revelation 22:6-10)

**And he said unto me, These sayings are faithful and true: and the Lord God of the holy prophets sent his angel to shew unto his servants the things which must shortly be done. Behold, I come quickly: blessed is he that keepeth the sayings of the prophecy of this book. And I John saw these things, and heard them. And when I had heard and seen, I fell down to worship before the feet of the angel which shewed me these things. Then saith he unto me, See thou do it not: for I am thy fellowservant, and of thy brethren the prophets, and of them which keep the sayings of this book: worship God. And he saith unto me, Seal not the sayings of the prophecy of this book: for the time is at hand.**

Verse 6 begins with one of the seven angels who held one of the seven bowls previously mentioned (see 21:9). This angel told John that the words he had received were "faithful and true," a reference to the reliability of the entire book. The phrase is used two other times in the book of Revelation (see 3:14; 19:11), where Jesus is riding on a great white horse. The words are faithful and true because they come from the One who is faithful and true. God is absolutely reliable and trustworthy. He is the One who never fails nor forsakes (see Joshua 1:5; 1 Corinthians 1:9; 10:13).

The first portion of the second phrase in verse 6—"and the Lord God of the holy prophets. . ."—is a variant rendering from other English versions of the New Testament.

What did John mean by "the holy prophets"? The phrase is found in Luke 1:70, Acts 3:21 and 2 Peter 3:2 to point out the truthfulness of the message that has come from God and was uttered through His messengers. The prophets spoke only that which God had authorized; their words were not their own (see Isaiah 6:5-7; Amos 7:14-15). What John saw were the things which were about to come to pass. The book ends on the same note on which it began—by pointing to the things that must shortly happen and which are part of the larger vision of the end times (1:1; 4:1).

The next voice John heard was Jesus Christ: "Behold, I come quickly" (verse 7). At long last the waiting was over; the Lord Himself would come with a great shout and the trump of God. Up to this point John had witnessed the mighty angels coming, speaking, and doing God's bidding, but now the Son of Man—the Lamb of God—would come. He was coming quickly, which was a warning to the saints to be ever ready and always watchful (see Matthew 24:42, 44; 25:13; 1 Thessalonians 4:16-17; Acts 1:5). The saints of Asia had suffered long enough under the tyranny of Rome. God had fixed a time and season to bring them to be with Himself in the New Jerusalem.

Who are the truly blessed ones? They are those who are faithful and obedient to the words of this prophecy. It is not enough to be a great talker about one's faithfulness to God; one must live it out daily. Faithfulness to Jesus Christ is a central theme of the book of Revelation. Only those who are faithful unto death will receive the crown of life (2:10). John specifically reminded the saints that the words of the Revelation were to be strictly kept. Hence, in each of the letters to the seven churches, those who overcame received the rewards.

John again attested to what he saw and heard. The witness that he recorded was not secondhand; rather, he saw, heard, and was commanded to write them down. Throughout the book of Revelation, John was repeating what he saw and what he heard (4:1, 4; 5:1-2, 6, 11; 6:1; 7:1, 4; 8:2). The point is that throughout the prophecy, John saw and heard the words of God, even though they came at times from angels or from one of the four living creatures. Therefore, what he has reported in the prophecy is authentic.

For a second time, John tried to worship at the feet of the angel of God. The first instance occurred in 19:10. He fell at the feet of the one who had revealed the words of the prophecy to him. The angel did not receive his praise or worship. Rather, he reminded John that he was just like him, a fellow bondservant and prophet of the Lord God. God is the One who must be worshiped and not created beings. There is a clear message for the church of every age, and this age in particular, especially when we have made celebrities out of the messengers of God. Preachers today run the risk of being impressed by their own abilities to reach millions over the airwaves and begin to believe that the ministry is about them. Unwittingly they can become consumed by the praises and plaudits of men and women and regard themselves more highly than they ought.

John was told not to seal up the words of the Book. Unlike Daniel, who was told to seal up the words of the Book, this was not John's mandate (see Daniel 12:4, 9). Why not seal them up? The answer is plain: God's will for the end of time had been hidden from the foundation of the world (see Ephesians 3:3-4, 9). The end was near; there would be no need to keep the revelation of God's will hidden from the saints.

Many Christians consider Revelation to be a mysterious book because of the many strange and bizarre images that are depicted throughout—the seven seals, trumpets, and bowls. But for the people of John's day, there was no doubt in their minds as to what those images and symbols meant. Though we stand nearly 1,900 years removed from that era, we can still know the truth and appreciate the richness of these wonderful words of encouragement in troubled times. There will always be a need for encouragement for the saints until Jesus Christ does come again.

## B. The Lord Is Coming
*(Revelation 22:12-13)*

**And, behold, I come quickly; and my reward is with me, to give every man according as his work shall be. I am Alpha and Omega, the beginning and the end, the first and the last.**

The coming of the Lord will signal a time of judgment for the unrepentant, but for the saints who have been faithful it will be a time of reward. The coming of the Lord will be so sudden that there will be no down-to-the-wire time to "get right with God" (see Matthew 24:36-44). The opportunity to repent and turn from unrighteousness will have been lost forever. In whatever state persons find themselves on that day, they will have no alibi. The message of the church today is that now is the day of salvation, for the very next moment could be too late (see Romans 13:11-12). Clearly, the call to sense the immediacy of the Lord's coming is before the reader of Revelation. At any moment Jesus Christ could return, and only those who have been faithful to the end will go back with Him.

Jesus speaks again—the second time in the epilogue that the statement "Behold, I come quickly" is found. The Lord is not only coming unannounced; moreover, in His coming the saints will be compensated for their faithfulness to Him. Saints will receive rewards according to what they have done. John echoes much of the teaching of the apostle Paul regarding reward and punishment. We will all appear before the judgment seat of Christ to answer for the way we have lived, whether it has been good or bad (see 2 Corinthians 5:10).

Here, we have the sobering fact of individual responsibility before God. The Christian faith is lived in a gathered community of other believers, yet each one is responsible for how he or she has lived (see Galatians 6:4-5). The reward is based upon one's own service and not what others have done or said. We are constantly called upon day by day to carry out the mandate of mission and ministry. In the teachings of Jesus, the Great White Throne judgment will be a time in which the nations will be called upon to account for how they have treated the least of the earth. Were the nations attuned to their cries and pain? Moreover, were they responsive to their needs? (See Matthew 25:31-46.)

Is there a correlation between works and reward? Clearly there is in Revelation. There can be no reward without a faithful commitment to the One who is Himself the faithful and true One. He has been faithful in His self-sacrifice on the Cross; thus, those who follow Him must likewise be the same (see Mark 8:34-38). Remember, the New Testament does not dismiss works as uncharacteristic of the believer's life. In fact, our works reveal our faith (see James 2:14-20). Works are not the only test of authenticity, but they are not to be discarded either (see Ephesians 2:8-10). We are saved by grace, but we also are saved to do good works and to be engaged in the work of the ministry (see Ephesians 4:11-12).

What is the reward? It is eternal life, which is a life that is free from the tyranny of Rome. Eternal life far exceeds the human mind's capacity to conceive and describe. The saints John saw in heaven and before the throne lived in a state of perfect bliss, surrounded by the very presence of the Lamb, free from trouble, tears, sickness, pain, darkness—and assured of never having to face death again. The pain of death included not only the act of dying, but also how many of the saints of that day died.

There is a further self-description of Jesus as the Alpha and Omega, the beginning and the end—the first and the last (see 1:8; 21:6). Here, there is the absolute attestation of the deity of Christ and His sovereignty over the universe. Everything begins with Him and concludes with Him. Thus, He governs all of the events of life and those in between as well. Nothing happens in the created universe of which He is not aware. Even the sparrow that falls from the sky comes to the attention of God. Even the hairs on our heads are numbered (see Luke 12:6-7).

### C. Come, Lord Jesus
*(Revelation 22:16-21)*

**I Jesus have sent mine angel to testify unto you these things in the churches. I am the root and the offspring of David, and the bright and morning star. And the Spirit and the bride say, Come. And let him that heareth say, Come. And let him that is athirst come. And whosoever will, let him take the water of life freely. For I testify unto every man that heareth the words of the prophecy of this book, If any man shall add unto these things, God shall add unto him the plagues that are written in this book: And if any man shall take away from the words of the book of this prophecy, God shall take away his part out of the book of life, and out of the holy city, and from the things which are written in this book. He which testifieth these things saith, Surely I come quickly. Amen. Even so, come, Lord Jesus. The grace of our Lord Jesus Christ be with you all. Amen.**

The angel sent with the message that John recorded came from Jesus. He came to testify to the seven churches about the coming of Jesus Christ. In this verse, Jesus gives another name for Himself. He is the root and the offspring of David and the bright and morning star. Several beliefs about the Jewish Messiah developed in ancient Judaism. The most prominent was the belief that He would be a Warrior-King in the lineage and heritage of David (see 2 Samuel 7:12-14). In Isaiah, the Messiah was a root out of dry ground and from the stem of Jesse (see Isaiah 11:1-2; 53:2). The title "Bright and Morning Star" was another of the messianic beliefs that developed over time and is found primarily in the book of Numbers: "I shall see him, but not now: I shall behold him, but not nigh: there shall come a Star out of Jacob, and a Sceptre shall rise out of Israel, and shall smite the corners of Moab, and destroy all the children of Sheth" (24:17). But, the Messiah in Revelation is not one who is a Warrior but a Lamb, who conquers not with a sword, but with the shedding of His blood.

The invitation is extended to all who thirst for righteousness. The river of the water of life can satisfy one's thirst as no other can. This water is free and gives life to all who drink (see Isaiah 55:1). These words cannot be added to nor can anything be taken from them. Whoever adds anything to the words of this prophecy will endure the same plagues as those in the Book. Also, to anyone who takes something from the Book, God will take away his or her part from the Tree of Life. Hence, the Book cannot be added to nor subtracted from; it is complete within itself.

## III. Concluding Reflections

Revelation is one of the most misunderstood and misinterpreted books in the Bible. Its value as a source of instruction and exhortation has not always been appreciated, yet it remains one of the most important books in the New Testament. Through its pages we have witnessed some of the things that were most prominent in the churches in the latter days of the first Christian century. In the days when Revelation was written, it was clearly one of the greatest sources of encouragement for saints who lived under the sweltering weight of persecution. They looked with an eye of expectancy to God, who called them to a life of unquestionable faithfulness.

This is our challenge today. How do we encourage faithfulness to God among a people who have achieved much and whose lives are more governed by their possessions than their relationship with Christ?

## WORD POWER

**I come (Greek: *erchomai*)**—is in middle voice, which means "the Speaker" (Jesus Christ) is the one who is performing the action. He is the coming King. The word "come" (erchomai) is followed by the emphatic participle "quickly." The emphasis is that there will be no delay in His coming and it will be sudden. Quickly is better rendered "sudden."

## HOME DAILY BIBLE READINGS

for the week of May 27, 2007
*Christ Will Return*

May 21, Monday
　—John 16:17-24
　—Pain Becomes Joy
May 22, Tuesday
　—John 16:25-33
　—Jesus Overcomes
May 23, Wednesday
　—Ephesians 4:1-6
　—One Body, One Spirit
May 24, Thursday
　—Colossians 3:12-17
　—May Christ Rule Your Hearts
May 25, Friday
　—Revelation 22:6-11
　—Worship God
May 26, Saturday
　—Revelation 22:12-16
　—The Reward for Faithfulness
May 27, Sunday
　—Revelation 22:17-21
　—The Invitation

## PRAYER

*Lord God, Creator of all that is, teach us to trust more in You than in the things we have. Your grace has been more than sufficient for every need. Forgive us for failing to walk faithfully and be committed to You. May we from this day live in the full assurance of Your abiding presence. In the name of Jesus Christ, we pray. Amen.*

# SUMMER QUARTER—June, July, August 2007

## *Committed to Doing Right*

### GENERAL INTRODUCTION

The three units in this quarter consider a number of Old Testament prophets in nearly chronological order. Most of the lessons set the prophet's message in historical context by also providing supporting texts from 2 Kings or 2 Chronicles. Although the prophets' careers spanned several hundred years, their messages were consistent: Being related to God through faith imposes certain requirements upon God's people. One such requirement is to do what is right.

**Unit I,** *Life as God's People,* has four lessons. These examine the need for justice, the people's accountability for their own wrongdoing, the nature of true worship, and the abundant life that God offers. The texts come from the books of Amos, Hosea, Isaiah, and 2 Kings. Lesson 1—many people experience injustice in today's world. What accounts for this and what does it have to do with Christians? Amos says that injustice stems from one part of society ignoring the needs of another, and that, as God's people, we are called to fight against such attitudes and behaviors. Lesson 2—people sometimes act callously and selfishly, even when they know better. What is the result when God's people act this way? Hosea says that God holds us accountable for our actions, even though God also always works for our redemption. Lesson 3—sincere believers who seek a worship experience want it to be pure and meaningful. How can we have a pure and meaningful experience when we worship God? Isaiah implies that there is a connection between how we live and how we worship. His own call is an example of how one can experience God's presence in true worship. Lesson 4—most people want an abundance of good things in their lives. What is the source of such abundance for believers? Using the image of a great feast to which all persons are invited, Isaiah says that God is the one who generously provides all good things for His children. Luke makes a similar point in the parable of the feast.

**Unit II,** *What Does God Require?,* has five lessons. The first lesson provides us with a panoramic view of God's requirements for righteous living. The next four lessons then relate this to God's justice, God's judgment, the people's disobedience, and the need for trust in God. The texts come from Micah, Zephaniah, Habakkuk, Jeremiah, 2 Kings, and 2 Chronicles. Lesson 5—most people want to do what is right. How do we know what the right thing is? Micah gives us solid help by highlighting justice, kindness, and love of God as standards to guide our actions. Lesson 6—people sometimes act wrongly without thinking of the consequences to themselves and others. What consequences result when God's people act wrongly? Zephaniah says that God will behave justly, bringing both punishment and redemption. The prophet also says that we will have reason in the end to praise God for all God's actions. Lesson 7— people want a reason to hope when all seems wrong with the world, or in their lives. What reason do we have to hope during adverse situations? Habakkuk's response is that the God who will not tolerate injustice is the same God who works for salvation, and this is the source of our hope. Lesson 8—some people act with impunity, believing they will always be protected from the consequences of their actions. Are Christians to have such a mindset? Jeremiah states that God holds us accountable, so we will not escape the consequences of our behavior. At the same time, Jeremiah says that God responds to our good actions and to true worship with faithfulness. Lesson 9—in the midst of loss and pain, people sometimes willingly believe something untrue because it makes them feel better. How can we guard against such a mistake? Jeremiah urges us to hold to our trust in God and to wait patiently for God's healing, which will come in God's own time.

**Unit III,** *How Shall We Respond?,* has four lessons. The first three lessons emphasize hope, personal responsibility, and repentance as appropriate responses for those who are committed to doing right. This unit closes with the reassurance that God's judgment is just. Texts in this unit come from Lamentations, 2 Kings, Ezekiel, Zechariah, and Malachi. Lesson 10—painful events occur in everyone's life. How are we to respond when such times come to us? The writer of Lamentations says that we have reason to hope in the midst of despair, because of God's unfailing love and care. The psalmist makes the same point in Psalm 23. Lesson 11—some people do not take responsibility for their actions; they seek to blame others instead. To what extent are we accountable for what we do? Ezekiel says that each of us is responsible for our deeds. Lesson 12—people yearn for wholeness and happiness in their lives. Where do we find such fulfillment? Zechariah says that when we return to the Lord, the wholeness and happiness we will have in God's new age will become available to us now, as well as then. Lesson 13—most people feel good when justice and good triumph in the events of their daily lives. What reason do we have to anticipate such a celebration on a cosmic level? Malachi affirms that God will come one day to judge the world and to set all things right. He also confirms the fact that God will bless true worshipers when that day comes.

## Lesson 1

# Amos Challenges Injustice

**ADULT TOPIC:** Committed to Doing Right
**YOUTH TOPIC:** God Has High Expectations
**CHILDREN'S TOPIC:** God Wants Us to Live Fairly

**DEVOTIONAL READING:** Psalm 82
**BACKGROUND SCRIPTURE:** Amos 5:10-15, 21-24; 8:4-12; 2 Kings 13:23-25
**PRINT PASSAGE:** Amos 5:10-15, 21-24

### Amos 5:10-15, 21-24—KJV

10 They hate him that rebuketh in the gate, and they abhor him that speaketh uprightly.

11 Forasmuch therefore as your treading is upon the poor, and ye take from him burdens of wheat: ye have built houses of hewn stone, but ye shall not dwell in them; ye have planted pleasant vineyards, but ye shall not drink wine of them.

12 For I know your manifold transgressions and your mighty sins: they afflict the just, they take a bribe, and they turn aside the poor in the gate from their right.

13 Therefore the prudent shall keep silence in that time; for it is an evil time.

14 Seek good, and not evil, that ye may live: and so the LORD, the God of hosts, shall be with you, as ye have spoken.

15 Hate the evil, and love the good, and establish judgment in the gate: it may be that the LORD God of hosts will be gracious unto the remnant of Joseph.

. . . . .

21 I hate, I despise your feast days, and I will not smell in your solemn assemblies.

22 Though ye offer me burnt offerings and your meat offerings, I will not accept them: neither will I regard the peace offerings of your fat beasts.

23 Take thou away from me the noise of thy songs; for I will not hear the melody of thy viols.

24 But let judgment run down as waters, and righteousness as a mighty stream.

---

**June 3, 2007**

**UNIT I**
Life as God's People

**CHILDREN'S UNIT**
Life as God's People

### KEY VERSE

But let judgment run down as waters, and righteousness as a mighty stream.—Amos 5:24

### OBJECTIVES

**Upon completion of this lesson, the students are expected to:**

1. Understand that God holds His people to a different standard, as set forth in His Word;
2. Recognize that social justice is to be practiced among all people with a common standard—the Word of God; and,
3. Understand that elaborate ceremonies and rituals do not impress God.

## UNIFYING LESSON PRINCIPLE

Many people experience injustice in today's world. What accounts for this, and what does it have to do with us? Amos says that injustice stems from one part of society ignoring the needs of another, and that, as God's people, we are called to fight such attitudes and behaviors.

## POINTS TO BE EMPHASIZED
### ADULTS/YOUTH

**Adult/Youth Key Verse:** Amos 5:24
**Print Passage:** Amos 5:10-15, 21-24

—Amos denounces those who oppress the poor, and the corruption of those who administer justice.
—Amos continuously urges people to denounce injustice and oppression.
—God requires righteous living not empty rituals.
—Amos denounces the injustice of religious leaders and rich people who oppress the poor.
—Amos urges people to seek good, not evil, and to turn their hearts to God and live in accordance with God's demand for justice.
—Amos identifies living righteously in economic terms.
—God judges injustice and demands accountability on behalf of those in need.

### CHILDREN

**Key Verse:** Amos 5:15
**Print Passage:** Amos 1:1; 3:1-2; 7:14-16

—Amos brought the people a message of God's condemnation of their unfair treatment of the poor and powerless.
—Amos was a shepherd when God called him to speak against injustice.
—God expects people to act justly toward others and to be responsible for their actions.
—How can children partner with God to help "establish justice"?

## TOPICAL OUTLINE OF THE LESSON

I. **INTRODUCTION**
   A. Life as God's People: Committed to Do Right
   B. Biblical Background

II. **EXPOSITION AND APPLICATION OF THE SCRIPTURE**
   A. The Indictment Against God's People *(Amos 5:10-13)*
   B. Remedy for God's People *(Amos 5:14-15)*
   C. God's Rejection of Insincere Worship *(Amos 5:21-23)*
   D. God's Demand for Repentance *(Amos 5:24)*

III. **CONCLUDING REFLECTIONS**

## I. INTRODUCTION
### A. Life as God's People: Committed to Do Right

The issue of justice is a common thread in the works of Dr. Martin Luther King, Jr. Most often, however, the issues of justice that he addressed are associated with equality between the races. While racial justice and equality were the pivotal concerns of Dr. King and the Civil Rights Movement, prior to his assassination the issue of economic justice began taking the spotlight.

The issues of justice and fair treatment of the poor are strongly rooted in the prophecy of Amos. In his writings and his speeches, Dr. King addressed the proclamation of Amos, especially Amos 5:24 (NRSV): "Let justice roll down…."

It is a sad commentary that Dr. King's writings and speeches were not directed at the unchurched, but rather to those professing membership in the household of faith. The majority of the White Christian community, and indeed many in the Black church community, were hard-hearted and stubborn regarding his message to do what is right. They were unwilling to give up their privileges, or even to lend themselves to self-examination, in order that justice would be served for the underprivileged. The majority of Whites were unwilling to let go of a social stratum in which they were the clear and obvious beneficiaries. Meanwhile, many blacks who were not bearing the heaviest weight of oppression did not want Dr. King making life difficult for them by "stirring up trouble" with his outcry for justice and equality. But Dr. King and his compatriots in the Movement continued in the struggle, knowing that God has called and holds His people to a different standard—a higher standard—as set forth in His Word. Claiming heritage in God without obedience to God is offensive to God; the book of Amos seeks to disclose this message.

### B. Biblical Background

Little is known about the prophet Amos. His name was probably uncommon in those days—as Amos appears only seven times in this book (and once in the gospel of Luke, where it referred to someone other than the prophet). The name Amos is believed to mean "burdened" or "burden bearer."

Amos' ministry occurred during the reign of Jeroboam II. It was a time of economic boom and political stability and peace, which brought on the evolution of ostentatious living. The rich were getting richer while the unfortunate poor were languishing in abject poverty—and the lethargic leadership seemed unconcerned. Amos castigated the rich and warned them of their impending doom. Worship of the Most High was meant for the poor, they believed; the rich had no time for God. Is life any different in our time? Many people are so caught up with living "the good life" that they appear unconcerned with living "the God life"—a life that is pleasing in His sight. Israel's moral decadence was an example of their unbridled idolatry. Thus, Amos issued an urgent call to repentance as the only escape for the impending judgment of God. Amos was the first of all God's messengers to prophecy regarding the demise of the kingdom of Israel.

The theme of the book of Amos is social injustice and religious infidelity. It addresses social evils of the people, as well as their paganized worship practices. In his message, Amos stretched beyond the covenantal relationship between God and Israel. To him, Yahweh was far greater than the covenant God of Israel; He was God of the entire world.

## II. Exposition and Application of the Scripture

### A. The Indictment Against God's People (Amos 5:10-13)

**They hate him that rebuketh in the gate,**

and they abhor him that speaketh uprightly. Forasmuch therefore as your treading is upon the poor, and ye take from him burdens of wheat: ye have built houses of hewn stone, but ye shall not dwell in them; ye have planted pleasant vineyards, but ye shall not drink wine of them. For I know your manifold transgressions and your mighty sins: they afflict the just, they take a bribe, and they turn aside the poor in the gate from their right. Therefore the prudent shall keep silence in that time; for it is an evil time.

In this particular lesson, Amos makes an accusation against God's people. He accuses them of:
- Having a negative attitude toward justice and righteousness;
- Being oppressive;
- Being dishonest; and,
- Loving luxury at the expense of the poor

Amos's accusation against God's people came in response to the social injustice that he witnessed as well as the hollow worship that they offered to God. Amos was a righteous man who was critical of their treatment of the poor and the downtrodden. He also condemned their hypocritical worship practices—offering sacrifices without obedience.

The accusations of Amos started with the negative opinions of those who spoke against social justice; they were hated. Why? They were maligned and despised because in advocating for the poor they revealed the corruption that was taking place among the privileged. This widespread social injustice had to be confronted before God's people could be blessed. It is impossible for people to be what God wants them to be by oppressing others. In order to be committed to doing the right thing, God's people had to rid themselves of the contempt in their hearts for those who sought justice, and exhibit fairness toward those who were sorely mistreated.

God gets no pleasure from the exploitation of any among His creation. Plainly put, God is angered when people choose to oppress, suppress, and exploit others. God had grown weary of the ill-treatment of some among them. Although they were poor, they still were created in the image of God. In fact, before the Flood (see Genesis 6:3), God stated that "My spirit shall not always strive with man"—that is to say, God will not always put up with human rebellion against His Word and His will. However, God always gives humanity a chance to repent (see Psalm 89:14). God does not mete out His judgment before He extends His mercy to those who are in a sinful state.

Christians should never be guilty of oppressive practices, or exploiting the poor to prosper themselves. Christians are obligated to stand for justice and equality for those whose voices are weak and those whose hopes have been dashed. Christians should stand for righteousness no matter the cost, for they are driven by a higher authority than the materialistic things of this world. They are driven by God's Word and should be attracted to obedience.

### B. Remedy for God's People
*(Amos 5:14-15)*

Seek good, and not evil, that ye may live: and so the LORD, the God of hosts, shall be with you, as ye have spoken. Hate the evil, and love the good, and establish judgment in the gate: it may be that the LORD God of hosts will be gracious unto the remnant of Joseph.

Amos not only communicates the indictment against the people, he details the corrective measures necessary to prevent them from experiencing the wrath of God. One of God's attributes is mercy; without mercy we all would receive the judgment we deserve. God's mercy can be seen through Amos's admonishment concerning what the people could do to have the charges against them dropped. First, he said to seek good. There is no earthly way one should see the oppression of other human beings as good. God did not intend for human beings to oppress each other. Therefore, Amos stated that the motives and actions of God's people must lead to good, and not to evil. Amos said that when the people sought to do good and not evil, they could be assured that God was with them. From Amos's perspective, nothing would be more gratifying than to have the presence of God with you in your well doing.

In fact, Amos stated that by following the instruction to seek good and not evil, not only would God be with them, but He would also make them live. This should be the goal of every believer—to live and not die. When people receive the truth and are willing to walk in it, they can be confident that the road they are traveling leads to life everlasting!

The next remedy for God's people, according to Amos, was that they begin to hate evil, and do good deeds. Amos followed up his admonishment with a suggestion of the kind of attitude that God's people should have. Their attitude should be the same as God's—which is an attitude of hating sin. Therefore, those who are God's should have the same attitude toward sin. Injustice should infuriate God's people; from Amos's perspective, it should be unacceptable and, therefore, confronted. Additionally, note that there should be people in place to hold all people accountable for their practices on social injustice. Although Amos realized that certain penalties already had been established in the Law for the fair treatment of others, there also needed to be an enforcement of those penalties to ensure the equal treatment of all people. There should be those who are guardians of fairness and equal treatment. It is not enough to talk about social justice and shine the light on it. There ought to be people who are willing to speak up for social justice, and who hold others accountable for acting justly and doing what is right. When one loves good rather than evil, one should be willing to champion the cause of the less fortunate and those who have no one to speak for them.

### C. God's Rejection of Insincere Worship *(Amos 5:21-23)*

**I hate, I despise your feast days, and I will not smell in your solemn assemblies. Though ye offer me burnt offerings and your meat offerings, I will not accept them: neither will I regard the peace offerings of your fat beasts. Take thou away from me the noise of thy songs; for I will not hear the melody of thy viols.**

Amos understood that worship is mandatory for God's people; however, if one's attitude toward sin is in question, it stands to reason that there will be a problem with that person's worship practices.

God denounced Israel's worship in strong terms: "I hate, I despise…I will not smell in your solemn assemblies" (verse 21). Sin had lodged in Israel's heart like shrapnel, and for that reason God despised them. Amos doesn't spare the truth, telling them that their songs of praise were merely noise to the ears of God. Their songs possessed no harmony and no intentional melody; therefore, God was rejecting their feeble attempts at worship.

God has no time to listen to those who are simply going through the motions of worship; His ears seek worship that is sincere. The holy God cannot receive a practicing sinner's songs—for such songs are filled with contempt, malice, and hatred for the things of God. When a person treats others unfairly and oppresses the poor, his or her worship is—as Paul declares in 1 Corinthians 13—a noisy gong or clanging cymbal: it makes a lot of noise but there is no music. One has to come before a holy God in a holy manner. God rejected the worship of Israel because of their sinful practices; therefore, they were missing the mark. He told them that their feast days were hated by God and their burnt offerings were unacceptable; in essence, God cared nothing for their ceremonies. However, He did care about their treatment of others, as well as their obedience to His Word. Ceremonies and rituals are meaningless to God if there is no love for that which is good, wholesome, and righteous. All the bulls, the goats, the turtle doves, and the lambs that they sacrificed to God meant nothing to Him if the people's hearts were far from Him.

God's rejection of the worship practices of the Israelites was significant. Worship was how they showed their allegiance to God; therefore, when God rejected their worship, which had become a stench to Him, this inferred that they were hypocrites and unfit to offer worship to God. Elaborate ceremonies and rituals do not impress God; He wants His people to be obedient to His Word (1 Samuel 15:22). When His people are in line with His Word, only then will He accept the worship offerings given to Him.

### D. God's Demand for Repentance (Amos 5:24)

**But let judgment run down as waters, and righteousness as a mighty stream.**

Amos paints a powerful word picture in verse 24: "Let judgment run down as waters"—which suggests that justice and righteousness are to be powerful forces in our lives. Water is one of the most powerful elements known to humankind. It can be both destructive and life-giving. Water can destroy whole towns and villages, but water also can bring life to a parched body. Likewise, justice in the wrong hands can be destructive; it can destroy lives and abort dreams; however, justice in the right hands can unlock doors that have been closed, and offer hope in the midst of hopelessness. Amos said, "let justice run down" to everyone, so that everyone can be refreshed by the powerful and refreshing streams of justice.

In this verse, Amos also proclaimed God's directive that righteousness be like a mighty stream. In other words, righteousness should empower God's people to do the right thing. This stream is constant, and obstacles do not impede it. It is free to flow and move mightily. Amos wanted them to become a free-flowing stream of righteousness. In doing this they would please God as well as avert judgment.

## III. Concluding Reflections

This lesson demonstrates that no matter how bad things are, God always has someone who will stand up against wrong and not give in to popular opinion. Amos observed the sinfulness of God's people and confronted them. His stance was not popular, but this is not what God calls His people to be. God is angered when "the haves" seek to oppress the less fortunate, or the "have nots." God calls people to be faithful and obedient.

Amos can be considered a champion for social justice issues. His stance on the treatment of the poor is an issue that contemporary society also must address. The message as it was then is still the same. The clarion call is: "Hear the Word of the Lord, modern-day people of God. It is time to stand up and do what is right!"

## WORD POWER

**Seek (Hebrew: *darash*)** (Amos 5:14)—this verb indicates an order, because it is cast in the imperative mood. A response to this command is expected from the hearer. It asks the hearer to seek with a sense of diligence and purpose.

**Hate (Hebrew: *saw-nay*)**—this verb also is in the imperative mood. It commands the hearers to make evil their enemy. Both of these verbs are not words of advice that the hearer may take or not. The superior (God) issued these orders; therefore, the subordinates (we) must carry them out.

## HOME DAILY BIBLE READINGS

for the week of June 3, 2007
*Amos Challenges Injustice*

May 28, Monday
—Psalm 82:1-8
—A Plea for Justice

May 29, Tuesday
—Isaiah 59:9-15
—Where Is Justice and Truth?

May 30, Wednesday
—Jeremiah 22:1-5
—Do What Is Just

May 31, Thursday
—Amos 3:1-10
—God Admonishes Israel

June 1, Friday
—Amos 8:4-8
—Protect the Poor

June 2, Saturday
—Amos 5:10-15
—Seek Good, Not Evil

June 3, Sunday
—Amos 5:20-25
—Let Justice Roll Down

## PRAYER

*Father, Creator and Maker of everything, we come humbly before You asking that You would search our hearts; if we have oppressed or treated anyone unfairly, please forgive us and purge our hearts of such sin. We need You to make plain our way, so that we may love Your laws, and meditate on Your Word. We thank You for what You can and will do for us according to Your Word. In Jesus' name, we pray. Amen.*

**June 10, 2007**

Lesson 2

**UNIT I**
Life as God's People

**CHILDREN'S UNIT**
Life as God's People

# Hosea Preaches God's Accusation Against Israel

**ADULT TOPIC:** God's Indictment of Israel
**YOUTH TOPIC:** Living Up to God's Higher Expectation
**CHILDREN'S TOPIC:** We Can Be Forgiven

**KEY VERSE**

Hear the word of the LORD, ye children of Israel: for the LORD hath a controversy with the inhabitants of the land, because there is no truth, nor mercy, nor knowledge of God in the land.
—Hosea 4:1

**DEVOTIONAL READING:** Hosea 14
**BACKGROUND SCRIPTURE:** Hosea 4:1-4; 7:1-2; 12:7-9; 14:1-3; 2 Kings 15:8-10
**PRINT PASSAGE:** Hosea 4:1-4; 7:1-2; 12:8-9

**OBJECTIVES**

Upon completion of this lesson, the students are expected to:
1. Explore the concept of God's unfailing love to an unfaithful people;
2. Recognize that God's message to Israel to return to Him is rooted in His steadfast love for them; and,
3. Understand that God promised to bless the land if the people obeyed Him, and punish the land if the people disobeyed Him.

### Hosea 4:1-4; 7:1-2; 12:8-9—KJV

HEAR THE word of the LORD, ye children of Israel: for the LORD hath a controversy with the inhabitants of the land, because there is no truth, nor mercy, nor knowledge of God in the land.

2 By swearing, and lying, and killing, and stealing, and committing adultery, they break out, and blood toucheth blood.

3 Therefore shall the land mourn, and every one that dwelleth therein shall languish, with the beasts of the field, and with the fowls of heaven; yea, the fishes of the sea also shall be taken away.

4 Yet let no man strive, nor reprove another: for thy people are as they that strive with the priest.

· · · · ·

WHEN I would have healed Israel, then the iniquity of Ephraim was discovered, and the wickedness of Samaria: for they commit falsehood; and the thief cometh in, and the troop of robbers spoileth without.

2 And they consider not in their hearts that I remember all their wickedness: now their own doings have beset them about; they are before my face.

· · · · ·

8 And Ephraim said, Yet I am become rich, I have found me out substance: in all my labours they shall find none iniquity in me that were sin.

**9 And I that am the L**ORD **thy God from the land of Egypt will yet make thee to dwell in tabernacles, as in the days of the solemn feast.**

## UNIFYING LESSON PRINCIPLE

People sometimes act callously and selfishly, even when they know better. What is the result when God's people act this way? Hosea says that God holds us accountable for our actions, even though God also always works for our redemption.

## POINTS TO BE EMPHASIZED
## ADULTS/YOUTH

**Adult/Youth Key Verse:** Hosea 4:1

**Print Passage:** Hosea 4:1-4; 7:1-2; 12:8-9

—Hosea uses the language of a trial court to bring an indictment against Israel.
—What specific transgressions did Israel commit against God?
—Faithfulness, loyalty, and knowledge of God designate key elements of the covenant faith.
—Hosea ministered during a time of great social upheaval and political intrigue.

## CHILDREN

**Key Verses:** Hosea 11:3-4

**Print Passage:** Hosea 1:1; 11:1-2, 3-4, 10-11

—Hosea demonstrated God's ongoing love through his own actions within his family.
—Hosea was chosen by God to deliver a special message on forgiveness and accountability.

## TOPICAL OUTLINE OF THE LESSON

### I. INTRODUCTION
  A. A Message from God for Israel
  B. Biblical Background

### II. EXPOSITION AND APPLICATION OF THE SCRIPTURE
  A. God's Controversy Against His People *(Hosea 4:1-4)*
  B. The People's Response to God's Charge *(Hosea 7:1-2)*
  C. Misguided by Arrogance and Deceit *(Hosea 12:8-9)*

### III. CONCLUDING REFLECTIONS

### I. INTRODUCTION
### A. A Message from God for Israel

When Pop/R&B diva Tina Turner released the song, "What's Love Got to Do with It?", it topped music charts; many believed she was inspired to sing the song following the demise of her abusive marriage to Ike Turner. Although Turner did not write the lyrics, many resonated with the question asked of love gone awry. The prophet Hosea could have asked that same question regarding his marriage to an adulterous woman.

The book of Hosea portrays a love relationship that has gone awry because of infidelity. God, who initiated this love relationship, used Hosea's adulterous marriage as an example to Israel of love that commits and endures, even in the face of infidelity. God's love relationship had been thwarted by His lover, Israel. Out of His great love, however, God allowed them another chance by extending mercy to them, so that they might be restored.

Hosea was chosen by God to give Israel a message of God's unfailing love to an unfaithful people. It shows God's relentless pursuit of His people, trying to get them back on track. This was illustrated by the love that Hosea had for his adulterous wife, Gomer.

In this lesson, God's message to Israel is to return to Him because of His steadfast love for them. Their return was not without repentance, for Israel could not come back the same way she left—there had to be a change of heart. This is an important lesson to learn for anyone who has been unfaithful to the Lord. No one who returns to God can come back the same way—repentance is necessary.

### B. Biblical Background

The name Hosea means "salvation" or "deliverance." Hosea began his ministry to Israel during the final days of Jeroboam II. Under his reign, Israel enjoyed both political peace and material prosperity, but the period was marred by moral corruption and spiritual bankruptcy. Hosea had a lengthy period of ministry, prophesying during the reigns of Uzziah, Jotham, Ahaz, and Hezekiah in Judah, and Jeroboam II in Israel.

Hosea is the first of the twelve Minor Prophets. "Minor" refers to the brevity of the prophecies, not their substance or significance. Hosea pictured the relationship between a faithful husband (Hosea, God) and an unfaithful wife (Gomer, Israel.) Hosea married Gomer, and she bore him children. He gave them names that were prophetically and historically meaningful: a son, Jezreel ("The Lord sows"); a daughter, Lo-ruhamah, ("no more mercy"); and another son, Lo-ammi ("not my people"). The theme of Hosea is God's loyal love for His covenant people, Israel, despite their idolatry.

## II. Exposition and Application of the Scripture
### A. God's Controversy Against His People (Hosea 4:1-4)

**HEAR THE word of the Lord, ye children of Israel: for the Lord hath a controversy with the inhabitants of the land, because there is no truth, nor mercy, nor knowledge of God in the land. By swearing, and lying, and killing, and stealing, and committing adultery, they break out, and blood toucheth blood. Therefore shall the land mourn, and every one that dwelleth therein shall languish, with the beasts of the field, and with the fowls of heaven; yea, the fishes of the sea also shall be taken away. Yet let no man strive, nor reprove another: for thy people are as they that strive with the priest.**

Using the language of a trial court, Hosea begins this section with an indictment of the people of Israel for their failure to exhibit love and faithfulness to God and their failure to acknowledge God as their covenant Lord. The basis of judgment against Israel was unfaithfulness. Just as Gomer was unfaithful and went to live with another man, Israel was unfaithful and had turned to pagan idols. Because they had abandoned the precepts of God, all the ethical norms were thrown out. Therefore, there was no mercy in the land, no love for one's neighbor, and no compassion for the poor and needy. The people were false-hearted toward

God and hard-hearted toward one another. When people reject God's covenant, they begin to exploit each other.

Hosea referenced the Ten Commandments in reminding the people of how they had violated God's law by pronouncing curses, telling lies, murdering, stealing, and committing adultery. As a result, they had brought suffering to themselves, to the land, and even to the animals. God's covenantal promise was that He would bless the land if the people obeyed Him, and He would punish the land if the people disobeyed Him. Hosea reminded the people that it was their sin that polluted the land and caused natural calamities, like famines and droughts. It is interesting to note that when God judges a nation, the land itself is involved; even the beasts and fowl of the air are affected by God's judgment. As a result of their transgressions against God, Hosea reminded the people that they were living with the consequences of their behavior.

The priests who were faithful to God had fled to Judah when Jeroboam I set up his own religious system in Israel. Jeroboam I had ordained his own priests who knew neither the Lord nor His Law. Their primary interest was having a job that would provide them with food, clothing, and pleasure. Hosea cautioned the corrupt priests not to blame the people for what was happening because the people were only following the priests' bad example. Their basic sin was hard-heartedness: it wasn't that they didn't know what God said, but rather, they were ignoring what God had said. Part of the pursuit of knowing is obeying (Hosea 6:3). In Luke 6:46, Jesus addressed this very issue of willful ignorance when He said, "Why call ye me, Lord, Lord, and do not the things which I say?" Second Peter 3:5 says, "For this they willingly are ignorant…." This ignorance does not mean that they didn't know; they willfully ignored what God said.

The controversy that God had with His people was in the area of relationship. Although ignorance and disobedience are two symptoms of a disconnected relationship, the main impetus for either of these symptoms was a strained, disjointed relationship. God's people had turned away from the truth, and forsook the connection they had with God. They should have known that God wanted an intimate and personal relationship with His people. Here, Hosea captured the source of the problem between God and Israel. Hosea 4:1 states that they had no knowledge of God. The intimate bond that was initiated by God had soured, not because of anything that God did, but because of the adulterous ways of His chosen people.

God values the relationship He has with His people—and for that reason, God woos people and seeks to reestablish the relationship. All He demands is that His people repent before they can experience intimacy with Him. Our modern society, with all of its ceremonies, is missing the point that God is making through Hosea: one cannot have an intimate relationship with God without repentance. Israel must come back to God with a remorseful attitude. Israel could not come back the same way she left; she had to return knowing that she had sinned and was now willing to follow God. Willfully ignoring God leads to fulfilling selfish desires, and it is the death of a right relationship with

Him. Faithfulness to God requires more than knowing what is right; it includes commitment to doing what is right.

### B. The People's Response to God's Charge *(Hosea 7:1-2)*

**WHEN I would have healed Israel, then the iniquity of Ephraim was discovered, and the wickedness of Samaria: for they commit falsehood; and the thief cometh in, and the troop of robbers spoileth without. And they consider not in their hearts that I remember all their wickedness: now their own doings have beset them about; they are before my face.**

Some scholars argue that it is probable that the last statement in Hosea 6:11 should be joined with Hosea 7:1 to read, "When I have returned the captivity of my people, When I would have healed Israel, then the iniquity of Ephraim was discovered…" This clause seems to highlight the pain and dissatisfaction of God with a people who were very persistent in their sinful ways, despite God's attempt to restore them. The corruption of Ephraim was tremendous: fraud, wicked deeds, drunkenness, adultery, and robberies were the norm. Both the people and the leaders were inflamed with lustful passions. Unfortunately, the people's desire for God to act on their terms instead of under the conditions of His holy covenant prevented God from helping them. They thought that they could get away with their sins, but God had seen them all and remembered them all. Their sins that had been covered were now being uncovered. That which they had been doing secretly was now done openly. Sadly, there was no shame, no conviction, and no conscience relative to their sin. The Lord would forgive them of their iniquity if they would only repent and return to Him. Unfortunately, they persisted in their wickedness and went farther and farther into rebellion and disobedience.

It is unfortunate that today sin seems to be paraded openly and flaunted shamelessly before the world, under the guise of a "new morality" and unbridled freedom. This term simply means humanity's standard versus God's standard; humanity's standard sees what is wrong in the sight of God as being acceptable. However, God's standard has set parameters that designate what is good and what is evil. Hosea did not attempt to become legalistic; he simply sought a response from those who had benefited from the goodness of God. When a life has no standards or principles to govern it, then it is dangerous, especially if one is a Christian.

In Judges 17:6 and 21:25, the writer says, "In those days there was no king in Israel: every man did that which was right in his own eyes." When there are no standards, chaos is created. Notice that in our Scripture, no matter how bad the people were, God did not give up on them. God found a way to bring them back to Himself. That is not to say that a person can sin and get away with it; to the contrary, God's love seeks to bring people back into right relationship with Him. This is the essence of the book of Hosea: God's willingness to be in a right relationship with people. It is not God's policy to cast the crown of His creation into hell's fire. His will is that all people would come to repentance (2 Peter 3:9). Hosea was making his case to the people for repentance; however, their response was contempt and selfish desire. They rejected God's offer to return to Him through repentance; the consequences of not returning would be painful.

## C. Misguided by Arrogance and Deceit
(Hosea 12:8-9)

**And Ephraim said, Yet I am become rich, I have found me out substance: in all my labours they shall find none iniquity in me that were sin. And I that am the LORD thy God from the land of Egypt will yet make thee to dwell in tabernacles, as in the days of the solemn feast.**

Ephraim was the largest tribe that made up the population of Israel; therefore, the prophets often referred to Israel as Ephraim. The prophet Hosea uses this expression for Israel some thirty-seven times. Sometimes "Ephraim" is a synonym for the whole Northern Kingdom. He is referred to as someone who thought himself to be immune from the detection of sin. Ephraim had presumed on the mercies of God. His position was that the fruits of his labor was proof that he was not guilty (see Ecclesiastes 8:9-13). But the Lord would remind him that all of Ephraim's possessions and prosperity were owed to the one who delivered him out of Egypt (verse 9).

The deceitfulness of riches was not suggesting that Israel didn't actually have the riches, but that the riches had made them feel self-sufficient—and Israel's sense of self-sufficiency had given way to an attitude of arrogance. Being misguided by arrogance and deceit can be seen in the terms of the deceitfulness of riches. The attitude of Ephraim in this verse would suggest that the accumulation of wealth advocates a mindset of self-sufficiency and a false sense of security, not needing God. "Yet I am become rich…" reflects arrogance. Ephraim is declaring independence from God by saying he has no regard for the sayings of the prophet of God "in all [his] labours." Again, Ephraim believed that his strength had gotten him the prosperity that was now his and Israel's. In the same verse, Ephraim says, "they shall find none iniquity…that were sin"—that none would find any fault in him that would bring down the penalty of sin. However, one can be rich and still be poor; that is to say, a person can have wealth and still be spiritually poor, such as the church of Laodicea mentioned in Revelation 3:17. This was a rich church; however, God accused them of being wretched, miserable, poor, blind, and naked, despite their abundance of material wealth. This charge would suggest that material things don't impress God, but that an obedient life does. God's continual plea was a plea of obedience. If Ephraim would simply obey, God would then allow him to dwell back in the tent, as they did in the days of the Feast of Tabernacles.

God does not approve of dishonesty in business. Perhaps Ephraim believed that he was able to buy his way with his seeming success, not knowing that he was being blessed by God. There are many people who place their hope in the accumulation of possessions in order to find satisfaction and purpose in life. Some compromise their spiritual values in order to accumulate possessions and accommodate the expectations of others. Tragically, they forget that they will be held accountable for their actions and that lasting joy and happiness can never be found in the accumulation of things. Faithfulness and loyalty to God produce an everlasting joy and contentment.

## III. Concluding Reflections

Hosea depicted God as just and loving. But as we see in the children of Hosea, their names reveal the displeasure of God against His people. Christians have assumed that because they are under grace, they have license to sin indiscriminately. Under the cloak of grace, many are wallowing in sin and coming to church on Sundays for absolution. Many pastors preach sermons that fail to rebuke the sinful lifestyle of their members. Members are pleased as long as the sermon does not touch their area of personal weakness. God, who judged Israel for their sins, is still on the throne, and He will not continue to hold His peace when there is no remorse for sin.

God is just and faithful to forgive us. God desired that the people of Israel repent and return home in spite of their many transgressions. He has that same desire for us today. He wants us to grow in faithfulness, loyalty, and knowledge toward Him. We must always remember that an ignorance of God will lead to a sinful life, and that knowledge of God will lead to an intimate communion with Him.

## WORD POWER

**Hear (Hebrew:** *shama)*—the first word in the Key Verse, "hear"—shama, is cast in the imperative mood. It is a command. God issued a command to the Israelites through Hosea. They had to hear intelligently because the Lord had a controversy—they had abandoned the precepts of God. This word, "hear" (shama) implies "to hear" and "to comply" No room is left for negotiation. It is a call that demands instant obedience. For example, when a military commander issues an order, the soldiers must obey. This is a call to obey.

## HOME DAILY BIBLE READINGS

for the week of June 10, 2007
*Hosea Preaches God's Accusation Against Israel*

June 4, Monday
   —2 Kings 15:8-12
   —The Fourth Generation
June 5, Tuesday
   —Hosea 14
   —Repentance Brings Blessing
June 6, Wednesday
   —Hosea 11:1-5
   —God's Love for Israel
June 7, Thursday
   —Hosea 11:6-11
   —God Cares
June 8, Friday
   —Hosea 4:1-5
   —A Nation Sins
June 9, Saturday
   —Hosea 7:1-7
   —Evil Deeds Remembered
June 10, Sunday
   —Hosea 12:5-10
   —Return to Your God

## PRAYER

*Eternal God, our Father, as we live in a selfish and self-centered world, may we always be mindful of Your continued work of redemption on our behalf. In Jesus' name, we pray. Amen.*

**Lesson 3**

# Isaiah Calls for True Worship

**ADULT TOPIC:** True Worship!
**YOUTH TOPIC:** The Heart of Worship
**CHILDREN'S TOPIC:** We Can Worship

**DEVOTIONAL READING:** Isaiah 58:6-12
**BACKGROUND SCRIPTURE:** Isaiah 1:10-20; 2 Kings 15:32-35
**PRINT PASSAGE:** Isaiah 1:10-11, 14-20

### Isaiah 1:10-11, 14-20—KJV

10 Hear the word of the LORD, ye rulers of Sodom; give ear unto the law of our God, ye people of Gomorrah.

11 To what purpose is the multitude of your sacrifices unto me? saith the LORD: I am full of the burnt offerings of rams, and the fat of fed beasts; and I delight not in the blood of bullocks, or of lambs, or of he goats.

.....

14 Your new moons and your appointed feasts my soul hateth: they are a trouble unto me; I am weary to bear them.

15 And when ye spread forth your hands, I will hide mine eyes from you: yea, when ye make many prayers, I will not hear: your hands are full of blood.

16 Wash you, make you clean; put away the evil of your doings from before mine eyes; cease to do evil;

17 Learn to do well; seek judgment, relieve the oppressed, judge the fatherless, plead for the widow.

18 Come now, and let us reason together, saith the LORD: though your sins be as scarlet, they shall be as white as snow; though they be red like crimson, they shall be as wool.

19 If ye be willing and obedient, ye shall eat the good of the land:

20 But if ye refuse and rebel, ye shall be devoured with the sword: for the mouth of the LORD hath spoken it.

---

**June 17, 2007**

**UNIT I**
Life as God's People

**CHILDREN'S UNIT**
Life as God's People

**KEY VERSE**
Learn to do well; seek judgment, relieve the oppressed, judge the fatherless, plead for the widow.
—Isaiah 1:17

**OBJECTIVES**
Upon completion of this lesson, the students are expected to:
1. Recognize that God is never pleased with His people when they choose to disobey Him, yet still seek to worship Him;
2. Understand that God looks upon the heart as a person seeks to worship Him; and,
3. Recognize that true worship pleases God and is not ritualistic; it must be done with a clean, sincere heart.

## UNIFYING LESSON PRINCIPLE

Most people who seek a worshipful experience want it to be pure and meaningful. How can we have a pure and meaningful experience when we worship God? Isaiah implies that there is a connection between how we live and how we worship. His own call is an example of how one can experience God's presence in true worship.

## POINTS TO BE EMPHASIZED ADULTS/YOUTH

**Adult/Youth Key Verse:** Isaiah 1:17
**Print Passage:** Isaiah 1:10-11, 14-20

—True worship has reverence for the moral character of God.
—God calls people to obedience, requiring that they act justly.
—God is more concerned with our behavior in social relationships than with the formal rituals of worship.
—True worship must be the expression and symbol of reverence for the moral character of God.
—Serving God requires us to seek God's justice and relieve the oppressed.
—God's mercy is always present, even in judgment.

## CHILDREN

**Key Verse:** Isaiah 6:8
**Print Passage:** Isaiah 6:1-8; 1:14-17

—Worship includes a realization of who God is and who we are.
—Real worship changes us and makes a difference in our lives.
—Isaiah recognized his shortcomings, yet he yielded to God.
—What does this passage teach us about how to worship?

## TOPICAL OUTLINE OF THE LESSON

I. **INTRODUCTION**
  A. True Worship
  B. Biblical Background

II. **EXPOSITION AND APPLICATION OF THE SCRIPTURE**
  A. God's Displeasure with Empty Worship *(Isaiah 1:10-11)*
  B. God's Displeasure with Ceremonial Display *(Isaiah 1:14-15)*
  C. Preparation for True Worship *(Isaiah 1:16-20)*

III. **CONCLUDING REFLECTIONS**

## I. INTRODUCTION
### A. True Worship

What is worship? It is a reverent devotion and allegiance pledged to God. The word "worship" comes from the old English term "worth ship," which denotes the worthiness of God. In Christian understanding, God is the soul object of worship. He is worthy to be worshiped for who He is, for what He has done, for what He continues to do, and for what He will do ultimately.

What is true worship? How do we know that our worship is acceptable to God? Is it when we sweat and dance that we know we have truly worshiped?

We need to understand that God is the object of the believers' worship. The Bible declares that, "God is a Spirit: and they that worship him must worship him in spirit and in truth" (John 4:24).

### B. Biblical Background

In the Old Testament, when God spoke

to Abraham, he erected several altars where he worshiped God. When God delivered the Israelites from the bondage of Pharaoh, they worshiped God. Worship became the foundation of Israel's way of life. Unfortunately, when they got to the Promised Land, Israelites adopted foreign gods, which they worshiped.

The spiritual condition of Israel and Judah at this time was at an all-time low. The spiritual condition of God's chosen people cannot be described any better than in Isaiah 1:4: "Ah sinful nation, a people laden with iniquity, a seed of evil-doers…they have forsaken the LORD…they are gone away backward." In this state they continued to worship God, but their worship was rejected. This is evidence that God does not accept just any worship. He accepts worship that is given with sincerity and truth. Thus, this lesson is entitled "True Worship."

## II. Exposition and Application of the Scripture
### A. God's Displeasure with Empty Worship (Isaiah 1:10-11)

**Hear the word of the LORD, ye rulers of Sodom; give ear unto the law of our God, ye people of Gomorrah. To what purpose is the multitude of your sacrifices unto me? saith the LORD: I am full of the burnt offerings of rams, and the fat of fed beasts; and I delight not in the blood of bullocks, or of lambs, or of he goats.**

Water and oil do not mix; neither do worship and disobedience. Therefore, God is never pleased when His people choose to disobey Him and then seek to worship Him. In Isaiah's time, God's people suffered from a heart condition of sinfulness, selfishness, and corruption. The prophet compared them to Sodom and Gomorrah because they completely rejected God. This made their worship empty and without the proper focus. The prophet Isaiah made a grim, yet proper, determination, that God's people were similar to the inhabitants of Sodom and Gomorrah. Their sinfulness and corruption reminded Isaiah of the people living in those wicked cities. God's Law demanded righteousness as a prerequisite for burnt offerings and sacrifices (Deuteronomy 33:19). Their offerings, sacrifices, feasts, festivals, and prayers had become empty rituals and a stench to the nostrils of God. Their worship was empty because God was not the object. God is not impressed by worship offered without reverence, adoration, and love. He is not impressed with sacrifices that are offered without obedience. In 1 Samuel 15:22 Samuel confronted King Saul by saying, "Hath the LORD as great delight in burnt offerings and sacrifices, as in obeying the voice of the LORD? Behold, to obey is better than sacrifice, and to hearken than the fat of rams." This is to say that worship means nothing to God if one does not obey His Word from the heart. This obedience ought to be done out of love and not because it is mandated.

Isaiah makes it clear that rebellion draws one away from God and prohibits a person from experiencing the intimacy of worship. Isaiah started out his prophecy speaking first to the rulers and judges because they had allowed the people to corporately rebel against God. Their rebellion displeased God, along with their sacrifices. As a result of their rebellion, God rejected their sacrifice.

A vital component to worship is the attitude of the worshiper. God looks upon the heart of the person seeking to worship Him. He sees whatever is in the heart of the worshiper and determines whether love for God is there. Love for God is the impetus of true worship. God does not delight in the ritualistic process of worship; He desires worship from a sincere heart. The people of Israel resisted the teachings and holy practices of God. They turned their backs on the God who promised to dwell in their midst. They threw away the opportunity to have an intimate relationship with God. They were a rebellious nation.

### B. God's Displeasure with Ceremonial Display *(Isaiah 1:14-15)*

**Your new moons and your appointed feasts my soul hateth: they are a trouble unto me; I am weary to bear them. And when ye spread forth your hands, I will hide mine eyes from you: yea, when ye make many prayers, I will not hear: your hands are full of blood.**

In the Israelites' rituals there were appointed feasts: Sabbath, Passover, Pentecost, Day of Atonement, and Feast of Tabernacles. These appointed and hallowed ceremonies meant nothing to God anymore because they had become perfunctory and ostentatious. In verse 14, God says that His soul (Hebrew: *nephesh*)—that is, the very essence of God—detests the hollow worship of the Israelites. The word "hate" (Hebrew: *sane*) here means "to regard something as loathsome." God is love; but here we see His hatred for hypocritical worship. God's words, "They are a trouble unto me…," denote a burden. Receiving the Israelites' worship is likened to carrying lead (the heaviest metal). God could no longer bear it. He was displeased and disappointed with their sinfulness and corruption, as well as with their motives for keeping the festivals. God was not impressed by their ritualistic ceremonies; God wanted His people to be in sync with His Word. People can keep the Commandments; however, if they are not doing it out of love, their expression of worship is empty. The hypocritical display of Judah and Israel seemed to incite the ire of God, so much so that He had grown weary of bearing them. God is not moved or impressed by performance and ritual, but by the obedience of a sincere heart.

Isaiah identified the problem—the people had tried to divert God's attention from their unholy lifestyles and shine the light on their acts of worship, keeping their appointed feasts (verse 14). These ceremonial displays were meaningless and laced with insincerity, seeking to ease and appease their collective conscience rather than really looking at how far down they had fallen. The ceremonies were a form of worship without power. The people even raised their hands in worship, but God hid His eyes from them and closed His ears to their prayers (verse 15). In fact, God stated that their hands were "full of blood." This symbolism suggests that they were unclean, not worthy to offer an acceptable worship.

### C. Preparation for True Worship *(Isaiah 1:16-20)*

**Wash you, make you clean; put away the evil of your doings from before mine eyes; cease to do evil; Learn to do well; seek judgment, relieve the oppressed, judge the fatherless, plead for the widow. Come now,**

and let us reason together, saith the LORD: though your sins be as scarlet, they shall be as white as snow; though they be red like crimson, they shall be as wool. If ye be willing and obedient, ye shall eat the good of the land: But if ye refuse and rebel, ye shall be devoured with the sword: for the mouth of the LORD hath spoken it.

The worship of God takes preparation. Isaiah begins verse 16 by saying "Wash you, make you clean." Cleansing makes the heart right. God seeks clean hearts and hands to worship Him. It is through acknowledging that one is unclean that God can then begin the process of cleansing. Unfortunately, many people don't want to admit that their hearts are not clean. What makes a person's heart unclean is unwillingness to obey God. The necessity for a clean heart means that preparing to worship must be intentional. The purpose behind this preparation is to actively clean from one's heart that which prevents acceptable worship. It is a demand because a pure heart is required before one can worship God. A congregation may be doing all the right things, but if the hearts of the people are not right, their worship is not acceptable to God.

Cleansing is only the first prerequisite to participation in true worship. The second is to stop doing evil. God demands that evil practices cease; willful disobedience has to stop if true worship is to take place. Both Judah and Israel were guilty of actively practicing evil, which displeased God. They were not ashamed of their evil; however, God gave them some steps to follow if they wanted to worship Him in truth. In verse 17, God reveals: "Learn to do well; seek judgment, relieve the oppressed, judge the fatherless, plead for the widow." This verse contains five verbs, each set in command mood. To understand the "well" in verse 17, it is important to turn to Genesis 4:7, where God says, "If thou doest well, shalt thou not be accepted? and if thou doest not well, sin lieth at the door." The "well" there refers to what causes the sacrifice to be accepted, which is doing God's will, God's way. God expressed His compassion and mercy even before the people repented.

In verses 19 and 20, God gives an alternative: "If ye be willing and obedient, ye shall eat the good of the land: But if ye refuse and rebel, ye shall be devoured with the sword: for the mouth of the LORD hath spoken it." The choice before the people was simple: obey or rebel. Multiple-choice examination was not new to that generation. God gave a multiple-choice examination to His people with a reward attached. They needed to understand that there is a blessing for willing obedience, and consequences for rebellion.

Preparation is necessary for true worship to take place. Only when we are able to meet the requirements of willing obedience and show our love for God is our worship made acceptable to God.

### III. CONCLUDING REFLECTIONS

What constitutes true worship? This lesson clearly shows that God is not pleased with religious ceremony and observances that ignore justice, goodness, truth, and mercy. Worship involves more than correct words; it involves courageous works of justice that extend beyond the walls of the church building. True worship must revere God through the attitude of the worshipers.

God wants His people to exhibit attitudes of obedience and faithfulness.

True worship stems from the heart. The Bible says, "And by this we will know that we are from the truth and will reassure our hearts before him whenever our hearts condemn us; for God is greater than our hearts" (1 John 3:19-20, NRSV). The condition of our hearts is important to God whenever we worship Him individually or corporately.

Do you want to know whether your worship is acceptable? Simply check the state of your heart. If your heart or conscience is speaking to you, pay attention; God may be saying something to you. The time has come when true worshipers must worship the Father in spirit and truth; therefore, repentance is necessary for those who seek to worship God. When one seeks repentance, he or she must cease to do evil, because God requires that one has clean hands and a pure heart in order to worship Him.

## WORD POWER

In the Key Verse, there are six verbs—and five of them are cast in imperative mood (command) with different verb stems.

**Learn (Hebrew: *lamad*)**—they must learn to do well. They must develop a heart attitude to always do well.

**Seek (Hebrew: *darash*)**—they must seek with diligence and must be frequent with intentional action.

**Relieve (Hebrew: *ashar*)**—they must help the oppressed and poor.

**Judge (Hebrew: *shaphat*)**—they must judge as God would judge and act as God would act to the fatherless.

**Plead (Hebrew: *reeb*)**—they must strive and contend rigorously for the widow, because widows were powerless in a patriarchal society.

## HOME DAILY BIBLE READINGS

for the week of June 17, 2007
*Isaiah Calls for True Worship*

June 11, Monday
　—Psalm 65:1-8
　—Praise for God's Goodness
June 12, Tuesday
　—2 Kings 15:32-36
　—Doing Right in God's Sight
June 13, Wednesday
　—Isaiah 6:1-8
　—Here Am I; Send Me
June 14, Thursday
　—Isaiah 58:6-12
　—The Fast that Pleases God
June 15, Friday
　—Isaiah 40:1-5
　—Comfort for God's People
June 16, Saturday
　—Isaiah 1:10-14
　—Not Desiring Sacrifices
June 17, Sunday
　—Isaiah 1:15-20
　—Learn to Do Good

## PRAYER

*Eternal God, our Father, we lift our hands, souls, and lives to Thee. We submit ourselves to You as sacrifices. Cleanse us through the blood of Your Son Jesus that we may worship You with our hearts and not just our words. Help us to see the connection between worship and our daily lives. Teach us to worship you with honest hearts. In Jesus' name, we pray. Amen.*

# Lesson 4

# Isaiah Invites Us to God's Feast

**June 24, 2007**

**Adult Topic:** Finding Satisfaction
**Youth Topic:** The Promise Is Real
**Children's Topic:** We Can Be Thankful

**Devotional Reading:** 2 Corinthians 9:10-15
**Background Scripture:** Isaiah 55:1-11
**Print Passage:** Isaiah 55:1-3a, 6-11

### Isaiah 55:1-3a, 6-11—KJV

HO, EVERY one that thirsteth, come ye to the waters, and he that hath no money; come ye, buy, and eat; yea, come, buy wine and milk without money and without price.

2 Wherefore do ye spend money for that which is not bread? and your labour for that which satisfieth not? hearken diligently unto me, and eat ye that which is good, and let your soul delight itself in fatness.

3 Incline your ear, and come unto me: hear, and your soul shall live.

.....

6 Seek ye the Lord while he may be found, call ye upon him while he is near:

7 Let the wicked forsake his way, and the unrighteous man his thoughts: and let him return unto the Lord, and he will have mercy upon him; and to our God, for he will abundantly pardon.

8 For my thoughts are not your thoughts, neither are your ways my ways, saith the Lord.

9 For as the heavens are higher than the earth, so are my ways higher than your ways, and my thoughts than your thoughts.

10 For as the rain cometh down, and the snow from heaven, and returneth not thither, but watereth the earth, and maketh it bring forth and bud, that it may give seed to the sower, and bread to the eater:

11 So shall my word be that goeth forth out of my mouth: it shall not return unto me void, but it shall accomplish that which I please, and it shall prosper in the thing whereto I sent it.

**UNIT I**
Life as God's People

**CHILDREN'S UNIT**
Life as God's People

### KEY VERSE
Seek ye the Lord while he may be found, call ye upon him while he is near.
—Isaiah 55:6

### OBJECTIVES
Upon completion of this lesson, the students are expected to:
1. Learn that the only real satisfaction in life is found in the Lord;
2. Recognize that God issues an invitation to anyone and everyone to turn to Him as the One who is able to provide for their needs; and,
3. Understand that returning to God gives people the assurance that His mercy and loving-kindness are not a concept but a reality that leads to satisfaction.

## UNIFYING LESSON PRINCIPLE

Most people want an abundance of good things in their lives. What is the source of such abundance for us? Using the image of a great feast to which we are invited, Isaiah says that God is the one who generously provides all good things for us. Luke makes a similar point in the parable of the feast.

## POINTS TO BE EMPHASIZED
## ADULTS/YOUTH

**Adult/Youth Key Verse:** Isaiah 55:6
**Print Passage:** Isaiah 55:1-3a, 6-11

—Isaiah symbolizes the new covenant by using the metaphor of free food and drink.
—God's faithfulness invites us to trust God's purposes even when we cannot fully understand them.
—God's forgiveness and love are available to all.
—The invitation to come and get free food and drink recalls earlier biblical themes such as the provision of manna and water in the desert.
—Isaiah is a prophet of hope. Whatever happens, God's plan and desire will prevail on behalf of His people.
—To trust God, even when we do not fully understand His purpose, is the way to a life of true goodness.

## CHILDREN

**Key Verse:** Isaiah 55:1
**Print Passage:** Luke 14:15-24; Isaiah 55:1

—God's feast is for everyone who will come, including children.
—What does this passage say to those who have little of this world's goods?

—How do we develop an attitude of gratitude?
—Making excuses can sometimes keep people from receiving God's blessings.

## TOPICAL OUTLINE OF THE LESSON

I. **INTRODUCTION**
   A. Satisfaction
   B. Biblical Background

II. **EXPOSITION AND APPLICATION OF THE SCRIPTURE**
   A. Universal Invitation *(Isaiah 55:1-3a)*
   B. Respond Now! *(Isaiah 55:6-7)*
   C. An Acknowledgment of the Sovereignty of God *(Isaiah 55:8-11)*

III. **CONCLUDING REFLECTIONS**

## I. INTRODUCTION
### A. Satisfaction

Every human being is looking for satisfaction. We want to be satisfied with our financial condition, and for that reason we look for ways to satisfy that urge. Employers want their employees to do a satisfactory job and help the company to remain profitable. Parents want their children to do well in school, and they get satisfaction knowing their children are getting prepared for the future. Pastors want their members to be present and on time at each gathering of the church, because that will cause the church to grow. The methods of attaining satisfaction are endless, as is its pursuit of it.

Rock star Mick Jagger, lead singer of the legendary British singing group The Rolling Stones, penned most of the words to their popular hit single, "I Can't Get No Satisfaction." The lyrics deal with what Jagger saw as the two sides of America, the real and phony. He wrote about a man looking for authenticity while trying to filter through all of the hype and commercialism of American life.

How do we get our human urges satisfied? The only real satisfaction in life is found in the "salvation of the Lord." Any satisfaction outside of Christ is not real; it will not last and it will lead to a dead end. Many people are eagerly seeking satisfaction in various ways but not according to God's way. Solomon says, "There is a way which seemeth right unto a man, but the end thereof are the ways of death" (Proverbs 14:12).

In Isaiah 55:1, the word "come" is an invitation, but is cast in a command form. It means that one has to give up one's present lifestyle and abandon a godless lifestyle—that has no purpose other than the pursuit of personal satisfaction and pleasure—and rely on God instead. This is an act of self-denial and obedience and is the first step to true satisfaction.

## B. Biblical Background

Names are important in Hebrew culture. A name symbolizes an event in the life of the parents. Noah's name signifies "this one shall give relief or rest." The name Isaiah means "Jehovah is salvation." His name reflects his messages. Isaiah, the son of Amoz, was born in Judah, most likely Jerusalem, around 760 B.C. He enjoyed a significant position in the contemporary society and had a close relationship with the ruling kings of his day. His education is evident in the sophistication of his writing, which has distinguished him in Hebrew literature. From his writings it is evident that Isaiah possessed a thorough grasp of political history and had the courage to voice unpopular views regarding the state and the economy. His knowledge of the religious heritage of Israel and his unique theological contributions are inspiring. Even Jesus quoted from Isaiah when defining His own calling and ministry (see Luke 4 and Isaiah 61). Isaiah was in touch with the pulse of his world—keenly aware of events transpiring in the court, in the marketplace, among the shallow in high society, and in the political frustrations of the nation.

Isaiah was called to be a prophet of Yahweh in remarkable visions that he experienced in the temple the year that the aged Judean king Uzziah died, around 740 B.C. (see Isaiah 6:1). The elements in that vision forecast the major themes of his preaching, particularly the magnificent nature of Yahweh, which may serve as a modern translation of Hebraic "holiness." God warned Isaiah that his ministry would meet with disappointment and limited results. Despite this, God assured the prophet that forgiveness would be granted in exchange for Israel's repentance and that the ultimate promises of God would be realized.

God offered the children of Israel a new beginning. They would be free from bondage. However, God told them that if this were to happen, they must seek Him while He might be found and call on Him while He was near. God called them to a deeper relationship with Him.

## II. Exposition and Application of the Scripture
### A. Universal Invitation *(Isaiah 55:1-3a)*

**Ho, every one that thirsteth, come ye to the waters, and he that hath no money; come ye, buy, and eat; yea, come, buy wine and milk without money and without price. Wherefore do ye spend money for that which is not bread? and your labour for that which satisfieth not? hearken diligently unto me, and eat ye that which is good, and let your soul delight itself in fatness. Incline your ear, and come unto me: hear.**

The expression "Ho" is designed to call attention to an important matter. It is a way of drawing earnest attention. It is a great call extended without partiality. The only category of people that is mentioned here is those who thirst. In God's economy of grace and mercy, there is no discrimination. Hence, the word "everyone" is employed. This invitation is inclusive—the nobility, the peasantry, the poor, the homeless, the lepers, the lame, the sick, the hopeless, males, females, and children are all invited. These groups are the only important guests. This is an invitation to the banquet of God. However, the invitation presupposes readiness for the banquet. God will not invite people to partake of a banquet which is not ready. This is not a charade; that is the reason for the opening word, "Ho." God is ready to invigorate His people and to bless them.

Even though everyone is invited, the invitation is narrowed down to those who are thirsty; the self-sufficient may likely ignore the invitation. The prophet uses two of the strongest human urges, drinking and eating, to highlight Israel's need for God. A person can live for a few days without water and for about forty-five days without food. In ancient Palestine, the climate was hot, arid, and unpleasant, yet people and animals often had to travel great distances under the open sun. Having a sufficient water supply during a desert journey was very important. Not having enough water was an invitation to death. In Isaiah's time, being thirsty but having no water was no light matter. Therefore, Isaiah employed the imageries that resonated with the people: "...Come ye to the waters...."

The word "buy" (Hebrew: *shaaba*) means "to break in order to purchase." It would be like breaking a silo for the grain to pour out without measure. In our time, we tell our guests to "dig in" when we invite them to a sumptuous meal. On such occasions, nothing is withheld. Our guests are invited to feast on what we have provided for them. In Isaiah 55, the call is to buy wine, which symbolizes blessings of salvation; milk, in Scripture, is used as an image of nourishment. The people were invited to purchase these commodities without money. The rich ones with their gold could not brag, and the poor ones without money did not have to stay back, because the spiritual food is free. This is a picture of salvation that Christ has made possible for all who will come to Him. Isaiah considers the fact that even though salvation is free there is a cost, which, for the believer, is self-denial. Self-denial must be exercised on the part of the believer if one is going to enjoy the good of the land (Isaiah 1:19).

In last week's lesson, we learned that if the people wanted to worship God in truth they had to be willing to obey. Just as there is a cost associated with true worship, there is also a cost associated with finding spiritual satisfaction. Only the things that come from God will sustain the soul. Matthew 5:6 (NIV) records: "Blessed are those who hunger and thirst for righteousness, for they will be filled." In John 4:13-14, Jesus tells the salacious woman at the well, "Everyone who drinks this water will be thirsty again, but whoever drinks the water I give him will never thirst. Indeed, the water I give him will become in him a spring of water welling up to eternal life" (NIV). That is why Isaiah exclaims "Ho"—because he wants everyone to hear and accept this invitation to come and drink from the fountain that will never run dry. Anyone who comes will not be disappointed.

Isaiah's appeal in the latter part of these verses is somewhat reminiscent of an announcer for a television commercial: "Why keep spending your hard-earned money on things that cannot bring you satisfaction?"

## B. Respond Now! *(Isaiah 55:6-7)*

**Seek ye the Lord while he may be found, call ye upon him while he is near: Let the wicked forsake his way, and the unrighteous man his thoughts: and let him return unto the Lord, and he will have mercy upon him; and to our God, for he will abundantly pardon.**

For every invitation there is a time to respond. We respond in two ways: "Yes, I will be there," or "No, I'm sorry, I have another appointment." Having already extended the invitation to receive salvation freely, the people have to make up their minds. The word "ye" is plural, meaning "you all" seek the Lord. "Seek" used here denotes frequency and the purpose of worship. It is a call to diligently inquire. In seeking, one must be willing and obedient if one is to receive this gift. The recipients of this gift are assured that they will be satisfied. Here, Isaiah mentions that this pursuit could be lost if one fails to take advantage of its openness. "Seek the Lord while He may be found." The implication of this statement is that God may be found now, and this opportunity may not come again.

The Hebrew word translated here as "call" was used primarily in three ways. First, it was used as a call from humanity to God asking for help. Second, it was used to describe one person asking for assistance from another. Third, it was used to describe the cry of an animal, mortally wounded and crying in pain. Just as an animal with its foot stuck in a steel trap cries out in pain, so we are to come before the Lord with a broken and repentant heart, crying out for God's salvation.

The Lord appealed to Israel to recognize their pitiful condition, turn, and repent while they had the opportunity. Not only did the Lord appeal to them to seize the moment to pursue Him, He compelled them to seek Him while He was near! This pursuit is one that would free God's people to experience satisfaction.

Verse 7 gives us an explanation of the call to repentance and how it is to be obeyed. In order for penitence to be effective, it must be complete. There is to be a total abandonment of sin and a return to a righteous life. Repentance then must take place in thought as well as in deed.

The prophet calls for a radical reversal of conduct and thought. To return to God, as signified by both action and thought, implies a complete change of heart. The return

## C. An Acknowledgment of the Sovereignty of God *(Isaiah 55:8-11)*

**For my thoughts are not your thoughts, neither are your ways my ways, saith the Lord. For as the heavens are higher than the earth, so are my ways higher than your ways, and my thoughts than your thoughts. For as the rain cometh down, and the snow from heaven, and returneth not thither, but watereth the earth, and maketh it bring forth and bud, that it may give seed to the sower, and bread to the eater: So shall my word be that goeth forth out of my mouth: it shall not return unto me void, but it shall accomplish that which I please, and it shall prosper in the thing whereto I sent it.**

God's gracious plan and ways exceed all human imagination! No one can fathom the depth of His wisdom. His compassion for those who turn to Him comes because His thoughts and ways are far superior to human thoughts and ways. Although humanity is made in the image and likeness of God, the nature of God is, in every way, infinitely greater than that of humankind. Our ways are not God's ways. Human beings see things dimly because we have finite minds. Only God possesses infinite sight. It is through Him that humanity receives and understands mercy. The Creator and Ruler conducts His affairs contrary to what any human mind can conceive.

Peter asked Jesus the question, "How many times shall I forgive my brother—as many as seven times?" (see Matthew 18:21). While Peter believed he was being generous with his offers of forgiveness, his query is illustrative of the fact that the human capacity for tolerance is limited. Our willingness to extend forgiveness is usually worn thin if the offense is repeated two or three times. Further, when we forgive, we do not always forget. Thankfully, this is not so with the almighty God. Churches have been destroyed because of an unforgiving spirit. Families and marriages have been separated because of deep-rooted malice and long-held resentments—but not so with God. As far as the east is from the west, so has He removed our transgression away from us (see Psalm 103:12). We human beings cannot tolerate those whose behavior we deem inappropriate, but God endures all our idiosyncrasies with love and patience.

The remaining two verses allude to when we allow the Word of God to take on flesh and dwell in us. This indwelling will bring about a foretaste of heaven. When rain and snow come down on the ground, with time they will soak the ground and plants will sprout. Like the refreshment of rain upon the soil, the Word of God will not return void. The purpose for which the words are sent will be accomplished. This is why Isaiah is so persistent in proclaiming that God's ways are not our ways. The answers to life's perplexing problems often lie beyond the human ability to solve. The Jews were faced with a number of decisions, issues, and problems. Because God had not protected them from the Babylonian invasion, they may have decided to take their future into their own hands instead of trusting in Him. However, Israel faced problems that far exceeded their capacity to solve; they needed Yahweh (God), who had delivered them from so many difficulties in times past.

## III. Concluding Reflections

The lesson raises a relevant question for every generation: "Why invest so much in the ways of life that cannot satisfy?" Why work so hard and so long in ways that give no satisfaction? We spend a disproportionate amount of our talent, time, and resources on things that promise to give satisfaction to our physical and psychological needs; meanwhile, the social indexes of a morally-bankrupt society are rising. It is interesting to note that, while our national per capita and pleasure-seeking pursuits have increased, there has been a corresponding rise in suicides, crime, violence, depression, drug addiction, and chemical dependency. Could it be that we are seekers, but of the wrong things? The generous invitation to salvation is the best gift that we could ever receive. If we remain apart from God, life can prove to be quite unsatisfying. The wisdom of Solomon reminds us, "There is a way which seemeth right unto a man, but the end thereof are the ways of death" (Proverbs 14:12).

Each of us must ask ourselves, "Who is the author of my life?" The answer must be God. However, do we allow God to be God? Augustine of Hippo said long ago, "If God is not God of all, He is not God at all."

## WORD POWER

**Seek (Hebrew:** *darash*)—this word is a command as opposed to a simple statement. One should not look at Isaiah 55:6 as an invitation in which the invitee has a choice; it is a command. However, the invitee has the volition to reject the offer. The reason for the command is because there are conditions and limits in obtaining spiritual benefits. There is a time limit for every offer, even for spiritual matters. Embedded in this word is the idea of frequency. The one seeking is urged to do it frequently.

## HOME DAILY BIBLE READINGS

for the week of June 24, 2007
*Isaiah Invites Us to God's Feast*
June 18, Monday
—Luke 14:15-24
—Parable of the Great Banquet
June 19, Tuesday
—Isaiah 25:6-10a
—God's Banquet
June 20, Wednesday
—Isaiah 61:1-6
—The Year of the Lord
June 21, Thursday
—Isaiah 61:7-11
—Delight in the Lord
June 22, Friday
—2 Corinthians 9:10-15
—Blessed to Bless
June 23, Saturday
—Isaiah 55:1-5
—God Invites Us
June 24, Sunday
—Isaiah 55:6-11
—Seek the Lord

## PRAYER

*Eternal God, our Father, our souls are barren until they are replenished with water from Your eternal stream. This is the only thing that can truly satisfy and refresh us. When we wither because of bad choices that we make, draw us close to Thee; cleanse us, strengthen us, and empower and guide us to the place where You will have us to do only those things that are pleasing in your sight. In Jesus' name, we pray. Amen.*

**July 1, 2007**

**UNIT II**
What Does God Require?

**CHILDREN'S UNIT**
What Does God Want?

**KEY VERSE**
He hath shewed thee, O man, what is good; and what doth the LORD require of thee, but to do justly, and to love mercy, and to walk humbly with thy God? —Micah 6:8

**OBJECTIVES**
Upon completion of this lesson, the students are expected to:
1. Recognize that God has set believers free and has called us to show kindness, love, and mercy towards others;
2. Underscore the fact that showing mercy, fighting for the poor, and humbly walking with God are the essential requirements of faith; and,
3. Discover that God is pleased with our material offerings only when our lives reflect His holiness.

Lesson 5

# Micah Announces God's Requirements

**ADULT TOPIC:** Doing the Right Thing
**YOUTH TOPIC:** What Does God Want, Anyway?
**CHILDREN'S TOPIC:** God Wants Us to Do What Is Right

**DEVOTIONAL READING:** Hebrews 12:6-12
**BACKGROUND SCRIPTURE:** Micah 2:1-4; 3:1-5, 8-12; 6:6-8
**PRINT PASSAGE:** Micah 3:1-4; 6:6-8

### Micah 3:1-4; 6:6-8—KJV

AND I said, Hear, I pray you, O heads of Jacob, and ye princes of the house of Israel; Is it not for you to know judgment?

2 Who hate the good, and love the evil; who pluck off their skin from off them, and their flesh from off their bones;

3 Who also eat the flesh of my people, and flay their skin from off them; and they break their bones, and chop them in pieces, as for the pot, and as flesh within the caldron.

4 Then shall they cry unto the Lord, but he will not hear them: he will even hide his face from them at that time, as they have behaved themselves ill in their doings.

. . . . .

6 Wherewith shall I come before the Lord, and bow myself before the high God? shall I come before him with burnt offerings, with calves of a year old?

7 Will the Lord be pleased with thousands of rams, or with ten thousands of rivers of oil? shall I give my firstborn for my transgression, the fruit of my body for the sin of my soul?

8 He hath shewed thee, O man, what is good; and what doth the Lord require of thee, but to do justly, and to love mercy, and to walk humbly with thy God?

## UNIFYING LESSON PRINCIPLE

Most people want to do what is right. How do we know what the right thing is? Micah gives us solid help by highlighting justice, kindness, and the love of God as standards to guide our actions.

## POINTS TO BE EMPHASIZED
## ADULTS/YOUTH

**Adult/Youth Key Verse:** Micah 6:8
**Print Passage:** Micah 3:1-4; 6:6-8

—Micah prophesied in the kingdom of Judah during the reigns of Jotham, Ahaz, and Hezekiah.
—Micah focused his prophecy on the crimes of corrupt officials (political and religious): priests, prophets, and judges.
—Micah prophesied during the last half of 700 B.C. and focused on the corrupt lives of those in authority.
—Micah emphasized that living in God's justice was more important than performing the correct sacrificial ritual.
—Like his contemporary Isaiah, Micah preached about worshiping God, social justice, judgment, and forgiveness.
—God expects believers to act justly, love tenderly, and serve God with humility.

## CHILDREN

**Key Verse:** Micah 6:8
**Print Passage:** Micah 1:1; 4:1-2; 6:6-8

—God is more interested in how we treat one another than in our tithes and offerings.
—God expects believers to act justly, love tenderly, and serve Him with humility.

—Micah preached about worshiping God, social justice, judgment, and forgiveness.
—Because of corrupt officials, Micah pre-

## TOPICAL OUTLINE OF THE LESSON

I. **INTRODUCTION**
   A. In Search of Absolute Truth
   B. Biblical Background

II. **EXPOSITION AND APPLICATION OF THE SCRIPTURE**
   A. The Ways of the Wicked *(Micah 3:1-4)*
   B. Man's Routine *(Micah 6:6-7)*
   C. God's Requirements *(Micah 6:8)*

III. **CONCLUDING REFLECTIONS**

## I. INTRODUCTION
### A. In Search of Absolute Truth

The modern philosophy of situational ethics was pioneered by Episcopal priest Joseph Fletcher (1905-1991). According to Fletcher's model, all decision making should be based upon the circumstances of a particular situation. As long as love is the intention, the end justifies the means. Fletcher based his model upon 1 John 4:8, which states, "God is love." While Fletcher's approach appears reasonable at first glance, its flaw soon becomes apparent. Fletcher holds that any commandment may be broken in good conscience if love is the motive; however, the Bible states that to love God is to obey God's commandments (1 John 5:3).

Throughout the ages, humanity has sought ways to make truth relative to our circumstances. People want to define truth according to their own standards. Truth has become relative, being altered to fit the circumstances. Throughout the Old Testament, Israel was engaged in a struggle to do what is right in God's eyes. Judges 21:25 reveals, "In those days there was no king in Israel: every man did that which was right in his own eyes." Our world is no different. Contemporary society behaves as if there is no God and no Law. But no matter how we manipulate truth—playing a game of moral gymnastics— God's truth cannot be compromised.

## B. Biblical Background

The name Micah means, "Who is like the Lord?" (Hebrew: *Mikayahu*). The prophet Micah was a contemporary of Isaiah's. He was a native of Moresheth, about twenty miles southwest of Jerusalem. The book of Micah predicts the fall of Samaria, which occurred in 722 B.C. at the hands of Sargon of Assyria. Micah was especially concerned with the sins of the people. He was an evangelist and a social reformer.

The message of Micah varies between condemnation of present sins of the people and God's purpose of ultimate blessings for them. Micah was a common man of the fields—a rustic and a village man. Less educated than the erudite Isaiah, who was a prophet to the upper echelon, Micah addressed the common people. He focused primarily on the crimes of corrupt officials, both political and religious. Micah echoed the profound theme that living in God's justice is more important than performing the correct sacrificial rituals before God. He taught that showing mercy, fighting for the poor, and humbly walking with God are the essential requirements of faith.

Using a courtroom-type format, Israel heard the charges that God had leveled against her through the prophet Micah.

## II. Exposition and Application of the Scripture
### A. The Ways of the Wicked
(Micah 3:1-4)

**AND I said, Hear, I pray you, O heads of Jacob, and ye princes of the house of Israel; Is it not for you to know judgment? Who hate the good, and love the evil; who pluck off their skin from off them, and their flesh from off their bones; Who also eat the flesh of my people, and flay their skin from off them; and they break their bones, and chop them in pieces, as for the pot, and as flesh within the caldron. Then shall they cry unto the Lord, but he will not hear them: he will even hide his face from them at that time, as they have behaved themselves ill in their doings.**

Micah leveled strong charges of wrongdoing against the political and governmental leaders of Judah in the latter half of the eighth century B.C. According to him, the people should have known justice, should have loved good, and should have hated evil. However, they had done just the opposite. They had enriched themselves at the expense of the common people.

Micah described the people's wrongdoings in horrifying terms. They were viciously criminal in their mistreatment of the common people. Their unjust governmental practices had, in effect, broken down the people. When the time of judgment came upon them, the leaders would cry out to the Lord for help, but there would be no answer. Micah not only indicted the political classes, but he also pointed out that even the prophets had failed to do their duty. They had been bought and paid for by the political leaders so that their messages of peace and prosperity were in line with the political leaders' own agendas. However, to the people they claimed that their ranting messages were from God. Shakespeare wrote, "Those who pay the piper dictate the tune." In effect, the priests and prophets participated in injustices by teaching and preaching what they were paid to preach and teach. The religious leaders had sold their consciences. The welfare of the common people had been sacrificed at the altar of Beelzebub.

The ways of the wicked are always destructive: they are depictions of premeditated evil; they are deliberate and intentional, according to Micah. Their pleasure produces pain for others. They operate out of greed and lust. They have little common sense and possess callous consciences. They are immoral and exalt themselves with disregard for almighty God. They take from their neighbors and do not stop to consider the power of God. They fail to even acknowledge that it was God who strengthened their limbs and allowed them to walk the path of wickedness.

The wicked not only steal from their neighbors, they also steal the heritage of their children and their children's children. They think no one will catch up with them, and that they will not be judged. Solomon says, "Because sentence against an evil work is not executed speedily, therefore the heart of the sons of men is fully set in them to do evil" (Ecclesiastes 8:11). Wicked people in Micah's time—as they do now—flagrantly ignored the omnipresent God, who was beholding the good and the evil things they did.

### B. Man's Routine *(Micah 6:6-7)*

**Wherewith shall I come before the Lord, and bow myself before the high God? shall I come before him with burnt offerings, with calves of a year old? Will the Lord be pleased with thousands of rams, or with ten thousands of rivers of oil? shall I give my firstborn for my transgression, the fruit of my body for the sin of my soul?**

Micah seems to put himself in the position of the people as they responded to the charges that God brought against them. What must they do to please the Lord? What did He want? A series of possible answers are put forth. First are burnt offerings. The burnt offerings were commanded in the Law of Moses (Leviticus 1). Animals that were a year old (including calves) were suggested. These types of animals were often required for sacrifices (Leviticus 9:2). Second in line were thousands of rams. Perhaps the people believed that God was more interested in quantity of sacrifices than quality. Third were ten thousand rivers of oil, which frequently accompanied certain offerings, such as those described in Leviticus 2. Finally, if the sacrifices mentioned would not appease God, the first-born was suggested as an alternative. None of these suggestions were adequate alternatives. Nothing could atone for their sin.

The people were naively trying to demonstrate how they were doing all of the things that the Law required of them regarding religion and more. Their sacrifices had become larger and more frequent, and their rituals more elaborate. They had even added temple prostitution to their worship (see Amos 2:7-8), and human sacrifices were still being made (see Isaiah 57:5; Jeremiah 7:31; 2 Kings 16:3; 21:2). Human sacrifice was the most extreme form of religious zeal. It is likely with a note of sarcasm that they suggested they could satisfy God with their firstborn for their transgressions, the fruit of their bodies for the sin of their souls. Sadly, they were so consumed with the rituals of religion that they had forgotten about the heart of religion. It is much easier to do religion than to be religious.

In our contemporary world, many Christians seek to make up for their wrongdoings by doing something. In an effort to compensate and give restitution for sin, they seek to bring God various offerings. Many want to purchase their pardon by engaging in more activities. They want to somehow "make it up to" God for what they have done, but these efforts are useless. The cattle on a thousand hills already belong to God. Thus, these offerings cannot satisfy Him. God is pleased with material offerings only when our lives reflect holiness. Hebrews 12:14 states, "Follow peace with all men, and holiness, without which no man shall see the Lord."

### C. God's Requirements *(Micah 6:8)*

**He hath shewed thee, O man, what is good; and what doth the Lord require of thee, but to do justly, and to love mercy, and to walk humbly with thy God?**

In contrast to what the people proposed, Micah offered a radically different solution. He was not implying that the people of Judah were not to offer the sacrifices that God had commanded in the Law. Rather, his point was that all of those sacrifices were meaningless without the people's love and their obedience to what God considered important: seeking justice, showing mercy, and walking humbly before God. These three requirements had not been kept secret from the people; as Micah said, "He hath showed you what is good." This means that the requirement of justice and fair play was not hidden, but that the people chose to ignore these concerns. Micah was pointing out that they had no excuse for having lost their relationship with God in religiousness. They seemed to believe that it was easier to follow prescribed rituals than it was to live out one's faith in everyday settings. God consistently warned His people about the danger of trusting in their rituals apart from being just, loving, and kind (Psalm 51:16-17).

These requirements in Micah 6:8 set the highest standards for righteous living. To act justly means to treat others with honesty, integrity, and equity. To love mercy means to be loyal to God and kind to others. This should not be done sporadically but, rather, as a consistent part of our lives. To walk humbly with God means to be circumspect in what we say and modest in our demeanor. We must willingly choose to follow the Lord and submit to His will.

God's requirements are not to be

fulfilled only when and where the church meets, but also in the public arenas of life—where people live, work, run businesses, and play. Doing justice, living in loving-kindness, and walking humbly with God are to be done in public life; that is where the opportunities for making a difference lay, and also where the opposition to such actions is the greatest. It should be uppermost in the mind of every believer to be conscious of God's presence every moment.

Micah's question—"What doth the Lord require of thee?"—represents the essence of the eighth-century prophet's message. The verb used for "require" is the Hebrew word *doresh,* an active participle. This verb form demonstrates action being done in an uninterrupted state—it neither starts nor stops. It is never-ending, showing that the action defined by the verb has been going on all of the time. Since God had delivered Israel in the Exodus, through every generation, God had expected His chosen people to remain in covenant with Him, obeying His law. He had not issued a new set of regulations nor changed His expectations of His people. God's standard, throughout the generations, had remained unchanged—as it is today.

God has not issued a new standard of truth nor has it been altered by Him. His Word has stood the test of time. No matter how we seek to manipulate God's truth— seeking our own level of comfortableness—in His sight, right is right and wrong is still wrong. God does not seek elaborate sacrifices, offerings, or institutions from us. He desires people who will do what is right, be kind to others, and walk humbly with Him. It is only when we are in right standing with others, through practicing justice and faithful love, that we are postured to walk humbly before God.

Micah and his contemporaries thrust moral conduct directly under the scope of divine reality. They demonstrated that there is no difference between duty toward humanity and duty toward God. Religion and worship must be much more than a series of perfunctory deeds. Rather, they encompass a lifestyle that is honorable and pleasing in His sight.

## III. Concluding Reflections

Any person who has been a church member knows that there are some who do all of the right things—attend worship and Bible study regularly, participate in the life of the church, and give tithes and offerings to support the ministries of the church—yet, these same people demonstrate little compassion or regard for others, and little humility before God. The apostle Paul said, "If I speak in the tongues of mortals and of angels, but do not have love, I am a noisy gong or a clanging cymbal" (1 Corinthians 13:1, NRSV).

Like the Pharisees whom Jesus criticized, they carry themselves with a false sense of their righteousness in the eyes of God. In Luke 18, Jesus told a parable about two men, one who presumed himself righteous in the eyes of God and another who came before God, humbly acknowledging his sinful condition. Jesus proclaimed that only the humble man went back home justified, "for all who exalt themselves will be humbled, but all who humble themselves will be exalted" (Luke 18:14, NRSV).

God's basic requirements for those who would serve Him have not changed. The question raised in Micah 6:8 is one to which Christians must give serious consideration. None of what God deems as important involves elaborate rituals or colorful ceremonies. Living a godly life requires commitment to those things God values.

It is a common saying that "knowledge is power," which is partially true. However, the statement should be interpreted, applied knowledge is power. What is the use of acquiring an education if one refuses to use it? What good is a medical degree when one is unconcerned about improving quality of life? What use is pastoral training when there is no love or passion to shepherd a congregation? How does Christian education prosper when one is not ready to apply the knowledge received?

The people of Judah in Micah's day had become obsessed with rites, rituals, and ceremonies, while forgetting God's primary agenda for them. They were substituting formal sacrifices and programmed pomp and circumstance for a humble walk with God and a heartfelt compassion for others. The major objectives of religion—obedience to God and love for humanity—had ceased to be their major objectives.

## WORD POWER

**Shewed (Hebrew: *Nagad*)**—Embedded in this word is the idea that God has caused His requirements to be made known. God acted on divine initiatives to let His creatures know His express will. The word "shewed" is used in the perfect tense, which denotes a completed action. God's commands still stand, without further collaboration. The action required from the past still stands (see Micah 6:8)—that is, that God's people should walk humbly.

## HOME DAILY BIBLE READINGS

for the week of July 1, 2007
*Micah Announces God's Requirements*

June 25, Monday
    —Deuteronomy 10:12-22
    —Fear the Lord
June 26, Tuesday
    —Hebrews 12:6-12
    —The Disciplined Life
June 27, Wednesday
    —Micah 2:1-5
    —Human Plans and God's
June 28, Thursday
    —Micah 3:1-7
    —Sins Denounced
June 29, Friday
    —Micah 3:8-12
    —Micah Speaks Out
June 30, Saturday
    —Micah 4:1-5
    —Water Flows Upstream
July 1, Sunday
    —Micah 6:3-8
    —What Does God Require?

## PRAYER

*Eternal God, our Father, help us to live in love, peace, happiness, and prosperity. Give us the gift of discernment that in the midst of the noise of this world we may clearly and distinctly hear Your voice. Hasten the time when the wicked will no longer rise up and implement their evil plans against the righteous. Enable us to be witnesses to Your omnipotent power. Undergird us with Your strength that we may be examples of Your justice and mercy as we humbly walk with Thee. In Jesus' name, we pray. Amen.*

**Lesson 6**

**July 8, 2007**

# Zephaniah Announces God's Justice

**ADULT TOPIC:** Getting Ready for Judgment
**YOUTH TOPIC:** Think About It!
**CHILDREN'S TOPIC:** God Wants Us to Offer Praise

**DEVOTIONAL READING:** Psalm 27:7-14
**BACKGROUND SCRIPTURE:** Zephaniah 3:1-13; 2 Chronicles 34:1-3
**PRINT PASSAGE:** Zephaniah 3:1-5, 8-9

**UNIT II**
What Does God Require?

**CHILDREN'S UNIT**
What Does God Want?

**KEY VERSE**

Therefore wait ye upon me, saith the LORD, until the day that I rise up to the prey: for my determination is to gather the nations, that I may assemble the kingdoms, to pour upon them mine indignation, even all my fierce anger: for all the earth shall be devoured with the fire of my jealousy.
—Zephaniah 3:8

### Zephaniah 3:1-5, 8-9—KJV

WOE TO her that is filthy and polluted, to the oppressing city!

2 She obeyed not the voice; she received not correction; she trusted not in the Lord; she drew not near to her God.

3 Her princes within her are roaring lions; her judges are evening wolves; they gnaw not the bones till the morrow.

4 Her prophets are light and treacherous persons: her priests have polluted the sanctuary, they have done violence to the law.

5 The just Lord is in the midst thereof; he will not do iniquity: every morning doth he bring his judgment to light, he faileth not; but the unjust knoweth no shame.

. . . . .

8 Therefore wait ye upon me, saith the Lord, until the day that I rise up to the prey: for my determination is to gather the nations, that I may assemble the kingdoms, to pour upon them mine indignation, even all my fierce anger: for all the earth shall be devoured with the fire of my jealousy.

9 For then will I turn to the people a pure language, that they may all call upon the name of the Lord, to serve him with one consent.

**OBJECTIVES**

Upon completion of this lesson, the students are expected to:

1. Know that God's justice includes both punishment and redemption;
2. Understand that there are consequences to disobeying God; and,
3. Discover that one day God will be supreme accord.

## UNIFYING LESSON PRINCIPLE

People sometimes act wrongly without thinking of the consequences to themselves or others. What consequences result when God's people behave wrongly? Zephaniah says that God will act justly, bringing both punishment and redemption. The prophet also says that we will have reason in the end to praise God for all God's actions.

## POINTS TO BE EMPHASIZED
### ADULTS /YOUTH
**Adult Key Verse:** Zephaniah 3:8
**Youth Key Verses:** Zephaniah 3:8-9
**Print Passage:** Zephaniah 3:1-5, 8-9
—Zephaniah's ministry took place during the reign of Josiah and may have influenced the reforms mandated by the king.
—Zephaniah developed the theme "the day of the Lord" as a day of punishment for those who did wrong.
—Zephaniah condemned the religious and political leadership.
—Before the reforms of King Josiah, people in Jerusalem seem to have worshiped the gods of Canaan (Baal), Assyria (host of heaven), and Ammon (Milcom) alongside God (Yahweh).
— "Day of the Lord" traditions are used to bring a message of judgment against Judah, but the judgment offers hope for the future.
—The promise of God is resident in the "just remnant" that will serve the Lord.

## CHILDREN
**Key Verse:** Zephaniah 3:9

**Print Passage:** Zephaniah 1:1; 3:8, 9, 16-18
—Zephaniah preached, like his ancestor Hezekiah, the importance of the pure worship of God.
—Zephaniah's public ministry occurred during Josiah's reign, and he prophesied before Josiah began his religious reform movement.
—God still disciplines those who defy biblical truths and/or include non-Christian practices in their acts of worship.

## TOPICAL OUTLINE OF THE LESSON
I. INTRODUCTION
   A. Is Justice Blind?
   B. Biblical Background

II. EXPOSITION AND APPLICATION OF THE SCRIPTURE
   A. The People's Refusal to Heed the Warnings of God *(Zephaniah 3:1-2)*
   B. The Leaders' Failure *(Zephaniah 3:3-4)*
   C. The Two Sides of God: Judgment and Mercy *(Zephaniah 3:5, 8-9)*

III. CONCLUDING REFLECTIONS

## I. INTRODUCTION
### A. Is Justice Blind?

An old cliché suggests that "justice is blind." The female symbol of blind justice that adorns courthouses around the world goes by these names: Lady Justice, Scales of Justice, and Blind Justice. The statue dates back to ancient Greek and Roman times to Themis, the goddess of justice and law. She typically holds a sword in one hand and scales in the other. The scales represent the impartiality with which justice is served. Her sword signifies the power that is held by those making the decision. During the sixteenth century, artists started showing the lady blindfolded to show that justice is not subject to influence. This ideal depicts justice as being dispensed without bias; however, a quick examination of our judicial system reveals that justice is anything but blind.

Many factors influence the dispensation of justice in our nation, most notably race and socioeconomics. Often, it does appear as though justice is for sale—as one's ability to pay for legal representation often affects the outcome of the trial. The wealthy, who can afford the best representation, often escape the severest of punishment.

Fortunately, in divine judgment, factors such as race, education, and income do not matter. In the courtroom of God, justice is not simply an ideal, it is the actual practice of a righteous God. Yet, contemporary society tends to de-emphasize the standards of God regarding immorality, choosing instead to focus on His love. But even God's justice is rooted in love, as it always has human redemption as its goal. It is important to remember that God's justice is not like human justice. There will be a day when everyone will give an account of his or her deeds.

### B. Biblical Background

Zephaniah means, "The Lord hides." This contemporary of Jeremiah is believed to be the last of the prophets before the captivity. Zephaniah could trace his lineage back to Hezekiah, king of Judah; therefore, we can conclude that Zephaniah's lineage was possibly of a royal line. Additionally, the prophet's father was a Cushite (Ethiopian), thus making Zephaniah a prophet of direct African descent.

Zephaniah prophesied to the nation of Israel during the reign of King Josiah. He was instrumental in Josiah's revival (see 2 Kings 22-23). At the time of Zephaniah's prophecy, Israel was in the midst of political upheaval; her unrighteous religious leaders were languishing in idolatry and wickedness.

The thrust of the book of Zephaniah is that judgment will come upon the entire world (Zephaniah 1:2-3). God will destroy all idol worshipers and despisers of God in Judah and Jerusalem. According to Zephaniah, this terrible judgment would surely come upon the inhabitants of the earth.

The people of Judah were corrupt and callous. Zephaniah challenged the injustices and immoral ways of the people in an effort to show how they had turned their backs on God. His desire was to lead them back to God before they experienced the severity of God's justice.

## II. Exposition and Application of the Scripture
### A. The People's Refusal to Heed the Warnings of God (Zephaniah 3:1-2)

**WOE TO her that is filthy and polluted, to the oppressing city! She obeyed not the voice; she received not correction; she trusted not in the Lord; she drew not near to her God.**

Zephaniah spoke strongly about the

defiled morals of Jerusalem. The holy city had become a land of oppressors—where the rich and powerful people trampled upon the rights of the poor and the helpless. The city could not plead ignorance of God's will, however, because God had been speaking to her through Zephaniah and His other prophets. God was eager to correct her wrongdoings, but she refused correction and did not obey anyone. God wanted to bless and help the city. He longed for a closer fellowship with the people, but Jerusalem repeatedly chose to go her own unclean way. Zephaniah's words seemed to have fallen on deaf ears.

Zephaniah began his prophecy by denouncing the entire population of Jerusalem. He listed four negatives which described the spiritual condition of the people of Jerusalem. Four negatives (nots) in verse 2 specify Jerusalem's dereliction of duty. First, "She obeyed not," meaning that the people refused to obey the words of God from the former prophets. They had sealed their consciences to the truth. Second, they did not receive correction. God had sent some mild punishments as corrective measures, yet they were not persuaded. They exhibited no repentance from His merciful chastisement. Third, they trusted not. They had replaced their trust in God with their present state of prosperity. Finally, they drew not near to God, meaning that they did not worship Him. They did not walk in His ways, nor did they make prayers to Him. Terrible things awaited Jerusalem because she disobeyed the voice of God—not trusting in the Lord despite the many promises, signs, and blessings God had guaranteed her; and not responding to God's outstretched hands, pleading "Come unto Me."

Let us look at the practical application of Jerusalem's refusal to repent. It was not the evil they had done, but, rather, the good left undone that would prove to be their undoing at the court of eternal justice. It would not be the vices avoided, but the virtues left uncultivated that would condemn them. When Jesus previewed the scenes of the Judgment Day (Matthew 25), He said that those who inherit the Kingdom will do so because they had seen hunger and fed the hungry; they had seen the naked and clothed them; they had heard the cries of the lonely and visited them. It is interesting to note that only their active charity was mentioned as opposed to their lack of sins. On the other hand, those who were disinherited were cast into outer darkness—not because of great evils committed, but rather because they had done no positive deeds.

**B. The Leaders' Failure**
*(Zephaniah 3:3-4)*

**Her princes within her are roaring lions; her judges are evening wolves; they gnaw not the bones till the morrow. Her prophets are light and treacherous persons: her priests have polluted the sanctuary, they have done violence to the law.**

Zephaniah charged the leaders, officials, rulers, prophets, and priests with ruling like gangsters. The metaphors employed to describe the leaders were graphic and unkind. The princes within her were roaring lions. They had destroyed the people like a lion destroys his prey. The political, social, and religious climates of Jerusalem were corrupt. Their ferocious appetite for self-enrichment made the officials behave like "roaring lions" (cf. Ezekiel 23:34). In Zephaniah 3:3, the judges are likened to evening wolves. This class of rulers practiced their unjust dealings from evening until morning. They did not sleep until they carried out injustice. They gnawed not the bone until morning, meaning they were completely immersed in doing evil. They spent their days dedicated to completing whatever evil had been left behind in the night. They thwarted justice by shedding innocent blood. Sadly, human life had been reduced to raw materials which leaders used at will.

In Zephaniah 3:4, their prophets were described as light and treacherous persons. Essentially, the prophets held no deep conviction of their calling, no concern for the immortal souls of the people under their spiritual charge. Their being treacherous in this instance means that they had betrayed the souls of the people for worldly honor. As the great preacher Charles Spurgeon once said, "These are ministers sailing under false colors."

In an indirect way, Zephaniah warned King Josiah not to trust the officials and religious leaders of Jerusalem. Zephaniah indicated that if Josiah was to successfully break away from the perverse pattern set by his father and grandfather, he would have to forego the counsel of those who were in power and return to God. Unlike the officials and religious leaders of Jerusalem, God is righteous, just, and faithful. And since God was unique in those qualities, He alone was qualified to judge the people.

It is a leadership principle that those in charge are responsible for all that their followers do or fail to do. Though everyone will give an individual account before God, the Bible reveals that those who stand in the high places and sacred offices of leadership will have a stricter account to give (Deuteronomy 15:20; James 3:1). After all, to whom much is given, much is required. In our world today, Zephaniah's message is still relevant for our people and our leaders, and we dare not ignore it.

The princes represented the government. The government had a duty: to protect the entire citizenry; to champion the cause of those who had no voice in high places; and to give every person a chance at life and liberty. The judges represented the lawmakers and the law enforcement communities: magistrates, sheriffs, police, justices of the peace, constables, the city council, the political leaders, and judges at all levels. Zephaniah's description of the leadership here is applicable to all civilized people. God will judge any nation that lives in such reproach. But, even in judgment, God does not willfully wreck nations. His goal is always redemption.

### C. The Two Sides of God: Judgment and Mercy *(Zephaniah 3:5, 8-9)*

**The just Lord is in the midst thereof; he will not do iniquity: every morning doth he bring his judgment to light, he faileth not; but the unjust knoweth no shame…Therefore wait ye upon me, saith the Lord, until the day that I rise up to the prey: for my determination is to gather the nations, that I may assemble the kingdoms, to pour upon them mine indignation, even all my fierce anger: for all the earth shall be devoured with the fire of my jealousy. For then will I turn to the people a pure language, that they may all call**

**upon the name of the Lord, to serve him with one consent.**

There are those who regard any discussion of sin as trivial and irrelevant. They argue that any ideas about punishment are incongruent with a loving God. But the Bible does not retreat from the fact that for every sin there is a price tag. And those of us who use the Bible as our guide book know that God is a God of justice. He will punish unrepentant sinners.

The word "then" in verse 9 signifies a major shift in Zephaniah's message, both in tone and in content. Zephaniah shifts here from frightful forecasts of destruction to prophecies of blessing and peace. Zephaniah's prophecy of restoration extends far beyond the return of the exiles. The prophet foretells of a broad group of peoples, of dispersed peoples, returning to the temple in Jerusalem. And this process begins with a return to proper worship. A return to the proper worship of God is the beginning of repentance. God restores a pure language, and proper offerings. God would give His people a pure language, which literally means "lip." Their speech would be different, reflecting a new encounter with God. The story of the Old Testament is really the story of divine redemption—in which God interacts with humankind and judges people and nations in His own time.

After destroying the nation's armies, God would then restore the nation to His favor. Instead of horrifying threats, God would comfort the people with promises of love and restoration. Zephaniah had already predicted the fall of Philistia, Moab, Ammon, and Assyria. Now he was calling upon the people to look at the record of the past and learn from it. God's response to the wickedness of Jerusalem was to declare His judgment. He would use other nations to punish the city for its rebellion. The faithful remnant of Judah was encouraged to wait for God until He destroyed all of His foes.

Zephaniah portrayed the judgment as lying just beyond the horizon. According to him, God was going to come soon and gather the nations together, witnessing against them. Because Judah was scarcely different from the nations, she too would encounter the awesome judgment of the Day of the Lord. On the Day of the Lord, the future of the kingdoms of the world would be determined. Zephaniah predicted that one day all people would eventually serve God on one accord, and that the nations would be renewed both spiritually and morally. The term "one consent" here literally means "(with) one shoulder" and would have been familiar to them as a nation of herders. Oxen in those days were linked shoulder to shoulder with a single yoke so that they pulled together in their work, thus making the team stronger. Perhaps, being united in pure speech, Zephaniah envisioned that God's people would then walk together in the same direction as people of God.

### III. CONCLUDING REFLECTIONS

It was heartbreaking for Zephaniah to see such spiritual deterioration among his people, and we too as Christians today must be alarmed about the spiritual decadence of our society to the extent that we are willing to take action.

The contemporary church has been an unfortunate principal in obliterating the line that separates righteousness from unrighteousness. Fewer congregations seem to maintain stricter moral expectations for our clergy. Out of fear of losing members, we no longer expect Christians to act and speak differently from their unchurched neighbors. Still, that does not dismiss our mandate to walk according to a higher calling. We are called to be holy and separate because we belong to our God. It is God that we make our first priority, and we pledge our lives in this fellowship.

Should we fail to do this, persons should not be surprised to see the anger of God upon His chosen ones. Zephaniah helps us to understand that the whole world will face God's wrath. His promise of blessings for faithfulness is just as piercing as the prophet's projections of doom for disobedience. Even though Judah and Jerusalem would have to suffer the consequences of their sinfulness, Zephaniah would see the day when the Lord (with His gift of joy) would bless a remnant of God's people and they would all dwell together on one accord.

## WORD POWER

**Wait (Hebrew: *Chaka*—chaw-kaw)**—the word is set in a commanding tone. The prophet is commanded to wait and see what the Lord will do. This waiting implies constant readiness; the One who made the promise would honor His word, and the prophet would not be caught unawares. The waiting is defined by the word "until" (adverb of time). There is no Hebrew word for "until"; it was added for editorial convenience.

## HOME DAILY BIBLE READINGS

for the week of July 8, 2007
*Zephaniah Announces God's Justice*
July 2, Monday
—Psalm 27:7-14
—Prayer for Help
July 3, Tuesday
—Isaiah 2:12-22
—The Day of the Lord
July 4, Wednesday
—Psalm 33:1-11
—God's Eternal Counsel
July 5, Thursday
—2 Chronicles 34:1-7
—Young Josiah's Reforms
July 6, Friday
—Zephaniah 3:1-7
—Woe to Wrongdoers
July 7, Saturday
—Zephaniah 3:8-13
—Deliverance Will Come
July 8, Sunday
—Zephaniah 3:14-20
—The Call to Rejoice

## PRAYER

*Eternal God, claim our hearts with Thy redemptive grace, that we may perceive others as objects of Your concern. May Your love constrain us to walk with Thee. In Jesus' name, we pray. Amen.*

**July 15, 2007**

Lesson 7

# Habakkuk Announces the Doom of the Unrighteous

**UNIT II**
What Does God Require?

**CHILDREN'S UNIT**
What Does God Want?

**ADULT TOPIC:** A Reason to Hope
**YOUTH TOPIC:** Reason to Hope
**CHILDREN'S TOPIC:** God Wants Us to Have Hope

**KEY VERSE**
For the earth shall be filled with the knowledge of the glory of the Lord, as the waters cover the sea.
—Habakkuk 2:14

**DEVOTIONAL READING:** Psalm 37:27-34
**BACKGROUND SCRIPTURE:** Habakkuk 2:1-20; 2 Kings 23:35-37
**PRINT PASSAGE:** Habakkuk 2:6-14

**OBJECTIVES**

Upon completion of this lesson, the students are expected to:
1. Recognize that God has a plan for each of our lives;
2. Learn that people must never think that injustice will go unheeded by God; and,
3. Understand that anything humans build without the blessing of God can never last and will eventually fall.

### Habakkuk 2:6-14—KJV

6 Shall not all these take up a parable against him, and a taunting proverb against him, and say, Woe to him that increaseth that which is not his! how long? and to him that ladeth himself with thick clay!

7 Shall they not rise up suddenly that shall bite thee, and awake that shall vex thee, and thou shalt be for booties unto them?

8 Because thou hast spoiled many nations, all the remnant of the people shall spoil thee; because of men's blood, and for the violence of the land, of the city, and of all that dwell therein.

9 Woe to him that coveteth an evil covetousness to his house, that he may set his nest on high, that he may be delivered from the power of evil!

10 Thou hast consulted shame to thy house by cutting off many people, and hast sinned against thy soul.

11 For the stone shall cry out of the wall, and the beam out of the timber shall answer it.

12 Woe to him that buildeth a town with blood, and stablisheth a city by iniquity!

13 Behold, is it not of the LORD of hosts that the people shall labour in the very fire, and the people shall weary themselves for very vanity?

14 For the earth shall be filled with the knowledge of the glory of the LORD, as the waters cover the sea.

## UNIFYING LESSON PRINCIPLE

When all seems wrong in the world or in their lives, people want a reason to hope. What reason do we have to hope during such situations? Habakkuk's response is that the God who will not tolerate injustice is the same God who works for salvation, and this is the source of our hope.

## POINTS TO BE EMPHASIZED
## ADULTS/YOUTH

**Adult/Youth Key Verse:** Habakkuk 2:14
**Print Passage:** Habakkuk 2:6-14
—Habakkuk affirms that the righteous live by their faith.
—Habakkuk is willing to sit in silence and wait for the action of God.
—Habakkuk believes in the ultimate triumph of the reign of God.
—Habakkuk struggles with the faith problem created by God's apparent lack of response to obvious evil and violence.
—Habakkuk describes the misdeeds that are condemned by God.
—The Lord teaches Habakkuk tenacity in hope; ultimately, God's justice will prevail.

## CHILDREN

**Key Verse:** Habakkuk 2:2
**Print Passage:** Habakkuk 1:1; 2:1-4; 3:17-19
—Although the righteous may experience difficulties, they continue to recognize and praise God's goodness and mercy in their lives.
—God is listening to the problems and concerns of the righteous even when He does not respond immediately.
—Although the wicked might take advantage of the righteous, God will deal with the wicked.
—There is a difference between visions and dreams.

## TOPICAL OUTLINE OF THE LESSON

I. INTRODUCTION
  A. I Have a Question
  B. Biblical Background

II. EXPOSITION AND APPLICATION OF THE SCRIPTURE
  A. Hope in the Midst of Hopelessness *(Habakkuk 2:6-8)*
  B. Warning Against Laying False Foundation *(Habakkuk 2:9-11)*
  C. Hope in God's Glory *(Habakkuk 2:12-14)*

III. CONCLUDING REFLECTIONS

## I. INTRODUCTION
### A. I Have a Question

God has a plan for each of our lives, and often we must endure hardships and frustrations before that plan can become a reality. It is the hardships and the frustrations of life that define a person's true character. While we know that we must endure these situations and circumstances of life, this knowledge does not remove our desire to question God from time to time. Many believers have gone through a period in their lives when they find themselves wondering, "Why is God doing this to me or allowing this to happen to me? What have I done?"

Perhaps a more relevant theological question is: How can God's patience with evil line up with His holiness? Faith that is not tested will not develop. The trials of our lives are opportunities for us to exercise our faith. Trials serve as a fertile ground through which faith grows and strengthens. However, many times when we are faced with trials, we quickly jump to the conclusion that we are out of favor with God.

### B. Biblical Background

Habakkuk found it difficult to understand how a kind and just God could punish the sins of Judah by using a wicked nation like Babylon as His instrument for chastisement. Habakkuk also wrestled with the spiritual decline of the nation and wondered why God was not doing anything about it. Habakkuk wanted to see the people revived (Habakkuk 3:2), but God wasn't answering his prayers right away. Habakkuk expressed his concerns to God and then listened as God replied to his concerns. God has now responded a second time to the questions posed by Habakkuk.

## II. Exposition and Application of the Scripture
### A. Hope in the Midst of Hopelessness
*(Habakkuk 2:6-8)*

**Shall not all these take up a parable against him, and a taunting proverb against him, and say, Woe to him that increaseth that which is not his! how long? and to him that ladeth himself with thick clay! Shall they not rise up suddenly that shall bite thee, and awake that shall vex thee, and thou shalt be for booties unto them? Because thou hast spoiled many nations, all the remnant of the people shall spoil thee; because of men's blood, and for the violence of the land, of the city, and of all that dwell therein.**

God told Habakkuk that, contrary to popular belief, Babylon's reign would not be long. "Shall not all these take up a parable against him…?" This is a rhetorical question; in effect, the people of God would soon see the fall of Babylon. The phrase "against him" means that when Babylon is dislodged from its position of prominence, the inhabitants of Jerusalem will rejoice. Babylon's sin was pride and arrogance. Babylon built her prestige on her own merit. But Babylon could not retain her wealth for a long time, because the oppressed were crying out against these people. Therefore, her punishment would be complete humiliation and dishonor by those who had been victims of her oppression. Habakkuk said Babylon covered itself with thick clay. In other words, all that Babylon thought of as wealth was only dirt, and it would soon be gone. The end of Babylon's prominence and avarice would be sudden, which answers the question, "How long?"

The Babylonians would receive the same brutality it had inflicted on Jerusalem. In the realm of divine justice, the very people who were abused may become His instruments of judgment. The common cliché "What goes around, comes around" is a more contemporary rendering of Galatians 6:7.

Habakkuk said in verse 8, "Because thou hast spoiled many nations, all the remnant of the people shall spoil thee." The leaders of Babylon believed that they had brought all the other nations down so low that there was no way that any of them could ever recover and become a threat to the Babylonian reign of terror. Habakkuk said the remnants that were left as feeble people would suffice to inflict vengeance upon Babylon. Human power and might are no match for God. Over and over, the Bible reveals God as being the avenger of the weak and the oppressed. This same message was given to Edom by the prophet Obadiah. No matter how powerful a person or nation appears to be, God can bring them down by any means He chooses.

God's plan to revenge the people's blood and the violence of the land were further indications that Babylon's time was quickly running out. This proves that there is every reason for oppressed children of God to have faith and hold on to their hope, especially when their circumstances appear hopeless. In God's own time, He will mete out justice.

### B. Warning Against Laying False Foundation (Habakkuk 2:9-11)

**Woe to him that coveteth an evil covetousness to his house, that he may set his nest on high, that he may be delivered from the power of evil! Thou hast consulted shame to thy house by cutting off many people, and hast sinned against thy soul. For the stone shall cry out of the wall, and the beam out of the timber shall answer it.**

Babylon possessed an attitude of greed and covetousness. The Babylonians were never satisfied, and they always sought more riches. Covetousness was embedded into their consciousness, and it led to excessive greed. They were not satisfied with what they possessed; they were piling up their ill-gotten gains for their progeny. They were like greedy dogs that protect what they have and still run for more. They became proud; Habakkuk compared their prideful attitude to an eagle who sets his nest in a high place. Babylon thought that building walls around their wealth would render them invincible. But Habakkuk described their attitudes as determination to perpetrate more evil. Sitting on high places as eagles projects an attitude of false protection. However, the very stones of their palaces would cry out against them. As the stones cried out, the crossbeam or main rafters would echo back. This is Habakkuk's way of saying that Babylon would have no rest. Babylon would sleep no more. The blood of their victims would not allow them to rest. When Cain killed his brother, the blood of Abel was walking in silent vengeance in his mind. The message here is that shame will be the end of Babylon's reign.

God desires us to have possessions and good things, but He also desires us to have an attitude of gratitude for those things that we have. People who look out only for themselves and are oblivious to the needs and desires of others are like a sour stench in the nostrils of the Lord. Those who manipulate others to advance themselves in evil ways will not go unnoticed by God. Covetousness leads to a dead end, but those who trust in the Lord will find out that God is able to meet all our needs. Habakkuk reminds us that greediness—the urge to get more at all costs—is a hopeless pursuit. A city, church, life, or business built on greed cannot stand. It may appear successful for a while, but it will crumble. We should remember that Babylon was built on such greed and it did not last. Babylon did fall, just as Habakkuk had prophesied.

### C. Hope in God's Glory
(Habakkuk 2:12-14)

**Woe to him that buildeth a town with blood, and stablisheth a city by iniquity! Behold, is it not of the Lord of hosts that the people shall labour in the very fire, and the people shall weary themselves for very vanity? For the earth shall be filled with the knowledge of the glory of the Lord, as the waters cover the sea.**

This is the third proclamation of woe used in chapter 2 (see also verses 6 and 9). Used a total of five times in this chapter alone, the prophet was calling attention to the evil ways of Babylon. It should serve as a deterrent to those who want to pursue prestige by building their lives on the blood and sweat of others. It gives hope to the oppressed that wickedness does not thrive perpetually. God has an end in view for every form of wickedness (see Ecclesiastes 3). Habakkuk believed that Babylon labored for what would be food for fire. This is a graphic way of saying that every structure built by the ill-gotten gain of extortion would be burnt to ashes. It is a classic way to describe wasteful energy. Only what we do for Christ will last.

Verse 13 clearly states that those who labor in pursuit of worldly wealth and honor exhaust themselves in vain. Babylon was built through the bloodshed of innocent victims—prisoners of war, slaves, and unappreciated servants. Babylon may have been proud of what it had built, but God classified it as only fuel for the fire. The city is believed to have been an example of architectural beauty, but this did not matter; Babylon, in all of its architectural splendor, was completely destroyed. All that remains of Babylon is confined to museums and replicas.

Verse 14 is important because it gives hope to the hopeless. It was first applied to Babylon, who crushed Jerusalem almost to ashes and eventually was destroyed by God. King Nebuchadnezzar, the monarch of Babylon, was finally humiliated (see Daniel 4:37). The defeat of Babylon was a precursor of good things to come to all the children of God. It reminds us that the earth is filled with the glory of the Lord for all who want to acknowledge it. Finally, God revealed that through the destruction of the Babylonian Empire (ca. 539 B.C.), He would get the ultimate honor. The glory of Babylon didn't last, but the glory of God will last forever. The Gospel is still spreading all over the world. In March 2006, Abdul Rahman, an Afghani man who converted to Christianity, was arrested for renouncing Islam, but he refused to deny Christ. The authorities had planned to execute him according to Islamic law; fortunately, Rahman was offered asylum in Rome. Babylon was destroyed long ago, but the glory of God continues to fill the earth. This is the hope we have as Christians. No matter the pain, God is there, and He will deliver and His name will be glorified.

### III. Concluding Reflections

God is the author of hope, and for that reason every child of God can trust that God will not abandon His creatures. He is constantly mindful of our circumstances. The psalmist declares that the One who keeps Israel does not sleep nor slumber (Psalm 121:4). The fall of Babylon should remind us that what human hands build without

God can never last. We cannot exploit and demean people made in the image of God for our personal benefit and believe that we will escape the judgment of God.

Babylon's fall from power serves as a reminder to us that God will ultimately triumph both here on earth and in heaven. Throughout human history, despotic rulers and prideful nations have risen and fallen. Meanwhile, God has continued to lift up the lowly of this world from oppression to liberation.

Nelson Mandela was jailed for almost thirty years, yet he did not emerge from the experience a bitter man. Mandela readily credits his personal maturity to his faith, which he allowed to grow into a vision during those years of forced contemplation. In just a few short years, Mandela moved from prisoner to president.

No matter what is going on in the world around them, those who put their trust in God and who faithfully seek to maintain a morally and spiritually steadfast life will make it through. As believers, we must remain steadfast that God will always be true to His character, no matter how things are going around us. Fraught with his own troubles, Habakkuk was still able to offer a hopeful reminder to all generations: "The just shall live by his faith" (Habakkuk 2:4).

## WORD POWER

**Fill (Hebrew: *male* [maw-lay])**—in the Key Verse, the word "fill" is used in a passive statement, meaning that it is God who is going to cause the earth to be filled with His knowledge as the waters cover the sea. It is also an imperfect tense in Hebrew.

Therefore, the filling will be a continuous event. There will be no time when God is not known throughout history. Ministers and church leaders may become unfaithful—and they have done so—but God will not fail.

## HOME DAILY BIBLE READINGS

for the week of July 15, 2007
*Habakkuk Announces the Doom of the Unrighteous*

July 9, Monday
   —Psalm 37:27-34
   —The Lord Loves Justice
July 10, Tuesday
   —2 Kings 23:31-37
   —Judah Becomes Egypt's Vassal
July 11, Wednesday
   —Habakkuk 1:12-17
   —Habakkuk's Complaint
July 12, Thursday
   —Habakkuk 2:1-5
   —The Lord Answers
July 13, Friday
   —Habakkuk 2:6-14
   —Woes Reported
July 14, Saturday
   —Habakkuk 2:15-20
   —The Lord Will Act
July 15, Sunday
   —Habakkuk 3:13-19
   —The Lord Is Our Strength

## PRAYER

*Eternal God, our Father, help us to be reminded that Your "all-seeing" eye is upon the land, and that we can find hope in the fact that You will not tolerate injustice forever. Remind us that You are working for the deliverance of Your people from evil. In Jesus' name, we pray. Amen.*

July 22, 2007

UNIT II
What Does God Require?

CHILDREN'S UNIT
What Does God Want?

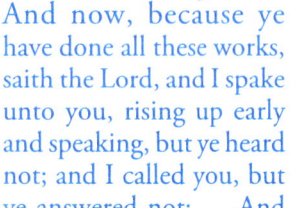

**KEY VERSES**
And now, because ye have done all these works, saith the Lord, and I spake unto you, rising up early and speaking, but ye heard not; and I called you, but ye answered not; ... And I will cast you out of my sight, as I have cast out all your brethren, even the whole seed of Ephraim.
—Jeremiah 7:13, 15

**OBJECTIVES**
Upon completion of this lesson, the students are expected to:
1. Understand that actions have consequences;
2. Recognize that God will not tolerate hypocrisy; and,
3. Learn that God requires accountability.

Lesson 8

# Jeremiah Announces the Consequences of Disobedience

**ADULT TOPIC:** Your Actions, Your Consequences
**YOUTH TOPIC:** What Goes Around, Comes Around
**CHILDREN'S TOPIC:** God Wants True Worship

**DEVOTIONAL READING:** 2 Chronicles 7:11-16
**BACKGROUND SCRIPTURE:** Jeremiah 7:11-15; 2 Kings 23:36-37
**PRINT PASSAGE:** Jeremiah 7:11-15; 2 Kings 23:36-37

### Jeremiah 7:11-15; 2 Kings 23:36-37—KJV

11 Is this house, which is called by my name, become a den of robbers in your eyes? Behold, even I have seen it, saith the LORD.

12 But go ye now unto my place which was in Shiloh, where I set my name at the first, and see what I did to it for the wickedness of my people Israel.

13 And now, because ye have done all these works, saith the LORD, and I spake unto you, rising up early and speaking, but ye heard not; and I called you, but ye answered not;

14 Therefore will I do unto this house, which is called by my name, wherein ye trust, and unto the place which I gave to you and to your fathers, as I have done to Shiloh.

15 And I will cast you out of my sight, as I have cast out all your brethren, even the whole seed of Ephraim.

.....

36 Jehoiakim was twenty and five years old when he began to reign; and he reigned eleven years in Jerusalem. And his mother's name was Zebudah, the daughter of Pedaiah of Rumah.

37 And he did that which was evil in the sight of the LORD, according to all that his fathers had done.

## UNIFYING LESSON PRINCIPLE

Some people act with impunity, believing they will always be protected from the consequences of their actions. Are Christians to have such views? Jeremiah states that God holds us accountable, so we will not escape the consequences of what we do. At the same time, Jeremiah says, God responds to our good actions and to true worship with faithfulness.

## POINTS TO BE EMPHASIZED ADULTS/YOUTH

**Adult/Youth Key Verse:** Jeremiah 7:13, 15

**Print Passage:** Jeremiah 7:11-15; 2 Kings 23:36-37

—Jeremiah's message followed the death of Josiah, the religious reformer.
—The false hopes raised by false prophets only assured Judah's doom.
—The focus of Jeremiah's message is that Israel's worship reveals a false religion.
—Obedience to the commandments and the covenant is Judah's only hope for survival.
—Jeremiah is traditionally understood as being a young man when he was called by God to prophesy.

## CHILDREN

**Key Verse:** Jeremiah 7:4
**Print Passage:** Jeremiah 7:1-15

—Some Christian believers still worship their possessions and other inanimate objects rather than the true and living God.
—Many believers are not living the life they profess in church.
—God requires a change in the morality of all Christian believers.

## TOPICAL OUTLINE OF THE LESSON

I. **INTRODUCTION**
   A. The Meaning of Consequences and Disobedience
   B. Biblical Background

II. **EXPOSITION AND APPLICATION OF THE SCRIPTURE**
   A. The Defilement of God's House (Jeremiah 7:11a)
   B. The Watchful Eye of God (Jeremiah 7:11b-12)
   C. The Constancy of Judgment (Jeremiah 7:13-15)
   D. Passing the Evil Torch (2 Kings 23:36-37)

III. **CONCLUDING REFLECTIONS**

## I. INTRODUCTION
### A. The Meaning of Consequences and Disobedience

A consequence can be defined as "the result of an action, word, or deed." In agriculture, there is a time of sowing and a time of harvesting. There are three basic rules that regulate sowing and reaping. First, what is reaped in the harvest is a reflection of what has been sown, or planted. If we plant apples, we harvest apples. It is impossible to harvest an orange from an apple seed. In nature, we reap exactly what we sow; likewise, if our character is offensive, we become offensive to others. Second, the harvest is always greater than what has been sown. If a person plants an apple seed, countless apples may one day generate from that single seed. The planter cannot know how many apples there are in one seed, but he or she can see that the consequences of his or her seed involve a return of far more than what was planted. Third, we harvest at different seasons. If one plants an apple seed today, it will take some years before a person begins to harvest the fruits from the seed. These laws of agriculture are closely associated with the consequences of any actions we take. This lesson will remind everyone to be cautious when they are making choices in life. A person going through a painful experience needs to do some personal reflection with a view to calling on God for help.

We are given the choice of whether or not to obey God's commandments. Samuel told Saul, "Behold, to obey is better than sacrifice" (1 Samuel 15:22). Disobedience is a byproduct of a hardened heart. When the Israelites were in bondage under Pharaoh, they cried unto the Lord. God sent Moses to them, but Pharaoh disobeyed. Then Pharaoh and his army perished. Obedience, therefore, is a prerequisite of the journey of faith.

### B. Biblical Background

Jeremiah, the son of Hilkiah, lived in the town of Anathoth in the land of Benjamin in Judah. According to Scripture, he was called to be a prophet by God while still in his mother's womb. Jeremiah preached in Jerusalem from about 628 B.C. to 586 B.C. His ministry began during the reign of Josiah, and continued through the reigns of Jehoiakim, Jehoiachin, and Zedekiah. During that time, the Babylonian Empire took control of Jerusalem. Jeremiah lived through the invasions by the Babylonian armies, the deportations of his people, the slaughter of Jews living in Jerusalem, and the destruction of the temple. Jeremiah warned the people of Jerusalem that they would be punished harshly for their sins. He pleaded with the people to turn from sin back to God; however, they did not respond to his plea. In return for their disobedience, Jerusalem was destroyed by the Babylonians. The inhabitants were carried into exile, as prophesied by Jeremiah. When the people of Jerusalem were being deported, Jeremiah was given a choice of either staying in Judah or going to Babylon. He chose to stay in Judah.

The book of Jeremiah primarily focuses on the relationship between God and His covenant people, as embodied in the surviving kingdom of Judah. At the core of Jeremiah's being was his concern for the relationship between God and His people. The book of Jeremiah essentially consists of a collection of prophecies against Judah and Jerusalem. Jeremiah was concerned with reward and punishment, good and evil, faithfulness and disobedience. He was critical of Judah for worshiping gods other than Yahweh. He urged God's people to return to Him. Jeremiah gave a stern warning against the inevitable destruction of the Babylonian captivity (Jeremiah 25:1-14). The material in the book is not in chronological order; nevertheless, it clearly depicts Jeremiah's spiritual struggle with God's will for his life.

## II. Exposition and Application of the Scripture

### A. The Defilement of God's House
*(Jeremiah 7:11a)*

**Is this house, which is called by my name, become a den of robbers in your eyes?**

We are able to immediately extract from our Bible reading in Jeremiah 7:11 that the people of Judah lived as though God could not see their actions when they were away from the temple. The Amplified Bible brings out clearly that the people of Israel had one lifestyle when they were at the temple and another way of living at home. God asked them if the place that was called by His name, the temple, had become a den of robbers in their eyes. When we think of a den, we think of a place where one relaxes and feels quite comfortable in the home. Notwithstanding the comfort of the den, even there one should not do what cannot be done openly. That was not the case with the people of Judah. The people of Judah turned the temple of the Lord into a shelter for thieves. The place was originally consecrated to God, but it had degenerated into a harbor for robbers and idol worshipers. How did they get so far off course? They commissioned, and listened to, false prophets (Jeremiah 7:4) who told them that God would overlook their sin and not destroy Jerusalem because His temple was there. Thus, the people lived wickedly all week long and then entered the holy temple gates for worship as though nothing was wrong.

They preferred to listen to the false prophets because their fanciful prediction, disguised as divinely-rooted prophesies, made the people feel comfortable in their sins. The people felt that they could continue in their sinful ways of oppressing their neighbors and still be blessed by God. Some of those oppressed included transients, aliens, the fatherless, and widows. The people even shed innocent blood (Jeremiah 7:5-6). They did these things outside the temple, while inside the temple they committed acts of adultery and murder, swore falsely, and burned incense to Baal (Jeremiah 7:9). This resulted in the defilement of God's house and revealed how far God's people had strayed away from Him. When these wrongs were perpetuated over the generations, suffering, trouble, and failure were inevitable.

These are the consequences of being alienated from God; but that was not God's plan for His people. God told Israel that He would cast them out of His house (Jeremiah 7:15). The people learned that disobedience comes with a price. Living in sin and coming to worship God as if nothing has happened is hypocrisy, a dishonor to God.

### B. The Watchful Eye of God
*(Jeremiah 7:11b-12)*

**Behold, even I have seen it, saith the Lord. But go ye now unto my place which was in Shiloh, where I set my name at the first, and see what I did to it for the wickedness of my people Israel.**

The ever-seeing eye of God is always present. His eyes go to and fro, beholding the works of humanity. God had warned the people of Israel, who oversaw the temple, that He had seen their misdeeds and those acts were an abomination to Him. Even though they could hide from other humans, they could not hide from the omnipresent God. He reminded them that He was watching their actions. He saw their hypocrisy. He saw their deeds inside the temple and their deeds while they were away from the temple. God is not limited by distance or space.

God's statement, "I have seen it" (verse 7), is used in the perfect tense. God had perfect knowledge of their deeds. God, who is a just judge, extended an invitation for them to go to Shiloh, the location of His former temple. At Shiloh, they could see what He had done because of the wickedness of the people there. God caused His tabernacle to be set up in Shiloh in Joshua's day. During Eli's time, the ark of the Lord rested in Shiloh, but because of their actions the Lord empowered the Philistines to take the ark away. The people of Shiloh provoked God to anger with their graven images; as a result, God forsook Shiloh (Psalm 78:56-61). This forsaking was to show the people that if God would destroy the place where His name first dwelt because of their wickedness, surely He would not hesitate to do the same to them. God will not be mocked. Perhaps God's invitation to see the destruction of the temple in Shiloh was intended to shock them into a new realization. God had an unequivocal determination to bring His people to ruin because of their rebellion and sin.

### C. The Constancy of Judgment
*(Jeremiah 7:13-15)*

**And now, because ye have done all these works, saith the LORD, and I spake unto you, rising up early and speaking, but ye heard not; and I called you, but ye answered not; Therefore will I do unto this house, which is called by my name, wherein ye trust, and unto the place which I gave to you and to your fathers, as I have done to Shiloh. And I will cast you out of my sight, as I have cast out all your brethren, even the whole seed of Ephraim.**

God is the same yesterday, today, and tomorrow. The things that were repugnant to Him in one generation are also repugnant to Him in other generations. God does not change. Unfortunately, He has to bring human beings into accountability every day. We must set our hearts to obey God. His ways are best and are the only ways that matter. Because of the hardness of our hearts, we tend to place ourselves and the desire for monetary gain above God. God is just and judges both the righteous and unrighteous alike. Persons will eventually feel the repercussions of their wrongful doings. Some will blame these consequences on luck, and others simply may think hardship is inevitable. Regardless of how we interpret God's judgment, God will reprimand us for our unrighteous behavior, desiring that His punishment will bring us into submission and obedience. God does not want any of His children to perish. He wants us to repent and stop sinning so that we may live and enjoy His blessings. God forever calls sinners away from their transgressions. He punishes our wrongdoings in an effort to get us to turn to Him and be forever blessed.

In our texts, God spoke to the children of Judah—not once, but constantly; however, they did not listen. God persistently called them individually into repentance, but they ignored Him. The phrase "rising up early and speaking" is a biblical expression for speaking zealously and earnestly. God not only called the present generation, but He also had made similar appeals to their ancestors. Even now, God is steadfast in seeking His children. However, the children of Israel perpetually ignored God; they inevitably suffered the consequences of their actions. We can learn from Israel's example and choose not to ignore Him today.

### D. Passing the Evil Torch
*(2 Kings 23:36-37)*

**Jehoiakim was twenty and five years old when he began to reign; and he reigned eleven years in Jerusalem. And his mother's name was Zebudah, the daughter of Pedaiah of Rumah. And he did that which was evil in the sight of the LORD, according to all that his fathers had done.**

The torch is of heritage, and history is passed from one generation to another, which can include both good behavior and bad behavior. The reign of Jehoiakim is an example of sin being passed from the father to the son. In modern-day speech we say, "The apple does not fall far from the tree." The cycle of sinful behavior continued with Jehoiakim. In verse 36, his mother's name is mentioned; the writer wanted to show that she, too, had done evil in the sight of the Lord. Eliakim was renamed Jehoiakim when Pharaoh Neco made him a puppet king of Judah.

Jehoiakim ruled Judah for eleven years. He was subservient to Pharaoh Neco for the first four years and to Babylon's Nebuchadnezzar for three more years, until he was temporarily able to oust the Babylonians. Jehoiakim's regime was marked by violence, greed, dishonesty, and oppression. He murdered the prophet Uriah. He would have killed Jeremiah and his companion Baruch, were it not for the protection of friends within Jehoiakim's regime. Jeremiah denounced the ways of Jehoiakim and Judah and predicted their downfall in the prophetic scrolls he dictated to Baruch. Apparently thinking he could overrule the prophecy, Jehoiakim shredded and burned the scrolls but had Jeremiah dictate his prophecy to his secretary word for word. Jehoiakim died violently and was given "the burial of a donkey"—dragged off and thrown out beyond the gates of Jerusalem (Jeremiah 22:19).

Jehoiakim reigned for eleven years. The length of his reign was recorded so that we would know that for an eleven-year span the people continuously did as they pleased. They were allowed to do so because the person in power encouraged it by his own disregard for God's Law and God's prophet. He led his people astray, but he reaped the consequences of his actions. Sadly, Jehoiakim was not alone in his defiance toward God. Even with eons of history giving witness to this truth, people still behave as though they can commit heinous, sinful acts with impunity, having no regard for divine retribution.

### III. CONCLUDING REFLECTIONS

The God who judged both Israel and Jehoiakim is still on the throne. God will not be ignored, He will not tolerate hypocrisy, and He will not allow His children to desecrate His holy temple without calling them to repentance. If they refuse to repent, the consequences will be grave. Many religious activities are held in God's name but do not truly honor God. We can avoid hypocrisy by exposing our hearts to truth revealed through the Spirit of God. Right worship can lead us into a right relationship with God.

Many people behave as though they will escape the consequences of their actions. However, God has a continuously watchful eye and His judgment is unwavering. He calls both the just and unjust into judgment. There are consequences for disobedience. Yet, when we sin, God's grace abounds. Still, we must be extra careful about willful rebellion against Him; obedience is the key to a successful Christian life. A person will always reap what he or she sows. Sometimes, obedience to God and His law may require disobedience to earthly powers. Acting righteously in the house of God but doing evil outside the four walls of the church is indicative of an unrepentant heart. Others may be impressed or swayed by hypocritical acts of righteousness at church, but God is neither deceived nor mocked. A time of judgment for all sin will come.

Many come to church, yet their hearts are hardened to the Word of God. Sermons have no transforming effect in their lives. This lesson calls for sober reflection. As we see today, rebellion against God can be cyclical and multigenerational, passing to the children from their parents. If the parents disregard authority, the children may do worse. If parents disobey spiritual authority, their children may become thorns in the flesh of the body of Christ.

## WORD POWER

**Cast (Hebrew: *shalak*—[shaw-lak])**—this is a strong word to be used for a declared enemy, a known enemy. The word "cast" could also mean: to throw out, hurl away, pluck out of from the place of origin, or cast down like a sick sheep waiting for the shepherd. The word describes the action of God done to the Israelites when Babylon invaded their land. The gravity of the word cannot be fathomed by us, but this was the reason why Jeremiah lamented when he saw the casting off of his people by God.

## HOME DAILY BIBLE READINGS

for the week of July 22, 2007
*Jeremiah Announces the Consequences of Disobedience*

July 16, Monday
—Hebrews 2:1-4
—Pay Greater Attention
July 17, Tuesday
—2 Chronicles 7:11-16
—Forgiveness Is Possible
July 18, Wednesday
—1 Kings 9:1-9
—Choices of Consequences
July 19, Thursday
—Jeremiah 19:1-6
—Disaster Is Coming
July 20, Friday
—Jeremiah 26:1-6
—Downfall Threatened
July 21, Saturday
—Jeremiah 7:1-7
—Amend Your Ways
July 22, Sunday
—Jeremiah 7:8-15
—Judgment of the Wicked

## PRAYER

*Eternal God, our Father, You have called each of us to be a minister. Thus, the responsibility for protecting Your house of worship falls on each of us. Forgive us when we desecrate Your house of worship. Show us Your way, that we may not suffer the consequences of our evil deeds. In Jesus' name, we pray. Amen.*

**Lesson 9**

# Jeremiah Invites Jews in Babylon to Trust God

**ADULT TOPIC:** Getting Through the Pain
**YOUTH TOPIC:** Have I Got a Plan for You!
**CHILDREN'S TOPIC:** God Wants Our Trust

---

**DEVOTIONAL READING:** Psalm 145:13b-21
**BACKGROUND SCRIPTURE:** Jeremiah 29:1-14
**PRINT PASSAGE:** Jeremiah 29:1-14

### Jeremiah 29:1-14—KJV

NOW THESE are the words of the letter that Jeremiah the prophet sent from Jerusalem unto the residue of the elders which were carried away captives, and to the priests, and to the prophets, and to all the people whom Nebuchadnezzar had carried away captive from Jerusalem to Babylon;

2 (After that Jeconiah the king, and the queen, and the eunuchs, the princes of Judah and Jerusalem, and the carpenters, and the smiths, were departed from Jerusalem;)

3 By the hand of Elasah the son of Shaphan, and Gemariah the son of Hilkiah, (whom Zedekiah king of Judah sent unto Babylon to Nebuchadnezzar king of Babylon) saying,

4 Thus saith the LORD of hosts, the God of Israel, unto all that are carried away captives, whom I have caused to be carried away from Jerusalem unto Babylon;

5 Build ye houses, and dwell in them; and plant gardens, and eat the fruit of them;

6 Take ye wives, and beget sons and daughters; and take wives for your sons, and give your daughters to husbands, that they may bear sons and daughters; that ye may be increased there, and not diminished.

7 And seek the peace of the city whither I have caused you to be carried away captives, and pray unto the Lord for it: for in the peace thereof shall ye have peace.

---

**July 29, 2007**

**UNIT II**
What Does God Require?

**CHILDREN'S UNIT**
What Does God Want?

### KEY VERSE

For I know the thoughts that I think toward you, saith the LORD, thoughts of peace, and not of evil, to give you an expected end.
—Jeremiah 29:11

### OBJECTIVES

Upon completion of this lesson, the students are expected to:

1. Learn that God has a divine plan and purpose for each of us;
2. Recognize that God is able to deliver us from any situation or circumstance when we continue to trust and believe Him; and,
3. Understand that God's desire is that we trust Him completely.

**8** For thus saith the Lord of hosts, the God of Israel; Let not your prophets and your diviners, that be in the midst of you, deceive you, neither hearken to your dreams which ye cause to be dreamed.

**9** For they prophesy falsely unto you in my name: I have not sent them, saith the Lord.

**10** For thus saith the Lord, That after seventy years be accomplished at Babylon I will visit you, and perform my good word toward you, in causing you to return to this place.

**11** For I know the thoughts that I think toward you, saith the Lord, thoughts of peace, and not of evil, to give you an expected end.

**12** Then shall ye call upon me, and ye shall go and pray unto me, and I will hearken unto you.

**13** And ye shall seek me, and find me, when ye shall search for me with all your heart.

**14** And I will be found of you, saith the Lord: and I will turn away your captivity, and I will gather you from all the nations, and from all the places whither I have driven you, saith the Lord; and I will bring you again into the place whence I caused you to be carried away captive.

## UNIFYING LESSON PRINCIPLE

In the midst of loss and pain, people will sometimes willingly believe something untrue because it makes them feel better. How can we guard against such a mistake? Jeremiah urges us to hold to our trust in God and to wait patiently for God's healing,

## POINTS TO BE EMPHASIZED ADULTS/YOUTH

**Adult/Youth Key Verse:** Jeremiah 29:11
**Print Passage:** Jeremiah 29:1-14

—The Babylonians permitted Jeremiah to remain in Judah after the destruction and exile of 587 BC.

—The remnants of both Israel and Judah are about to enter into a new relationship with God.

—Jeremiah instructed the exiles not to listen to the false prophets.

—Jeremiah encouraged the exiles to settle in Babylon and to wait patiently for God's restoration.

## CHILDREN

**Key Verse:** Jeremiah 29:11
**Print Passage:** Jeremiah 29:1-14

—Through Jeremiah, God tells the exiles to pray for the welfare of Babylon because their prosperity was closely aligned to Babylon's future.

—God's people are able to prosper in dire circumstances, if they remain faithful to God's Word.

—Sometimes, it is difficult to know who is speaking for God, and godly wisdom is needed to discern who are the true spokespersons.

## TOPICAL OUTLINE OF THE LESSON

I. **Introduction**
   A. Going in and Coming Out
   B. Biblical Background

II. **Exposition and Application of the Scripture**
   A. Don't Stop Living *(Jeremiah 29:1-6)*
   B. Don't Fight It *(Jeremiah 29:7-9)*
   C. God's Timetable *(Jeremiah 29:10-11)*

D. The Demands of God
(Jeremiah 29:12-14)

III. **Concluding Reflections**

# I. Introduction
## A. Going In and Coming Out

It has often been said that in order to get to something, we must first go through something. Life is not static—there is movement everywhere. The earth revolves around the sun. Many people who fail on a mission are unsuccessful simply because they have not been willing to move on to another venture. We all have dreams, aspirations, wants, and desires. Often, what distinguishes people who are successful in achieving their goals from those who are not is that successful people are willing to endure the frustrations of the journey on the road to becoming what they always believed they could be. God has a divine plan and purpose for each of us. He has something set before us that only we can do. He made us with a purpose in mind and He knows what obstacles stand in our way. He knows the difficulties that we will have to face, and wherever He leads, we surely will make it through if we follow Him.

Although the Israelites had to suffer the consequences of their rebellion against God, God did not abandon His people in Babylon. He eventually brought them out and settled them back in their homeland.

## B. Biblical Background

Jeremiah means "the Lord exalts." He came from the lineage of Abiathar the priest. Abiathar was banished by Solomon to Anathoth for supporting Adonijah to become king instead of Solomon. Jeremiah's ministry was directed mostly to the people of Judah. He appealed to the people of Judah to repent and avoid God's judgment.

His message was scathing and challenging to his listeners. Jeremiah warned of Babylonian victory, but the people of Judah would not listen. They failed to repent and turn to God. Because of their disobedience, Judah suffered a serious military defeat and was exiled into Babylonian captivity. The children of Israel found themselves in a devastating and dreadful situation. They had been exiled from the Promised Land into a heathen land. To them, their situation was not just embarrassing, but downright unbearable. They longed for a report that promised only a brief stay in Babylon, so they listened to false prophecies. God's true prophet Jeremiah would only give them the truth: their current circumstances would not be permanent, but they would be there long enough to get settled and establish some roots. Meanwhile, they would need to keep hope alive.

# II. Exposition and Application of the Scripture
## A. Don't Stop Living (Jeremiah 29:1-6)

**NOW THESE are the words of the letter that Jeremiah the prophet sent from Jerusalem unto the residue of the elders which were carried away captives, and to the priests, and to the prophets, and to all the people whom Nebuchadnezzar had carried away captive from Jerusalem to Babylon; (After that Jeconiah the king, and the queen, and the eunuchs, the princes of Judah and Jerusalem, and the carpenters, and the smiths, were departed from Jerusalem;) By the hand**

of Elasah the son of Shaphan, and Gemariah the son of Hilkiah, (whom Zedekiah king of Judah sent unto Babylon to Nebuchadnezzar king of Babylon) saying, Thus saith the LORD of hosts, the God of Israel, unto all that are carried away captives, whom I have caused to be carried away from Jerusalem unto Babylon; Build ye houses, and dwell in them; and plant gardens, and eat the fruit of them; Take ye wives, and beget sons and daughters; and take wives for your sons, and give your daughters to husbands, that they may bear sons and daughters; that ye may be increased there, and not diminished.**

Jeremiah gave an interesting message to the Israelite exiles who found themselves in Babylonian captivity: "Don't stop living." Chapter 28 helps us to know the reason for the letter we nestled in Jeremiah 29. Hananiah, a false prophet, had given the exiles this message: "Thus speaketh the LORD of hosts, the God of Israel, saying, I have broken the yoke of the king of Babylon. Within two full years will I bring again into this place [Jerusalem] all the vessels of the LORD's house" (Jeremiah 28:2-3). Hananiah ascribed his own prophecy to God. Jeremiah countered him and the contest became fierce. However, God vindicated Jeremiah, and Hananiah died a violent death a few months later (Jeremiah 28:17). It appears that the captives were in a state of confusion. They believed that the captivity would soon be over—within two years. But Jeremiah encouraged them to submit to their new conditions and start to make a life for themselves there in Babylon.

Jeremiah knew that the morale of the people was low because they had believed Hananiah. So, Jeremiah encouraged the people to make the best of a bad situation. His message to them was to go ahead and plan for their future, get married, and establish their homes—because they would be in captivity for seventy years.

God is faithful. Often when people find themselves in situations that are tumultuous, they throw up their hands and decide to give up. Most people tend to look for an easy way out. Some so-called Christians have fallen into the hands of false preachers and prophets who promise an easy way. False preachers don't last; they are like soap foam that appears suddenly and dwindles down to a thin layer of suds. Some people who experience hardships act as if life is no longer worth living. However, every believer should be able to testify that even though trouble is sure to come, it does not last always. For the hopeful, there will come a time when things can and will get better. Sometimes God allows us to get into situations that are uncomfortable or undesirable in order for greater things to happen to our faith. Jeremiah's words of wisdom express the fact that regardless of where we may be on the road of life, it does go on. With God all things are possible, to those who believe. God is able to deliver us from any situation when we continue to trust and believe Him.

### B. Don't Fight It *(Jeremiah 29:7-9)*

**And seek the peace of the city whither I have caused you to be carried away captives, and pray unto the LORD for it: for in the peace thereof shall ye have peace. For thus saith the LORD of hosts, the God of Israel; Let not your prophets and your diviners, that be in the midst of you, deceive you, neither hearken to your dreams which ye cause to**

be dreamed. For they prophesy falsely unto you in my name: I have not sent them, saith the LORD.

Jeremiah understood the frustrations of his people. He knew their resentment toward their captors. Knowing these frustrations, he wrote an extensive letter to the elders, priests, prophets, and people who were in Babylon. They were commanded to seek the peace of the city. Essentially, Jeremiah's message was: "Don't fight it. Make the most of it because you are going to be there for a while." To seek the peace of the city is tantamount to saying that the peace of the city was its own peace. They were not only to bear the burdens of the Babylonians patiently, but also to pray for their yoke masters who were appointed over them. They were not to allow disaffection to appear in word or act that might cause more pain for them.

In a similar way, the place where we live today and have daily nourishment and support is our country. If things go well with our country, the goodness will affect everyone. When everyone works together for the good of the land, the entire nation benefits. Jeremiah knew that the lives of the exiles were better than the lives of the remnant in Judea, who had to contend with famine. To rebel for seventy years would have been a fruitless endeavor. God wanted the Israelites to see that living rebelliously would not help anything, but, rather, would only make their circumstances worse.

God wanted them to understand that with an attitude of praise they would find victory in the midst of defeat. When we learn to give God the praise, even in the midst of our worst circumstances, we are demonstrating that we have more faith in Him than we do in our predicament. Our situation cannot change our God, but our God can change our situation.

### C. God's Timetable *(Jeremiah 29:10-11)*

**For thus saith the LORD, That after seventy years be accomplished at Babylon I will visit you, and perform my good word toward you, in causing you to return to this place. For I know the thoughts that I think toward you, saith the LORD, thoughts of peace, and not of evil, to give you an expected end.**

*For thus saith the LORD....* Jeremiah wrote a letter to the captives, urging them not to foment any trouble. Here, Jeremiah is speaking from the Lord. This is to help the people to reflect over their condition and the plan of God for them. "Thus saith the Lord" is a formula to get attention. Many prophets used the same formula to get the attention of their people, but what was the word from the Lord? *After seventy years be accomplished at Babylon....* God would move the people back to Jerusalem, but not for seventy years. The specification of the time period was to curb the impatience of the captives so that they did not make a senseless decision to return to Jerusalem. Seventy years of exile must be accomplished or else Jeremiah would be a false prophet. The time of God's visitation would be after seventy years. The promise of God was, "I will visit you" (Jeremiah 29:10). The word "visit" indicates a deliberate act of God in this context. God's visitation would bring about their freedom. God would be the one to cause their return to Jerusalem. God did not tell them whom He would use to effect these changes. All they needed to know at that time was that He would orchestrate their release.

After their release was described, God issued a manifesto of His plan. *For I know* meant "I alone," not the false prophets who had never been in the council of God. What were God's thoughts? They included several components. First, visions of peace were among His thoughts. Peace was first on the list because the exiles were just going back to settle in Jerusalem after seventy years. Having been through their ordeal with their captors, they needed to hear the word "peace" from God. Second, there was no thought of evil against them. This was an assurance that no evil would befall them. God would guard them on all sides. Finally, God's thoughts included an expected end. There are two words here that we need to pay close attention to: *end* and *expected.* The end that the Israelites wished for was their captivity experience; their expectation was a return to their homeland. These things would come, eventually, but not as soon as they had hoped. God's visitation would involve prosperity for them. These two things were guaranteed under the manifesto of God. God did not hide His plans for the people. Also, His revelation of His plan encouraged them to know that He was with them throughout their entire ordeal.

### D. The Demands of God
(Jeremiah 29:12-14)

Then shall ye call upon me, and ye shall go and pray unto me, and I will hearken unto you. And ye shall seek me, and find me, when ye shall search for me with all your heart. And I will be found of you, saith the Lord: **and I will turn away your captivity, and I will gather you from all the nations, and from all the places whither I have driven you, saith the Lord; and I will bring you again into the place whence I caused you to be carried away captive.**

God wants His people to live in hope. The release of the Israelites was guaranteed, but they were told to usher it in with prayers. The seeking must not be flippant; they must seek Him with all their hearts and souls. When the exiles prayed with all their hearts, God's promise was, I will hear. Before they went into exile they had neglected the worship of God. They worshiped other gods and behaved in ways that were displeasing to Him. Jeremiah had warned against the consequences of their action, but they refused to listen to him. They did not rely on prayer.

After their punishment, God would deliver them, but they had their own part to play. God demanded total submission from their hearts, just as He does with us today.

God never hides from us; but we don't always see Him because we are not looking for Him. We must find the courage to look away from the problems around us and look toward the solutions to our problems. Jeremiah encouraged the people to walk toward the Lord; their propensity to walk away from God had caused them to fall into captivity. In the midst of our trials and tribulations, we should move closer to God, rather than walking away from Him as though we can find our own way.

### III. Concluding Reflections

When we are in the midst of trouble, it may feel as if we are never going to come out of it. It may appear that we will be captive to our condition forever. However, in God's own time, He brings us through our troubles. That is good news for those who believe; we can look forward to the end of the trouble. We can stand with our heads held high because we know that God will deliver us.

Israel's suffering was a result of their willful rebellion against God. Yet, trials and tribulations are not always an indictment of sin. How we react when we find ourselves in the midst of an uncomfortable situation is an indictment of our character and faith. As we experience difficulties in life our true character is revealed. What do we do when we find ourselves in pain? Will we remain true to our God, or will we succumb to the enemy?

Today's lesson offers us hope in the midst of sorrow and guilt. It lets us know that no matter where we are, God is with us. God is able to work with us in any situation. We must remain cognizant of the fact that God knows our ending and our beginning. By faithfully following God, we are destined for greatness. By walking away from God and wallowing in the waters of despair and depression, we are doomed to destruction.

## WORD POWER

**Know (Hebrew: *Yada*)**—it means "to know for sure, to understand completely." This word "know" (yada), as it is used by God here, means that God alone knows the plans He has in store for His people. False prophets have no knowledge of God's plans.

This Hebrew word could be reserved for God alone. Human beings know in part; God knows (yada) completely.

## HOME DAILY BIBLE READINGS

for the week of July 29, 2007
*Jeremiah Invites Jews in Babylon to Trust God*

July 23, Monday
    —Psalm 145:13b-21
    —The Goodness of the Lord
July 24, Tuesday
    —Jeremiah 30:18-22
    —God Restores
July 25, Wednesday
    —Jeremiah 31:1-9
    —Loved with an Everlasting Love
July 26, Thursday
    —Jeremiah 31:10-14
    —Shepherd of the Flock
July 27, Friday
    —Jeremiah 31:33-37
    —They Shall Be My People
July 28, Saturday
    —Jeremiah 29:1-9
    —Jeremiah Writes the Exiles
July 29, Sunday
    —Jeremiah 29:10-14
    —God's Good Plans

## PRAYER

*Eternal God of heaven, thank You for being a God of direction and deliverance. Grant us the courage to go wherever You direct. Give us the ability to realize that when You allow us to go into situations that appear to be dangerous or detrimental, that You will—in Your own due time—provide a way of escape. In Jesus' name, we pray. Amen.*

August 5, 2007

Lesson 10

# Lamentations Urges Hope in God

**UNIT III**
How Shall We Respond?

**CHILDREN'S UNIT**
What Will We Do?

**ADULT TOPIC:** Maintaining Hope!
**YOUTH TOPIC:** Despair and Hope
**CHILDREN'S TOPIC:** God Receives Our Trust

**KEY VERSE**

It is good that a man should both hope and quietly wait for the salvation of the LORD.
— Lamentations 3:26

**DEVOTIONAL READING:** Psalm 23
**BACKGROUND SCRIPTURE:** 2 Kings 25:1-2, 5-7; Lamentations 3:25-33, 55-58
**PRINT PASSAGE:** Lamentations 3:25-33, 55-58

**OBJECTIVES**

Upon completion of this lesson, the students are expected to:
1. Learn that by faith we must have confidence to hope in God;
2. Discover that God takes pleasure in our desire to be in His presence; and,
3. Recognize that God's goodness shines brightest in the midst of affliction.

### Lamentations 3:25-33, 55-58—KJV

25 The LORD is good unto them that wait for him, to the soul that seeketh him.

26 It is good that a man should both hope and quietly wait for the salvation of the LORD.

27 It is good for a man that he bear the yoke in his youth.

28 He sitteth alone and keepeth silence, because he hath borne it upon him.

29 He putteth his mouth in the dust; if so be there may be hope.

30 He giveth his cheek to him that smiteth him: he is filled full with reproach.

31 For the LORD will not cast off for ever:

32 But though he cause grief, yet will he have compassion according to the multitude of his mercies.

33 For he doth not afflict willingly nor grieve the children of men.

.....

55 I called upon thy name, O LORD, out of the low dungeon.

56 Thou hast heard my voice: hide not thine ear at my breathing, at my cry.

57 Thou drewest near in the day that I called upon thee: thou saidst, Fear not.

58 O LORD, thou hast pleaded the causes of my soul; thou hast redeemed my life.

## UNIFYING LESSON PRINCIPLE

Painful events occur in everyone's life. How are we to respond when such times come to us? The writer of Lamentations says that we have reason to hope in the midst of despair because of God's unfailing love and care. The psalmist makes the same point in Psalm 23.

## POINTS TO BE EMPHASIZED ADULTS /YOUTH

**Adult/Youth Key Verse:**
Lamentations 3:26

**Print Passage:** Lamentations 3:25-33, 55-58

—Lamentations 3:20-21 marks the transition from despair to hope.
—Assurance of divine mercy is given to those who will seek it.
—Even in the depths of despair, the element of hope is present.
—God is not indifferent to our suffering, even if we merit it.

## CHILDREN

**Key Verse:** Psalm 23:4

**Print Passage:** Psalm 23; Lamentations 3:21-25

—The Scripture provides an assurance that God's provisions are recurring.
—God provides for all areas of human need: physical, emotional, social, and the like.
—The greatness of God's power to provide earns our hope and trust.
—God's faithfulness is consistent and motivates one to trust Him.

## TOPICAL OUTLINE OF THE LESSON

I. **INTRODUCTION**
   A. The Meaning of Lamentations
   B. Biblical Background

II. **EXPOSITION AND APPLICATION OF THE SCRIPTURE**
   A. The Reward of Trust
      (Lamentations 3:25-27)
   B. Suffering in Silence
      (Lamentations 3:28-30)
   C. The Mercy of God
      (Lamentations 3:31-33)
   D. Kept by God's Love
      (Lamentations 3:55-58)

III. **CONCLUDING REFLECTIONS**

## I. INTRODUCTION
### A. The Meaning of Lamentations

A lamentation is a wailing expression of sorrow. Such mourning is often a gesture to express deep grief or regret. Jeremiah challenged the elders of the city by saying, "Arise, cry out in the night…lift up thy hands…in the top of every street" (Lamentations 2:19). In the contemporary world, we hardly hear the word lament. We deem ourselves too civilized to grieve openly over situations in the world. In our country, we see our young ones turning away from their Creator, and it does not seem to matter to us.

Judgment as found in Scripture refers to the pronouncement of a formal opinion or decision by human beings, but more often it indicates a calamity sent by God. It is a punishment or a sentence from God as the Judge of all. God is going to judge us all one day. There are all sorts of Bible teachers who assert that there is no day of judgment—and many people have been influenced by them. However, the Bible teaches us, "And as it is appointed unto men once to die, but after this the judgment" (Hebrews 9:27).

Hope is not merely expectation and desire; rather, it is a confident assurance about unseen things (1 Peter 3:15). It is a gift of the holy God—God being the source of that hope. In the Lamentations of Jeremiah, hope was held high. Jeremiah knew that God would eventually bring His people back to their homeland. As he consoled the people, he consoled himself as well (see Lamentations 3:26).

Trust is confidence and reliance that good qualities, especially fairness, truth, and honor, will prevail. When our faith becomes weak, we can maintain trust in God because we have confidence, based on what God has done in the past and on what God will do in the future.

Mercy is compassion. It is one of the cardinal virtues of a true Christian and is one of the determinants of God's treatment towards us (see Matthew 5:7).

Love is an attribute of God. It is an earnest desire for an active and beneficent interest in the well-being of the one loved. It causes individuals and nations to act fairly with integrity and forgiveness. Biblically, it calls us to live out the image of God for which we were created.

### B. Biblical Background

This book, written by the prophet Jeremiah, is a sequel to the book of Jeremiah. This smaller book of prophecy reveals the pain and anguish Jeremiah experienced when he saw the beautiful Jerusalem tumbling down, and the temple being completely burned to ashes. The book of Lamentations is comprised of five poems regarding the desolation that seized the Holy City in 586 B.C. It mourns not only the destruction of Jerusalem but also the condition of its inhabitants. There is a poignant confession of sin on behalf of the people and their leaders that acknowledges complex submission to the divine will of God. Petitions are offered for God to again show them favor and restore them to a right relationship with Him.

The destruction of Jerusalem's walls was a final act of humiliation for the inhabitants. In biblical times, a city without walls was doomed, having protection from neither animals nor enemy. Second Kings 27 reveals that King Nebuchadnezzar had ruled Babylon for nine years when he and his entire army came against King Zedekiah of Jerusalem in battle. The city of Jerusalem remained under siege for nearly two years, which was the eleventh year of King Zedekiah's reign. King Nebuchadnezzar's army did not fight and retreat; they stayed in Jerusalem and built forts around the capital city. Judea fell to the Chaldeans in 586 B.C. Sadly, God had sent numerous prophets to warn the people of such a fate and His impending judgment if they did not repent. They did not repent and had to suffer the consequences of their rebellion.

When the Chaldean army pursued and overtook King Zedekiah of Jerusalem in the plains of Jericho, all of King Zedekiah's army was scattered. Therefore, it was quite easy for the Chaldeans to capture King Zedekiah. The enemy judged him, and King Nebuchadnezzar passed sentence on him. As we have seen in our previous text, not only did he come under judgment, but his sons were punished also. Nebuchadnezzar's men plucked out King Zedekiah's eyes after he watched the slaying of his sons. At this, the foretold prophesy of Jeremiah 34:3 and Ezekiel 12:13 had been fulfilled.

## II. Exposition and Application of the Scripture
### A. The Reward of Trust
(Lamentations 3:25-27)

**The Lord is good unto them that wait for him, to the soul that seeketh him. It is good that a man should both hope and quietly wait for the salvation of the Lord. It is good for a man that he bear the yoke in his youth.**

Jeremiah, the author of Lamentations, was a teenager when God called him to be a prophet. In the original Hebrew text, lamentations means "beating the breast" or "playing an instrument." Merriam-Webster's Collegiate Dictionary defines Lamentations as a poetic book about the fall of Jerusalem in Jewish and Christian Scripture. It defines the root word lament as a grief-stricken cry. Jeremiah is known as "the weeping prophet" as he was well-acquainted with grief. He was given the vision of the kingdom of Judah being captured and scattered. Due to this foreknowledge, many times Jeremiah had to deliver the message of what was considered "doom and gloom" to the rebellious people of Jerusalem. Despite his ominous prophesies, Jeremiah did not lose hope. He was not angry at God for calling him at such a young age to be a prophet to the nations. Jeremiah's sorrow was not personal; he grieved over the people's steadfast rebellion against God and their worship of idol gods. He was a true intercessor; he continually prayed for the people. Since he felt this was not a burden, he was willing to do whatever was necessary to move the people from hardheartedness to righteousness.

Jeremiah's stance and confession was, "The Lord is good unto them that wait for him, to the soul that seeketh him" (verse 25). He thought it was appropriate for people to have both expectation and hope. One must have confidence to hope in God (Hebrews 10:35). Hope is akin to faith. Hope is expectation for the unseen. It is a cherished expectation of fulfillment. Jeremiah expected the people to hear his prophesy and be convicted in their hearts. He believed that they would abandon their ways and wholeheartedly turn back to God. Jeremiah is seen as an encourager. He tells us that it is good that a man bear the yoke while he is young. This may have been his rationalization that sustained him when God called him into ministry at such a young age. Many would describe this as "taking his childhood away." Instead, Jeremiah considered that it was good to be yoked with God early in life and encouraged the captives to see their plight as early labor for their eventual release in the "evening." He waited quietly for the salvation of the Lord (Lamentations 3:26-27).

To wait on the Lord during an extreme situation is a mark of strong belief in the existence of God. God is unseen, but God's activities are obvious to believers. When Jeremiah saw the devastation that brought down Judah, his strong conviction was realized that the only course of action for people was to hope in God. Actually, the word "wait" is in the imperative, meaning it was a command. God's people were commanded to wait, because Jeremiah knew that God eventually would give them the plan of final restoration. To "wait" in this context suggests silence and lack of complaint.

### B. Suffering in Silence
(Lamentations 3:28-30)

**He sitteth alone and keepeth silence, because he hath borne it upon him. He putteth his mouth in the dust; if so be there may be hope. He giveth his cheek to him that smiteth him: he is filled full with reproach.**

We see here that Jeremiah was patient under the yoke God placed on him. Jeremiah learned the lesson of resignation, but not as a powerless man. Rather, his hope was in God—who brought about the burden. To bear a burden alone is to submit to the will of the almighty God. Jeremiah knew the Source of the burden, and for that reason he put his mouth in the dust. "[M]outh in the dust" is an attitude of humble submission to the strokes of God. He believed hope was on the horizon. Many people today are patient when they know that their punishment is from God, but when another human being wrongs them, they take it to heart. However, as one waits for the salvation of the Lord, a person must be able to withstand the reproach of others. For example, we see Jeremiah assuming a meek posture. Strength comes when one goes to God alone in silence. One is then able to understand that God will not put more on a person than he or she can bear. The Amplified Bible records that God had laid the yoke upon Jeremiah for his benefit. Romans 8:28 reads, "And we know that all things work together for good to them that love God, to them who are the called according to his purpose."

Just as Jesus Christ suffered in silence on the cross at Calvary, Jeremiah suffered reproach and shame silently. One is able to accept reproach when one spends time in intimate prayer with God. There is no record that Jeremiah complained to others regarding the burden the Lord laid on him. He knew that his yoke was of God. Rather than complain against the plans and purposes of God, he put his "mouth in the dust" (Lamentations 3:29).

Jeremiah was not hidden alone in the desert; he was among his family, friends, and even his enemies. Verse 30 reads that Jeremiah gave his cheek to the smiter and was filled with insults. He was filled with reproach and smitten because the people did not want to submit to holiness. Jeremiah was living his life in the fear of the Lord; he was working and interceding for his family and countrymen who had gone back and ignored the knowledge of God. He remained steadfast in prayer—weeping, working, and interceding to God, because he never let go of hope. He continued to hope and expect that the people would someday return to God.

### C. The Mercy of God
(Lamentations 3:31-33)

**For the Lord will not cast off for ever: But though he cause grief, yet will he have compassion according to the multitude of his mercies. For he doth not afflict willingly nor grieve the children of men.**

God is full of mercy and compassion. The weeping prophet Jeremiah had already given assurance in Lamentations 3:23 that

God's mercies are new every morning, and great is His faithfulness. Moreover, it is because of the Lord's mercies that we are not consumed; His compassion does not fail (verse 22). The reason for his resignation—as pointed out in the former section—is made plain here. "[T]he Lord will not cast off for ever." God does not from His heart afflict His creatures. He takes no delight in our pain and misery. Good, earthly parents do not willingly inflict pain on their children, even when the children are stubborn or rebellious. God, as our heavenly Father, knows better than we do, and His love is everlasting.

God is always calling to the unsaved; He calls them to salvation. He calls the saved to have a more intimate relationship with Him. It is only human for us to fret in the time of crisis, but we cannot get stuck in that mindset and allow fear, anxiety, and doubt to dominate us and cripple our faith. Jesus understood these emotions when He told His disciples that He would send the Holy Spirit to be with them. Those who feel alone can take assurance in knowing that God is beside them always.

Jeremiah tells us that God will not cast us aside forever. He will not abandon His heritage (see Psalm 94:14). He takes pleasure in our desire to be in His presence. He invites us to come and learn of Him. God is a God of love, mercy, and justice. Although He chastises us when we are disobedient, He welcomes us back to Him. God's mercy is tender. He is moved with compassion and remembers that we are weak. Jesus said that "I and the Father are one. When you have seen me you have seen the Father." At the death of Lazarus, it is recorded: "Jesus wept" (John 11:35). This is an indication that God mourns with us when our loved ones depart. We must trust God in our times of loneliness and sorrow.

### D. Kept by God's Love
*(Lamentations 3:55-58)*

**I called upon thy name, O LORD, out of the low dungeon. Thou hast heard my voice: hide not thine ear at my breathing, at my cry. Thou drewest near in the day that I called upon thee: thou saidst, Fear not. O Lord, thou hast pleaded the causes of my soul; thou hast redeemed my life.**

Verse 55 of our text reads, "out of the low dungeon." The dungeon is found in Jeremiah 38:6: "They let down Jeremiah with cords…there was no water, but mire." Yet, Jeremiah had confidence in God. In the midst of persecution, he remained confident that God was his stronghold, and that God would keep him. Jeremiah had struggled with faith, fear, and hope; fortunately, faith won out. God heard his prayer and emphatically answered "Fear not."

God's goodness shines brightest in the midst of affliction. God did not abandon Jeremiah in the dry well. Ebed-melech heard about the harsh treatment of Jeremiah and took his case to the king—and the king ordered Jeremiah to be taken out of the well (see Jeremiah 38:7-12). When a person follows King David's example and proclaims the Lord his Shepherd, that person can even walk close to death and fear no evil. God does not give us the spirit of fear; He gives us love and sound minds (2 Timothy 1:7). Though Jeremiah was sorrowful, he did not cease to pray.

## III. Concluding Reflections

Because of the mobility of our culture, many people find themselves living apart from their families. This has caused some to feel a deep sense of isolation. Like Jeremiah, we must know that God is always present and can be called upon at any time. We should never blame God for our grief and pain, though He is compassionate and understands when we do. Rather, like Jeremiah, we must examine our circumstances to determine whether God is trying to discipline us to draw us closer to Him.

Jeremiah did not blame God for the demise of Jerusalem and the inhabitants or the temple; rather, he blamed his own people. He said, "Let us search and try our ways, and turn again to the LORD" (Lamentations 3:40). Some theologians contend that persons are continuously plagued with tribulations until they learn the spiritual lesson those situations are designed to teach. Once learned, we can readily go from despair to hope.

No matter what choices we make in life, it is comforting to know that God's love remains constant and reliable. He is always sympathetic and responsive to our suffering. The blessings of God never run out. However, we must constantly be on the alert so that we do not run into sin. The God of mercy is also the God of justice, and He hates sin but loves a repentant sinner.

## WORD POWER

**Wait (Hebrew: *duwmam*)**—it means "to be in silent expectation, and to be quiet under afflictions." It involves resting and meditating in the promises of God. This waiting is the believer's heart attitude. To wait is to believe that God is going to carry out what He has promised. In the context of this lesson, Jeremiah admonished the captives to patiently bear the brunt of the oppressors' burdens and repose themselves in almighty God.

## HOME DAILY BIBLE READINGS

for the week of August 5, 2007
*Lamentations Urges Hope in God*

July 30, Monday
　—Isaiah 30:15-19
　—Promise of Deliverance
July 31, Tuesday
　—2 Kings 25:1-2, 5-7
　—Jerusalem Destroyed
Aug. 1, Wednesday
　—Psalm 33:12-22
　—God Is Our Hope
Aug. 2, Thursday
　—Psalm 130
　—My Soul Waits
Aug. 3, Friday
　—Lamentations 3:19-24
　—God Is Faithful
Aug. 4, Saturday
　—Lamentations 3:25-33
　—Wait for the Lord
Aug. 5, Sunday
　—Lamentations 3:55-59
　—God Hears My Plea

## PRAYER

*God, we thank You for reminding us of Your steadfast love. When we are in despair You are our source of hope. When pursued by enemies, teach us to quietly wait and see Your salvation. Make us mindful that we are never alone and that You are a deliverer of those who diligently seek You. In Jesus' name, we pray. Amen.*

## Lesson 11

# Ezekiel Preaches About Individual Responsibility

**ADULT TOPIC:** Personal Consequences of Sin!
**YOUTH TOPIC:** Turn and Live!
**CHILDREN'S TOPIC:** God Wants Responsible Actions

---

**DEVOTIONAL READING:** Psalm 18:20-24
**BACKGROUND SCRIPTURE:** Ezekiel 18
**PRINT PASSAGE:** Ezekiel 18:4, 20-23, 30-32

### Ezekiel 18:4, 20-23, 30-32—KJV

4 Behold, all souls are mine; as the soul of the father, so also the soul of the son is mine: the soul that sinneth, it shall die.

· · · · ·

20 The soul that sinneth, it shall die. The son shall not bear the iniquity of the father, neither shall the father bear the iniquity of the son: the righteousness of the righteous shall be upon him, and the wickedness of the wicked shall be upon him.

21 But if the wicked will turn from all his sins that he hath committed, and keep all my statutes, and do that which is lawful and right, he shall surely live, he shall not die.

22 All his transgressions that he hath committed, they shall not be mentioned unto him: in his righteousness that he hath done he shall live.

23 Have I any pleasure at all that the wicked should die? saith the Lord GOD: and not that he should return from his ways, and live?

· · · · ·

30 Therefore I will judge you, O house of Israel, every one according to his ways, saith the Lord GOD. Repent, and turn yourselves from all your transgressions; so iniquity shall not be your ruin.

31 Cast away from you all your transgressions, whereby ye have transgressed; and make you a new heart and a new spirit: for why will ye die, O house of Israel?

---

**August 12, 2007**

**UNIT III**
How Shall We Respond?

**CHILDREN'S UNIT**
What Will We Do?

**KEY VERSE**

For I have no pleasure in the death of him that dieth, saith the Lord GOD: wherefore turn yourselves, and live ye.
—Ezekiel 18:32

**OBJECTIVES**

Upon completion of this lesson, the students are expected to:
1. Recognize that each of us has our own ethical responsibility;
2. Learn that God desires that all turn away from their wicked ways and live in the fullness of Him; and,
3. Understand that only God can give a person a new heart.

**32** For I have no pleasure in the death of him that dieth, saith the Lord God: wherefore turn yourselves, and live ye.

## UNIFYING LESSON PRINCIPLE

Some people do not take responsibility for their actions; they seek to blame others instead. To what extent are we accountable for what we do? Ezekiel says that each of us is responsible for our own deeds.

## POINTS TO BE EMPHASIZED
### ADULTS /YOUTH
**Adult/Youth Key Verse:** Ezekiel 18:32
**Print Passage**: Ezekiel 18:4, 20-23, 30-32
—Ezekiel's argument was that the exiles could not change what their parents had done, even though the consequences of their parents' sin had been visited on them.
—Instead of complaining about suffering, the exiles need to examine their own conduct and see how their sins were contributing to their suffering.
—Although Ezekiel recognizes the validity of corporate guilt, his emphasis was on individual, personal guilt and responsibility.
—Ezekiel is concerned with righteousness and propriety and purity and holiness among the prophets and priests.
—Ezekiel's message was directed to both those who are with him in exile and those who remained in Judah.
—The glory of the Lord had departed from the Temple because of defilement. Once the defilement was removed, a new Temple with new regulations would provide the focus for a restored Israel.

—While there is justice for the individual person, provisions for unlimited liability of covenant punishment extends well beyond the individual violating a stipulation—"to the third and fourth generation."

### CHILDREN
**Key Verse:** Ezekiel 18:30
**Print Passage:** Ezekiel 18:1-5, 7-13, 19-20
—God looks at the behavior of individual persons.
—God does not hold children responsible for the things that their parents do.
—Scripture lets us know that a person is responsible for his or her own wickedness.
—Scripture tells us what is right for us in the sight of God.

## TOPICAL OUTLINE OF THE LESSON
  I. INTRODUCTION
     A. The Meaning of Responsibility
     B. Biblical Background

  II. EXPOSITION AND APPLICATION OF THE SCRIPTURE
     A. A Stern Warning *(Ezekiel 18:4)*
     B. Individual Responsibility *(Ezekiel 18:20-23)*
     C. Turn and Live *(Ezekiel 18:30-32)*

III. CONCLUDING REFLECTIONS

## I. INTRODUCTION
### A. The Meaning of Responsibility

Theologian H. Richard Niebuhr, in *The Responsible Self* (New York: Harper and Row, 1963), wrote: "A responsible person does not only act, but thinks about the consequences of his actions before he does them." Responsibility involves the capacity to make both ethical and moral decisions.

Few people seem willing to accept responsibility for their own behavioral choices. In the 1950s, psychologist Stanton Samenow and psychiatrist Samuel Yochelson shared the conventional wisdom that the tendency toward criminal behavior is rooted in one's environment. The men set out to prove their point by undertaking a seventeen-year study involving thousands of hours of clinical testing of 250 prison inmates. To their astonishment, they discovered that the cause of crime cannot be directly linked to environment, poverty, or oppression. Instead, crime is the result of individuals making wrong moral choices. In 1987, Harvard professors James Q. Wilson and Richard J. Herrnstein came to similar conclusions in their book *Crime and Human Nature* (Free Press). They determined that the cause of crime is a lack of proper moral training among young people during the morally formative years, particularly ages one to six.[1]

God does not blame the innocent but definitely does not allow the guilty to go free. Can one generation affect the other? Yes! But this was not Israel's problem. God admonished them to assume responsibility for their own spiritual immorality.

## B. Biblical Background

The name Ezekiel means "God strengthens." This prophet was the son of Zadok and was a young man when he was deported to Babylon in 597 B.C. He received his calling to become a prophet while in exile, and that is why Bible scholars refer to him as an exilic prophet. Ezekiel functioned as both a prophet and a priest to the Hebrew people in exile, as well as to those who were still in Judea. His name, "God strengthens," testifies to his character. He was one of the major prophets of the Old Testament, along with Isaiah, Jeremiah, and Daniel. Ezekiel was concerned with both prophetic issues and priestly issues: righteousness, religious propriety, purity, and holiness.

The historical context of Ezekiel chapter 18 starts to unfold in 609 B.C., with an event that took place in 2 Kings 23:28-29. Pharaoh Neco of Egypt had killed Josiah when they met at Megiddo. Egypt ruled Judah for about four years until it was defeated at Carchemish by the Babylonian king, Nebuchadnezzar, in 605 B.C., and many Jews were taken into exile.

Ezekiel directed his message to the Jews in Babylon, warning them of God's judgment for their sin and rebellion. Under the leadership of several evil kings, Judah had deserted the Lord, had begun worshiping foreign gods, and had defiled the temple. Ezekiel foresaw the destruction of Jerusalem and its temple. His message was harsh at times, but it was given with the hope that the people would be delivered from evil and restored to God.

To a nation that had abandoned their God and given themselves to the idols of foreign nations, Ezekiel had one central message, which he repeated seventy times: "And you shall know that I am the LORD" (Ezekiel 6:13, NRSV). Ezekiel called the

---

[1] From *Christianity Today*, "Environment or Choice," August 16, 1993, p. 30.

people to repentance. The Israelites, however, were not the sole focus of his prophecies. Ezekiel also addressed surrounding nations that ravaged and ransacked Israel. Further, the book of Ezekiel consists of several messages that were enhanced by Ezekiel's visions.

As this lesson opens, the Israelites had tried to abdicate their responsibility for moral living and for the immoral choices that they had made by relying on an old, worn proverb. They wanted to rid themselves of guilt by blaming their ancestors for the predicament in which they found themselves—living in exile. They said, "The fathers have eaten sour grapes, and the children's teeth are set on edge" (Ezekiel 18:2). They used this to rationalize what they thought was God's unfair practice. They placed the blame for their predicament on their ancestors' wrongdoings.

The entire eighteenth chapter of Ezekiel is a diatribe against their way of thinking.

## II. Exposition and Application of the Scripture
### A. A Stern Warning *(Ezekiel 18:4)*

**Behold, all souls are mine; as the soul of the father, so also the soul of the son is mine: the soul that sinneth, it shall die.**

In verse 4, God emphasizes that He is the Creator of all flesh, and will deal accordingly with the whole. We should never think that our existence on earth is by chance, as some people have claimed. A human life is not a product of random selection; God is the Creator of all. He has a purpose for every person He has made. As the Creator, He has the absolute right to deal with us as He wishes.

A prayer of John Wesley echoes the understanding that we belong to our Creator and not to ourselves: "I am no longer my own, but yours. Put me to what you will, rank me with whom you will; put me to doing, put me to suffering; let me be employed for you or laid aside for you, exalted for you or brought low for you; let me be full, let me be empty; let me have all things, let me have nothing; I freely and heartily yield all things to your pleasure and disposal."

Every living soul belongs to God the Father, as well as to the Son. God will not punish a righteous person. God is not blind or unjust; God judges justly. Very few people seem willing to accept responsibility for their actions; it is easy to blame others. This is not to say that there are not situations where persons have been harmed because of the acts of another in a previous generation (i.e., drug addiction, alcoholism, abuse, and so forth).

God says that no one will die for another's crimes and no one will be saved by another's righteousness. Though we inherited our sinful nature, and God is aware of that, there is a point at which the individual must begin to take personal responsibility for sinful and careless actions. Ironically, many who blame their troubles on a former generation are less anxious to give credit to someone else's righteousness when they receive blessings. God says that each of us has our own ethical responsibility. The past does not determine our future, and our future is not locked into the present.

### B. Individual Responsibility *(Ezekiel 18:20-23)*

**The soul that sinneth, it shall die. The**

son shall not bear the iniquity of the father, neither shall the father bear the iniquity of the son: the righteousness of the righteous shall be upon him, and the wickedness of the wicked shall be upon him. But if the wicked will turn from all his sins that he hath committed, and keep all my statutes, and do that which is lawful and right, he shall surely live, he shall not die. All his transgressions that he hath committed, they shall not be mentioned unto him: in his righteousness that he hath done he shall live. Have I any pleasure at all that the wicked should die? saith the Lord GOD: and not that he should return from his ways, and live?

In litigation language, we often hear the phrase "burden of proof." This concept is the crux of this section. Ezekiel taught that each person must take responsibility for his or her own actions. There should be no blame shifting. There is a natural tendency for children to follow the lifestyle of their parents and share in the parents' troubles. Sadam Hussein was toppled from the highest position of authority in his country and his sons suffered violent deaths. Evidence has revealed that all of them were commonly engaged in heinous and inhumane activity. Apparently, Hussein's sons had observed his behavior and had been raised to believe that they could act without retribution. But each of the sons made a choice regarding his actions. Children will not bear the guilt of their parents; conversely, neither will the parents bear the guilt of their children. The soul that sins will be punished. The righteous will be rewarded with good and the wicked will get their "just desserts" in evil. The Lord, however, does not take pleasure in punishing the wicked and does not want them to die. Everyone must bear his or her own burden of responsibility for personal choices made.

God desires that all people turn away from their wicked ways and live. God abhors transgression. A "transgression" is a rebellion or a trespass. *Pesha* is the Hebrew word for *transgression,* which means "to revolt," "to rebel," and "to trespass." Whether used as a noun or verb, "trespass" has to do with revolting against the law. The people to whom Ezekiel spoke had rebelled against the Word of God. Despite their willful rebellion, the Israelites wanted to make excuses for their sins so that they did not have to be held accountable. They believed that righteousness was unattainable and that they were destined to lead lives of sin. But the opposite was true, both then and today. We can choose righteousness. God gives us freedom to choose life or death. To hold on to the "sour grape" mentality is to be perpetually held captive to sin and stifles one's desire to live a righteous life. Such a stance automatically condemns people to death. The people of God must be willing to examine their own conduct and see how their own sins have contributed to their suffering.

### C. Turn and Live *(Ezekiel 18:30-32)*

**Therefore I will judge you, O house of Israel, every one according to his ways, saith the Lord GOD. Repent, and turn yourselves from all your transgressions; so iniquity shall not be your ruin. Cast away from you all your transgressions, whereby ye have transgressed; and make you a new heart and a new spirit: for why will ye die, O house of Israel? For I have no pleasure in the death of him that dieth, saith the Lord GOD: wherefore turn yourselves, and live ye.**

The love of God is always manifested through His words. Here, we see God issuing a warning before judgment falls. The judgment would not be sudden so that the people could accuse God of inconsiderate judgment. He tells them not to assume that there will be corporate or group judgment; rather, every individual would bear the brunt of his or her sins. The first statement is a declaration: "I will judge you." The judgment might be reversed, however, based on certain conditions, like repentance and turning away from sin. It is one thing to repent, and another thing to turn to God wholeheartedly. The people must also cast away their transgressions. To "cast away" is to throw away an object with the mindset of not getting it back. Also, the people were implored to wear new hearts. David prayed in Psalm 51:10, "Create in me a clean heart, O God; and renew a right spirit within me." Finally, God says: "I have no pleasure in the death of him that dieth" (verse 32). This means that God is not pleased when a sinner dies in his or her sins. The final appeal is, "Turn yourselves, and live ye" (verse 32). The verb "turn" is in the imperative mood here, which means this is not an advisement but a command—a command from a loving heart.

God wants us all to live. This, however, necessitates that we abandon our sinful ways. If we contend that we are all born by sin into sin, then we know that to change from sin requires a power beyond us. Henri J. M. Nouwen, in *The Way of the Heart* (Seabury Press, 1981), states, "We are speaking about a mystery for which words are inadequate….It is a mystery that God transforms the heart, which is the center of our being, into His own heart, a heart large enough to embrace the entire universe. Through prayer we can carry in our hearts all human pain and sorrow, all conflicts and agonies, all torture and war, all hunger, loneliness, and misery, not because of some great psychological or emotional capacity, but because God's heart has become one with ours." Only God can give us new hearts. But we must make the choice to turn away from sin and rid ourselves of the offenses that we have committed.

When God gives us new hearts and new spirits, we cease being part of the "living dead." We will not die but live. Death is the consequence of sin. Too many people are part of the living dead because they are riddled with sin.

### III. Concluding Reflections

A few decades ago, comedian Flip Wilson popularized a female character named Geraldine who was fond of saying, "The devil made me do it." It is convenient to have someone to blame for our misdeeds. But does the devil really cause our actions, or do we simply choose of our own volition to do wrong?

Saying "the fathers have eaten sour grapes and the children's teeth are set on edge" (Ezekiel 18:2) was the Israelites' way of avoiding responsibility for their own sins. Their mindset reflected an incorrect idea about the goodness of God. Ezekiel came and gave the people both a warning and hope. He told them to repent and live because God is on the side of the righteous and on the side of creation in general.

God does not blame the innocent but definitely does not allow the guilty to go free. Can one generation affect another? Yes! The eighteenth chapter of Ezekiel reveals that God heard this proverb expounded by Israel over time and did not want to continue hearing it. God said this saying did not apply to the Israelites in exile; their interpretation of the proverb was not accurate. God admonished them to assume responsibility for their own spiritual immorality.

One major fact stands out in the Key Verse and calls for our attention. God's statement that He has no pleasure in the death of anyone should give comfort to every child of God. God will give enough time and opportunities for people to return to Him. The death of a wicked individual is painful to the Lord. By contrast, the psalmist reminds us that "precious in the sight of the LORD is the death of His saints" (Psalm 116:15). In other words, God is happy to receive His righteous children when they die.

Taking personal responsibility was and is necessary in people's lives—particularly those who have claimed to have an encounter with the Lord Jesus Christ. Paul says, "If any man be in Christ, he is a new creature: old things are passed away; behold, all things are become new" (2 Corinthians 5:17).

## WORD POWER

**Turn (Hebrew: *shuwb*)**—it is used in a commanding tone, having military connotations, like a superior officer commanding the others under him to carry out an order. God issued an order to His people, commanding them to return. This word, *shuwb*, belongs to a stem in Hebrew which means "They have all it takes within them to carry out His order."

## HOME DAILY BIBLE READINGS

for the week of August 12, 2007
*Ezekiel Preaches About Individual Responsibility*

Aug. 6, Monday
—1 Timothy 2:1-6
—One God and One Mediator
Aug. 7, Tuesday
—Psalm 18:20-24
—God Rewards the Righteous
Aug. 8, Wednesday
—Ezekiel 33:12–20
—God Judges Each One's Ways
Aug. 9, Thursday
—Ezekiel 18:1-4
—Those Who Sin Will Die
Aug. 10, Friday
—Ezekiel 18:5-9
—The Righteous Will Live
Aug. 11, Saturday
—Ezekiel 18:19-23
—Those Who Repent Will Live
Aug. 12, Sunday
—Ezekiel 18:25-32
—God Judges Each of Us

## PRAYER

*Eternal God, our Father, develop clean hearts in us. Open our eyes to see our own faults and shortcomings. Strengthen us to accept our own responsibility for righteous living. We repent of our wrongdoings and commit our lives anew to Your way. Teach us to follow righteousness and mercy that we may find life. In Jesus' name, we pray. Amen.*

**August 19, 2007**

Lesson 12

**UNIT III**
How Shall We Respond?

**CHILDREN'S UNIT**
What Will We Do?

# Zechariah Calls for a Return to God

**KEY VERSE**

Therefore say thou unto them, Thus saith the LORD of hosts; Turn ye unto me, saith the LORD of hosts, and I will turn unto you, saith the LORD of hosts.
—Zechariah 1:3

**ADULT TOPIC:** Call for Repentance
**YOUTH TOPIC:** Grow Up, Take Responsibility, and Speak the Truth
**CHILDREN'S TOPIC:** God Promises to Restore

**DEVOTIONAL READING:** Isaiah 12
**BACKGROUND SCRIPTURE:** Zechariah 1:1-6; 7:8-14; 8:16-17, 20-21, 23
**PRINT PASSAGE:** Zechariah 1:1-6; 7:8-14

**OBJECTIVES**

Upon completion of this lesson, the students are expected to:

1. Learn that we must take responsibility for our actions in order for God to grant us restoration;
2. Recognize God's promise that if we turn back to Him, He will in turn come back to us; and,
3. Affirm that God can deliver us from the difficulties to show that they will not lead to our demise but contribute to our development.

### Zechariah 1:1-6; 7:8-14—KJV

IN THE eighth month, in the second year of Darius, came the word of the LORD unto Zechariah, the son of Berechiah, the son of Iddo the prophet, saying,

2 The LORD hath been sore displeased with your fathers.

3 Therefore say thou unto them, Thus saith the LORD of hosts; Turn ye unto me, saith the LORD of hosts, and I will turn unto you, saith the LORD of hosts.

4 Be ye not as your fathers, unto whom the former prophets have cried, saying, Thus saith the LORD of hosts; Turn ye now from your evil ways, and from your evil doings: but they did not hear, nor hearken unto me, saith the LORD.

5 Your fathers, where are they? and the prophets, do they live for ever?

6 But my words and my statutes, which I commanded my servants the prophets, did they not take hold of your fathers? and they returned and said, Like as the LORD of hosts thought to do unto us, according to our ways, and according to our doings, so hath he dealt with us.

•••••

8 And the word of the LORD came unto Zechariah, saying,

9 Thus speaketh the LORD of hosts, saying, Execute true judgment, and shew mercy and compassions every man to his brother:

10 And oppress not the widow, nor the fatherless, the stranger, nor the poor; and let none of you imagine evil against his brother in your heart.

11 But they refused to hearken, and pulled away the shoulder, and stopped their ears, that they should not hear.

12 Yea, they made their hearts as an adamant stone, lest they should hear the law, and the words which the LORD of hosts hath sent in his spirit by the former prophets: therefore came a great wrath from the LORD of hosts.

13 Therefore it is come to pass, that as he cried, and they would not hear; so they cried, and I would not hear, saith the LORD of hosts:

14 But I scattered them with a whirlwind among all the nations whom they knew not. Thus the land was desolate after them, that no man passed through nor returned: for they laid the pleasant land desolate.

## UNIFYING LESSON PRINCIPLE

People yearn for wholeness and happiness in their lives. Where do we find such fulfillment? Zechariah says that when we return to the Lord, the wholeness and happiness we will have in God's new age will become available to us now, as well as then.

## POINTS TO BE EMPHASIZED
## ADULTS/YOUTH

**Adult Key Verse:** Zechariah 1:3
**Youth Key Verses**: Zechariah 8:16-17
**Print Passage:** Zechariah 1:1-6; 7:8-14

—Rebuilding of the Temple would allow the restored community of Judah to enjoy the God-given provisions for right relationship and right worship.
—Zechariah as well as Haggai encouraged the reconstruction of the Temple in Jerusalem.
—Zechariah links the salvation of Israel with the return of the Lord.
—The restored community of Judah was to be rooted in justice and truth.

## CHILDREN

**Key Verse:** Zechariah 8:5
**Print Passage:** Zechariah 8:1-8

—The presence of God in our midst makes a difference in our happiness.
—Happiness is not present where God is not present.
—We become faithful and righteous when we live where God abides.
—Zechariah was a prophet selected to deliver a message of hope.

## TOPICAL OUTLINE OF THE LESSON

I. **INTRODUCTION**
   A. I Am Sorry
   B. Biblical Background

II. **EXPOSITION AND APPLICATION OF THE SCRIPTURE**
   A. Zechariah's Exhortation (Zechariah 1:1-2)
   B. Necessary Action (Zechariah 1:3-6)
   C. Reason for Captivity (Zechariah 7:8-14)

III. **CONCLUDING REFLECTIONS**

## I. INTRODUCTION
### A. I Am Sorry

A story is told about a child who was having problems with his father. The father decided to put the child in a closet for a few minutes to see whether his son would admit his mistakes by saying he was sorry. After a little while, the father called the lad to the sitting room and demanded that the son say, "Sorry, Dad." The lad looked at his father and said, "While I was there I used a razor blade to tear your winter coat and, as I stand here, only my head is bent down, but my heart is up!"

The words "I am sorry" seem to be some of the hardest to say. Many people erroneously believe that saying "I'm sorry" is a sign of weakness and vulnerability. However, it takes a strong person to admit fault and apologize for the wrong that he or she has done. Many relationships are broken, many futures are fractured, and many hopes and dreams are damaged because our pride hinders us from admitting that we are wrong and apologizing.

In Christianity, repentance is a prerequisite for entering into a relationship with Jesus Christ. If an individual finds it very difficult to say "I'm sorry," it will be difficult for that person to understand the true meaning of repentance or his or her need for divine forgiveness. What we do on a social level has a correlation to our spiritual lives. If we do not have a loving relationship on the horizontal level, we will not have a good relationship on a vertical level.

The children of Israel, who were at a crossroads in their existence, were returning to their homeland after seventy years of bondage in Babylonian exile, and God wanted to restore them to their past prominence. However, in order for God to restore them to the glory of days gone by, they had to first apologize and repent of their sins.

## B. Biblical Background

Zechariah means "Whom the Lord Remembers," and is one of the most common names in the Bible. There are at least twenty-seven characters in the Bible who bear this name. The Zechariah we are studying about today identifies himself as the son of Berekiah, the son of Iddo (Zechariah 1:1, 7). Like Jeremiah and Ezekiel, Zechariah was also from a priestly lineage. Zechariah was a member of the Great Synagogue, which later developed into the group of ruling elders known as the Sanhedrin Council.

He was born in Babylon and was among the group of exiles who first returned to Jerusalem under the leadership of Zerubbabel and Joshua, the high priest (Nehemiah 12:1, 4). Zechariah's main mission was to call people to repentance and motivate them to rebuild the temple of God. His prophecy is unique in the sense that it emphasizes events connected to the First and Second Advent of Christ. Bible scholars have referred to it as the most messianic book among the prophets.

The prophet Zechariah was a contemporary of the prophet Haggai; they both encouraged the returning exiles to focus on rebuilding the temple. Zechariah was truly a prophet sent by God, because future things were revealed to him. In Zechariah 9:13, Zechariah saw the future prominence of Greece. Moreover, because his ministry started in 520 B.C., Bible scholars believe that he witnessed the important victories gained by Greece over Persia. Because of his messianic emphasis, he helps us as contemporary Christians to look forward to the coming of Jesus Christ.

## II. Exposition and Application of the Scripture
### A. Zechariah's Exhortation (Zechariah 1:1-2)

**In the eighth month, in the second year of Darius, came the word of the Lord unto Zechariah, the son of Berechiah, the son of Iddo the prophet, saying, The Lord hath been sore displeased with your fathers.**

In the eight month, in the second year of Darius (Zechariah 1:1) helps us to understand that Zechariah began to prophesy two months after Haggai did. These two prophets became companions in ministry, and because of that they were able to move the people to action. The Word of the Lord first came to Zechariah. Certainly, he would not have been effective as a prophet if he had not received the message from the Lord. Receiving a word from the Lord authenticated both the prophet and the prophecy.

This was a time of extreme difficulty for the Israelites, who were bewildered about rebuilding the temple. Their captivity had ended. God called His people to repent. God commanded Zechariah to tell the people that there was a reason why they had been in bondage. God had been extremely displeased with their forebears. They had sinned against God and turned their backs on Him; therefore, God had punished them with captivity. This lets us know that there is a judgment for the deeds that we do.

Although God allowed the Israelites to be taken into bondage because of their sins, God was still merciful enough to bring them out of bondage in order to restore them. God warned the present Israelites of the consequences of following in the footsteps of their fathers.

Just as it was in Ezekiel's day, it is now incumbent upon each of us to look critically at the mistakes that were made by our ancestors to avoid repeating them. Zechariah told the Israelites, "The Lord was very angry with your forefathers" (1:2, NIV). No sane generation would deliberately incur the anger and wrath of the Lord. However, the previous generations of Israelites had failed God at every point, despite repeated warnings from prophets.

### B. Necessary Action (Zechariah 1:3-6)

**Therefore say thou unto them, Thus saith the Lord of hosts; Turn ye unto me, saith the Lord of hosts, and I will turn unto you, saith the Lord of hosts. Be ye not as your fathers, unto whom the former prophets have cried, saying, Thus saith the Lord of hosts; Turn ye now from your evil ways, and from your evil doings: but they did not hear, nor hearken unto me, saith the Lord. Your fathers, where are they? and the prophets, do they live for ever? But my words and my statutes, which I commanded my servants the prophets, did they not take hold of your fathers? and they returned and said, Like as the Lord of hosts thought to do unto us, according to our ways, and according to our doings, so hath he dealt with us.**

"Thus saith the Lord of hosts" is a statement of encouragement common to Haggai and Zechariah. It is also an attention-getting statement in the sense that it identifies the source of the word. How encouraging will it be today if ministers of God can identify the source of their messages? We are bombarded today with all kinds of talk shows and self-help books laced with Bible verses quoted out of context. The necessary action is stated here: "Turn ye unto me." This shows that the ability to turn, or return to God, resided in the Israelites, if only they would take this action.

God encouraged Israel by sharing His promise with them that if they turned back to Him, He would in time turn back to them. God had left His people on their own when they decided to turn against Him, and this was the reason why they were experiencing so much turmoil and trouble. God wanted them to understand that if they drew near to Him, they would experience total forgiveness. Being close to God changes us, and inevitably changes our situations and our circumstances. God desired a change in the state of the Israelites; therefore, He called them to draw close to Him.

God then gave them a stern warning. He explained to them that their fathers had paid no attention to the prophets who were sent by God. They had refused to listen to God's prophets. Their blatant disregard for God's Word and warning resulted in years of captivity, frustration, and despair for them. Because the fathers had refused to turn their lives back to God, God had done as God had promised—they were punished for their rebellious attitudes.

Any time we harden our hearts to the Word of God, we are destined for a life of unhappiness. It does not matter whether we like what the prophet (pastor, preacher) is saying; it behooves us to hearken to the Word of the Lord. There we find mercy and salvation if we turn to Him.

As believers, we must acknowledge the power of repentance. Our repentance allows God to wipe our slates clean and gives us another chance. God can work more easily with a person who is wrong and willing to repent than a person who is wrong and remains adamant in his or her wrongdoings. Once we repent, we can then take responsibility for our actions.

Too many people have the propensity to blame their mistakes and wrongdoings on someone or something else. We must take responsibility for our actions in order for God to grant us absolution and restoration. God has the ability and the willingness to restore us, to rebuild us—to bring us back to the place of goodness that we have rejected.

## C. Reason for Captivity
*(Zechariah 7:8-14)*

**And the word of the Lord came unto Zechariah, saying, Thus speaketh the Lord of hosts, saying, Execute true judgment, and show mercy and compassions every man to his brother: And oppress not the widow, nor the fatherless, the stranger, nor the poor; and let none of you imagine evil against his brother in your heart. But they refused to hearken, and pulled away the shoulder, and stopped their ears, that they should not hear. Yea, they made their hearts as an adamant stone, lest they should hear the law, and the words which the Lord of hosts hath sent in his spirit by the former prophets: therefore came a great wrath from the Lord of hosts. Therefore it is come to pass, that as he cried, and they would not hear; so they cried, and I would not hear, saith the Lord of hosts: But I scattered them with a whirlwind among all the nations whom they knew not. Thus the land was desolate after them, that no man passed through nor returned: for they laid the pleasant land desolate.**

Zechariah was not ignorant as to what led to Israel's captivity. "[T]he word of the Lord came to him," perhaps as he was reflecting over the plight of the captives. Having been told the reasons for their captivity, Zechariah reminded the people of the way their forebears practiced their religion but failed to obey God's Word. God was, and still is, concerned with the plight of the poor, the widows, the orphans, and the strangers. The Israelites' "religion" was beautiful outside—a façade that masked their ugly inward hearts. Through His prophets, God commanded the people to practice justice, but the leaders were exploitative for personal gain. The rulers of the nation had ignored the Law of Moses and had no compassion toward the less fortunate. Today, as in Zechariah's day, God was not and is not as interested in our sacrifices as He is in our obedience.

The danger of tradition is that it can quickly come to rule us. "Tradition is the living faith of the dead," wrote theologian Jerislav Pelikan, and "traditionalism is the dead faith of the living." Traditionalism dictates that we subscribe to regimented outward motions, with no inward change in our hearts. It refers to being part of a religious event, but failing to have a spiritual experience. The children of Israel became so obsessed with their vain tricks and traditions that they refused to listen to the voice of God and simply shrugged their shoulders and stopped their ears. God's commandments did not matter to them; they were only concerned with doing what they had always done.

Today, we often fall into the same tragic traps of following traditions; we do not follow the Spirit of God, but, rather, do what we have always done. Someone once said, "If you do what you've always done, you are going to get what you've always gotten." Tradition has its place and is necessary; however, when it becomes a stumbling block to serving the Lord, it is time to let go. God does not change, but God changes things. Through God's Word, with faith and obedience on our side we can help others change their lives for the better. Through God's Word, captives can be set free; and through God's Word, people's circumstances may get better.

Often, God has to get our attention and bring us back to His fold by allowing us to experience suffering. Israel had drifted so far away from God that He had no recourse other than to scatter them among all the nations like a whirlwind would. God had to take them out of their comfort zone and make them uncomfortable in order to turn them from their wicked ways. What often appear to be trials and tribulations in our lives are actually blessings in disguise. Very often, God literally has to save us from ourselves. He may accomplish this task by placing us in uncomfortable situations and then bringing our repentant souls out of these situations with His grace and mercy.

### III. CONCLUDING REFLECTIONS

We sometimes find ourselves dealing with difficulties that appear to be leading to a bad ending. But many times when God delivers us from these difficulties, we find that the situation did not lead to our demise, but, rather, contributed to our development as people of God. In His infinite wisdom and knowledge, God will sometimes allow us to get into a situation that looks like a mess on one side, but becomes a miracle on the other side. We have learned from our lesson today that when we repent and are remorseful for our sins and shortcomings, God has the ability to bless us and allow us to be a blessing to others.

What is repentance? It is turning away from sin, rebellion, and disobedience, and turning to God saying, "Here I am." A classic example of true repentance is that of King David, which is recorded in Psalm 51. David realized that he had sinned against Uriah, against Bathsheba, against his community, and, ultimately, against God. In the New Testament, we see John the Baptist calling people to repent and return to God (Matthew 3:8). In the ministry of Jesus, repentance played an important role. The only condition for entering into the kingdom of God is repentance and faith in Jesus Christ (see Matthew 18:3). "Unless you repent, you will all perish as they did" (Luke 13:3, NRSV). After Jesus ascended to heaven, the disciples continued His message of repentance and faith. Repentance is not a doctrine that should be relegated to the back burner of any church life. It must be a central part of the preaching ministry and should be taught quite often.

## WORD POWER

**Hosts (Hebrew:** *tsaba*)—refers to an organized army that is always on errands for God. Contextually, this word was appropriate, since the Israelites were still under bondage. However, the Lord of Hosts (tsaba) commanded them to return, and He too would return with hosts of heaven to destroy their captors. God promised them that He would return if they returned to Him.

## HOME DAILY BIBLE READINGS

for the week of August 19, 2007
*Zechariah Calls for a Return to God*

Aug. 13, Monday
 —James 4:6-10
 —How to Return to God
Aug. 14, Tuesday
 —Psalm 103:8-18
 —God's Everlasting Love
Aug. 15, Wednesday
 —Isaiah 12
 —God Is My Salvation
Aug. 16, Thursday
 —Zechariah 1:1-6
 —Return to God
Aug. 17, Friday
 —Zechariah 7:8-14
 —The People Refuse God
Aug. 18, Saturday
 —Zechariah 8:1-8
 —Divine Deliverance for God's People
Aug. 19, Sunday
 —Zechariah 8:14-17, 20-23
 —Seek the Lord

## PRAYER

*God of our past and of our future, we thank You for Your loving-kindness and grace that has brought us from days gone by en route to days to come. We acknowledge our sins and transgressions against Thee and Thee alone; we request Your forgiveness and Your mercy. Allow us another opportunity to become the people that You pre-ordained us to be through Your Son, Jesus the Christ. In Jesus' name, we pray. Amen.*

Lesson 13

**August 26, 2007**

# Malachi Describes God's Just Judgment

**ADULT TOPIC:** Living Responsibly in the Community of Faith
**YOUTH TOPIC:** Here Comes the Son
**CHILDREN'S TOPIC:** God Wants Obedience

**DEVOTIONAL READING:** Psalm 34:11-22
**BACKGROUND SCRIPTURE:** Malachi 2:17–4:3
**PRINT PASSAGE:** Malachi 2:17–3:5; 4:1

### Malachi 2:17–3:5; 4:1—KJV

17 Ye have wearied the LORD with your words. Yet ye say, Wherein have we wearied him? When ye say, Every one that doeth evil is good in the sight of the LORD, and he delighteth in them; or, Where is the God of judgment?

. . . . .

BEHOLD, I will send my messenger, and he shall prepare the way before me: and the Lord, whom ye seek, shall suddenly come to his temple, even the messenger of the covenant, whom ye delight in: behold, he shall come, saith the LORD of hosts.

2 But who may abide the day of his coming? and who shall stand when he appeareth? for he is like a refiner's fire, and like fullers' soap.

3 And he shall sit as a refiner and purifier of silver: and he shall purify the sons of Levi, and purge them as gold and silver, that they may offer unto the LORD an offering in righteousness.

4 Then shall the offering of Judah and Jerusalem be pleasant unto the LORD, as in the days of old, and as in former years.

5 And I will come near to you to judgment; and I will be a swift witness against the sorcerers, and against the adulterers, and against false swearers, and against those that oppress the hireling in his wages, the widow, and the fatherless, and that turn aside the stranger from his right, and fear not me, saith the LORD of hosts.

. . . . .

FOR, BEHOLD, the day cometh, that shall burn as an oven; and all the proud, yea, and all that do wickedly, shall be stubble:

**UNIT III**
How Shall We Respond?

**CHILDREN'S UNIT**
What Will We Do?

## KEY VERSES

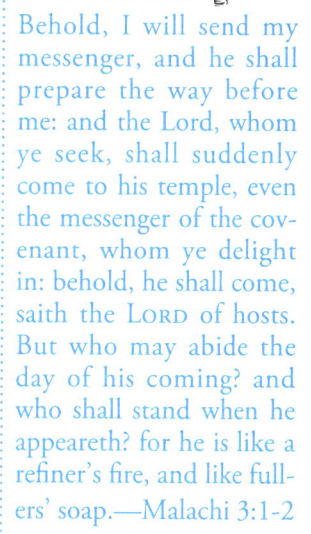

Behold, I will send my messenger, and he shall prepare the way before me: and the Lord, whom ye seek, shall suddenly come to his temple, even the messenger of the covenant, whom ye delight in: behold, he shall come, saith the LORD of hosts. But who may abide the day of his coming? and who shall stand when he appeareth? for he is like a refiner's fire, and like fullers' soap.—Malachi 3:1-2

## OBJECTIVES

**Upon completion of this lesson, the students are expected to:**
1. Affirm that God desires pure worship;
2. Recognize that God defends the downtrodden and oppressed; and,
3. Discover that God exercises correction after due warning.

**and the day that cometh shall burn them up, saith the LORD of hosts, that it shall leave them neither root nor branch.**

## UNIFYING LESSON PRINCIPLE

Most people feel good when justice and good triumph in the events of daily life. What reason do we have to anticipate such a celebration on a cosmic level? Malachi affirms that God will come one day to judge the world and to set all things right. He also affirms that God will bless true worshipers when that day comes.

## POINTS TO BE EMPHASIZED ADULTS/YOUTH

**Adult Key Verses:** Malachi 3:1-2
**Youth Key Verse:** Malachi 4:2
**Print Passage:** Malachi 2:17–3:5; 4:1

—Malachi was concerned with personal conduct and the integrity of the priests.
—Malachi affirms that God is about to send a messenger who will reunite and purify all Israel.
—In early Christian thought, the advent of Christ is thought to be the first of the culminating events of history promised by the prophet Malachi.
—The day of the Lord is both a Day of Judgment and a day of salvation.

## CHILDREN

**Key Verse:** Malachi 3:18
**Print Passage:** Malachi 3:6-18

—Malachi teaches that God requires persons to return to Him a portion of what they receive.
—Being obedient is our way of putting God to the test and seeing that God responds positively to it.
—God keeps a record of our righteous and unrighteous acts.
—Being obedient to God results in God's blessings.

## TOPICAL OUTLINE OF THE LESSON

### I. INTRODUCTION
   A. The Meaning of Messenger and Judgment
   B. Biblical Background

### II. EXPOSITION AND APPLICATION OF THE SCRIPTURE
   A. What Do You Mean, "Wearied the Lord"? *(Malachi 2:17)*
   B. A Messenger: Sent to Prepare for Judgment *(Malachi 3:1-5)*
   C. The Coming Judgment of the Wicked *(Malachi 4:1)*

### III. CONCLUDING REFLECTIONS

## I. INTRODUCTION
### A. The Meaning of Messenger and Judgment

A messenger is someone who carries information between two entities. The lesson for today centers on the message of Malachi to the Jews. His message was relevant then and is still relevant today.

This lesson deals with individual accountability. Is it possible to avoid judgment in our time? No! But it is not only America that God will judge; He will judge the whole world. He remains the same God, impartial and just.

### B. Biblical Background

Malachi's message is described as an oracle (burden, KJV). In the Old Testament, when a prophet's words are condemnatory and threaten the people with God's judgment, the word "oracle" conveys a burden, as in the King James Version (see Jeremiah 23:33-40).

The book of Malachi reflects a political situation where church and state were separate; therefore, the prophet's concern was not with national politics but with the personal conduct of God's people. There was much political and economic upheaval during the time of Malachi.

Malachi was concerned not only with the personal conduct of the people, but also with the integrity of the priests. Because of the evildoings of the priests, the people had acted out their despair through moral decadence and religious apathy. Even the faithful had become skeptics. If intimacy between God and God's people was to be restored, the people and the priests had to repent.

## II. Exposition and Application of the Scripture
### A. What Do You Mean, "Wearied the Lord"? *(Malachi 2:17)*

**Ye have wearied the Lord with your words. Yet ye say, Wherein have we wearied him? When ye say, Every one that doeth evil is good in the sight of the Lord, and he delighteth in them; or, Where is the God of judgment?**

God is not like us, having a flesh-and-blood body. How then is it possible for us to weary the Lord? What then makes God weary? This portion of the text goes to the heart of this lesson. The Jews had wearied the Lord with their words. Their words reflected unbelief and mistrust. They had blasphemed by doubting the existence of God. They were questioning the fairness of God.

The question they asked was, "Does God love the wicked?" If not, why did God fail to mete out immediate judgment? The disillusioned Jews had just returned from Babylon, and they saw wicked nations living in peace and prosperity. So they asked, "Where is the fairness of God?" Because of their frame of mind, the priests and people had caused God grief. Their view of God had been contrary to the laws of God. This was a miserable period in time for them. During this time, God had withheld His blessings. Both the people and priests had begun to lose faith in God. Even the God-fearing among them had become skeptics. It appeared to them that God favored the wicked and allowed them to prosper. Those who had remained faithful began to ask, "Where is the God of justice?"

God sought to bring correction to His people through His prophet Malachi. The problem with the people of Judah and Jerusalem was that they had existed in a state of rebellion for so long that they thought God would continue to overlook the way they neglected and mistreated Him.

When God called Malachi, the temple had already been rebuilt. People's spirits were broken because they were tired—both physically and spiritually. They had reverted to their former wicked ways. The priests had even allowed the people to commit sin in the temple. They allowed this sinfulness because they too were living unholy lives and had profaned the house of God. They had gotten so steeped in their sinful lifestyle that sinning in the temple no longer bothered them.

Since the priests had allowed polluted food upon the altar, the people thought that God must allow this practice (see Malachi 1:7-8). The people actually were more afraid of the governor than they were of God. They did not bring the governor lame or blind animals for payment of their taxes because they feared him, but they were willing to sacrifice blemished animals to God.

Where was the God of judgment? Are we asking that today? If we continue living in sin, our continued acts of transgression would cause us to answer in the affirmative.

### B. A Messenger: Sent to Prepare for Judgment *(Malachi 3:1-5)*

**Behold, I will send my messenger, and he shall prepare the way before me: and the Lord, whom ye seek, shall suddenly come to his temple, even the messenger of the covenant, whom ye delight in: behold, he shall come, saith the LORD of hosts. But who may abide the day of his coming? and who shall stand when he appeareth? for he is like a refiner's fire, and like fullers' soap. And he shall sit as a refiner and purifier of silver: and he shall purify the sons of Levi, and purge them as gold and silver, that they may offer unto the LORD an offering in righteousness. Then shall the offering of Judah and Jerusalem be pleasant unto the LORD, as in the days of old, and as in former years. And I will come near to you to judgment; and I will be a swift witness against the sorcerers, and against the adulterers, and against false swearers, and against those that oppress the hireling in his wages, the widow, and the fatherless, and that turn aside the stranger from his right, and fear not me, saith the LORD of hosts.**

"I will send my messenger...." Malachi foretells here of John the Baptist, although the messenger's identity in Malachi is not specific. The Synoptic Gospel writers seem to support that John is the prophesied messenger of the Lord (see Matthew 11:10-11; Mark 1:2-4; Luke 7:27-28). The messenger would prepare a way for the Messiah, who would remove obstacles and correct civil abuses. Other scholars consider that the messenger is identified with Elijah or is a symbolic representation of the line of prophets sent by God.

The people had been waiting for a long time for the Redeemer, but according to Malachi, the Redeemer would appear suddenly in the temple. Through Malachi, we know God wanted then and wants now to prepare God's people for judgment. God sent Malachi to warn the people about their cold hearts and defiant acts, because He wanted them to be refined, or saved. Malachi said, in Malachi 3:3, that God would "sit...and... purify the sons of Levi" so that they might make an offering in righteousness. The sons of Levi must, like all others, live responsibly so that they would not be judged.

Unlike Amos's prophesy, Malachi's does not portray God's judgment as destructive—neither for the leaders nor the people. For Malachi, the judgment of God would be for the purpose of cleansing and purifying. Both prophets envisioned the day of the Lord that would mark the presence of One before whom no one could stand as justified.

God's judgment and correction are not vengeful. Instead, they are a purifying process. Perfect praise cannot come forth from polluted temples, whether the temples are churches or individuals. God's ultimate purpose is to change our hearts in order to reflect His presence in our lives. When one walks the path of righteousness, goodness and mercy will follow.

God gives time and opportunity to everyone to be forgiven before God punishes them. Malachi warned the people because they had grown accustomed to sorcery and other magical arts in Babylon. Although He had been patient, the day would come when the proud and arrogant would be burnt up by the refining fire, and neither the branch nor the root would be left.

### C. The Coming Judgment of the Wicked *(Malachi 4:1)*

**For, behold, the day cometh, that shall burn as an oven; and all the proud, yea, and all that do wickedly, shall be stubble: and the day that cometh shall burn them up, saith the Lord of hosts, that it shall leave them neither root nor branch.**

This chapter tells us that the day of final judgment is coming. There will be no escape route; no alibi or argument will avail. There will be no postponement or appeal. This will be a day reserved for the wicked and the unrepentant. This judgment will be different from that mentioned in Malachi 3:2. The previously-mentioned judgment is "refining fire," which applies to God's people—particularly the Levites. The refining fire will purify them so that they can do their normal work. The judgment in verse 1 is described as an oven fire.

The candidates for this eternal inferno are mentioned: the proud and all that do wickedly. The proud are those who see themselves as above the knowledge of God and resist efforts of conversion. They will meet their match on the final day. The wicked ones are the ones who are continuously involved in doing evil. They have no regard for common decency. The oppressors will be nothing more than mere stubble. They will be consumed. No one will be able to see them anymore. Nothing about them will remain. Their roots will be destroyed and their branches will be cut away.

The last portion of Malachi 4:1 says, "[They] shall leave them neither root nor branch." This passage means that they will have no hope of returning to life. The roots are the life of any plant. Job 14:7 says, "There is hope of a tree, if it be cut down, that it will sprout again, and that the tender branch thereof will not cease." But in the case of the wicked, their lives will be uprooted and cast into the oven. So Malachi is saying that the hope of sinners will perish.

God used Malachi to alert His people and prepare them for the coming Day of Judgment. There is an old saying: "Forewarned is forearmed." God was giving His people time to get ready for the day when the righteous shall be distinguished from the wicked.

### III. Concluding Reflections

It is incumbent upon all believers in Christ to lead a life worthy of emulation. There will be times when it seems that God is not involved in our personal lives or in the affairs of the world. John the Baptist doubted when he was in jail. He sent his disciples to Jesus to ask Him whether or not He was the Messiah. Pangs of doubt are part of the human psyche. However, to doubt to the point of denying the existence of God is sin.

The people of God in the Old Testament doubted God to the point of worshiping other gods; therefore, they incurred the wrath of God. Not acknowledging God's divinity is a collapse of faith, which points to agnosticism or atheism. The psalmist is correct in saying, "Fools say in their hearts, 'There is no God.'" (Psalms 14:1, 53:1, NRSV).

Judgment Day is sure to come. God means what He says. His Word affirms over and over that those who do wrong will be destroyed. They will perish and burn in God's oven of fire. Further, the Lord will leave those who do evil no root or branch to use to continue in their transgressions.

Sometimes, we are reluctant to acknowledge God's kindness, and we ignore His judgment. We try to mollify our sin and disguise it with more palatable terms. There are two sides of God. God is a good and just God, and, at the same time, God is a God of judgment. But God's judgment is fair and just. Out of mercy He has given us time and a way to prepare for that day to which some will look forward and others will dread.

## WORD POWER

**Suddenly (Hebrew:** *pith-owm)*—it means "appearing unexpectedly or surprisingly, in order to put an end to old things and bring new things." This is where we get the English word for "petals."

## HOME DAILY BIBLE READINGS

for the week of August 26, 2007
*Malachi Describes God's Just Judgment*

Aug. 20, Monday
  —Psalm 34:11-22
  —God's Concern for the People
Aug. 21, Tuesday
  —1 Corinthians 3:10-15
  —Our Works Are Tested
Aug. 22, Wednesday
  —1 Corinthians 4:1-5
  —God Judges Our Hearts
Aug. 23, Thursday
  —Malachi 2:17-3:7
  —God Will Judge
Aug. 24, Friday
  —Malachi 3:8-12
  —Will Anyone Rob God?
Aug. 25, Saturday
  —Malachi 3:13-18
  —Choosing Between Good and Evil
Aug. 26, Sunday
  —Malachi 4:1-6
  —The Day of the Lord

## PRAYER

*Eternal God our Father, help us to live each day in light of Your coming judgment. Help us to realize that Your judgment is fair and just. In Jesus' name, we pray. Amen.*

# GLOSSARY OF TERMS

**Apocalyptic Writings**—a genre of prophetical writing that developed in post-exilic Jewish culture. "Apocalypse" is from the Greek word for "revelation." The book of Daniel is a fully-matured and classic example of this genre of literature.

**Aramaic**—a Semitic language known since the ninth century B.C. as the speech of the Aramaeans and later used extensively in southwest Asia as a commercial and governmental language. It was adopted as a customary speech by various non-Aramaean peoples, including the Jews after the Babylonian exile.

**Ark of the Covenant**—a rectangular chest containing the Ten Commandments, Aaron's budding rod, and a sample of manna; it symbolized the presence of God. Moses made the ark and placed a pair of cherubim facing each other atop the ark, whose wings touched.

**Atone/Atonement**—satisfaction of a debt created by sin by which forgiveness is attained.

**Babylonian Exile**—a seventy-year period in which the tribes of Judah, Benjamin, and half-tribe of Manasseh were taken by force to Babylon by King Nebuchadnezzar. This began around 605 B.C. under King Jehoiakim and was followed by the overthrow and destruction of Jerusalem around 586 B.C. under Zedekiah. The Babylonian Exile ended when Babylon was conquered by King Cyrus and the Persian Empire.

**Blasphemy**—speaking evil of God; punishable by death in biblical times. The Jews during Jesus' time did not accept Jesus as the Messiah. Therefore, Jesus' claims of equality with the Father were taken as blasphemous.

**Co-existence**—contemporary with God from eternity; only Jesus Christ is spoken of in this manner.

**Council of Chalcedon**—This was the fourth ecumenical (worldwide) council of the church and was held in A.D. 451. In particular, it declared that Jesus had two natures from birth: one divine and one human. These were combined in equal portions within the single being of Jesus.

**Council of Nicea**—the first church council; it was called by Emperor Constantine in A.D. 325 It decisively ruled that Jesus was both human and divine and equivalent to (literally, "of the same substance as") God the Father. As a result Aryanism was declared heresy.

**Day of Atonement**—this annual Jewish rite signified that the life of the people, the loss of which they had merited by their sins, was offered to God in the blood as the life of the victim, and that God by this ceremony was appeased and their sins expiated.

**Docetism**—the belief, regarded by most Christian theologians as heretical, that Jesus did not have a physical body; rather, it was believed that His body was an illusion, as was His crucifixion.

**Dualism**—the belief that there are two basic opposing principles in operation in the world, such as good and evil. There are also the contrasts of light versus darkness, love versus hate, obedience versus disobedience, and worldliness versus holiness.

*Ekklesia*— pronounced, EK-luh-SEE-ah. Greek, "called out"; the church.

**Eschatology**—the study of end times. A large portion of the understanding of Christian eschatology comes from the book of Revelation.

**Existential**—an outlook, or a perspective, on life that pursues the question of the meaning of life or the meaning of existence. This question is seen as being of paramount importance, above all other scientific and philosophical pursuits.

**Expiatory**—serving to make amends or atonement for offense or sin; serving to cancel the debt created by sin.

**Godhead**—God the Father, God the Son, and God the Holy Spirit.

**Gnosticism**—a heretical view during early Christianity. They disagreed that a human being was sinful by nature, but believed a person erred through ignorance; by knowledge, an individual could correct his or her ways and gain salvation. The special knowledge, which the Gnostics subscribed to, was known as "gnosis," an intuitive or reflexive type of knowledge, which came from the study of humanity's inner self or soul. Any other knowledge did not concern the Gnostics.

**Heretical**—teaching or doctrine in the church that is inconsistent with authentic Christian doctrine and belief.

**Holy War**—a war in which one or more sides claim to have been led by or authorized by God.

**Imagio dei**— Latin; literally, "the image of God." This term is generally used in reference to the creation of human beings, that we are created in God's image.

**Incarnation**—the embodiment of God in human form as Jesus Christ; the union of divinity with humanity in Jesus Christ.

**Islamic jihad**—a holy war waged on behalf of Islam as a religious duty.

**Jewish Torah**—the body of wisdom and law contained in Jewish Scripture; the five books of Moses—also called the Pentateuch.

**Liberation Theology**—an important, sometimes controversial, school of theological thought. It focuses on those who are oppressed and/or poor and the ways in which Jesus urged His disciples to seek freedom for all people. It is often cited as a form of Christian socialism, and it has had particularly widespread influence in Latin America and among the Jesuits, although its influence has diminished within Catholicism in the past decade. The current Pope, Benedict XVI, has been long-known as a fierce opponent of liberation theology.

**Orthodox Jews**—Judaism that adheres to the Torah and Talmud as interpreted in an authoritative rabbinic law code and applies their principles and regulations to modern living.

**Pantheism**—a doctrine that equates God with the forces and laws of the universe; the worship of all gods of different creeds, cults, or peoples indifferently.

**Pre-existence**—a state of being that dates before creation. The Godhead is eternally preexistent; the angelic host is immediately preexistent.

**Propitiation**—an atoning sacrifice that gains or regains God's favor or goodwill.

**Revisionist**—an advocate of the revision and understanding of an accepted, usually long-standing view, theory, or doctrine, especially of historical events and movements.

**Sanhedrin Court**—the supreme council and tribunal of the Jews during postexilic times headed by a high priest and having religious, civil, and criminal jurisdiction.

**Shekinah of God**—a manifestation of the presence of God.

**Syncretism**—the combination of different forms of belief or practice

**Synoptics**—the first three Gospels.

**Theocracy**—government of a state by God's immediate guidance or by officials who are regarded as guided by God.

**Transliterate**—to spell a foreign word with characters of similar sound from another alphabet.

**Uni-plural**—a collective noun (such as family, team, congregation, or group) used primarily in religious or theological circles to denote the Trinitarian nature of the Godhead.

**United Kingdom**—the kingdom of Israel under Saul, David, and Solomon. Jerusalem served as the capital and center of worship. Solomon built the famed temple there during his reign.